INTRODUCTION TO
WOMEN'S AND GENDER STUDIES

INTRODUCTION TO WOMEN'S AND GENDER STUDIES

An Interdisciplinary Approach

Melissa J. Gillis

Andrew T. Jacobs

NEW YORK   OXFORD
OXFORD UNIVERSITY PRESS

Oxford University Press is a department of the University of Oxford.
It furthers the University's objective of excellence in research, scholarship,
and education by publishing worldwide. Oxford is a registered trade mark
of Oxford University Press in the UK and certain other countries.

Published in the United States of America by
Oxford University Press
198 Madison Avenue, New York, NY 10016,
United States of America.

For titles covered by Section 112 of the US Higher Education
Opportunity Act, please visit www.oup.com/us/he for the
latest information about pricing and alternate formats.

Library of Congress Cataloging-in-Publication Data

Names: Gillis, Melissa, author. | Jacobs, Andrew, author.
Title: Introduction to women's and gender studies : an interdisciplinary
    approach / Melissa J. Gillis, Andrew T. Jacobs.
Description: New York : Oxford University Press, [2017] | Includes
    bibliographical references and index.
Identifiers: LCCN 2016024544| ISBN 9780199315468 (pbk. : alk. paper) | ISBN
    9780190633974 (eISBN)
Subjects: LCSH: Women's studies--Textbooks. | Sex role--Textbooks. |
    Feminism--Textbooks.
Classification: LCC HQ1180 .G555 2017 | DDC 305.4--dc23 LC record available
    at https://lccn.loc.gov/2016024544

9 8 7 6 5 4 3 2 1
Printed by LSC Communications, United States of America

We dedicate this book with love to our parents,
Sharon and Alan and Claire and Caroll,
and to our children, Lily and Emma.

Brief Contents

Contents

5   Constructions of Homosexualities: Past and Present   117

12   Feminisms: Theories and Practices   353

Preface

Introduction to Women's and Gender Studies: An Interdisciplinary Approach is a primary text for the introductory course in women's, gender, and sexuality studies (WGSS). We created this interdisciplinary textbook because, although we loved using anthologies of primary sources, we were frustrated at having to provide the context and background necessary for students to situate those primary sources and come to a comprehensive understanding of the subject. Anthologies always left significant gaps in student knowledge, but textbooks were too dry to convey the richness of the subject matter. *Introduction to Women's and Gender Studies: An Interdisciplinary Approach* is our solution. The text covers frequently anthologized issues and is written in a more engaging and narrative style than traditional textbooks. At the same time, it systematically covers core interdisciplinary concepts in WGSS. As such, our text aims to draw on the strengths of both anthologies and textbooks.

OUR APPROACH

Most WGSS textbooks are written primarily from a sociological point of view (especially focusing on analyses of institutions such as family or religion). However, many WGSS instructors (like us) come from other disciplines. And, regardless of our primary discipline, many WGSS instructors want to teach this course from an interdisciplinary perspective. *Introduction to Women's and Gender Studies: An Interdisciplinary Approach* is designed to appeal to instructors who come from a broader range of disciplinary perspectives. All of the chapters feature concepts from a variety of disciplines, and the thematic organization of the text moves beyond the standard sociological chapters. An interdisciplinary approach also emphasizes the relevance of WGSS perspectives and inquiries to students who may be majoring in other disciplines.

Key elements of our approach include the following:

- **A genuinely interdisciplinary approach** that draws both on social sciences and humanities such as art, communication studies, English, history, and philosophy. Students will be given an overview of the field of WGSS and be prepared for common upper-level courses.

- **Full chapters on race and international women's issues** so that people of color move from margin to center in terms of the thematic organization of the text. In addition, discussions of global issues and race are integrated throughout the text.
- **Two chapters devoted to LGBTQQIAA people, history, and social issues**, including one devoted to explaining the LGBTQQIAA alphabetic string, conceptions of sexual orientation (such as the Kinsey Scale and Klein Grid), and how homophobia operates in society. The second LGBTQQIAA chapter surveys how same-sex desire, sexual activity, and relationships have functioned through history and the rise of modern notions of lesbianism and male homosexuality. The second chapter also provides an account of the Stonewall uprising and the advent of the LGBTQ liberation movement.
- **An inductive approach** to the exegesis of material (that is, the text often begins with examples and then moves to general statements rather than vice versa). This approach allows students to engage more readily with the material. Instructors have less background work to do in class and can move students more quickly to more advanced material.
- **A sophisticated level of analysis** that begins with basic exposition of terms and necessary background information. Although we agree with the prevailing view in WGSS that all definitions are suspect, beginning with definitions and deconstructing them as the discussion progresses facilitates student learning.
- **Comprehensive coverage and discussion of material**, which makes this text a flexible tool not only for students of varying levels in traditional classrooms but also for flipped classrooms and online learning. For students who need textual material reinforced in a traditional classroom setting, this text is designed to support traditional lectures and guided classroom discussion. The movement of the text from basic terms and concepts to more fine-grained analysis and extended discussion makes this a useful text for classes composed of students of varying academic levels. For students who are good independent learners, the comprehensive treatment of material can free up time for classroom activities and discussions in flipped classrooms. Comprehensive coverage and discussion of material will also support online learning where lecture time is reduced or absent.
- **An engaging approach to difficult ideas**, which overcomes student resistance to core ideas in WGSS (such as the term "feminism," the nature of oppression, and the persistence of racism and sexism). Strategies based on communication principles and honed over 20 years in the introductory

WGSS classroom allow students to assimilate challenging ideas more quickly, transforming unproductive classroom conflict into constructive dialogue.

- **Recursive pedagogy** allows students to build a more complex, multifaceted understanding of material and reinforces key concepts. Features such as "Recap of Terms" allow students to see the value of WGSS core concepts as they are utilized as analytical tools in a variety of contexts.

FEATURES

Each chapter includes an engaging array of features, including thematic boxes and images that encourage students to appreciate the urgency and diversity of WGSS issues and inquiries to lives in a global context. Features include the following:

- **Breaking the Frame** draws from the research of the cognitive linguist George Lakoff, which indicates that it can be difficult for people to accept certain ideas because of the linguistic frame in which such ideas are usually presented. This feature, which reveals and then breaks the faulty linguistic frame that interferes with understanding certain ideas, is a useful pedagogical tool to encourage students to challenge and "break" their own preconceived ideas that interfere with or prompt resistance to difficult or provocative new ideas.
- **More About . . .** boxes extend the discussion of complex and challenging issues in the chapter through the introduction of additional voices and perspectives.

PEDAGOGY

The pedagogical apparatus of each chapter supports and appeals to diverse learning styles. Engaging images, as well as tables and line art, provide a visual perspective on key WGSS concepts. In addition, each chapter includes the following:

- **Introductory narratives** that frame the chapter's key concepts within a relatable biographical, cultural, or other context.
- **Key terms** critical to WGSS study appear in **boldface** when first used in the text, are collected for review at the end of each chapter, and are defined in a glossary at the end of the book. In addition, terms not necessarily

specific to WGSS (but still essential to understanding a WGSS issue in a particular context) are seamlessly integrated within the chapter's main text, so that explanations can be more sophisticated but still accessible.

- **Recap of Terms** reminds students of key concepts from earlier chapters and sets them within the context of the current chapter. This modular design gives instructors the freedom to choose chapters and a chapter sequence that makes sense for their class.
- **Citations** (in a modified APA style) are used throughout the chapters, providing students with a model of scholarly conventions. A full reference list appears at the end of the book, providing a valuable resource for students' own work.

SUPPLEMENTARY ONLINE MATERIAL

The **Student Website** (www.oup.com/us/gillis-jacobs) features the following:

- **On the Web** readings discuss chapter-related subjects (often contemporary issues) and can be used as handouts, prompts for student research papers, and/or supplementary reading.
- **Taking Stock, Taking Action** prompts and activities encourage students to apply concepts, initiate inquiries, and take action on campus and in the broader community around WGSS issues and concepts.
- **Recommended Readings and Multimedia Resources** including scholarly and literary works, documentaries, feature films, podcasts and more, to enrich the in- and out-of-classroom experience.

The **Ancillary Resource Center** (ARC) provides secure access to materials designed exclusively for instructors, including the following: instructor's manual, PowerPoint slides, comprehensive test bank, and other resources. It also allows OUP to inform instructors when new content becomes available. The ARC can be accessed online at www.oup-arc.com through individual user accounts.

OUR INDUCTIVE APPROACH

One unusual element of this text is the placement of Chapter 11, "History of Women's Activism in the United States," and Chapter 12, "Feminisms: Theories and Practices," at the end of the book (although we would note that feminism is defined in Chapter 3, which for some will be the first chapter assigned, and feminist theory and activism are discussed throughout the text). Most WGSS textbooks put discussions of forms of feminism and a history of feminist activism in the introductory chapters. By contrast, our back-loading of this framework is unconventional. For reasons we will explain below, we find this approach meshes with our pedagogical approach and with the learning styles of our first- and second-year students.

We believe identifying as feminists in the classroom is important both to clarify our analytical framework and as a way to model ethical engagement with the world. For us, feminist analysis is the wellspring of our thinking about WGSS issues and has shaped the entire text. The discussions of feminist activism and feminisms are the culmination of the text (for reasons we will discuss further below). However, if this structure does not suit your approach or your students' needs, we encourage you to assign these chapters as early as you see fit. In fact, the text has been designed to give you just such freedom of sequencing.

Why such a radically different default organization for this text? In our experience, two factors make the conventional approach, which we call theoretical front-loading, more difficult for many introductory WGSS students. The first factor is the relative youth and lack of life experience of many first-year students. Many of our students have a less than comprehensive understanding of various historical periods and have relatively little personal experience with a variety of issues, such as workplace discrimination or varying cultural conceptions of the place of gender in society. In this context, we have found that beginning a course with a discussion of forms of feminism and feminist activism can be both overwhelming and frustrating. Many students simply do not have the background knowledge and personal experience to fruitfully situate first and second wave feminism in political, economic, and social context, to understand the ways intersectional identities complicate experiences of advantage or disadvantage, or to understand how global feminist perspectives are a response to colonial and postcolonial regimes of control. Our classes are diverse—and this characterization is not true for all our students and probably not true for all of yours, but we find these gaps in knowledge and experience are frequent enough to be important pedagogical challenges.

The second factor that makes theoretical front-loading problematic is the resistance to the very word *feminism*. Although many who plan on majoring in WGSS embrace the word, your WGSS course—if it is like ours—is likely to include nonmajors as well, at least some of whom have the preconception that feminism is simply an outdated and cranky doctrine. Moreover, this cohort may be suspicious the course will be primarily PC indoctrination. In this context, beginning the course with the necessarily subtle and complex theoretical framework of feminist theory and history can trigger emotional resistance, which is reinforced by understandable sets of misunderstandings about issues including race, sex, class, and sexual orientation, all of which can collude in preventing a fair reading of feminist theory and feminist activism (not to mention whatever follows in the course).

We have found that moving the in-depth discussion of feminist theory and history of activism to the end of the course is pedagogically more effective for our students and is in keeping with the inductive approach of the text. This may seem counterintuitive because so much of academic work is presented deductively with theoretical claims presented first. For example, academics are likely to advance a broad claim such as "radical feminism claims the primary form of oppression is the oppression of women" and follow it with supporting statements such as "the division of labor between the sexes resulted in the first form of systematic inequality in some societies" and that "the sexual division of labor continues to result in inequality for women as a group." The form and substance of such argumentation are unsurprising to WGSS academics but have proven overwhelming to many of our students who have strong emotional reactions to words like "radical" and "feminism" and the claim that women are oppressed. Moreover, our students often lack personal experience and the academic background to see, for example, how a sexual division of labor is the result of systemic forces rather than unproblematic "free" choices of women.

Again, this description of some (but certainly not all) of our students may not reflect your experience in the classroom. We recognize many student populations are sophisticated in terms of their experiences and educational background. It is also true that many students with less experience in these subjects are open to the material in WGSS classes and may have strong activist bents. If this is the case in your WGSS class, we would encourage you to assign the chapters in the order that best fits your situation. However, if you experience significant resistance to or misunderstanding of feminist theory, particularly early on in your course, consider our inductive approach. We have found the problem of resistance is surmountable if we delay the introduction of complex theoretical claims and first introduce students to the series of problems that are related to sex, gender, sexual orientation, race, and class in society. For example, in the first few chapters students will confront the following questions: Are there really only two sexes? Why aren't sexed and gendered terms like stud and slut parallel in terms of connotation? Why is homophobia often expressed as the hatred of feminine qualities in men? Why are women and men of certain racial groups seen as more feminine or more masculine than others? As students experience these societal puzzles, they develop the rich background and analytical skills necessary to interrogate them. They will be faced with concrete examples of how a variety of issues affect people of various intersectional identities and (we hope) come to empathize with them. They will systematically unlearn binaries associated with sex, gender, and sexual orientation and master the vocabulary and analytical tools necessary to think about a variety of WGSS issues in a more complex way.

In keeping with this approach, we introduce the word feminism for the first time in Chapter 3, "Gender and In/Equality" (which may be assigned to students in sequence or could be introduced earlier). A fair amount of ink is devoted to unpacking the idea. After this introduction, the word is used increasingly and in increasingly complex ways as chapters progress; examples of feminist activism are integrated throughout the text. Finally, Chapter 11, "History of Activism in the United States," and Chapter 12, "Feminisms: Theories and Practices," offer the most nuanced explications, which students can understand within the context of all that they have learned.

HOW TO USE THIS TEXT

We would like to make a few observations about the structure of the text and a few suggestions about how to tailor the text for your particular class.

Use the chapters as they work best for you—Although there is an intentional logical flow from Chapter 1 through Chapter 12, each chapter is also designed to be self-contained. This gives you the freedom to omit or reorder chapters as befits your class objectives.

Treat the material in box features as central rather than peripheral—As with pull-quotes (those larger typeface quotes from newspaper and magazine articles that draw attention to an article), box features are often read before the "central" text. This means that box-feature material is often highlighted in the minds of students. We created the box features with this fact in mind; this material is not meant to be conceptually marginal.

Consider using this textbook more like an anthology—Because the chapters are dense, there may be more material than can be fruitfully covered in a semester; assign a selection of these chapters or portions of chapters and/or test on a subset of this material. This approach gives you flexibility more akin to selecting readings from an anthology.

- *Consider Chapters 1, 3, 4, 6, 8, 9, 10, and 12 the "core" chapters*—These chapters cover themes common to an introductory interdisciplinary WGSS course, including sex, gender, sexual orientation, race, work, violence, international issues, and feminist theory.
- *Consider Chapters 2, 5, 7, and 11 the more "specialized" chapters*—These chapters include the themes of language and communication; history of sexual orientation; fashion, beauty, and viewership; and the history of U.S. feminist activism. These chapters may play to your disciplinary strengths or, depending on your approach to the WGSS class, you may think of some of this material as essential for your students. Select from these chapters with these approaches in mind.
- *Consider using the text with additional readings*—Since the chapters are meant to serve as primers for a variety of subjects, they can be assigned in combination with outside books, essays, video, etc. The annotated bibliographies available online include works that will help with both the affective and the intellectual dimensions of learning.

Chapter 12 can be used in a variety of ways. Chapter 12 is somewhat stylistically different from the other chapters. Rather than presenting an overarching argument or set of arguments, it introduces a variety of feminist viewpoints. Moreover, it is meant to be a chapter that is read and re-read—as students reflect on previous chapters and as a reference point for majors who return to the chapter in light of other courses. Our hope is that just as an architectural capstone is often a unique element that serves a specific purpose, so too this capstone chapter serves a special role.

Consider using it in a variety of ways:

- *As a capstone chapter*—Chapter 12 (and also Chapter 11) requires the most background knowledge, has the most theoretical claims, and relies on concepts (like feminism) that may require systematic unlearning before they can be seriously studied. Particularly if you experience resistance to the idea of feminism in your classroom (and even if you do not), we urge you to seriously consider this approach. Let students experience the problems people face regarding sex, gender, sexual orientation, race, and class without first focusing on the theoretical framework. Let students think about and "discover" the framework for themselves. We think you will be pleasantly surprised at how this reduces resistance to learning (especially in nonmajors) and facilitates deeper appreciation of feminist theory and history of feminist activism for all students.

- *With cognate chapters*—Alternatively, each form of feminism discussed in Chapter 12 could be assigned with a related chapter. Here is a possible lineup:

Chapter 3, "Gender and In/Equality"	Liberal Feminism
Chapter 4, "LGBTQQIAA Identities and Challenges"	Radical Feminism and/or Postmodern/Queer Theory
Chapter 5, "Constructions of Homosexualities"	Postmodern/Queer Theory
Chapter 6, "Beyond the Mythical Norm"	U.S. Intersectional Feminism
Chapter 8, "Work, Inequality, and Neoliberalism"	Marxist/Socialist Feminism
Chapter 10, "Human Rights and Global Activism"	Transnational Feminism

- *As a foundational chapter*—For those who want to use a deductive approach and foreground discussions of feminism, Chapters 11 and/or 12 could be assigned at the beginning of the course, along with Chapter 1 or Chapter 3. Appendix C, Feminisms in Brief, could then be used as a quick reference as the semester progresses (more on Appendix C below).

Utilize the appendices throughout your course. Appendices A, B, and C are designed to enrich and expand the coverage of the textbook.

- *Appendix A, Basic Terms*, provides a review of terms from Chapter 1. If your course begins with other than Chapter 1, use this appendix to provide/review foundational terms. (See the section "Consider creating WGSS 101 and 102 courses" for other chapter sequencing options.)
- *Appendix B, Names for People and Places*, discusses identity terms (such as African American, Black, and Native American) and places (such as Global North and Third World). This appendix provides an in-depth discussion of why some terms are preferred or disfavored and guidance on usage.
- *Appendix C, Feminisms in Brief*, offers a short introduction to the forms of feminism covered in Chapter 12. For each form of feminism it offers a "Thumbnail Description" and "Sources of Inequality," which are highly condensed from the "Feminist Theory" discussions in Chapter 12.

Appendix C also includes "Some Problems and Solutions" and "Advances Toward Feminist Goals," which go beyond the material in Chapter 12 and provide concrete examples of feminist practice. (It does not recap the "History of Feminist Theory" sections from Chapter 12.)

Appendix C may be used in a variety of ways:

- *As a study aid along with Chapter 12*—We recommend assigning it after assigning Chapter 12. Remind students it is not a wholesale recap of Chapter 12.
- *In combination with parts of Chapter 12*—The Chapter 12 introductory material and "Feminist Theory" sections can be assigned with Appendix C, allowing instructors to omit the "History of . . ." each form of feminism from Chapter 12. This approach will lessen the reading load, so it is particularly recommended if you feel Chapter 12 might be too long for your students. We are sensitive to the fact that a substantial number of students have non-academic responsibilities and challenges, such as work and caregiving commitments, that can make long reading assignments difficult. Yet we firmly believe that feminism should be made accessible to everyone. We are striving to provide ways to tailor reading and workloads to make that possible.
- *As a stand-alone resource/reference*—Appendix C may also be used in place of Chapter 12 or as a quick reference tool throughout the semester, as a resource for discussions of feminism in upper-level classes, or as an ancilla for independent reading.

Consider creating WGSS 101 and 102 courses. We believe there is enough material in this text to support a two-course introduction to WGSS. We would envision either 101 or 102 fulfilling the distribution requirement normally fulfilled by the single WGSS course. The two-course sequence could work as Western Civilization 101 and 102 function at many colleges—where students can take either or both courses, in any order. Both courses could be required of WGSS majors. With that in mind, Chapter 1 and Chapter 3 have been designed for use as potential introductory chapters (Chapter 3 should be supplemented with a brief overview of the basic terms from Chapter 1, which can be found in Appendix A). Chapters 11 and 12 could serve as capstone chapters. The two courses could cover different thematic elements such as the following:

WGSS 101: Chapters 1, 3 (first half), 4, 6, 8, 9, 12

WGSS 102: Appendix A, Chapters 2, 3, (second half), 7, 10, 11

(This sequence utilizes all chapters except 5.)

Or:

WGSS 101: Chapters 1, 4, 6, 8 (first or second half), 9, 12

WGSS 102: Appendix A, Chapters 3, 5, 7, 8 (first or second half), 10, 11

(This sequence utilizes all chapters except 2.)

Alternatively, the courses could divide material into a U.S.-oriented 101 and internationally oriented 102.

We hope this book aids your teaching of your WGSS course. We would very much like to hear about how you use the text, what works, and what could be done to improve the text for you and your students. Please email us at ajacobs@sunyrockland.edu.

ABOUT THE AUTHORS

Melissa J. Gillis has taught the WGSS course at SUNY Rockland, developed and taught a Women and Violence in Literature course at John Jay College through a competitive grant, and taught composition. She has worked for various United Nations programs and nongovernmental organizations, often focusing on global women's issues. She is a writer and editor, having written more than three dozen publications, including many devoted to women's issues, such as *When We Are All Strong Together: Understanding Gender Discrimination, Building Gender Justice* (a book co-authored with Jennifer Butler). She authored *Disarmament: A Basic Guide* for the United Nations and was editor of *Disarmament Times*, a quarterly UN-NGO publication on disarmament, peace, and security issues for six years.

She is ABD in English literature from CUNY and holds a master's degree in interdisciplinary studies (focusing on women's studies) from New York University's Gallatin School. At the undergraduate level she was summa cum laude in English at DePauw University.

Andrew T. Jacobs co-developed the introductory WGSS course at SUNY Rockland and has taught it for more than 20 years. His publications include peer-reviewed work and essays for a popular audience. His master's degree is in speech communication from Syracuse University and his bachelor's degree is in philosophy from Cornell University. His graduate work in speech communication focused on rhetoric and he has 25 years of experience teaching persuasion and coaching academic debate.

ACKNOWLEDGMENTS

We thank Sherith Pankratz and her assistants, Cari Heicklen, Katy Albis, and especially Meredith Keffer, for all their support. Thanks to those who gave us advice and support on the business of publishing, including the Text and Academic Author's Association, our attorney Michael R. Lennie, and Joann Miller.

Thanks to New York University for their Semester Scholar-in-Residence program through the Faculty Resource Network. Special thanks to FRN Associate Director, Anne L. Ward, copyright and scholarly communications librarian, Melissa A. Brown, and professor Gayatri Gopinath.

Thanks to all the reviewers of our text. We deeply appreciate the thoughtful criticism, which we believe resulted in a better book.

Tanya Sarjof Bakhru, San Jose State University
Dana Berkowitz, Louisiana State University
Jenn Brandt, High Point University
Steven F. Butterman, University of Miami
Stephanie D'Auria, Vanguard University
Dawn Rae Davis, Illinois State University
Gretchen DeHart, Washington State University, Johnson State College,
    Commnity College of Vermont
Robyn Stein DeLuca, Stony Brook University
Kathleen Farrell, Colby-Sawyer College
Lindsey Feitz, University of Denver
Laura Franey, Millsaps College
Bethany Gizzi, Monroe Community College
Tanya Harasym, Columbia College Chicago
Terri L. Hardwick, Eastern Kentucky University
Desiree Henderson, University of Texas at Arlington
Deborah Anne Hooker, North Carolina State University
Elizabeth A. Hubble, University of Montana
Natalie Jolly, University of Washington
Rachel Bailey Jones, Nazareth College
Kathryn Linder, Suffolk University
Cristina Lombardi-Diop, Loyola University Chicago
Irene López, Kenyon College
Hedda Marcus, Nassau Community College
Deanna H. Mihaly, Eastern Michigan University
Celeste Montoya, University of Colorado Boulder

Maire Mullins, Pepperdine University
Michael J. Murphy, University of Illinois Springfield
Jennifer Musial, Northern Arizona University
Kathryn J. Norlock, Trent University
María Ochoa, San Jose State University
Risikat Okedeyi, Prince George's Community College
Abigail L. Palko, University of Notre Dame
Yosálida C. Rivero-Zaritzky, Mercer University
Danielle Roth-Johnson, University of Nevada, Las Vegas
Michelle V. Rowley, University of Maryland
David Rubin, University of South Florida
Shannon Schipper, Arizona State University
Megan Sinnott, Georgia State University
Sharon L. Sullivan, Washburn University
Susan Talburt, Georgia State University
Kumru F. Toktamis, Pratt University and Brooklyn College, CUNY
Mary Valentine, College of the Canyons
M. Catherine Vann, Towson University
Andrea Walsh, MIT
Guang-Zhen Wang, University of Texas-Pan American
Kimberly Welch, University of Redlands
Kathryn A. Ziegler, Eastern Michigan University
4 anonymous reviewers

Thanks to everyone at Rockland Community College (now and in the past) who has been supportive of our project. Thanks to President Cliff L. Wood, Vice President Susan Deer, the sabbatical leave committee, and Wilma Frank for their support of Andrew's sabbatical. Thanks to David Lucander, Chaya Rachel Nove, and Christina Stern for their feedback on chapters. Thanks to the students of Andrew's women's and gender studies class who read chapters with enthusiasm and a critical eye. Very special thanks to Sarah Levy—a great librarian at a great little library.

SEX, GENDER, AND SOCIAL CONSTRUCTION

"Once upon a time," Lois Gould (1992) began her fable, *X: A Fabulous Child's Story,* "a baby named X was born. This baby was named X so that nobody could tell whether it was a boy or a girl" (p. 9). Gould, who originally published *X* in 1978, went on to tell the story of a "Secret Science Xperiment" (sic) to find out what would happen if you raised a child without revealing its sex to anyone (other than the parents, of course). In the course of the experiment, scientists subjected "thousands of volunteers" to "thousands of tests" to find just the right parents to raise Baby X. "Almost everybody failed," wrote Gould, "because as it turned out, almost everybody really wanted either a baby boy or a baby girl, and not Baby X at all" (p. 9). At last, "the scientists found the Joneses, who really wanted to raise an X more than any other kind of baby" (p. 10).

When the Joneses brought X home, friends and family came over to see the baby. (None had been clued into the Secret Science Xperiment.) The first thing they asked was whether X was a girl or a boy. When the Joneses replied, "'It's an X,'" the visitors were stymied into silence, then became uncomfortable, and, finally, angry. They did not know how to talk to X; they did not know what to buy X. They stopped visiting. But, "the Official Instruction Manual" had warned this would happen, so X's parents didn't worry too much and went about treating X as prescribed.

The Joneses were careful to bounce *and* cuddle X in equal measure, so as not to treat X too much like a girl or too much like a boy. They dressed X in blue pajamas and flowered underwear and, for school, red and white checked overalls. X had a pageboy haircut (which would be considered appropriate for a girl or a boy) and was taught how to throw a football (by X's mother), as well as how to throw a tea party (by X's father).

One purpose of Gould's "fabulous" story (meaning, in this case, based on a fable, that is, a fictional story intended to enforce a truth or teach a lesson) was to point out just how much our lives, from the earliest moments, are structured around ideas about what is appropriate for a girl and what is appropriate for a boy and to raise questions: What would happen if a child were raised without revealing whether the child is a girl or a boy (or a third category)? Would such a child, if it were a girl, "naturally" turn out to be "girlish"? Or, if it were a boy, would it naturally turn out to be "boyish"? If the child belonged (or chose to belong) to a third category, what then? Would a Baby X somehow suffer from confusion and be ill-adapted to the world? Or would such a child be freer to develop into the child's "true" self?

You may have heard the phrase *"is it nature or is it nurture?"* in relation to these kind of issues, which is a sort of shorthand for asking how much of our behaviors are innate or can be attributed to biology (nature) and how much can be attributed to social forces or socialization (nurture). These questions (which, as it turns out, have no simple answers) will be central to this book. What does it matter whether girls are girlish and boys are boyish (or the reverse, if girls are boyish and boys are girlish)? What about those who fall outside the girl/boy binary? Or those whose self-conceptions are fluid and changing? Can and should we try to influence the behavior of individuals within society? How and when?

Before we go further, we must establish a vocabulary as a way of understanding basic concepts to help us think about the many issues raised by Baby X.

SEX

In *X: A Fabulous Child's Story*, Baby X's sex (female, male, something else) at birth—based presumably on X's external genitalia—was a secret. Only the parents knew X's sex—although of course, it will become known to (or

Phosphoros: ℞ = Ph

FIGURE 1.1

The female symbol was originally the symbol for Venus (the goddess and planet). Sometimes known as the mirror of Venus, it is more likely a contraction of the initial Greek letter for Venus (known as Phosphoros).

understood by) Baby X eventually. **Sex** is *traditionally* defined as "anatomical or biological characteristics" used to classify a person as female or male (Moradi et al., 2009), which might include external and internal sex organs, chromosomes, hormones, and perhaps brain structure, as well as secondary sex characteristics such as breasts and facial hair.

Although many of us have no trouble checking a box for either "female" or "male," not everyone falls neatly into one of these two categories. There are a variety of reasons for this. Some people choose, whether or not they have the biological characteristics most often used to classify a person as female or male, not to identify as female or male (Meerkamper, 2013). For others, the categories female and male may not be adequate because they are in fact **intersex**—that is, they have sex characteristics that make them different from predominant notions of biological femaleness and maleness. Understanding intersex is important for a number of reasons, but in particular it helps us to understand in a concrete way the inadequacy of the female/male binary.

Intersex

Intersex people may have genitalia that are not typically female or male—that is, genitals that seem somewhat like female genitals and somewhat like male genitals. Some intersex people may have enlarged clitorises that resemble penises or smaller penises that resemble clitorises or genitals that intersex people do not want classified as resembling female or male genitals. These genitals may or may not be accompanied by vaginal openings. In other cases, intersex people may have external genitalia that seem typically female or male but may have internal sex organs or a genetic makeup more typical of a

Thouros: Θ = Th ρ = r

FIGURE 1.2
The male symbol was originally the symbol for Mars (the god and planet).
Sometimes known as the shield and spear of Mars, it is more likely a contraction
of the initial Greek letter for Mars (known as Thouros).

different sex. Intersex people may sometimes have a mix of sex organs (for example, instead of two ovaries or two testes, they may have one ovary and one testis or ovo-testes that are a combination). Intersex people may also have varied secondary sex characteristics (for example a "feminine" or a "masculine" build and/or facial hair) that do not typically accompany their primary sex characteristics.

It may be apparent at an infant's birth that the child is intersex or it may become apparent only later at puberty or as an adult. It is also possible for intersex people to go their entire lives without anyone (even themselves) knowing they are intersex, because most intersex people have typical-looking genitalia and are atypical in terms of chromosomes, hormone levels, and/or other reproductive features that are not readily apparent (Hinkle & Viloria, n.d.). The biologist Anne Fausto-Sterling (2000) conducted the first assessment of biological data to determine the rate of intersex conditions in the population and estimated that roughly 1.7 percent of the population (or 17 of 1,000 people) is to some degree intersex. But experts' estimates of the number of intersex people vary widely, in part because many people are born with subtle biological variations that are not apparent until later in life (Harper, 2007). There is clearly a need for more extensive and better data collection.

In the past, intersex people were sometimes called hermaphrodites after the Greek myth of Hermaphroditus, who had female and male attributes. Fausto-Sterling stated that what she calls "true hermaphrodites" who are capable of both female and male reproduction are rare, "possibly one in 100,000" (p. 22). By contrast, Organisation Intersex International Australia (2014) stated that having "fully functioning sets of 'male' and 'female' sex organs . . . is impossible for mammals" (p. 2). Today, intersex is usually the preferred term and the term hermaphrodite is considered offensive to many in the intersex community—although some have taken on the label to fight the stigma associated with it (Harper; Organisation Intersex International Australia).

The Social Construction of Sex

Determining who is female, male, and intersex is complicated, as the Intersex Society of North America (ISNA) (2008b) explained:

> Which variations of sexual anatomy count as intersex? In practice, different people have different answers to that question. That's not surprising, because intersex isn't a discreet or natural category. . . . Intersex is a socially constructed category that reflects real biological variation. . . . Nature presents us with sex anatomy spectrums. Breasts, penises, clitorises, scrotums, labia, gonads—all of these vary in size and shape and morphology. So-called "sex" chromosomes can vary quite a bit, too. (para. 3)

Fausto-Sterling noted that it may seem "natural" to imagine intersex people "as living midway between the poles of male and female" (p. 22). But, she argued, female, male, and intersex should not be seen as falling along "some kind of continuum" (p. 22). They are better imagined "as points in a multi-dimensional space" that can account for the myriad combinations of genes, hormones, and anatomy that make up individuals (Fausto-Sterling, p. 22). And that point may not be such a stable one. One's understanding (or the physical presentation) of one's sex may change over time.

How do we make sense of this amazing sexual diversity? Often difference is overlooked or oversimplified. However it is classified, the process of categorization turns out to be more than a question of nature alone, as the ISNA (2008b) made clear:

> But in human cultures, sex categories get simplified into male, female, and sometimes intersex, in order to simplify social interactions, express what we know and feel, and maintain order. So nature doesn't decide where the category of "male" ends and the category of "intersex" begins, or where the category of "intersex" ends and the category of "female" begins. **Humans decide**. Humans (today, typically doctors) decide how small a penis has to be, or how unusual a combination of parts has to be, before it counts as intersex. Humans decide whether a person with XXY chromosomes or XY chromosomes and androgen insensitivity will count as intersex. (para. 3)

FIGURE 1.3

Tony Briffa was the first openly intersex mayor (Hobsons Bay, Australia). Briffa, who has partial androgen insensitivity syndrome, has XY chromosomes (usually male) but did not develop in a "typically" male way. Briffa said: "I am not male or female, but both." Briffa suffered unwanted sex assignment surgery as a child.

If we accept the idea that "humans decide," in other words, that intersex is a socially constructed category, then we must also take seriously the notion that female, male, and even "sex" itself are to some degree socially constructed (Muehlehard & Peterson, 2011). A **social construct** is a "concept or perception of something based on the collective views developed and maintained within a society or social group . . . as opposed to existing inherently or naturally" (Oxford English Dictionary [OED]). When we say something is socially constructed, we are saying it is created by people and, therefore, that it varies across cultures and history. Returning to the topic of sex, one's sex, then, is determined not only by biology but also by human activity and human choice. These activities and choices include political, economic, and cultural factors. The recognition of the social construction of sex has led many to abandon the term "biological sex" in favor of "**assigned sex**," which recognizes that sexual categorization is not simply a matter of objective biological fact but also a matter of human decision (Butler, 2006).

Indeed, we believe all categories are socially constructed; they exist because we create them as useful sorting tools in our incredibly complex world. But as useful as they can be, categories can also be problematic—because they can be overly simplistic, are (often) not entirely accurate, and involve judgments that can lead to mistreatment of individuals or groups. The process of social construction is extremely complex and involves many factors. We will continue to examine it in Chapter 3, "Gender and In/Equality."

Sex Identity

Regardless of sexual characteristics, people in Western culture (that is, the cultures of Europe and North America) generally identify as either female or male—although not always. (See Appendix B, Names for People and Places for a definition of Western.) Sometimes people's **sex identity** (what people understand their sex to be) can be at odds with their assigned sex or other sex characteristics. When this happens, a person may (or may not) decide to undergo a **sex reassignment process**, which may include surgery and/or hormone treatment to bring a person's body more into biological alignment with their sex identity. People who undergo sex reassignment are sometimes called **transsexual** (Denny, 2006), although some no longer prefer this term and instead identify as **transgender** (or trans), an umbrella term that includes "transsexual" and other identities. (Transgender, trans, and transsexual are adjectives, for example, transgender person, trans woman, transsexual man.) (See Appendix B, Names for People and Places for a discussion of transgender people and the term transsexual. More on transsexual and transgender will also be presented in Chapter 4, "LGBTQQIAA Identities and Challenges.")

In light of our discussion of sex, let us return to our initial definition: Sex is *traditionally* defined as anatomical or biological characteristics used to classify a person as female or male. A more nuanced view of sex would, for one, recognize that people and other organisms are not simply female or male. The categories female, male, third sex, and even intersex imply an easy divisibility that simply does not exist. As the sociologist Michael Kimmel (2013) has argued, a better descriptor of sex is that it is related to "our chromosomal, chemical, anatomical organization" (p. 3). But it is also more than simply physiological. Human choice is involved, meaning sex is to some degree socially constructed. For example, what must a structure be before we label it a penis rather than a clitoris—or something that is neither (what length, shape, etc.)? Biology does not provide an answer; humans decide. This means the so-called "biological" categories of female, male, and intersex are human constructions. We prefer the term assigned sex to biological sex because it acknowledges that social constructedness.

GENDER

Sexual diversity notwithstanding, it seems that in the story of Baby X, Gould intended for us to think of Baby X's sex as either female or male. Despite having been assigned the female or male sex, X looked and behaved in ways that did not allow others to pin down exactly who X was. X's clothes (red and white checked overalls), haircut (short for a girl or long for a boy), and games (X plays ball and house, equally well) baffled the other parents because they did not provide the usual clues as to whether X was a girl or a boy. These attributes regarding appearance and behavior are traits related to **gender**, which has *traditionally* been thought of as "the non-physiological aspects" of oneself, expectations of femininity and masculinity (Lips, 2005, p. 5). These include clothing, hairstyle, activities, and behaviors that mark one as feminine, masculine, or something else. Because of its simplicity, this is a good starting point for our discussion, but gender, like sex, turns out to be more complex and more difficult to define than this conception suggests.

In Western culture, gender, like sex, is seen as permanent (Devor, 1992). That is, just as one is always female or male, one is always **feminine** or **masculine**. Moreover, in Western culture sex entails gender, that is, if you are female, you "should be" stereotypically feminine, and if you are male, you should be stereotypically masculine. Of course individuals can be gender nonconforming, but Western culture generally views gender nonconformity as a problem.

Gender Polarization

Researchers have found that ideas about gender are surprisingly similar across many different cultures, although they are certainly not the same. In a wide range of cultures, people recognize two genders, feminine and masculine, which are often thought of as being in binary opposition to one another (thus the notion of "opposite" sexes). Deborah Best (2009) reported that in a study of adults from 25 countries, participants showed considerable agreement about psychological characteristics associated with women on the one hand and men on the other. Keep in mind, these characteristics were identified as stereotypically feminine and masculine; they were not self-descriptions. [A stereotype is a "preconceived and oversimplified idea of the characteristics which typify a person, situation, etc." (OED).] Numerous studies have demonstrated that female stereotypes tend to emphasize nurturance, affiliation, and abasement, whereas male stereotypes tend to emphasize dominance, autonomy, and aggression (Table 1.1; see, for example, J. Williams et al., 1999). John Williams and colleagues noted that researchers often find only a "weak echo" of gender stereotypes in people's self-concepts (p. 524). Furthermore, the developmental psychologist Deborah Best (2009) found that

> *fluctuations in average gender are greater within a person than variations in gender between people, with the smallest differences found between the sexes.... Not only are there some men who are feminine, but almost all men are feminine at some times. Similarly, not only are there some women who are masculine, almost all women are sometimes more masculine than most men.* (p. 344)

The psychologist Sandra Bem (1993) labeled the notion that femininity and masculinity are polar opposites "**gender polarization**" and wrote,

> *Gender polarization operates in two related ways. First, it defines mutually exclusive scripts for being male and female. Second, it defines any person or behavior that deviates from these scripts as problematic—as unnatural or*

TABLE 1.1
Gender Stereotypes/Gender Polarization

Women	Men
Feminine	Masculine
Passive	Active
Dependent	Independent
Weak	Strong
Sentimental/soft-hearted	Tough
Sophisticated	Coarse
Fickle	Steady
Emotional	Unemotional
Submissive	Aggressive
Cooperative	Competitive
Petite/dainty	Brawny/burly
Creative	Analytical
Verbally skilled	Quantitatively skilled

In 1975, Williams and Bennett gave 100 college students in the United States (50 women, 50 men) a list of 200 adjectives and asked them to identify the words as describing either women or men (or neither). Seventy-five percent of the study participants agreed on 30 adjectives describing women and 33 describing men. The information in this table is based on the results of that study and later studies (see, for example, J. Williams et al., 1999). The results demonstrate what Bem (1993) called gender polarization.

immoral from a religious perspective or as biologically anomalous or psychologically pathological from a scientific perspective. (pp. 80–81)

Any social or individual system of sex and gender that imposes rigid and opposing categories of sex, gender, gender identity, and gender roles on people is a gender-polarizing system.

Western culture tends to conflate sex and gender, that is, to think of them as the same or interchangeable. In common usage, gender is often used as a synonym for sex. For example, most everyone has filled out a form asking them to check a box indicating gender—in most cases the form is not asking about femininity, masculinity, or some other gendered category, but about sex.

Another set of words that are more or less synonymous with feminine and masculine are the earthier vernacular (that is, informal or colloquial) terms **femme** and **butch**. Within gay and lesbian subcultures, women who are gender conforming (who appear and act more feminine) are frequently described as femme and those who are gender nonconforming (who appear and act in a more

breaking the frame
The Concepts of Sex and Gender Blur

Prior to the development of women's, gender, and sexuality studies, the terms "sex" and "gender" tended to be used interchangeably, usually to refer to "biological" females and males (Scott, 1986). The prevailing view at the time was that females and males were fundamentally different because of their biology. Statements about biological differences were often used to justify claims of women's inferiority. However, many women's rights activists believed that women's unequal status was rooted not in biological difference but in differences in socialization as well as discrimination.

Women's studies scholars began to use the terms sex (for biological characteristics) and gender (for nonphysiological aspects) to tease apart the roles of biology and socialization (Scott). The existence of these distinct terms and the recognition of the roles of both biology and socialization have helped to advance scholarly analysis in women's, gender, and sexuality studies.

However, as we have discussed, much of sex assignment is based on human values and judgments and so sex is not entirely biological, and gender (which may be influenced by biology) is probably not entirely socially or individually determined. What has this meant for scholars of sex and gender? Despite the blurring of the categories of sex and gender, we will continue to use the two terms because they have been useful terms for analysis. Whenever they appear, it may be helpful to imagine them as appearing in quotation marks. When we use the term sex we are referring to characteristics used to classify a person as female, male, intersex, or another category, which are *more* biological in their scope. And when we use the term gender, we are referring to the *less* physiological aspects of being feminine or masculine (or another category). Ultimately, we recognize that sex and gender as categories are not entirely distinct.

masculine fashion) are called butch. The terms are often also applied to men: butch to gender-conforming men and femme to gender-nonconforming men.

Doing Sex and Gender Across Cultures

Although researchers have identified similar concepts about sex and gender across many cultures, there is variation both within and between cultures, not only in what is considered female and male, feminine and masculine, but also in how sex and gender as categories work. Although most societies recognize two sexes and two genders (Nanda & Warms, 2010), some recognize four or even more social categories or groups based on what we call sex and gender (Gailey, 1987; Graham, 2004). The Bugis of Indonesia, for example, recognize five groups: *calabai'* (sex assigned male, identifies female), *calalai'* (sex assigned female, identifies male), *makunrai* (sex assigned female, identifies female), *oroane* (sex assigned male, identifies male), and *bissu* (sex assigned male, female, or ambiguous, considered to embody male and female elements) (Graham).

Some kinship societies (societies that use actual or perceived biological relations as the primary basis for ordering social relations) recognize four social groups based primarily on what we call sex: females of childbearing age, males of childbearing age, females before they are able to reproduce, and males before they are able to reproduce (Gailey). Each has its own gender roles. In other kinship societies, older people (beyond their reproductive years) are seen as outside what we might consider traditional notions of sex and gender. There are (or were) kinship societies where men traditionally do the cooking and routinely care for and play with infants (Gailey). There are also societies where women have taken on activities we mostly associate with men. Iroquois women, for example, decided whether the men would go to war and conducted the torture of male war captives (Gailey).

The Hua people (who live in the highlands of Papua New Guinea, which is north of Australia in the South Pacific Ocean) assign qualities that run contrary to dominant Western ways of thinking about sex and gender (femaleness, for example, is said to make one "invulnerable") and have more fluid expectations of how sex and gender work (females and males, for example, are said to switch sex and gender roles after their reproductive years). Although there is hierarchy within this system, women and men each exercise authority at different times in their lives (Gailey).

Multiple Femininities and Masculinities

Much recent scholarship examines the idea of multiple femininities and masculinities that exist not only across time and space but also within a "single cultural and temporal context" (Reeser, 2010, p. 3). R. W. Connell and James Messerschmidt (2005), researchers particularly interested in multiple masculinities, have posited that some masculinities are dominant and some subordinate and that different expectations about masculinity may be associated with different contexts and identities. So, a middle-class

MORE ABOUT...

Hua Society

The anthropologist Christine Gailey wrote about conceptions of sex and gender in Hua society that are contrary to Western notions. In Hua society, according to Gailey,

> people with large quantities of femaleness are invulnerable, but polluted, and thus dangerous; people with maleness have high status, but they are vulnerable. . . . All children are born at least partially female and polluted. Male children are given more masculine substance through growth rituals conducted by adult men. Girl children are seen as healthier and faster growing because they are female and less vulnerable.

Among adult Hua, wrote Gailey,

> Women lose their female substance through menstruation and childbirth. The Hua say men become pregnant if they eat certain red-colored foods or anything that has been touched by a menstruating woman. But men are vulnerable: Women can give birth safely; pregnancy in a man is fatal. By the time a woman has borne three children, she is effectively no longer polluted and is inducted into the men's society. She can then live in the men's house, take part in men's discussions and rituals. . . . Men lose their masculine substance through time, in the process of helping boys acquire masculinity. Older men become female . . . [and] work with the young married women in the fields, but they have little social authority. Older women have considerable say in social arrangements. (pp. 35–36)

Source: Gailey, C. W. (1987). Evolutionary Perspectives on Gender Hierarchy. In B. B. Hess & M. M. Ferree (Eds.), Analyzing Gender: A Handbook of Social Science Research (pp. 32–67). Newbury Park, CA: Sage.

male college professor might enact masculinity by displaying intellectual mastery of his subject area and using standard English as he lectures to his students, whereas a working-class male factory worker might enact masculinity by being tough, strong, and unemotional while on the job and using nonstandard English to talk with his fellow workers. (Working class refers to a person who has an income and social position below that of a middle-class person.) Indeed, the college professor and the factory worker may have different conceptions of what masculinity is; thus scholars also describe gender as "contested." Finally, scholars such as Jack Halberstam (1998) are interested in "alternative" ways of being gendered, including "female masculinity" and "male femininity," which challenge the dominant notion that sex entails gender.

Gender Ideology

A set of interrelated ideas about something (like masculinity or politics) is known as an ideology. Much work in women's, gender, and sexuality studies includes an exploration of **gender ideology**, which, drawing on Ronald Levant and colleagues (2007), we define as a set of interrelated, internalized cultural beliefs about gender. In Western society, gender ideology is often subdivided into masculinity ideology and femininity ideology.

Various scales have been developed to measure conformity to or endorsement of traditional masculinity ideology and femininity ideology (internalization of traditional cultural beliefs about masculinity and femininity, respectively.) We will briefly discuss two scales developed by Levant and colleagues.

The **Male Role Norms Inventory–Revised** measures seven norms of traditional masculinity:

1. Avoidance of femininity (e.g., a man should prefer action movies to romance novels)
2. Negativity toward sexual minorities (e.g., homosexuals should never marry)
3. Self-reliance through mechanical skills (a man should be able to fix most things around the house)
4. Toughness (a man should try to be physically tough even if he's not big)
5. Dominance (a man should always be the boss)
6. Importance of sex (a man should always be ready for sex)
7. Restrictive emotionality (men should not be too quick to tell others they care about them)
   (Levant et al., 2010)

Studies conducted in the United States have found that young, single males generally endorse traditional masculinity ideology to a greater degree than other groups. Some studies have also found that African Americans and Latinos "endorse traditional masculinity ideology to a greater extent" than European Americans (Levant & Richmond, 2007, p. 134). American men "endorse traditional masculinity ideology to a greater extent" than American women in all ethnic groups studied, and the effect of gender is larger than that of race (Levant & Richmond, p. 135). Cross-national studies have found that women and men in China, Russia, and Pakistan tended to endorse traditional masculinity ideology to a greater extent than women and men in the United States.

The researchers hypothesized that "these nation-level differences in endorsement of traditional masculinity ideology may reflect differences in gender empowerment between these countries" (i.e., relatively higher gender empowerment in the United States versus China, Russia, and Pakistan) (Levant et al., 2013, p. 229). The endorsement of traditional masculinity ideology has been found to be associated with a number of "problematic" variables, including "fear of intimacy, lower relationship satisfaction, more negative beliefs about the fathers' role" in child care, "negative attitudes toward racial diversity and women's equality," "self-reports of sexual aggression," and difficulty identifying and describing one's feelings (Levant & Richmond, p. 142). (To be clear, "to be associated with" is not the same as "to cause." "Associated with" simply means the two variables are related but does not imply that one has been proven to cause the other.)

The **Femininity Ideology Scale** measures five norms of traditional femininity:

1. Stereotypic image and activities (e.g., women should adhere to thin body ideals)
2. Dependence/deference (e.g., women should play a dependent role in relation to their husbands)
3. Purity (women should be chaste—or sexually pure—and play a passive sexual role)
4. Caretaking (motherhood should be woman's ultimate fulfillment)
5. Emotionality (women should have emotional affinity for domestic-related work and may be sensitive)
   (Levant et al., 2007)

In studies, the component of femininity ideology endorsed most strongly by both women and men is caretaking (the expectation that women will be the main caretakers for children and other family members) (Levant et al., 2007). More traditional femininity ideology has been associated with lower-body appreciation (more negative feelings about one's body) among young women, although more study is warranted (Swami & Abbasnejad, 2010).

Androgyny

Because Baby X appeared and acted in both feminine and masculine ways, Baby X could be called **androgynous**. The word androgyny comes from the Greek root *andr*, which means man or male, and the root *gyn*, meaning woman. Androgyny, then, is the state of having female and male characteristics,

Popular Culture's Embrace of Androgyny

A number of public figures across history have played with sex and gender and cultivated androgynous looks and mannerisms, from the female author George Sand in the 19th century to the actors Quentin Crisp and Marlene Dietrich in the mid-20th century to a whole slew of artists from the 1970s forward—David Bowie, Michael Jackson, Prince, Tilda Swinton, Adam Lambert, Milla Jovovich, and Lady Gaga, to name only a few. In the 1990s and 2000s, androgynous looks began to pop up increasingly often in ads and on runways and magazine covers. Ruth La Ferla (2009) asserted about self-consciously androgynous looks, "At one time, such artfully calibrated ambiguity might have been the expression of a renegade mind. Today it seems scarcely more subversive than wearing black, just the latest countercultural gesture to be tugged into the mainstream."

MORE ABOUT...

interests, etc. In this case, it does not mean to have biological sex characteristics of females and males at once (although in the field of biology and other contexts it can mean that as well); rather, it means to behave and/or appear in both feminine and masculine ways.

Most people probably conceive of gender as a continuum, with femininity and masculinity representing the poles and androgyny occupying the middle position. Bem (1993) argued that it is more helpful to view femininity and masculinity as independent attributes. That is, an individual can have both stereotypical feminine and masculine attributes at the same time. Because these attributes are independent of one another, an individual can be either high or low in femininity and high or low in masculinity. Individuals who are high in both measures are considered androgynous. Individuals who are low in terms of both measures are called undifferentiated. It is important to note that although Western society often assumes that masculinity and femininity are binary opposites (gender polarization), Bem's research has suggested that this is not actually the case. (To see how you score, take the Bem Sex Role Inventory at garote.bdmonkeys.net/bsri.html.)

Sex and Gender as Cognitive Schemas

When people perceive the world, they automatically take in the information that they perceive (often called sense data) and immediately begin to categorize it. If you see something fluttering through the air, you immediately try to categorize it—is it a butterfly? A leaf? When looks confound, we often press harder. Take the example of Andreja Pejic. When Andrej Pejic began modeling (identifying as a male), he had difficulty finding work because his looks were not easily identifiable as female or male. Pejic said, "No one knew whether they should put me on the women's boards or the men's boards. . . . There was a lot of uncertainty about my commercial viability" (Robehmed, 2014). Pejic ended up walking runways in both women's and men's wear before having sex reassignment surgery in 2014. Pejic, who changed her name to Andreja, now plans to model only women's wear. (In an ironic twist, Andreja will likely make more as a female model than Andrej did as a male model. Modeling is one of the few businesses where women are routinely paid more than men.)

Any system of categorization involves a mental system of organization known as a **cognitive schema**. Most societies use sex and gender as major cognitive schemas in their perception of the world. Not only are people schematized as female/male or feminine/masculine, but also other things can be organized according to these categories. For example, the color pink, butterflies, and cats are often schematized as feminine. This example illustrates Bem's (1981) statement that a schema is "a network of associations that organizes and guides an individual's perception" (p. 355). She also described a schema as an "anticipatory structure," meaning that when we identify certain attributes in something, we impose the schema on it (p. 355). So, for example, if we see an animal that is sufficiently catlike, we are likely to view it as feminine. Research has revealed that by the age of 2, children can usually identify themselves by the socially appropriate gender grouping, which shows that children use gender schematization to understand themselves (Devor).

Gender Roles

In the story of Baby X, Gould suggested that the sex of Baby X was irrelevant through most of childhood. By way of the story, Gould argued that by the time Baby X's sex mattered, it would become apparent through natural secondary sexual development. The parents of Baby X's classmates disagreed, however; they suggested that something was wrong with Baby X and that X be tested. Their belief was that Baby X should behave as either a girl *or* a boy is traditionally expected to behave (but not both). A set of social expectations about how one should appear and behave within a specific culture based on one's sex and gender is called a **gender role**.

As we have said, notions of gender and gender roles vary within and between cultures, although scholars have identified some general patterns that hold true across many sites globally. In the majority of cultures, for example, women have had greater responsibility for housework and child-rearing than men, and men have traditionally been considered the "breadwinners" in families. Researchers have also reported that many, if not all, societies assign characteristics and tasks using sex as a basis and accord men superior status to women. In fact, Best (2004) asserted that "in no society is the status of women superior to that of men" (p. 208).

Researchers classify beliefs about sex, gender, and gender roles along a continuum from what they term "traditional" to "modern." In this context, "traditional ideologies maintain that men are more 'important' than women and that it is appropriate for men to control and dominate women" (Best, 2002, p. 280). Conversely, modern ideologies maintain "that women and men are equally important, and dominance of one sex over the other is inappropriate" (Best, 2002, p. 280). Based on these definitions, studies by Williams and Best found the most modern ideologies in the Netherlands, Germany, Finland, and England and the most traditional ideologies in Nigeria, Pakistan, India, Japan, and Malaysia. The United States fell in the middle (Best, 2002). Best (2002) also noted that women generally have been found to have more "modern" views than men, but that women's and men's scores were similar in any single country. In other words, women's and men's beliefs within a country were more alike (in general) than women's beliefs (or men's) compared across cultures. Thus culture was found to have a greater effect than sex on one's beliefs about appropriate gender roles for women and men (Best, 2002).

Changing Ideas About Gender

Ideas about gender vary not only across the globe but also across time. Expectations of and roles played by women and men have changed dramatically even in the last half century. In the United States, for example, women now earn the majority of college degrees at all levels (associate's, bachelor's, master's, and doctor's) (National Center for Education Statistics, 2012). The number of American women working for pay has increased dramatically. In 1950, 18 million women in the United States were in the labor force. Today that number is around 72 million women who are working or actively seeking work (Bureau of Labor Statistics, 2012). The number of men who are stay-at-home dads has doubled in the past decade alone, but stay-at-home dads remain a small minority—3.4 percent of stay-at-home parents (U.S. Census Bureau, 2011). Another telling example: newspaper help-wanted ads as late as the 1960s were divided into jobs for women and jobs for men (Pedriana & Abraham, 2006). Today that is illegal. Researchers have also found that over the years more people have accepted women's rights, although women are still more likely to endorse egalitarianism than men (Steil, 2001).

Intersectionality

Ideas about and experiences of gender often vary significantly depending on race, ethnicity, class, sexual orientation, and sex (among other factors), as well as on the interplay among these factors. The idea that people's experiences are shaped by the convergence of these sorts of multiple factors in specific contexts and that a full understanding of people's lives requires the simultaneous analysis of these various elements is known as **intersectionality**. A good case in point is the advantages and disadvantages people face in the workplace based on sex and race. In the 1970s, research found that people who were in the extreme minority in their work situations (in this case, women who worked in overwhelmingly male workplaces or men who worked in female-dominated workplaces) had a harder time blending into their organizations and faced significant barriers to promotion (Kanter, 1977). Later studies refined these findings, showing that although women in male-dominated corporate settings were disadvantaged, men in female-dominated workplaces in fact had more opportunities, not less (a phenomenon labeled the "glass escalator") (C. Williams, 1992). Subsequent studies refined the results even further, showing that although white men often experienced significant advantages in female-dominated workplaces, men of color did not (Wingfield, 2009). What these results illustrated is that multiple factors are often at play in any given situation. In this example, considering gender and race and the interactions between the two changed the answers to the questions being asked. It would be interesting to add socioeconomic status to this picture as an additional variable and see what effect that might have. (Intersectionality is a complex notion with more facets than we have outlined here. We will discuss it in more detail in Chapter 3, "Gender and In/Equality," and Chapter 12, "Feminisms.")

Gender Identity

Some might argue that children should be encouraged to adopt the gendered behaviors traditional to their sex so that they can develop the appropriate **gender identity**. This seems to have been one of the concerns of the adults who were alarmed at Baby X's upbringing. Gender identity can be defined as one's perception of the gender that is appropriate to oneself. Traditionally, girls and women are expected to identify as feminine and boys and men are expected to identify as masculine. This is known as being sex-typed (Bem, 1981). A term that is used to describe people whose gender identity is in traditional alignment with their assigned sex at birth is **cisgender** (pronounced "sis" gender). Thus, a cisgender woman would view herself as feminine and a cisgender man would view himself as masculine. A related term is **gender expression** (or **gender presentation**), which is one's outward expression of gender, for example, how one dresses, the length of one's hair, the way one acts, moves, or speaks, and whether or how one wears or does not wear make-up.

Gender Nonconforming

There are a variety of ways to be **gender variant** or **gender nonconforming**—to have one's gender expression in nontraditional alignment with one's assigned sex at birth. These various identities are often covered by the umbrella term transgender. People who identify as transgender can include people of one sex who choose to take on the gender that society considers traditional or appropriate for another sex. Transgender people may or may not have sex reassignment surgery or hormonal treatment to bring their bodies more into traditional alignment with another sex. Laverne Cox and Caitlyn Jenner are two contemporary examples of prominent transgender people. Gender nonconformity encompasses a wide variety of practices, including heterosexual cross-dressing and gay drag (Currah, 2006; Stryker, 1994).

Increasingly, people recognize that gender is not a stable or unchanging marker of identity and reject binary notions about gender. These people may describe themselves as **genderqueer**, genderfluid, or pangender or by another identifier. Those who choose to "queer" gender, that is, express gender nonnormatively, may wish to stress the idea that one's gender can change over time or is constantly in flux. They often resist or reject the idea of gender as binary or even as an authentic category at all.

In light of this discussion, how do we refine or reform our definition of gender? A good beginning would be to recognize that gender is not necessarily an either/or proposition, a choice between feminine or masculine. Nor is it stable, either at the individual or at the societal levels. So today one could present oneself as feminine and tomorrow as masculine. Or one could reject established categories and adopt a nonnormative category—or none at all. Although gender is often described as the nonphysiological aspects of being feminine or masculine, a better descriptor, which recognizes the close ties between sex and gender, might be *less* physiological aspects related to femininity, masculinity, and other associated categories. Gender concerns ways of presenting oneself that are constructed and reconstructed through what one does, how one looks, how one behaves, etc.

The definition of gender, like gender itself (and sex, for that matter), is unstable and open to change. Trying to define categories like gender and sex presents us with the real problem inherent in categorization itself, that is, that categories are bound to fall short of capturing the complexity of real life.

BABY X: THE CONCLUSION

ON THE
web

Read about a Canadian family inspired by Baby X to raise their child without revealing the child's sex on the Student Website: www .oup.com/us/gillis-jacobs

At the conclusion of *X: A Fabulous Child's Story*, Baby X was tested to see whether s/he had suffered from her/his androgynous upbringing. After hours and hundreds of questions, the door opened. "Everyone crowded around to hear the results. X didn't look any different. . . . But the Psychiatrist looked terrible. He looked as if he was crying!" (Gould, p. 15). Wiping his eyes, he pronounced the verdict: young X is "just about the *least* mixed-up child I've ever Xamined" (p. 15, emphasis in original). Here Gould was clearly suggesting that not forcing children to conform to rigid gender binaries and traditional feminine and masculine gender roles not only was freeing, but also allowed children to develop their full, human potential.

Gould's fabulous story raises a number of interesting questions. Although it might seem impossible to do, would it be beneficial to raise an "X" instead of a "girl" or a "boy"? What would be learned in the process? Is sex innately linked to gender? Even if sex does not entail gender—that is, even if being a certain sex does not always require a person to have the traditionally accompanying gender—do people have a naturally occurring gender? In other words, is it possible that some boys are naturally more feminine and some girls naturally more masculine?

What effect would the masking of one's sex have on, say, second-grade crushes? Would such masking affect the development of sexual orientation? Would raising children androgynously and without the constraints of traditional gender roles give them more freedom to develop their human potential, as Gould suggested? Or would it lead to sex identity and gender identity "confusion" or even social chaos? The answers to these questions are complex and no doubt depend on many variables.

SEXUAL ORIENTATION

Whatever one's sex, sex identity, gender, or gender role, most people have a **sexual orientation**, which, for this chapter, will simply be defined as the attraction one has to others based on one's sex and/or gender in relation to another's sex and/or gender. Like sex, sexual orientation is more complicated and involves more than the binary, heterosexual and homosexual. It may be conceived of as a continuum with bisexuality in the middle, but there are other conceptions as well. More sophisticated conceptions of sexual orientation not only reject the heterosexual/homosexual binary but also reject sexual orientation as a static category (that is, reject it as unchanging over the course of people's lives).

There is also increasing recognition that some people are **asexual**. In biology, asexuality generally refers to a lack of sex-specific organs (that is, the lack of female or male sex organs), but in this context, asexuality refers to someone who "experiences little or no sexual attraction" to other people (AVEN, 2012). (Sexual orientation and asexuality will be discussed in Chapter 4.)

The prevailing view in gender studies is that being born with particular sex characteristics does not entail a particular sex identity, gender, gender identity, gender role, or sexual orientation. All of these qualities are independent of one another. As you can see from the chart below, a person could, for example, be assigned the male sex at birth, identify as a woman, undergo sex reassignment, live as a butch woman, and identify as a lesbian. The possible permutations are numerous, but to present just one more, a person could be assigned the female sex at birth, not undergo sex reassignment, live as a feminine woman, and

Sex, Gender, and Sexual Orientation

Here is the terminology for the sex, sex identity, gender, gender identity, and sexual orientation of a person who was "born" male (assigned male at birth), identifies as a woman, undergoes sex reassignment, lives as a butch woman, and identifies as a lesbian:

"Born" male
Identifies as a woman
Sex reassignment
Lives as a butch woman
Identifies as a lesbian

Assigned sex: male
Sex identity: female
Reassigned sex: female
Gender and gender identity: masculine/butch
Sexual orientation: lesbian

MORE ABOUT...

identify as a lesbian. It is important to recognize that different societies throughout history have expected and allowed different identities and roles and that individuals have often taken on various combinations of these identities and roles.

THIRD SEX / THIRD GENDER

Despite recent developments, generally in the West, one's sex is "supposed" to entail a particular gender, gender identity, gender role, and sexual orientation. Being female "requires" being feminine and taking on female gender roles, as well as being heterosexual; and being male requires being masculine and taking on male gender roles, as well as being heterosexual (Bem, 1993; Bohan, 1996; M. A. Gilbert, 2009). However, as we have seen, some societies do not have the same expectations. Some cultures have a category that in the past was

FIGURE 1.4
We'wha (WAY-wah), a Zuni Indian who lived during the latter half of the 1800s, was a two-spirit person, living outside Western conceptions of binary sex and gender.

called "berdache," in which individuals are allowed to go outside what we think of as the usual sex and gender boundaries. Because berdache is now recognized as offensive to many who have been labeled as such (S. E. Jacobs et al., 1997), many are now using the term **third sex** (or **third gender**) as an umbrella term for people across various cultures who go outside usual (normative) sex and gender boundaries (see, for example, Herdt, 1994; Littlewood, 2002). As Herdt stated, "the code of 'thirdness' should not be taken literally to mean that in all times and places there are only three categories possible in human classification. . . . the third is emblematic of other possible combinations that transcend" sex and gender binaries (pp. 19–20). People within the third sex category are also sometimes referred to as transgender (Currah).

Many Native American tribes within the United States and First Nations within Canada have or had such a category. In these cases, women and men sometimes took on gender role duties traditional to the other sex. A person whose assigned sex at birth was female could live as a man and sometimes even take a wife, or a person whose assigned sex at birth was male could live as a woman and sometimes take a husband. Roscoe (1994) argued that in American Indian nations, such people occupied distinct third ("men" who lived as "women") and fourth ("women" who lived as "men") gender categories. Roscoe stated that females who became fourth gender performed roles that were usually not mirror images of males who became third gender. Because these roles were different for those assigned female and male at birth, Roscoe argued Native people conceived third and fourth sex categories as two distinct genders in Native culture. Generalizations about a third sex/third gender within Native American cultures are difficult to make because the roles vary or varied from tribe to tribe.

Sometimes people choose to live as a third sex/third gender because they feel more comfortable in that role and sometimes circumstances may require the gender transformation. In Albania, there has been a practice, now nearly extinct, where females take on the gender role of males in families where there is no male. These females are known as *virgjinesha*, sworn virgins (Figure 1.5; Littlewood). Because Albanian society had rigid gender expectations, males were expected to provide for and protect the family. If there was no male to perform these functions, a female was sometimes selected to undergo the transformation to maleness, not through sex reassignment, but by adopting a masculine gender role. The girl or woman would dress as a male, do the work of a male, be referred to as a male, and socialize as a male. She would also swear to abstain from sex; hence the term sworn virgin. Young (2000) estimated that there were approximately 100 *virgjinesha* alive in mostly Northern Albania in

FIGURE 1.5

Qamile Stema was assigned female at birth and has taken on the gender role and identity of a man. Known as "uncle," he is wearing a *qeleshe*, a white cap traditionally worn by Albanian men.

2000 (the youngest was in his twenties when Young met him). However, it seems girls are no longer becoming sworn virgins. (Hijras are also often included in discussions of third sex/third gender. We will discuss hijras in Chapter 5, "Constructions of Homosexualities.")

Modern Native people in North America often use the phrase **two-spirit** to describe third sex people. This term was coined by Native American people at the third Native American/First Nations gay and lesbian conference in Winnipeg in 1990 (S. E. Jacobs et al.). It is an English term and not a translation of a tribe-specific third sex name. Two-spirit serves as an umbrella term that includes contemporary Native people who identify as lesbian or gay, Native people who

Native American Third Sex/Third Gender

The scholar and activist Will Roscoe has written extensively on Native American third sex/third gender people, as well as on non-Native homosexuality. Here is his overview of the features of the third sex/third gender category among Native Americans:

Male berdaches have been documented in nearly 150 North American societies. In nearly half of these groups, a social status also has been documented for females who undertook a man's life-style. . . .

The key features of male and female berdache roles were, in order of importance, productive specialization (crafts and domestic work for male berdaches and warfare, hunting and leadership roles in the case of female berdaches), supernatural sanction (in the form of authorization, and/or bestowal of powers from extrasocietal sources) and gender variation (in relation to normative cultural expectations for male and female genders). In the case of gender variation, cross-dressing was the most common and visible marker, but it has proven a more variable and less reliable indicator of berdache status than previously assumed . . . in some tribes male berdaches dressed distinctly from both men and women. In other cases, berdaches did not cross dress at all, or only partly. In the case of female berdaches, cross dressing was even more variable. Often, female berdaches wore men's clothes only when hunting or participating in warfare.

The sexual behavior of male and female berdaches was also variable . . . the partners of berdaches were usually non-berdache members of the same sex—that is, berdaches were homosexual, if we define the term narrowly in terms of behavior and anatomy. Some berdaches, however, appear to have been bisexual or heterosexual. (pp. 330–335)

Source: Roscoe, W. (1994). How to Become a Berdache: Toward a Unified Analysis of Gender Diversity. In Herdt, G. (Ed.). Third Sex, Third Gender: Beyond Sexual Dimorphism in Culture and History (pp. 329–372). New York, NY: Zone Books.

MORE ABOUT...

identify as belonging to contemporary Native gender categories, Native people who identify as belonging to traditional Native third sex categories, people who identify as belonging to third sex categories beyond Native American culture, and people who identify as transgender (Jacobs et al.). Two-spirit people may be conceived of as not being female or male (whatever sex organs or secondary sex characteristics they may or may not possess). They may also be conceived of as occupying a gender and gender role beyond feminine and masculine.

CONCLUSION

The fictional story of Baby X's androgynous upbringing raises questions about the connection between sex and gender (and illustrates the anxieties that androgyny can produce). Perhaps the most central question it raises is the degree to which we are shaped by biology and by socialization. Proper exploration of both this and other questions (and related anxieties) requires an understanding of basic terminology including sex, assigned sex, intersex, sex identity, gender, gender roles, and sexual orientation.

Our exploration of intersex reveals that even sexual categorization is a social construction. Our introduction to gender indicates that although people tend to think of gender as polarized with feminine and masculine as the only socially appropriate options that entail certain gender scripts, insights from the fields of psychology and anthropology reveal much greater variation in the world.

Ideas about gender are not isolated from other beliefs but are embedded in broader ways of thinking about society. The research on traditional and modern gender ideologies indicates that views about gender tend to be heavily influenced by one's culture rather than being the outgrowth of individual thinking on the issue. Because gender roles vary not only across cultures and time but also within cultures, intersectional analysis of gender based on a variety of axes such as race, class, and sexual orientation is critical for a full understanding of how gender operates in the world. Last, it is important to recognize that sex, sex identity, gender, gender identity, and sexual orientation are free-floating categories and that identification with one category does not entail any particular identification with another category.

 THINK, LEARN, ACT

The following resources are available on the Student Website: www.oup.com/us /gillis-jacobs

Taking Stock, Taking Action prompts and activities. Apply what you've learned to take action on campus and in the broader community.

Recommended Readings and Multimedia Resources, including scholarly and literary works, documentaries, feature films, podcasts and more, to enrich the in- and out-of-classroom experience.

2

LANGUAGE AND COMMUNICATION

Here is a riddle: one afternoon a man and his son go for a drive through the country. After an hour or so they get into a terrible car crash. The father dies instantly. The son is taken by helicopter to the nearest hospital, where a prominent surgeon is called in to help save the boy's life. Immediately on entering the operating room and looking at the boy, the surgeon exclaims, "I can't possibly operate on this boy . . . he's my son!"

Who is the surgeon?

This riddle is fairly old—perhaps dating to the 1960s—although we do not know exactly when or where it originated (Coontz, 2013b; Padavic & Reskin, 2002; Paludi, 2004). Perhaps you have heard it before or perhaps you figured out an answer easily.

In 2012, the researchers Mikaela Wapman and Deborah Belle posed the riddle to Boston University students, many of whom were flummoxed by the question and some of whom reached for "inventive" answers: the "father" in the car was actually a priest, the surgeon was confused, the scenario was a dream (Barlow,

2014). Among the students, only 14 percent answered that the surgeon was the boy's mother. More students in fact answered that the surgeon was the boy's second gay father than that she was his mother (Barlow).

What made imagining a female surgeon so difficult? The wording of the riddle itself may steer you off course because the language refers only to males (man, son, father, boy, he). Perhaps this nudges you to think "male" rather than female. But the researchers concluded that the biggest factor was the way stereotypes of women and men tend to shape our thinking about the world (Barlow). Although we "know" women can be surgeons, the predominant image—the stereotype—is that surgeons (and doctors more generally) are men. So the possibility of a female surgeon does not come easily to us. Nor does the idea of a male nurse, apparently. When the researchers presented a different version of the riddle, a mother is killed, her daughter is sent to the hospital, and a nurse declines to attend the patient because "that girl is my daughter," only a few people guessed that the nurse was the child's father (Barlow).

Not being able to answer an old riddle may seem trivial, but the difficulty many have with this particular riddle illuminates the power of the sex and gender binaries to shape what and how we think (and do not think). The ways we think about sex and gender influence many aspects of our lives, including the language we use and the ways we communicate. But the reverse is also true: the ways we use language and communicate also influence how we (can) think about sex and gender. In this chapter, we will be examining the complex relationships that exist among language, communication, gender, and sex and the ways that language and communication both reflect and produce gender in Western society. We will also be looking at a variety of other intersections that affect communication, most prominently socioeconomic class.

WHAT LANGUAGE REVEALS, CONCEALS, AND IMPOSES

What can conventions of grammar and terminology reveal about gender in society? Let's take the example of the use of the **generic he** or universal he by English speakers. What is the generic he? Suppose there is a student in a gender studies class and he wants to write a paper on gender and language. In the previous sentence, the nonspecific student could be female or male, but the default pronoun is male (he). Although the generic he may be falling out of favor (major style guides such as those produced by the American Psychological Association and the Modern Language Association recommend against using it), many English speakers continue to deploy it. The style guides counsel rewriting to avoid needing a singular pronoun, an answer that works much but not all of the time. Another strategy for avoiding the generic he is to replace it with "he or she," but many people object to this usage because they find it awkward—and note that even the substitution he or she places "he" first. Still another alternative is to substitute the plural "they," although this often means tolerating what is still considered by many incorrect grammar (a mismatch of a singular antecedent and a plural pronoun as in *a person writes a women's studies paper and they choose a language topic*"). (We have used "they" in place of "he or she" in the text.)

The generic he is not the only male-focused element of language. The words "man," "men," or "mankind" are similarly male centered. Neil Armstrong, in his famous moon landing statement, "That's one small step for [a] man, one giant leap for mankind," presumably meant to include women as well, but his language was gendered (E. M. Jones, 1995; Kaplan, 2013). Similarly, the word "guy" is often used colloquially (informally) to refer to both females and males—as in "Come on guys!" or "Hi guys!" These sorts of sex-specific terms that are supposed to apply to people regardless of sex are called **male generic terms** (J. T. Wood, 2013). **Gender-neutral terms** include people, humanity,

FIGURES 2.1 and 2.2
"People Working" is a gender-neutral alternative to the traditional "Men Working" sign.

or humankind. The word man can also be found in names for professions ending in the suffix -man (e.g., policeman, fireman, mailman). A number of gender-neutral words can be substituted for each of these names, including police officer, firefighter, and postal worker. (At this point it is worth pointing out that, strictly speaking, these gender-neutral alternatives are actually *sex*-neutral alternatives, given the distinction we made between sex and gender in Chapter 1. The term "gender-neutral language" was created before the distinction between sex and gender as used in this text caught on in academic circles and it is likely that the term gender-neutral will continue to be used despite this inconsistency.)

One recent survey showed that the use of at least some sexist language has decreased since 1970 and the use of some nonsexist language has increased sharply (Earp, 2012). In this case, the researcher looked specifically at the use of the word mankind, which decreased, and the use of the word "humankind," which increased, in academic and popular writing since 1970. However, despite this trend, mankind continued to be used more often than humankind in the samples studied. The researcher also compared the use of the generic he pronoun and the use of the phrase he or she in academic and popular writing from the same time period. Again, the use of the generic he pronoun decreased, whereas the use of the phrase he or she increased. However, as with mankind, the use of generic he continued to outrank the use of the phrase he or she. So, although the use of nonsexist language seems to be advancing, it does not seem to have yet caught up with the use of male generic terms.

Why the fuss over male gendered language? If speakers default to using the generic he, it seems reasonable that when they picture a generic person in their mind's eye, they picture a male. It is, for example, possible to imagine someone trying to puzzle out the answer to the riddle we posed at the beginning of the chapter and saying, "Who could *he* be?" Linguistic research also shows that people who encounter he/man generic terms "are more likely to think of *male* human beings as the referents of those terms" (Earp, p. 6). Thus, asserted the cognitive scientist Brian Earp, sexist language has "the effect of minimizing women's importance and diverting attention away from their very existence" (p. 6). In other words, the use of male generic terms **elides** females. To elide is "to strike out, suppress or pass over in silence" (OED). It also seems to encourage more sex-typed thinking. In a related finding, subjects have been found to think about the appropriateness of particular careers for female and male candidates in more sex-stereotyped ways after exposure to sexist language (Earp).

Gender-Neutral Pronoun *Yo* Emerges in Baltimore

In 2004, several Baltimore, Maryland, school teachers reported that many of their students were using *yo* as a gender-neutral pronoun. Further research by Elaine M. Stotko and Margaret Troyer (2007) found that students would use *yo* in the following kinds of sentences:

Yo handin' out papers = She (the teacher) is handing out papers.

Peep yo! = Look at him!

Yo wearing a new coat = She's wearing a new coat

The students came from schools that were almost entirely African American. Some African Americans (and some people from other ethnic groups) speak a form of English known as African American Vernacular English (AAVE), which is also known as Black English or Ebonics. The researchers did not say that *yo* was unique to AAVE, but when sample sentences were consistent with AAVE grammar, students found the use more acceptable.

Many attempts have been made to introduce gender-neutral pronouns into English in a top-down way but none has gained general acceptance. It is significant that a gender-neutral pronoun has emerged spontaneously within urban Baltimore.

MORE ABOUT...

The Primacy of Males and Masculine Terms

Even when language includes females, terms for women and girls usually follow after those for men and boys. Usually we speak of "men and women," "boys and girls," or "males and females," rather than the reverse order of "women and men," etc. This seems to reflect a deeper theme in Western culture of the primacy of males, that is, "the state of being first in order, rank, importance or authority" (OED). The primacy of males is even found in the first book of the Bible, Genesis. First, God created man; then He created the animals; and finally He created woman out of the rib of man as a helper for him (Gen. 2).

Not everyone who uses the traditional ordering of male and female intends to suggest that females are secondary in importance (and some would object to interpreting Genesis as suggesting this). However, like the generic he, one could argue that there is a subtle but important effect in always giving males precedence.

Simone de Beauvoir (1949/1989) contended that Western society conceives of males as the norm or primary and females as the **second sex**. "Humanity is male and man defines woman not in herself but as relative to him," wrote de Beauvoir (p. xxi).

De Beauvoir asserted that because men are the primary sex, "the Subject," women become "incidental . . . inessential," (p. xxii); women are the **other**, the group that exists in opposition to the norm, the group that exhibits difference. By contrast, men are **unmarked**. An unmarked category is a group that is conceived of as the norm and lacks distinguishing characteristics (Brekhus, 1998). So, when it comes to sex, men are "normal" or "regular people" (unmarked) and women are conceived of as "different" or outside the norm (**marked**).

The pervasive conception of males as the norm has far-reaching consequences. Consider, for example, that prior to 1994, women were routinely excluded from

MORE ABOUT...

He and She in Mandarin

In Mandarin Chinese, the spoken pronoun *tā* is gender neutral, referring to she, he, or it. The written word for *tā*, however, has feminine and masculine forms (and a different form for "it").

The written form of "she" contains two characters: the character 女 on the left, which means "female," and the character 也 on the right, which means "also." Together 女 (female) + 也 (also) = 她 (she).

If the written form of "he" were parallel to the written form of she, one would expect he to contain the character for "male" on the left (男) and the character for also (也) on the right. But the two are not parallel. Instead, the written form of he contains the character 亻 on the left, which means person, and, as expected, the character 也 (also) on the right. So, together 亻 (person) + 也 (also) = 他 (he).

Thus, in written Mandarin, she is marked as female but he is unmarked, simply a "person."

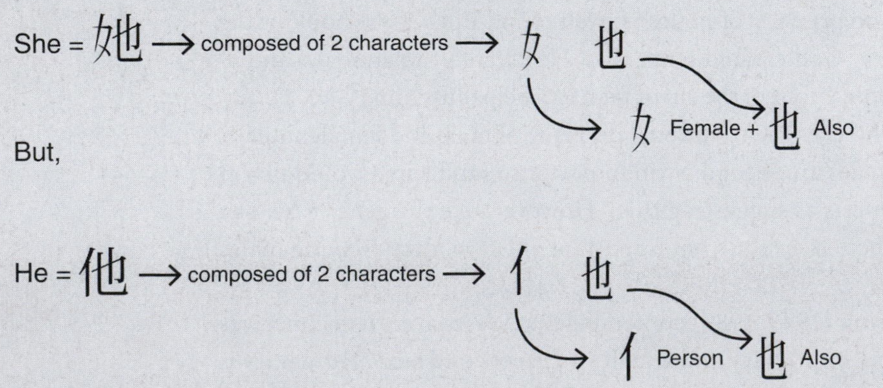

She = 她 → composed of 2 characters → 女 也 → 女 Female + 也 Also

But,

He = 他 → composed of 2 characters → 亻 也 → 亻 Person → 也 Also

FIGURE 2.3

early studies of most drugs (because their physiology differed from that of men). Recent analyses show that despite new laws to ensure women's participation in medical studies, "significant barriers" to the inclusion of women in clinical trials persist (Holdcroft, 2007, p. 2). Even when it comes to animal-model research, male animals are mostly used (Beery & Zucker, 2011; Pitts & Phillips, 1998). It seems possible that viewing males as the norm has led to what is called male-only thinking and caused the elision of females in scientific investigations. This kind of thinking may also be called **androcentric** (from the Greek "andro," or male), meaning focused on males or men. Female-focused thinking is called **gynocentric** (from the Greek "gyne," female or women).

One could argue that the generic he and other elements of language use reinforce the unmarked status of men and reinforce the markedness or othering of women. Many groups are unmarked in Western society. For example, being middle class is perceived as the norm and frequently we assume people in generic examples are just "regular" middle-class people. Other unmarked categories include being white, able-bodied, Christian, heterosexual, and from the Western world. Those who are other, then, include those who are beyond these categories: people of color, people with dis/abilities, people of different religious beliefs (or no religious belief), gay people, and/or people from different parts of the world (to name just a few categories).

FIGURE 2.4
Simone de Beauvoir (1908–1986), a feminist and philosopher, published *The Second Sex* in 1949, in which she sought to answer the question, "How is it that this world has always belonged to the men . . . ?" (p. xxvii).

The Sex and Gender of Things

As we discussed in Chapter 1, we use cognitive schemas to organize our experience of the world and these cognitive schemas are reflected in our language. Sex and gender are pervasive concepts and important schemas that influence many aspects of our lives. Naming and schematizing our experience of the world not only helps us understand the world but also actually shapes how we experience the world; thus it is important to explore how the schemas of sex and gender permeate our language.

One important schema for English speakers is the schema of sex. English speakers use the singular subject pronouns she, he, and it when referring to people and objects. She or he is used when referring to a person (and

recap of terms:
Cognitive Schemas

Any system of categorization involves a mental system of organization known as a **cognitive schema**. Most societies use sex and gender as major cognitive schemas in their perception of the world. Not only are people schematized as female/male or feminine/masculine, but also other things can be organized according to these categories. For example, the color pink, butterflies, and cats are often schematized as feminine. This example illustrates Bem's (1981) statement that a schema is "a network of associations that organizes and guides an individual's perception" (p. 355). She also described a schema as an "anticipatory structure," meaning that when we identify certain attributes in something, we impose the schema on it (p. 355). So, for example, if we see an animal that is sufficiently catlike, we are likely to view it as feminine.

From Chapter 1, "Sex, Gender, and Social Construction."

Pronouns -- A How to Guide

Subject: ___1___ laughed at the notion of a gender binary.

Object: They tried to convince ___2___ that asexuality does not exist.

Possessive: ___3___ favorite color is unknown.

Possessive Pronoun: The pronoun card is ___4___.

Reflexive: ___1___ thinks highly of ___5___.

The pronoun list on the reverse is not an exhaustive list.
It is good practice to ask which pronouns a person uses.

© 2011 UW-Milwaukee LGBT Resource Center

1	2	3	4	5
e/ey	em	eir	eirs	eirself
he	him	his	his	himself
[name]	[name]	[name]'s	[name]'s	[name]'s self
per	per	pers	pers	perself
she	her	her	hers	herself
sie	sir	hir	hirs	hirself
they	them	their	theirs	themself
ve	ver	vis	vers	verself
zie	zim	zir	zirs	zirself

FIGURE 2.5

Pocket-size guide to gender-neutral pronouns (LGBT Resource Center, University of Wisconsin, Milwaukee). Although gender-neutral pronouns in English have proven most popular on college campuses, in Sweden the gender-neutral pronoun "hen" has been adopted by a broad swath of Swedish society.

some objects), whereas it is used for an object (but generally not for people; such usage is considered dehumanizing). The fact that people are traditionally thought of as female (she) or male (he) underscores the importance of the sexual binary (that is, our tendency to think of female and male as in opposition to one another or as "opposite" sexes). In English, there simply are not any widely accepted ways to schematize people other than in the polarized schemas of female and male (and gender binaries of feminine and masculine). However, if you speak a language other than English, you may be aware that not all languages use gendered pronouns. For example, Azerbaijani, Basque, Finnish, Hindi, Hungarian, and Swahili all have the same pronouns for she and he. The existence of languages with gender-neutral pronouns offers up the possibility of other ways of schematizing English pronouns.

Not only are people gendered, but also even language more generally can be gendered. Latin nouns are masculine, feminine, or neuter, and Romance languages descended from Latin such as French and Spanish have gendered words. In English, some nouns are gendered; boats and cars are referred to as she. We use the expressions "mother country" and "mother earth," and one's college is called one's "alma mater" (meaning "nourishing mother" in Latin). The femininity of the latter words seems to be tied to the nurturing capacity of these things.

Connectors and fasteners such as those used in electrical and plumbing work are often designated female and male. Male electrical plugs go into female sockets and male threaded pipes screw into female threaded pipes. Sigmund Freud (1933/1994) noted that we generally conceive of masculinity as fundamentally about being active and femininity as fundamentally about being passive and that this thinking is an extension of our conception of heterosexual intercourse involving males as penetrators and females as penetrated. It is worth noting that although Freud (1933/1994) recognized that this schematization was embedded in Western culture, he himself believed it was a mistake to view males as fundamentally more active than females.

Freud's (1933/1994) observation suggests that of the binary pairs of stereotypical traits discussed in Chapter 1, the active/passive distinction is particularly powerful in shaping people's experience of sex and gender. Frequently this

Female Names for Soldiers' Guns

What about the practice of some soldiers in U.S. boot camps giving their weapons female names? This seems to contradict the cultural logic of feminine objects as nurturing, but perhaps it can be explained by the need for soldiers to be especially attentive to the maintenance of their weapons. The traditionally male soldier would thus see himself as a male protector or provider—a traditionally masculine role. This might also explain the use of the phrase, "she's a beauty," which is often used to refer to equipment that is traditionally maintained by men. This phrase also captures the sense that feminine things are objects that one can admire.

This is not meant to deny the fact that guns often function as phallic symbols (symbols representing or resembling a penis)—and giving a phallic symbol a female name seems peculiar. Perhaps this simply highlights the fact that the logic of symbolism has its limits and does not always yield a consistent system.

MORE ABOUT...

distinction is expressed by the idea that masculinity is about doing or acting and that femininity is about being or being acted on. (This conception of masculinity and femininity will be discussed further in Chapter 7, "Embodiment, Beauty, and the Viewer.")

Parallel Language

Sometimes the difficulty with our language is not in the built-in gendering of language, but in the way we use language. For example, many gendered words have **parallel terms**—words that are equivalent for females and males, such as "ladies" and "gentlemen." In movies and on television, drill sergeants and sports coaches sometimes derisively call their male charges ladies. Yet, if a drill sergeant or coach called a group of women gentlemen, which is the parallel masculine term, it would be nonsensical as a put-down. This suggests that parallel terms are sometimes parallel in terms of denotation (the literal meaning of a word) but not in terms of connotation (the suggested or associated meaning apart from its literal meaning). What are the associations we have with the term "lady?" Contextually, we can infer that ladies are feminine in the negative sense of being less capable and fragile (see Lakoff, 1975). Not everyone shares the view that lady has negative connotations. Connotations are, after all, associations people have with words, and not everyone makes the same associations; but it does appear that the words lady and gentleman are often used asymmetrically.

Another example of nonparallel usage involves the phrase "guys and girls." In college, people often refer to students as guys and girls rather than using the parallel terms, "boys and girls." Undoubtedly this is the case because the phrase boys and girls makes college students sound like little children when they are not. And no one uses the alternative parallel phrase, "guys and gals," because it sounds dated. The trouble with using guys together with girls in this context is that they are not parallel terms. A guy can be of almost any age. You could say "Hi little guy!" to a 2-year-old boy or refer to a 90-year-old man as "that guy." By contrast, a girl is, by definition, a child. Particularly for women, who are often valued in society based on their youthfulness, there can be a downside to moving away from being referred to as a girl, but it does seem preferable (at least to us) for college women to claim their status as adults (with the power and authority it confers) rather than be referred to as girls (Lakoff).

Some of the most striking asymmetries in language can be seen in derogatory terms that are gendered. The gendered put-down "slut," for example, seems to lack a meaningful parallel term. Students sometimes suggest "stud" as the parallel term, but this word has a positive connotation, whereas slut is entirely negative. Another possible parallel term is "male slut" (which seems to be gaining strength as a term of derision for males), but by tacking on the word male, this term implies that being a slut is essentially a feminine quality that occasionally applies to males. Asymmetries in derogatory language suggest that one group is vulnerable to negative labeling, whereas another group is less vulnerable. The slut/stud asymmetry is a case in point; women are more vulnerable to charges of sexual promiscuity than men.

FIGURE 2.6

Mr., Miss, Mrs., and Ms.

Another case of nonparallelism involves Mr., Miss, and Mrs. The title Mr. (which was an abbreviation of "master") is applied to both married and unmarried men (C. Miller & Swift, 1976). Miss, originally an abbreviation of "mistress" (which originally referred to the female master of the house), has come to mean an unmarried woman (C. Miller & Swift, 1976). Mrs. was also originally an abbreviation of mistress, but is now used solely for married women. Once again, we see that Miss and Mrs. are not parallel to Mr. The use of Mr. reveals no information about marital status, whereas Miss and Mrs. do (Lakoff). Put bluntly, information is power. Why should titles reveal the marital status of women but not of men? This can be particularly problematic when women go for job interviews. Employers may be reluctant to hire a woman who is unmarried, thinking she will soon get married and quit. Employers may also be reluctant to hire a married woman, thinking her career may come second to her spouse and that she may have primary responsibility for child care, which may interfere with her career. Although discriminating against an employee on the basis of marital status is illegal, it is often a concern. The use of Ms. avoids drawing attention to marital status and puts women on the same footing as men, who do not reveal their marital status with the title of Mr.

Spanish is the third most spoken language in the world (counting second-language speakers) behind Mandarin Chinese and English ("Chinese, Mandarin," 2015; "English," 2015; "Spanish," 2015). In Spanish there is no widely used equivalent of Ms. The honorific "Señorita" (abbreviated Srta.) is used as the equivalent of Miss (Vega, 2010). "Señora" (abbreviated Sra.) is traditionally used for married women and is equivalent to Mrs. (Vega). Interestingly, Google Translate provides "Sra. García" as the translation for Ms. Garcia (February 11, 2015). Miranda Stewart (1999) noted that the abbreviation "Sa." was proposed as the Spanish equivalent to Ms., but it does not appear to have caught on.

FIGURE 2.7

A campaign in France to eliminate the use of "mademoiselle" (used for single women) has been successful in removing the term from government forms. The honorific "madame" (traditionally used for married women) will be used for all women to parallel the use of "monsieur" for all men.

LANGUAGE, COMMUNICATION, AND SEMANTIC CHANGE

It may seem strange, but in the 7th century the daughter of an English monarch was described as "a wonderful man" (C. Miller & Swift, 2000). In 1597, Bishop John King stated that Adam and Eve were the only people in the Garden of Eden by saying, "The Lord had but one paire of men in paradise" (OED). Although these references seem odd today, the word man was

ON THE web

Read about the **origin and evolution of the term Ms.** on the Student Website: www.oup.com/us/gillis-jacobs

FIGURE 2.8
The first regular issue of *Ms.* was published in July 1972, "the first national magazine to make feminist voices audible, feminist journalism tenable, and a feminist worldview available to the public" ("Her Story: 1971 – Present," n.d., para. 8). Gloria Steinem was a founding editor.

originally a generic word meaning person or human being. In Old English, *wer* meant an adult male and *wif* meant adult female (although the Oxford English Dictionary states that the *were* in werewolf is probably unrelated). *Waepman* meant adult male person and *wifman* meant adult female person. *Wifman* became the modern word "woman" and also gave rise to the word "wife." As part of this shift, man was no longer used to refer to a woman (C. Miller & Swift, 2000).

These shifts highlight the fact that words do not have universal or permanent meanings but undergo **semantic change**. That is, words develop new meanings and associations and also lose old meanings and associations. Additionally, new words are coined to carry new meanings or replace old words. There is a saying in the field of communication studies that meanings are in people, not in words, implying that words can mean different things depending on who says them and the context in which they are said. The Russian philosopher and semiotician Mikhail Bakhtin (1929/1990) argued that to understand what and how words mean, we must examine the way they are actually used rather than viewing them abstractly. Words, according to Bakhtin, are imbued or infused with meaning by the relationship between a speaker (or writer) and a listener (or reader) as they are found in a particular context.

At this point it is worth pointing out that most of this chapter has been an exploration of **language**. Adler et al. (2012) defined language as "a collection of symbols, governed by rules, and used to convey messages between individuals" (p. 98). We have analyzed a number of symbols (such as the generic he, Mrs., man) and examined the rules for their usage. Our discussion is now shifting from an account of language to a discussion of **communication**, which can be defined as "the process of creating meaning through symbolic interaction" (Adler et al., p. 5). As Bakhtin pointed out, "a word is a bridge thrown between myself and another" (p. 933). Meaning is not found in the word, but is created through our understanding of one another within a particular context. For example, the word "queer" originally meant "strange, odd, peculiar, eccentric. Also: of questionable character; suspicious, dubious" (OED) and then was used to refer, usually in a derogatory way, to people who were homosexual. Today, queer is still used as a slur for gay people but it has also been appropriated (that is, taken possession of for one's own) by some in the gay community as a neutral term and even a term of pride (OED). How does one know whether queer is meant as an insult or a badge of pride? The word may be read as a badge of pride if speakers mark themselves as gay; if the audience identifies as queer; if the context involves positive statements about gay pride; and/or if any number of other features of the speaker or speaker's language or audience or situation cues the word queer as positively inflected. (And, of course, any of the previous elements may be present but still fail to clearly mark the word as positive. Cues in any communicative situation are vastly more rich and subtle than our ability to lay them out for examination in a paragraph like this one). Put simply, how one appropriately interprets the use of queer depends on more contextual variables (and individual interpretation) than we can spell out in advance.

The case of the use of queer underscores the linguistic idea that there are no "bad words" in the sense that words cannot be intrinsically bad. Words are only bad in context. This does not mean that we should not be careful with words—indeed, just the opposite is often the case. So many elements go into creating meaning that misinterpretation is easy—especially when it comes to charged subjects such as sexual orientation, sex, and race. The word queer is just one example of a multilayered term that may be deployed and interpreted in a variety of ways. (See Appendix B, Names for People and Places for a more detailed discussion of naming and definitions for a variety of terms.)

Appropriation of Stigmatized Names

Although replacing a stigmatized name (a name marked by disgrace) with a euphemism (a mild, agreeable, or inoffensive word) can be an effective strategy to improve the status of a group, some groups choose a different tactic: appropriating the stigmatized name as a badge of honor, as with the word queer, which we discussed above. "Dyke" is also a word that has been appropriated by some lesbians. Michel Foucault (1978/1980) referred to this kind of oppositional way of naming and valuing things as a **reverse discourse**. Another example is the word "bitch," which has been appropriated by the magazine *Bitch*, which advocates for women. The publishers of *Bitch* note on their website, "We know that not everyone's down with the term. . . . But we stand firm in our belief that if we choose to reappropriate the word, it loses its power to hurt us. And if we can get people thinking about what they're saying when they use the word, that's even better" (Bitchmedia, 2015). Although these kinds of appropriations are often described as "reclaiming" stigmatized identities with the goal of wiping away the stigma of the name, it seems more accurate to say that often these appropriations derive their force from the very existence of the derogatory usage. The power of calling oneself queer or a dyke or a bitch stems precisely from identifying with and valuing the outsider status

FIGURE 2.9

A young woman demonstrating the reclamation of stigmatized words often used to blame victims of rape. SlutWalks featuring such language have become a global phenomenon. (See Additional Resources: Nonfiction/Scholarly Works on the Student Website for more on the SlutWalk controversy.)

associated with the stigmatized identity. The appropriated use, then, actually requires the existence of the derogatory use to have force as an oppositional identity (A. T. Jacobs, 2002). Appropriation of stigmatized names is often controversial and may be supported by some within a group, but opposed by others. There is no way to judge this method as "right" or "wrong" and in fact it may be both—at once.

Communication and Reception Theory

Given our discussion, it is clear that language use shifts over time. It is also true that language use varies across places and groups and even within groups, where members sometimes disagree about language (for example, whether it is desirable to appropriate stigmatized terms). This brings us to another important facet of how language works: communication theorists recognize that ultimately all symbols, including names, are arbitrary. There is no necessary connection between a name and the person or thing named (de Saussure, 1916/1966). As we have said, words in themselves do not carry meaning.

Meanings exist in people, and those meanings develop through the context of their use. If we use a word like queer in an insulting context, the word is likely to be received as an insult. If others label themselves queer in a context that suggests pride in the identity, it is likely to be received as a positive name. To complicate things even further, different groups may receive the name differently depending on their perspective. Communication theorists often speak of meaning as being co-created by senders and receivers. The study of how symbols or messages are received is sometimes known as **reception theory**.

To broaden our discussion, recall that our definition of communication includes not only written and spoken words but also any "symbolic interaction," so communication also includes other forms of symbolic interaction such as signed languages, fashion, movement, painting, and music (Zeshan, 2002).

Because symbolic communication beyond words is so important for women's and gender studies, let's look at one kind of symbol: hair. Among Black women, wearing hair in a particular style can be an important statement concerning fashion and identity. For African American women who have tightly curled hair (often called kinky hair), the decision to wear their hair in what is called "a natural" (where it remains tightly curled) can be intended as a statement about valuing Black women's natural beauty. From this perspective, using hair products to straighten hair may be seen as giving in to a white standard of beauty. Other Black women who choose to straighten their hair may view their choice as unrelated to white beauty standards and as part of a long and culturally appropriate tradition of African American women manipulating their hair as they see fit. What does wearing a natural or straightened hair symbolize? No analysis of the symbol in itself will yield the answer. As with any symbol, how we receive it is often related to our orientation toward the symbol—our values, our experience, our sense of being-in-the-world. We will further explore the symbolism of beauty and fashion in Chapter 7.

SEX, GENDER, AND COMMUNICATION

Already our discussion has begun to move from an exploration of language, specifically the meanings of words related to gender and other social categories, to the broader realm of how gender and other categories are related to communication—"the process of creating meaning through symbolic interaction" (Adler et al.). In this section we will explore how communication sometimes reflects and even helps to constitute or create gender and other differences in everyday speech as well as in fashion symbolism.

Gender, Class, and Speech

In the field of linguistics several early studies suggested that women use more standard language than men (see Eisikovits, 2011). Standard language is language that is generally considered more "correct" (Mooney & Evans, 2015). So, for example, pronouncing the "g" in words like "going" rather than dropping the "g" and saying "goin'" is an example of standard language. Preferring standard grammatical constructions such as "they can't say anything" to the use of double negatives such as "they can't say nothing" is another example of standard language use. According to these studies, women are much more likely to use standard language and men are much more likely to use nonstandard language (Eisikovits). Why the variation?

The linguist Edina Eisikovits and others studying sex differences in places such as Australia, England, and the United States contended that males (especially working-class males) demonstrate their masculinity by using nonstandard language, which is associated with physical power, toughness, violence, and an antiauthority persona (see for example, Eisikovits; Kiesling, 1998; Labov, 1966/2006; MacRuairc, 2011; Trudgill, 1972). These attributes in turn generally signal a working-class orientation. Thus men often derive power and prestige from using more working-class speech, which is seen as masculine, rather than from middle-class speech, which is viewed as more correct. Women, by contrast, derive status from using more middle-class speech, which is in keeping with traditional feminine attributes such as refinement and sophistication (Trudgill).

The linguist Penelope Eckert (2011) conducted a study of high school students in a Detroit suburb in the 1980s. Eckert (2011) found another interesting variance—a group of young women using more nonstandard speech than their male peers. In this high school, which she called "Belten High" (a fictitious name), many students routinely referred to each other as "jocks" and "burnouts." Jocks were middle-class students who planned on attending college and expected to have white-collar jobs (office or professional jobs such as lawyers or business executives) as adults. Jock boys proved their masculinity primarily by participating in high school athletic events and jock girls gained social status by participating in social activities, including "student government, cheerleading, organizing dances—all of which are seen as secondary or even auxiliary, to boys' varsity athletics" (Eckert, 2011, p. 62).

Burnout boys took vocational classes that prepared them for working-class jobs (doing manual labor such as construction or factory work) and did not aspire to college or white-collar jobs. Burnout boys proved their masculinity by minimizing their time in school, "rumbling" (getting into fights) in Detroit, dirt-biking, or working on their cars. Burnout girls had fewer ways to demonstrate their burnout femininity because they were supposed to spurn school social events but also did not engage in the burnout boys' activities. As a result, according to Eckert (2011), "burnout girls gain[ed] status through their social skill, their networks and their reputation for daring and fun" (p. 62).

Given the earlier studies of gender and language, we would expect jock girls to have more standard speech than jock boys and burnout girls to have more standard speech than burnout boys. However, Eckert (2011) found that jock girls were only slightly more standard in their speech than the jock boys; most surprisingly, she found that burnout girls spoke the most nonstandard English of all the groups. Eckert (2011) surmised that since both jock and burnout boys can gain status through their "actions and abilities," there is less of a need to prove status through the use of standard English (in the case of jock boys) or through the use of nonstandard English (in the case of burnout boys) (p. 64). However, for the girls the situation was different. Jock girls gained some status through second-class school activities (such as cheerleading), which explained why they used slightly more standard English than jock boys. Burnout girls, in contrast, had little way to prove their status through traditional activities and were forced to resort to creating their identity mostly through language (and other symbols such as clothing) to achieve their status (Eckert, 2012).

Eckert (2011) argued that this is typical of women's situation more generally because "men develop a sense of themselves and find a place in the world on the basis of their actions and abilities, [but] women have to focus on the production of selves" through symbol use such as speech and dress (p. 64). This seems to be another example of the stereotypical active/passive binary at work.

Still other studies of socioeconomic class and speech suggest that women sometimes adopt more standard speech when it gives them economic mobility. A study in rural coastal South Carolina (Nichols, 2011) found that African American women who had access to better-paying white-collar jobs spoke more standard forms of English, whereas African American women (and men) who did not have access to these jobs used more forms of speech associated with a language known as Gullah, which is a mix of West African languages and English ("Gullah," 2008).

By contrast, in a study of women and men 80 miles east of Mexico City, Jane H. Hill (1994), an anthropologist and linguist, found that the women in the area spoke a mix of Nahuatl (the indigenous language) and Spanish, but the women's mix differed from the men's mix and was paradoxically perceived as both less Nahuatl and less Spanish than the men's speech. Hill asserted that these rural women, who did not have access to working-class industrial jobs (as the men did) and also did not have high status in their rural communities (which the men also did), were not able to gain status and economic mobility by speaking more Spanish, nor could they gain status by speaking more Nahuatl. As a result, women were constrained to speak a mixed form that failed to provide status either way.

What do all these studies of gender, class, and language tell us? First, there is no simple connection between how people speak and their sex or gender identity. Sometimes girls and women use what are perceived to be more middle-class forms of speech than boys and men, but frequently other factors lead to different speech patterns. Even with the addition of other variables such as socioeconomic status to the equation, the results are not always easy to predict. Second, despite the messiness of the results, gender can be an important variable—just not the sole important variable. Third, people do not simply *have* a gender identity, but through their symbolic activity they continually *create* their gender identity.

Performativity

What does it mean to say that a person's identity is *created*, *produced*, or *enacted* through interaction with others, as we described in the case of Eckert's Belten High School adolescents? This idea is meant to suggest that one does not have a

breaking the frame
Speech Is Action

The definition of communication provided earlier in this chapter noted that communication occurs through "symbolic interaction." Although symbolic inter*action*—whether in the form of words, gestures, imagery, fashion, etc.—is an activity, an action, Western society tends to think of communication as passive and to distinguish between "words" and "deeds." This creates the false impression that expression is somehow inactive. In fact, symbolic expression is an active process that is an important part of gender presentation—acts that result in a public expression of gender.

Not only is speech (and expression more broadly) a form of action but also traditional deeds often have an expressive component. Playing football, for example, is an action but it can also be a way to express one's masculinity, one's allegiance to one's school, or any number of things.

Although it is sometimes appropriate to distinguish between words (or expression) and deeds, in many instances it is more useful to see speech as a form of action and traditional action as expressive. This is particularly useful when it comes to notions of gender. The sociologists Candace West and Don Zimmerman (1987) proposed that people's gender is not a given; instead, people's gender is always a work in progress. West and Zimmerman asserted that we are always "doing gender" rather than having a gender. Understanding that our speech and other forms of expression are actions helps us see how the ongoing process of expression creates gender.

preformed identity that one brings to a communication setting. For example, women are not simply feminine women who come to a communication situation ready to communicate in feminine ways, and men are not simply masculine men who are ready to communicate in masculine ways. Instead, one's identity comes into being by "doing" the identity. The burnout girls of Belten High did not show up in school or social situations with their communication strategies already formed. Instead, they arrived in a setting (such as school); developed a goal of identifying (in this case, as a burnout girl); and then developed ways for expressing that gendered socioeconomic class identity. The philosopher and gender theorist Judith Butler called this **performativity**. According to Butler

(1990/1999), identities such as gender identities come into being through "a stylized repetition of acts" (p. 179). A stylized act is an act that is conventional or widely accepted. For example, in movies in the mid-20th century, smoking was a stylized act (performed in a conventional way) that signaled that the smoker was cool and sophisticated.

Here is another example: wearing earrings was largely a feminine form of adornment in the early 20th century in the United States. But beginning in the 1960s, this began to change when gay men and hippies took up the style. Earrings became part of punk style in the 1970s, and soon after, a number of male rock stars, rappers, and athletes began to pierce their ears as well (DeMello, 2007). Today, earrings are sported by many men, gay, straight, and beyond (Figures 2.10 and 2.11).

How did this happen? How did a feminine accessory become a masculine accessory as well? One can think of dress, bodily movement, and ways of speaking as ways to perform masculinity. When a rock singer who already is

FIGURES 2.10 and 2.11

What do earrings signify? Earrings worn by a woman in the 1950s and by LeBron James in the 2000s.

FIGURE 2.12
You are likely to have seen the artist and performer RuPaul in drag so often that seeing him in men's clothing seems odd. The repeated stylized representations of RuPaul as feminine change our expectations. The feminist theorist Judith Butler (1990/1999) contended that what seems normal or natural is simply the result of repeated associations.

coded or perceived as masculine donned an earring in the 1980s, it may have initially seemed out of place, but because all the other symbols of his clothing, bodily movement, and vocal performance were read as masculine, over time the earring began to be read as masculine as well. The key to the performative aspect of identity is that our interpretation of symbols shifts through stylized repetition. This is in keeping with the communication principle that symbols have no inherent meaning; they develop meaning through our associations with other things that have symbolic meaning. So an earring worn by a 1980s rock star, along with his leather jacket and black boots, is read as a masculine, antiauthority look. The earrings worn by a 1950s housewife wearing high heels and a bob hairdo are read as a conventionally feminine look.

Over time, the concept of femininity or masculinity might change because of the performative aspect of gender. Gender is not a prefabricated thing; it is a notion based on a constantly changing series of acts. Put another way, because we enact gender, we have the power to shift how gender is perceived; but because this power comes from choosing among a repertoire of already existing conventional acts, our power to change the enactment of gender is still limited by society. In the case of burnout girls, for example, they could not choose to communicate their "burnout-hood" by working on cars or getting into fights—because such activities were considered inappropriate for girls and would presumably have resulted in the girls being penalized socially. An avenue that was available to them, however, was the conventional act of speaking nonstandard English.

Butler (1990/1999) asserted that although we have some freedom to perform gender (and other aspects of our identity) in new ways, the strategies available to us are still limited. She argued that there is a "**rigid regulatory frame**" that always limits the performative strategies available to us (p. 43). Butler did not define this term but we take her to mean that a rigid regulatory frame is the set of social conventions operating at any given moment that limit what it is acceptable to do. However, even if this regulatory frame is rigid at any particular moment, the frame that limits us does shift over time—sometimes allowing what was previously forbidden or forbidding what was previously allowed.

A popular misunderstanding of performativity takes Butler to mean that gender is simply a performance—a role that one takes on as one would take on a role in a play. This misconception assumes that gender is, to use Butler's (1990/1999) word, "exterior" to us and masks our true selves. Our performance of gender usually does not feel artificial to us and the changes in our conception of gender usually occur slowly as our gender enactments evolve (through repetition and subtle shifts in the understanding of these gendered acts).

Despite any feeling we may have that our gender feels natural or genuine, Butler (1990/1999) rejected the notion that we have a one, true self; performativity relies on the notion that we are a sum of our actions, which have symbolic meaning. These acts then are not a false performance, but that does not imply these acts are "natural" or inevitable. For the purposes of this chapter, the idea of performativity is significant because it suggests that although we are not prisoners of preexisting meanings of symbols (because we can shift the meaning of words and other symbols), we are not entirely free to control symbolism either (because these shifts are constrained by a web of other preexisting meanings—symbolism, conventions, etc.).

Women, Men, and Communities of Practice

Many scholars have argued that the different experiences of females and males have given rise to different ways of communicating. The linguist Robin Lakoff referred to these forms as women's language and men's language (although she also referred to a third form as neutral language). Julia T. Wood (2013), a communication scholar, has said that women and men "tend to be socialized into different speech communities" that she calls feminine and masculine speech communities (p. 137). J. T. Wood (2013), drawing on the work of the linguist William Labov, defined a **speech community** as "a group of people who share norms about communication" (p. 126). J. T. Wood (2013) explained: "a speech community exists when people share understandings about goals of communication, strategies for enacting those goals, and ways of interpreting communication" (p. 126). Similarly, Deborah Tannen, a linguist, asserted that the communication styles of women and men are so different that conversation between them is like "cross-cultural communication" (1990). Wood and Tannen claimed not only that female and male communication styles are generally different, but also that females and males value their respective styles of communication over the other style. In addition to this scholarship, there have been popular books that claim major differences between women's and men's communication. Perhaps the most well-known nonacademic book is John Gray's bestseller, *Men Are From Mars, Women Are From Venus*, published in 1992 (J. T. Wood, 2002). Gray appeared to be making the claim that women's and men's differences are not only significant but also innate—which is a much stronger claim than that made by Lakoff, Wood, or Tannen. In fact, J. T. Wood (2002) criticized Gray's book as "innocent of scholarly methods and modes of thought"—which we take to mean unsupported by research or rigorous thinking.

Although Lakoff, Wood, and Tannen make somewhat different arguments about sex and/or gender differences, we will refer to their similar overarching claims as the "**different cultures thesis**" (MacGeorge et al., 2004). We take the different cultures thesis to be the claim that many (but not all) females and males are socialized into two fairly distinctive groups that often have different goals when communicating, different strategies for achieving those goals, and different approaches to interpreting communication.

As we have seen with middle- and working-class speech, however, the idea that females as a group speak differently than males is not supported by at least some research. Eckert and Kiesling found that speech often varies within groups of females and males based on socioeconomic class—and even these generalizations are just that, generalizations that are not true for all females or males. Communication differences are also influenced by a number of other intersectional factors, such as age, ethnicity, region, and religion. Once we take these features of identity into account, we are likely to find even greater variation in human communication.

We also must take into account how communication may vary between groups. Do women communicate differently with men than they do with each other? Do upper-class women communicate differently with working-class women? The variables are virtually endless. Some researchers, such as linguists, attempt to deal with this diversity by narrowing their studies of communication to concrete settings. For example, Eckert studied the speech of adolescents in a Midwestern suburban high school and Kiesling studied men in a U.S. fraternity. These researchers do not claim that their findings necessarily apply when the same suburban teenagers are speaking to their parents at home or when the fraternity men are speaking with their girlfriends or boyfriends. According to this view, each setting could yield unique results. These researchers tend to describe these settings as **communities of practice**: a group of people "who come together around mutual engagement in some common endeavor" (Eckert & McConnell-Ginet, 2011, p. 578).

So, once we take into account all these variables, does the research indicate that females and males communicate differently? The short and oversimplified answer is that females and males *sometimes* communicate differently—but not very differently. A meta-analysis of studies of communication and gender that examined more than 1,200 studies of sex differences in communication found that only 1 percent of the variance could be accounted for by sex—and even

Variables That May Affect Communication

There are a wide variety of variables that may affect communication, including the following:

Traditional intersectional variables: age, sex, race, ethnicity, socioeconomic class, nationality, and/or religion

Communication across intersections: male–female communication, interethnic communication, interreligious communication

Types of communication: interpersonal communication, small group communication, public speaking

Formal role: boss or employee, teacher or student, judge, prosecutor, or expert witness

this variance was sometimes affected by other factors (like socioeconomic class) (Canary & Hause, 1993). The researchers Daniel Canary and Kimberley Hause concluded that in general "we should not expect to find substantial sex differences in communication" (p. 140). Unfortunately, we tend to think about females and males as binary opposites (as we discussed earlier) and this feeds our expectations of sex differences in communication (Canary & Hause). Even our examination of gender and standard language use has focused on the ways female and male communication varies—and this may obscure the fact that often even female and male communication with regard to standard language may overlap a great deal in many instances.

CONCLUSION

Our language and ways we communicate both reflect and create who we are and how we perceive the world. Language can also conceal from us possibilities about the world and impose ways of thinking that reinforce traditionally gendered perspectives. These perspectives can reinforce the primacy of males in our thought and buttress traditional binaries of femininity and masculinity as well as other gendered schemas. Despite the sometimes conservative influence of language, we do have the power to change it. For example, various

Key Terms

sexual, racial, and ethnic groups and/or people with dis/abilities have broken with old labels and adopted new ones, even claiming previously derogatory terms.

In this chapter we have also seen that gender can influence communication because we use speech and other symbolic activity as a way of enacting our gender identity. However, our approaches to communication are also a way of enacting other intersecting elements of our identity, such as race and/or socio-economic class, and it can be hard to predict how a person will communicate based on one, two, or even three of these variables. The situation is complicated further by an emerging consensus that people do not simply have static identities; instead, identities are performative, which makes them fluid and hard to pin down. Furthermore, meta-analyses of communication studies suggest that only about 1 percent of the variance in our communication is caused by sex and there is frequently more overlap between female and male communication than there is difference.

THINK, LEARN, ACT

The following resources are available on the Student Website: www.oup.com/us /gillis-jacobs

Taking Stock, Taking Action prompts and activities. Apply what you've learned to take action on campus and in the broader community.

Recommended Readings and Multimedia Resources, including scholarly and literary works, documentaries, feature films, podcasts and more, to enrich the in- and out-of-classroom experience.

GENDER AND IN/EQUALITY

"On her first day of preschool, at age two, [my daughter, Daisy] wore her favorite outfit—her 'engineers' (a pair of pin-striped overalls)—and proudly toted her Thomas the Tank Engine lunchbox," wrote Peggy Orenstein (2011) in *Cinderella Ate My Daughter*. Orenstein went on to explain that she complained "to anyone who would listen" about how the makers of Thomas pictured only boys on their packaging and made the only girl engine, Lady, smaller than the others. "Really, though," said Orenstein, "my bitching was a form of bragging. *My* daughter had transcended typecasting" (p. 2, italics in original). But fast forward just a bit and "Oh, how the mighty fall." Orenstein wrote:

> All it took was one boy who, while whizzing past her on the play-ground, yelled, "Girls *don't* like trains!" and Thomas was shoved to the bottom of the toy chest. Within a month, Daisy threw a tantrum when I tried to wrestle her into pants. As if by osmosis she had learned the names and gown colors of every Disney

Princess. . . . She gazed longingly into the tulle-draped windows of the local toys stores and for her third birthday begged for a "real princess dress" with matching plastic high heels. Meanwhile, one of her classmates, the one with Two Mommies, showed up to school every single day dressed in a Cinderella gown. With a bridal veil. (pp. 2–3)

What was going on here? asked Orenstein. Was her little girl, Daisy, not to mention the boy who chastised her for liking trains, a Baby X gone off the rails? (See Chapter 1, "Sex, Gender, and Social Construction"). How did this come about? Sooner or later—in many cases sooner—we all come face to face with ideas about gender and gender roles, that is, the idea that one should appear and behave in a certain way and perform particular tasks based on one's sex and gender. Long before we have heard the word stereotype, we can identify gender stereotypes and are made aware, whether subtly (*Don't you look pretty?*) or bluntly (*Girls don't like trains!*) of our place in a gendered society. It is not a coincidence that Thomas the Train packages picture only boys or that Daisy knew the names and gown colors of the Disney princesses.

This is a process that starts at birth, or if you count all those pink and blue baby showers, even before birth. It is no accident that sex and gender are important and pervasive in Western culture. Janet Taylor Spence (1984) argued, in fact, that gender is the "earliest, most central and most active organizing component of one's self concept." When a baby is born today, one can easily imagine the doctor announcing the sex of the baby—"It's a girl!" A birth certificate is filled out listing the sex and given name of the child—a "girl's" name or a "boy's" name. Friends and family might dote on a baby girl, highlighting her feminine characteristics: "What a pretty girl!" "What delicate fingers!" and "How sweet!" or on a baby boy, highlighting his masculine characteristics: "What a big boy!" "How strong!" and "So handsome!" It is to this process that Simone de Beauvoir (1949/1989) referred when she wrote, "One is not born, but rather becomes, a woman" (p. 267). Although this may not be the exact script your family or friends will follow, chances are good that this sounds familiar. This is just the beginning of the social construction of gender, a process that will continue throughout life.

What is the big deal? you might wonder. So what if she wears pink ruffled dresses and plays only with baby dolls? So what if he wears football jerseys and plays only with trucks and balls? So what if they rarely play together? Girls will be girls, right? Perhaps. To some degree.

recap of terms:
Social Construct

A **social construct** is a "concept or perception of something based on the collective views developed and maintained within a society or social group . . . as opposed to existing inherently or naturally" (OED).

From Chapter 1, "Sex, Gender, and Social Construction."

But to what degree will *girls be girls* and *boys be boys,* and to what degree does society push, pull, and convince girls and boys (and those who will come to think of themselves as neither girls nor boys) to conform to our ideas of girls and boys? And what are the consequences in the short and long term? Where do these ideas come from? How do we learn them? How much do they change over time and across different cultures and locations? Do society's conceptions of sex and gender unduly restrict who we are allowed to be? Do ideas about sex and gender systematically generate power imbalances in society? These are the questions we will be exploring.

THE SOCIAL CONSTRUCTION OF GENDER

The push and pull of societal forces is what we mean by social construction. The forces of social construction are many, including families, peers, the media and popular culture (television, movies, books, music, fashion, social media), and corporations (marketing and advertising, much of it aimed at children and young people).

Let's step back and think about why it is important to understand sex and gender as socially constructed. First, it emphasizes that society plays a part in making our identities; in other words, gender and assigned sex are at least partially the result of human choice rather than being (pre)determined by nature or biology. Society affects, but does not wholly determine, who we *can* become and who we *do* become with regard to sex and gender. A second reason it is important to understand sex and gender as socially constructed is that constructedness implies the possibility, even the inevitability, of change. Sex and gender are categories in flux, constantly being made and remade. Yet our ideas about them can also be stubbornly resistant to change.

Gender Construction in Children

The push of social forces can be significant, shaping both how we see ourselves and how we see others. Think of the preschool-age boy from the beginning of this chapter who declared, "Girls don't like trains!" He had already developed specific ideas about how boys and girls are supposed to act, and in that he is probably not unusual. Gender plays a big part in our lives from a very young age. Researchers report that already between the ages of 6 and 12 months, many

recap of terms:
Sex and Gender

The term **sex** refers to the more physiological characteristics used to classify a person as female, male, intersex, third sex, or other related category. Since human choice is always involved, sex classification always involves more than biological characteristics and is always socially constructed. In recognition of this fact, many have abandoned the term "biological sex" in favor of "assigned sex."

The term **gender** refers to the less physiological aspects related to femininity, masculinity, androgyny, and other associated categories; ways of presenting oneself that are constructed and reconstructed through what one does, how one looks, how one behaves, etc.

From Chapter 1, "Sex, Gender, and Social Construction."

"Mom, Dad, I prefer to gather."

FIGURE 3.1

children are able to divide people by gender (Leinbach & Fagot, 1993). A study of children of European Canadian, Asian Canadian, and West Indian descent found that 18- and 24-month-old female infants match girls' faces to dolls and boys' faces to vehicles (Serbin et al., 2001). The psychologist Sandra Bem (1993) reported that "fully 80 percent of American two-year-olds can readily distinguish males from females on the basis of purely cultural cues like hairstyle and clothing" (p. 114). Yet, Bem (1993) also noted that "as many as 50 percent of American three- and four-year-olds still fail to distinguish females and males if all they have to go on are biologically 'natural' cues like genitalia and body physique. In other words, it is not biological sex differences that young American children find so perceptually and emotionally compelling but culturally constructed gender differences" (p. 114). Bem (1993) also noted that "American culture is so gender polarizing in its discourse and its social institutions, children come to be **gender schematic** (or gender polarizing)," which leads in turn to their becoming "conventionally sex-typed" (p. 125). (See Chapter 1 for more on gender polarization.) As such, "children evaluate different ways of behaving in terms of the cultural definitions of gender appropriateness and reject any way of behaving that does not match their sex" (pp. 125–126).

So, even as young children, we "know" that girls are supposed to wear pink and boys are supposed to wear blue. And the adults in our lives often reconfirm this for us in small and large ways. Don't think it is so? Try taking a baby girl out sometime in a blue snowsuit. We know parents who have had the experience of taking their infant daughters out in blue clothes and received "What a cute little boy" comments. Likewise, try letting your small son's hair grow long, and he will likely become "a lovely little girl" to strangers on the street. We have found that only in rare instances will people actually ask rather than presume based on these cues.

Because gender is socially constructed, however, notions about it can (and do) change over time. They also vary from culture to culture and even within cultures, depending on factors such as region, racial and ethnic background, socioeconomic status, and age. Consider, for example, something as basic as the idea that blue is for boys and pink is for girls. This is a notion that is bound both by geography and by time. In South Korea, for example, black (charcoal) is used to announce the birth of a girl and red (chili peppers) a boy. Orenstein noted that up until the early 20th century, most babies in the United States wore white, primarily because it was practical; the laundry, before washing machines, was all boiled together to clean it. In addition, both boys and girls wore dresses, which were thought of as gender-neutral (and no doubt more practical for access to wet diapers). Even today you can buy what amount to dresses for infant girls and boys—just do not use the d-word. Rather than dresses, they are known as sleepers or sleep sacks, and they come in appropriately color-coded pink and blue.

In fact, pink and blue themselves have seemingly switched allegiances. When the idea of colors for babies' rooms was first introduced, pink was thought to be the more masculine color (being a version of red, which symbolized strength) and blue (which was associated with the Virgin Mary) was thought to represent femininity (Orenstein). As late as the 1930s, one in four adults still identified blue with girls and pink with boys (Orenstein).

Although much differs across cultural and national boundaries, there are also striking similarities among young children. John Williams and Deborah Best (1982/1990) found that 5-year-olds in the 25 countries they studied held similar stereotypes about characteristics associated with females and males. They also found that female and male stereotypes were more differentiated in younger children and became more flexible as children grew older. Williams and Best did not speculate why similar notions of gender traits exist across different cultures (some cross-cultural studies of adults have recorded similar results). A number of factors are at work here, and in the future, globalization may have an even greater homogenizing effect on our notions of gender.

As children become older, the influence of peers grows. Would children make fun of a boy who enjoyed knitting or had a fondness for pink? Would a girl who disliked dolls or playing house but liked G.I. Joe be considered strange? In the United States and cross culturally as early as age 3, children tend "to seek out same-sex playmates and to avoid other-sex children. This tendency strengthens throughout grade school" (Best, 2009, p. 348). Boys' play in general is more "active," "boisterous," and "risk-taking" and also more "separate from adult culture" (Best, 2009, p. 348). Girls' play, in contrast, is in general more "cooperative" and "egalitarian" (Best, 2009, p. 348). Interestingly, in early childhood both girls and boys "think their own sex is the better one" (Best, 2009, p. 348). Although it might be tempting to extrapolate from this that females and males are fundamentally different, as Michael Kimmel (2013) has noted, "In fact, in virtually all the research that has been done on the attributes associated with masculinity or femininity, the differences among women and among men are far greater than the mean [average] differences between women and men" (p. 14).

Even the exceptions to gender norms are revealing. For example, it is true that many girls have happy childhoods breaking elements of the girl's gender role; these "tomboys" favor traditionally male activities, often without facing overly negative repercussions. By contrast, a boy's masculinity might be suspect if he played hopscotch or jump rope too much. Girls can often avoid traditionally female clothing like dresses, but a skirt on a boy would generally mark that boy as "unmasculine" and unacceptable. Boys, it seems, are much more at risk of being ostracized, bullied, or worse if they fail to be "real boys."

Research supports the notion of more rigid gender roles for boys. Bem (1993) reported that by 20 to 24 months of age "preschool children generate much more restrictive gender rules for their male peers than for their females peers, an asymmetry for which there is no obvious source in either cognitive development or biology but for which there is an obvious source in culture, which prescribes much harsher treatment for male gender deviance ('sissies') than for female deviance ('tomboys')" (p. 114). Even the lack of parallel terms is telling. Why do we have the female category of tomboy (now with often positive connotations) but no parallel term for boys? If we tried to create a parallel term for boys (janegirl, anyone?), would such a term have positive connotations? Even for girls, however, this freedom is often expected to be a childhood phase. After all, although we have the socially accepted category of tomboy, we do not have a socially accepted equivalent category for women.

Peers and popular culture are important and pervasive influences on children and adults. Television, movies, music, social media, video games, toys, magazines, newspapers, and advertising teach many lessons about gender. What do we learn when we repeatedly see brave and daring male heroes save women in danger in movies and video games? What do we learn from Barbie? One study has shown, in fact, that after playing with Barbie, girls "appear to believe that there are more careers for boys than for themselves" (Sherman & Zurbriggen, 2014, p. 206). (Researchers found this to be true for both "Fashion Barbie" and "Doctor Barbie.") The researchers theorized that Barbie communicated messages of objectification and sexualization to girls at a time in their lives when they were rapidly developing self-concepts. These messages deeply influence how girls (and probably boys as well) engage with gendered stereotypes and have been shown to affect how girls assess their skills (as less competent) and their bodies (as less satisfactory), among other things.

breaking the frame
Throw Like a Girl

[Fill in the blank] like a girl. What does it mean to you? Research has shown that many girls lose confidence at puberty, that *[blank-ing] like a girl* comes to mean something negative, weak, passive. But the phrase is getting some rethinking these days, even in popular culture, where brands as diverse as Chevy, Nike, Always, and *Sports Illustrated* have ads or covers featuring girls who are strong, fast, and aggressive. The brand Always has a "Like a girl" video featuring young women, who when asked to "run like a girl," "run" with arms and legs flopping and akimbo. But when young *girls* are asked to do the same, they run straight, strong, and sure. One girl, when asked is "like a girl" a good thing, says "I actually don't know if it's a bad thing or a good thing." Mo'ne Davis, who was the first girl to throw a shutout in the Little League World Series and the first Little Leaguer to be featured on the cover of *Sports Illustrated*, is also the subject of an ad (directed by Spike Lee) in which she says, "I stand for girls who want to play sports with the boys. . . . I throw 70 miles per hour. That's throwing like a girl!" Troubling messages to and about girls still show up regularly in popular culture; perhaps these positive images can begin to counter some of the negative ones.

Think of your life. Are your experiences with gender roles similar to the ones suggested here? Many people experience a much more complicated set of forces than the stereotypical vision just described. "Society," after all, is not a monolithic entity. For example, you may have had grandparents with less traditional gender role expectations or parents with more traditional expectations. It is also often true that people have traditional gender role expectations in some areas of their lives but not others, for example, traditional views about clothing but not sports. Whatever your experiences, however, one thing is likely to be true: whether you endorse societal beliefs about gender or not, you are likely to be able to identify those beliefs—and chances are whether you want to or not, to some degree, you rely on gender stereotypes when thinking about yourself and others.

THE SOCIAL COSTS OF TRADITIONAL FEMININITY AND MASCULINITY

When we ask our gender studies classes, "Which set of characteristics, the feminine or masculine ones, is most valued by our society?" they invariably say the attributes of masculinity. Obviously (at least we hope it is obvious), some of the qualities stereotypically associated with femininity are at times desirable and some of the qualities associated with masculinity are at times undesirable. For example, the stereotypically feminine qualities of cooperativeness, expressing emotion, and willingness to talk in interpersonal settings are traits that should be encouraged in all people. The traditionally masculine traits of competitiveness, aggression, and independence are frequently overemphasized and can create problems, including for those who exhibit such traits. Interestingly, Best (2009) reported that in only half of the countries she and her colleagues examined was "the male stereotype rated more favorably than the female and the reverse was true in the remaining countries" (p. 346). She did not speculate why this might be true.

During the course of such discussions, many students recognize the value in being androgynous, or acting in both feminine and masculine ways. However, many people still believe that men and boys should display traditional masculine characteristics and behavior and women and girls should display traditional feminine characteristics and behavior. In other words, to some degree they endorse a traditional gender ideology (a set of interrelated, internalized cultural beliefs about gender).

It seems clear that the attributes traditionally associated with masculinity allow a person to vie for a dominant position in society, whereas within our current cultural milieu, traditional femininity relegates a person to a nondominant or subordinate position. This works out well for males, at least for those who are able to enact what R. W. Connell and James Messerschmidt (2005) have called **hegemonic masculinity**, which they defined as the "currently most honored way of being a man" (p. 832). Connell and Messerschmidt theorized that there exist a "plurality of masculinities" arranged hierarchically; hegemonic masculinity occupies the top spot and thus is associated with authority and social power. Models of hegemonic masculinity "express widespread ideals, fantasies, and desires" about what men should be (p. 838). The characteristics associated with hegemonic masculinity are not "fixed" or "transhistorical" but rather specific to particular locations and historical times; in this sense, hegemonic masculinity is "not a certain type of man but, rather, a way that men position themselves" (Connell & Messerschmidt, pp. 840–841). Hegemonic masculinity includes the possibility of both "positive" traits (e.g., "bringing home a wage") and "negative" traits (e.g., "violence, aggression") (p. 840) and should not be thought of as "normal" but "normative" (something to be emulated). Connell and Messerschmidt wrote that hegemonic masculinity requires "all other men to position themselves in relation to it, and it [currently] ideologically legitimate[s] the global subordination of women to men" (p. 832).

The female companion to hegemonic masculinity is **emphasized femininity**, the form of femininity given "the most cultural and ideological support at present" (Connell, 1987, p. 187). Emphasized femininity is oriented around the idea that women should accommodate "the interests and desires of [heterosexual] men" (Connell, p. 183.) Its central features are "compliance, nurturance and empathy" (p. 188). Unlike hegemonic masculinity, emphasized femininity does not seek to "negate or subordinate other forms of femininity," so the two terms are not "symmetrical." Connell noted that "this kind of femininity is performed, and performed especially to men" (p. 188). Related to this is the idea of a **patriarchal bargain**, which the sociologist Lisa Wade (2010) defined as "a decision [by some females] to accept gender rules that disadvantage women in exchange for whatever power one can wrest from the system. It is an individual strategy designed to manipulate the system to one's best advantage, but one that leaves the system itself intact" (para. 4). Wade cited Kim Kardashian as an example of someone who has made a patriarchal bargain and gotten "a good deal for herself" (para. 5). By trading on her sexual allure she is accommodating the desires of men—which benefits her individually—but perpetuates a system that disadvantages and objectifies women (Figure 3.2).

FIGURE 3.2

The sociologist Lisa Wade posed the question: Why is Kim Kardashian so famous? Her answer—for so successfully striking the patriarchal bargain.

Conforming to or endorsing traditional gender ideologies often has serious consequences. For example, adherence to traditional gender ideology can lead to lower expectations for women at work. Thus, male job applicants have been shown to be preferred compared with female applicants (Chang, 2012; Davison & Burke, 2000). Men more than women are assigned more of the critical work assignments that lead to workplace advancement (Silva et al., 2012). Research has also shown that women in sales are assigned inferior accounts when compared with men and, as a result, make 30 percent less than their male counterparts (Madden, 2012). Women who work on Wall Street receive more positive evaluations than men but are less likely to be considered partner material (Biernat et al., 2012).

If traditional femininity limits girls and women, couldn't they simply opt for masculinity? They could, but there are costs to this approach. According to a recent study, women who were "agentic" or display "masculinity" in the workplace (for example, aggressiveness and assertiveness) were not rewarded professionally and may be sanctioned economically and socially, which researchers called "a backlash effect" (O'Neill & O'Reilly, 2011; Rudman & Phelan, 2008). Male managers who displayed similarly assertive behavior seemed to suffer no backlash effect (Heilman & Wallen, 2010). A woman who is too strong, independent, competitive, and active may be harshly portrayed and criticized as not only unlikable but also unnatural, that is, not truly a woman (i.e., a lesbian). This fact illustrates that in our society traditional femininity is connected not only to passivity, weakness, and softness, but also to a demand for women and girls to be heterosexual. In fact, the whole notion of the traditional, male-headed family depends particularly on women to reproduce (that is, have children) within a heterosexual, married relationship.

Women who resist traditional notions of gender are often labeled "dykes," suggesting that gender norms or stereotypes are deeply related to homophobia in society (an issue we will we will take up more fully in Chapter 4). This puts women and girls in a **double bind**—a lose–lose (or no-win) situation (Heilman et al., 1998). They either conform to the demand to be feminine, which limits the respect and power they have, or become gender nonconforming and open themselves up to ridicule, discrimination, and homophobic attacks.

Many women's rights advocates have argued that for women to achieve equality, rigid notions of gender and gender roles must be eliminated and that essential to this effort is the fight for social acceptance of and rights for lesbians and gay men. Until all people are free to choose how they express themselves as gendered beings without fear of negative labeling or much worse, then really none of us is free to choose who we will be.

Double Binds

Because of societal expectations, women seem particularly vulnerable to double binds. Here are three circumstances in which women are often penalized no matter what they do:

Work and Motherhood Double Bind— Mothers who choose to work outside the home risk being called neglectful mothers or selfish. Mothers who choose to stay at home full-time risk being denigrated as "not working" and "just a housewife."

Leadership Double Bind—Women who lead risk being called "unfeminine," "aggressive," "bitchy," or "lesbians." Women who choose not to lead risk being seen as "weak," "passive," and "ineffective."

Sexual Double Bind—If women are sexually active they are considered "sluts." If they are not sexually active they are "prudes," "frigid," or "lesbians."

MORE ABOUT....

Not only do women routinely face double binds, but also they face **double standards**, a rule or set of rules that applies differently to different groups. For example, women face a sexual double standard: a different standard of sexual permissiveness for females than for males. There is evidence that fewer people subscribe to a sexual double standard than in years past, but according to Crawford and Popp (2003), who conducted a review of 20 years of studies on the issue, sexual double standards still come into play. According to one study in their review, "Women may be judged more negatively than men for having had sex with many partners in the past, having sex outside of a committed relationship, or for having sexual experience at an early age" (Crawford & Popp, p. 23). According to another study, "sexually permissive women may be preferred as dating partners; however, those who say no to casual sex may be more acceptable for long-term relationships" (Crawford & Popp, p. 23). Kathleen A. Bogle (2008) asserted that "rule number one for women is: do not act like men in the sexual arena" (p. 103).

Women also face a double standard when it comes to aging, with people believing women reach age milestones, such as middle and old age, earlier than men. Women are also thought to decline at a younger age than men do, although women live longer than men in general (Kite, 2001). Because cultural ideals of beauty are applied to women more than men, older women are more likely than older men to be viewed negatively regarding appearance and are more likely to be seen as falling short of beauty ideals (Weil, 2008).

Given the bias against older people in general in our society, this can have serious consequences for women, particularly regarding their career opportunities. For example, although both female and male actors receive fewer film roles and have less star presence as they grow older, women are disproportionately affected by this trend (Lincoln & Allen, 2004).

Sexism: A Special Case of Prejudice

Sexism is typically thought of as prejudice, that is, "a preconceived opinion not based on reason or actual experience" (OED), in this case based on sex. This can translate into hostility toward women in general, although as the psychologists Peter Glick and Susan Fiske (1996) pointed out, sexism need not be overtly hostile. In fact, sexism is at times expressed more subtly, in what might be characterized as "benevolent" ways. As the term benevolent is used here, however, it should not be confused with positive or harmless.

Glick and Fiske have called sexism against women a "special case of prejudice" marked not only by overt hostility toward women, but also by ambivalence, that is, contradictory emotions or attitudes about women. **Hostile sexism** against women, which most people recognize as sexism, is based on the notion that men are more competent than women and therefore deserve higher status and more power than women (Glick et al., 2000). (Glick is dealing here only with sexism against women, but hostile sexism could be aimed at men or other sexes.) Hostile sexism against women is often coupled with a fear that women use sex/sexuality to gain power over men, for example, the idea that once a woman gets a man to commit to her, she often attempts to put him on a short leash, or that women enjoy teasing men sexually and then refusing their advances. Hostile sexist beliefs often go hand in hand with negative perceptions of feminism and feminists, for example, the belief that when women say they are seeking equality, what they really want are special favors to give them advantages over men in the workplace, or the idea that women often complain about discrimination when none exists. Hostile sexism is marked by a belief in negative stereotypes of women (Glick et al.). Examples of hostile sexism include sexist name-calling, sexual harassment, and employment discrimination based on sex.

Benevolent sexism against women, by contrast, is less likely to be identified as sexism by both the doer and the receiver (Glick et al.). This is because it may appear to be affectionate or chivalrous. Examples include believing women are morally better than men, believing women are deserving of men's protection, or carrying heavy objects or opening doors for women (when one would not make a similar gesture to a man in the same situation). If you routinely hold the door open for others *regardless of their sex,* that is not benevolent sexism. If you would hold the door open for a woman but not a man in the same circumstance, that is benevolent sexism. No one is saying that you should not be polite to others or that you should avoid gracious gestures to others, but that these acts should be carried out regardless of the sex of the recipient.

Because benevolent sexism may appear to be positive, many people have difficulty believing it is actually harmful—or indeed that it should be called sexism at all. What is important to remember is that underpinning benevolent sexism are traditional stereotypes and the idea of masculine dominance. As with hostile sexism, benevolent sexism at its core involves the belief that women are not as capable as men, although it is often couched in terms that seem unthreatening or even flattering.

Benevolent sexism may be experienced as positive or negative by the recipient, but regardless of how it is perceived, its consequences can be negative. In fact, benevolent sexism can be even more detrimental than hostile sexism. One study showed that benevolent sexism negatively affected women's performance, whereas hostile sexism or no sexism at all had no effect on performance, perhaps because women could become defiant in the face of hostile sexism, whereas benevolent sexism was more difficult to identify and consciously resist (Dardenne et al., 2007). Another study found that the presence of benevolent sexism made it less likely that women would engage in social action for gender equality, whereas the presence of hostile sexism made it more likely women would engage in such action (Becker & Wright, 2011).

Misogyny

The fact that stereotypically feminine attributes are so widely devalued suggests that women themselves are often devalued. Many argue that society suffers from **misogyny**, that is, "hatred or dislike of, or prejudice against women" (OED). However, misogynists usually do not hate women in ways that make them want to completely avoid women. A misogynist might marry a woman or be attracted to women but simultaneously think less of women than men. For example, a man might think that a woman should not be president but still enjoy his relationship with his wife. Cooper Thompson (1992) has insightfully argued that the hatred of feminine qualities in women is the defining element of misogyny. It is not that misogynists hate women per se, which is why they may still enjoy the company of women; but they devalue the qualities traditionally required of women.

Devaluing femininity is also limiting to boys and men, who risk triggering homophobic reactions if they display attributes associated with femininity. In many ways, being a "fag" seems to be the ultimate put-down for a man. Why is this? C. Thompson (1992) has written that misogyny and homophobia are deeply related. Traditionally, **homophobia** is defined as "fear or hatred of homosexuals and homosexuality" (OED). When it comes to men, C. Thompson (1992) argued that homophobia boils down to the hatred of feminine qualities *in men*. To be a "real man" is to exhibit masculine qualities and to be devoid of feminine ones. In sports, boys do not want to "throw like a girl." Boys and men must not be "girly men." C. Thompson (1992) even reported that U.S. Marine training used to be described as the process of "killing the woman in men" (p. 79).

One could argue that homophobia in C. Thompson's (1992) sense restricts the freedom of all boys and men. Being seen as too sensitive, too caring, too unwilling to use violence, or too interested in the wrong playtime activities can lead to ostracization, social isolation, and even death. According to statistics from the Federal Bureau of Investigation, almost 1,400 hate crimes against people because of their sexual orientation were reported in 2012, the second most frequent hate crime committed after crimes based on race. The majority (53.9 percent) were reported as anti–male homosexual (12.7 percent were classified as anti–female homosexual bias and most others were classified as simply antihomosexual bias) (Federal Bureau of Investigation, 2013). Many gay and transgender rights advocates suspect the number is actually much higher because such crimes often go unreported as bias crimes. (We will discuss homophobia directed at lesbians later in this chapter and anti-lesbian, gay, bisexual, and transgender crimes and attitudes in Chapter 4.)

Political and Economic Inequality

Given our exploration in this chapter it should seem apparent that women and girls often do not have the same status as men and boys in society. Not only do females face social constraints based on gender, but also they are at a disadvantage in many other ways, including politically and economically.

In terms of political power, consider these facts:

In 2012, there were 9 women heads of state and 15 women heads of government globally (UN Women, 2014). Although women have headed governments in countries as diverse as Argentina, Germany, India, Israel, Liberia, and Nicaragua, Only one woman, Hillary Rodham Clinton, has ever been nominated by a major political party to run for president of the United States. (As of this writing in 2016, Clinton may win the presidency). Only 2 women have ever been nominated by a major political party as vice president (Geraldine Ferraro and Sarah Palin); neither was part of the winning ticket.

Women make up just over 20 percent of parliaments worldwide. The Nordic countries (Denmark, Finland, Iceland, Norway, and Sweden) have the highest percentage of women in parliament, at 42 percent; the Middle East and North Africa have the lowest, at almost 16 percent. Rwanda has the highest percentage of women in any single house of parliament, with 64 percent of its lower house made up of women (UN Women, 2014).

In the 114th U.S. Congress (2015), there were a record number of women—108. Yet women still constituted slightly less than 20 percent of the House and Senate (but 64 percent of the electorate); only 3 of the 9 U.S. Supreme Court Justices are women. As of 2015, only 1 woman of color had ever served in the U.S. Senate, Carol Moseley Braun (Democrat, Illinois), who is African American, and 59 women of color have served in the House (10 Asian Pacific Americans, 11 Hispanic Americans, 38 African Americans, and 0 Native Americans) (U.S. House of Representatives, 2015).

Consider these facts about economic power:

FIGURE 3.3

Patsy Takemoto Mink was the first woman of color elected to the U.S. Congress, in 1965, from Hawaii. She was the coauthor of Title IX, which prohibits sex discrimination in federally funded education programs.

Female paid labor force participation is about 50 percent globally (Elborgh-Woytek et al., 2013; Kim, 2012). Yet women make only 70 to 90 percent of what men make in a majority of countries globally (United Nations, 2010). In the United States, women working full-time outside the home make on average only 78 cents for every dollar a man does (Hegewisch & Hartmann, 2014). The difference is even more pronounced for African American women, who earn just 64 cents for every dollar white men earn, and for Hispanic women, who make only 54 cents for every dollar white men earn. (African American and Hispanic men also face a racial earnings gap when compared with white men. More on the earnings gap will be presented in Chapter 8, "Work, Inequality, and Neoliberalism.")

According to Forbes (2014), only 47 of the top 400 wealthiest individuals in the U.S. are women. In 2014, only slightly more than 5 percent of Fortune 500 and Fortune 1000 companies were headed by women (Catalyst, 2014). In 2013, two-thirds of Fortune 500 companies had no women of color as board members (Catalyst, 2013).

Patriarchy

Given all that we have been discussing to this point, it hardly seems controversial to say that women as a group face hurdles to equality. When discussing the systematic nature of prejudice and discrimination against women, we often

ON THE web

Read about **gender quotas in politics** on the Student Website: www.oup.com/us /gillis-jacobs

talk about **patriarchy**, which literally means rule of the fathers, but for our purposes refers to much more than the father exercising control over his family and its affairs. Just how prevalent is patriarchy? Although anthropologists do not agree whether male dominance plays a defining role in all human cultures, they do agree it is common across many different cultures (Stockard & Johnson, 1992).

Susan Basow (2001) described patriarchy as "a sociopolitical system in which men and their experience have power over women and their experience" (p. 125). Allan Johnson (2004) noted that patriarchy is a "male-dominated, male-identified, and male-centered" system that is above all about control and domination (p. 29). The power relations that constitute patriarchy take many forms, "from the sexual division of labor and the social organization of procreation to the internalized norms of femininity by which we live" (Weedon, 1987, p. 2). In other words, many factors, from stereotypes about women and men, to the fact that women as a group are still most responsible for caring for the family, to the ways the workplace and politics are structured to accommodate the male experience work together to make it harder for women to achieve equality with men. Think, for example, of how professional work is often structured to require long, at times unpredictable, hours. This can be difficult for women if they are the main caregivers—or responsible for arranging care—of children and other family members. Similarly, career advancement often requires years of uninterrupted work, although this can be difficult for women who, more often than men, interrupt their careers to have children or care for others. Yet arrangements and policies that might help such women, like job sharing, flex time, and the availability of high-quality, affordable child care, although they are more common in places like Canada, Germany, France, and the Scandinavian countries, have not gained much traction in the United States.

It is important to remember that patriarchy is not an individual or even a group of individuals but a complex system: "an it, not a he, a them, or an us" (A. G. Johnson, p. 25). As such, it shapes our values and behaviors; it may reward us when we perpetuate it and sanction us when we resist. Like gender, race, and class, it is socially constructed (and thus can be deconstructed). Although patriarchy generally advantages men over women, not all men benefit equally (more on this later). Women (and other sexes beyond male) may also perpetuate patriarchy (think of how emphasized femininity and engaging in the patriarchal bargain may reinforce patriarchy). Although it is nearly impossible to remain free of its values and judgments, patriarchy does not "run us" (A. G. Johnson, p. 29), nor does it order every aspect of our lives. We have a degree of freedom within the system to break the rules. So, our choices can perpetuate or resist patriarchy. As A. G. Johnson concluded, it is within our control to choose *how* we participate in patriarchy.

Patriarchy at Home—Although patriarchy is not confined to the private realm of the home, women's status in marriage historically provides an especially illuminating example of the way that patriarchy works. "Marriage, for women, has historically meant a loss of individual identity," wrote Basow (p. 133). Under the doctrine known as **coverture** in English common law (on which many U.S. laws were based), "no female person had a legal identity" (Allgor, n.d.). When a female was born, she was "covered" by her father's identity and, if she married, by her husband's. Let us be clear, however, that coverture, prior to the abolition of enslavement, applied only to free-born women. (Black women and men who were enslaved could not legally marry.)

In the simplest terms, "the doctrine of coverture fused husband and wife into one legal entity—and the one was the husband" (Wilhoit, 1979, p. 191). The husband was responsible for his wife and bound to protect her. In return, she was supposed to obey him. The law gave him control of his wife's property and she was not permitted to testify against him in criminal cases (Wilhoit). (By contrast, Spanish/Mexican women living on the Mexican frontier could own property, a right they lost when the frontier became part of the United States after the Mexican–American War.)

A married woman was treated as a child under the law. She was in most places unable to enter into contracts or sue. Any income of the wife belonged to the husband and the custody of the children belonged to the father, who could refuse contact between a mother and her children. It was legal for husbands to rape their wives. Wife beating too was generally seen as the husband's prerogative. Women nearly everywhere were denied the right to vote. Catherine Allgor noted that coverture as actually practiced was "not as restrictive" as the letter of the law (para. 6); nonetheless, it disadvantaged most females to a great degree.

It was not until the 20th century in the United States that most married women were able to sign contracts or hold property in their own names. Women did not gain the right to vote in federal elections until 1920 in the United States, with the passage of the 19th Amendment (although many women and men of color remained disenfranchised for decades longer). In England, women did not achieve that right until 1928. In Saudi Arabia, women were able to vote and run for office for the first time in 2015 (but still were not allowed to drive). Women in Vatican City (the country where the Pope resides) cannot vote. It was not until the 1960s that women in the United States were regularly allowed on juries and not until 1975 that married women in the United States were entitled to credit in their own names. Marital rape was not a crime in the United States until the 1980s. So, coverture in the United States has been eroded "bit by bit," wrote Allgor, but never fully or formally abolished. Indeed, its remnants persist. Allgor, who is a women's studies professor, wrote for example of recently applying for a home loan with her husband. She made more money, had longer work experience, and had owned more homes than her husband, yet the loan officer insisted on listing her husband as the primary borrower and Allgor as the co-borrower. Why? The lawyers would "fuss" and insist on the "traditional" order anyway, the loan officer reported; "It's a man's world."

Globally, the status of women is improving but women must still clear incredible hurdles to achieving equality. Although 136 countries explicitly guarantee equality and nondiscrimination for women and men in their constitutions (the United States not among them), women worldwide face persistent discrimination with sometimes dire results. (For more on the struggle to pass an Equal Rights Amendment in the United States, see Chapter 11, "History of Women's Activism in the United States.")

The burdens of combining work and family life continue to fall more predominantly on women. "Men have traditionally combined work and family life by having the wife be in charge of the latter," asserted Basow (p. 133). According to a study by the Institute for Social Research at the University of Michigan, husbands created an extra 7 hours a week of housework for wives, whereas wives saved husbands from about an hour of housework a week (Mixon, 2008). If they have children, the burden for women usually increases. Although women are generally doing less housework than they did 50 years ago and men are doing more, women still work longer total hours, paid and unpaid, than men nearly everywhere, except perhaps Norway and Sweden (Antonopolous, 2009).

Elderly women too are vulnerable, particularly if they have spent most of their lives as unpaid homemakers or in low-paying jobs with few benefits. Such women rarely have pensions of their own and only 10 percent receive pension benefits from their husband's plans if they outlive them (Basow). "The result is that 40 percent of all women over 60 years of age have incomes below or only slightly above poverty level," reported Basow (p. 134).

As this brief description makes clear, the struggle for women's equality globally—including in the United States—is far from ancient history; indeed, it is far from over. Women in the United States have enjoyed basic legal rights—such as the right to vote—for less than 100 years (many people of color for less than 60 years). Women globally continue to lag behind men in the recognition of their basic human rights. Laws, of course, do not guarantee equal treatment, and discrimination on a number of fronts persists.

Feminism

The "F" word! **Feminist**. This is probably the most difficult of all the words in this textbook to unpack—not because the definition is hard to understand, but because the preconceptions about feminism and feminists are so strong and often so far off the mark. Let's begin with a simple question: Do you believe in the political, economic, and social equality of all people? This is not a trick question. If you believe that all people should have the same opportunities and rights in these three areas, you are in agreement with a basic tenet of feminism. A very basic definition of a feminist, then, is someone who believes in or advocates for the political, economic, and social equality of all people regardless of sex.

Another question: name three leading feminist figures. In our experience, many students have difficulty naming people who are feminists, yet many also report that the word "feminist" seems negative to them. This may in large part be because in the mass media, it is common to hear commentators railing against feminists. Feminists seem to be the boogey "men" of our time, often mentioned in the media but rarely seen. When we ask students to paint a picture of a stereotypical feminist (not necessarily a true picture), they may describe a "bitter," "angry," "man-hating," "fat," "hairy-legged" "dyke." But as the definition of feminism indicates and a quick Google search of who identifies as a feminist shows, this is, like all stereotypes, a caricature. You do not have to be a woman to be a feminist; anyone can be a feminist. You do not have to be a lesbian to be a feminist. You certainly do not have to be bitter or hate men to be a feminist. You do not have to be a woman with hairy legs to be a feminist. (But you can be.)

FIGURES 3.4–3.6

The author Chimamanda Ngozi Adichie (left), actors Tina Fey and Amy Poehler (middle), and actor Rosario Dawson (right) identify as feminists.

We have provided a simple, easy to understand definition of feminism, and although it accurately describes many feminists and provides a good jumping-off point for discussion, it leaves important questions unanswered. For example, what is political, economic, and social equality? How do we achieve it? Is equality of the sexes a sufficient end? Different feminists have different answers to these questions. As a result, there are many different forms of feminism, which often overlap and intersect. Although we will explore many of these in the following chapters, we would like to discuss one more definition of feminism here, that espoused by the feminist theorist bell hooks (2000/2014):

> *Simply put, feminism is a movement to end sexism, sexist exploitation, and oppression. This was a definition of feminism I offered in* Feminist Theory: From Margin to Center *more than 10 years ago. It was my hope at the time that it would become a common definition everyone would use. I liked this definition because it did not imply that men were the enemy. By naming sexism as the problem it went directly to the heart of the matter. Practically, it is a definition which implies that all sexist thinking and action is the problem, whether those who perpetuate it are female or male, child or adult. It is also broad enough to include an understanding of systemic institutionalized sexism. As a definition it is open-ended. To understand feminism it implies one has to necessarily understand sexism. (p. 1)*

hooks and many other feminists wish to push feminism beyond the goal of equality between women and men, saying that altering the current system so that women have more rights is insufficient (in part because this approach does not sufficiently recognize race and class oppressions that subjugate many women and men). Much deeper change is necessary, wrote hooks (2000/2014), nothing short of restructuring society to end patriarchy and sexism.

FIGURE 3.7
Frederick Douglass, an abolitionist writer and orator, supported women's rights and was a feminist. He wrote (1892/2001), "I have never yet been able to find one consideration, one argument, or suggestion in favor of man's right to participate in civil government which did not equally apply to the right of woman."

THE "MYTHICAL NORM"

Throughout the text so far, we have been discussing "women" and "men" as if such generic figures exist. And in fact, as you have been reading, you have probably pictured such a woman or man. She or he could be anyone, right?— Or more accurately, no one in particular? Well, as it turns out, the answer is likely no. Research has shown that most Americans, when asked to describe a stereotypical woman—or man, for that matter—do not exactly think in generic terms. In fact, they think in rather specific terms, and most often (unless asked to do otherwise) the woman they conjure is white and middle class; likewise for the man. So, the stereotypical woman has not only a race (white) but also a socioeconomic status (middle class) and probably some other traits as well. She is probably moderately attractive, of medium build, and able bodied. These are characteristics that most of us assume.

The poet and feminist activist Audre Lorde (1978/1984) gave a name to such stereotypical figures: the **mythical norm**. Lorde wrote, "Somewhere, on the edge of consciousness, there is what I call a *mythical norm*. . . . In america, (*sic*) this norm is usually defined as white, thin, male, young, heterosexual, christian, and financially secure. It is with this mythical norm that the trappings of power reside within this society" (p. 116). Unsurprisingly, for those outside Lorde's mythical norm (where she placed herself as a Black, lesbian, woman poet), there are serious consequences beyond invisibility. Women, men, and others whose identities lie at the intersection of categories other than white, male, heterosexual, and able bodied (and potentially many other categories, depending on the context) may be disadvantaged in unique ways.

Intersectionality

In the late 1980s the feminist and legal scholar Kimberlé Crenshaw, building on the work of other Black feminists, introduced the term intersectionality to describe a method of analysis that examined the "ways in which gender and race interact to shape the multiple dimensions" of experience (Crenshaw, 1991, p. 1244). (We discussed this term briefly in Chapter 1.) Intersectionality, asserted Crenshaw (1989), was meant to counter the "tendency to treat race and gender as mutually exclusive categories" (p. 39)—that is, the tendency to think about one without considering the influence of the other. Although Crenshaw emphasized the categories of gender and race in her early work, intersectional analysis is in no way limited to these categories and may also consider categories such as socioeconomic status/class, sexuality/sexual identity, age, language, immigration status, religion, disability, and more, depending on the context.

Crenshaw (1989) described intersectionality using the analogy of the traffic intersection: just as traffic flows in many ways at a four-way intersection, so discrimination can come from many directions based on race, sex, or other factors. Crenshaw (1989) also asserted that discrimination faced by those with intersectional identities was not additive, that is, it did not simply equal race discrimination plus sex discrimination. In the case of Black women, Crenshaw (1989) explained,

Black women sometimes experience discrimination in ways similar to white women's experiences; sometimes they share very similar experiences with Black men. Yet often they experience double-discrimination—the combined effects of practices which discriminate on the basis of race, and on the basis of sex. And sometimes, they experience discrimination as Black women—not the sum of race and sex discrimination, but as Black women. (p. 44)

Discrimination, in our view, can vary depending on several factors: (1) the unique combination of characteristics of the person or group being discriminated against (their race, sex, class, sexual orientation, etc.); (2) the unique combination of characteristics of the person or group doing the discrimination (their race, sex, class, sexual orientation, etc.); and (3) the context in which the discrimination occurs. In a related discussion of oppression, the sociologist Patricia Hill Collins (1990/2002) noted, "Depending on the context, individuals and groups may be alternately oppressors in some settings, oppressed in others, or simultaneously oppressing and oppressed in still others" (p. 246). For example, a middle-class Asian American female may face discrimination at home from her husband because he wants her to conform to traditional conceptions of femininity and female gender roles and also face sexual harassment from her white boss who stereotypes Asian American women as sexually exotic. At the same time, this woman may discriminate against lesbians and gay men in her own hiring decisions at work.

In Crenshaw's later work, she emphasized that although intersectionality begins with "the infinite combinations and implications of overlapping identities," it does not end there (Cho et al., 2013, p. 797). It is also concerned with the processes that advantage some while disadvantaging others. We will explore further layers of intersectionality theory in Chapter 12, "Feminisms."

OPPRESSION

So far in this chapter we have covered a lot of territory about gender, inequality, and the struggle for equality. To try to put this all together we would like to explore another important concept in women's, gender, and sexuality studies (which bell hooks [2000/2014] employs in her definition of feminism)—the concept of **oppression**.

Marilyn Frye (1983), a philosopher and feminist theorist, has examined the situation of women and has argued that all women, regardless of race and class, are oppressed as women. Frye looked to the root of the word, "press," to understand the meaning of the word oppression. To be pressed is to be caught between opposing forces. Building on this, she stated that oppression is a network of forces that together restrict the freedom of individuals. The position of women, she argued, is analogous to a bird in a cage. Each wire of the cage represents one of the forces that restrict women's freedom. As Frye said, each individual wire is relatively inconsequential. A bird could fly around any given wire, but together, these restrictions form a network that prevents the bird from escaping. Frye would argue that many of the limitations that we have explored in this chapter are analogous to these wires. Women are paid less for equal work, they face double binds and double standards, feminine qualities are devalued in women (and men), women who are not feminine enough are subject to a backlash, and more. Individually, these impediments may be relatively minor, but taken as a whole they form an oppressive network of forces that limits women.

Frye contended that oppression can occur only because one is a member of an oppressed class. Thus, Frye argued, women are oppressed *as women*. That is, simply because women belong to the class, women, they face the systemic restrictive forces we have discussed. In particular, she said that all women, regardless of race and class, are expected to perform one special class of work: they must perform **service work** for men. This can be thought of as the responsibilities of caretaking, nurturing, supporting, and assisting. Frye divided this work into three forms of service: personal service, including the work of "maids, butlers, cooks, personal secretaries"; sexual service, which includes not only pleasing men through sex but also childbearing and pleasing men by being attractive and pleasant; and ego service, which includes "encouragement, support, praise and attention" (p. 9).

One might hope that in a heterosexual relationship both women and men would care for, nurture, and support one another in these ways. Frye was not suggesting that in itself it is wrong for women (or men) to do service work; what she objected to is the lopsided nature of this service. As Frye said, "But at every race/class level and even across race/class lines men do not serve women as women serve men." She went on to say that "women's sphere" (or women's place) "may be understood as the service sector" in the deepest sense of the phrase (p. 10). Although there may be exceptions to Frye's broad claim about service work, the gender roles we have discussed do suggest that girls and women are generally required to do more kinds of service and to a greater extent than boys and men.

One might wonder whether upper-class women have the same burden of service as middle- and working-class women. Frye stated that at higher class levels, women may not have to do all this service work but they often oversee the hiring of service workers and supervise their work. A good example might be the "first lady" of the United States. Although first ladies do not hang drapes in the White House or cook dinners for visiting heads of state, they traditionally oversee the decoration of the White House and state dinners. So, for example, the media reported that Michelle Obama organized the first state dinner of the Obama presidency and chose a new pattern for the White House china (Superville, 2015). Of the latter, she said, "I think . . . that's part of the job" (Malcolm, 2009) (Figure 3.8).

Frye stated that there are many oppressed classes of people. It is not hard to imagine that a person could be oppressed because of one's race, sexual orientation, economic class, age, etc. However, Frye asserted that men are not oppressed *as men*. They could be oppressed because they are gay men or Black men,

FIGURE 3.8
Michelle Obama's White House biography describes her "first and foremost" as a mom and a daughter. She is also a Yale and Harvard graduate, a lawyer, and a university administrator. Public images of Ms. Obama often represent her as a mother figure, as here.

but it is their homosexuality or race that is the reason for their oppression, not their maleness. To illustrate this, Frye described a rich, white South African playboy who broke his leg on a European ski slope. Was he miserable? Certainly. But he was not caught in a network of forces that caused his misery. If anything, his status as a rich, white man enabled him to deal with his situation in the best way possible, with the best possible care and comforts. To Frye, misery is a state of unhappiness that is not the result of a network of forces, but an *accidental* state, that is, it happens by chance without foresight or expectation. Developing an illness, breaking a bone, or financial misfortune can all be accidental events.

Frye's hypothetical example of a rich, white South African playboy is telling. At the time she published this piece in 1983, South Africa enforced a system of racial segregation known as apartheid (which, coincidentally, is pronounced by South Africans as "apart-hate"). The example of the white South African playboy was meant to bring to mind this system, which oppressed Blacks and other people of color. In Frye's hypothetical situation, the South African play-boy became wealthy by investing in a diamond mine. Although Frye did not carry the example further, we would note that the dangerous work of mining was done by Black South Africans who were poorly paid, exposed to numerous dangers, and had no access to decent medical care. If a Black man working in this playboy's diamond mine broke his leg, he would be more than miserable. Although the injury may have been "accidental" in the immediate sense (no one may have foreseen the particular rock that fell and crushed his leg), it cer-tainly is foreseeable that diamond mine workers would suffer accidents in their dangerous occupation, especially given that there were few safety protections. The fact that he has no access to decent medical care and the fact that his leg may never heal properly and that he may never be able to work in the mines again is certainly something we could foresee. This Black South African man suffers then, not by accident, but because of the network of forces that conspire to cause him to suffer. In short, he is oppressed because he is a *Black* man; it is being Black that catches him up in the network of oppressive forces.

Reading Frye's analysis of the oppression of women, you might mistakenly assume that she is arguing that there is a vast conspiracy on the part of men to create this network of oppressive forces. Although Frye did believe that men as a whole benefit from the oppressive system, she was not saying that it is a con-scious conspiracy on the part of all men to subjugate women. In fact, it is pos-sible that most men are unaware of the network of forces that are in place. Despite this ignorance, Frye asserted that men perpetuate the system that ben-efits them. If you think about notions of gender and gender roles, it is easy to see how we all perpetuate them when our behavior supports traditional gender ideology and gender role expectations. It is not the individual actors who consciously engage in a conspiracy to oppress women that are the problem, but the sum total of our actions that affirm the "rightness" of gender and gender role norms. In this view, even women can contribute to the oppression of women.

What About the Oppression of Men?

One could disagree with Frye's conception of oppression on a number of fronts. One objection is to point out that men are oppressed, too. For example, in a letter to *The Humanist* magazine, a writer named Jerry Boggs (1996) objected to an article that presumed that "all men are awash in power and privilege" (2). He listed eight ways that men are oppressed, many focusing on the United States:

> Most people holding 25 of the 26 worst jobs are men.
>
> The overwhelming majority of those killed on the job are men.
>
> Men are more likely to be alcoholic and use illegal drugs than women.
>
> The vast majority of the prison population is male.
>
> Most homeless people are men.
>
> The suicide rate for men is higher than women.
>
> For centuries males have been enslaved by the military and have been killed by the millions.
>
> More men are murdered than women.

This list suggests that men frequently suffer and there is certainly truth that these harms are often related to gender. Warfare, for example, has historically been the province of men (at least as soldiers, although women have frequently been killed, maimed, raped, and starved in their role as "noncombatants"). Defenders of Frye's view of oppression might argue that many of these harms befall men not *as men* but as a kind of man. For example, poor men are more likely to be homeless and hold the worst jobs. The network of forces that restricts men in this case is not really operative on all men *as men* but on some men because they are *working-class or poor* men. Supporters of Frye's view might also argue that the beneficiaries of the systematic oppression of the men are, by and large, other men. This does not excuse ill treatment, but if we are to solve it we must accurately diagnose the cause.

Still another rejoinder to Boggs is that men's vulnerability to some forms of harm is simply the cost of having power in the first place. Frye took up just such an argument when she described the social pressure that men face to refrain from crying. She argued that men can cry "in the company of women" (p. 14) (she is probably thinking of men who cry in private in front of their girlfriends or wives), but that they suffer consequences for crying in the company of other men. She acknowledged that this may be painful but argued that it is a self-imposed constraint. Men could cry in the company of other men, but they choose not to. Why? Frye wrote that "the man who maintains a steely or tough or laid-back demeanor (all are forms which suggest invulnerability) marks himself as a member of the male community and is esteemed by men" (p. 14). Since men benefit by the "practice [of] this discipline," it is not really an involuntary restriction but a trade-off that gives men status (p. 15).

Not All Discrimination Is Oppression

Another objection to Frye can be found in the work of Wendy Kaminer, a lawyer, social critic, and feminist writer. Kaminer (1997), in the short essay "A Civic Duty to Annoy," proudly proclaimed herself to be a feminist who enjoys irritating her "more orthodox feminist colleagues" (p. 16). She stated that she disavows "any personal guilt at being born white and middle class" and, being based at Radcliffe College, she scoffs "every time I hear a Harvard student complain that she's oppressed" (p. 16). Despite Kaminer's view that Harvard students are incredibly privileged people, she qualified her criticism by saying,

> I don't mean to scoff at the discrimination that a young woman of any color may have experienced or is likely to experience someday. I do want to remind her that as a student at Harvard/Radcliffe or any other elite university she enjoys many more advantages than a working class white male attending a community college. And that the kind of discrimination that students are apt to encounter at Harvard—relatively subtle and occasional—is not "oppression." It does not systematically deprive people of basic civil rights and liberties, and is not generally sanctioned by the administration. (p. 16)

Although Kaminer did not address Frye and her argument directly, hers is an interesting counterpoint to Frye's position. Kaminer asserted that the label of oppression should be reserved only for the denial of basic civil rights and liberties: restrictions on freedom of speech, the denial of the right to vote, and the like. By contrast, Frye believed that a woman at Harvard/Radcliffe, despite her advantages, could face a network of subtle forms of discrimination that together limit her (like being in a birdcage) and that this should be called oppression.

Kaminer acknowledged that women can and do face discrimination; in the essay she described women objecting to offensive T-shirts worn by men or encountering derogatory remarks about women online. However, she argued that these forms of expression, uncomfortable though they may be, particularly if they are not aimed at an individual, should not be categorized as oppression. Her point was that to claim that a woman at an elite university is oppressed trivializes the notion of oppression. As Kaminer wrote, "What's lost is a sense of perspective. If attending Harvard is oppression, what was slavery?" (p. 18).

Kaminer, who is a strong free speech advocate, appeared to be fearful that if we classify derogatory speech about women as "oppressive" and then move to censor it, we will move society to a position where upon feeling hurt or upset by any speech, we will simply censor it (note, Frye did not advocate this). Kaminer believed that such a societal attitude actually endangers the rights of women to advocate for women's rights. It is not that she approves of derogatory remarks about women, but if you insist on suppressing them, you must allow the suppression of remarks by women's rights advocates that may offend others. And Kaminer stated, "There would be no feminist movement if women never dared to give offense" (p. 18).

It is certainly true that the fight for women's equality has been a contentious one that has offended the sensibilities of many. Kaminer further argued that "communities are built on compromise, and compromise presupposes disagreement" (p. 18). If democracy is about the vigorous clash of ideas and perspectives, then ultimately our most important duty is not to paper over our differences but rather to foster vigorous debate. Thus, Kaminer said, we have "a civic duty to annoy."

Frye and Kaminer's disagreement about the definition of oppression is significant for several reasons. First, it raises the issue of how damaging various forms of social pressure and societal norms are to the freedom of women. It would be a mistake to think that Kaminer was saying that no social pressures can ever be oppressive, but she was suggesting that sometimes these pressures, uncomfortable though they may be, are not genuinely oppressive in the way that slavery or disenfranchisement (being denied the right to vote) is oppressive. In contrast, Frye's analysis suggested that social pressures can be both subtle and profoundly limiting. She might argue that Kaminer has failed to take a wider view: individual restrictions women face (offensive T-shirts, derogatory remarks online, etc.), when added together, create a network of forces that are stronger than the sum of their parts. Kaminer might counter that for some elite women, their status and power prevent this network of forces from being truly oppressive.

Frye and Kaminer's disagreement is also significant because it raises the importance of intersectional analysis, that is, the idea that individuals must not be reduced to a single facet of their identity (such as their sex) but that to understand a person's position you must examine the intersection of various elements. Frye's anecdote and Kaminer's examples about the issue of oppression deliberately inject race/racism and class/class exploitation into our awareness and our discussion. We have begun to explore a number of social categories in this chapter, but as we proceed, we will explore them in more depth so that you are equipped with the information and theories you need to employ intersectional analysis.

CONCLUSION

In this chapter we have examined the social construction of gender. Because of gender polarization in U.S. society, from a very young age, children learn to distinguish gender based on social cues and become gender schematic. In childhood, boys are prescribed more rigid gender roles but as girls grow, acceptable choices for gendered behavior become narrower.

Traditional gender ideologies (often exemplified by emphasized femininity and hegemonic masculinity) have social costs especially for women, who are often disadvantaged socially, economically, and politically. Because of such gender ideologies, women face double binds and double standards. Women are also subject to sexism, which is grounded in the idea of masculine dominance. Misogyny is "a hatred or dislike of, or prejudice against women" (OED) or, more precisely, feminine qualities in women. It is closely related to homophobia, which involves the hatred of feminine qualities in men.

Patriarchy is a system under which women are subordinated to men in society. One response to patriarchy is feminism, which, in the simplest terms, is the belief in the political, economic, and social equality of all people. bell hooks (2000/2014) defined feminism as "a movement to end sexism, sexist exploitation, and oppression." Audre Lorde's (1978/1984) idea of the mythical norm reminds us that gender is not the only basis for subjugation within society. The intersection of gender with race, class, ethnicity, religion, language, disability, age, and other factors must also be considered.

Marilyn Frye has argued that all women, regardless of race and class, face oppression, a network of forces that together restrict women's freedom. Wendy

Key Terms

Kaminer, however, cautioned that not all discrimination is oppression, a label that should be reserved only for the denial of basic civil rights and liberties. Both Frye and Kaminer made compelling arguments and provide a useful example of how feminists can constructively disagree while working toward common goals.

THINK, LEARN, ACT

The following resources are available on the Student Website: www.oup.com/us /gillis-jacobs

Taking Stock, Taking Action prompts and activities. Apply what you've learned to take action on campus and in the broader community.

Recommended Readings and Multimedia Resources, including scholarly and literary works, documentaries, feature films, podcasts and more, to enrich the in- and out-of-classroom experience.

LGBTQQIAA IDENTITIES AND CHALLENGES

Imagine a man named Juan who has been married to a woman for 25 years and has had three children who are biologically his with his wife. Now imagine that for his entire life he has felt sexual attraction to men and not to women; however, because the society he lives in does not accept same-sex attraction, he has hidden his true feelings and never engaged in same-sex sexual activity. Most of us would likely classify this man as a homosexual or gay man. We would probably regard him as "in the closet"—someone who conceals his sexual orientation from others.

By contrast, imagine a man named John who identifies himself as heterosexual who goes to prison for 25 years. Although he would like to have sex with women, because he has no opportunity to do so, he engages in sex with men. Is this man straight? Some might insist that John is really gay because he is having sex with men. Under this conception, if a man has sex with men, no matter what the circumstances, then he is truly gay. In the case of Juan, the closeted gay man, he has only had heterosexual sex (including sex to the point of orgasm on at least the three occasions that yielded his children) and yet most people have no trouble classifying him as gay. Given that the "desire" of both Juan and John is toward someone whom they are not having sex with, couldn't one argue that the cases are parallel and that classifying John as gay represents a double standard?

You will recall that in Chapter 1, "Sex, Gender, and Social Construction," we defined sexual orientation simply as the attraction one has to others based on one's sex and/or gender in relation to another's sex and/or gender. But we noted that sexual orientation (like sex and gender) is more complicated and that more sophisticated conceptions reject both the heterosexual/homosexual binary and sexual orientation as a static category. The above scenarios demonstrate some of the complexity of clearly defining sexual orientation. In this chapter we will explore why a universally accepted definition of sexual orientation remains elusive, how Western society has sometimes constructed and schematized (systematically arranged) sexual orientation, and the many identities associated with it.

MEASURING SEXUAL ORIENTATION

Some of the earliest measures of sexual orientation divided people into one of two categories: homosexual or heterosexual. The sex researcher Alfred Kinsey and his associates opposed this either/or dichotomy, saying,

> *The world is not to be divided into sheep and goats. Not all things are black nor all things white. It is a fundamental of taxonomy [the systematic classification of living organisms (OED)] that nature rarely deals with discrete categories. Only the human mind invents categories and tries to force facts into separated pigeon-holes. The living world is a continuum in each and every one of its aspects. The sooner we learn this concerning human sexual behavior the sooner we shall reach a sound understanding of the realities of sex. . . .*

> *It is characteristic of the human mind that it tries to dichotomize [divide into two parts] in its classification of phenomena. Things are either so, or they are not so. Sexual behavior is either normal or abnormal, socially acceptable or unacceptable, heterosexual or homosexual; and many persons do not want to believe that there are gradations in these matters from one to the other extreme. (as cited in Sell, 1997, p. 651) [brackets not in Sell]*

Kinsey Scale

In keeping with his philosophy, Kinsey developed a 7-point scale known as the Kinsey Heterosexual–Homosexual Rating Scale, or **Kinsey Scale**, in which individuals were assigned ratings from exclusively heterosexual to exclusively homosexual. The 5 points in between allowed for what we today call varying degrees of bisexuality (attraction to more than one sex). (Figure 4.1.) In 1948, Kinsey added an X category to account for those with "no socio-sexual contacts or reactions" (Kinsey et al., 1948/1998, p. 656), which today we call asexual (AVEN, 2012). It is interesting to note that Kinsey disagreed with the "use of the terms heterosexual and homosexual . . . as nouns" (Kinsey et al., p. 657). He himself used the terms as adjectives to indicate that he did not think

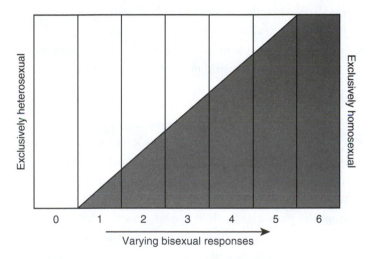

The Meaning of the Ratings:

0—Exclusively heterosexual with no homosexual

1—Predominantly heterosexual, only incidentally homosexual

2—Predominantly heterosexual, but more than incidentally homosexual

3—Equally heterosexual and homosexual

4—Predominantly homosexual, but more than incidentally heterosexual

5—Predominantly homosexual, only incidentally heterosexual

6—Exclusively homosexual

X—No socio-sexual contacts or reactions (category added in Kinsey reports of 1948 and 1953)

Source: Kinsey, A. C., Pomeroy, W. B., & Martin, C. E. (1948/1998).

Sexual Behavior in the Human Male. Bloomington, IN: Indiana University Press.

FIGURE 4.1

of homosexuals or heterosexuals as identifiable sexual types (Weinrich, 2014b).

Although Kinsey's scale is a step forward from the binary division of people into gay or straight, some experts believe it still does not capture the range of human sexual orientation. For example, in the scenarios of Juan and John described at the beginning of this chapter, both could be described as bisexual on the Kinsey Scale but this misses an important distinction between the two men. Regardless of their sexual experiences, Juan would rather have sex with a man and John would rather have sex with a woman. A problem with the Kinsey Scale, which Kinsey himself acknowledged, is that it merges two aspects of sexuality that many believe should be measured separately: what Kinsey called "overt sexual experience"—or actual sexual experience—and "psychosexual reactions" (cited in Sell, p. 652). Wenrich (2014b) referred to the latter as "erotic responsiveness" (p. 323). Juan's overt sexual experience is sex with a woman, whereas John's overt sexual experience is sex with women (before prison) and men (in prison). In terms of psychosexual reactions, Juan would prefer to have sex with men and John would prefer to have sex with women.

Klein Grid

Fritz Klein (1993) attempted to address this shortcoming of the Kinsey Scale by developing the Klein Sexual Orientation Grid, or **Klein Grid**, which assesses seven dimensions: (1) sexual attraction, (2) sexual behavior, (3) sexual fantasies, (4) emotional preference, (5) social preference, (6) self-identification, and (7) heterosexual/homosexual lifestyle. The Klein Grid also adds another important dimension: the potential to change over time. Each of these factors is self-assessed during the past, the present, and the person's ideal. (Figure 4.2.) In both the Kinsey Scale and the Klein Grid the numbers do not yield any further conclusion; that is, the numbers are not processed further to yield a final summary "answer" to a person's sexual orientation. The purpose of plotting people is simply to become aware of the nuances of sexual orientation.

Although the Klein Grid appears to be an improvement over the Kinsey Scale, the researcher Randall Sell noted several concerns regarding the model. First, researchers studying sexual orientation find it difficult to use such a complicated multidimensional scale in their research. Imagine creating a questionnaire with dozens of items that you want to collect data about and then having to combine them with all the additional questions about sexual orientation from the Klein Grid. Such surveys could become unmanageable. A second concern is that the various dimensions have not yet been

The Klein Sexuality Grid

	Variable	Past	Present	Ideal
A	Sexual Attraction			
B	Sexual Behavior			
C	Sexual Fantasies			
D	Emotional Preference			
E	Social Preference			
F	Heterosexual/Homosexual Lifestyle			
G	Self-identification			

For variables A to E:

1 = Other sex only
2 = Other sex mostly
3 = Other sex somewhat more
4 = Both sexes
5 = Same sex somewhat more
6 = Same sex mostly
7 = Same sex only

For variables F to G:

1 = Heterosexual only
2 = Heterosexual mostly
3 = Heterosexual somewhat more
4 = Hetero/Gay-Lesbian equally
5 = Gay-Lesbian somewhat more
6 = Gay-Lesbian mostly
7 = Gay-Lesbian only

FIGURE 4.2

systematically studied to determine whether they are truly important and distinct dimensions of sexual orientation.

Homosociality—One interesting element of the Klein Grid is social preference, or the sex of those with whom you socialize. There are a variety of social relationships between people of the same sex within society. These relationships are known as **homosocial** relationships. The professor and queer theorist Eve Kosofsky Sedgwick (1985) distinguished the term homosocial from homosexual, noting that homosocial "is a word occasionally used in history and the social sciences where it describes social bonds between persons of the same sex . . . it is applied to such activities as 'male bonding,' which may, as in our society, be characterized by intense homophobia, fear and hatred of homosexuality" (p. 1). Homosocial behavior can include "a boys' (or girls') night out," same-sex fraternity or sorority activities, same-sex sports activities, etc.

These and other homosocial activities may occur in homosexual or non-homosexual contexts. Many who study sexual orientation in culture believe that homosociality is often an important element of how sexual orientations manifest themselves in society. For example, some subcultures of gay men socialize almost exclusively with men. In contrast, many straight male groups such as fraternities stress homosocial bonding as integral to their heterosexual identity. Homosociality, then, is a complex and widespread form of bonding that can be used to reinforce a variety of subcultural perspectives on sexual orientation.

Storms's Scale

The psychologist Michael D. Storms proposed a modification of Kinsey's bipolar scale (which, you will remember, places heterosexuality and homosexuality on opposite ends of a single continuum). **Storms's Scale** is based on Kinsey's idea that sexual orientation should be based on the "type, extent, and frequency" of a person's "erotic fantasies" (Storms, 1980, p. 784). So, unlike the Klein Grid, the degree of homoeroticism and heteroeroticism are the only dimensions. This results in an orthogonal chart (a square chart with two axes)—the horizontal axis measures heteroeroticism (low to high, measured left to right) and the vertical axis measures homoeroticism (low to high, measured bottom to top). The resulting chart, then, has four categories (represented by four boxes): homosexuals (upper left), who are classified as high in homoeroticism and low in heteroeroticism; bisexuals (upper right), who are high in homoeroticism and high in heteroeroticism; asexuals (bottom left), who are low in homoeroticism and low in heteroeroticism; and heterosexuals (bottom right), who are low in homoeroticism and high in heteroeroticism (Storms).

Just as the feminist psychologist Sandra Bem (1993) argued that femininity and masculinity may vary independently, so a person could be high in both masculinity and femininity, high in one and low in another, or low in both (see Chapter 3, "Gender and In/Equality"), Storms's Scale allowed for a person to be highly erotically oriented toward males and females, high toward only one, or low toward both. One clear advantage of this chart, apart from treating homoeroticism and heteroeroticism as varying independently, is that it also allows for the recognition of a fourth category: asexuals—people who have little or no erotic attraction to others (see the section "A/Asexual"). James D. Weinrich (2014b), who was a colleague of Fritz Klein, called Storms's Scale compelling, but noted that there has been almost no research using this approach, perhaps because the scale has been misunderstood.

Looking Back, Looking Forward

Sexual orientation has been studied for more than 150 years, yet it "remains an elusive concept" (Galupo et al., 2014, p. 404). Despite the development of the measuring tools we have discussed here (and others), "there is still little consensus on how the term 'sexual orientation'" is best defined and measured (Lovelock, 2014, p. 457). Weinrich (2014a) has noted the need for new measuring tools, specifically scales that measure sex with or attraction to women and men separately (as Storms's does) and offer ways to record sexual fluidity, that is, the idea that one's orientation may be a range, undefined, or something else altogether. In the end, concluded Weinrich (2014a), there is still "a lot of methodological work to do" (p. 555).

What can we say about sexual orientation then? Like our definitions of sex and gender, our definition of sexual orientation is provisional and open to change. Sexual orientation describes people's attractions (sexual and/or romantic) and sexual activities. Sexual orientation is not static or stable; it can change over time, as does our understanding of it.

LGBTQQIAA IDENTITIES

Many involved in counseling, teaching, and activism about sexual orientation speak of terms related to sexual orientation that can be abbreviated as LGBTQQIAA—although it is frequently represented as LGBT.

L/Lesbian

The "L" that begins the alphabetic string stands for lesbian, a female who is attracted to other females. Given that there is no generally accepted definition of sexual orientation, we are deliberately using the relatively vague word attraction in our definition of the term lesbian. Attraction can be thought of as including any of the seven Klein Grid factors: (1) sexual attraction to females, (2) sexual activity with females, (3) sexual fantasies about females, (4) emotional preference for females, (5) social preference for females, (6) lesbian lifestyle, and (7) lesbian identification. As the Klein Grid suggests, lesbianism need not be conceived of as a permanent state of being; a lesbian sexual orientation may change over time. (Note that as with our discussion of the terms sex and gender, we consider "sexual orientation" a social construct; so this definition of lesbian is provisional, as are all of the definitions in this chapter related to the LGBTQQIAA string. See the section on Q/Queer for more on our perspective).

The placement of lesbian first in this string is not accidental. As we discussed in Chapter 2, "Language and Communication," males are often the primary

FIGURE 4.3
LGBT Pride March, New York City, June 24, 2007.

focus in society. When it comes to discussing sexual orientation and homosexuality, this focus persists and attention often shifts from homosexuality in general to male homosexuals in particular. Putting lesbian first in this string is an attempt to correct the elision, or the action of dropping out or suppressing lesbians.

G/Gay

"G" stands for gay males. Although it is true that both of the words homosexual and gay are umbrella terms that refer to both females and males, gay is also often used specifically to refer to gay males. As with lesbianism, we will define male homosexuality broadly as male same-sex attraction.

B/Bisexual

"B" stands for **bisexual**. Given that there is a degree of sexual fluidity in human beings, what does it mean to be bisexual? Some have claimed that everyone is to some degree bisexual (such as Sigmund Freud, 1916/1920). Even if this were true, many believe that declaring everyone bisexual dilutes the meaning of the term and that the word should be used to refer to people who demonstrate more significant bisexual desire and/or behavior.

The legal scholar Kenji Yoshino (2000) clarified further, arguing that the term bisexual should be reserved for people who have sexual desire for both sexes that is more than occasional or incidental. Yoshino did not assert that the desire for both sexes must be equal in strength or experienced at the same time. According to his view, a woman who has only had serious relationships with women but consistently experiences sexual desires for men should be considered bisexual. His definition would exclude people who have "experimented" with homosexual sex and subsequently engaged only in heterosexual sex for the remainder of their lives. It would also exclude a woman who engages in same-sex activity purely to excite a boyfriend. His definition would also exclude gay people who have similarly experimented with heterosexual sex.

Other definitions of bisexuality may include dimensions other than sexual desire. Definitions may include attraction more broadly (both sexual attraction and romantic desire) as well as sexual behavior and sexual self-identification. The Klein Grid is an example of a way of mapping sexual orientation that takes all three of these factors into account. Robin Ochs (2014), in contrast to Yoshino, defined a bisexual as someone who has "the potential to be attracted— romantically and/or sexually—to people of more than one sex and/or gender, not necessarily at the same time, not necessarily in the same way, and not necessarily to the same degree" (para. 1).

Regardless of the definition of bisexuality, it appears to be more common than homosexuality. Yoshino, for example, noted that using his relatively narrow definition of bisexuality to analyze five major sexuality studies (by Kinsey, Masters and Johnson, Janus and Janus, Laumann, and Wellings) indicated that bisexuals make up "from 0.2 percent to 15 percent" of the population and that in all the studies the frequency of bisexuality was greater or equal to the incidence of homosexuality (p. 13).

Although the number of bisexuals appears equal to or greater than the number of homosexuals, society seems less willing to recognize the existence of bisexuality, and so bisexuals remain hidden. When sexual orientation is raised as a subject for public discussion, it is usually conceived as an issue of heterosexuality *or* homosexuality. For example, when the issue of sexual orientation comes up in class or on the news, it may include a discussion of discrimination against gays or gay rights more generally, but it is less likely to include mention of discrimination against bisexuals or bisexual rights. The schematization of sexual orientation as a binary (homosexual/heterosexual) has the

FIGURE 4.4

Bisexual Network Marchers at Gay Pride March. Small placards read "Queer Is as Queer Does," "Don't Assume I'm Gay," and "Don't Assume I'm Straight."

effect of erasing bisexuality (known as bisexual erasure) from our thinking and public discussion of sexual orientation. So, just as women and lesbians are vulnerable to elision or erasure in society, so too are bisexuals.

T/Transgender

"T" stands for transgender (also known as gender variant or gender noncon-forming, among other identifiers). When it was first coined, the term referred to crossing gender boundaries. The transgender activist Virginia Prince is "often recognized as the person who brought the term *transgenderist* into wide usage" (Currah, 2006, p. 3). Prince used the term to mean someone who crossed the "gender barrier" (that is, expressed gender nonnormatively) but did not attempt to change their assigned sex (Currah, p. 3). A man who dresses as a woman (but does not undergo a sex reassignment process) would fit Prince's definition of crossing the gender barrier. Prince was involved with several organizations devoted to cross-dressers—people who express gender nonnormatively by dressing in clothes generally considered appropriate to a different sex than their assigned sex. Prince's organizations were exclusively for heterosexual cross-dressers and it is important to note that cross-dressing is not necessarily related to sexual orientation. A person who cross-dresses is also sometimes called a transvestite (from the latin *trans,* to cross over, and *vestire,* to dress) and cross-dressing is called transvestitism; however, because of its associations with the medical community the term is sometimes considered derogatory (Venus, 2011).

In the early 1950s, an American ex-G.I. named George Jorgensen, whose assigned sex at birth was male, underwent surgery and hormone treatment in Denmark to transition from male to female. Her return to the United States as Christine Jorgensen became a media sensation and created popular awareness of what was then called "transsexualism." GLAAD (2015) noted that "transsexual" is "an older term that originated in the medical and psychological communities" (in this sense, it is like the term homosexual) and is "still preferred by some people who have permanently changed—or seek to change—their bodies through medical interventions" such as hormones and/or surgeries. Unlike "transgender," however, transsexual is "not an umbrella term. Many transgender people do not identify as transsexual" (even if they have had medical interventions) (GLAAD). GLAAD advised that "it is best to ask which term an individual prefers." (We will use it when a specific person self-identifies as transsexual or when we need to refer specifically to people who have undergone the sex reassignment process. Transsexual, like "transgender," is used as an adjective, for example, transsexual woman.)

Christine Jorgensen was not the first person to undergo modern sex reassignment surgery but she was the first to draw such widespread public attention. Today, there are various terms used to describe transgender-related surgeries, including gender or sex reassignment surgery, and gender-affirming or gender-confirming surgery (Chyten-Brennan, 2014). (The term "sex change" is now considered a derogatory term.)

By the mid-20th century, the medical establishment recognized both cross-dressing and transsexualism but considered them separate categories. To be diagnosed as transsexual, people not only had to feel an affinity for different-sex clothing but also had to feel like they were "born in the wrong body" and have a desire to express different-gender characteristics in stereotypical ways.

In 1991, the trans activist and author Holly Boswell wrote an influential article called "The Transgender Alternative" that argued transgender people had a healthy need to diverge from stereotypical gender norms and that a

breaking the frame
Acknowledging Trans Identity

FIGURE 4.5

The transgender activist Laverne Cox, star of *Orange Is the New Black*, was left off *Time*'s 100 most influential people list in 2014, despite receiving the fifth highest number of online votes. After an outcry, *Time* put Cox on its cover, calling the struggle for transgender rights "America's next civil rights frontier."

Jules Chyten-Brennan (2014) has written, "How anyone's gender is perceived on a daily basis is not related to our genitals at all—we never see, or even think about, most people's genitals, and yet we manage to relate to people as a certain gender without knowing this information. However, when our trans identity is revealed, our surgical status becomes crucial to others to place us in a new box." The curiosity about genital surgery, wrote Chyten-Brennan, also "has to do with the belief that we need to be able to fulfill particular sexual roles" (p. 265).

"As trans people, we are often asked whether we have had 'the surgery,' continued Chyten-Brennan. "Our surgical status as 'pre-op' or pre-operative versus 'post-op' or post-operative is also often used to judge whether we have 'completed' transition" (p. 265). When Katie Couric interviewed the trans activists Carmen Carrera and Laverne Cox in 2014, she pressed both about their physical transitions. Carrera told Couric she did not want to talk about such a personal matter. Cox explained: "I feel like the preoccupation with transition and with surgery objectifies trans people." She went on: "And then we don't really get the lived experiences and reality of trans people's lives."

"Perhaps when the world can consider that sexual orientation and gender identity exist as natural healthy spectrums, we will not hear this question quite so often," concluded Chyten-Brennan (p. 265).

Source: Chyten-Brennan, J. (2014). Surgical Transition. In L. Erickson-Schroth (Ed.), Trans Bodies, Trans Selves: A Resource for the Transgender Community (pp. 265–290). New York, NY: Oxford University Press.

path between cross-dressing and "transsexualism" was appropriate for many transgender people. By the 1990s this view had become well accepted within the transgender community, and as Dallas Denny (2006), a leader in the transgender rights movement, noted, "the cross dresser/transsexual dichotomy had been replaced by a model in which individuals could structure their lives, appearances, and genders along a continuum" (p. 180).

As a result of this shift in thinking, the term transgender took on meanings beyond the cross-dressing component originally intended by Virginia Prince. The political science and transgender studies professor Paisley Currah noted in *Transgender Rights* that today transgender is an umbrella term that covers a variety of gender identities and practices that seem to be "endlessly proliferating" (p. 5). As we noted in Chapter 1, this could mean people of one sex who choose to have sex reassignment surgery or hormonal treatment to bring their bodies more into alignment with another sex (Currah). It can also include people of one sex who choose to take on the gender that society considers traditionally appropriate for another sex. Among other practices, it can include heterosexual cross-dressing and gay drag. It also covers identities including butch lesbianism, American Indian third sex/third gender, and Hijras. (See Chapter 1 for a discussion of third sex/third gender and Chapter 5, "Constructions of Homosexualities," for a discussion of Hijras.) The gender studies professor Susan Stryker stated that transgender "refers to all identities or practices that cross over, cut across, move between, or otherwise queer socially constructed sex/gender boundaries" (as cited in Currrah, p. 4).

Oftentimes the word transgender is shortened to "trans"—which, like the word transgender, functions as an umbrella term. Some now also include an asterisk with the term, trans*, which is taken from computer search code where * represents a wildcard; a search for trans* would return any result beginning with trans, such as transgender and transsexual (Delaney, 2014; Ryan, 2014). Laine Delaney explained that "that little asterisk represents an inclusive stance" that could include "genderqueer, genderfluid, gender non-conforming, intersex" people and many others (p. 24). (See Appendix B, Names for People and Places for more.)

Although people who identify (or are identified) as transgender are not necessarily gay, the transgender movement is often closely linked with the gay community and gay activism. The civil rights attorney Shannon Price Minter (2006) wrote,

Many transgender people consider the gay community to be their only viable social and political home. In part . . . because a sizable percentage of transgender people also identify as lesbian, gay, or bisexual. More fundamentally, it is

FIGURE 4.6
The sign held by this
TransLatina features a
popular transgender
symbol that combines
elements of both the
female and the male
symbols.

because homophobia and transphobia are tightly intertwined, and because antigay bias often takes the form of violence against those who are seen as transgressing gender norms. (p. 142)

ON THE
web

For more information about
**transgender people and
military service**, see the
Student Website: www.oup
.com/us/gillis-jacobs

Minter also noted that transgender people are among the most "visible and vulnerable members of gay communities," at higher risk than others for being victims of violence, discrimination, being branded deviant, and being institutionalized in hospitals and prisons (p. 142). Transgender people played an important role at Stonewall—the uprising that is considered the beginning of the modern gay rights movement in the United States (See Chapter 5 for more on the Stonewall uprising.)

Q/Queer

"Q" refers to queer. Like transgender, queer has many meanings. Before it became part of this alphabetic string, queer originally meant "strange, odd, peculiar, eccentric. Also, of questionable character; suspicious, dubious" (OED). Eventually, it became a pejorative word for gay people. By the 1980s, however, it was being appropriated in a "gay affirmative" sense (Halperin, 2003, p. 339). Perhaps the group that did the most to popularize the term was Queer Nation, founded in 1990, whose activists would often shout at street demonstrations, "We're here, we're queer. Get used to it!" (Escoffier, 1998, p. 216).

Sometimes the term queer is used as an umbrella term for all LGBTQQIAA people. In another usage, to identify as queer is best thought of as an anti-identity that opposes the binary thinking of sex, gender, sexual orientation, and any number of other categories. In this respect, to be queer is to be fundamentally antinormative—that is, to be against the norms of sexual classification and all that goes with it. People who identify as queer may have sexual desires and/or engage in sexual practices that do not fall neatly into the LGBTQQIA system, but this is not always the case. For example, a person who could be classified as straight may choose to identify as queer because they oppose labeling or categorization generally or in solidarity with people of different sexual orientations. Cherríe Moraga (2000), a playwright, activist, and professor of comparative studies in race and ethnicity, argued that as long as a straight person is willing to take on the disenfranchised identity of being queer in all circumstances and is willing to lose something because of it, then "regardless of who you are sleeping with," it is acceptable to identify as queer (p. 75).

Queer has also become a verb. Recall that in the discussion of the term transgender, Stryker asserted that transgender "refers to all identities or practices that cross over, cut across, move between, or otherwise queer socially constructed sex/gender boundaries." The English professor Lynda Goldstein stated that

> to queer identity, nation or theory is to subvert expectations, open up possibilities for multiplicity, erase lines of division by repositioning the debate. No more ownership of identities or discourses. No borders. No ethnic models of identity as a basis for formulating a coherent politics. No coherence. No utopias. Bi? Trans? Straight? Gay? Lesbian? Whatever, queer theory responds. Get over categories. (as cited in Hafen, 2004, p. 187)

The term **queer theory** was coined by the Italian feminist Teresa de Lauretis in 1990, but according to the queer theory scholar Annamarie Jagose (1996), she gave up the term only 3 years later because "it had been taken over by those mainstream forces and institutions it had been coined to resist" (p. 127).

Texts that gave rise to queer theory are often said to include Cherríe Moraga's and Gloria Anzaldúa's *This Bridge Called My Back: Writings by Radical Women of Color* (1981/1983), Anzaldúa's *Borderlands/La Frontera: The New Mestiza* (1987), Judith Butler's *Gender Trouble* (1990/1999), and Eve Kosofsky Sedgwick's *Epistemology of the Closet* (1990)—although all were written before the term queer theory was in use (Halperin, 2003; Keating, 2009; Soto, 2013). One might define queer theory as "an approach to social and cultural study which seeks to challenge or deconstruct traditional ideas of sexuality and gender, esp. the acceptance of heterosexuality as normative and the perception of a rigid dichotomy of male and female traits" (OED). Jagose explained: "Broadly speaking, queer describes those gestures or analytical models which dramatise incoherencies in the allegedly stable relations between chromosomal sex, gender and sexual desire" (p. 3). By now it should be clear that this text attempts to raise questions concerning most categories (including notions of the stability of sex, gender, and sexual orientation) and attempts to suggest that sex, gender, and sexual orientation are not necessarily connected in traditional ways. This is in keeping with a queer theoretical approach.

David M. Halperin (2003) argued that although queer theory has been "immensely valuable" (p. 343), it also has had some negative effects, including moving academia away from studying the concrete circumstances of lesbian and gay male culture. Because queer theory is often so concerned with "theory"—the critiquing of traditional ideas including those related to sexuality and gender—queer theoretical analysis sometimes fails to explore actual lesbian and gay male culture and students of queer theory may fail to learn or understand much about actual lesbian and gay people. (See Chapter 12, "Feminisms," and Appendix C, Feminisms in Brief for more on queer theory.)

Q/Questioning

The second letter "Q" stands for **questioning**. As various models suggest, sexual orientation is not necessarily fixed and for various reasons people may question their sexual identity. The inclusion of questioning opens up space for people who do not fit neatly into one box and are seeking to explore their identification.

I/Intersex

"I" refers to intersex. As we discussed in Chapter 1, intersex people have sex characteristics that make them different from predominant notions of biological femaleness and maleness. Sometimes this letter is omitted from the LGBTQQIAA string. Some argue that intersexuality, like transgender, is not about sexual orientation and thus does not belong under this alphabetic umbrella. Others argue that intersex people fall within the term transgender. Recall that Currah's definition of transgender included "any person whose *anatomy . . .* diverges from or is perceived to diverge from prevailing social norms about gender." Because intersex people "cross over, cut across, move between" or otherwise disrupt socially constructed sex/gender categories, intersex people could be considered transgendered. A broader question one could ask is, why include sexual variation in a discussion of sexual orientation? We think this inclusion is important for a few reasons. First, the LGBTQQIAA alphabetic string is a useful teaching tool despite its shortcomings and it is often the best opportunity to discuss transgender and intersex issues. Second, because sex and gender are often intimately connected with conceptions of sexual orientation, it seems fitting to include it within this context. Third, the LGBTQQIAA string is often an activist's tool used to highlight common interests and build coalitions, and it is certainly true that intersex and other LGBTQQAA people often feel the need to work together on related causes. However, we agree that the attempt to merge an ever-expanding array of identities and practices within what was supposed to be a short string of letters is imperfect; it can be unwieldy and may gloss over important differences between groups.

A/Asexual

The letter "A" stands for asexual. As noted in Chapter 1, in the field of biology, asexuality generally refers to a lack of sex-specific sex organs, but in the context of sexual orientation, being asexual means something different. Some define asexuality as having "no sexual attraction" to persons of any sex (Bogaert, 2004, p. 279). Others, such as Storms, define asexuality as low in heteroeroticism and homoeroticism. According to the Asexual Visibility and Education Network, or AVEN, an asexual person is someone who "experiences little or no sexual attraction" to other people. AVEN also notes that sexual orientation can be fluid and that if a person experiences "little or no sexual attraction to other people now, then [a person] can choose to identify as asexual." A study done by the professor Anthony F. Bogaert (2004) in Britain suggested that about 1 percent of the population are lifelong asexuals and that more women than men are asexual.

The American Psychological Association's (APA) *Diagnostic and Statistical Manual of Mental Disorders* recognized the possibility that a lack of sexual desire can be a mental disorder (for example, female sexual interest/arousal disorder or male hypoactive sexual desire disorder). The APA noted that for a diagnosis of these disorders, "clinically significant distress must accompany" symptoms (see also Bogaert, 2006; Brotto, 2010). The APA also noted that "if a lifelong lack of sexual desire is better explained by one's self-identification as 'asexual,'" then a diagnosis of female sexual interest/arousal disorder or male hypoactive sexual desire disorder is not made (see also Brotto). The diagnosis of sexual disorder must occur in the absence of certain medical conditions such as depression and medications that are known to reduce sexual desire. Because a lack of desire can be caused by medications or medical conditions, AVEN recommends that anyone who experiences "a sudden decline in sexual interest or attraction" should consult a doctor.

Asexuals differ from people who are celibate in that asexuals have a lack of sexual attraction, whereas celibates refrain from sex despite having sexual desire for others. Despite this lack of sexual attraction, asexuals can be romantically attracted to others, feel affection for others, find others beautiful, and even fall in love, but they are not motivated to have sex because of these things. Some asexuals masturbate but others do not (remember that the definition of asexuality involves a lack of sexual attraction to *others,* so autoerotic activity is in keeping with the definition). Because asexuals can feel attractions that are nonsexual to others (such as romantic or emotional attraction), some asexuals identify as lesbian, gay, or bisexual. Some think of asexuality as queer. David Jay, the founder of AVEN, noted that some asexuals may have sex out of curiosity, experimentation, or "as an expression of romantic or emotional attraction (love) rather than because they are driven to do so by a sex drive" and that this "need not contradict an asexual identity." AVEN's website also states that "certain aspects of sex might be sensual and enjoyable . . . even without sexual attraction or drive." However, "most asexual people feel completely neutral about sex or perhaps tried it and found it very disappointing. Others find the idea of participating in sexual activity absolutely repulsive."

AVEN suggests that asexuals are opening up new forms of sociality and that asexuals "form many kinds of relationships, from close friendships to romantic couplings to other kinds of bonds which our society doesn't have words for."

A/Ally

The second "A" stands for **ally**. LGBTQQIA groups often welcome non-LGBTQQIA people who are supporters of LGBTQQIA rights. Although making common cause with diverse groups of people can be challenging (for example, it may water down a group's message or sense of identity), activists such as Audre Lorde, a Black lesbian, have noted the necessity of community and turning differences to strength. Lorde (1978/1984) wrote (about women, specifically): "As women, we have been taught either to ignore our differences, or to view them as causes for separation and suspicion rather than as forces for change" (p. 112). But "without community," wrote Lorde, "there is no liberation" (p. 112). Lorde stressed, however, that community was not about "shedding" differences or pretending they did not exist. To Lorde, community was especially important for those who

> *stand outside the circle of this society's definition of acceptable women; those of us who have been forged in the crucibles of difference—those of us who are poor, who are lesbians, who are Black, who are older—know that survival is not an academic skill. (p. 112)*

Lorde emphasized the importance of making "common cause" with other outsiders in order to "flourish" (p. 112). She concluded, "For the master's tools will never dismantle the master's house. They may allow us to temporarily beat him at his own game, but they will never enable us to bring about genuine change" (p. 112) (Figure 4.7).

FIGURE 4.7
Audre Lorde (1934–1992) identified as a "Black, lesbian, mother, warrior, poet." She said as a poet she had a duty "to speak the truth as I see it and to share not just my triumphs . . . but the pain, the intense, often unmitigating pain" (1978/1984).

THE PROBLEM OF HETEROSEXUAL FOCUS

People who identify as LGBTQQIA face great obstacles to being recognized and accepted in society. Many gender studies theorists have identified mainstream ways of thinking that impede broader societal awareness and acceptance of LGBTQQIA people, some of which we discussed in Chapters 1 and 3. It should be clear by now that adherence to traditional gender ideologies (interrelated, internalized cultural beliefs about gender), which often includes a belief in gender polarization or gender binaries, makes it difficult to recognize the existence of LGBTQQIA people and to accept them.

Many identify heterosexism as part of the problem. If sexism is "prejudice, stereotyping, or discrimination, typically against women, on the basis of sex" (OED), then it makes sense to think of **heterosexism** as prejudice, stereotyping, or discrimination on the basis of not being heterosexual. Lorde defined heterosexism as "the belief in the inherent superiority of one pattern of loving and thereby its right to dominance" (p. 45). An important element of heterosexism is **heterocentrism**, the belief that heterosexuality should be central

MORE ABOUT...

Pansexual

Some have advocated for the inclusion of additional terms and letters in the LGBTQQIAA alphabetic string. One term and letter that has received support popularly and somewhat in the academic literature is **pansexual**, which has been defined as "a person who is sexually attracted to people regardless of their gender identity, gender expression or biological sex" ("Bisexual/Pansexual Basics," 2015, p. 18). Some have argued that pansexuals are distinct from bisexuals in that bisexuals (from the prefix, *bi* meaning two) are attracted to only two sexes—women and men (see, for example, "Bisexual/Pansexual Basics"). Supporters of this position sometimes argue that the term bisexual is inadequate since there are more than two sexes and genders. Since, for example, there are intersex and transgender people who do not identify as female or male, it would appear that the term bisexual would exclude attraction to them. In this context, using the term bisexual seems to reinforce the very idea of a sex/gender binary—which in turn erases those beyond the binary. Following this line of reasoning, the term pansexual is a more inclusive term (Elizabeth, 2013, p. 335). In popular usage, pansexual is used in just this way; bisexuality is often presumed to fall within the sex/gender binary and consequently pansexual identification is often used to signal rejection of attraction based on the sex/gender binary (Gonel, 2013).

However, prominent people and groups in the bisexual community consider the bisexual/pansexual distinction a mischaracterization of bisexuality. As noted earlier, Ochs defined a bisexual as someone who is "attracted, romantically and/or sexually, to people *of more than one sex*" (para. 1, italics not in original)—not simply attraction to females and males. Moreover, the Bisexual Resource Center asserted that the meaning of the word bisexual has evolved over time and that "for many bisexuals, the 'bi' in 'bisexual' refers not to male plus female, but to attraction to genders like our own, plus attraction to genders different from our own. In other words, it's the ability to move in two directions along a continuum of multiple genders" ("Way Beyond the Binary," n.d.). (It should be noted that the use of the term gender in this context includes sex as defined in this text.) Given these broad definitions of bisexuality, some bisexuals may only be attracted to women and men but others may have attraction to other sex/gender configurations as well.

and normal in contrast to other sexual orientations that are marginal, abnormal, and inferior. Part of a heterocentric outlook is the assumption that everyone is straight until proven otherwise.

The poet and activist Adrienne Rich (1980) noted that society also enforces **compulsory heterosexuality**, a concept she explored in detail in her essay, "Compulsory Heterosexuality and Lesbian Existence." Rich wrote that society has used a variety of economic, social, and political forces that "have enforced or insured the coupling of women with men" (p. 636). Think about the pressure on females to date males and males to date females or the "traditional" definition of marriage as being between a woman and a man. Think of the traditional pressure on young women and men to marry and provide their parents with biologically related grandchildren. All of these kinds of pressures constitute compulsory heterosexuality (Figure 4.8).

Rich further explained that in the case of women, compulsory heterosexuality had also "obstructed or penalized our coupling or allying in independent groups with other women" (p. 636). Here Rich was arguing that compulsory heterosexuality not only interferes with relationships between women that include a "genital sexual" component (that is, are lesbian relationships in the popular sense of the term) but also interferes with relationships that include "many more forms of primary intensity between

> ### recap of terms:
> #### Gender Polarization
> The feminist psychologist Sandra Bem (1993) labeled the notion that masculinity and femininity are polar opposites, **gender polarization**. According to Bem (1993), "Gender polarization . . . defines mutually exclusive scripts for being male and female [and] . . . defines any person or behavior that deviates from these scripts as problematic—as unnatural or immoral from a religious perspective or psychologically pathological from a scientific perspective" (pp. 80–81). Any social or individual system of sex and gender that imposes rigid and opposing categories of sex, gender, gender identity, and gender roles on people would be a gender polarizing system.
> From Chapter 1, "Sex, Gender, and Social Construction."
> *Source: Bem, S. L. (1993). The Lenses of Gender. New Haven, CT: Yale University Press.*

FIGURE 4.8

Adrienne Rich (1929–2012) was a poet and essayist whose work explored issues of identity, sexuality, and politics. In *On Lies, Secrets, and Silence* (1995), she wrote, "In a world where language and naming are power, silence is oppression, is violence" (p. 203).

and among women, including the sharing of a rich inner life, the bonding against male tyranny, the giving and receiving of practical and political support" (pp. 648–649). Rich considered these intense relationships part of what she called the **lesbian continuum**, "a range—through each woman's life and throughout history—of woman-identified experience" (p. 648). Rich's open-ended notion of a lesbian continuum can be seen as a way of honoring the importance of a variety of homosocial bonds, including nonsexual ones, that she found threatened by compulsory heterosexuality.

A term related to heterocentrism and compulsory heterosexuality is **heteronormativity**, which was coined by Michael Warner, a professor of English who has written about publics and social movements and has been a major contributor to queer theory. In describing heteronormativity, Warner (1993/2007) stated, "Het[erosexual] culture thinks of itself as the elemental form of human association, as the very model of inter-gender relations, as the indivisible basis of all community, and as the means of reproduction without which society wouldn't exist" (p. xxi). Warner credited Monique Wittig (1992/2002) with having this notion when she wrote, "To live in society is to live in heterosexuality. . . . Heterosexuality is always already there within all mental categories. It has sneaked into dialectical thought (or thought of differences) as its main category" (pp. 40, 43).

Conceptually, heteronormativity shares much in common with heterocentrism and compulsory heterosexuality. Even if Warner was not breaking new ground with this term, it has become popular, particularly in queer theory. The psychologist Gregory M. Herek (2004), an authority on prejudice against lesbians and gay men and hate crimes, stated that the term heteronormativity is valuable because it focuses attention on the heterosexual–homosexual binary that informs society's notions of sexual orientation.

Most important for this text, compulsory heterosexuality and heteronormativity remind us that society is composed of norms or patterns of social behavior that are accepted or expected of a group. These include the many social activities, customs, and institutions that generate these forms of behavior—senior proms, traditional marriage, popular movies, children's games, etc. These activities, customs, and institutions affect our way of thinking about heterosexuality and create in us the idea that heterosexuality is the basic form of human interaction. Warner and Rich also believed that society makes heterosexual reproduction unduly central, which, among other things, reinforces the centrality of heterosexual relationships. The activist intellectual Gary Kinsman (1987/1992) contended that we need "to develop alternative visions and experiences that will help all people understand how their lives could be organized without heterosexuality as the institutionalized norm. Such a goal is a radically transformed society in which everyone will be able to gain control of his or her own body, desires and life" (p. 96).

The Lesbian Continuum and Marriage Resistance in Southern China

A fascinating example of female homosociality, which served as resistance to heterocentrism, involves a practice of marriage resistance that occurred in the Pearl River delta region of southern China during the 19th and early 20th centuries. Here, girls who reached the age of puberty often slept in houses separate from their parents because it was considered inauspicious for young women to marry straight from their birth homes. These houses could be big with large numbers of girls in formal associations or a few girls living more informally in the home of an elderly couple or widow (Sankar, 1986).

Historically in China, married couples took up residence with the husband's family, a custom that anthropologists call **patrilocality**. This arrangement generally separated women from their birth families except on certain special occasions. Marriages were often arranged such that the wife would not meet her husband until the wedding. Many young girls found the prospect of the marriage arrangement unappealing because living under a mother-in-law's roof often meant being treated as a servant, lacking freedom, and having to compete with concubines (other lower-status "wives") of her husband. Often, the obligation to raise and marry off a daughter was also a burden to the birth family. Because girls were destined to serve a husband's family and were usually of no economic value to their birth family, they were considered "goods on which one loses"—an investment of time and resources that would have to be given away with no reward (Topley, 1975, p. 78).

The status of women in the Pearl River Delta region was different, however. Young women often worked in the thriving silk industry, earned their own money, and were economically valuable to their parents. Unlike in other areas of China, girls and women had more freedom to travel beyond their homes. Given these factors, the restrictions of marriage often appeared even more onerous. In particular, girls who seemed to dislike marriage or were notable for their intelligence might be considered to have a "non-marrying fate"— something that could be confirmed by a horoscope reader (Topley, pp. 81–82). A socially approved alternative was to go through a *sou hei* **ceremony**, which was like a marriage ceremony. Such women took a vow to be celibate and to remain unmarried. They joined sisterhoods, usually groups of 5 to 6 women who lived together for mutual support; although they sometimes lived in spinsters' houses or in larger groups of up to 40 people in Buddhist vegetarian halls (Sankar; Topley). Because they often worked in the silk industry, these women were literally spinsters—females who spin (in this case silk)—whose income and living arrangements made it possible to avoid a traditional heterosexual family structure (Figure 4.9). The spinsters would often stay in close

FIGURE 4.9

Women spinning silk thread in Hong Kong in the 1880s.

contact with their families, contribute money from their factory labor to their brothers' families, and be cared for by nieces and nephews in old age (Sankar).

Sometimes two or three women would have an especially strong bond and become "sworn sisters" (Topley, p. 76). These bonds were sometimes called **Golden Orchid Associations** and could be sexual relationships (Topley). Andrea Sankar, who interviewed women who came from mainland China but lived in a surviving vegetarian hall in the 1980s in Hong Kong, found same-sex relationships among the members. She stated that "larger sisterhoods may have contained several couples or ménages a trois"—that is, threesomes (p. 78). Marjorie Topley's research seems to suggest that same-sex sexual relationships were considered unremarkable and were sometimes described in religious terms; according to one explanation, if your fated partner from another life is reborn in the body of the female sex, it was logical that there would still be an attraction even if both were female (Topley).

Because neither the general existence of sisterhoods nor particular lesbian relationships interfered with patriarchal privilege and often was beneficial to families with spinster daughters, this marriage resistance movement appears to have flourished. Sankar asserted that this seems to fit with a broader Chinese societal response to lesbianism in history that was generally to ignore or even tacitly condone it. Sankar also contended that some Confucian texts even suggest lesbianism is a way to keep wives content. This tolerance was not shared by all, however. Vivien Ng (1997) cited a passage from the *Nuren jing* or *Canon for Women* in which a commentator referred to Golden Orchid Associations as "blasphemous" and stated with incredulity that "they believe that father-in-law, mother-in-law, husband, children, etc. bind their bodies and deprive them of their freedom . . . [which is] suffocating bondage and even death!" (p. 202).

This marriage resistance, which opposed the broader heteronormative practices in Chinese society, came about because of unique economic and social conditions that allowed marriage resisters and their families to find a socially acceptable alternative to the dominant patriarchal system. This movement is an excellent example of women living on Adrienne Rich's lesbian continuum, which included "many . . . forms of primary intensity between and among women, including the sharing of a rich inner life, the bonding against male tyranny, the giving and receiving of practical and political support" (pp. 648–649) and, of course, same-sex sexual relationships. The practice of sisterhoods largely ended with the collapse of industrial work for women, including the silk industry in the depression of the 1930s, and the remaining spinster halls in mainland China were phased out when the Communists came to power in 1949 (Topley).

ANTI-LGBT ATTITUDES

A Gallup poll conducted in 2014 indicated that 38 percent of people in the United States believed that "gay and lesbian relations" were "morally wrong"—and although this number is part of a declining trend of negative attitudes, it still represents significant disapproval of gay and lesbian relationships (Gallup, 2014). What drives disapproval of gays and lesbians and, by extension, discrimination against LGBTQQIA people? Although the causes are still being investigated, many experts have identified important sources of anti-LGBTQQIA feeling and behavior. Since the research indicates that negative attitudes and behavior can vary depending on the subgroup, we will explore each group separately

As we discussed in Chapter 3, homophobia can be defined as "fear or hatred of homosexuals and homosexuality" (OED). Some critics of the term argue that since homophobia is often not a phobia (an irrational, pathological fear of gay people), there is a need for a different name. Some use the term **homonegativity**, which can be defined as negative attitudes about gay people. Gregory M. Herek (2007), a professor of psychology, has argued for the term **sexual stigma**, which he defined as "the negative regard, inferior status, and relative power-lessness that society collectively accords to any nonheterosexual behavior, identity, relationship, or community. Sexual stigma is socially shared knowledge about homosexuality's devalued status in society" (pp. 906–907). Because all three terms are used in the literature, we will use them interchangeably in this text. Related to sexual stigma is heterosexual privilege. The activist Charlotte Bunch said, "What makes heterosexuality work is heterosexual privilege—and if you don't have a sense of what privilege is, I suggest you go home and announce to everybody you know . . . that you're queer. Try being queer for a week" (as cited in Kinsman, p. 86).

One factor that seems to reduce the likelihood of homophobic attitudes is contact with gay people. Studies have indicated that the more contact straight people have with gay people, the less homophobic they are (Herek, 2007). It is possible that that the causality is the reverse: the less homophobic someone is, the more contact with gay people they are likely to have; however, researchers hypothesize that greater contact with gay people is likely to reduce homonegativity.

On the flip side, at least one study has found that acceptance by straight people contributed to the well-being of LGB youth (Dane & MacDonald, 2009). The study, conducted in Australia, examined the effects of acceptance by four groups of straight people: one's mother, one's father, straight friends, and contacts (such as neighbors, teachers, and coworkers). The acceptance of "contacts" was most strongly predictive of well-being among LGB youth. The researchers speculated that

> *perhaps for [LGB youth] who have already crossed the hurdles associated with "coming out" to family and friends, overcoming hurdles within the wider community takes on new importance; disclosure to contacts is a continuous lifetime process and is a key to establishing new friendships. (p. 672)*

Researchers have begun to investigate many potential causes of homophobia, some of which we will explore here. Homophobia exists at both the individual level and the societal level and can be divided into three categories (see, for example, Tully, 2000). The first category is **internalized homophobia** (also called internalized heterosexism), which we will broadly define as homonegative attitudes directed toward oneself. The second category is simply homophobia (also called sexual prejudice), which we will define as homonegative attitudes expressed by individuals toward others. The third category is **institutional homophobia** (also called institutional heterosexism), which we will define as "a cultural ideology that is embodied in institutional practices that work to the disadvantage of sexual minority groups even in the absence of individual prejudice or discrimination" (Herek, 2009b, p. 442). The failure to allow same-sex marriage or criminalizing homosexual sex are examples of institutional homophobia; both disadvantage gay people in ways that straight people are not disadvantaged. Shockingly, five countries still have the death penalty for same-sex relationships: Iran, Mauritania, Saudi Arabia, Sudan, and Yemen. Homosexuality is also punishable by the death penalty in parts of Nigeria and Somalia (BBC, 2014). Uganda considered such legislation in 2014 but ultimately settled on life imprisonment for some homosexual acts (Karimi & Thompson, 2014).

Herek (1986) has suggested that individual homophobia can be divided into three kinds. First is **defensive-expressive homophobia**, in which individuals (men, in this case) express homophobia as a way to cope with anxiety over their own heterosexual masculinity. The second kind is **social-expressive homophobia**, in which individuals try to gain the approval of others and enhance their own self-esteem by expressing homophobia. The third kind is **value-expressive homophobia**, in which individuals express homophobia as part of a broader value system of right and wrong, such as a conservative religious ideology.

Two attitudes that correlate with homonegativity are adherence to right-wing authoritarianism and belief in traditional gender roles. Individuals who adhere to right-wing authoritarianism believe in traditional values and norms, are willing to submit to authority, and are willing to use aggression against people who are disapproved of by established authorities (Basow & Johnson, 2000). Beyond these correlations, researchers have found interesting differences between the homophobic attitudes of straight women and men.

Straight Male Homonegativity Regarding Gay Men

As we discussed in Chapter 3, misogyny can be defined as hatred of, dislike of, or prejudice against women. We also noted that Cooper Thompson (1992) contended that the root of misogyny is the hatred of feminine qualities in women and that homophobia against men can be thought of as the hatred of feminine qualities in men. Research has indicated that gay men face homonegativity for precisely this reason—their perceived violation of masculine gender norms. As the psychologist Scott Keiller (2010) noted, gay men are often believed to have "stereotypically feminine personality traits, interests, skills and behaviors" (p. 39)—a condition known as gender inversion, where a person of one sex displays traits usually considered appropriate for a different sex. Many studies have indicated that boys and men face strong pressure to conform to traditional gender roles and behavior, and anti-gay male attitudes are linked to a fear of being perceived as feminine. Research has also indicated that men who generally conform to traditional masculinity ideology are more likely to have negative attitudes toward gay men (Keiller). One specific masculine norm, known as Power Over Women, is particularly linked to homonegativity. Research has shown that men who preferred situations in which they or other men had control over women were more likely to display anti-gay male attitudes. Keiller concluded that "these findings suggest that men most invested in traditional masculinity perceive gay men . . . as threats to patriarchal privilege and status" (p. 48). Similarly, the researchers Peter Theodore and Susan Basow (2000) found that the men who have the most insecurity about their own masculinity are the most likely to be homophobic toward gay men. This is an example of defensive-expressive homophobia (see above), where men express homophobia to prove their masculinity.

Straight Male Homonegativity Regarding Lesbians

Although conformity to masculine norms in straight men was correlated with negative attitudes toward gay men, Keiller and others have found that general adherence to masculine norms is *not* related to anti-lesbian attitudes.

On the contrary, there is evidence that some masculine norms were correlated with *favorable* attitudes toward lesbian women. The strongest example of this involves men who adhere to the Playboy norm. These men, as Keiller described them, prefer "casual sexual adventures with multiple women, without commitment or emotional involvement" (p. 41). Adherence to the Playboy norm is correlated with more positive attitudes about lesbians (in comparison to gay men). Such positive attitudes, however, should not be confused with genuine acceptance of lesbianism. Research has suggested that these positive attitudes are the result of the eroticization of lesbians by straight men. That is, men think of lesbians in sexual terms and find the thought of lesbian sex to be sexually arousing. Thus, these heterosexual men are not respecting lesbianism as an identity assumed by women to be more fully themselves. Instead, it is part of a straight male attitude that trivializes or reduces the significance of lesbian sexuality by bringing it into the orbit of male heterosexuality. Put another way, these Playboy men appear to be viewing lesbianism through the lens of their own heterosexual desire (Louderback & Whitley, 1997). In fact, if you factor out the positive attitude resulting from eroticization, straight men have much the same negative attitude about lesbians as they do about gay men.

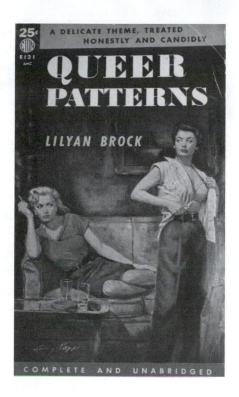

FIGURE 4.10
Lesbian pulp fiction from the 1950s and 1960s appealed to straight men as well as lesbians. In its appeal to straight men, it is an example of the eroticization of lesbians.

Straight Female Homonegativity Regarding Gay Men and Lesbians

Straight women seem to have less intense homophobic attitudes than straight men, and whereas men exhibit more intense homophobia toward gay men than lesbians, straight women have been found to have equally less intense negative attitudes toward both gay men and lesbians (see, for example, Basow & Johnson and Louderback & Whitley). This can be partly explained by research that shows women do not express homophobia as a defensive-expressive strategy to prove their femininity (whereas certain men do express homophobia to prove their masculinity) (Basow & Johnson; Theodore & Basow).

The lack of a defensive-expressive function for homophobia in straight women is revealing about how masculinity and femininity operate in straight people. As Basow and Johnson stated, masculinity in men appears to be rigidly defined and must be constantly proven. By contrast, femininity in females is "less rigid than masculinity in men and less tied to heterosexuality" (Basow &

Johnson, "Discussion," para. 2). Femininity is also something that is assumed in women rather than a quality that must be proven.

Negative Attitudes Regarding Bisexuals

A nationwide study by Herek (2002) about attitudes of heterosexuals toward bisexuals revealed attitudes similar to those that heterosexuals have toward lesbians and gay men. Being politically conservative, authoritarian, and religious were all correlated with negative attitudes toward bisexuals. (The findings also suggested that other, as yet undiscovered factors were related to negative attitudes toward bisexuals.) Overall, heterosexual women and men had less positive feelings about bisexual women and men than they did about lesbians and gay men (Herek, 2002). Straight men felt more unfavorably about both bisexual men and gay men than they did about bisexual women and lesbians.

A recurring theme in writing about bisexuality is that bisexual people face discrimination not only from some straight people who view them negatively because of their homosexual desires and activity, but also from some gay people who view them negatively because they are viewed as not homosexual enough. Binegativity from **monosexuals**—people with a sexual orientation toward only one sex (homosexual or heterosexual)—can be a big problem for bisexuals.

Rebecca Shuster (1987) argued that heterosexist society defines bisexual women (and we could add bisexual men) based on their homosexuality. But, she wrote, bisexual people "are not 50 percent oppressed" (p. 59). In contrast, gay people may view bisexuals as insufficiently committed politically or socially to gay people. There is sometimes a concern that bisexuals can always retreat to heterosexual relationships if being in a same-sex relationship becomes difficult. Because a bisexual person's bisexuality cannot be seen when they are in a different-sex relationship, there is also sometimes the concern that bisexuals are not sufficiently out of the closet as nonheterosexual. (Hartman [2013] found that some bisexual women attempt to counter this by "displaying" their bisexuality through androgynous looks, assertive manners, etc.) Both gay and straight people may also view bisexuality as simply "a phase" that is insignificant, a form of fence-sitting, or merely a half-way point to their "true" homosexuality. All of these negative views can make the expression of bisexuality difficult.

Negative Attitudes Regarding Transgender People

The researcher Eiko Sugano and colleagues (2006) defined **transphobia** as "societal discrimination and stigma of individuals who do not conform to traditional norms of sex and gender" (p. 217). This definition would include transgender people in the broadest sense of the term, "including cross dressers, feminine men, and masculine women" (Nagoshi et al., 2008, p. 521). Although transphobia has not been extensively researched, findings thus far suggest that transphobia in straight people is correlated with many of the same factors as homophobia in straight women and men. For both women and men, transphobia is correlated with "right-wing authoritarianism," "religious fundamentalism," and "hostile sexism" (Nagoshi et al., p. 521). As with homophobia, men are more likely to be more transphobic than women. Benevolent sexism (which, as discussed in Chapter 3, includes protective paternalistic attitudes and the idealization of women) is more correlated with transphobia than homophobia, especially in women. Nagoshi and colleagues explained this is "reflective of supporting gender roles."

Racism and Homophobia Against LGBT People of Color

As one might expect, studies indicate that LGBT people of color face racism in dating relationships, social networks, and LGBT communities (Balsam et al., 2011). Additionally, LGBT people of color face homonegativity in their racial/ethnic minority communities. For example, Latinos and African American men have reported greater rates of gay-related prejudice than European Americans (Balsam et al.). In the case of African American men, such homonegativity may cause them to conceal their sexual orientation to avoid such prejudice (Balsam et al.). Balsam and colleagues also noted that LGBT Asian Americans may conceal their sexual orientation for the same reason—particularly in Chinese and Japanese cultures where "there are sexual limitations and restrictions on gender roles" (p. 164).

Microagressions Against LGBT People of Color

Although racism and homonegativity are sometimes expressed in blatant ways such as hate crime, they can also be expressed in subtle and sometimes unintentional ways called **microaggressions**. Derald Wing Sue et al. (2007) define microaggressions as "brief and commonplace daily verbal, behavioral, or environmental indignities, whether intentional or unintentional, that communicate hostile, derogatory, or negative slights and insults" (p. 271). For LGBT people of color, microaggressions might include racism within the LGBT community: being excluded from LGBT spaces (such as gay bars that refuse entry to African Americans); experiencing racism in dating relationships (like personal ads for "white people only"); and being sexually objectified because of race by other LGBT people. LGBT people of color may also experience heterosexism within their racial/ethnic communities. For example, some Asian

FIGURE 4.11

Scholars argue that Bayard Rustin, an advisor to Martin Luther King Jr., did not get the credit he deserved for organizing the 1964 Civil Rights March on Washington because of public criticism of his homosexuality.

Americans view lesbianism as a Western concept not associated with individuals from their cultures (Balsam et al.).

Researchers who conducted a survey of 297 self-identified LGBT people of color found that among people of color, lesbians and gay men reported greater distress regarding microaggressions than bisexual women and men (Balsam et al.). This is in keeping with other research that has suggested that "LGBT identity and same-sex relationships may be more central for lesbians and gay men than bisexuals" (Balsam et al., p. 171). In addition, the study found that Asian American men reported experiencing more relationship racism than African American and Latino/a LGBT people. This fits with other research, which found that Asian American men were viewed as the "least sexually desirable by gay men of other races/ethnicities" and "less desirable by other Asian-American gay men" (Balsam et al., p. 171). Another interesting finding was that microaggressions did not vary by income and education, but occurred "regardless of social class or other types of privilege" (Balsam et al., p. 171). (Note: we discuss the movement for gay rights in Chapter 5, "Constructions of Homosexualities," violence against LGBTQQ people in Chapter 9, "Gender-Based Violence," and LGBTQQ human rights in Chapter 10, "Human Rights and Global Activism.")

GAY COMMUNITY AND SOCIAL SUPPORT

Most gay and lesbian people are psychologically healthy, but some experience what is known as gay-related stress because of social stigma, discrimination, and other factors (Fingerhut et al., 2010). E. J. Graff (1993), an investigative journalist, captured the importance of gay community to well-being when she wrote,

> Because communities do build self-esteem and pride, I don't want to live too far from Boston, its annual parades, its queer newspapers and magazines, the lobbyists at the City Council and the State House. The hatemongers are almost right when they say we recruit. Not in the vampirish sense of creating gays where there were none before but in the sense of giving each other the courage to be true to our selves. [sic] (So draining is the effort to suppress

evidence of our lives that I'm startled when lesbians and gay men are called flagrant—for resting a moment and allowing themselves to be seen.) (p. 14)

Graff noted that part of the stress that gay people (and we believe other LGBTQQIA people) face is the stress of simply being themselves, which forces them to be constantly on guard for negative reactions. Social science research backs up Graff's observation that gay community is an important antidote to gay-related stress. Some studies have indicated that those who have a "positive" lesbian or gay identity and "strong connections to the LGB community" do better in terms of psychological well-being (Fingerhut et al., p. 103). Studies have also shown, however, that having a strong lesbian or gay identity is associated with an increased likelihood of discrimination, which appears to occur because people with positive gay identities are more likely to be out; increased visibility puts lesbians and gay men at risk for discrimination. Despite this, having a positive lesbian or gay identity is linked with feeling less stigmatized as a gay person.

Research on bisexual identity is limited. In one small Australian study of 47 lesbian, bisexual, and queer identified women who considered themselves "flourishing," interviewees suggested that lesbian women participated in more extensive communities and had stronger ties to those communities than bisexual women (Heath & Mulligan, 2008). These researchers indicated that bisexuals felt less constrained by the norms of their communities (which included lesbians) and could more easily be themselves but also had less access to resources and networks in comparison with the lesbians, who were more embedded in extensive gay communities. Another theme of these bisexual women was the feeling that they were less accepted because of their bisexuality and experienced "compulsory monosexuality"—in this case, pressure to be lesbian.

There is also little research on gay people of color and community. One study found that immigrant and U.S.-born Latinas/os who had greater social support also had higher personal self-esteem (Zea et al., 1999). Researchers noted that in the case of Latina/o lesbians and gays, this social support tended to come from friends more than family because negative attitudes about homosexuality tended to be more prevalent in Latino families. The researchers also noted that those Latinas/os who evaluated Latina/o lesbian and gay community positively "had lower levels of depression" and Latinas/os who had a "high sense of worth as members of the [Latina/o] lesbian and gay community had higher self-esteem" (Zea et al., p. 377).

A study of LGB people age 50 and older found that most were out to their social networks (93 percent said that all members definitely knew they were

ON THE web

For more information about the **It Gets Better Project** and social support for LGBT youth, see the Student Website: www.oup.com/us /gillis-jacobs

FIGURE 4.12

Harvey Milk High School in New York City is a school for LGBTQ youth. It is named after the gay rights advocate and politician Harvey Milk, who was assassinated in 1978.

lesbian, gay, or bisexual) and that close friends and partners were more likely than family members to provide "emotional, practical, advice, and socializing support" (Masini & Barrett, 2008, p. 104). The researchers also found that "support from friends predicted higher mental quality of life, and lower depression, anxiety, and internalized homophobia, illustrating the protective mental health effects of friendships" (p. 104). The researchers concluded that "this finding speaks to the importance of networks that extend beyond the traditional familial boundaries" (p. 104).

CONCLUSION

A clear definition of sexual orientation remains elusive, and despite the development of several scales to measure sexual orientation, more and/or better measuring tools are needed.

Terms related to sexual orientation are often abbreviated by the alphabetic string LGBTQQIAA. People who identify as LGBTQQIA face great obstacles to being recognized and accepted in society. Heterosexism and heterocentrism both contribute to this problem.

The Pearl River Delta region of Southern China provides an interesting example of marriage resistance and female homosociality (that is, female–female social bonding). In the 19th and early 20th centuries, many young women here lived away from home and worked in the silk industry. Some remained unmarried and formed lesbian relationships, which were accepted at least by some in the society.

Anti-LGBT attitudes (sometimes called homophobia, homonegativity, or sexual stigma), although they are declining in the United States, are still expressed by a significant minority of the population. Homonegativity varies depending on both the person expressing homonegativity and the person toward whom it is directed. LGBT people of color face both homonegativity and racism, expressed both blatantly (e.g., hate crimes) and subtly (microaggressions). Studies have shown the importance of gay community as an antidote to gay-related stress caused by sexual stigma.

THINK, LEARN, ACT

The following resources are available on the Student Website: www.oup.com/us/gillis-jacobs

Taking Stock, Taking Action prompts and activities. Apply what you've learned to take action on campus and in the broader community.

Recommended Readings and Multimedia Resources, including scholarly and literary works, documentaries, feature films, podcasts and more, to enrich the in- and out-of-classroom experience.

CHAPTER 5

CONSTRUCTIONS OF HOMOSEXUALITIES

Past and Present

According to Michel Foucault (1976/1980), for most of human history there were no homosexuals. Lesbians and gay men were not to be found in ancient Greece or Rome; nor did they exist in the Middle Ages. Foucault located the point where and when homosexuals first came into existence in the late 19th century in Europe. To be clear, Foucault was not suggesting that prior to this period people did not have same-sex desire. Instead, he contended that it was only at this time that homosexuals were recognized as a distinct kind of person—and labeled as such. According to Foucault, before the 1860s people recognized same-sex desire existed but did not assume it was limited to certain people—anyone might have such desire (although it was generally condemned). However, in the 1860s this changed. Along with the recognition of this kind of person, the word homosexual was coined to refer to people with same-sex desire and the word heterosexual was coined to refer to people with "opposite-sex" desire. For the first time in history, people could identify themselves or be labeled by others as homosexual or heterosexual. Foucault was also making the broader claim that this supposedly objectively true medical category is really a social construction. Put another way, we created homosexuals (and heterosexuals) where there were none before.

Roughly 100 years after the term homosexual was coined, on a June night in 1969, police were shutting down a lesbian, gay, and transgender bar called the Stonewall Inn in New York City—usually a routine procedure to which employees and patrons submitted peacefully. But on this night a man in the crowd outside the bar grew upset. He yelled "Gay power!" riffing off of the well-known slogan of Black power (Carter, 2010, p. 147). "Gay power!" was then shouted a few times by others before it ended in laughter—this new slogan seemed too silly to be taken seriously, even by the LGBT crowd. Before the night was over, however, the crowd would erupt in violence, marking the beginning of the modern gay rights movement in the United States and an important milestone in transgender history.

This is a remarkable (and highly abridged) story of what some call the emergence of the modern homosexual. This story has two components: the creation of a publicly recognized category of sexuality (the homosexual) and the later widespread pride in and declaration of this identity by gay people. But can we really say that homosexuality (and, by extension, heterosexuality and other categories such as bisexuality) came into existence in the late 19th century? If yes, the implication would seem to be that the category of sexual orientation is in fact socially constructed. What are the ramifications of this? These are not easy questions to answer, nor is the answer universally agreed on. Most of this chapter will be devoted to providing the background necessary to understand and evaluate Foucault's story of the creation of the modern homosexual category. This background will include an exploration of how same-sex desire, same-sex sexual activity, and same-sex relationships have been constructed through history and across cultures beginning in ancient Greece and Rome, including current-day Latin America and early modern England. We will also discuss Foucault's story of the emergence of the homosexual, ending with the Stonewall uprising and the beginning of the modern gay rights movement in the United States.

By way of comparison, we will examine same-sex desire and sexual activity in some African cultures and how Indian *Hijras*'s desire and sexual activity resist being classified either as homosexual/gay or even as *same*-sex desire and sexual activity. The social construction of same-sex desire, sexual activity, and relationships is deeply intertwined with conceptions of heterosexual desire, activity, and relationships; so this chapter is also an account of the construction of heterosexualities and other conceptions of sexuality (including bisexuality).

One note on terminology in this chapter: most scholars who support the social constructionist position use the terms "same-sex" and "opposite-sex" rather than homosexual/gay or heterosexual/straight. However, you will remember from the discussion of biological variation of sexes and the discussion of intersexuality that the idea that there are only two sexes and that they are "opposite" is a deeply problematic one (See Chapter 1, "Sex, Gender, and Socialization"). Although we would rather not use terms like *same*-sex and *opposite*-sex, they are the terms currently used in this field of scholarship. We ask you to take these terms with a grain of salt and recognize there is much more sexual diversity than these terms suggest—a point we will take up with the discussion of *Hijras* at the end of the chapter.

ANCIENT GREECE

In ancient Greek there is no word for homosexuals (either female or male) or for the idea of homosexuality (Blundell, 1995; Crompton, 2003). As we have noted, this is not to say that people did not have same-sex desires or act on those desires, but the category of homosexual seems not to have been a significant social grouping for the ancient Greeks.

How then, did the ancient Greeks think about same-sex desire? Or opposite-sex desire? Answering these broad questions is problematic; there is no generic answer that will do. So we will narrow our scope to a specific time (the Classical Age, 508–322 BCE) and place (Athens) and imagine an upper-class male youth of about 17 who we will call Leagros. Such a young man would have many opportunities to socialize with other male youths and men but would have virtually no contact with upper-class women who were kept in seclusion from men (Blundell; O'Neal, 1993; Percy, 2005).

A youth like Leagros might be approached by an adult male, perhaps 20 to 30 years old, who was attracted to his youthful beauty. By social convention, such a man would not yet be married (delayed marriage was used to control population). If Leagros became involved with this man, the relationship might or might not be sexual in nature, but in any case it would likely involve much more than sex, including educational guidance and perhaps military training. Many elite Athenians viewed these relationships as important on a number of levels, even for the flourishing of democracy itself (Percy).

This practice was known as **pederasty**. Unlike pedophilia, which involves sexual attraction to children who are generally 13 years old or younger, the

FIGURE 5.1
Aristogeiton (left) and Harmodius were legendary pederastic lovers who supposedly ended a tyranny. Their story epitomized the importance of male love for the flourishing of democracy. The bronze statues were as associated with Athens as the Statue of Liberty is with New York (Crompton).

ancient Greek tradition of pederasty involved attraction to youths who had at least begun puberty (roughly 14 years of age) and extended to youths in their 20s (Hubbard, 2004; Rice, 2008; Risen, 2004). Scholars generally agree that pederasty was an upper-class practice (Rice) but less is known about whether it was practiced more widely—some scholars contend it was not (see, for example, Ludwig, 1996).

As Leagros left the age of youthful beauty, he himself might take a younger male as his beloved, but at the age of 30, Leagros, like all upper-class men, would be expected to marry a woman and become a father. This was important because having sons could ensure a man's estate remained intact and his ancestors' graves were properly tended (Beaumont, 1996; Blundell). So, over the course of his lifetime, Leagros might engage in what we would today call bisexual behavior—sexual activity with both females and males (see Chapter 4, "LGBTQQIAA Identities and Challenges," for a discussion of bisexual behavior). In fact, the scholar Louis Crompton asserted that the practice of "bisexuality [was] taken for granted" (p. 21) in Classical Greek society and there was widespread approval of "male love." But if approval was widespread, it was not universal, nor was there acceptance of all sexual practices. The Greek playwright Aristophanes made sexual jokes in his plays that denigrated men for being penetrated by other men. This was in keeping with the general Classical Athenian view that even if same-sex sexual contact was acceptable, being penetrated by another man was shameful (Crompton). Moreover, the philosopher Plato supported but then later rejected homosexuality. This is hardly surprising. Societies are not monolithic regarding almost any belief, including attitudes about sexual desire and activity. In fact, it is from such contrary conceptions and practices that societal change often springs.

ON THE
web
Read about **Plato's views on same-sex sexuality** on the Student Website: www.oup.com/us/gillis-jacobs

Within the Classical Athenian context, it is not at all clear that Leagros would have much reason to concern himself with whether he would rather have sex with females or males. As a matter of course, on the one hand, some male youths who preferred sex with females may have had sex with other males because females were unavailable or may have entered pederastic relationships, which may or may not have involved sex, for camaraderie and mentorship. On the other hand, if a young man preferred sex and sexual relationships with males, outlets for same-sex desire existed. But at the same time, the need for opposite-sex sexual relations within marriage would have been recognized as an important duty. Given these circumstances, there would not be much use in Leagros identifying as homosexual or heterosexual—or even as bisexual. These terms simply would not have illuminated the relationships he formed.

This account supports Foucault's contention that same-sex desire, sexual activity, and relationships prior to the 1860s were socially constructed in such a radically different way from modern relationships that the modern identity terms, homosexual, gay, and lesbian, just do not apply. Theorists who see Classical Athenian and other cultures as having fundamentally different schematizations for same- and opposite-sex desire are said to hold the social constructionist position. Some theorists prefer the term **historicism**, which suggests that these schematizations must always be considered within their unique historical and cultural contexts. Some theorists speak of varying **homosexualities** across time and cultures—different schemas of same-sex desire, same-sex sexual activity, and same-sex relationships rather than a universal, unchanging category of homosexuality (see, for example, Epprecht, 2005; Msibi, 2011).

recap of terms:

Homosocial

Homosocial behavior is any social behavior between people of the same sex. This can include "a boys' (or girls') night out," same-sex fraternity or sorority activities, same-sex sports activities, etc. These and other homosocial activities may occur in homosexual or non-homosexual contexts. Many who study sexual orientation in culture believe that homosociality is often an important element of how sexual orientations manifest themselves in society. For example, some subcultures of gay men socialize almost exclusively with men. In contrast, many straight male groups such as fraternities stress homosocial bonding as integral to their heterosexual identity. Homosociality, then, is a complex and widespread form of bonding that can be used to reinforce a variety of subcultural perspectives on sexual orientation. From Chapter 4, "LGBTQQIAA Identities and Challenges"

The varying schemas of homosexuality often reflect culturally specific notions of how gender is supposed to be tied to homosocial activity, same-sex desire, and same-sex sexual activity. So, for example, upper-class classical Athenians' conceptions of masculinity not only led many of them to condone pederasty and same-sex desire among men, but also many viewed these practices as productive in the development of a youth's manly potential. Today, by contrast, some hegemonic masculinities require men to distance themselves from same-sex desire and to regard homosexuality as unmanly or effeminate (E. Anderson, 2011). Recall, for example, that Cooper Thompson (1992) described homophobia as the hatred of female characteristics in men, and homophobia is often associated with the stereotypical belief that gay men are feminine (see discussions of homophobia in Chapter 3, "Gender and In/Equality," and Chapter 4).

Sappho and Female Same-Sex Sexuality

To what extent female same-sex sexual relationships occurred in ancient Greece and how much they were accepted is much more difficult to determine because almost all the visual art and written material that survives from ancient Greece was produced by men (Rupp, 2009). There are no accounts by women of female same-sex sexual relationships, with perhaps the exception of the poet Sappho (c. 600 BCE), who lived on the island of Lesbos (from which we get the word lesbian), which is in the Aegean Sea off the coast of Turkey (Sappho, 1999).

Sappho is often considered one of the greatest poets of the ancient world (Figure 5.2). Plato, for example, called her "the tenth muse" (Percy, p. 24). It is easy to imagine that some of the surviving fragments of her lush poetry are autobiographical accounts of her love of women. "Ode to Anactoria" is a good example of a poem that could be interpreted as an expression of same-sex desire. The poem begins, "He seems as fortunate as the gods to me, / The man who sits opposite you" (lines 1–2). The writer goes on to say that just looking at "you," "My tongue has snapped" (line 7), "a subtle fire" (line 8) has taken hold and "I am a little short of dying" (line 12). (Campbell, 1982).

Although many want to read Sappho's poems as autobiographical and evidence for the existence of a lesbian subculture, one must be cautious. Little is known for certain about Sappho and scholars disagree about how to read her poetry. Percy believed the surviving evidence is too thin to be certain the poetry attributed to Sappho was even written by her. The poems are written in the first person but it is not necessarily clear that Sappho is writing about herself; nor is it clear what her relationship to the women or girls in the poems is. Klinck (2005) asserted that her poetry is homoerotic but acknowledged it is *possible* to read the poetry addressed to females as following a literary convention that may not have been meant to be read literally. It may well be that Sappho and her poetry will forever remain enigmas.

ANCIENT ROME

Ancient Roman culture spans a time of more than a thousand years, but we will be examining a 400-year period that includes the Roman republic (circa 500 BCE to 27 BCE) and Roman empire (27 BCE to 476 CE) (Graeco-Roman Heritage, 2005; Roman Empire, 2002; C. A. Williams, 2010). This time period overlaps with the Classical Athenian period (508–322 BCE) and extends beyond it. As in ancient Greek culture, sex between males was often acceptable in Roman culture, including sex with youths; however, the Romans did not have a tradition of pederasty (meaning a mentoring relationship, sexual or nonsexual, between a free-born man and a free-born male youth).

FIGURE 5.2

A representation of Sappho by the French painter Léon Perrault, 1891.

Male Same-Sex Relations

As in ancient Greece, Ancient Romans had no word for homosexual or heterosexual, according to the professor of classics Craig A. Williams. Although Roman men could engage in same-sex sexual activity, how one engaged in such sex was critical to demonstrating one's masculinity. Williams stated that an adult male citizen of Rome would follow what we will call the two masculine rules of Roman sexual conduct. The first, which Williams called the **prime directive of masculine sexual behavior**, is to "always give the appearance of playing the insertive role in penetrative acts, and not the receptive role" with either female or male sexual partners (p. 18). Williams believed that Roman masculinity was linked to dominance, and penetration was perceived as an essential act of masculine dominance. In contrast, to be penetrated made one unmanly—feminine in the case of females or effeminate in the case of males.

The second rule of Roman sexual conduct we will call the **rule of masculine self-restraint**. According to this rule, a free-born man would ideally limit sexual activity to his wife or, if outside of marriage, to noncitizens (female or male), such as slaves or prostitutes. To have sex with a free-born (citizen) female or male interfered with the rights of adult male citizens to control their family members and, because it was thought to demonstrate an unmanly loss of self-control, was considered shameful.

The prime directive of masculine behavior is interesting for a number of reasons. First, it did not stigmatize people as gay in the modern sense of the term—only the penetrated partner was stigmatized. Second, it shows how hierarchical (especially in terms of class) and misogynistic Roman culture was. Third, this conception of male sexual activity is echoed in modern society in a number of ways. As in Roman culture, many modern cultures stereotypically regard men as "active" and women as "passive"—think of the stereotypical notions of sex and gender discussed in the first three chapters of this text. Modern Western culture also frequently conceives of certain sexual practices as a form of domination that is emasculating or feminizing (for an interesting feminist analysis of the disturbing similarities between Roman sexual culture and modern Western culture, see Richlin, 1992). Consider the way people joke about men going to prison and becoming someone else's "girlfriend." The theme of prison rape is about humiliation through emasculation and sexual subordination. Females are also symbolically subordinated through similar modern insults and conceptualizations of sexual acts. Moreover, modern straight male homophobia regarding gay men may at times be based on a fear of being sexually dominated; homophobia more generally often rests on stereotypes of gay men as fundamentally effeminate (Finkel-Konigsberg, 2010; Keiller, 2010) (see Chapter 4).

Female Same-Sex Relations

Unlike male same-sex sexual activity, female same-sex sexual activity was rarely written about in the material that survives from ancient Rome. For example, there are no known examples of women in ancient Rome who engaged in same-sex sexual activity (Butrica, 2005). There are writings by men about women who have sex with women, but it is unclear whether these reflect the actual activities of women or are entirely fictional accounts (Butrica).

One plausible explanation for the lack of historical evidence about real women who had sex with women is that the men who did most of the writing in Roman times and the historians who preserved these writings simply may not have cared much about what women did. The classicist James Butrica argued that there was "near total indifference" to female same-sex sexual activity "except as a source of humour" (p. 238). Butrica noted that references to same-sex sexual activity are mostly found in sexually explicit poems by the Roman poet Martial (40 CE—between 102 and 104 CE) that humorously describe women who mimic men's sexual appetites and take the insertive role in sex with both boys and women. Butrica noted there were no laws against female same-sex sexual activity and that even laws related to adultery did not mention or result in the punishment of female same-sex adultery—presumably because there was no danger of the creation of illegitimate offspring. For Butrica, the absence of laws to suppress female same-sex sexual activity indicates male unconcern with it. It is possible that sex without a penis may generally have been conceived as not really being sex at all; as such, lesbian sexual activity may not have rated mention. Whatever the reason, once again women's lives are elided (struck out or passed over in silence), this time in the writing of history.

MALE SAME-SEX SEXUAL RELATIONS IN LATIN AMERICAN CULTURES

There is a parallel to the Roman prime directive of masculine sexual behavior in many Latin American cultures today. Sometimes in these cultures, among men who have sex with men, the man who plays the insertive role (what is called the *activo* **sex role**) is considered masculine and may be considered a "normal" man, not "truly gay" (for normalcy, see Nesvig, 2001, p. 724; regarding not being gay, see, for example, Carrillo, 2002, pp. 37–39; Lancaster, 1988, p. 113); he may also view and present himself as macho (see, for example, Carrillo; Lancaster). By contrast, the man who is penetrated (what is called the *pasivo* **sex role**) may be considered effeminate and suffer the stigma associated with same-sex sexual activity (see Carrillo; Lancaster; Nesvig); he may also view or present himself as feminine, sometimes appearing as a woman or an effeminate man (see, for example, Carrillo; Lancaster). (For a discussion of macho behavior or *machismo*, see Chapter 6, "Beyond the Mythical Norm.")

The sociologist Héctor Carrillo, a native of Mexico who studied sexuality in Guadalajara, Mexico, explained that this model "validates the notion, often associated with machismo, that the realm of the masculine dominates over the feminine (and by extension that men are superior to women)" (p. 39). This model is called the **gender-based model of sexual identity** (based on the gender enactment, rather than sex, of individuals) as opposed to the **object choice model of sexual identity** (where homosexuality, bisexuality, and heterosexuality are determined based on the sex of the person who is attracted to another and the sex of the object [person] one is attracted to) (see Carrillo). The fact that people who engage in same-sex sexual activity sometimes do not conceive of themselves as engaging in homosexual behavior has given rise to the terms "men who have sex with men" (or MSM) and "women who have sex with women."

The historian Martin Nesvig, who reviewed studies of Latin American MSM, argued that although there is sometimes an *activo/pasivo* distinction, it is not accurate to say that *activos* escape all sexual stigma. It seems that *activos*, according to Nesvig, escape stigma within MSM communities but can run into problems in the broader heterosexual community and therefore tend to remain silent beyond their MSM communities. Carrillo explained:

> *Men can easily remain "normal" by choosing to respect, at least publicly, social expectations of masculinity. They most likely have to conceal their sexual behaviors with men in order to maintain their status, but in some instances they might still be able to maintain their status even when others know about their same-sex attraction. They might also find a few spaces and social networks—those made up mostly of other men "who understand" and whose discretion can be trusted. . . . And, in any case, they would need to take some steps to protect their masculinity. . . . Should their same-sex behavior become publicly known, people around these men could assume, at least initially, that there must have been special circumstances—"he was drunk" or "he was too* caliente *[horny]"—and that they were the insertive, or dominant, partners in the sexual interaction. But the information would nonetheless create some kind of scandal and gossip. (pp. 56–57, brackets in original)*

The anthropologist Roger Lancaster, who studied MSM in Nicaragua, found that it was acceptable to boast among men (including heterosexual men) of one's sexual exploits, including playing the active role with other men. Lancaster contended,

> *Desire is not at issue here and it is irrelevant to what degree one is attracted sexually to members of one's own sex. What matters is the manner in which one is attracted to other males. It is expected that one would naturally be aroused by the idea of anally penetrating another male.*

> *This is not to say that active homosexual pursuits are encouraged or even approved in all social contexts. Like adultery and heterosexual promiscuity, the active role in homosexual intercourse is seen as an infraction. That is, from the point of view of civil-religious authority, and from the point of view of women, it is indeed a sin (*pecado *[sin] or* mal *[wrong]). But like its equivalent forms of adultery or promiscuity, the sodomizing act is a relatively minor*

sin. And in male–male social relations, any number of peccadillos (heavy drinking, promiscuity, the active role in same-sex intercourse) become status markers of male honor. (p. 113, brackets not in original)

A further complication concerns how socioeconomic class and geography intersect with sexual practices. The sociologist James Thing (2010), who interviewed Mexican American immigrants in Los Angeles, found that men from "poor and working-class origins, rural communities or smaller provincial cities" (p. 816) usually observed the *activo/pasivo* divide, whereas men who were lower-middle class or middle class and came almost exclusively from urban areas did not identify as *activo* or *pasivo*. Instead, these urban lower-middle and middle-class men were more likely to follow an object choice model of sexual identity and practice mutual oral sex or anal penetration.

Carrillo stated that among the Mexicans he studied, the new terms of urban, middle-class, same-sex identity are homosexual, to a lesser extent, gay, and, even more rarely, bisexual. Carrillo contended there is a mixing of these modern terms with current MSM terms. That is, there is a blending of the use of gender-based terms for sexuality (including *activo, pasivo,* and *normal*) with object-based terms for sexuality (gay, homosexual, and heterosexual). As a result, a Mexican man might divide men into normal and heterosexual (drawing from both sets of terms) or think of himself as gay, *pasivo,* and a woman.

The Gender-Based Model of Sexual Identity and Women

Carrillo noted that in the gender-based model of sexual identity, Mexican women are divided into two groups. One is masculine women (*machorras* or other derogatory labels) who are presumed to reject men and desire women. The other category is "women" or "normal women" (*mujeres/mujeres normales*) who are feminine and who are attracted to women and/or men (p. 38).

Carrillo further noted that in this model bisexuality is not recognized as a distinct category "because individuals considered *normal* are given some latitude to transgress and have sex with members of their own sex without losing their status" (p. 39).

MORE ABOUT...

Carrillo noted that mixing such terms may seem "paradoxical" but in fact reflects the uniqueness of Mexican sexual identities (p. 80). It is possible that this blending of categories is part of a transition to modern sexual identity categories identified by Foucault, but Carrillo asserted it is more likely a reflection of the distinctiveness of current-day Mexican sexual identities. Carrillo is suggesting that the so-called "modern" categories of homosexual, heterosexual, and bisexual are not naturally the best descriptors in Mexican culture, nor will they inevitably replace traditional gender-based identity categories or current-day hybrid identities.

THE EMERGENCE OF THE MODERN HOMOSEXUAL

If ancient Greeks and Romans did not neatly divide the world into homosexuals and heterosexuals and echoes of the Roman schematization of same-sex sexuality and masculinity still exist, how and when did modern notions of homosexuality and heterosexuality come about? Theorists of the history of sexuality argue that social and economic transformations brought about the modern conception of homosexual identity. Our historical survey will pass over the Middle Ages and focus on early modern England and then move to modern Europe in the 19th century.

Marriage in Early Modern England

One key to understanding the emergence of modern homosexuality is the varying ways that marriage has functioned in Western society. During the early 17th century in England, for example, marriage among the upper classes was a way of protecting property and blood lineage. Intense bonds of friendship between women were seen as appropriate channels for women's energy, particularly because women had to remain virgins before marriage to ensure the purity of their husband's lineage, which was necessary to pass on inheritance and titles (Traub, 2002). In the literature of the period, these female friendships were celebrated and declarations of love and even physical intimacy were considered appropriate. As Valerie Traub, a professor of English and women's studies, explained, drawing on Bach, "marriage was compulsory for most people" but heterosexuality in the modern sense of the term, including romantic and sexual desire, was not (p. 266). In this context, erotic desire and activity between women was seen not only as harmless to the institution of marriage but also as a way of preserving the chastity of women with regard to men. Traub referred to this vision of women's close and sometimes sexual relationships as **chaste femme love**. By using the word femme, Traub was suggesting such women were perceived as appropriately feminine. "Chaste" has several meanings, including being sexually pure, sexually restrained, or celibate—all of which capture how these relationships were considered inconsequential as they related to the marriage of women to men, despite sometimes being sexual in nature.

The insignificance of female same-sex sexual activity is emblematic of early modern Europe's thinking about sex, which was often phallocentric—**phallocentrism** is an attitude in which attention revolves around the phallus or penis. Women of the time who engaged in erotic activity that did not involve a penis often were not recognized as engaging in sex at all (as may also have been the case in ancient Rome, which we discussed earlier). As such, female same-sex sexual activity was rarely punished and, when it was, it fell under sodomy laws. Sodomy laws prohibited any number of immoral and "unnatural" sexual acts, including anal sex, rape, sex with animals, masturbation, and child molestation (Traub). Sodomy laws sometimes included penetrative sex between two women, including by the use of a dildo or by the use of an unusually large clitoris on the part of one woman who was known as a **tribade** because of her unique anatomy (some of these individuals may have been what we call intersex today). Court testimony suggests that women were more likely to be punished if one partner cross-dressed and passed as a man and if the women attempted to live as a married couple because these were seen as threats to patriarchal power.

Provided that women did not engage in penetrative sex or cross-dressing, however, their physical intimacies were generally not seen as a threat to patriarchal status. This began to change as a new vision of marriage emerged by the late 17th century that emphasized what Traub called **domestic heterosexuality**. As part of this new vision, erotic desire became necessary for marriage. Moreover, women and men were expected to "invest more of their emotional life into their domestic partners, and . . . express it through sex" (Traub, p. 269). Traub wrote, "it might not be pushing my argument too far to say that under the regime of domestic heterosexuality, heterosexual desire was constructed" (p. 269). With this new way of thinking about marriage, intense romantic relationships between women were no longer seen as proper; instead chaste femme love began to be seen as unchaste and a threat to marital bonding, a process Traub called the **perversion of lesbian desire**. Traub viewed this as an important element in the creation of the modern lesbian identity category.

Traub argued that elements of female same-sex desire and activity undergo **cycles of salience**, "recurring moments [in history] when certain definitional elements crop up as particularly meaningful to understandings of eroticism" (p. 358). Put another way, different aspects of female same-sex relationships become more prominent in specific historical periods. So sometimes chaste femme love is the predominant way of viewing same-sex relationships between women and the relationships are immune to charges of sexual deviance, but at other times almost any same-sex relationship can be suspect. In other circumstances, certain markers of female masculinity are prominent in thinking about female same-sex sexuality, such as female cross-dressing or certain forms of female same-sex sexual activity such as penetrative sex.

Traub's research on early modern England suggested three recurrent themes regarding what we think of as modern lesbianism: **(im)possibility, (in)signif-icance**, and **(in)visibility**. At times and in certain configurations lesbian sex is either: impossible or possible, insignificant or significant, invisible or visible.

(Im)possibility—Under the phallocentric perspective of early modern England it is simply impossible for most women (except for sodomites and tribades) to have "sex" with one another because they lack a phallus. This also seemed to be the perspective of ancient Roman culture, where sex between women was viewed as humorous for precisely the same reason. However, sometimes lesbian sex does seem to be a cultural possibility—as when women were tribades or used dildos or assumed masculine gender roles.

(In)significance/(In)visibility—Sometimes certain forms of sexual activity are simply trivial, as was the case in early modern England before domestic heterosexuality took hold. When marriage was compulsory and heterosexual sex was important for producing legitimate children who could inherit titles and property, female same-sex sexual activity was not significant and was often invisible as sexual activity. However, with the rise of domestic heterosexuality, the sexual and emotional connection between women became a visible threat to marriage.

Social Relations in Modern Europe

Another key to understanding the rise of modern homosexuality involves a series of social changes that occurred in modern Europe. The sociologist Gary Kinsman (1987/1992), elaborating on the work of Michel Foucault, described them as follows.

The Rise of Capitalist Social Relations—From the 15th to the 19th centuries, as capitalism replaced a primarily rural economic system, the family was

Boston Marriage

In late-19th-century New England it was not uncommon for two women to live together in a long-term relationship known as a **Boston marriage** (Gritz, 2012). Many women in such relationships were so-called New Women who took up professions as social restrictions on women loosened in turn-of-the-century America (Faderman, 1981, 1993). (See Chapter 7, "Embodiment, Beauty, and the Viewer," and Chapter 11, "History of Women's Activism in the United States," for related discussions about the New Woman and first wave feminism.) It seems that some women in Boston marriages were sexually intimate, whereas others were not. It is tempting to label such relationships lesbian, but even in those relationships that were sexually intimate, such a label is problematic primarily because the women in such relationships and the society they lived in understood same-sex relationships and desire so differently than we do today. Same-sex intimacy was "accepted at the time as a natural part of heterosexuality," wrote Jennie Rothenberg Gritz (2012). In addition, women were perceived as nonsexual beings, said Peggy Wishart (as cited in Gritz, para. 10). She added, "Most people assumed that if they didn't have husbands, they wouldn't have any interest in sex." All of this began to change as the century turned (think of Traub's cycles of salience). In Traub's terms, what had been seen as chaste gradually came to be seen as perverted. Why? Gritz noted two factors. One was Oscar Wilde's trial and conviction on sodomy charges in 1895 (newspapers focused on salacious details about Wilde's life). "The other game-changer," wrote Gritz, "was Sigmund Freud." Since Freud, we tend to view life through a "sexualized lens," concluded Gritz (para. 12).

MORE ABOUT....

displaced as the basic economic unit. Prior to capitalism, families would farm together; marriage and child-rearing were crucial to survival because children were necessary to perform agricultural labor and to take care of parents in old age. Even if people had same-sex desire they would usually be forced by economic necessity into opposite-sex marriages. With capitalism and industrialization, cities grew and men (and increasingly women) could earn wages in urban jobs independent of their families. As women and men gathered in cities, they could socialize together in taverns, restaurants, and other venues and have an outlet for same-sex desire (Kinsman). (See Chapter 4 for a related discussion of how industrialization opened up possibilities for female same-sex relationships in China.)

The Modern Regime of Sexuality—According to Kinsman, the second factor responsible for the emergence of the modern homosexual is what we term the

modern regime of sexuality. Under the old regime of sexuality, Foucault argued, same-sex sexual activity was viewed as an act that anyone might commit (a conception similar to that of ancient Greek, Roman, and certain current-day Latin American conceptions of male same-sex desire). Laws under the old regime punished homosexual *acts* but did not recognize the existence of a unique *kind* of person (namely, homosexuals) who would commit such acts. For example, in the Bible, the book of Leviticus condemns acts of sodomy but does not refer to or condemn a kind of person (the homosexual) who commits such acts. Just as anyone might be tempted to steal and be a thief, anyone might be tempted to commit sodomy and be a sodomite. The modern Western conception drew a line around those who engaged in same-sex sexual activity and/or had same-sex desire and created what Foucault calls a "personage" (a person with special status): the homosexual. The LGBTI scholar Thabo Msibi called this the **personification of homosexuality**.

During the modern capitalist period, new fields of study emerged, including psychiatry and sexology (the study of sex). Experts in these fields were aware of the emerging urban gay subcultures and tried to categorize and coin terms for people engaging in same-sex sexual activity. In 1868, Károly Mária Kertbeny (who was also known by the last name Benkert) used the terms heterosexuality and homosexuality for the first time in history in a private draft of a letter to the sexologist Karl Heinrich Ulrichs (Katz, 1997). Although Kertbeny hoped

FIGURE 5.3

Men in a Nazi concentration camp wearing pink triangles, the Nazi symbol for homosexual prisoners.

that the coining of these terms would help people see that everyone is naturally homosexual or heterosexual and our desires are simply the normal outgrowth of who we are, the term homosexual was quickly used to classify and repress gay people as abnormal and sick. Previously, homosexual activity had been suppressed as criminal and sinful, but now homosexuality became increasingly medicalized (that is, treated as a medical or psychiatric condition) and pathologized (treated as a disease or psychological abnormality). For Foucault, this was the beginning of the modern regime of sexuality and the birth of the category of homosexual as part of our modern cognitive schema.

Homosexual Identity as a Movement—The third factor responsible for the emergence of the modern homosexual, according to Kinsman, is what we term **homosexual identity as a movement**. As we have seen, prior to the emergence of capitalism, between the 14th and 19th centuries, there were few opportunities for people with same-sex desires to live in community with one another and no widespread recognition of themselves as being a distinct group with its own cultural norms and practices. Foucault argued that once homosexuals faced repression under the medical category of homosexual, they could band together as a group and resist that repression. The medical language or discourse that condemned homosexuality also gave rise to a " 'reverse discourse': homosexuality began to speak in [sic] its own behalf, to demand that its legitimacy or 'naturality' be acknowledged, often in the same vocabulary, using the same categories by which it was medically disqualified" (Foucault, p. 101). To put it another way, the very category that was used to stigmatize homosexuality became a flag under which gay people could build a sense of identity and rally to demand equality (Figures 5.3 and 5.4).

FIGURE 5.4

The up-ended pink triangle became an element of the reverse discourse of gay rights and is especially associated with ACT UP's SILENCE = DEATH campaign about the AIDS crisis and the necessity for gay or queer activism.

THE STONEWALL UPRISING AND LGBTQ LIBERATION IN THE UNITED STATES

Although homosexual activism did occur in the late 1800s in Europe, even as late as the mid-20th century there was no mass movement for LGBTQ rights in the United States. The 1960s saw the rise of a number of movements, including the women's movement (the so-called second wave of feminism), the Black civil rights movement, the anti-war movement (against the war in

FIGURE 5.5

Activists outside the Stonewall Inn after riots the weekend of June 28, 1969. This uprising marked the start of the modern gay rights movement in the United States and an important moment in transgender history.

Vietnam), and others (see Chapter 11 and Chapter 12, "Feminisms"). The modern gay rights movement would be launched on a June night in 1969, with the Stonewall Riots in the neighborhood of Greenwich Village in New York City (Figure 5.5).

The writer David Carter (2009) noted that in 1961 homosexuality was negatively sanctioned in a variety of ways in the United States. States had legal penalties for engaging in consensual homosexual sex that ranged from small fines to many years or even life in prison. Many states had "sex psychopath" laws that allowed for the detention of gay people, and California authorized lobotomies and castration for those convicted of consensual sodomy. Most states permitted professional licenses to be revoked because of homosexuality. New York State used an antilabor law from the 1800s, originally meant to prevent demonstrators from disguising themselves as the "opposite" sex, to arrest transvestites who wore "fewer than three articles of clothing appropriate to their sex" (Carter, 2010, p. 15). Carter (2009) asserted that religious groups "universally" condemned homosexuality as sinful (p. 11). Furthermore, gay people were often arrested for "'homosexual solicitation' as a result of police entrapment" (Carter, 2010, p. 18). They faced jail time, loss of their jobs, and shake-downs by corrupt attorneys.

Given the antihomosexual climate, it is no surprise that few people were brave enough to join the existing gay rights organizations, or **homophile organizations**, as they were called. The most notable of these homophile groups were the Mattachine Society and the Daughters of Bilitis. Instead of activist organizations, gay bars were the center of gay life into the 1960s (Carter, 2010). Given that New York City had the largest gay population in the United States, one might imagine a thriving gay scene; but in fact all but one legal gay bar had been closed down in a 1960 crackdown (despite any specific law against them) and the Mafia moved in to replace them with illegally operated bars (Carter, 2010). Most illegally operated gay bars in New York

Historicizing Homosexualities

Our survey of same-sex sexuality through Western history suggests that a modern public homosexual or gay identity is a relatively new phenomenon. However, some scholars disagree with Foucault's claim that the socially constructed category of homosexual people did not exist prior to the 19th century. Opponents of Foucault's position are often referred to as essentialists—in this case, people who believe that homosexuality is a category with fixed and commonly shared characteristics that existed through time (for more on essentialism, see Chapter 6).

Those who disagree with Foucault often refer to the existence of the gender-based model of sexual activity that distinguishes between a masculine penetrator and an effeminate or feminine penetrated person (the model that applied in ancient Rome and in some Latin American contexts). Essentialists often claim that at least the penetrated person is recognizably a kind of homosexual person. This would seem to us an overly narrow definition of homosexuality by modern standards and suggests that such societies had a distinctive view of same-sex desire, activity, and relationships. (Essentialists have also raised other objections too lengthy to explore here. See, for example, Clarke, 2005; S. O. Murray, 1995; Norton, 1997.) Despite essentialists' claims, we lean heavily toward the historicist position. Our survey of history and culture suggests to us that same-sex sexual activity and same-sex relationships have been configured in different ways across time and place and that a nuanced understanding will recognize the cultural and historical distinctiveness of same-sex sexuality. At the same time, we recognize the validity of a point often raised by essentialists: there are recurring themes and cycles of salience through history and across cultures.

MORE ABOUT...

were concentrated in the neighborhood known as Greenwich Village (or simply the Village) and the Stonewall Inn, a long established favorite among many segments of the gay community, was located in the center of the neighborhood (Carter, 2010).

On the hot night of Friday, June 27, 1969, the police Public Morals division attempted to close down the Stonewall Inn to stop a Mafia-run extortion racket targeting gay people that operated out of the bar. The clientele of the bar was mixed, including lesbians, gay men, and trans people (in full or partial drag). There were businessmen and homeless street youth. A back room, occupied by younger patrons, was sometimes called the "black room" or "Puerto-Rican room" because of the ethnic and racial mix of people who congregated there (Carter, 2010, p. 73). On that June night, the police arrested Mafia members and non-Mafia employees as well as selected transvestites who initially resisted attempts "to be 'examined'" in the bathrooms (Carter, 2010, p. 140). The patrons exiting the bar and the growing crowd outside initially reacted with humor and camping (which in this context is "ostentatious, affected theatrical; effeminate" or gay posing) (OED). But in clearing the bar of the 200 patrons, the police faced increasing resistance; first from a drag queen who hit a police officer with her purse after being shoved and, at a turning point in the evening, from at least one butch lesbian who resisted arrest. The crowd turned ugly and then violent as the lesbian patron was manhandled by police, who were forced to retreat into the bar as bottles and paving stones were thrown by those outside. Then Molotov cocktails were hurled as the police were trapped inside (Carter, 2009).

Blue-helmeted riot police equipped with batons, guns, and riot shields, who were veterans of 1960s race riots, descended on the scene and attempted to clear the streets. Racially and ethnically mixed rioters taunted and attacked the police. Most notable was a group of effeminate street youths who formed Rockette-style kick-lines in the street daring the police to attack—which they did. The rioting continued on and off over a 6-day period (Carter, 2009).

The Stonewall Riots are widely considered a pivotal or founding moment for the modern gay liberation movement in the United States. Although gay people had begun to organize over the previous hundred years, Carter (2009) argued that the riots had a galvanizing effect that "transformed the small homophile movement into a mass movement" (p. 13). Frank Kameny, the founder of the Washington, DC, chapter of the Mattachine Society and a gay activist for 50 years, stated that around the time of Stonewall, there were 50–60 gay rights groups; within a year that number grew to about 1,500 groups; within 2 years the number was around 2,500—"that was the impact of Stonewall" (as cited in Carter, 2009, p. 13; Eaklor, 2008).

Carter argued that the Stonewall Riots were symbolically important because they were violent. He wrote, "just as nonviolence allowed African Americans to overturn racist images of Blacks as violence-prone and achieve a measure of moral superiority, the use of violence by gay men subverted the stereotype of homosexuals as ineffectual and lacking in courage or masculine qualities" (2009, p. 13).

Carter also argued that the Stonewall Riots were pivotal for the self-image of gay people. His research indicated that the riots were ignited by the resistance of transvestites and at least one butch lesbian, as well as effeminate homeless gay youths, who were on the front lines of the rioting over the 6-day course of the conflict. Carter elaborated: "the Stonewall Riots were instigated and led by the most despised and marginal elements of the lesbian, gay, bisexual and transgendered community" (Carter, 2010, p. 262). Carter (2010) concluded that it is significant that "gender transgression" was the common characteristic of "those who resisted first and fought the hardest" in the riots (p. 261). The Stonewall Riots then, were not simply about gay liberation (although that would be significant enough); they were also about injustices created by the prevailing views of sex and gender.

The Stonewall uprising was not the first violent response to discrimination against LGBTQ people. Fighting erupted at Cooper's Donuts in Los Angeles in 1959; and there was a riot at Compton's Cafeteria in San Francisco in 1966 (Stryker, 2008). The transgender scholar Susan Stryker (2008) noted that transgender people figured prominently in these incidents (as well as in Stonewall) and that nonviolent transgender activism in "working-class districts of major U.S. cities" overlapped with gay activism. Stryker (2008) wrote that "by the early 1970's transgender political activism had progressed in ways scarcely imaginable when the 1960's had begun" (p. 89).

The story of the emergence of the homosexual may seem neatly concluded with Stonewall's generation of a modern gay rights movement that has since grown into a global movement. However, this is a single strand of the Western story of homosexuality, not the story of all homosexualities within the West

FIGURE 5.6
The Stonewall Inn as it appears today.

or other cultures. We should not forget, for example, that Latin American gender-based models of sexuality do not fit neatly into a story of the emergence of modern Western homosexuality. We will now turn to other conceptions of homosexualities in Africa and Asia that are reminiscent of some elements of Western homosexualities and in other respects vary from Western ways of conceiving of same-sex desire, sexual activity, and relationships.

HOMOSEXUALITIES IN AFRICA

Marc Epprecht (2005), a professor of history and global development studies, has written that "most African soci-eties traditionally placed a high value on heterosexual marriage leading to many children" (p. 139) and "remain powerfully heteronormative with little public social space or unambiguous vocabularies for people who did not conform to the virile and fecund [fertile] marital ideals" (p. 162, brackets not in original). Yet despite this, Epprecht (2005) said, "African cultures also had ways to explain and accommodate those men and women who did not fit the social ideal" (p. 139). Most people did not acknowledge these practices as homo-sexual or bisexual, but Epprecht (2008) asserted that often they could reason-ably be considered as such. Africa is a huge continent composed of many different cultures and same-sex sexual practices have varied over time and across the continent. We will discuss just a few forms of same-sex sexuality in African cultures.

Boy-Wives and *Bagburu* Relationships

The Azande people live in areas of Sudan, the Democratic Republic of Congo, and the Central African Republic (Azande, 2003). In 1930, the social anthro-pologist Edward Evans-Pritchard (1970) interviewed Azande men about the extinct practice of a man taking a **boy-wife**, as well as the traditional and ongoing practice of female homosexuality within *bagburu* **relationships**. Evans-Pritchard explained that because the Azande people practiced polyg-amy (men marrying more than one woman), it reduced the availability of marriageable women. It was difficult for most men to accumulate enough wealth to pay a bride-price to acquire a wife and so most men married late (in their 20s and 30s). Furthermore, adultery was severely punished and so sexual outlets for unmarried men were limited. However, a man could pay a lower bride-price to acquire a male youth, perhaps between the ages of 12 and 20, who would take on the gender role of wife, including cooking, drawing water, and other household chores (and was even encouraged to speak softly as women were supposed to do). Boy-wives and male husbands would share a bed and husbands would have intercrural sex with their boy-wives. Intercrural sex, also called thigh-sex, is where a person puts his penis between the thighs of another person. Intercrural sex was also an ancient Greek pederastic practice. Evans-Pritchard compared the custom of taking a boy-wife to ancient Greek pederasty, saying that such relationships were also "apprenticeships" and that when boy-wives grew up, both the "wife" and the male husband would eventually take female wives (p. 1430).

Although taking a boy-wife was widely accepted among the Azande, female homosexuality was viewed with "horror" (Evans-Pritchard, p. 1432). According to Azande men, lesbian behavior existed because polygamy limited the opportunity of women to have sex with their husbands. However, a woman could obtain permission to enter into a *bagburu* relationship, which is a formal bond of friendship with another woman. These relationships could provide "respectable cover" for female same-sex sexual activity (Evans-Pritchard, p. 1432).

Mummy–Baby Relationships

A more modern example of female same-sex sexual activity sometimes takes place in what are known as **mummy–baby relationships**. These are relatively formal relationships between adolescent girls and young women in which one takes on the role of "mommy" and the other takes on the role of "baby." Such relationships appear to have begun as early as the 1950s in Lesotho, a country entirely surrounded by South Africa (Gay, 1986). Mummy–baby relationships have also been documented in Swaziland and Kenya (Gunkel, 2009). These relationships are often formed between schoolgirls, with the older taking on the role of mommy and the younger that of baby. In these relationships babies receive small gifts and maternal guidance—including how to handle boys and heterosexual dating. Both mummies and babies are emotionally and physically intimate, cuddling, touching, and kissing. Parents often approve of these relationships as a way to postpone heterosexual sexual activity. However, mummy–baby relationships sometimes go beyond sensual intimacies typical of mothers and young children and become erotic relationships.

Much like *bagburu* relationships, mummy–baby relationships may provide a respectable cover for same-sex sexual intimacy. Despite any same-sex sexual intimacy, mummies and babies typically also engage in heterosexual dating

FIGURE 5.7
Khnumhotep and
Niankhkhnum, men of
equal rank in ancient
Egypt, were buried
together along with their
wives; however, instead
of depictions of intimate
embraces with their wives,
the tomb only depicts the
male couple in embraces
with each other that are
typical of married couples.

and marriage. Mummy-baby relationships may continue into adulthood (although most women say they outgrow the mummy–baby frame and may develop mature adult relationships with their partners) and can provide continued cover for same-sex sexual activity. As one woman put it, "if a husband comes home and finds you in bed with a woman, he won't mind. But if he finds you in bed with another man, he may kill someone" (Gay, p. 111).

Homosexuality as Un-African

Epprecht (2008), Msibi, and others have expressed concern over the move by many across Africa to label homosexual activity as "un-African." Epprecht (2008) explained that a variety of forces have fostered the myth of same-sex sexuality as un-African. We will explore just a few of these influences. One source of this sentiment is Western views of Africans. Westerners who colonized Africa often viewed homosexuality as a decadent vice of civilization and believed that "primitive" (that is, "uncivilized") Africans could not suffer from this moral decay; even when Westerners collected evidence to the contrary, Epprecht (2008) contended, it was "easily overlooked" (p. 164). Modern Western stereotypes of Africans as heterosexually promiscuous have also elided the existence of same-sex sexual activity (Epprecht, 2008, p. 2). Another source of these views is nationalist and anticolonialist sentiment within Africa. Msibi noted that several African leaders have claimed that homosexuality was brought to Africa from the West and goes against African religions and traditions; for example, the president of Zimbabwe, Robert Mugabe, has said that homosexuality was "a scourge planted by the white man on a pure continent" (Msibi, p. 62). However, Murray and Will stated, "The colonialists did not introduce homosexuality to Africa but rather an intolerance of it—and systems of surveillance and regulation for suppressing it" (as cited in Msibi, p. 66). Of the 53 countries in Africa, 38 have laws that punish homosexual activity, most of them derived from colonial era laws (Msibi).

Personification of Homosexuality

Although Msibi was alarmed at the argument that homosexuality is un-African and explained how same-sex sexuality has been a historical feature in many African cultures, he also stated that "homosexuality is a concept that does *not* come out of Africa" (p. 56, emphasis added). Msibi and Epprecht (2008)

FIGURE 5.8
Protestors oppose anti-gay legislation in Uganda.

asserted that it is inaccurate to characterize people who engaged in traditional African same-sex practices as homosexual or gay. Msibi argued that these Western words reflect the personification of homosexuality (and heterosexuality, we would add). As Epprecht (2005) explained at the beginning of our discussion of African homosexualities, because same-sex sexuality often took place in a way that did not interfere with marriage and childbearing, African cultures had ways of explaining and accommodating such behavior. Epprecht (2005) added that traditional and even some modern Africans who engage in same-sex sexual activity do not see their same-sex sexual activity as homosexual or gay; sometimes it is not considered sex at all. Such activity simply is not important or visible as long as heterosexual behavior and relationships are maintained.

Msibi argued that the term homosexual was a Western creation used "to control social relations, while labeling those engaged in same sex relations as deviant" (p. 56). Likewise, Msibi, citing Gamson, contended that a gay identity is a "public collective identity"—a movement that emerged in the West with "its own cultural and political institutions, festivals, neighborhoods, and even its own flag" (p. 56). Comparatively recently, gay identity and activism have also begun to emerge in Africa. Significant successes for the movement include an equality clause prohibiting discrimination based on sexual orientation in the South African constitution in 1996—the first such clause in the world (Cock, 2003). With the rise of this public identity in Africa, however, there has also been an increasingly hostile response, including a number of recent anti-gay laws in places like Uganda and Nigeria (Quinn, 2014). Graeme Reid of Human Rights Watch said of the anti-gay laws: "I think it's a backlash against an increased visibility and activism [among LGBT people] throughout sub-Saharan Africa that we have seen over the last 20 years" (as cited in Quinn). He continued, "There's been an emergence of an African LGBT movement and it's much more visible and much more vocal. So I think . . . there's a link between the two."

Msibi argued that Africans who adopt a specifically gay identity are for the first time thinking of and presenting themselves as a kind of person—a homosexual person—and that such a public, collective identity threatens the enforcement of heteronormativity because it does not fit the norms of heterosexual marriage and fertility. Msibi also contended that visible gay identity threatens patriarchy for a variety of reasons, including that gay men pose a threat to the power of men derived from heterosexual masculinity and that lesbians undermine men's status by violating perceived gender norms and not adhering to the heterosexual ideal of reproduction.

ON THE
web

Read about **Article 377 of India's penal code**, which criminalizes "carnal intercourse against the order of nature" on the Student Website: www.oup.com/us/gillis-jacobs

INDIA'S *HIJRAS*: TROUBLING SAME- AND OPPOSITE-SEX SCHEMAS

Lakshmi, a young **Hijra** dancer, explained that she became a *Hijra* because "I was born a man but not a perfect man" (Nanda, 1993, p. 544). This is a typical explanation of why (mostly) males adopt female dress (at least on some occasions), ideally renounce sexual desire (and sex), and undergo the removal of their penis and testicles in a sacrifice dedicated to the Hindu goddess Bahuchara Mata (Nanda, 1993; Reddy, 2005). *Hijras* often explain that they were "imperfect" men—meaning that either their genitals were insufficiently male-looking in physical appearance (that is, they are intersex or simply vary from the physical male norm) or that their genitals failed to work properly (meaning they were unable to experience sexual arousal toward women). In fact, the word *Hijra*, which comes from the Urdu language, is often translated

FIGURE 5.9
Hijras in Pushkar, India.

as eunuch (a person who is castrated—had his testicles removed) or hermaphrodite (which we call intersex today). *Hijras* are widely considered a "quintessential" example of a third sex category (Reddy, p. 2) (See Chapter 1 for a
discussion of the third sex category). *Hijras* are found in India, Pakistan, and
Bangladesh, although we will focus solely on Indian *Hijras* (Nanda, 2014).

Although most *Hijras* begin life with the assigned sex of male, the anthropologist Serena Nanda (1993) reported that some *Hijras* are raised as girls but
become *Hijras* after they do not develop secondary female sex characteristics.
In fact, it is claimed one of the founders of the *Hijra* group was "a woman, but
not a normal woman, she did not menstruate" (Nanda, 1993, p. 544). In most
cases, however, *Hijras* are assumed to have begun life as males. Because of the
differences from other men, *Hijras* are viewed as "not men" or, as O'Flaherty
describes them, "man minus man" (as cited in Nanda, 1993, p. 544).

Nanda (1993, 2014) explained that *Hijras* take female names and wear female clothing—some exclusively wear female attire and others only on some occasions. *Hijras* have also asked to be included on the census as women (Nanda, 1993, 2014). In this respect, Nanda (2014) described *Hijras* as not only "man minus man" but also "man plus woman" (p. 29). *Hijras* also often take on exaggerated female mannerisms and behave in ways that are considered sexually inappropriate and outrageous by the usual standards of "demure and restrained femininity" (Nanda, 1993, p. 546). In terms of physiology, *Hijras* lack female reproductive ability (as emasculated men or as intersex individuals assigned female at birth). These qualities make *Hijras* "like women" but "also not women." Ultimately, Nanda (2014) contended that *Hijras* are considered "as 'neither man nor woman'" (p. 28).

Hijras are primarily associated with Hinduism and worship the Hindu goddess Bahuchara Mata. Today *Hijras* are considered to have the power to bless married couples and children with fertility (Nanda, 2014). A *Hijra*'s curse, by contrast, is thought to harm a man's virility or fertility (Nanda, 2014). *Hijras* also claim a connection to Islam through the Moghul emperors' tradition of having eunuchs who had important status in their courts and Muslim rulers who were supportive of *Hijras* (Nanda, 1993). Nanda explained that today *Hijras'* appearances at marriages and births are viewed with ambivalence. *Hijras* inspire fear through their ability to curse a family and because of what Nanda calls India's "virility complex," which associates manhood with semen and male sexual performance—which *Hijras* lack as "'failed' men" (Nanda, 2014, p. 35). In contrast, *Hijras* are respected as part of a Hindu religious tradition that includes numerous myths about Gods who change sex and because of *Hijras'* association with procreative power.

Hijras are ideally supposed to renounce sexual desire, sexual activity, and procreative family life. However, *Hijras* often admit to being sexually attracted to men and some engage in sex with men. Some *Hijras* enter into long-term relationships with men who they refer to as their "husbands" (Nanda, 2014, p. 34). It is also true that for hundreds of years and still today, *Hijras* have engaged in prostitution (Nanda, 2014). Nanda (1993) noted that the word *Hijra* does not mean homosexual. *Hijra* identity is not based on sexual desire for men; the hallmark of being a *Hijra* is male impotence, not sexual attraction (Nanda, 1993, 2014).

We include *Hijras* in this chapter not because they neatly fit into the array of other homosexualities described herein, but precisely because they resist even the broadest schematizations of same-sex desire, sexual activity, and relationships. This suggests that sexual desire, sexual activity, and sexual

breaking the frame
Hijras as a Third Sex Category

The category of the *Hijra* is an expansive one that includes people who in the West we would divide into "eunuchs, homosexuals, transsexuals, [intersex people] . . . transvestites" (Nanda, 1993, p. 547)—and we would add, perhaps asexual people. (See Chapter 4 for a discussion of transsexual people, transvestites, and asexual people.) The category of *Hijra*, then, is not a category that is primarily about sexual desire for males.

Even more fundamentally, it is not a category about *male same*-sex desire. *Hijras* by definition are "neither man nor woman" so even when they desire men, they would not be considered to have *same*-sex desire—they instead constitute a third sex that may desire men. This status makes it problematic to speak of *Hijras* as men who have sex with men or even to speak of their category as a historically specific form of homosexuality. Moreover, *Hijra* communities are highly organized and usually involve communal living in households of 5 to 20 people. This, along with their sacred status in India, gives them a unique cultural role that distinguishes them from people who have a modern transnational gay identity.

relationships—"same-sex" and otherwise—are culturally and historically constructed in often radically different ways.

CONCLUSION

Human understanding of same-sex and opposite-sex sexuality has varied across time and cultures. In ancient Greece, male same-sex relations, including pederasty, were sometimes tolerated and even celebrated. Our knowledge of ancient Greek female same-sex practices is scanty; Sappho may be the only documented example of a woman in ancient Greece who had sex with women.

Male same-sex sexual activity in ancient Roman culture was accepted, but how a man engaged in such activity could either reinforce or threaten his masculine status. The total absence of Roman historical examples of female same-sex sexual activity is telling, suggesting a remarkable indifference and perhaps blindness to such activity.

Key Terms

The *activo/pasivo* distinction in many Latin American cultures appears to echo the Roman prime directive of masculine sexual behavior and, as in ancient Rome, results in a gendered model of sexual activity that gives higher status to masculine men over effeminate men and women. It appears in some instances this gender-based model of sexual identity is now blending with the increasingly globalized object choice model of sexual identity, creating a unique hybrid model of identity.

Traub has identified the rise of the ideal of domestic heterosexuality and the disappearance of chaste femme love through the perversion of lesbian desire as important developments in the emergence of the modern homosexual female in early modern England. She further contended that so-called lesbianism undergoes cycles of salience—sometimes it is possible, significant, and visible and at other times (and in other forms) it is impossible, insignificant, and invisible.

Kinsman fleshed out the emergence of the modern homosexual in modern Europe by explaining several factors identified by Foucault. Carter noted that the pivotal moment in the United States that transformed gay rights activism into a modern mass movement occurred a century later in 1969, when the most marginalized members of LGBT communities instigated and led the Stonewall uprising in the Village in New York City.

African societies have generally been strongly heteronormative but have often left space for same-sex sexuality. Examples include the precolonial practice in Azande culture of men taking boy-wives, the Azande custom of establishing *bagburu* relationships between women, and the modern practice of female mummy–baby relationships. These indigenously African same-sex practices demonstrate that same-sex sexual activity and relationships are indeed African but, as Msibi stated, the people who engage in them could not be appropriately called homosexual. The personification of homosexuality, Msibi stated, is originally a Western notion.

Indian *Hijras* provide another example of how sexuality can be constructed in ways that are culturally unique. Ultimately as "neither man nor woman," *Hijras'* sexual desire, behavior, and relationships resist classification as homosexual or even as same-sex sexuality.

The history of sexual orientation is complex because how we have conceived of sexuality has varied significantly across time and cultures (and even within cultures). There are interesting cycles of salience that emerge from time to time. However, these occur in the midst of a matrix of difference. Every culture and time period deserves attention for what it reveals about the diversity and uniqueness of human sexual expression.

THINK, LEARN, ACT

The following resources are available on the Student Website: www.oup.com/us/gillis-jacobs

Taking Stock, Taking Action prompts and activities. Apply what you've learned to take action on campus and in the broader community.

Recommended Readings and Multimedia Resources, including scholarly and literary works, documentaries, feature films, podcasts and more, to enrich the in- and out-of-classroom experience.

CHAPTER 6

BEYOND THE MYTHICAL NORM

Considering Race, Class, and Gender

In 1751, when Benjamin Franklin was still a loyal British subject, he wrote an essay about immigration and population in British America. In that essay he expressed concern about people of color establishing themselves in America and worried in particular about an alien racial group that was swarming into Pennsylvania. Here is what he said:

> Why should the Palatine Boors [Germans roughly from a German state known as the Palatinate] be suffered to swarm into our Settlements, and by herding together, establish their Language and Manners to the Exclusion of ours? Why should Pennsylvania, founded by the English, become a Colony of Aliens, who will shortly be so numerous as to Germanize us instead of our Anglifying them, and will never adopt our Language or Customs, any more than they can acquire our Complexion.

Which leads me to add one Remark: That the Number of purely white People in the World is proportionably very small. All Africa is black or tawny [orange-brown or yellowish brown]; Asia chiefly tawny. America (exclusive of the new Comers) wholly so. And in Europe, the Spaniards, Italians, French, Russians and Swedes, are generally of what we call a swarthy Complexion [of a dark hue; black or blackish; dusky (OED)]; as are the Germans also, the Saxons [a group supposedly of Germanic origin] only excepted, who, with the English, make the principal Body of White People on the Face of the Earth. I could wish their Numbers were increased . . . why should we . . . darken [America's] People? Why increase the Sons of Africa, by Planting them in America, where we have so fair an Opportunity, by excluding all Blacks and Tawnys, of increasing the lovely White and Red? But perhaps I am partial to the Complexion of my Country, for such Kind of Partiality is natural to Mankind.

(Bracketed comments not in original) (Franklin, 1751/1936, paras. 23–24)

Given the times, it is not surprising that Franklin expressed a desire to exclude Africans and Asians from America. What is peculiar by modern standards is who else he wanted to exclude because of their non-white status; the list included some Germans as well as Spaniards, Italians, French, Russians, and Swedes. Today it would be hard to imagine, as Franklin did, that Germans are an "alien" people who could "never adopt our language and customs," and it seems nonsensical to claim they cannot "acquire [a white] complexion" since we generally think of most Germans as white by any contemporary standard. Benjamin Franklin's racial categories, however, were not unusual for the age. In fact, racial categorization is a relatively new schema in Western history and these categories have shifted dramatically over time (M. James, 2012; Painter, 2010).

This chapter will begin with an exploration of the concepts of race, ethnicity, and racial categorization. We will then explore the intersection of sex and gender with socioeconomic class and racial/ethnic categories (Asian Americans and Pacific Islanders, Blacks, Latina/os, American Indians, and multiracial people). Last, we will investigate the concept of discrimination and the idea of white privilege.

recap of terms:
Mythical Norm

The poet and activist Audre Lorde (1978/1984) wrote, "Somewhere, on the edge of consciousness, there is what I call a *mythical norm*. . . . In america, [*sic*] this norm is usually defined as white, thin, male, young, heterosexual, christian, and financially secure. It is with this mythical norm that the trappings of power reside within this society" (p. 116).

From Chapter 3, "Gender and In/Equality."

A note about terminology: explanations for many of the terms used in this chapter, including people of color and the names of different racial and ethnic groups, are defined and discussed in Appendix B, Names for Peoples and Places.

EXAMINING RACE

Many racial theories have divided humans into a wide variety of racial categories. Some rely on skin color like Franklin's and others stress other racial configurations so that people we might consider racially white today were previously divided into different races. For example, in the 19th century, the Irish (or Celts) were popularly thought to be a different racial group from the Anglo-Saxon English (Painter). Robert Knox, a medical doctor and anatomist (1791–1862), believed that intermarriage between these groups went against nature as much as marriage between Saxons and Black Africans known as Hottentots (the Khoikhoi of southern Africa) (Painter). Painter noted that in the United States, groups such as Jews, Italians, and the Irish only gradually lost their status as separate races from white Anglo-Saxons.

This raises the question, what is **race**? And what can we say about people of different racial groups? Despite Benjamin Franklin's peculiar view of who belongs to the white race, he does seem to have a traditional conception of what race itself means. Traditionally the term race has been used to refer to a group of people who all share inherited biological features not shared by other races that account for how they look (such as skin color, bone structure, or nose shape) and sometimes for their behavior, character, and cultural predispositions (M. James, 2012). For example, Franklin believed that some Germans (the Palatine Boors) were dark-skinned people incapable of adopting white/American customs because of racial (that is, presumably biological) differences that influenced their cultural behavior.

Franklin's view fits the standard definition of **racism**: "The belief that all members of each race possess characteristics, abilities, or qualities specific to that race, especially so as to distinguish it as inferior or superior to another race or races" (OED). However, we would note that Franklin did not express here the belief in racial superiority—only racial difference.

Among contemporary scholars there is broad agreement that races do not universally share behavior, character, and cultural predispositions that are unique to their race and that there is no basis for believing in the superiority or inferiority of races. However, today, like Franklin, people still categorize by race. Is there a basis for dividing people into different races? If there is, these divisions might be based on observable characteristics such as skin tone or skull shape. In biology, observable physical characteristics and behaviors are known as **phenotypical traits** ("all of an organism's observable characteristics are known as a phenotype, which are dictated by genetic and environmental influences" ["Phenotype," 2012]). It is also possible that racial distinctions could be made based on underlying genetic characteristics that are not directly observable (OED). Before we turn to the phenotypic and direct genetic evidence for racial classification, we must explore an important philosophical concept used for classification: essentialism.

Essentialism

Broadly speaking, an **essence** is "the property of a thing without which the thing could not be what it is" ("Essence," 2004). **Essentialism** (or more specifically a standard account of Aristotelian species essentialism) is the doctrine that at least some things have a common nature, a fixed and unchanging property or set of properties that necessarily make something or some organism what it is (see Stoljar, 1995; Witt, 1989). These properties are called **essential properties**. Entities may have other properties that do not make them what they are; these are called **accidental properties**. An entity could lack an accidental property and still be what it is. For example, a triangle could have three sides and be painted red; having three sides is essential to being a triangle but being red is an inessential or accidental feature.

When scientists look for phenotypical or genetic characteristics that distinguish races from one another, they are often looking for essential properties. For a property or properties (such as genes) to be essential to a race they would need to be shared by all members of the race and only shared by that race. So, do races have essential phenotypic or genetic traits?

Biology and Racial Classification

It does not take much reflection to realize that people cannot be classified by race based on phenotypical characteristics. For example, not all Black people are black—some may be albino (lacking any dark pigmentation) or very light skinned. The same is true for other phenotypical characteristics such as eye color or nose shape. Andreasen (2005) has noted that according to our "common sense" notions of race based on phenotype, Asians are a racial group distinct from Europeans; however, genetic analysis of these populations suggests that Northeast Asians are actually more closely related to Europeans than to Southeast Asians. Thus, according to generalizations about ancestral descent, Europeans and Northeast Asians are "racially" more similar to each other than to Southeast Asians. All this evidence suggests that coherent notions of race cannot be based on observable racial differences. Furthermore, no racial group is known to universally and exclusively possess a gene or set of genes in common, so even genetics is not a sound basis for racial categorization.

At this point it should be clear that races have no essential properties, be they phenotypic (physical or behavioral) or genetic essence(s). With a little reflection you might agree that other categories we have discussed in this text also lack essential properties including sexes, genders, and sexual orientations (none of which can be neatly divided into clear and exclusive categories).

FIGURE 6.1

Fraternal twins born to parents identified as mixed race: each parent has a white mother and a Black father. Such families demonstrate the problem with the idea of distinct races.

MORE ABOUT...

Understanding Essentialism

Within the field of philosophy there is considerable disagreement about how to define essentialism (see Stoljar and Witt). Our definition is admittedly overly simplistic but is a good starting point. If you are interested in philosophy or the philosophy of feminism, you should explore more sophisticated conceptions in upper-level college courses. We disagree with essentialism in all its formulations and this book has an antiessentialist approach—as do many scholars in women's and gender studies. Unfortunately, essentialism has been associated with racism, sexism, and transphobia, among other unpopular beliefs. It is true, for example, that essentialism can be part of a belief in racial categories and therefore support a racist belief system or used to argue for rigid sex categories (which might also be used to oppose the legitimacy of transgender identity) and a sexist belief system, but this does not have to be the case. In fact, there are some committed feminists who call themselves essentialists (see for example Richlin, 1992; Stoljar).

If you agree, then you are an antiessentialist (at least with regard to these categories). This provides philosophical support for the idea that these categories are imagined and without physical basis.

Abandoning the Race Concept

Some scholars, such as Kwame Anthony Appiah and Naomi Zack, believe that since race as it is commonly understood does not exist, we should abandon the term race entirely (M. James, 2012). Using the term merely reinforces racist thinking. Put another way, using the term race inappropriately suggests races have essential properties when they do not. This is often called reifying race (reify comes from the Latin word *res*, meaning thing; to reify is "to regard or treat (an idea, concept, etc.) as if having material existence" [OED]). Appiah and Zack would agree that using the term race reifies it—that is, inappropriately implies that race refers to properties that have material existence.

Given that racial categories are socially constructed, many scholars increasingly refer not to race but to **racialization**. The term recognizes that becoming marked by race is an action—something that happens to people rather than something they are (Moore, 2003).

Keeping Race to Aid Activism

Other scholars believe that although race is a fiction, it would be problematic to abandon the concept entirely. Even if races do not really exist, they are still popularly believed to exist and this has real-world consequences. If, on the one hand, so-called Black men are being stopped and frisked by police in cases where so-called whites are not, it would do little good for a so-called Black person to object by pulling out this text and explaining that race does not exist. On the other hand, if people who are perceived to be Black rally together as Black people who oppose discriminatory stop-and-frisk policies, they may mobilize enough support to stop the inappropriate police behavior. Racial labels then may be socially constructed fictions, but they may also be useful labels to mobilize resistance to the discrimination that the labels create. This is an example of what Gayatri Chakravorty Spivak has called **strategic essentialism**, the use of essentialist labels although they are recognized to be inaccurate because they help achieve important short-term political objectives (Heyes, 2012).

ETHNICITY

Benjamin Franklin's concerns for America were rooted in anxieties about race, but they were linked to concerns about preserving the English language and Anglo-American customs (recall that he was worried the Palatine Boors would "establish their language and manners" and would "Germanize us instead of our Anglifying [that is, "English-ifying"] them"). In Franklin's view, racial difference was not the only problem; cultural and linguistic differences between English settlers and the more recent German ones were also a cause for anxiety. These differences are often summed up as ethnic differences.

Ethnicity is another term that defies precise definition. Sian Jones defined an **ethnic group** as any "group of people who set themselves apart and/or are set apart by others with whom they interact or co-exist on the basis of their perceptions or cultural differentiation and/or common ancestry" (as cited in Baumann, 2004, pp. 12–13). Cultural elements that set ethnic groups apart from others often include religion, language (or varieties of language), and customs. As with many conceptions of ethnicity, Jones's definition allows overlap with the notion of race (indicated by her phrase "common ancestry"); some use race and ethnicity somewhat interchangeably, whereas others view ethnicity as distinct from race (that is, having nothing to do with phenotypic or other biological traits). The Irish, Basques (indigenous people from the Basque region of Spain), Cherokee Indians, and Cajun people (descendants of French Canadians living mostly in Louisiana) are often classified as ethnic groups.

Related to nonbiological concepts of ethnicity are the concepts of culture and subculture (a culture within a culture). Some of the groups we discuss in this text can be described as subcultures, such as the marriage resistance

FIGURE 6.2

movement in southern China and the Mexican subculture of MSM (see Chapter 5, "Constructions of Homosexualities").

US AND THEM

The French feminist philosopher Simone de Beauvoir (1949/1989) described women as being the "Other," the "second sex." Because men are the norm or primary in Western culture, she said that when we think of humanity we think of men ("us"), not of women ("them" or the "other"). Just as sexual distinctions have made women other, the process of making racial and ethnic distinctions also results in **othering** people. Othering can be described as the "perception or representation of a person or group of people as fundamentally alien from another, frequently more powerful, group" (OED) (Figure 6.2). Because we are the norm, or the unmarked group, racial and ethnic othering focuses on the differences of the others. We, by contrast, are plain, ordinary. In the United States, white, middle-class people often consider themselves without ethnicity or distinctive culture; they have unmarked status.

GENDER, RACE, AND ETHNICITY ARE SOCIALLY CONSTRUCTED

Why is this extended discussion of race, ethnicity, othering, and markedness important for our purposes? Once again, we see that a major set of categories (including race and ethnicity) that many of us deploy in our everyday lives is socially constructed. Understanding the social construction of race and related categories makes it clear that much of classification is really about the use of power to create in-groups and out-groups. In the rest of this chapter we explore intersections of race, ethnicity, class, gender, and other categories and examine myths, struggles, and advocacy by those considered "other" in American society.

STEREOTYPES

As defined in Chapter 1, a stereotype is a "preconceived and oversimplified idea of the characteristics which typify a person, situation, etc." (OED). Stereotypes are often directed at those perceived as other. In our discussion of race and racialization, we will examine some common stereotypes of those outside the "mythical norm." As you read, we urge you to ask yourself not so much what these stereotypes reveal about those to whom they refer (perhaps not much, certainly not about any particular individual), but what they reveal about the society that produces and employs them.

SOCIOECONOMIC STATUS IN AMERICA

The United States is a country with a staggering—and growing—divide between rich and poor. The top 1 percent of Americans control 43 percent of the wealth in this country; the top 5 percent, 72 percent of the wealth (Domhoff, 2013). The share of national income going to the top 1 percent in the United States has followed what the economist Paul Krugman (2014) called "a great U-shaped arc" in the 20th century. The 1 percent's share peaked in the Gilded Age (early in the 20th century), dropped by more than half by 1950, and has climbed precipitously since 1980, back to where it was a century ago, prompting some economists to declare that we have entered a "second Gilded Age" (Krugman; Piketty, 2014). Child poverty in the United States has also risen dramatically; half of all public school students in the United States now come from families living in poverty (Southern Education Foundation, 2015).

The consequences of inequality can be difficult to pin down, but the growing concentration of income seems to have slowed income growth for people in the middle and the bottom. Rising inequality in the United States has also "allowed the one percent to take control of the political system" and promote their own interests (Porter, 2014). Both poverty and income inequality are correlated with negative health outcomes for adults and children (Olson et al., 2010).

FIGURE 6.3

Oprah Winfrey, whose media empire has made her a billionaire, defies the stereotype that Black women are poor.

Socioeconomic status is "commonly conceptualized as the social standing or class of an individual or group . . . often measured as a combination of education, income and occupation" (American Psychological Association, 2014). Several studies have shown that even young children are aware of wealth disparities in the United States (Weinger, 2000). It is commonly assumed that "people are the class they deserve to be" and those in higher classes work harder and are smarter (Lott & Saxon, 2002). The intersection of class with gender and race produces a variety of stereotypes of the poor, who are often seen as lazy, dysfunctional, less intelligent, sloppy, and unmotivated (Bullock, 1995).

Although working-class women have been the focus of little research, several studies have found that working-class women are judged to be more irresponsible, hostile, illogical, incoherent, superstitious, and crude than middle-class women (Landrine, 1985; Lott & Saxon). By contrast, middle-class women are seen as more ambitious, competent, happy, intelligent, self-confident, vain, and warm (Landrine). One serious consequence is that working-class women are more often seen as unsuitable for positions that require competence (such as officers in a parent–teacher association) (Lott & Saxon).

One study has also found overlap between stereotypes of Black women and working-class women on the one hand and white women and middle-class women on the other, suggesting that when we think of race we are unconsciously thinking of social class as well (Landrine). Specifically, when we think of Black women in general, we think of them as poor, and when we think of white women, we think of them as middle class.

Working-class men in the United States are the subject of contradictory representations. On the one hand, such men have long been portrayed in the media (particularly television) as buffoons—loud, stupid, trashy, and often fat, sometimes racist (Fleras & Dixon, 2011). Ralph Kramden of the *Honeymooners* and Archie Bunker of *All in the Family* are classic television examples; Homer from *The Simpsons*, Doug from *The King of Queens*, and Peter from *Family Guy* are contemporary versions (Ryle, 2015). In such media representations, gender status is often "inverted" (Fleras & Dixon); women/wives are seen as competent (if not in the most flattering light), whereas men/husbands are portrayed as idiots. In contrast, working-class men are also sometimes valorized as hard-working, honest, authentic Americans (Fleras & Dixon). This split might be characterized as the poor versus the working class, with the poor seen as unmotivated, unproductive, and undeserving (and often implicitly non-white, although the "white trash" stereotype is undoubtedly strong), versus the working class, who are seen as the builders and backbone of our country (and often implicitly white). The reality this split elides, however, is that in the United States today the working class (often) is poor (and decidedly mixed as far as race is concerned), and the poor, by and large, work, but often do not make enough to get by.

"America is witnessing a kind of renaissance of working-class culture" (Desmond, 2009, p. 69). Reality shows featuring working-class men are proliferating (*Deadliest Catch*, *Ice Road Truckers*, *Ax Men*); "working-class

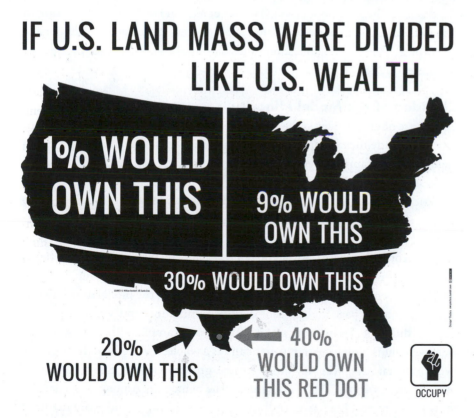

FIGURE 6.4

ON THE
web
Read about **economic immobility in the United States** on the Student Website: www.oup .com/us/gillis-jacobs

garb" and "working-class beer" (Fleras & Dixon, p. 583) are all the rage (sales of Carhartt and Pabst Blue Ribbon have been buoyed by hipster fans). It is, however, a paradoxical trend: "the simultaneous erosion of blue-collar work and the adulation of blue-collar culture . . . [a] nationwide longing for the industrial society" that no longer exists (Desmond, p. 71).

ASIAN AMERICANS AND PACIFIC ISLANDERS IN AMERICA

Asians in America include more than 50 different groups, some such as Chinese, Filipinos, and Asian Indians whose nationality groups are also composed of different linguistic and ethnic groups. Others, such as the Hmong, are ethnic groups not related to one particular country (Schaefer, 2011). The U.S. population also includes Pacific Islanders (Hawaiians, Samoans, Tongans, and other smaller groups). In 2010, there were some 15.2 million Asian, Native Hawaiian, and other Pacific Islanders in the United States—just over 5 percent of the U.S. population (Humes et al., 2011). Despite numbering in the millions, Asian Americans "often feel ignored" because they fall outside the typical Black/white (and sometimes Latino/a) framing of race in America (Schaefer, p. 285).

The Idea of the Model Minority

Asians are often considered the "**model minority**" in the United States—hard working, academically superior, particularly in math and technically oriented fields, loyal to family, obedient to authority, soft-spoken, and professionally successful (Chu & Kwan, 2007). There is a widespread perception that Asian Americans have "made it" in the United States—and statistics would seem to bolster that claim. Asians graduate from college at a higher rate than any other ethnic group in the United States, including whites, and earn a higher median family income. But these statistics do not reveal the full picture. Asian Americans are such a diverse group that "generalizations are often unhelpful" (Cohen, 2012c). Uncritical acceptance of the ideas inherent in the model minority stereotype ignores past and present-day discrimination and wide disparities among different Asian groups (Li, 2014). For example, although academic achievement is high for Asian Americans as a whole, it varies widely by group, with high rates of illiteracy among some groups (such as Southeast Asian Americans) (Varma, 2004). The same is true of income. Among the 10 largest Asian groups, 5 (Japanese, Indian, Chinese, Filipino, and Korean) have incomes above the U.S. average and 5 (Vietnamese, Pakistani, Laotian,

Cambodian, and Hmong) have incomes below that average (Cohen, 2012c). The idea of the model minority is also used "to legitimize the oppression of other minority groups" and to oppose policies such as affirmative action, which creates resentment among different ethnic groups (Li, p. 157).

One clear example of discrimination against Asian Americans is the existence of a **bamboo ceiling** in the workplace, which results in Asian Americans being overrepresented in technical positions but underrepresented in managerial and government posts (Varma). In 2010, for example, Asian Americans held only 2.1 percent of seats on Fortune 500 corporate boards. Whites held more than 90 percent of such seats. This may result from commonly held negative ideas about the leadership abilities of Asians, including that they are competent but lacking in warmth and social skills and too technically oriented to manage effectively (Li; Ong & Hee, 1993).

History of Discrimination

U.S. history is replete with examples of discrimination against Asian Americans. From the time of their arrival in the United States in the early 1800s as a source of cheap labor, Asians were systematically excluded from the rights of citizenship. The Chinese Exclusion Act of 1882, for example, suspended the immigration of Chinese laborers for 10 years and barred Chinese immigrants from naturalizing. At the time, they were also excluded from white public education and could not own property. As a result of persistent discrimination, many Asian American men in the 19th and early 20th century were concentrated in occupations perceived as unmasculine, including cooking, laundry, and housekeeping. This, along with the fact that Asian men were prohibited from bringing their wives to the United States and from marrying white women, contributed to perceptions of Asian American men as emasculated, asexual, effeminate, and gay (Wong et al., 2012), a stereotype that persists even today.

Another persistent stereotype of Asian American men is that of the perpetual foreigner (Wong et al.). Asian American men are commonly perceived as strongly connected to their cultures of origin and as unassimilable. Such a view contributed to the decision to detain 120,000 Japanese Americans in internment camps during World War II, many of them U.S. citizens and legal permanent residents, half of them children (PBS, 1999). Although the internment was justified as a matter of "military necessity" to protect against domestic espionage, a later investigation determined the actions were in fact "motivated largely by racial prejudice, wartime hysteria, and a failure of political leadership" (PBS, 1999).

The barriers and discrimination that Asian American women face are in many ways distinct from those faced by Asian American men and grounded in the specific history of Asian American women in the United States. The first wave of Asian American women (mostly Chinese) coming to the United States in the 19th century were predominantly prostitutes, many of them indentured, brought to serve first white men and then, later, Chinese men as well (Perez, 2003). (At the time, antimiscegenation laws outlawed romantic or sexual relationships between Asian men and white women). Because of this, Asian women in the United States came to be seen in primarily sexual terms, as either "lotus blossoms" or "dragon ladies," the former thought to be passive and ultrafeminine and the latter "aggressive, conniving and predatory" (Li, p. 151). Contemporary stereotypes of Asian American women as meek, shy, and child-like on the one hand, yet "surprising in their sexual prowess" on the other, are rooted in 19th-century images (Li, p. 153).

Complex portrayals of Asian American women in popular culture and the media are "few and far between," asserted Li, although increasing numbers of Asian American women writers are garnering awards and gaining commercial success for just such portrayals, including Amy Tan, Maxine Hong Kingston, Bharati Mukherjee, Joy Kogawa, Gish Jen, and Jhumpa Lahiri.

BLACK PEOPLE IN THE UNITED STATES

In the 2010 U.S. census, nearly 39 million people identified themselves as Black or African American, representing 13 percent of the U.S. population (Humes et al.). Most live in cities, and in recent years, more Blacks have moved to the South than are departing that region, reversing a historic trend (Feagin & Feagin, 2011). More Blacks than ever are going to college; in fact, the percentage of Blacks and whites who enter college is similar, but young Black people graduate and attain degrees at only half the rate of young white people (Casselman, 2014). A larger segment of Black Americans than ever before holds better-paying jobs and has greater economic stability. Nearly 40 percent of Black families in the United States have incomes at or above $50,000, placing them solidly in the middle class (Parrillo, 2011). Yet more than one-quarter of Blacks live in poverty (compared with about 10 percent of non-Hispanic whites and 12 percent of Asians) ("Poverty in the United States," 2016). Blacks continue to face housing discrimination that denies them the opportunity to buy into high-value areas that could provide better educations for children and better return on investments (*New York Times* editorial board, 2015).

The Myth of the Strong Black Woman

In *Behind the Mask of the Strong Black Woman*, Tamara Beauboeuf-Lafontant (2009) contended that "the defining quality of Black womanhood is strength." Within African American communities there has long been a sense that Black women are especially resilient, tireless, caring, and able to shoulder the heavy burdens of racism and hard, low-status work (Beauboeuf-Lafontant). This notion is often captured by the phrase "the strong Black woman" and, previously, "the Black superwoman" (see for example, Collins, 1990/2002; hooks, 1989; Wallace, 1978/1999; Woods-Giscombé, 2010). This has fed the belief that Black women can do it all on their own. Being called a strong Black woman is meant to be a tribute to African American women (Beauboeuf-Lafontant, p. 2). Yet, many scholars (see for example, Collins; hooks, 1989; Wallace; Woods-Giscombé) have asserted this label has negative consequences, obscuring the suffering of Black women and intensifying the demands on them.

There has been much attention paid to the "plight" of the single Black woman and the single Black mother both by sympathetic scholars (many of them Black feminists) and by unsympathetic scholars, politicians, and members of the media. Much has been made of low marriage rates among Black women and men and the relative unavailability of Black men for marriage in part because of disproportionately high rates of unemployment and incarceration. Data reported by the sociologist Philip Cohen (2015), however, indicated that the rates of Black and white women who marry are not all that different—78 percent versus 85 percent, respectively. Cohen (2015) found that *young* Black women have lower marriage rates than *young* white women, but that as Black women age, they marry at higher rates, resulting in a "surprisingly small" gap in marriage rates between the two groups (para. 10).

The Black feminist Patricia Hill Collins noted that the sexual politics between Black women and men can be complicated and that meeting gendered expectations may be difficult for both—for Black men because they may feel emasculated when they cannot play the role of provider and for Black women who, in maintaining families without husbands, may be described as "aggressive [and] assertive" and labeled unfeminine (p. 77). Collins argued that moving beyond reductive thinking requires understanding that two underlying dynamics are at work: an interpersonal dynamic driven by gendered expectations and "overarching structures of power" that foster racism, high unemployment, and low wages (p. 155).

Some scholars have contended that framing single Black womanhood as a problem to be solved through marriage is itself problematic (Marsh, 2012.) Marsh and others have noted a trend in the Black middle class, the growth of households of Black people who are single and living alone, whom they call the **Love Jones cohort** after the romantic comedy of the same name (Marsh et al., 2007). The Love Jones cohort is predominantly female and professional and represents 20 percent of the Black middle class (Marsh). Rather than seeing these singles as a problem to be solved through marriage, Marsh argued that the Love Jones cohort should be celebrated for stabilizing and even increasing the proportion of Blacks in the middle class.

Black Men, Black Women, and Public Surveillance

"My first victim was a woman—white, well-dressed, probably in her early twenties. I came upon her late one evening on a deserted street in Hyde Park, a relatively affluent neighborhood . . . of Chicago," wrote Brent Staples (1998). Although Staples attempted to keep a "discrete, uninflammatory distance" between himself and the woman, she "cast back a worried glance. To her, the youngish Black man—a broad six feet two inches with a beard and billowing hair . . .—seemed menacingly close." She picked up her pace, disappearing into a cross street. Staples, a graduate student at the time, was "stalking sleep, not defenseless wayfarers" (p. 40). But his experience is all too common for Black males. Staples and other Black men (for example, L. Thomas, 1990; Yancy, 2013) have described hearing the "thunk, thunk, thunk" of car doors being locked by "Black, white, male or female" drivers as they walk past (Staples, p. 40).

Fear of Black men is not limited to whites. Indeed, Staples noted that even Black people may prejudge other Black people. Moreover, Staples suggested that this fear is sometimes warranted. He noted, for example, that "women are particularly vulnerable to street violence, and young Black males are drastically overrepresented among the perpetrators of violence" (p. 40). Staples contended that Black men may be seduced by their power to intimidate. "It is after all, only manly to frighten and intimidate" (p. 41). However, he said, "poor powerless men" mistake this apparent power for real power—and the consequences are often lethal. Staples recounted burying a cousin, a childhood friend, and a brother because they consummated the "male romance with the power to intimidate" (p. 41).

The problem of public surveillance extends to the police, who disproportionately detain, stop, frisk, and arrest not only Black men but also Black women in comparison to other racial groups. The idea that Black people are being unruly merely walking in public has been called the "crime" of **walking while Black**. This term itself is a spin-off of the expression driving while Black—police racially profiling and stopping Black drivers simply because they are Black. Black people also report suffering from surveillance, suspicion, and rude behavior while shopping. In one high-profile case, the actor Rob Brown, star of *Treme*, was arrested after buying a $1,000 watch for his mother. These sorts of cases have given rise to still another term—shopping while Black.

Kimberlé Crenshaw and Andrea Ritchie (2015) have noted that too often Black women are "unseen" in national discussions of "racial profiling, police brutality, and lethal force" (para. 6). They continued,

Yet Black women are policed similar to other members of our communities.... [They are also subject to] other forms and contexts of police violence such as sexual assault by police, police abuse of pregnant women, profiling and abusive treatment of lesbian, bisexual, transgender, and gender nonconforming Black women, and police brutality in the context of responses to violence. (para. 6)

Laurence Thomas (1990) suggested that for Black people, the cumulative effect of public surveillance can be devastating. Thomas, a professor who is himself Black, recalled walking down the aisle of a grocery store with a full basket in each hand only to have a white woman rush to her pocketbook left in her grocery cart. He imagined she must have been thinking, "He won't fool me with that old basket-in-each-hand-trick" (1990, p. 84). Thomas (1990), who teaches ethics, suggested enjoying the public trust is important to human flourishing and that Black people suffer "a very deep psychic scar of relentless moral disconfirmation" (p. 84). Thomas (1990) imagined that it is easier for men like him, who because of his social and economic position have the resources to cope with such slights, but the consequences for other less fortunate Black people may be more adverse. Indeed, research has shown the cumulative effect of such slights can lead to a sense of powerlessness, anger, and low self-esteem (Sue et al., 2008).

In the wake of recent examples of Black people killed in encounters with police, it is difficult to feel optimistic about the future. Yet as nationwide demonstrations have also shown, there are many voices proclaiming that "Black lives matter." Those in the movement for change note not only "profound injustice" but also "extraordinary resilience" in the Black community (Black Lives Matter, 2015). The group Black Lives Matter says of its work, "We have stood united in demanding a new system of policing and a vision for Black lives, lived fully and with dignity. Gains have been made, but we who believe in freedom know we cannot rest until justice is won."

breaking the frame
Black Men Valuing Fatherhood

While doing research for their book on fatherhood in the inner city, Kathryn Edin and Timothy Nelson (2014) conducted interviews with dozens of young men, many of them Black, all facing economic struggles. What was fatherhood like for them? the researchers wanted to know. Many reported that fatherhood was one of the best things that had ever happened to them. Most desired a life for their children that differed sharply from their own. Although only a few had primary or even equal responsibility for their children, many did "the best they could" to contribute and desired to do more if circumstances improved. The obstacles these men faced were many and complex. Perhaps most devastating, most had little or no access to "on-the-books" jobs that might pay a living wage. Lack of quality education, prior incarceration, and ongoing discrimination were formidable barriers to stability. Most also had only fragile ties to the mothers of their children before the children were born. In contrast to the ways dominant culture often thinks of Black fatherhood, these young Black men desired to be more involved in their children's lives and were acutely aware of their own shortcomings. They were also hopeful that they could make a positive difference in the lives of their children.

Representations of Black People

Black woman and men in the United States are the objects of a discourse that is deeply entangled with the history of enslavement and ongoing racism in this country. In the case of African American women, contemporary representations can be traced back to images and perceptions of enslaved African American women as either asexual Mammies (subservient, loyal and giving) or overtly sexual Jezebels (independent and aggressive) (Morton, 1991; S. Porter & Parks, 2011). Today, stereotypes grounded in these images include the welfare queen (poor, lazy, exploitative), the matriarch (controlling, emasculating), and the angry Black woman or Sapphire (fiery, unapologetic, perhaps successful) (S. Porter & Parks).

Although media representations of Black women often draw heavily on these stereotypes, S. Porter and Parks have asserted that Michelle Obama has largely escaped such pigeon-holing. Although representations of Michelle Obama as "unpatriotic" and angry emerged early in her husband's first presidential campaign (and contributed to low favorability ratings for her), the coverage she received later in the campaign and following the election was much more positive, representing Obama as a devoted mother, fashion and fitness icon, and respectable First Lady (Brannon, 2011). These representations run directly counter to predominant images of Black women in the media, a positive development, but Michelle Obama remains the exception, not the rule, when it comes to portrayals of Black women in the media (Hobson, 2012).

A number of studies have shown that Black women (like women of low socioeconomic status) are seen as less stereotypically feminine than white women. This may be partly because of the fact that since the postslavery era African American women have been more likely to work outside the home than their European American female counterparts. Even as early as 1890, nearly two in five Black females were employed outside their homes—often as domestic servants (Malveaux, 1984). Others have noted that African American women, during slavery, developed multiple roles, both stereotypically masculine and feminine, to enable their survival (Burgess, 1994), which may also influence stereotypes about Black women today. One study has shown that Black women are more likely to reject culturally dominant views of femininity and to support the women's movement (K. Dugger, 1991).

Black men have been the site of multiple and often contradictory stereotypes—as hypersexual (Ward, 2005), emasculated, and lazy or shiftless (Phillips et al., 2011). Along with the "sexualized Black male" (too cool or aloof to hold down an authentic relationship), Majors and Billson (1992) described two other stereotypes that are often ascribed to Black men: what we might call the cool man (well-dressed with a cool car) and the Black athlete (who turns to physical activity to express his masculinity and become rich and famous).

Mirza (1999) pointed out that we read regularly about Black male exclusion in school, the disproportionate incarceration of young Black men, and their higher than average rates of unemployment. She concluded that, as a result, we as a society focus on these: "Unthinkingly, in our everyday discourse, we have come to associate Black men with absent fathers, violent deaths, drugs and crime" (p. 137).

The ways Black men see themselves has been the topic of a small but significant body of research. Some studies (although not all) have shown that African American men endorse traditional notions of masculinity to a greater extent than both Latina/os and European Americans (Levant & Richmond, 2007). Related to this, researchers have theorized that Black men, in part "to vent . . . frustration" and "shor[e] up a sense of identity in an uncertain social world" act in a hypermasculine way (gangsta rappers being an example of this type of behavior) (Ward, pp. 498–499). Ward called Black hypermasculinity "an intensified, Black male cultural reflection" of negative aspects (sexism, materialism, homophobia) of wider U.S. society (p. 497). Majors and Billson theorized that young Black males may respond to societal prejudice and discrimination by striking a "**cool pose**," the appearance of aloofness and superiority, which is meant to convey pride, strength, control, and emotionlessness. The cool pose may be best understood as a coping strategy Black men use in the face of racism and lack of opportunity, as well as a way to express contempt and rage toward the dominant society (Majors & Billson).

LATINAS/OS

Latinas/os have come to the United States from more than a dozen countries, including Mexico, the countries of Central and South America, and the islands of the Caribbean. In 2010, there were 50.5 million Hispanics in the United States, comprising 16 percent of the total population, and their numbers are growing (Humes et al.). By 2050, Latinas/os are expected to comprise about 30 percent of the U.S. population (Schaefer). Latinas/os in the United States live mostly in cities (91 percent), and although they continue to be concentrated in the Southwest, many are moving away from traditional areas of settlement. In 2012, nearly two-thirds of Hispanics living in the United States were born in the United States (Krogstad & Lopez, 2014), and 49 percent of young Hispanic high school graduates were enrolled in college, a number that has been rising. By comparison, in 2012, 47 percent of white high school graduates were enrolled in college. Hispanics, however, have a higher high school dropout rate than whites (Lopez & Fry, 2013). Although Hispanic incomes and wealth in the United States are growing, Hispanics still earn significantly less, on average, than the typical American household (Ferdman, 2014).

A note about terminology: Latina/o and Hispanic are pan-ethnic names that are often used interchangeably by researchers and academics; we use the terms as we find them in the research. Latinas/os themselves, however, often prefer other terms. For those born outside the United States, more than half prefer to use their country of origin as a term of identity, whereas many Latinas/os born in the United States use first or only the term American to describe themselves (Schaefer).

The Latino Threat Narrative

Latinas/os have often been portrayed not only as "other" in U.S. discourse, but also as a threat to "America's traditional identity" (Samuel Huntington's phrase, as cited in L. R. Chavez, 2013, p. 24). Although recent calls to deport large numbers of immigrants may sound far-fetched, they are not without precedent. During the 1930s and 1940s "up to two million Mexicans and Mexican-Americans were deported or expelled" from the United States; by some estimates more than half were American citizens born in the United States (Florido, 2015). Even for legal residents today, wrote Schaefer, "the specter of people questioning Latinos about their legal status looms" large (p. 220).

U.S. immigration reform of the 1920s created a hierarchy of immigrants, with northern and western Europeans at the top and Asians, Africans, and Latin Americans at the bottom (Ngai, 2004). The immigration restrictions aimed at those at the bottom of the hierarchy "produced the illegal alien" where none had existed before (Ngai, p. 4). In time, Ngai explained, "walking (or wading) across the [U.S.] border emerged as the quintessential act of illegal immigration" (p. 89).

By the 1970s, some politicians, news magazines, and newspapers were promoting what Leo Chavez (2013) called the "**Latino threat narrative**," claiming that "illegal aliens" from Latin America were flooding the United States with the goal of reconquering the U.S. Southwest and returning it to Mexico (from which the United States had won it in the Mexican–American War of 1848).

Post 9/11, this narrative was recast with a focus on the southern border as a terrorist threat. As a result, "border walls have been constructed [and] unmanned drones dispatched" (G. Thompson, 2011). Deportation numbers have steadily increased while a number of states have passed harsh laws seeking to deny undocumented immigrants public services, including medical care and education (L. Chavez, 2013). It is not only undocumented immigrants who are affected by the Latino threat narrative. Latinas/os in U.S. society are often cast as an undifferentiated group, with little attention to their actual birthplace or legal status. For those who are undocumented, there are limited paths to citizenship and a patchwork of laws that make driving, working, and accessing education and health care challenging at best. In response, Latinas/os are increasingly organizing, making themselves visible, and influencing election outcomes locally and nationally.

Machismo and Marianismo

Latinas/os are often associated with the concepts of *machismo* and *marianismo*. *Machismo* is a measure of manhood based on inner strength, personal daring, bravado, leadership, and sexual prowess that stresses the role of the

recap of terms:

Benevolent Sexism

Benevolent sexism, because it appears to be affectionate or chivalrous in nature, is less likely to be identified as sexism than hostile sexism. Examples include believing women are morally superior to men, believing women are deserving of men's protection, or carrying heavy objects for women (when one would not make a similar gesture to a man). Although some have difficulty believing benevolent sexism is actually harmful, it is important to remember it rests on the notion of masculine dominance (Glick & Fiske, 1996).

From Chapter 3, "Gender and In/Equality."

man as provider and protector both within the family and within the culture at large (Schaefer). In reality, of course, Latino men may be dominating, submissive, or egalitarian, and characteristics associated with *machismo* are often attributed to men in many cultures (Torres et al., 2002).

Although *machismo* has often been characterized negatively by outsiders, recent research has suggested that machismo is in fact "dynamic and multidimensional," including both positive and negative traits (Torres et al., p. 166). Often-overlooked positive aspects include loyalty, compassion, generosity, and respect (Torres et al.). Torres and colleagues asserted that the sometimes contradictory characteristics attributed to *machismo* reflect an "incessant ambivalence among some Latino men" about changing male gender roles (p. 165).

Machismo is sometimes divided into two subcategories: traditional machismo ("aggressive, sexist, chauvinistic, and hypermasculine") and **caballerismo** ("nurturing, family-centered and chivalrous") (Arciniega et al., 2008, p. 29). The term *caballerismo* is derived from the Spanish word *caballero*, meaning horseman, and has come "to signify a Spanish gentleman with proper, respectful manners living by an ethical code of chivalry" (Arciniega et al., p. 20). Although *caballerismo* seems to entail a more positive set of traits, it is not entirely unproblematic because, like benevolent sexism, it appears to support the idea of masculine dominance.

Studies have found that the ideas inherent in *machismo* can have negative effects on the self-esteem and behavior of gay Latino men. Those who come out as gay may encounter negative consequences, resulting in feelings of detachment from other Latino men and Latino culture (Torres et al.).

Marianismo, the idea of the Latina as "submissive, self-sacrificing, humble, and modest" (Torres et al., p. 166), is (like *machismo*) a term with both positive and negative behavioral expectations (Castillo et al., 2010). "Although *la mujer buena* (the good woman) can be a strong and capable woman who takes a proactive role in her life," wrote Castillo et al., "she is limited to exerting her power within the home with primary focus on care and nurturance of her family" (p. 164). This idealized Latina is expected to be virtuous, humble, nonsexual, and spiritually superior to men (like the Virgin Mary, from which the term originates) (Castillo et al.). Niemann (2001) noted that although gender roles

Latinas and the Story of La Malinche

The idea of *la vendida*, the sellout, is often linked to the historical figure of *La Malinche*, the woman who acted as a translator for the Spanish conquistador Hernán Cortés in his conquest of Mexico beginning in 1519 (Figure 6.5). Little is known for sure about *La Malinche*, whose given name may have been Malinalli Tenepal. She was apparently given to Cortés as a tribute and took the role of *la lengua* (the tongue), serving as his interpreter and intermediary with indigenous Indian groups (Valdeón, 2013; Godayol, 2012). She also bore Cortés's son, although the dynamics of their personal relationship are unknown. For this she has earned the pejorative name *La Chingada*, which translates as "the fucked one," but she is also seen positively as the mother of a new race, *Mestizos*, which she "birthed" figuratively, as Cortes's go-between with the Indians and, literally, as the mother of Cortes's son.

La Malinche is an iconic symbol, both positive and negative, within Latina/o/Chicana/o culture—*la lengua, la vendida, la chingada*—but who was she really? Latina feminists have set out to answer this question for themselves. Carmen Tafolla (1993), in her poem "La Malinche," imagined Malinalli not as *La Chingada*, "Not tricked, not screwed, not traitor," but as a woman who speaks and acts for herself and a new future, a new people. In Tafolla's poem, *La Malinche* says: "I saw a dream / and I reached it. / Another world / . . . la raza. / La raaaaa—zaaaaa" (*La raza* literally means "the race" and is used as a term of ethnic pride.) Tafolla has repositioned *La Malinche* not as turncoat or "sexual victim" but as "mythical mother" (Godayol, p. 65).

Gloria Anzaldúa (1987) likewise rejected interpretations of *La Malinche* as "traitor" and "whore" and located betrayal not in *La Malinche*'s actions but in the dominant "male culture" that teaches women to "police the Indian in us, brutalize and condemn her" (p. 22). Anzaldúa proposed *La Malinche* as a model for "a new mestiza . . . Indian in Mexican culture . . . Mexican from an Anglo point of view" (p. 79). The new mestiza is "plural," wrote Anzaldúa, "she sustains contradictions" (p. 79).

FIGURE 6.5

In this image of Cortés from the History of Tlaxcala (1580s), *La Malinche* figures prominently, symbolized by her placement between the Spanish conquistadors and the indigenous Indians, and her posture, which mirrors that of Cortés.

for Latinas are becoming increasingly diverse, those who reject the conservative bounds prescribed by *marianismo* may risk being labeled **vendidas**, or sellouts. Cherríe Moraga (1983) linked the term *vendida* specifically to heterosexism or valorization of heterosexuality: "The woman who defies her role as subservient to her husband, father, brother, or son by taking control of her own sexual destiny is purported to be a 'traitor to her race' . . . she is corrupted by foreign influences which threaten to destroy her people" (p. 113).

Contrary to the notion of *marianismo* is the stereotype of the "hot Latina," a hypersexualized seductress (L. Chavez, 2013). The Colombian actor Sofía Vergara's character, Gloria, on the television program *Modern Family* is a popular example. Chavez (2013) asserted that related to the idea of the hot Latina is a discourse that focuses on supposed "limitless fertility" and "excessive reproduction" among Latinas. According to this discourse, Latina fertility in the United States and fertility among women in Latin America are the primary forces behind the "browning of America," which is seen as a negative phenomenon. Chavez (2013) noted that fear of immigrants' sexuality and reproductive capacity is not new. During the great migration to the United States from southern and eastern Europe in the late 19th century, for example, immigrant fertility was also viewed as dangerously high. The issue of Latina reproduction is the subject of a particularly alarmist discourse today because of the fact that babies born to undocumented persons in the United States (so-called "anchor babies") are granted citizenship. It should be noted, however, that giving birth to a baby in the United States does not confer citizenship rights on parents. To the contrary, many are deported along with their citizen children, who may return legally as adults.

What are the demographic trends behind the stereotype? Latinas do have a relatively high birth rate when compared with white women in the United States, but both groups have seen dramatic drops in fertility. L. Chavez (2013) reported that birth rates for U.S.-born Latinas and white women nationally are similar and that Latinas, like American women in general, have fewer children the more years of education they have.

AMERICAN INDIANS

There are approximately 2.9 million American Indians and Alaskan Natives living in the United States today (just less than 1 percent of total U.S. population) (Humes et al.), nearly a 1,000 percent increase from a century ago (the increase is the result of births as well as more people identifying as Native Americans). Overall, the Native American population skews younger than the

U.S. population and has a higher fertility rate as a result, meaning that population growth among Native Americans is likely to continue to outpace general population growth in the United States (Schaefer). The U.S. government recognizes 564 different Native American tribal entities speaking 175 different languages within its borders. In the past 25 years, 17 new tribal colleges have opened in the United States, bringing the total number to nearly 40, enrolling some 14,000 Native American students. Although reservations continue to play an important role in the lives of American Indians, today the majority of American Indians—70 percent, in fact—live in urban areas away from reservations.

Poverty remains a persistent problem for many Native Americans, with 27 percent living in poverty, nearly double the national average (U.S. Census Bureau, 2013), but there are a number of economic success stories among American Indian tribes and individuals involved in a wide variety of economic pursuits. The Southern Ute of southwest Colorado, for example, control the distribution of approximately 1 percent of the United States' natural gas supply and have a net worth of about $4 billion. They offer full scholarships and living stipends for the tribe's college students (Parrillo). The Mississippi Choctaw are one of the 10 largest employers in the state of Mississippi, with an annual payroll of about $100 million in diverse businesses that include a forestry management company, manufacturing, and tourism-related businesses. For more than 40 years, Cherokee Nation Industries has provided products and services to the commercial and defense aerospace industry and telecommunications companies.

An increasing number of American Indian writers and filmmakers—including Leslie Marmon Silko, Louise Erdrich, and Sherman Alexie—have achieved recognition and commercial success in recent years. Alexie, a Spokane/Coeur d'Alene tribal member, has won dozens of awards for his fiction and poetry, including the National Book Award for Young People's Literature and the PEN/Faulkner Award. Alexie also wrote and coproduced the movie *Smoke Signals*, which was released in 1998, the first all–Native American film production. Erdrich, who is of German, French, and Ojibwe descent, has also won dozens of prizes, including the National Book Award in 2012 for her novel *The Round House*.

We begin with the above examples not to suggest that all is right with American Indians—indeed, American Indians face many ongoing challenges, including higher than average rates of poverty, alcoholism, violence, and discrimination—we begin with these examples to remind you of the simple fact that American Indians are alive today, some thriving, some struggling, but all part of contemporary American society. (See Chapter 9, "Gender-Based Violence," for more on American Indians and gender-based violence.)

A Rich History Rife With Exploitation

Yet persistent ideas about American Indians would have it otherwise. One of the most widely held beliefs about American Indians is that they are disappearing (or have disappeared). American Indians are often thought of in the past tense, as artifacts or primitive figures, connected to historic events, rather than "present, modern, individualized people" (Antoine, 2011, p. 243). This strategy, asserted David Murray (2001), allows Americans to avoid confronting our own colonialism and continuing exploitation of American Indians.

The history of the exploitation of American Indians is long, but even longer is the history of Native Americans themselves. When Christopher Columbus landed on the shores of the "new" world in 1492, he "discovered" indigenous societies as old, or older than most European societies. The people of the "Americas" belonged to several hundred distinct tribes, many organized in highly complex ways, each with their own language and culture (Parrillo). In fact, many Native American societies at the time were more egalitarian and democratic than their European counterparts. Although Native American women and men had different roles, Native American women often had significantly more social status than European women. The Cherokee and Iroquois, for example, were matrilineal (meaning property and status derived from and were passed through the mother's family). Mankiller et al. (1998) wrote that Clan Mothers of the Iroquois Confederacy nominated Chiefs, served as advisers, could warn or remove Chiefs, and decided when young men should go into battle and peace terms. Contact with whites, in many cases, contributed to the decline in Native American women's status (Feagin & Feagin, 2011). (See Chapter 12 for more.)

An echo from colonial times can be found in the fact that outsiders today still often lump all Native Americans together although the hundreds of tribes differ considerably. Although it is not always possible to refer to American Indians by their specific tribal affiliations, it is always preferable when possible.

Other stereotypes also persist; Paula Gunn Allen (2005), a Laguna and Sioux poet and novelist, wrote,

> *No Indian can grow to any age without being informed that her people were "savages" who interfered with the march of progress pursued by respectable, loving, civilized white people. . . . We are absent from much of white history except when we are calmly, rationally, succinctly, and systematically dehumanized. On the few occasions we are noticed in any way other than as howling, bloodthirsty beings, we are acclaimed for our noble quaintness. In this definition, we are exotic curios. Our ancient arts and customs are used to*

draw tourist money to state coffers, into the pocketbooks and bank accounts of scholars, and into support of the American-in-Disneyland promoters' dream. (p. 85)

As with most groups, stereotypes of American Indians often vary by gender. Media representations of women have tended to fall into one of two categories—the princess or the "squaw." The princess, who often has distinctly European features, is portrayed as "exotic, powerful, dangerous and beautiful," whereas the squaw (which is considered a derogatory term) is, by contrast, often "darker, fatter and cruder," marked by drunkenness, stupidity, and thievery (Feagin & Feagin, p. 143).

FIGURE 6.6

Wilma Mankiller became the first female chief of the Cherokee Nation in 1985, serving until 1995. Mankiller is credited with reinvigorating the Cherokee Nation and transforming the Cherokee relationship with the U.S. government. A recipient of the Presidential Medal of Freedom, she died in 2010.

The most widely recognized female Native American figure is undoubtedly Pocahontas, whose story circulated as early as the 17th century. Little is known about the actual Pocahontas, and what is known comes entirely from accounts by European men, which are themselves inconsistent. There is some certainty, however, that Pocahontas (whose real names were Amonute and Matoaka) was around 10, 11, or 12 when she first encountered Europeans (Downs, 2008). She was eventually captured by the English, who attempted unsuccessfully to ransom her back to her father (a leader of the Algonquin people). Pocahontas remained in Jamestown, married an Englishman, John Rolfe, and traveled with him to England, where she died in 1617, probably not yet 30 years of age. This is not the legend that survives today, however, either in Disney films or even in textbooks, for the most part. "Every part of Pocahontas's identity has been appropriated by Europeans," according to Downs (p. 401). Pocahontas has been turned into the archetype of the Indian princess—young, virginal, and exotic; she is the embodiment of the American frontier (Downs). Representations of Pocahontas perpetuate both stereotypes and what Feagin and Feagin term "pseudo-history." The central action of that legend, Pocahontas's risking her own life to save John Smith's, is much debated. Did it actually happen? If it did, have her actions been misconstrued? No one knows for sure, but what is certain is that it became a potent symbol of self-sacrifice by an Indian woman on behalf of English colonialism. The real story was certainly more complicated and likely much harder to sell at the box office.

What then are American Indian women like? It is an impossibly broad question, of course. The poet and novelist Paula Gunn Allen wrote that Native American "women's roles are as diverse as tribal cultures in the Americas." Allen noted that women in some tribes are "devalued," whereas in others they "wield considerable power." "But in no tribal definitions," wrote Allen, "is she perceived in the same way as are women in western industrial and postindustrial cultures. . . . Sometimes [tribes] see women as fearful, sometimes peaceful, sometimes omnipotent and omniscient, but they never portray women as mindless, helpless, simple, or oppressed," although they "may be all these things" (p. 82).

Representations of Indian men are also largely built on pseudo-history that more closely resembles myth than reality. American Indian men are commonly seen as noble savages (uncorrupted children of nature), brutal warriors (terrorizing white settlers), or New Age mystics. The years of western expansion in particular have been represented in movies (and textbooks, for that matter) as a time of constant conflict between Indians and white settlers, but in reality the weather and terrain were much greater threats to white colonists than Indians, and white casualties at the hands of American Indians were relatively few in number.

More contemporary stereotypes include the "drunken Indian" and the "rich Indian," but as with all stereotypes, these overgeneralize. The stereotype of American Indians who get rich from casino gambling, for example, is contradicted by fact. Although a relatively small number of American Indian tribes have gained fortunes, most American Indian casinos are small, isolated, and unprofitable. Many Native Americans struggle with under- and unemployment. At least one recent study has shown a strong tendency among European Americans to see the negative socioeconomic conditions of Native Americans as self-inflicted, giving little credence to the hundreds of years of discrimination, forced displacement, broken treaties, and ethnic cleansing perpetrated against American Indians (Feagin & Feagin, 2011).

MULTIRACIAL AMERICA

Increasing numbers of Americans identify as mixed race or multiracial. Between the 2000 Census (the first to allow individuals to identify with more than one race) and the 2010 Census, the number of people in the United States who reported being multiracial increased by about one-third, to 9 million people. The four largest combinations reported on the 2010 census were the following:

Racial Designation	Number	Percentage Change 2000 to 2010
White and Black	1.8 million	+134%
White and some other race	1.7 million	−21%*
White and Asian	1.6 million	+87%
White and American Indian/Alaska Native	1.4 million	+32%

*Decrease may be partly caused by a counting error in the 2000 Census that resulted in overestimation in this category.

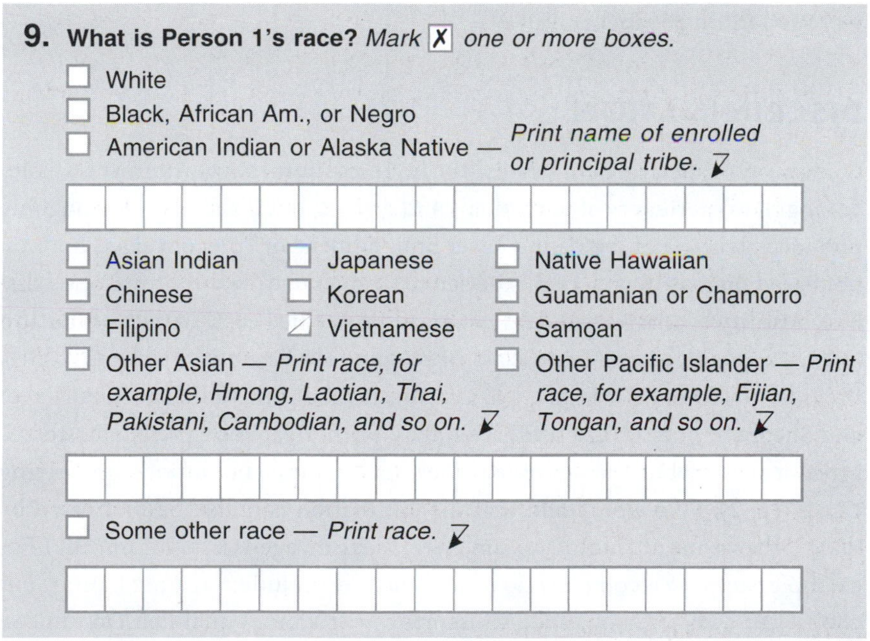

9. What is Person 1's race? *Mark* X *one or more boxes.*

☐ White
☐ Black, African Am., or Negro
☐ American Indian or Alaska Native — *Print name of enrolled or principal tribe.* ↗

[empty grid of boxes]

☐ Asian Indian   ☐ Japanese   ☐ Native Hawaiian
☐ Chinese   ☐ Korean   ☐ Guamanian or Chamorro
☐ Filipino   ☑ Vietnamese   ☐ Samoan
☐ Other Asian — *Print race, for example, Hmong, Laotian, Thai, Pakistani, Cambodian, and so on.* ↗   ☐ Other Pacific Islander — *Print race, for example, Fijian, Tongan, and so on.* ↗

[empty grid of boxes]

☐ Some other race — *Print race.* ↗

[empty grid of boxes]

FIGURE 6.7
2010 U.S. Census form.

The changing numbers are likely caused by multiple factors, including changing demographics (resulting from births, deaths, and migration) and changing perceptions of racial identity (N. Jones & Bullock, 2013). Given that one in seven new marriages in the United States is between spouses of different races or ethnicities and that the multiracial population is overwhelmingly young, the category is likely to continue growing rapidly (Saulny, 2011). Studies have shown not only that multiracial people vary greatly in how they identify, but also that they understand what it means to be multiracial in "conceptually complex" ways (Rockquemore & Brunsma, 2008). Researchers have found that multiracial people frequently describe themselves as having a "border identity" or "blended identity" distinct from its constituent parts. A significant number of multiracial people also indicate a desire to opt out of categorization altogether, which the researchers call a "transcendent identity" (Rockquemore & Brunsma). Many multiracial people have fluid notions of their own identities that change depending on the context. For example, one 20-year-old college junior when asked by a reporter how she marks her race on forms responded, "It depends on the day, and it depends on the options" (Saulny, 2011). Multiracial people are also more likely than monoracial people to challenge the validity of race as a concept and to view race as a social construction (Shih & Sanchez, 2009).

DISCRIMINATION

Our survey of social groups beyond the mythical norm suggests great diversity among the experiences of individuals and groups, but it also suggests ongoing prejudice, which can be defined as a prejudgment or "preconceived opinion not based on reason or actual experience," which may be an "unreasoned dislike, hostility or antagonism" against a class of people (OED). **Discrimination** is the unequal treatment of a class of people (see Pager & Shepherd, 2008). Prejudice is a mental attitude, whereas discrimination is a behavior. As Pager and Shepherd noted, "discrimination may be motivated by prejudice, stereotype, or racism, but the definition does not presume any unique underlying cause" (p. 2). (We would add that discrimination can also be motivated by many other -isms, including sexism, heterosexism, age-ism, able-ism, etc.) For example, suppose a company does not hold any prejudice against Latinos but chooses to hire a less qualified white male over a more qualified Dominican man because the company believes its clients would prefer to interact with a white man. In this case, the company's discrimination is not driven by racial animosity toward Latinos, but is discriminatory nonetheless.

Discrimination can be divided into two forms: **differential treatment** and **disparate impact**. Differential treatment is unequal treatment of a class of people, such as in the case of outlawing same-sex marriage. Disparate impact involves the equal treatment of people according to a set of rules and procedures that nonetheless are constructed in ways that disadvantage one class of people versus another (Pager & Shepherd). For example, voter identification laws have been passed with the supposed intent of reducing voter fraud (although such fraud is virtually nonexistent). Whatever the intent, these laws have resulted in the disenfranchisement (loss of the right to vote) of several groups of people who are less likely to have valid forms of identification without explicitly targeting them: the poor, the less educated, and people of color who are more likely to have lower incomes and less education than whites ("Voter ID," 2014). Voter identification laws, then, are a form of discrimination based on outcome regardless of intent.

Discrimination's legacy is a powerful one. The disadvantage caused to a group because of past discrimination can dramatically affect future generations. For example, past discrimination against African Americans has reduced the inherited wealth of African Americans today (Stanfield, 2011). Past discrimination can include factors like inferior schooling, poorer health care, inadequate counseling, the need to care for relatives, poor job record, and a lack of inherited wealth (Schaefer). The cumulative effect of these past disadvantages means that even when a group (such as the poor or people of color) is being treated fairly today, they will be at a disadvantage relative to other groups such as the wealthy or white people. Schaefer referred to the effect of current discrimination and past discrimination as **total discrimination** (Schaefer limited the definition to discrimination in the labor market but it seems useful to widen it).

Some might argue that life is not fair and it is not realistic to remedy all inequality in society. We agree; but it does seem morally appropriate for a society to do what it can to remedy deliberate past discrimination. It would also seem to be in our collective self-interest to create a society where talent and hard work are fairly rewarded.

If racism puts people of color at a disadvantage, the corollary of racism is what is known as **white privilege** (McIntosh, 1988). White privilege is built on a historical foundation of racial discrimination that casts a long shadow over contemporary America. Peggy McIntosh described it as an "invisible package of unearned assets" enjoyed by white people that advantages them over people of other races (p. 75). White people can count on the fact that the color of their skin is nearly always an asset rather than a liability. White people can shop, drive, bank, vote, attend school, move into a neighborhood, and use a credit card, all while feeling fairly assured that their whiteness will not arouse suspicion or animosity. Often, the advantage they garner from their race is invisible to them; they think of it as "neutral, normal and universally available" (McIntosh, p. 78). Except it is not.

Although white people clearly are advantaged by being able to live their daily lives with a general expectation of acceptance, to think of this as a state of "privilege" is somewhat misleading. We believe the label of rights is more helpful here. We all, regardless of race, have a right to shop, drive, bank, and vote without fear of discrimination. The label rights also makes clear that whether these are "earned" or "unearned" is beside the point. Rights by definition cannot and need not be earned. That white people have been advantaged in exercising these rights is undoubtedly true. The appropriate remedy then is to ensure that all are free to exercise these rights. In doing so, we need not disempower any individual or group but rather empower all groups equally.

"Privilege," according to McIntosh, also involves "negative advantages" that reinforce existing hierarchies. She gives the example that white people can remain oblivious to the languages, customs, and perspectives of people of color and not be penalized for it. McIntosh also said she is never "asked to speak for all the people of my racial group" (p. 77). The more general point is that white people are not asked to stand for, or thought of as standing for, their entire race, whereas Blacks, Latinas/os, and others are more often considered in an undifferentiated way as tokens, whether positively or negatively.

We want to turn to one more example of "privilege" that McIntosh cited to further complicate the notion of white privilege. McIntosh wrote that as a white person, she can "swear, dress in secondhand clothes, or not answer letters, without having people attribute these choices to the bad morals, the poverty, or the illiteracy of my race" (p. 77). We do not doubt the truth of this, but we would suggest that were Peggy McIntosh a working-class white woman, rather than an upper-middle-class white college professor, her choices might be seen as reflecting her working-class white background (which is not exactly the same as reflecting her Blackness were she Black, but is also not completely different). The point is that white privilege, like racism, is not static and undifferentiated. It affects different white people differently. It generally confers more advantage to some (the mythical norm) and less to others (the working class, those who fall under the LGBTQQIA rubric, and others outside the mythic norm). Just as there are interlocking systems of disadvantage or oppression, there are interlocking systems of advantage or privilege. How much white privilege does a white transgender person experience? A white working-class male? Individual white people may rightly feel that in their day-to-day lives they benefit little or not at all from their whiteness. They may also feel in any given situation that their whiteness is of little benefit. They may simply be in denial, or they may be making an accurate assessment. Without a deep understanding of the situation, we cannot predict.

CONCLUSION

How we have conceived of race has shifted dramatically over time and reveals how we have socially constructed race. Today, there is broad agreement that people of a particular "race" do not share any traits or sets of traits in common—and that races do not really exist. Nonetheless, we have a tendency to divide people into us and them—and racializing and stereotyping people are powerful tools for othering human beings.

The histories and current challenges of many of the groups beyond the mythical norm suggest that discrimination is an enduring problem. Even when groups do not face direct discrimination, rules and procedures may have a disparate impact on previously disadvantaged groups. To create a more just society, we should be aware of total discrimination that groups face and work to ensure the rights of groups who have been systematically disadvantaged. We should also be aware of forms of privilege that may operate in society such as white privilege or class privilege. At the same time, we should be careful to note that the intersectional nature of social categories complicates notions of advantage and privilege. Leveling the playing field will require introspection as well as action at the personal and societal levels.

THINK, LEARN, ACT

The following resources are available on the Student Website: www.oup.com/us/gillis-jacobs

Taking Stock, Taking Action prompts and activities. Apply what you've learned to take action on campus and in the broader community.

Recommended Readings and Multimedia Resources, including scholarly and literary works, documentaries, feature films, podcasts and more, to enrich the in- and out-of-classroom experience.

Key Terms

EMBODIMENT, BEAUTY, AND THE VIEWER

The ethnologist Marianne Thesander (1997) has written that "there is no totally natural or neutral body—even the naked body reflects the culture to which it belongs" (p. 19). From birth, Thesander concluded, "our bodies are a part of our culture's order" (p. 19). Thesander's argument that our bodies—whatever our biological predispositions—are shaped by our culture may be surprising. Thesander went on to say that many cultures engage in body modification, including piercing and tattooing. However, she is making a deeper claim: that no body is ever "just as it is" or completely natural. For example, what we eat and how much we exercise play a role in our body size, shape, and appearance. If we work outdoors doing construction work, we are likely to be more muscular and suntanned. If we work in an office doing paperwork, we are more likely to be less muscular and lighter skinned. If we eat inexpensive processed and fast food, we are more likely to be fatter; whereas if we consume whole foods—whole grains and fresh fruits and vegetables—we are more likely to be thinner. What we eat, however, is often not only a matter of preference, but also a matter of economics and availability. When our economic system influences what we eat, this counts as a social force or a social construction of our bodies.

As far back as the Paleolithic period, people seem to have been aware of the malleability of the human body and its relationship to social status. Stone figurines from the time depict fat women and emphasize their breasts, buttocks, stomachs, and vulvas (Soffer et al., 2000). Perhaps the most famous of these is the Venus of Willendorf, a limestone carving made about 25,000 BCE (Figure 7.1; Chare, 2009). It is not clear who these women were (perhaps fertility goddesses), but the imagery suggests that fat women may have been admired for their beauty. That prehistoric people's bodies were socially constructed gives weight to Thesander's view that there is no such thing as "a totally natural or neutral body." All bodies bear the imprint of culture.

If Thesander is right that we cannot escape style either in shaping our bodies or in choosing clothing or other adornments, this may be interesting, but does it matter? It is easy to dismiss style as simply superficial, but increasingly those in women's, gender, and sexuality studies believe that **embodiment**, or the way our bodies are and interact with the world to create social meaning, is not a trivial matter but is deeply intertwined with important social relationships and power in society. In this chapter we will explore one aspect of embodiment—how bodies are perceived as beautiful and the relationship of this idea to fashion, art, and the media.

FAT STUDIES AND ACTIVISM

Fat or fabulous? asked a recent advertising campaign. (See the Student Website to view the ad.) Fat activists (and others) might reply, why choose? Today fat studies scholars have produced an "aggressive, consistent, rigorous critique of the negative assumptions, stereotypes, and stigma placed on fat and the fat body" (Rothblum & Solovay, 2009, p. 2). A good place to begin an exploration of fat studies is with the word "fat" itself. Although terms like "overweight" and "obese" tend to be considered more acceptable or polite, fat is being reclaimed by some as a "preferred" word (Wann, 2009, p. xii). Overweight and obese, scholars argue, are problematic terms in part because they assume there is an abstract ideal weight for each person.

FIGURE 7.1
The Venus of Willendorf.

Today this ideal weight is usually based on calculation of one's body mass index, or BMI. Fat studies scholars point to many problems with BMI, including the poorly supported idea that everyone, regardless of body shape, should have the same BMI.

Although body weight is often used as a measure of health and longevity, Campos et al. (2006) argued it is an inaccurate measure at best. Studies have shown that one need not necessarily lose weight to reduce health risks, which might be more effectively alleviated through interventions such as seeking medical care, being physically active, and eating well, regardless of whether there is weight loss (Bjorntorpe et al., 1970, as cited in Burgard, 2009; H. Brown, 2012; LaMarche et. al, 1992). In fact, one analysis of studies linking obesity with health problems indicated that "91 percent of what accounts for a health outcome has *nothing to do with BMI*" (Burgard, p. 43, emphasis in original).

Many fat studies scholars and fat activists subscribe to the public health model known as **Health at Every Size** (HAES). According to Burgard, this model advocates

> *Enhancing health*—attending to emotional, physical, and spiritual well-being, without focusing on weight loss or achieving a specific "ideal weight."
>
> *Size and self-acceptance*—respecting and appreciating the wonderful diversity of body shapes, sizes and features . . . rather than pursuing an idealized weight, shape, or physical feature.
>
> *The pleasure of eating well*—eating based on internal cues of hunger, satiety, and appetite; individual nutritional needs; and enjoyment, rather than on external food plans or diets.
>
> *The joy of movement*—encouraging all physical activities for the associated pleasure and health benefits, rather than following a specific routine of regimented exercise for the primary purpose of weight loss or management.
>
> *An end to weight bias*—recognizing that body shape, size, or weight are not evidence of any particular way of eating, level of physical activity, personality, or psychological issue, or moral character; and confirming that there is beauty and worth in EVERY body. (Shuman & Kratina as cited in Burgard, pp. 42–43)

It is easy to misunderstand the HAES model (Burgard). For example, HAES advocates do think health is important and that fatness can be unhealthy. This

breaking the frame
Thin Can Be Unhealthy

We are awash in messages encouraging us to buy diet pills, subscribe to exercise programs, and seek weight-loss surgery. There is much profit to be made from our buying into the cult of thinness, but many of the "diets" being pedaled today are unhealthy, and some diet pills and programs have been linked to serious medical side effects, including death (Lyons, 2009). Chronic dieting and weight cycling (gaining and losing weight) have also been linked to medical problems (Lyons), and there is growing evidence that fatter patients with some chronic medical conditions live longer than so-called "normal weight" patients (H. Brown, 2012). So, thin is not always healthy and striving to be thin can be alarmingly unhealthy.

model assumes that people naturally have different appetites and their bodies naturally settle at different weights (although everyone can fluctuate in terms of weight). The model accepts that people can be too fat or too thin based on who they are (not an abstract number). HAES does not mean *everyone* is healthy at *any* size; rather, it means that there are healthy people at every size. HAES advocates are really "weight neutral." Gaining or losing weight is not the concern; instead developing "long-term health-enhancing behaviors" is the goal (Burgard, p. 49).

HISTORY OF WOMEN'S BODY SHAPE AND CLOTHING IN THE UNITED STATES

If we examine the history of women's bodies and fashion in the United States from the 19th through the 20th century, we see that the ideal of beauty has changed frequently. Scholars of the subject suggest that beauty standards do not change arbitrarily but instead change in relation to political, economic, and social conditions.

1890s: Shifting Ideals in a Shifting Social Climate

From the 1870s until at least the 1890s, the ideal of beauty in the United States was the "voluptuous woman" (Figure 7.2; Banner, p. 107). Corsets narrowed

FIGURE 7.2

Lillian Russell was the great beauty of the 1880s. One college student remarked, "She was a voluptuous beauty, and there was plenty of her to see. We liked that" (as cited in Banner, 1984, p. 136).

FIGURE 7.3

By the 1890s, women cyclists began wearing shirtwaist blouses and bifurcated skirts (as in this image). Invented in the 1860s, shirtwaists were more practical than constricting bodices (which accompanied corsets) that required lacing (Banner, 1984; FIDM Museum, 2010).

waists, pushing flesh upward and downward, creating an hourglass figure. But by the late 1890s the social climate for women began to change and middle-class women started taking part in the new bicycling craze (Figure 7.3). (They had begun playing tennis in the previous decade). Female exercise programs called calisthenics, the introduction of athletics into women's colleges, and the arguments of exercise advocates had helped prepare for this social shift (Banner).

The 1890s also saw the emergence of a new beauty ideal, the Gibson Girl, created by the illustrator Charles Dana Gibson. Lois Banner called her "symbolic of the hopeful changes of the age: the new movement of women into the work force, the new freedom of behavior between men and women, the new vogue of athletics promising healthier bodies" (p. 168). This ideal was summed up by the 1890s phrase, the New Woman. The Gibson Girl's figure was "thinner than that of the voluptuous woman, but she remained large of bosom and hips" (Banner, p. 154). Dieting became an important trend and even the full-figured Lillian Russell began a "career of dieting" in 1896 (Banner, p. 151). Yet until the 1900s there was still also a "taste for heavy, voluptuous women" (Banner, p. 151). Chorus girls with "balloon-like curves" were common and women displayed on cigarette cards (a form of popular erotic art) and in the *Police Gazette* magazine (a sort of *Playboy* of the day) were fat by today's standards (Banner, p. 151). These differing ideals suggest that what was considered beautiful was influenced not only by mainstream middle-class culture but also by the working-class ideal of full-figured beauty, as well as by medium (Banner).

Among African Americans, the decade saw a dramatic increase in migration to the North (primarily because of worsening conditions for Blacks in the South). This migration included members of the educated Black elite such as Ida B. Wells (because of her opposition to lynching), as well as working-class African Americans (Grossman, 1991). In response to fears that the increasing visibility of lower-class Blacks would threaten their social status, the African American middle class, through organizations such as the National Association of Colored Women, engaged in what Evelyn Brooks Higginbotham (1993) called the **"politics of respectability."** The campaign sought to inculcate in lower-class Blacks "allegiance to temperance (abstaining from drinking), industriousness, thrift, refined manners, and Victorian sexual morals" as a way to earn the respect of "white America" (Higginbotham, p. 14). This model of middle-class respectability required Black women to assimilate to white, middle-class standards of beauty and fashion (Figure 7.4). As part of this beauty standard, women of mixed Black and white heritage (known as "mulattos") with lighter skin were considered models of beauty.

1900s–1920s: The Age of the Boyish Flapper

In the early 1900s, the designer Paul Poiret developed a loose style that expressed femininity by "toning down . . . female curves" (Banner, p. 113). This style "became a symbol of physical liberation and freedom for women to move into areas that previously had been restricted to men" (Thesander, p. 113). By 1913, the newspaper *The New York World* labeled the new model of beauty, with her "straight, boyish shape, totally lacking in curves" (Thesander, p. 107), the flapper (Banner, p. 176). Ideally, flappers were flat chested with small hips. Bras of the time were used to flatten a woman's bust rather than to accentuate it. The roaring twenties—as the decade was known—was a time of economic prosperity in the United States and women enjoyed a great deal of freedom in comparison to earlier decades. The U.S. women's movement of the 1800s, which had pushed for more economic, political, and social freedom,

FIGURE 7.4

These models of middle class respectability are identified in the original caption as "5 female Negro officers of Women's League, Newport, R.I." Circa 1899.

culminated in women achieving the right to vote nationally with the ratification of the 19th Amendment in 1920.

From the 1910s through the end of World War II in 1945, "film stars . . . governed the definitions of ideal female beauty in the United States" (Banner, p. 283). The star of silent films (and later talkies), Clara Bow epitomized the flapper image. Myrtle Gonzalez, a native Mexican Californian, was another beauty of the era. Gonzalez, who may have been Hollywood's "first Latina star," often played the lead in westerns—frequently in the role of "vigorous

FIGURES 7.5–7.7

Clara Bow, Myrtle Gonzalez, and Nina Mae Mickinney (left to right). Mickinney was known as "the dusky Clara Bow" and later restyled in Europe as "the Black Garbo" (Manchel, 2007, p. 316).

outdoor heroines" (Rodríguez, 2004, pp. 32, 34). Another star who epitomized the flapper look was Nina Mae Mickinney, who starred in a number of all-Black films and has been called the first Black movie star (Manchel, 2007). The *New York Post* theater critic Richard Watts Jr. wrote that Mickinney was "assuredly one of the most beautiful women of our time" (Figures 7.5–7.7; D. Bogle, 1973, p. 33).

1930s: A Turn to Mature, Classical Beauty

The decade of the 1930s was a different time in the United States; the stock market crashed in 1929 and the Great Depression followed. With the right to vote secured, the U.S. women's movement lacked a single dramatic issue to serve as a rallying point and subsequently declined, although feminist activism did not disappear (Bolt, 1995; Laughlin et al., 2010). Alison Lurie (1981) wrote that the "childlike fashions of the twenties passed away far more rapidly than those of the previous century" and were made to "look silly and irrelevant" by the stock market crash and the ensuing economic depression (p. 77). Lurie continued, "In ages of anxiety . . . seriousness and maturity are in style; manly men and womanly (not girlish) women are admired" (p. 77). The ideal woman was older (in her 30s) and "classically handsome rather than childishly pretty: Greta Garbo had replaced Clara Bow" (Figure 7.8; Lurie, p. 77).

FIGURE 7.8
Greta Garbo. Rodríguez (2004) suggested that
the success of foreign actors, including Swedish
Garbo, German Marlene Dietrich, and early
"Latin" film stars Myrtle Gonzalez, Beatriz
Michelena, and Antonio Moreno, paved the
way for later Latina/o stars.

FIGURE 7.9
Anna May Wong in costume for a dramatic
adaptation of Puccini's *Turandot*, 1937.

Another beauty of the era was Fredi Washington, an African American actress who was cast opposite the Black film star Paul Robeson in *Emperor Jones*
and later, in *Imitation of Life*, played a tragic mulatto figure (a mixed-race
woman who is beautiful, light skinned with European features, but is condemned to unhappiness because of her mixed ancestry). Anna May Wong,
born Liu Tsong in Los Angeles to parents of Chinese descent, was also considered glamorous and exotic (Figure 7.9). Wong, who had roles in dozens of
movies in the 1920s and 1930s, was sometimes scantily clad in her earlier
films, but after a visit to China (where her immodesty was cause for concern),
she publicly associated herself with the *qipao* dress (pronounced chee-pow),
which evoked modesty and sophistication (Metzger, 2014). The Chinese

considered the *qipao* a symbol of the liberated Chinese woman but Westerners often viewed it as "traditional" Chinese fashion (Metzger).

The era also witnessed a "Latin invasion," including Lupe Velez and Dolores del Rio, both born in Mexico (Rodríguez, p. 57). Del Rio, who had leading roles in more than 50 films, was a Latin superstar, described by the press as "sophisticated," "aristocratic," and "refined" (Rodríguez, p. 54). (See "More About . . . Being "Latin" and the Latin Lover Craze" in this chapter for more about the use of the term "Latin" in this time period. See also Latina/o in Appendix B, Names for People and Places.)

1940s–1950s: Move to Glamorous Fuller Figures

In 1939, the year that Hitler invaded Poland and World War II began, notions of the ideal body shifted once again. "The decent female type of the 1930's gave way to a more glamorized type with greater sensual appeal and heavier make-up. The corset made the bust higher and more pointed, the waist more clearly defined and the slender hips became more rounded" (Thesander, p. 141).

Although World War II ended in 1945, the United States was still anxious about the Soviet Union and increasingly worried about Communists in the United States. This period would come to be known as the Red Scare or the McCarthy era and lasted into the 1950s. During this time, fashion and the ideal body shape took a severe turn. The year 1947 saw the introduction of the New Look, which included a narrower waist achieved by tighter corsets known as waspies, which cinched around a woman's waist so that she looked like a wasp (Thesander). Lurie remarked that "between 1940 and 1955, though clothes went through many changes, they remained the clothes of grownups. The postwar New Look with its longer skirts added years and dignity to women, and the sober, well-tailored Man in the Gray Flannel Suit was their fit companion" (p. 78).

Latin stars (female and male) increasingly had difficulty with their careers in the 1940s as an "antiethnic image of America came to prevail" (Rodríguez, p. 75). This resulted in a period of invisibility for Latin actresses and actors. No better example can be found than Rita Hayworth, who came to be known as the "Love Goddess" and "ethereal all-American girl" (Rodríguez, p.77). Hayworth was born Margarita Carmen Cansino; her father was a Spanish flamenco dancer and her mother a showgirl of Irish and English descent. But it was not until after she changed her name that her career took off and she became a popular pin-up girl with her hourglass figure.

The biggest African American star of the 1940s was Lena Horne, who was light skinned and also had an hourglass figure. By the 1950s, however, she was blacklisted because of her relationship with Paul Robeson (Bogle). (See

History of Men's Body Shape and Clothing in the United States in this chapter for more on Robeson).

The 1950s, a time of sexual conservatism, saw the rise of the sex idol Marilyn Monroe, who had large breasts and full hips (Thesander). It also saw the rise of light-skinned African American Dorothy Dandridge, "who was the first Black woman ever to be held in the arms of a white man in an American movie" (*Island in the Sun* in 1957) (Bogle, p. 171). Dandridge, like Fredi Washington in the 1930s, was often cast in the role of the tragic mulatto.

1960s–1970s: Return to the Thin Ideal

By the 1960s the world had changed dramatically. The United States was escalating involvement in Vietnam; the antiwar movement, the civil rights movement, and the women's movement, sometimes known as second wave feminism, were in full swing (Tortora & Eubank 1998; Pilcher & Whelehan, 2005). With these changes the ideal body type also changed drastically. Thesander described the new ideal as "a thin, little-girl type without any obvious female characteristics, similar to the lanky, tomboy fashion of the 1920's" (p. 179). This look was epitomized by the English model Lesley Hornby, better known as Twiggy (Figure 7.10). Beginning in the 1950s, "individual models became style setters in their own right" (Banner, p. 287). This trend and the rise of television ended film's dominance in defining beauty (Banner).

Banner also noted that "for the first time in American history, non-European models of beauty were not only extolled . . . but were actually presented as models for cultural emulation" (p. 289). The Black power movement and the "Black is beautiful" slogan gained widespread recognition (Banner; Blanco et al., 2008). Many Black females and males wore their hair in Afros or cornrow braids and wore dashiki shirts ("collarless, wide shirt[s] with kimono sleeves") and caftans (a similarly structured floor-length outfit) (Blanco et al.). Non-Western fashion influenced hippie dress, including American Indian–inspired headbands, sandals, ponchos, beads, and South Asian clothing (Blanco et al.).

Banner contended that there were still "voluptuous [white] blondes and elegant [white] brunettes" (p. 289)—such as Bridget Bardot (who was French) and Sofia Loren (who was Italian)—but "what is important about the 1960s is that the rigid standardization of physical appearance was broken to such an extent that, more than ever before, a variety of racial and ethnic looks could be seen as attractive" (p. 290). One example of the continuing appeal of

FIGURE 7.10
The English model Lesley Hornby, known as Twiggy. Note her signature short hair and dress, accentuating the straight line of her body.

voluptuous bodies was Raquel Welch, dubbed "today's sex symbol" by *Time* magazine. Welch was born Jo Raquel Tejada in Chicago to a father of Bolivian descent and a mother of English ancestry (Rodríguez). According to Bogle, Welch agreed to dye her hair blonde and changed her last name but refused to give up "Raquel." Although she claimed to have never hidden her heritage, Welch was afraid of being typecast and so became an "invisible" Latina (much as Hayworth's ethnicity had been invisible in the 1940s).

Ideals of beauty within African American communities changed during the 1960s as well. From the 19th century through the 1950s, middle-class Blacks, because of racism and segregation, built separate institutions such as Black social organizations, newspapers, colleges, and beauty contests (Craig, 2002). These institutions generally championed a light-skinned, respectable, middle-class model of beauty. Valuing women of lighter complexions was part of a broader ideology known as **colorism**, differential treatment based on skin tone that generally manifests itself as a preference for lighter colored skin (Hunter, 2005; Keith, 2009; M. S. Thompson & Keith, 2001). Colorism is a prejudice that continues to exist not only among African Americans, but also among many people of color and whites (Glenn, 2009; Hannon & DeFina, 2014).

In "contesting the racist devaluation of all blacks," middle-class models of beauty often reinforced ideas "that favored light-complexioned blacks" (Craig, p. 46). However, long before the 1960s there was resistance to colorism and the preference for stereotypically European facial features. Some of this dissent was inspired by Marcus Garvey and his back-to-Africa movement in the 1910s and 1920s and by the Nation of Islam (popularly known as the Black Muslims) beginning in the 1930s (Craig). Thus, "by 1950, even the middle class black press accepted that there were multiple ways to define Negro beauty and that the beauty standard included a spectrum of skin shades" (Craig, p. 58). All of this set the stage for the "Black is beautiful" movement of the mid-1960s.

One important factor that gave rise to widespread changes in African American fashion was a rejection of the politics of respectability. In the 1960s, many female African American civil rights activists still employed the politics of respectability as a way to win support for Black civil rights. Female protestors would appear in public in "dresses, cardigan [sweaters], pearls, pillbox hats, and gloves, with their hair straightened and neatly styled" (Ford, 2013, p. 651). Ford contended that

> by maintaining dignity and Christian values, even against the brutality of police billy clubs, attack dogs, and water hoses, African Americans aimed to expose the savagery of both white segregationists and segregation itself as it denied "well-behaved" African Americans their full citizenship rights. (p. 631)

MORE ABOUT...

Race, Colorism, and Beauty

Colorism is a problem for people of color throughout Africa, Asia, and the Americas. Although colorism most often manifests itself as a preference for lighter colored skin and so-called European or white features (such as straight, blonde hair, thin lips, light eyes, and narrow noses) (Hunter, 2005; Keith, 2009; M. S. Thompson & Keith, 2001), colorism can also result in prejudice against, rather than preference for, light-skinned women in particular. Despite generally being perceived as more attractive, such women may be considered problematic within their own communities of color. Within the African American community, for example, light-skinned women are sometimes seen as overtly sexual, independent, or snobbish (Thomas et al., 2011; Wilder, 2010), and among Asian Americans, light-skinned women may be seen as racially troubled, shallow, or irresponsible (Rondilla & Spickard, 2007).

Global research regarding colorism reveals the complexity of the issue. It has been found, for example, that the idea that beauty is light is generally more applicable to women than to men. But that may be changing. There are signs that the light ideal for men is increasingly important globally; for example, in emerging markets, sales of skin-lightening products for men are growing at a rate of 150 percent annually (Wax, 2008). The appeal of light skin, although global in reach, is not universal. For example, among African American men, light-colored skin seems less important as a marker of attractiveness (Hill, 2002; M. S. Thompson & Keith). Hunter found that some African American women even prefer darker-skinned males for at least two reasons: because they regard dark skin as a sign of ethnic authenticity or because they

accept "stereotypical images of dark skinned men as more sexually potent" (p. 87).

Hunter noted that darker-skinned men are increasingly visible in media campaigns, where they are often portrayed "as highly sexualized and attractive" (p. 87). Hunter warned that although this "may look like racial progress, this trend actually coincides with long-held beliefs of African American and Mexican American men as hyper-sexualized and sexually dangerous," threatening "the chastity of white women and white nationhood" (p. 87).

The global desire for lighter skin is "accelerating in places where modernization and the influence of Western capitalism and culture have been most prominent," concluded Glenn (p. 183). The skin cream Fair & Lovely, for example, the largest selling skin cream in India, is used by 60 million consumers throughout Asia (South, South East, and Central) and the Middle East (Runkle as cited in Glenn).

Many scholars suspect that global beauty standards are driven by hegemonic white beauty standards—that is, a ruling ideal of beauty that gives power/status to those with stereotypically European features at the expense of others (Glenn; Lenehan, 2011; Rondilla & Spickard). But the phenomenon is not as straightforward as it may seem. Scholars also note that "there is a lot of evidence for . . . longstanding preferences" for lightness in parts of Africa, Asia, Latin America, and the Middle East that predate contact with Europe (Rondilla & Spickard, p. 121). Still, "it is essential to understand," wrote Rondilla and Spickard,

that there is a whiteness move at work here, too, bound up in international celebrity culture and

(continued)

fed by a global capitalist marketing machine. There is particular strength, it seems, when ancient beauty imperatives are overlaid with and reinforced by colonially produced desires. (p. 121)

These forces draw on anxieties and fantasies about race, sex, and class to sell products—skin-lightening creams being a prime example. In the process, they help manufacture what Patricia Hill Collins (1990/2002) called controlling images—stereotypical or idealized images (Rondilla, 2009) that allow an elite group power over those depicted in the imagery. These controlling images do not so much reflect reality, as "disguise" or mystify social relations—that is, they obscure truths about social relations (Hazel Carby as cited in Collins, p. 69). Promoted by the capitalist marketing machine, whitening, then, is not uncomfortably related to racism and internalized racism; it is "like glowing from within," as a L'Oreal ad from the Philippines for White Perfect puts it (Rondilla, p. 75). As a result, wrote Collins, "these controlling images . . . make racism, sexism, poverty and other forms of social injustice appear natural, normal, and inevitable parts of everyday life" (p. 69).

Other female activists, however, including those who were part of the Student Non-Violent Coordinating Committee (SNCC, pronounced, "snick"), a youth organization founded by Ella Baker, grew increasingly concerned with how the politics of respectability created distance between middle-class Black activists and poor and working-class African Americans (Ford, p. 631).

SNCC women adopted the denim overalls and jeans typically worn by the rural southern working-class communities they were organizing (i.e., doing voter registration and the freedom rides to integrate southern buses) (Student Non-Violent Coordinating Committee, 2014). SNCC women with curly hair increasingly gave up chemical straightening and wore their hair in naturals (where their hair would be tightly curled or kinky). Both the clothing and the naturals were low-maintenance styles that were more practical in the rural environments they were working in. Ford contended that SNCC women of the 1960s played an important role in the establishment of "a Black aesthetic of dress, hair, and beauty that became fashionable for Black women of the 1970's" and also served as a model of "radical Black womanhood" (p. 655) for women like the activist Angela Davis, who came to prominence in 1969 (Craig). (See Chapter 12, "Feminisms," for more on Angela Davis.)

In 1967, Pearl Marsh, a student at a historically Black college, decided to give up straightening her hair after seeing Black militants on television wearing their hair in naturals. Marsh explained the repercussions:

> *Black is beautiful didn't overcome everything. The one thing it did overcome was shame. That we were ashamed that our hair was kinky. I mean the thought that a white person would ever see your hair not straightened was just inconceivable. . . .*
>
> *My father died when he saw it. He just died. I came home with my hair out there looking like this globe. "You look like an African!" That was pejorative. I said, "Yeah. So I look like an African. I am an African." (Ford, pp. 94–95)*

Although ethnicity was fashionable during the 1970s, Latina/os remained obscured (Rodríguez, p. 152). For example, few people knew that Lynda Carter, Miss USA in 1972 and the highest paid actress on television for her role as Wonder Woman (1975–1979), was born Lynda Jean Córdoba in Arizona and had "English, Irish, Mexican and Spanish ancestry" (Lynda Carter, n.d., para 14; Rodríguez; Sheridan, 2015).

The clothing style changed again in the early 1970s as the economic situation worsened and competition for jobs increased. Clothing became more masculine and a more mature ideal consisting of "suits, trousers and dresses in a rather severe classical style" became fashionable (Thesander, p. 197).

By the late 1970s, the television show *Charlie's Angels* made stars of Farrah Fawcett-Majors, Kate Jackson, and Jaclyn Smith and helped make the bronzed beach look popular ("Charlie's Angels," 2009; "The 70's," 2014). A pin-up poster of Farrah Fawcett sold more copies than one of Marilyn Monroe (McShane, 2009; S. Stewart, 2009). The model of beauty was natural, slim, and hair was generally worn long ("The 70's").

1980s: Return to the Hourglass Look

The 1980s saw a resurgence of conservatism; Ronald Reagan, an icon of the Republican Party, was president from 1981 to 1989. Susan Faludi (1991) famously called this period a time of backlash against women's rights. Faludi (1991) argued that just when women's rights issues were on the verge of successes (such as the Equal Rights Amendment, which was ultimately defeated) forces mobilized against them. The 1980s saw a return to the ideal of large-breasted women with slim waists and narrow hips, but this time the ideal was linked to a vision of a more athletic, toned body as fitness training and sports gained in popularity (Thesander). Jane Fonda, an actor who was well established in the 1960s and 1970s, became an exercise icon and model of beauty with her hourglass shape (S. Stewart, 2009; Thesander). Other icons of beauty included the supermodels Brooke Shields, Claudia Schiffer (German), Naomi Campbell (Black and English), Iman (Somali born), and Sonia Braga (Brazilian born) (Rodrígeuz; "The 80's," 2014).

1990s: Enter the Waif Look

The 1990s was a decade of visibility for gay people in the United States. The AIDS epidemic of the 1980s gave rise to a number of important gay rights organizations and in the 1990s President Bill Clinton signed "Don't Ask, Don't Tell," which was supposed to allow gay people to serve in the military provided they did not tell anyone they were gay. However, discharges for homosexuality increased every year until the U.S. war in Afghanistan in 2001 ("Don't Ask," 2014).

A popular model of beauty was the "glamazon super model" look, thin but more athletic and curvy ("The 90's," 2014). Naomi Campbell, Cindy Crawford, Linda Evangelista, Elle Macpherson, Claudia Schiffer, and Christy Turlington typified this look (Cokal, 2000' "The 90's"). Cokal contended that in the 1980s and 1990s fashion designers were changing their focus from the wealthy to a larger mass market by advertising on television, billboards, and bus shelters. Movie stars were less glamorous during this period and supermodels filled "America's hunger for opulence" (Cokal, p. 584).

Runway models were also beauty icons in the 1990s. The waif look, thin and small—like Twiggy in the 1960s—became an ideal, epitomized by Kate Moss (Figure 7.11; Cortese, 2007). Increasing attention was paid to anorexia and severely skinny female actors became more common, a trend that Erica Berman called the "Ally McBeal effect," citing the influence of the television show *Ally McBeal* (1997–2002), which featured extremely thin female actors such Calista Flockhart (Berman, 2014; "The 2000's," 2013).

By the end of the 1990s, Hispanic women were popular icons of beauty again, including the Spanish-born Penélope Cruz and Mexican-born Salma Hayek (who is of Lebanese and Mexican descent) (Rodríguez). But the biggest Hispanic star of the decade was Jennifer Lopez, who was born in

FIGURE 7.11
The model Kate Moss.

the Bronx, New York City, to Puerto Rican parents. Lopez was marketed as a mix of "ghetto fabulousness and middle-class respectability" (Rodríguez).

2000s–2010s: Slim and Hourglass Looks

In the 2000s, reality television became popular and the Internet grew as a mass medium, increasing avenues to fame. The ideal body size was still very slim to slim with large breasts ("The 2000s"). Tyra Banks, Gisele Bundchen, Penélope Cruz, Paris Hilton, Keira Knightley, Lucy Liu, and Britney Spears fit these physical ideals ("The 2000s"; Valdivia, 2007). In addition, women with a more hourglass shape also became famous for their beauty and sexual appeal, including the singer Beyoncé and actors Christina Hendricks (who played Joan Harris on *Mad Men*) and Catherine Zeta Jones ("The 2000s"). In 2003, Latinas/os in the United States officially outnumbered African Americans and the Latinization of the 1990s continued (Rodríguez). Among Latina stars, Jennifer Lopez was considered a "supernova"; in 2001, she had both the number one movie at the box office (*The Wedding Planner*) and the top selling album (*J. Lo*) (Rodríguez, p. 220). Lopez was not only a symbol of beauty for Latina/os, but also a crossover success with Anglo (non-Latina/o) audiences (Negrón-Muntaner, 2004; Valdivia). Media coverage of Lopez, who was named the "Sexiest Woman in the World" by *Playboy* (Negrón-Muntaner), often focused on her curves and more specifically her buttocks, which became "a cultural icon" (as cited in Mendible, 2009, para. 7).

Latina/o and African American culture has long celebrated a more full-figured body, including women with prominent rear ends (Mendible). "Urban" men's magazines like *King*, *Smooth*, and *Sweets* have traded on such imagery "turning 'booty love' into a sign of ethnic masculinity" (Mendible). Valdivia contended that because Lopez's figure was so at odds with prevailing white standards of beauty, "her butt represent[ed] ethnic difference," a racialized vision of beauty.

The 2000s and 2010s appear to have marked some opening of beauty standards. It has been suggested, for example, that as long as they are famous and sexy, women today can adhere to a number of ideal body types ("2013," 2013). Although this may represent an expansion of the ideals of beauty, these ideals are still far from unlimited and are often preferred based on class and racialized identification.

recap of terms
Racialization

Racialization recognizes that becoming marked by race is an action—something that happens to people rather than something they are.

From Chapter 6, "Beyond the Mythical Norm."

The Significance of Female Body Shape and Fashion

What does this brief and selective history of bodies and fashion reveal about social relations and power in our society? In the era of the Gibson Girl (1890s), a time of greater freedom for white women, female clothing was less restraining and women's bodies could appear in a more "natural," less stylized way. In the 20th century, when white women have asserted more political, economic, and social power, the ideal appears to be smaller (slimmer from bust to hips). This was true during the 1920s (the flapper era), the 1960s (the Twiggy look), and the 1990s (the waif look). As Thesander pointed out, this smaller ideal might be interpreted in at least two different ways: either as more "boyish" (with more masculine attire) or more "girlish" (as opposed to womanly). By contrast, during times that were more politically conservative (such as the 1930s–1950s and 1980s), the ideal body was larger (a more hourglass-shape figure with a larger bust, slim waist, and larger hips)—a figure that could be seen as more sexy and/or more maternal. Given these patterns, the question becomes how to interpret them. Were such ideals actively sought by women in concert with or reaction to social conditions or were they largely imposed on American women by the mainstream culture?

Scholars have offered various theories. Christine Smith (1997) speculated that it is not a coincidence "that a thin, restrictive beauty ideal, one that reduces women to a childlike appearance—has occurred during the same periods that women have sought power and control" (p. 118). However, she also offered the possibility that the opposite is true: women might seek the thin ideal as a way of stressing their girlish femininity and appearing less threatening to men, as "a way of saying to society, 'Don't worry, I don't want to be a man. See how feminine I look?'" (p. 118). Thesander made a different argument: that for women to be taken seriously in their effort to achieve rights traditionally granted men, they actively seek to take on a more masculine (boyish) body type and attire, the appropriation of masculine attributes, thereby allowing the appropriation of masculine power.

The question of whether the shift in the beauty ideal in the 20th century was forced on women by society or actively assumed by women as a strategy in the struggle for greater rights (or some combination of the two) raises an important question: how much of style is a result of gender ideology?

For women of color, popular ideals of beauty often parallel white ideals in terms of body shape, skin tone, and fashion, although we have seen exceptions such as Black women's ideals in the 1960s and, to some extent, Black and Hispanic ideals from the 2000s to today. For both white women and women of

ON THE web

View a **timeline of changes in women's body shape and fashion** on the Student Website: www.oup.com/us/gillis-jacobs

color, it appears that upper-class ideals of beauty are often thinner than working-class ideals.

Class

Thorstein Veblen (1912), an American economist and sociologist, asserted in *The Theory of the Leisure Class* that what is fashionable in terms of clothing and body shape is determined by wealth and power. Consider, for example, the idea that being fat is often a sign of beauty when food is scarce and so becomes an emblem of wealth and power. Veblen argued that fashion, in terms of both body shape and clothing, works in a similar way: the more expensive, complicated, and restrictive the fashion, the more desirable and higher class it becomes because of the expense associated with it. For example, as Thesander noted, "Wearing a corset . . . demonstrated that one could afford servants to do the housework (because being tightly corseted made housework too difficult); and the mere process of tying the laces required the assistance of a lady's maid" (p. 26). High-heeled shoes served a similar function both in Veblen's time and today; working-class women are less likely to wear high heels on a regular basis because they are too restrictive and impractical—and the most fashionable high-heeled shoes (brands like Manolo Blahnik) cost thousands of dollars (Clifford, 2011; L. Mohanty, 2014).

Veblen was arguing that part of what makes women's fashion high status is that it is incapacitating. The fact that a corset or high-heeled shoes make it hard to accomplish meaningful tasks is precisely what makes them high status. These mark the bearer as one who will not (and indeed cannot) perform low-status manual labor. To some degree, even professional men's clothing (including suits that must be dry cleaned and ironed and ties that are impractical for performing manual labor) serves this function. They mark the wearer as someone above physical labor and literally suited for more valued intellectual labor.

Veblen also noted the importance of conspicuous waste and conspicuous consumption as ways to display wealth and power. Upper-class women, according to Veblen, were expected to consume, and by doing so they became symbols of men's success. Power, however, rested not with the women, but with the men. Moreover, men who participated directly in conspicuous waste and conspicuous consumption were likely to be seen as *not* powerful. Veblen seems to be suggesting that a powerful man was presumed to have a strong work ethic and self-control. His role was to accrue power and wealth rather than to expend them.

HISTORY OF MEN'S BODY SHAPE AND CLOTHING IN THE UNITED STATES

To be a man in contemporary times has largely been equated with ignoring fashion (see, e.g., Chenoune, 1993). Today, a middle- or upper-class man who pays too much attention to fashion—or dresses too stylishly—risks being thought of as frivolous, effeminate, or gay. But this was not always so. In the early 17th century, both women and men dressed in colorful and ornate clothing. In this "old sartorial regime," as David Kuchta (2002) called it, conspicuous consumption by the aristocracy was seen as a mark of their superior status.

1666–1800s: Into the Great Masculine Renunciation

Kuchta marked the date of October 7, 1666, as the beginning of the end of the old sartorial regime of sumptuous dress for men. On this date, England's King Charles II set out to create a new fashion for clothes (and head off criticism of his court as decadent and tyrannous) by donning a vest (also called a waistcoat), a more restrained style than the traditional doublet (Kuchta; Tortora & Eubank). Doing so, he ushered in the era of the three-piece suit and modern masculinity. Since this time, according to Kuchta, "male gentility has been associated with modesty and plainness in dress" (p. 2).

Many have argued that what resulted was a turn in which "the social function of dress shifted from distinguishing the classes in the eighteenth century to distinguishing the sexes in the nineteenth" (Shannon, 2006, p. 15). John Carl Flugel (1930/1950) referred to the end of the era of flashy clothes for men as the "**great masculine renunciation**." Conspicuous consumption via ornate and expensive clothing for women remained appropriate, but for men, inconspicuous consumption became a marker of masculinity (Kuchta). Shannon pointed out that men did not really renounce fashion altogether; they mostly took up an understated style of dress as a fashion statement against fashion. As George Bryant Brummel, or "Beau" Brummell, a trendsetter of the early 1800s, explained, if one draws attention, one is either "too stiff, too tight or too fashionable" (Frantz, 2003, p. 166).

The great masculine renunciation begun by King Charles II was refashioned in the 19th century by the middle class as a rejection of aristocratic values and style and an embrace of democratic values and style. This shift took place as the middle class overtook the aristocracy as the major political and social force in Europe and the United States. The middle class championed values of thrift, self-control, and modesty while accusing the aristocracy of lacking these qualities, which were considered necessary for good government. The fancy dress of the aristocracy was seen as a sign that they had been "effeminated" by luxury, that they had lost masculine self-control and the modesty necessary to rule in a sober fashion. Increasingly, men who were conspicuously fashionable were viewed as effeminate, sexually suspect, and unsuited for political power. Similarly, women's fashionable dress was seen as an outward sign of their frivolous nature, a sign of being unsuited to participate in public discussion and political decision making. Kuchta asserted that because "masculinity was a pre-requisite to power . . . femininity itself . . . was reason enough to disqualify women from political participation" (p. 10). Kuchta contended that through the label of "effeminacy . . . politically legitimate masculinity was defined in opposition to three 'others'—the other gender, other sexual practices and other classes" (p. 11). One could also extend this argument to racialized others. In this context, one might see the numerous 19th-century photographic representations of the Black abolitionist Frederick Douglass in a three-piece suit as a way of appropriating and embodying politically legitimate masculinity, which was racialized as white (see Figure 3.7 in Chapter 3, "Gender and In/Equality").

1890s: Enter the Athletic, Muscular Man

As we discussed earlier, in the 1890s bicycling and tennis became the rage for women. Similarly, in the latter half of the 19th century, the rise in popularity of men's athletics—in the form of youth sports as well as college sports like football—resulted in a shift away from the portly older ideal toward a more youthful, muscular ideal for men. Eugene Sandow, a weight lifter, fit this masculine ideal, as did the boxer John L. Sullivan (Figure 7.12) and Charles Dana Gibson, the creator of the iconic Gibson Girl (Banner; Kimmel, 2003).

Still another exemplar of masculine beauty was the African American Paul Robeson (Figure 7.13). The physically imposing Robeson, who was a college football star and Phi Beta Kappa honor student, became a star of stage and screen, as well as a lawyer and activist for many causes, including civil rights, labor unions, and the peace movement (D. Bogle; "Paul Robeson," 2012).

Some historians contend that in the late 19th and early 20th century there was a crisis of masculinity for middle-class white men in the United States. This period saw the closing of the Western frontier as a place where men could go to prove themselves, increasing urbanization, and a move from entrepreneurial capitalism (where men were economically independent) to a more corporate capitalist economy (where men were dependent on company jobs) (Kimmel, 2003). The changing status of women is also said to have contributed to this crisis of masculinity. The New Women of the time were wearing tailor-made suits similar to men's suits and "were more active than their

FIGURE 7.12

John L. Sullivan was a popular American professional boxer and heavyweight champion who bridged the bareknuckle and gloved eras of boxing in the latter half of the 19th and early 20th centuries.

FIGURE 7.13
Paul Robeson as Othello with Uta Hagen as
Desdemona in the 1943/44 Broadway
production of *Othello*. Robeson was later
blacklisted and unable to work because of his
association with American Communists
("Robeson, Paul," 2014).

FIGURE 7.14
The Arrow Collar Man, like the Gibson
Girl, was a type rather than a specific
character so he could be represented as
different men at different stages of life in
advertisements (Turbin).

ON THE
web

Read about **zoot suits,**
Mexican American youth
culture, and the zoot suit
riots of 1943 on the Student
Website: www.oup.com/us/
gillis-jacobs

predecessors—they were more likely to take exercise, go to college, go to club
meetings, be gainfully employed and be actively involved in the social causes
of the day" (Cosbey, 2008, p. 24). Men needed ways of distinguishing themselves from women and increasingly muscularity and ritual combat in the form
of sports provided a way to recover masculinity (Cosbey; Kimmel, 2003).

1907–1950s: Continuation of the Broad-Shouldered Ideal

Between 1907 and 1931, J. C. Leyendecker's drawings of the Arrow Collar
Man—stylish, "tall, well built, with broad shoulders a strong jaw and chiseled
features and muscular hands"—graced advertisements for Arrow detachable
collars (Figure 7.14; Turbin, 2002, pp. 471–472). The Arrow Collar Man has
been described as the "visual representation of the New American Man and the

male equivalent of the Gibson Girl who represented the New Woman" (Turbin, p. 472). These images are in keeping with the ideal male bodies of the 1930s, 1940s, and 1950s, which featured tall, broad-shouldered men in suits—although these periods often emphasized an older ideal than the younger versions of the Arrow Collar Man. The masculine ideal was personified by movie stars such as Clark Gable (in the 1930s to 1940s), Cary Grant (from the 1930s to 1950s), and Rock Hudson (in the 1950s) (Benshoff & Griffin, 2009; Weinberg, 2015).

An exception to the broad-shouldered ideal was the Spanish-born "megastar" Antonio Moreno (Figure 7.15), who appeared in 146 films during his career, opposite stars like Gloria Swanson and Greta Garbo (Rodríguez, p. 45). Although he was known as a "Latin lover," he was not limited to Latin roles; he played the wealthy Anglo Cyrus T. Waltham in the blockbuster film *It* (1912) with Clara Bow.

In 1954, the U.S. Supreme Court in *Brown v. Board of Education* ruled that segregation was unconstitutional. D. Bogle contended that the handsome, broad-shouldered African American Sidney Poitier was the perfect star for

FIGURE 7.15

The film star Antonio Moreno had a show marriage but was known to be gay (Rodríguez).

Being "Latin" and the Latin Lover Craze

Clara E. Rodríguez (2004) noted that in the early 1900s the word "Latin" was used to refer to anyone from Italy, Spain, or Portuguese-speaking countries—as well as Latin America. In fact, "the original Latin lover, Rudolf Valentino, [whose movie career spanned 1914–1926] was from Italy" (p. 21). As with Antonio Moreno and other Latin film stars of the age, Valentino was not limited to Latin roles. The Latin lover craze was so great that in 1922 the Vienna-born Jacob Krantz was renamed Ricardo Cortez and with his "dark good looks" made 90 movies (Rodríguez, p. 19). Rodríguez stated, however, that Latino (and Latina) actors still had to conform to "European prototypes—perhaps to southern and eastern European prototypes [that is, they could be somewhat darker but not too dark skinned] but clearly in the evolving fold of what it meant to be 'white' (and upper class) in the United States at the time" (p. 28). On Valentino's early death of blood poisoning in 1926, other actors were marketed as replacements for Valentino. One such actor was the Mexico-born Ramon Novarro, who was dubbed the "new Valentino" after the success of the film *Ben Hur* in 1926 (Reinholtz, 2013, p. 569). Sadly, Novarro, who was gay, was the victim of an anti-gay murder in 1968. Within the independent Black film industry, the African American Lorenzo Tucker was promoted as the "black Valentino" to Black audiences by the prolific Black writer, producer, and director Oscar Micheaux (D. Bogle, 1973, p. 114).

MORE ABOUT...

the "integrationist age" (p. 175). He dressed conservatively, spoke standard American English, and played characters that were level headed and never challenged the system. This made him a "paragon of Black middle-class values and virtues," which played well with Black and white audiences alike (D. Bogle, p. 176).

1960s: Enter the Peacock

In terms of fashion, the period of the 1960s is known as the Peacock Revolution, in which men adopted bold colors and prints (Blanco et al.). Men's suits were cut to be slim. The 1960s also saw the rise of unisex fashions. In the 1970s, business suits became even less conservative and restrictive (Blanco et al.).

In 1966 in Mississippi, the SNCC member Stokely Carmichael (who later changed his name to Kwame Ture) gave a speech and led a chant of "Black power." As articulated by Carmichael, the Black Power movement was critical of the nonviolent protest movement's demands that Blacks remain vulnerable to attack as a demonstration of their middle-class respectability. The Black Power movement also took an early stand against the Vietnam War and demanded a radical restructuring of society to eliminate white supremacy and economic exploitation of both Blacks and whites (Carmichael, 1966). It is through the Black Power movement that the natural hairstyle—now termed the Afro—gained prominence in the media. (We noted earlier that SNCC women also wore naturals, but imagery of SNCC women was not disseminated in the media.)

FIGURE 7.16

An important icon of masculinity in the 1960s and 1970s was the Marlboro Man—a cowboy figure who personified rugged masculinity and smoked Marlboro cigarettes (which became the bestselling brand globally) ("Marlboro Man," 2003).

1970s: Continuation of the Peacock and Rugged Masculinity

Flamboyant clothing for men continued to be in style in the 1970s, including tie-dye shirts, bell-bottom pants, and military surplus clothing. Disco dancing was all the rage and men wore shirts with collars that were long and pointed. During the decade, three-piece suits came in a "bewildering variety of colors" (Trepanier, 2015, para. 19).

The 1970s also saw the rise of the Chinese American martial artist and movie star Bruce Lee (Figure 7.17), who according to Chan (2000), represented a heroic model of both Chinese and Chinese American manhood and at the same time presented a more complex vision of masculinity than the predominantly white stars of the time. Lee's film characters did not participate in compulsory heterosexuality or traditional dominance of women. They did, however, "create a male-centered . . . world" where masculinity involved the domination of "other men through violence" (Chan). But unlike other heroes (such as James Bond), Lee's characters were not shown in sexual relationships with women and were unconcerned with being sexually admired by gay male characters. Chan argued that Lee's characters, who relied solely on martial arts ability to prevail against whites and other racial groups (frequently armed with guns), served for some in the audience as a metaphor for the asymmetric warfare in Vietnam, where the less well-equipped Nationalist-Communist forces prevailed over technologically superior U.S. forces. This image was appealing to those who opposed the Vietnam War and those who supported anticolonialist and anti-imperialist movements, including Black people in the United States (Cha-Jua, 2008; Prashad, 2003).

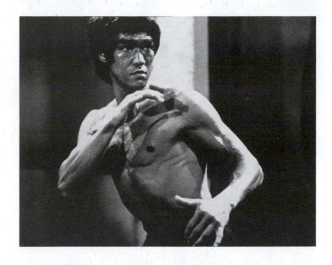

FIGURE 7.17
Bruce Lee in the movie *Enter the Dragon*, 1973.

1980s: Rise of the Hypermuscular Ideal

The 1980s saw the return of broad-shouldered men in suits, and branded clothing took off as the economy created wealth for the economic elite (Blanco et al). A number of Vietnam War–related films were released, including the action picture *Rambo: First Blood II* (1985), starring the heavily muscled Sylvester Stallone. Jonathan Rutherford (1988) referred to this kind of action hero as "Retributive Man," a character who attempts to "reassert a traditional masculinity, a tough independent authority," and uses a frenzy of violence to solve problems (p. 28). Rutherford saw the "hysterical assertions of maleness" by Rambo and Retributive Man more generally as a shift from traditional war films that presented war as "a rite of passage, an opportunity for men to find themselves, to prove their masculinity and their capacity to tame their bodies and physical fear" (p. 29). This traditional genre links masculinity, violence, and nationalism, where proving yourself to be a man and a good soldier and advancing the interests of your country all coincide. By contrast, in these new militaristic films, Retributive Man is a rogue figure who still fights for his country but lashes out against those in power who have compromised national honor (for example, by allowing our defeat in Vietnam). As Rutherford said, Retributive Man "confronts a world gone soft, pacified by traitors and cowards, dishonorable feminized men" (p. 28).

In addition to highly muscled action film heroes like Stallone and Arnold Schwarzenegger, advertising in the 1980s began to feature men with similar physiques in a nonmilitaristic context. This New Man "blends fashion consciousness with the hypermasculine concept represented in muscularity" (Freson & Arthur, 2008, p. 343) (not to be confused with the New American Man or New Man of the early 1900s). If there was a pivotal date for this New Man, it was 1982, when Calvin Klein began an advertising campaign for his line of underwear. The first ad featured Tom Hintnaus, broad shouldered, tanned, and muscular, lying in the sun wearing only a pair of cotton briefs. (See the Student Website to view the ad.) *American Photographer* magazine listed it as one of "10 pictures that changed America," stating that in creating the image, the photographer Bruce Weber "made men the focal point of sexual attention; for the first time, they were sold as sexual objects, not breadwinners or authority figures" ("10 Pictures," 1989, p. 36). Weber's Calvin Klein campaign also included iconic images of Kate Moss and Mark Wahlberg, and he continues to be well known for his Abercrombie & Fitch ads. Like the Arrow Collar Man, these ads had a homoerotic aesthetic very different from that of action hero figures, although they both featured men with classic V-shape muscular bodies, a shape that is wide at the shoulders and narrow at the hips, including well-defined abdominal muscles (Murnen, 2011). Some have speculated that this ideal, which persists today, is the outgrowth of a continuing crisis of masculinity brought on by women gaining in equality with men. Men traditionally distinguished themselves from women by being soldiers, providers, and athletes, but these no longer serve as adequate markers of masculinity. In response, men turn to hypermuscularity and leanness as a way of distinguishing themselves from women (Leit, Pope, & Gray, 2001; Mishkind et al., 1987).

1990s: Advent of the Metrosexual

Although large, muscular men were still an ideal of beauty in the 1990s (such as the Black supermodel Tyson Beckford of Jamaican and Chinese descent), the **metrosexual** model of masculinity also emerged (Coad, 2008). The name, coined by Mark Simpson in 1994, gained popularity in 2002 (Coad). A metrosexual is a kind of modern-day dandy, a man who devotes time to shopping, accessorizing, and using body products (Coad). Simpson described the typical metrosexual as a "single young man with high disposable income, living or working in the city" (as cited in Coad, p. 19). Metrosexuals can be of any sexual orientation, but the source of the ideal came from gay male imagery from the 1970s that was coded with a new sense of "eroticism and overt sexuality"

(Blachford, as cited in Cole, 2008, p. 280; Simpson, 2002). Simpson described the metrosexual as a kind of artificial creation of marketers, saying,

> *For some time now, old-fashioned (re)productive, repressed, unmoisturized heterosexuality has been given the pink slip by consumer capitalism. The stoic, self-denying, modest straight male didn't shop enough (his role was to earn money for his wife to spend), and so he had to be replaced by a new kind of man, one less certain of his identity and much more interested in his image—that's to say, one who was much more interested in being looked at. . . . A man, in other words, who is an advertiser's walking wet dream. (para. 8)*

Although marketers may have generated the metrosexual as a strategy to get men to function more as female consumers, the associations of metrosexuality with homosexuality and effeminacy (because of his fashion consciousness) have limited the appeal of this model as an ideal of masculine beauty. A modern-day example of a metrosexual is the character of Schmidt on the television show *New Girl*.

2000s–2010s: Popularization of the Slim Ideal

The 2000s to the present has seen an increase in the popularity of a slim body type for men. For example, *People* magazine's list of the sexiest men alive from 2000 to 2015 includes slim celebrities such as Johnny Depp, Bradley Cooper, Jude Law, Hugh Jackman, and Ben Affleck (although there are exceptions, such as Matt Damon and George Clooney) ("People Magazine's Sexiest Man Alive," 2016). *Latina* magazine's list of the sexiest men of 2014 included the soccer player James Rodriguez, Pedro Pascal, Enrique Iglesias, and Antonio Banderas (Arreola, 2014). Celebrated Black men include the model David Agbodji, the television star Shemar Moore, and two of the top grossing movie actors of 2014, Will Smith and Denzel Washington ("David Agbodji," n.d.; Leon, 2011; "Shemar Moore," 2015).

Many fashion sources note that the lean body ideal was driven by Hedi Slimane's high fashion collection in 2001 (see, for example, Milligan, 2012; Trebay, 2008; Vernon, 2010), which relied on very lean models and "hinged on razor-sharp, super-tight tailoring; and jeans so clinging that they almost qualified as . . . man leggings" (Vernon, para. 6). Vernon observed that this ideal gradually spread beyond high fashion, although she also noted it did not replace a larger, more muscular ideal; instead, the two "polarised ideals" exist side by side (para. 10).

The Significance of Male Body Shape and Fashion

What are we to make of the shifting ideals of male beauty and fashion in history? It is more difficult to draw conclusions about men's fashion than women's, at least in part because the body of research is much smaller. Therefore, our comments here should necessarily be seen as tentative and preliminary. That said, it appears that the ideal of the tall, athletic man dressed in a conservative suit has often held sway from the 1890s forward. Exceptions to this are the 1960s and 1970s, times of great political and social change and sexual liberation, when men's fashion became more open to bold colors and prints and less conservative silhouettes. The hypermuscularity of the 1980s (and continuing in the 1990s) seems to echo (and amplify) the athletic man of the 1890s—and both seem to be attempts to reassert traditional masculinity in response to perceived external threats (for example, the closing of the frontier and the changing status of women in society). The 1990s and 2000s have seen some degree of democratization of fashion and beauty ideals for men (and women), with a wider range of possibilities, perhaps in part because of wide access to social media and the incredible volume of images it produces and reproduces.

ON THE
web

View a **timeline of changes in men's body shape and fashion** on the Student Website: www.oup.com/us/ gillis-jacobs

VIEWING GENDERED BODIES

"Seeing comes before words," wrote John Berger (n.d., cover). In *Ways of Seeing* and the BBC television series he hosted, Berger argued that Western art (like trends in fashion and beauty) can reveal much about femininity and masculinity and the status of women and men in society. An artist and an art historian, he asserted that from the paintings of the Renaissance we can learn about how we are socialized into seeing, that is, how we learn to view others and ourselves, and how that experience is different for women and men.

Renaissance paintings, which were often commissioned by rich, powerful men, frequently depict women on display for the pleasure of the men. In many of these paintings the women are undressed and the men are clothed. Berger believed that this artistic tradition has not only shaped our **aesthetics** (that is, our ideas about what is beautiful or tasteful) but also influenced social behavior. Berger observed that often "men dream of women. Women dream of themselves being dreamt of. Men look at women. Women watch themselves being looked at" (Dibb, 1972). Central to Berger's view is the idea that women in art and society more generally are surveyed; women are evaluated primarily by how they look rather than what they can do. In the Renaissance artwork that Berger examined, the primary surveyors are the men who have commissioned these works of art and the men to whom the works were shown off. It seems clear that the painter has created the work for an **ideal viewer**—that is, a specific kind of imagined viewer—namely, a male who is expected to take heterosexual pleasure from the picture.

Modern media imagery seems to follow a similar pattern. The ideal viewer generally fits Audre Lorde's (1978/1984) mythical norm—"white, . . . male, young, heterosexual, [and] . . . Christian" (p. 116). The ideal beauty featured in the media parallels this—often young, female, very thin, and white. The beauty standards at work here mostly exclude women of color, fatter women, older women, non-Christian women and women with disabilities. And although a small number of women of color have achieved some prominence (for example, Beyoncé, Rihanna, Jennifer Lopez, and Jennifer Hudson), Lexie and Lindsay Kite (2011) pointed out that "media representations of these women have become increasingly 'anglicized' or 'whitewashed' over time, with lighter-colored, straighter hair, lighter make up, colored contacts and often, shrinking figures" (para. 5).

This dynamic uniquely affects people perceived as "disabled"—another group excluded from the ideal of beauty. As Garland-Thomson (2004) noted, "cultural stereotypes imagine disabled women as asexual, unfit to reproduce, overly dependent, unattractive—as generally removed from the sphere of true womanhood and feminine beauty" (p. 89). Regarding older women, Garland-Thomson also asserted that "aging is a form of disablement that disqualifies older women from the limited power allotted females who are young and meet the criteria for attracting men" (p. 89). For men, having a "disability" is inherently problematic to stereotypical notions of masculinity. Asch and Fine (as cited in Shuttleworth et al., 2012) explained that "having a disability [is] seen as synonymous with being dependent, childlike and helpless—an image fundamentally challenging all that is embodied in the ideal male: virility, autonomy and independence" (p. 175). (See "Dis/ability" in Appendix B, Names for People and Places for a discussion of how "disablement" is a consequence of social choices rather than inherent in people.)

People who do not fit the beauty ideal are sometimes **exoticized**—viewed as exotic, foreign, or unusual in an interesting way. Cashmore (2003) noted that women outside the racial norm have been exoticized in two ways—as "grotesquely sexual" or as "sexually inviting and seductively mysterious"—sometimes dangerously so (p. 50). An infamous example of the former is Sarah Baartman, an African woman from the Cape Colony that is part of present-day South Africa (Scully & Crais, 2008). Baartman was put on display in Paris and London from 1810 to 1815 as the Hottentot Venus. Exactly how she was exhibited is not entirely clear, but the display emphasized her large breasts and protruding buttocks (which are said to be common to women of some South

MORE ABOUT...

Veiling as Fetish Art

Muslimah Media Watch wrote about "veil fetish art" (Figure 7.18):

> The [earlier] view of Middle Eastern/Muslim women was that of a lazily sensual harem woman reclining on a couch. Most recently, it has morphed into a cowed housewife bullied by her religion and the men in her life. From these icons arises a newer image of Muslim women: one that combines the two.
>
> I'll term it "veil fetish art," because every featured woman has most or all of her face and her hair covered . . . the veil acts as a sexual catalyst: it brands the woman as forbidden. . . .
>
> In these pictures, the veil adds a dimension of oppression that cries out for western male help: you can almost hear the women breathe, "Liberate me!." . . .

The type of liberation these images imply is a sexual one: erotic poses and come-hither eyes imply that this veiled woman just wants the freedom to be the dirty, dirty girl that she is. This simultaneously reinforces Orientalist ideas that Muslim women are oppressed (sexually as well as socially or religiously) and hypersexual. It also supports the idea that covering oneself is oppressive, and that the only way to be a liberated woman is to show some skin.

Source: Muslimah Media Watch (2008, January 28). Oooh, Baby, Put It On: Ripping up Veil Fetish Art. *Retrieved November 26, 2012, from* http://www.patheos.com/blogs/mmw/2008/01/oooh-baby-put-it-on-ripping-up-veil-fetish-art-2/

FIGURE 7.18
A representation of a veiled woman with a come-hither gaze is common in commercial stock imagery.

African tribes) (Willis & Williams, 2002, pp. 59–63). Her story is an extreme but not unique example of the dehumanization of African people during this colonial period.

The Male Gaze

Because appearance is so vital to women's status, women constantly survey themselves and one another. In fact, when we discuss this idea in class, many of our students remark that women are often the most critical observers of themselves and other women. Even when women are the surveyors, however, this looking is done from the perspective of the ideal male viewer, meaning that women survey themselves to determine how men would view them. Laura Mulvey (1975/1997) referred to this as the **male gaze**.

FIGURE 7.19
Venus of Urbino by Titian (1538).

The principal quality of women in art and cinema is what Mulvey called "to-be-looked-at-ness," whereas men are most often actors (p. 837). This active/passive distinction is captured by Berger's phrase "men act and women appear"; men are judged primarily on what they can accomplish, whereas women are judged primarily on how they look. Men also play the part of **voyeur**, someone who takes sexual pleasure in looking.

One consequence of the "sexual imbalance" caused by this male gaze is the **objectification** of women (Mulvey, p. 442). According to Papadaki (2015), objectification can be roughly defined as "seeing and/or treating a person, usually a woman, *as an object*" (para. 1). Sandra Bartky (1990) further explained:

> *A person is sexually objectified when her sexual parts or her sexual functions are separated out from the rest of her personality and reduced to the status of mere instruments or else regarded as if they were capable of representing her. On this definition, then, the prostitute would be a victim of sexual objectification, as would the* Playboy *bunny, the female breeder, and the bathing beauty.* (p. 26)

Although it is still true, as Mulvey and Berger claimed, that women are more likely than men to be depicted as passive, there have been significant shifts in the portrayal of men in the media. As we discussed earlier in this chapter, the Calvin Klein underwear campaign began a new trend of portraying men as sexual objects rather than as active subjects. Susan Bordo (1999) referred somewhat jokingly to the men in this genre of advertisements as "leaners"; they are depicted in reclining postures rather than "more traditional representations, which pose the male body heroically upright, fully conscious looking bravely onto the world, ready for action" (p. 22). Today, Bordo continued,

> we are seeing more and more male bodies that do not assert themselves aggressively, but ask to be admired, loved, or sexually dominated . . . [as in a] . . . Calvin Klein "Escape" advertisement [that] depicts a young, sensuous-looking man leaning against a wall, dark underarm hair exposed. His eyes seek out the imagined viewer, soberly but flirtatiously. "Take Me," the copy reads. (p. 22)

This imagery increasingly pushes men to gaze at themselves in the way that historically they have been expected to gaze at women. Patterson and Elliot (2002) referred to this as the inversion of the male gaze. This new development seems to be a result of rising gay visibility and marketers' attempts to get men to function more like female consumers. Many identify these new objectifying images as part of a dual marketing strategy meant to appeal to both gay and straight men (Bordo; Rohlinger, 2002; Stabiner, 1982).

Not only does modern imagery objectify people (most often women), but also such images are frequently crafted to cause **fragmentation**—the reduction of a person to a particular body part. In much of the media, cameras focus on a particular body part and neglect the whole person. The Renaissance artist Albrecht Dürer approached his work similarly, believing that the ideal of beauty should be achieved by taking various ideally beautiful body parts from different women and combining them in one artistic rendering (Berger). This reflected a view that the artist's job was to *create* beauty rather than to reflect the beauty of actual women—an idea that seems pervasive in the media in the age of Photoshop. Beauty, then, is a Frankenstein's monster, an impossible ideal composed of body parts knit together by an artist or image editor. Berger argued that although this was supposed to glorify humans, it instead "presumed a remarkable indifference to who any one person really was" (p. 62). To be beautiful according to this conception is to lack individual character and to be conventional (conforming to an artificial standard that is not original, natural, or spontaneous).

To some extent, the conventionalization of beauty is what enables a Renaissance man to show off the beauty of his wife in an oil painting. Without some

ON THE web

Read about the **Bechdel test for representations of women in the media** on the Student Website: www.oup.com/us/gillis-jacobs

degree of standardization or uniformity of beauty standards, the Renaissance man cannot anticipate what others will find beautiful. Conventionalizing beauty (or ugliness or other traits such as coolness) is also important in the mass media; coding a person as beautiful or cool enables viewers to immediately understand in a 30-second ad that Axe body spray makes men attractive to beautiful women or to recognize while channel surfing that a character on a new sitcom is uncool and should be the object of laughter. The fact that this conventionality creates a remarkably unreal world populated with caricatures of actual people is unimportant to the goals of advertising and ad-driven media—but perhaps it should be important to us.

Objectification and fragmentation are important because they can have moral consequences. Generally speaking, objects do not have the same moral status as people. If you own an object, you can destroy it if you want—others may say it is foolish to do so, but you are within your rights to destroy it, nonetheless. Many theorists argue that the moral problem with objectification and fragmentation is that by reducing a person to a "mere instrument" (to use Bartky's phrase), you deny (among other things) the autonomy, agency (capacity to act), and subjectivity (feelings and experiences) of the person objectified or fragmented (Papadaki).

Related to objectification is **commodification**, turning something or someone into or treating something or someone as an object that can be bought, sold, and traded. An M&S bra advertisement that shows a woman wearing a revealing bra exemplifies this concept. In the ad, the model's head and the rest of her torso are not visible, only her chest. This objectified and fragmented image of breasts in a sexy bra is meant to appeal to women who imagine themselves in the position of the model, who herself appeals to the male gaze; thus the viewer is, to borrow Berger's words, a woman dreaming of herself being dreamt of. Moreover, the ad text, "Quality worth every penny," implies that both the bra and the breasts should be viewed as commodities that are worth spending money on (Lacey, 2009). (See the ad on the Student Website.)

Is objectification always bad? Some argue that objectification may not always be negative. In this view, it may be acceptable to appreciate people as objects of beauty or instruments of pleasure provided that it does not come at the expense of their status as beings whose subjectivity should be respected. Leslie Green (2000) for example, stated that

most people desperately want *to be of use to others, and they come to understand themselves partly through their uses. . . . Of course, they do not want only that, and they want to be of use and used subject to certain constraints—but the idea of being useful is in fact valued. Part of what is at stake when people age, when they are severely disabled, when they are chronically unemployed, is the fear that they are not, or are no longer, useful. . . . They miss not only their diminished agency, but also their diminished objectivity. In dire cases people may no longer see themselves as something desired, wanted, or useful at all, even as they retain their standing as civic subjects, applicants, supplicants, users or consumers. They become, to coin a term, subjectified. (pp. 45–46, italics in original)*

Others such as Andrea Dworkin and Catharine MacKinnon argue that objectification by definition disregards the humanity of people and is therefore never acceptable (Papadaki).

How do we oppose the move in media and society more generally that seeks to conventionalize beauty and put people (especially women) under an objectifying, fragmenting, and commodifying male gaze? We probably cannot do without conventions altogether, yet we need not give in to them totally. Berger argued that in our aesthetic we should aim to represent the particularity of individuals, even when it is at odds with the prevailing notions of beauty as a way to reflect their humanity. Berger's aesthetic also allows room for explicitly sexual representations. As long as sexually explicit imagery reflects the subjectivity of people—their feelings, opinions, and preferences—he believes it does not strip them of their humanity.

CONCLUSION

Our bodies have always been shaped by a variety of forces, and hopes of returning to a purely natural state or doing away with style as it relates to the presentation of our bodies seems impossible.

The history of female and male body shape and fashion are good examples of how political, economic, and social forces have left their mark on embodied style—although how much body shape and fashion are actively chosen or imposed on people seems to be an open question. Meaning is created not only by the wearer of the fashion, but also by the viewer of the fashion. Any number of factors including race, class, gender, and sense of national or ethnic identity of the bearer of the style and the viewer influence how fashion symbols are interpreted.

Understanding how we view gendered bodies and the consequences of the dominant cultural perspective of the male gaze is important if we are to develop a more humane aesthetic. The issues of colorism and fat studies are good cases in point. Surrendering to dominant cultural and economic forces often seems at odds with human happiness. But with the appropriate analytical tools, one has the possibility of forging a better world.

THINK, LEARN, ACT

The following resources are available on the Student Website: www.oup.com/us/gillis-jacobs

Taking Stock, Taking Action prompts and activities. Apply what you've learned to take action on campus and in the broader community.

Recommended Readings and Multimedia Resources, including scholarly and literary works, documentaries, feature films, podcasts and more, to enrich the in- and out-of-classroom experience.

KEY TERMS

Aesthetics 210

Colorism 194

Commodification 215

Embodiment 184

Exoticize 211

Fat 184

Fragmentation 214

Great masculine
  renunciation 202

Health at Every Size 185

Ideal viewer 211

Male gaze 213

Metrosexual 208

Objectification 213

Politics of
  respectability 188

Voyeur 213

WORK, INEQUALITY, AND NEOLIBERALISM

In *Beyond the Double Bind,* Kathleen Hall Jamieson (1995), a professor of communication, chronicled American women's struggles to overcome the "traps" that have been used to keep women in their places. These traps, or double binds, offer up false choices; women must be either "wombs or brains," must choose either "femininity or competence." They cannot have both or be both—and whatever they choose, wrote Jamieson, they lose. Jamieson included a brief autobiographical note, evidence of the double binds that have tied. She noted that her great-grandmother was denied access to higher education and that her mother, despite being the valedictorian of her high school class, did not attend college. But Jamieson and her two sisters all completed college and she went on to earn a PhD.

The first offer of a university job she ever had was withdrawn, she wrote, because she "had the poor judgment to tell" the department chair she was pregnant (Jamieson, p. viii). But the same university (different chair) hired her 2 years later, despite Jamieson's telling them she planned to have another child. "The world had changed," she asserted (p. viii). Affirmative action and other legal protections were in place that had not been previously. When Jamieson studied at the University of Wisconsin, there were no female members of the graduate faculty in her department. But by 1995, a woman chaired the department. She herself became a dean at the University of Pennsylvania, an Ivy League school (which in 1995 was also headed by a woman). In 1967, Jamieson was denied a fellowship because she was shortly to be married. In 1989, she received that fellowship, marriage ring and all. "Subtle and overt forms of sex discrimination persist," asserted Jamieson, but there are now avenues of redress, and not just for "the educated and well-to-do" but for all women (p. viii).

Jamieson's is just one story and we should not overgeneralize based on her experience, but if we each look back through our family histories, we will likely see that the relationship of women to work has changed, perhaps dramatically. Women in the United States today are more likely to go to college and more likely to seek and do paid work. Yet labor participation rates are still lower for women than men, and women are overrepresented in service-oriented jobs that often have low pay, no benefits, and little job security. Women still earn less than men for jobs that require substantially the same skills, and the number of women in leadership positions, particularly women of color, remains stubbornly low. In this chapter we will examine these issues, as well as the effects of globalization on workers worldwide.

EXAMINING UNEQUAL PAY

According to the International Labor Organization, women make 10 to 30 percent less globally than men (United Nations, 2010). The **pay gap** is similar in Europe (15 to 25 percent) and the United States (22 percent, when comparing annual earnings for full-time wage and salary workers) (Hegewisch et al., 2014).

Disaggregated data taking race and ethnicity into account reveal even larger pay gaps. In the United States, Hispanic women earn just 54 percent of what white men earn annually (but 90 percent of what Hispanic men earn). African American women earn 64 percent of what white men earn (but 91 percent of what African American men earn). Asian women and men in the United States have the highest median weekly earnings, but Asian American women earn only 79 cents for every dollar Asian American men earn (DeNavas-Walt & Proctor, 2014). The smaller pay gaps between African American and Hispanic women and men are a result of the fact that men in these groups earn substantially less—29 and 40 percent, respectively—than white men.

Although it is tempting to think of the gender pay gap as a "women's problem," that framing misses the real story. Unequal pay may most directly affect women, but many women have families and those families are also negatively affected. Unequal pay for women can also place more burden on the shoulders of "traditional breadwinners," that is, men, who face more pressure to work and less flexibility to take time off or act as caregivers when female partners do not earn a fair wage. Unequal pay, along with a culture of overwork, point not to a "women's problem" but a "work problem" (Slaughter, 2015). (A note on terminology: although the fact that women make less than men for waged work is called a "gender" or "gender-based" pay gap, it is, strictly speaking, a "sex-based" pay gap, that is, it is based on one's sex (being a woman), not on one's gender (being feminine). We use the term gender here because it is used in the research literature but recognize that sex or sex-based would be more accurate.)

Lesbian, gay, bisexual, and transgender people also experience significant pay gaps. Studies have shown, for example, that gay men make 10 to 32 percent less than heterosexual men. Men in same-sex couples also consistently earn less than men in female/male marriages, whereas women in same-sex couples generally earn the same or more than women in female/male marriages (but less than coupled gay men or men in female/male marriages) (Sears & Malloy, 2011).

Men and the Racial Earnings Gap

The racial earnings gap between Black men and white men decreased substantially between 1960 and 2000 (Semyonov & Lewin-Epstein, 2009). By 2013, however, gains were being reversed, with the racial earnings gap between Black men and white men growing slightly (DeNavas-Walt & Proctor). For Black men, there are significant differences between the public (government-related) and private sectors when it comes to the racial pay gap. In the public sector, the disparity in pay between Black men and white men has nearly disappeared, but in the private sector, it remains significant, roughly equivalent to where the public sector was 30 years ago. Organizational structure and regulations, unionization, and affirmative action policies likely explain pay equity in the public sector (Semyonov & Lewin-Epstein).

MORE ABOUT...

FIGURE 8.1

Going up? Studies show that companies with women in top roles earn higher profits than do companies with all-male leadership. Yet in one recent study, more than 50 percent of companies globally had no female executives (Victor, 2016).

Gender
Pay gap

Starting Out Behind, Staying Behind

The "gender" pay gap begins early in women's careers and grows as they age. In 2013, among full-time workers in the United States ages 16–19, women earned 88 percent of what men earned weekly. Among college graduates the gap is larger. In one study, women one year out of college working full time earned only 82 percent of what their male peers earned (C. Corbett & Hill, 2012). Although women make up some ground in their 20s and early 30s, the gap widens dramatically for most women after age 35. According to the U.S. Bureau of Labor Statistics (2013), women 35–44 years old earn just 78 percent of what men of the same age earn; women 45–54 years old earn just 75 percent. The situation is similar in Europe, with women under 30 experiencing a 7 percent pay gap, but women between the ages of 50 and 59 experiencing a 30 percent pay gap (United Nations).

Why do women start out behind? College major and type of job pursued after graduation are factors. Women are overrepresented in some college majors, like education, and underrepresented in others, like computer science. Although there was rapid sex-based desegregation of college majors from the 1970s to the mid-1980s, in some fields women have lost ground of late, including computer science, where 37 percent of degrees were awarded to women in 1985, but only 18 percent were awarded to women in 2014 (C. Miller, 2014a).

Choice of college major can explain some, but not all, of the gender pay gap. Researchers have shown that women tend to begin their careers earning less than men even when they have similar academic credentials (Weinberger, 2011). A recent study of science professors illustrates one way this may happen. In the study, professors in biology, chemistry, and physics departments at six universities were asked to evaluate the application of a recent graduate seeking a job as a laboratory manager. In half of the applications, the candidate was identified as female (Jennifer) and in the other half as male (John). The applications were otherwise identical. The science professors rated John higher than Jennifer and offered him an average starting salary of $30,328, whereas they offered Jennifer on average $26,508, for a pay gap of 13 percent (Chang, 2012).

Although women in the United States earn more associate's, bachelor's, and master's degrees then men, having a higher degree does not narrow the earnings gap for women. In fact, in some cases, the gender pay gap is larger at higher levels of education (American Association of University Women, 2016).

FIGURE 8.2

A woman must earn a PhD to earn as much on average as a man with a bachelor's degree (Jaffe, 2013).

Black men experience a similar phenomenon; the pay gap between Black men and white men with associate's degrees is 21 percent, whereas at the bachelor's and master's levels, the pay gap grows to 27 percent (Wilson, 2011). But a closer look at the data reveals a more complex picture. The racial pay gap varies by socioeconomic background (Pais, 2011). Pais found the largest gap between working- and lower-middle-class Black men and their white male counterparts, but found no evidence of an earnings gap between Black men and white men from upper-middle-class backgrounds. Coming from a low socioeconomic background seems to continue to disadvantage even Black men who have earned college degrees and work in white-collar occupations. Pais explained, "Blacks from working class backgrounds find it [much] . . . more difficult than whites from working class backgrounds to succeed in attaining access to, and prospering in, high paying career fields" (p. 48). Why? Upper-middle-class

ON THE
web

Read about what you should do **if you experience workplace discrimination** on the Student Website: www.oup.com/us/gillis-jacobs

Blacks may benefit more from affirmative action policies and work in environments that are generally less conducive to racial discrimination, whereas blue-collar workplaces may have more racial discrimination and fewer affirmative action policies (Pais).

The fact that women enter different occupations and different industries than men plays a "substantial role" in the gender wage gap (Blau & Kahn, 2016, p. 7). Pay is less in many fields where women outnumber men. Teaching is a good example of an occupation that is lower paying than occupations that require the same level of education—and the majority of teachers, particularly at the elementary school level, are women. Researchers have found that the difference in pay between female-dominated and male-dominated occupations cannot be fully explained by educational or skill requirements, but instead seems to result at least in part from gender stereotyping (Levanon et al., 2009). Because men are generally stereotyped as more competent and status worthy, the work they do is often assigned greater value. Conversely, work done by women is devalued, leading to lower pay (Levanon et al.). What about men who work in female-dominated fields such as nursing? Male nurses—about 10 percent of the field—make on average $5,100 more than female colleagues in similar positions (Saint Louis, 2015). The gap is larger in certain specialties, like nurse anesthetists, where women earn $17,290 less per year than men (Saint Louis). The pay gap also exists for women in traditionally male occupations; sometimes it is much greater in these occupations, such as in the financial sector; sometimes it is less, as in engineering.

As women's careers progress, the earnings gap with men grows. Why? One explanation has been that women are more likely to interrupt work to take on family responsibilities. In so doing, women lose ground in comparison to men in two areas that affect wages: they work fewer hours of paid labor than men per year and they have fewer years of job experience. In fact, the experience gap was a significant factor into the 1980s, but since then, women have greatly reduced this gap, explaining in part why the gender pay gap has also been reduced. So, although the experience gap used to be a particularly important factor, it is no longer as relevant (Blau & Kahn).

Studies have attempted to isolate the role of sex in the pay gap by controlling for as many other factors as possible. One study found that "after accounting for all variables known to affect earnings" including college major, occupation, employment sector, differences in the hours worked, college type and selectivity, grade point average, occupational segregation, race/ethnicity, geographic location, age, and marital status, an "unexplained wage gap" of 6.6 percent remained between women and men one year after college graduation

(C. Corbett & Hill, p. 39). Ten years after graduation, the unexplained difference in earnings grew to 12 percent (Dey & Hill, 2007). The economists Francine Blau and Lawrence Kahn concluded that the "persistence of an unexplained gender wage gap suggests, though it does not prove, that labor market discrimination continues to contribute to the gender wage gap" (p. 50). Other factors may include the greater tendency of women to forego workplace advancement in exchange for greater flexibility (U.S. General Accounting Office, 2003) and the fact that men are more likely than women to negotiate for their salaries may also contribute (AAUW).

The gender pay gap translates into thousands of dollars of lost wages for women and their families. A high school graduate who begins her career making $20,000 annually will lose $700,000 over the course of her career because of the wage gap; a college graduate with a starting salary of $30,000 will lose $1.2 million over the course of her career; and a professional school graduate with a starting salary of $70,000 will lose $2 million in her lifetime. Lower wages also mean lower retirement and social security benefits, which are based on the money earned over the course of a career (WAGE Project, 2012).

One way for women to make up for these lost wages may be to learn to negotiate. Research shows that women are less likely to negotiate salary than their male counterparts, yet this one act, done well, can make a big difference. Key tactics (that can work for women and men) include the following: never name a salary figure first (provide a range, not a number, if you are pressed); do not say what you made at your last job unless explicitly asked; consider initial offers just that, initial; and never say yes to an offer immediately. For women, when it comes to negotiating there is an important caveat—how women ask seems to be nearly as important as the asking itself. Research has shown that when women negotiate, they can be seen as aggressive and less likable unless they conform to feminine expectations. (Check out wageproject.org for more information.)

Negotiations

PAID WORK AND PARENTING

Mothers drop out of the workforce or move to part-time work at a much higher rate than fathers—40 percent of mothers versus just 3 percent of fathers (AAUW). And although the number of stay-at-home dads has doubled in the past decade, fathers still make up just more than 3 percent of all stay-at-home parents in the United States.

In a number of Western countries, women with children suffer a substantial **motherhood penalty** (Blau & Kahn; Misra et al., 2005; U.S. Government

FIGURE 8.3

In the United States, about 70 percent of women with children at home are in the labor force. Many end up on the "mommy track," doing part-time or more flexible work to try to achieve a work–family balance, which often negatively affects their earnings.

Accounting Office). In fact, in the United States among women under age 35, the pay gap is larger between mothers and nonmothers than it is between women and men. Research shows mothers are often rated as less competent, less committed, and less promotable than women without children and are less likely to be recommended for management positions (Correll et al., 2007). Studies taking race into consideration show a more complicated picture. One recent U.S. study found that Latinas suffer no motherhood wage penalty. Among African American women, only married women with more than two children seem to pay a wage penalty. For white women, however, both married and never-married mothers experience a pay penalty (Glauber, 2007).

Black, Latino, and white men, in contrast, seem to benefit from both a **marriage premium** and a **fatherhood premium**, although one study showed Latino and white men benefiting more than Black men (Correll et al.; Glauber, 2008). Studies have found that fathers are rated significantly more committed to their jobs and offered significantly higher salaries than nonfathers (Correll et al.; U.S. Government Accounting Office). The result of the fatherhood wage premium and motherhood wage penalty is to widen the gender gap in earnings over the course of women's and men's lives (Glauber, 2008).

What accounts for the motherhood penalty and the fatherhood premium? Researchers at Cornell University surmised that "cultural understandings of the motherhood role exist in tension with the cultural understandings of the 'ideal worker' role," but the roles of good father and good worker are not seen as incompatible. Although work interruptions, working part-time, and decreased seniority and experience can account for some of the motherhood penalty (about one-third), discrimination also seems to play a significant role (Budig & England, 2001; Correll et al.).

FIGURE 8.4
Black fathers seem to benefit less from the fatherhood wage premium than both white and Latino fathers.

Although gender roles are becoming more egalitarian and women increasingly contribute to the economic well-being of families, many men still feel pressure to be their families' primary financial providers. A considerable number of men also feel they should be more involved at home. Aumann et al. (2011) labeled this phenomenon the **new male mystique**, a play on the term **feminine mystique** coined by Betty Friedan in her 1963 book of the same title. In *The Feminine Mystique*, Friedan described what she called "the problem that has no name"—widespread unhappiness among "housewives" from middle- and upper-income (predominantly white) families in the 1950s and 1960s who lived comfortably yet felt they were missing something. Friedan cataloged how popular culture pushed the message that women were naturally fulfilled by devoting themselves to wife- and motherhood (an idea she termed the feminine mystique). (See Chapters 11 and 12 for more on Betty Friedan.)

Like some housewives of the 1950s and 1960s, some men today may feel caught between "old and new worlds," between "traditional views about their roles as breadwinners" and emerging gender roles "that encourage men to participate in family life" (Aumann et al., pp. 2–3). As a result, men report experiencing significantly more work–family conflict today than 30 years ago, whereas women do not; men who hold traditional gender role values are the most likely to experience such conflict (Aumann et al.).

FIGURE 8.5

In 2013, the U.S. secretary of defense rescinded the ban on women serving in ground combat units. Because women have been officially excluded from combat roles, they have had a more difficult time being promoted to leadership positions in the military.

WOMEN'S WORK, MEN'S WORK

Women and men in all regions of the world experience **sex segregation in employment** (also called occupational segregation). Globally, women are more concentrated in service-oriented occupations (clerks, professional service workers, shop and market sales), which require skills that are thought of as more feminine, the sorts of skills women often use at home to care for their families. Men, by contrast, are overrepresented among manual laborers, machine operators, industrial laborers, and managers, among other occupations. Although sex segregation in the U.S. labor force has decreased markedly over the past 40 years, its decline has been uneven; occupational segregation decreased sharply from the 1960s to the 1980s, more slowly in the 1990s, and hardly at all from 2000 to 2010 (AAUW; Cotter et al., 2012). Furthermore, most of the decline has happened in middle-class occupations, whereas working-class occupations remain nearly as segregated as in 1950 and have become more segregated since 1990 (Cotter et al.).

Overall in the United States, less than 6 percent of women work in traditionally male occupations and less than 5 percent of men work in traditionally female occupations (Table 8.1; Hegewisch et al., 2012). Historically, occupational segregation and the gender pay gap move in tandem. That is, as occupational segregation declines, so does the pay gap (Hegewisch et al., 2014).

There are varying degrees of occupational sex segregation within different racial and ethnic groups. Among different ethnic groups in the United States, Hispanic women and men are the least likely to work in the same occupations, whereas Asian American women and men are the most likely.

Segregation by race and ethnicity within occupations and individual workplaces is also common in the United States, where Blacks and ethnic minorities are often clustered at the bottom. One recent study found that differences in education could not account for segregation of Blacks in the workplace and suggested that further research should examine explanations unrelated to skills, including discrimination and residential segregation (the fact that Blacks and whites tend to live in different neighborhoods or places) (Hellerstein & Neumark, 2008). The same study found that ethnic segregation in the workplace

TABLE 8.1
Female-Dominated and Male-Dominated Occupations

WHERE WOMEN DOMINATE

Prekindergarten and kindergarten teachers	98 percent women
Secretaries	95 percent
Licensed practical nurses	92 percent
Receptionists	91 percent
Registered nurses	89 percent

WHERE MEN DOMINATE

Electricians	98 percent men
Construction laborers	97 percent
Truck drivers	96 percent
Groundskeepers	96 percent
Construction managers	92 percent

Source: U.S. Bureau of Labor Statistics, U.S. Department of Labor. (2013). Labor Force Statistics from the Current Population Survey. Retrieved February 15, 2013, from http://www.bls.gov/cps/cpsaat37.htm.

Silicon Valley's Diversity Problem

High-tech companies are dominated by white and Asian men. Among technical employees in particular, few are women (15 percent at Facebook, 17 percent at Google) and even fewer are Latino or Black (C. Miller, 2014a; *New York Times* editorial board, 2014a). Should it matter? Beyond issues of basic fairness, many studies show that more diverse companies tend to be more creative and profitable (Bajaj, 2015). Although tech companies are beginning to address these issues, there are challenges to recruiting and maintaining a diverse high-tech workforce. One major challenge is what some have characterized as "Silicon Valley's aggressive frat-boy culture" (Streitfeld, 2015, B2). Another is a shrinking number of female computer science majors. Among women who work in the high-tech industry, the dropout rate is high, in fact, twice as high as the rate for their male colleagues. Many women report leaving high-tech jobs because of extreme pressure and a hostile work environment (*New York Times* editorial board, 2014a).

MORE ABOUT....

is largely a result of language proficiency, but suggested that discrimination should also be examined as a factor (Hellerstein & Neumark).

Why does occupational segregation matter? Researchers have found that occupations with a higher percentage of females generally pay less than those with a higher percentage of males—and that this is true even when the occupations require substantially the same education and skills (Levanon et al.). They have also found that as women move into an occupational field in greater numbers—this is called **occupational feminization**—relative pay diminishes (Blau & Kahn; Levanon et al.). The same effect is demonstrated when racial and ethnic minorities move into a field. Overall in the United States, more than twice as many women as men work in occupations with median earnings for full-time work below the federal poverty level for a family of four (5.52 million women versus 2.3 million men) (Hegewisch et al., 2014); and although women make up just under half the U.S. workforce, they comprise nearly two-thirds of minimum wage workers and two-thirds of tipped workers; women of color alone comprise nearly one-fourth of minimum wage workers (Dube, 2013; Jaffe; National Women's Law Center, 2015). It is also interesting to note that whereas more than a quarter of minimum wage workers in 1979 were teenagers, today about 90 percent of such workers are adults, many of whom are trying to support families (Dube).

In 2015, the federal minimum wage in the United States was $7.25 per hour. At this rate, a full-time worker makes $14,500 per year, well below poverty level for a family of three (National Women's Law Center). Congress has raised the minimum wage only three times over the past 30 years. As a result, the minimum wage is worth 24 percent less today than it was in 1968 (National Women's Law Center). In response, workers nationwide are organizing for a living wage. For example, fast-food workers in more than 150 U.S. cities have engaged in strikes and civil disobedience to demand higher pay and the right to unionize (Greenhouse, 2014a). Hotel workers in Los Angeles won a wage increase to $15.37 per hour (Greenhouse, 2014c). In the wake of congressional inaction, more than half of states have enacted minimum wages higher than the federal standard, and major cities, including New York, Chicago, Los Angeles, San Francisco, and Seattle, have raised or are considering raising minimum wages as high as $15 per hour.

When compared with other developed countries globally, the U.S. minimum wage is near the bottom (Dube). In Denmark, for example, fast-food workers make the equivalent of $20 per hour, two and a half times what many fast-food workers in the United States earn (Alderman & Greenhouse, 2014).

One important question that must be faced is whether raising the minimum wage will lead to job losses. Several rigorous new studies suggest the number of jobs lost has been small, in some cases statistically indistinguishable from zero, in places where wage increases have taken place. Why is that? In the fast-food industry, for example, raising the price of a $3 burger by just a few pennies can cover much of the increased wage costs. Higher wages also tend to lower worker turnover, which saves businesses money (Dube). But local circumstances will affect job losses.

In what fields are women paid more equitably? In the traditionally male-dominated areas of science, technology, engineering, and mathematics (known collectively as STEM), the gender pay gap is smaller than that in the labor force as a whole; this is also true among federal government workers. Among female and male police and sheriff's patrol officers, there is almost parity, with women earning 99 percent of what men earn (Hegewisch et al., 2012). It seems likely that female federal workers and patrol officers do better because their wages are governed by union contracts. In fact, unionization raises women's wages by almost 13 percent, or $2.50 per hour, compared with nonunion women with similar characteristics. Female union members are also more likely to have employer-provided health insurance and an employer-provided pension than women who are not in unions (Schmitt & Woo, 2013). Increased unionization among female workers (relative to male workers) has been one factor in closing the gender wage gap (Blau & Kahn).

The gender pay gap in the United States has closed considerably over time, which is good news for women and families that increasingly depend on women's earnings. However, this good news has a downside. Women have closed the gap with men largely because real wages for men are virtually unchanged since 1975, whereas during the same time, women's real wages have risen 25 percent. Progress closing the gender gap has slowed considerably over time. From 1981 to 1990, the gap narrowed by more than 10 percent, but since 2001, the gender pay gap has narrowed by only 1 percent (Hegewisch et al., 2012).

FIGURE 8.6

Rosie the Riveter has become an iconic American figure, originally representing women who worked in factories during World War II.

FEWER WOMEN AND PEOPLE OF COLOR AT THE TOP

Even when women and men work within the same occupational field, they are often employed at different levels, a phenomenon known as **sex stratification in employment**. Men tend to be overrepresented in the top tier and often predominate in higher-paying, higher-prestige jobs, whereas women are often clustered in the middle and bottom, in lower-paying, lower-prestige jobs. Take the example of educators. Women overwhelmingly fill the ranks of preschool and elementary school teachers, whereas men predominate among full-time university professors (white men in particular make up the single largest group among university professors, another indicator of racial stratification).

It is not that women are never found in positions of power. Women make up 38 percent of the management workforce, for example. But many women are ghettoized in lower-paying, lower-status managerial positions such as day care managers (94 percent are women) and nursing home managers (75 percent are women). In blue-collar industries, women are still virtually invisible in management (Cohen, 2012a).

At the very highest levels, women are much more scarce. In fact, women make up only 25 percent of chief executive officers in the United States and only 4.2 percent in Fortune 500 companies (the top 500 companies in the United States as determined by gross revenues) (Catalyst, 2016; "Forbes 400," 2014). Similarly, in Europe, only 3.2 percent of the presidents and chairpersons of large companies are women (Castle, 2012). For women of color in the United States, the numbers are even starker. In 2012, African American women made up only 5.3 percent of all managers, professionals, and related occupations, Latinas 3.9 percent, and Asian American women only 2.7 percent. That same year among the Fortune 500 companies, one was headed by an African American woman and one by an Asian woman (Catalyst, 2012).

In the United States, men of color are also underrepresented in and slower to advance to managerial positions (see, for example, Maume, 1999), although at least one study has found that among Black men who are college graduates, the effect of race on promotions is eliminated (Maume). (The author noted, however, that young college graduates constitute less than 10 percent of the Black population.)

Why are women so rare at the very top? Women face multiple obstacles to advancement, including prejudice, resistance to women's leadership, and the pressures of balancing work and family (Eagly & Carli, 2007). Studies have repeatedly shown that promotions come more slowly for women than for men with equivalent qualifications. Adia Harvey Wingfield (2009) explained: "Gendered perceptions about men's roles, abilities and skills privilege them and facilitate their advancement" (p. 8). But, noted Wingfield, when race is also considered, the results become more nuanced. Studies have consistently shown that whereas white men have an advantage when they enter the labor market and in attaining managerial positions, Black and Latino men experience no such advantage. Even in female-dominated fields like nursing, white men ascend to supervisory positions more quickly than women in general and Black men, which has led some researchers to posit the existence of a **glass escalator** that is both gendered and racialized (Eagly & Carli; C. Williams, 2013; Wingfield). White trans men who achieved the most masculine presentations of themselves also benefited from the glass escalator. After transitioning, trans men were considered more competent, were able to exercise more authority, and received greater rewards compared with when they were women (C. Williams, 2013). By contrast, trans women experienced greater workplace discrimination, as did trans men who were not perceived as masculine (C. Williams, 2013). C. Williams (2013) posited that the glass escalator is also tied to class in that it applies to jobs that offer built-in opportunities for advancement, which are primarily middle class and professional in nature. C. Williams (2013) noted that given the shift away from stable, long-term employment toward on-demand, low-wage, high-turnover jobs, concepts such as the glass escalator may need to be replaced by new metaphors that critique the exploitation of the contemporary workplace.

Women Leaders in a Bind

Stereotypes that ascribe different characteristics to women and men have a strong pull in the workplace. According to such stereotypes, men are more agentic (assertive, ambitious, and individualistic) and women are more communal (friendly, gentle, and helpful). It is agentic characteristics that are most associated with effective leadership.

Women leaders (and men, too, to some extent) may fear social rejection and other negative consequences when they go outside expected behavioral norms. But when *women* are expected to be one way and *leaders* another, this puts women leaders in a difficult position. As a result, women in leadership positions can face double binds; they are "damned if they do and doomed if they don't" (Catalyst, 2007). Catalyst (2007) has identified two related but distinct double bind dilemmas for women leaders:

> *Too soft or too tough*: Women leaders are often seen as either too soft or too tough but rarely "just right."

FIGURE 8.7
Women leaders often face a double bind because the demands of being stereotypically feminine conflict with the desire to be independent or exercise control. Male leaders face no such double bind.

Competent or liked: Women leaders are seen as competent or likable, but rarely both.

Women face a series of disadvantages in the competition for leadership positions. They often work fewer hours and have less job experience, in part because women generally bear the brunt of housework and child care at home, even when they work outside the home. Even women who do not interrupt careers are often at a disadvantage because, in spending more time on family, they miss out on socializing with colleagues and building professional networks, which one study has found to be even more important than skills or job performance in career advancement (Eagly & Carli).

Recent research has asked, "What sorts of jobs are women given when they finally make it into senior

breaking the frame
Glass Ceiling or Labyrinth?

The underrepresentation of women and minorities in high-level occupations has been attributed to the existence of a **glass ceiling**, a term that first appeared in the *Wall Street Journal* in 1986 to describe an invisible barrier preventing women from reaching the highest levels of the corporate ladder. In addition to being underrepresented at the highest levels, when women do reach the top, they face a larger gender pay gap than middle- and lower-wage female workers (Blau & Kahn).

Eagly and Carli suggested that women do not bump up against a glass ceiling as they approach the top so much as they are forced to navigate a labyrinth throughout their careers, replete with obstacles they must overcome to make it to the upper ranks of any organization. The popular phrase "breaking through the glass ceiling" may suggest that success for women can be achieved by sheer force of effort or a single policy solution. The labyrinth metaphor more accurately captures the ongoing and intractable nature of the problem. (C. Williams (2013) reminds us that whether it is a ceiling or a labyrinth, these metaphors apply almost exclusively to professional work and addressing race-, class-, and sex-based exploitation in low-paying jobs requires a different focus altogether.)

leadership positions?" (Hewlett, 2008). The answer? More so than men, women are likely to break through to senior leadership if an organization is in crisis, thus finding themselves on what has been called the **glass cliff**. (One often-cited example is Marissa Mayer at Yahoo!) Such situations are inherently risky and women leaders may be more isolated than men and may find it more difficult to rally support in the face of difficulties (Hewlett).

THE POLITICS OF HOUSEWORK

"I want a wife," wrote Judy Syfers in the inaugural issue of *Ms. Magazine* (1972, reprint 1990), "a wife who will work and send me to school. And while I am going to school, I want a wife to take care of my children." She went on to catalog all that a wife would do for her—keep track of the children's appointments (and hers, too), arrange for the children's schooling, care, and social life, care

FIGURE 8.8

Women globally dedicate more time to domestic work than men. In the Global North, women average almost 5 hours per day versus 2.5 for men. In Asia, there is a particularly large gap between women's and men's domestic work, with women putting in four times as many hours as men (United Nations).

for the children when they are sick, take time away from work when the children have special needs, keep the house and clothes clean and mended, do the grocery shopping and cook the meals, take care of their social life, be a good listener, be sensitive to her sexual needs, and assume complete responsibility for birth control. "My God," concluded Syfers, "who wouldn't want a wife?"

That was more than 40 years ago. How much has changed today? Perhaps we should begin with the question, who does the "wife's" work at your house? If you are part of a family with two parents, then it is likely that both parents contribute significant time each week to household work. If your family consists of female and male partners, then it is also likely that the mother (perhaps with the help of other females in the household) does the bulk of the household chores, just as women did 4 decades ago (Bridgeman et al., 2012). Today, however, she is likely to do less housework than her counterpart in 1965 and she is more likely to do paid work outside the home. Your father is also likely to contribute more hours to housework than his 1965 counterpart.

Still, globally women shoulder much more of the burden of unpaid work than men, making women's total work day (paid and unpaid) on average longer than men's. The most balanced unpaid workloads are found in Norway, Sweden, and Denmark. In Norway, for example, women do 3.6 hours of unpaid work per day and men 3.1. In fact, in these countries, men's total work day (paid and unpaid) is slightly longer than women's total work day (Organization for Economic Cooperation and Development, 2016). In the United States, the comparable numbers are 4.1 hours of unpaid work per day for women versus 2.7 for men (Organization for Economic Cooperation and Development)—and U.S. women's total work day remains longer than men's. Although richer countries tend to have smaller time gaps for unpaid work than poorer countries, there are considerable differences across countries and even among economically similar countries. For example, compare Japan and South Korea with the Nordic countries discussed earlier. In Japan, women do 5 hours of unpaid work per day versus only 1 hour for men. Similarly, in South Korea, women do nearly 4 hours of unpaid work per day but men only 42 minutes.

The Value of All That Housework

"How ironic," wrote the economist Nancy Folbre (2012), "that the measure we call gross domestic product excludes the value of most domestic work" (that is, work that is done at home, most of which goes unpaid). She went on to explain that unless services are explicitly exchanged for money, they do not count as economic activity as far as official statistics are concerned.

What is all that "housework" worth? It is difficult to calculate the value of unpaid work primarily because many countries do not collect the data to make such a calculation. One recent study found that incorporating the value of nonmarket services (for example, cooking, cleaning, gardening, housework, shopping, and child care done by a household member for which no money is exchanged) into gross domestic product (GDP) raised the U.S. GDP by 26 percent (Bridgeman et al.). (The GDP is the total monetary value of all finished goods and services produced in a country in a year.) Other studies have put the value of unpaid work higher, at 42 percent of GDP for the United States and 45 percent of GDP for Canada (Antonopoulos). It is estimated that globally, the value of unpaid domestic work is between 20 and 60 percent of GDP (Antonopoulos, 2009). But currently unpaid work is rendered invisible.

Why Count Unpaid Work?

She doesn't work. She's just a housewife. She just stays home with the kids.

Have you ever thought of the monetary value of all the work "she" is doing while she is "not working"? Valuing unpaid work points out the fallacy in the notion that "she doesn't work." And that housework is, for the most part, necessary, facilitating learning, training, and paid work outside the home.

Unpaid work supports paid work in several ways. First, it lowers the cost of labor for employers because activities to maintain the laborer are done for free. Thus, business and government can pay workers less (and, in the case of business, retain greater profits). Without unpaid domestic labor, workers would need higher wages to maintain their current standards of living (reducing profits). Unpaid work, then, functions as a hidden subsidy to governments and business, which in turn feel less pressure to pay workers higher wages (Antonopoulos).

Second, unpaid work also makes up for goods and services that the public sector (government) should—but does not—make available (Antonopoulos). This is especially, but not exclusively, true in the Global South where unpaid care work often makes up for gaps in or the lack of public health, education, transportation, sanitation, and child-care programs. (See Appendix B, Names for People and Places for more on Global South.) Women (mostly) spend a tremendous amount of time (essentially a time tax) doing such tasks as gathering water and caring for children, the sick, and the elderly. This severely limits the time they can spend in paid employment, leisure and self-care, political activities, and education (Antonopoulos).

One result of this time tax is that women do not work outside the home or are more likely than men to work part-time. Indeed, the rise in women's employment globally over the past 20 years is largely a result of the creation and growth of a part-time female work force (United Nations). Women are at least twice as likely as men to work part time in three-quarters of countries (United Nations).

Although part-time work can be a boon for some women, it does not come without penalties. In Britain, for example, women working part-time earn 25 percent less per hour than women working full-time, amounting to a **part-time pay penalty** (Manning & Petrongolo, 2006). Researchers have found that the part-time pay penalty is larger for women than for men (Grimshaw & Rubery, 2007). Part-time work not only often translates into lower pay, lower retirement income, and less career advancement, but also contributes to the idea that women are not serious about work and reinforces the model of the male as breadwinner. In response to the part-time pay penalty, the European Union has instituted protections for workers, including prohibiting employers from paying part-time workers less per hour than full-time workers or excluding them from pension plans and paid leave policies (Coontz, 2013a). American workers, by contrast, enjoy none of these protections.

WORK, FAMILY, AND SOCIAL POLICY

Social policies related to work that directly affect children and families vary dramatically from country to country. They include family leave policies, which provide workers with time off (with or without pay) to care for children and other family members; working time regulations, which limit normal hours of employment and guarantee a minimum number of vacation days each year; and public provision of early childhood care and education, which increase the probability women will remain in the labor force (Gornick & Meyers, 2003).

Family leave policies are particularly important to achieving equality of opportunity for women. Such policies ensure that women of childbearing age have access to jobs, that they maintain their wages and benefits during maternity, and that they will not be dismissed if they become pregnant. Maternity

Women Workers in the Kaiser Shipyards

FIGURE 8.9
Welder-trainee Josie Lucille Owens was among nearly 1,000 African American women employed as burners, welders, scalers, and in other capacities at the Kaiser Shipyards in Richmond, California, during World War II.

MORE ABOUT...

In 1943, Kaiser, which built ships for the U.S. war effort, employed 12,000 women in its shipyards in Portland, Oregon, one-third of whom were mothers (Dowley, 2011). When the company found that absenteeism among mothers, largely caused by a lack of dependable child care, was causing production to slow, it did something no company had ever done. Kaiser, with the support of the U.S. Maritime Commission, built two huge child-care centers near the entrance to its shipyards. The centers were open 24 hours a day, 6 days a week (the same as the shipyards). For a nominal fee (75 cents a day), workers could drop off their children on the way to work and pick them up on the way home, along with a packaged hot meal and even their mending. The centers, which served more than 3,800 children, featured grass courtyards with wading pools, covered porches with play equipment, and windows overlooking the shipyards. Teachers all had college degrees. Each center had a nurse, social workers, and dieticians. Children could receive immunizations at the centers and haircuts too. Children whose parents worked the overnight shift were fed dinner, put to bed for the night, and awakened in the morning before their parents ended their shifts. Kaiser closed the child-care centers in 1945 as the war ended, the U.S. government withdrew support, and women were urged to leave the workplace to make way for men returning from war (Dowley).

leave also benefits children because it is associated with lower infant mortality rates (Bernard, 2013). About half the countries of the Global South and 95 percent of the countries of the Global North offer at least 14 weeks of maternity leave (United Nations). (See Appendix B, Names for People and Places for more on Global North.) Globally, only a handful of countries have failed to legislate for paid maternity leave, among them Suriname, Papua New Guinea, and the United States, which is the only "developed" country without paid maternity benefits (Coontz, 2013a).

One important shortfall of legal maternity protections globally is that many groups of women are excluded from these measures. In the United States, for example, almost half of all workers are employed at small companies that are not required to offer any leave at all (C. Miller, 2014b). In the Global South, the percentage of women excluded is often even higher. In the United States, there are also dramatic differences between the benefits offered new mothers who lack a high school diploma versus new mothers with at least a bachelor's degree. Of the former, only 18 percent have access to paid maternity leave compared with 66 percent of the latter (U.S. Census Bureau, 2011b).

To encourage more sharing of responsibilities among parents, paternity leave (or increasingly partner or primary caregiver leave, open to either parent) is becoming more common. Even with these new policies, however, women still utilize maternity and parental leave programs far more often than men, even in countries such as Iceland, Norway, and Sweden, where gender equality is the highest. To encourage more men to use family leave, Norway and Sweden have introduced a **paternity quota**, parental leave that can be used only by fathers and is lost if not used (United Nations). In the United States, the number of companies offering paternity leave declined from 2010 to 2014, and nearly one-third of men report they have no option to take leave, paid or unpaid, for the birth of a child. Those working in blue-collar jobs are the least likely to have access to paternity leave and other flexible work arrangements (C. Miller, 2014b; Sundbye & Hegewisch, 2011). Paternity leave may be particularly important to single fathers and gay couples, who are likely to have no other access to extended time off after the birth or adoption of a child.

There are undeniable benefits to paternity leave; fathers who take a more hands-on role early in children's lives are more likely to be involved later. In heterosexual couples, mothers also benefit when men take paternity leave, with increased career earnings and less postpartum depression. But for men there are tradeoffs, including lower pay, being passed over for promotions, and being stigmatized as weak and uncertain, similar to the penalties suffered by mothers in the workforce (C. Miller, 2014b).

It is not only in the area of parental leave that the United States falls behind when it comes to work–family policies (Table 8.2). Since 1990, wrote Stephanie

	TABLE 8.2 Family Leave Policies
Country	No. of Weeks of Family Leave With Full Pay
Norway	42
Sweden	42
Denmark	37
Finland	29
Netherlands	16
France	16
Germany	14
Belgium	12
United Kingdom	6*
United States	0

*Britain offers 90 percent of weekly earnings for the first 6 weeks of maternity leave.

Norway and Sweden offer families the equivalent of 42 weeks of leave at full pay when a child is born. By contrast, in the United States only employers with 50 or more employees are required to offer eligible employees 12 weeks of *un*paid leave.

Table modified from Gornick and Meyers (2003).

Coontz (2013a), other countries with comparable resources have taken a number of steps to help balance work and family requirements, including limiting normal hours of employment and providing high-quality, affordable (publicly funded) early childhood care. "When the United States' work–family policies are compared with those of countries at similar levels of economic and political development," wrote Coontz (2013a), "the United States comes in dead last" (SR 7). As a result, the percentage of women in the American work force has dropped since 1999, from 74 percent to 69 percent (women ages 25–54), whereas the percentage of women in the work force in countries like Switzerland, Australia, Germany, and France has continued to climb. American women are not choosing to leave their jobs, according to Anne-Marie Slaughter; they are being forced out "by the refusal of their bosses to make it possible for them to fit their family life and their work life together" (SR 1).

More than a dozen countries now have a higher percentage of women in the work force than the United States (C. Miller & Alderman, 2014). The lack of family-friendly policies can be particularly tough for working-class women in the United States, who sometimes choose not to work because the cost of child care exceeds the wages they are able to make (C. Miller & Alderman).

WORK IN A GLOBALIZING WORLD

Ever wonder who made that T-shirt you are wearing? Or the story of your cell phone from factory to store to you? What does made in _____ (fill in the blank: Vietnam, El Salvador, China, Guatemala, Bangladesh, and dozens of others) really mean? Today with a bit of research you can piece together a fairly complete story of much of the clothing and electronics found at major chain stores in your community (even if not *your* particular T-shirt or phone). And that story may reveal some uncomfortable truths.

Most textiles (cloth or woven fabric) and electronics, in fact most products you purchase, are likely not made in the United States (or in any country in the Global North). The reasons mostly come down to money. But the push to supply America's malls with fairly inexpensive (really, *un*fairly inexpensive) clothes, electronics, makeup, and other items often comes at a steep price to those making such items. It also comes at a price to workers in the United States, where thousands of manufacturing jobs have been lost as corporations move production overseas.

Documenting Life on the Global Assembly Line

In 1984, Barbara Ehrenreich and Annette Fuentes described the "**new international division of labor**" in an essay entitled "Life on the Global Assembly Line" published in *Ms. Magazine*. Among other things, Ehrenreich and Fuentes exposed the working conditions of women industrial workers who made up the backbone of this new international division of labor, a system in which production was moved to different parts of the "Third World" while the technology and control (and much of the profits) stayed in the "First World." (See Appendix B, Names for People and Places for more on First World, Third World, and other related terms.)

Ehrenreich and Fuentes noted in 1984 that the overwhelming majority of low-skilled assembly jobs in the Global South were performed by women, a change from earlier times when jobs from foreign corporations routinely went to men, raising their economic status. Ehrenreich and Fuentes explained: "It's an article of faith with management that only women can do, or will do, the monotonous, painstaking work that American business is exporting to the Third World" (para. 7). The authors went on to quote a management consultant, who described the situation thus: "The [factory] girls genuinely enjoy themselves. They're away from their families. They have spending money. Of course it's a regulated experience too—with dormitories to live in—so it's a healthful experience" (para. 8). Ehrenreich and Fuentes, however, described a much different reality.

Researchers found that transnational corporations were exporting the most tedious and hazardous work to the Global South and were often operating without interference from inspectors, trade unions, or local reformers. A prime example of this are the ***maquiladoras*** (factories located in **free trade zones**, sometimes also called special export zones) of Mexico and Central America, which in the 1980s employed mostly young, single, childless females, chosen for their supposed dexterity and docility (Figure 8.10; Fussell, 2000). Maquila work continues in this region, although as production in Mexican maquiladoras has become more technically complex, companies have hired more male workers, resulting in a "significant defeminization" of maquiladoras there (Dominguez et al., 2010, p. 187). In another shift, married women are increasingly viewed as better workers in Mexican maquiladoras, "more mature, reliable and less apt to jump from job to job." Employers justify hiring them by arguing that they are "helping to strengthen Mexican families" (Dominguez et al., p. 187).

According to many scholars, work in maquiladoras has not significantly improved the material lives of local women, nor has it raised their status within their communities and families. "Instead of representing a way of enhancing themselves, the income women earn in the maquiladoras seems only a means of economic survival," concluded Dominguez and colleagues (p. 188). There are some limited exceptions, for example, where unions are present that advocate for women's rights. But even these gains often quickly evaporate in harder economic times (Dominguez et al). And unionization is the rare exception rather than the rule, not only in Mexico and Central America, but also in free trade zones globally, where the bulk of such factories are located. It is not unusual for labor organizers to be banned, threatened, beaten up, or fired (see, for example, Human Rights Watch, 2014).

FIGURE 8.10

Workers in a Mexican maquiladora. In the 1980s, maquiladora workers in Mexico were overwhelmingly young and female, recruited for their dexterity and docility.

Maquiladora workers are routinely paid less than the legal minimum wage and many work extra hours or take on additional domestic work just to make ends meet. Workers often live in slum conditions, without basic services, such as dependable electricity, maintained roads, clean water and sanitation, and access to good hospitals and schools (Dominguez et al.). Sexual harassment and physical violence are significant problems, the "expression of a widespread gender ideology that undervalues women in general and women workers in particular" (Dominguez et al., p. 194).

Ehrenreich and Fuentes documented extremely hazardous work conditions in the South Korean garment industry in 1984, including forced overtime, rotating day and night shifts, and amphetamine injections so laborers could meet production quotas. More recently, the collapse of the Rana Plaza garment factory outside Dhaka, Bangladesh, which killed 1,100 workers making garments for export to the United States and Europe, is a reminder of how dangerous such work remains. Garment factories in Indonesia, Sri Lanka, and the Philippines (among other places) still subject workers to practices like those Ehrenreich and Fuentes identified more than 30 years ago. In these countries, garment workers, more than three-quarters of whom are women, are routinely forced to work up to 40 hours of overtime per week. If they fail to meet production quotas, they are subject to physical and mental abuse (M. Bunting, 2011).

It is not only workers who suffer. In Bangladesh, garment and textile factories supplying transnational corporations have been major contributors to a "water pollution disaster" (Yardley, 2013). Rice paddies are contaminated with toxic waste water and fish stocks are dying. Schoolchildren report being sickened by toxic fumes. One local official said he was powerless to stop the pollution. "These people who are setting up industries and factories are much more powerful than me," he said (as cited in Yardley). Activists have attributed the degradation of the environment by transnational corporations in places such as Bangladesh to **environmental racism**, a term used to describe the connection between racism and disproportionate environmental degradation in communities of color. Examples of environmental racism are not limited to the Global South; studies have shown that in the United States people of color are more likely than whites to be exposed to environmental hazards, including toxic waste sites in their neighborhoods and toxic chemical use in their workplaces. The result of environmental racism is that many people of color bear the costly burdens of environmental hazards on their health and well-being, while elites benefit through profit and protection.

It is not only transnational corporations promoting this global assembly line, according to Ehrenreich and Fuentes, but also host countries, where competition is fierce to attract foreign capital, although these sorts of transnationals rarely bring much revenue to the host government or country as a whole, largely because they pay little or no taxes in free trade zones set up specifically to attract transnational corporations. So who beyond the corporations themselves is profiting? The answer seems to be the owners of local businesses that subcontract with the corporations, those who work in management at large factories, and some government officials, who gain personally through bribes and connections.

Modern-Day Slavery

Today, labor practices in thread mills in southern India exemplify the ongoing exploitation of female workers in the name of transnational corporate profit. In the 1970s such mills employed largely male workforces where workers had won permanent contracts and benefits. However, in recent years, factories in southern India have stopped hiring men and begun to employ 13- to 18-year-old females, who work on 3-year contracts in what is known as the **Sumangali system** (Anti-Slavery International, 2012). It is estimated that more than half the *Sumangali* workers are from the lowest caste in the Indian social hierarchy, the Dalits (traditionally known as Untouchables, a term that is considered offensive by many today), who in practice have few or no rights, although discrimination is illegal in India. Under the *Sumangali* system, young female workers are paid only a small wage during their contract period, from which money is deducted by the employer to pay for food and housing. The girls and young women are promised a lump sum (between about $500 and $1,000) to be paid if they complete the 3-year contract without break or absence, which is apparently rare (Anti-Slavery International, 2012). The term *Sumangali*, which traditionally referred to an unmarried girl becoming a respectable woman by entering into married life, has now become synonymous with this type of labor.

Although the amount promised under these contracts varies somewhat, even the most generous offer only about two-thirds of the legal minimum wage in Tamil Nadu (in the southeastern tip of India). The conditions under which the girls and young women work and live are often intolerable. One worker described how 268 workers lived in a mill hostel with only six toilets among them. Workers are often assigned compulsory extra hours, many times without compensation. When they are not working, girls are confined to the mill grounds, allowed out only under supervision. According to the accounts of former *Sumangali*, workers rarely last the full term (many become ill from the poor conditions) and thus never see the lump sum payment they are promised. Even if they are able to work the 3 years, it is not unusual to be cheated out of wages or fired just before the end of the contract (Anti-Slavery International, 2012).

In 2007, an Indian court ruled the *Sumangali* scheme illegal, calling it a form of slavery. Some factories seem to be altering their practices in response to the court decision, for instance, eliminating the final lump sum payment and raising daily wages. However, workers' freedom of movement is still restricted and situations of forced labor remain. According to Anti-Slavery International (2012), "Many [businesses] seem to be dealing with the question of slavery in their supply chains as a public relations issue to be managed rather than a human rights issue to be addressed" (p. 40).

Conditions in Tamil Nadu, particularly high rates of poverty and conservative attitudes toward the role of females in society, make girls and young women there vulnerable to exploitative labor practices. But it is not only these conditions that contribute to girls' vulnerability. Demands by international companies for low costs and fast turnaround are "a significant catalyst in driving exploitative labor practices in Indian manufacture" (Anti-Slavery International, 2012, p. 22).

ON THE
web
Read about the **plight of**
female migrant workers on
the Student Website:
www.oup.com/us/gillis-jacobs

Neoliberalism and Globalization

Ehrenreich, Fuentes, and many transnational feminists like Chandra Mohanty (2003) have been critical not only of transnational corporations, but also of the United States and the European Union, as well as organizations like the World Bank and World Trade Organization, for promoting economic policies that undergird exploitative labor practices. Such policies are part of an ideology known as **neoliberalism**, which, among other things, prioritizes profit, discourages government regulation, and encourages competition over social solidarity. We will discuss the philosophy underpinning neoliberalism in more detail below, but first let us look at how neoliberal policies have played out in practical terms.

Under this system, many countries in the Global South have been loaned money, for example, by the World Bank, to build factories and necessary infrastructure (like roads, bridges, water and sewer systems, and power and telecommunications grids) often in free trade zones, all in the name of promoting economic growth or development. The infrastructure, it should be noted, often benefits mostly or solely the factories themselves but rarely reaches into surrounding communities. These zones frequently exempt transnational corporations from taxes and wage laws, as well as health and environmental regulations, and keep union organizers away. The work, as we noted above, is frequently low paying, tedious, and dangerous. If the factories in these zones fail, which may happen for various reasons including that transnationals relocate if the costs of production become too high, then jobs and income disappear and host countries are saddled with enormous debt. To pay off the debt or to be eligible for more loans, groups like the International Monetary Fund (IMF) and the World Bank insist that the indebted country implement structural adjustment programs. Structural adjustment programs require, among other things, that indebted countries spend less on social programs like health care, education, and social security to enable them to pay off loans. The responsibility for social welfare then shifts from the state to private households, where the burden falls disproportionately on poor women (C. Mohanty, 2003). Countries may also be pressured to sell off public-owned assets like electrical grids and water systems to raise needed cash, often increasing the costs of power and water to residents. Critics of neoliberalism, including many feminists, say these policies have enriched the countries of the Global North and their transnational corporations but further impoverished many nations in the Global South, particularly their poor, the majority of whom are women of color. (See Chapter 10 "Human Rights and Global Activism," for a discussion of Cochabamba, Bolivia's "water war" to protest the selling of their water system to a transnational corporation.)

The ideology that underlies much of what we have been discussing is neoliberalism, which is related to classical liberalism with its focus on individualism and individual rights and freedoms (see Chapter 12, "Feminisms," for more on liberalism). Jeremy Gilbert (2013) identified the basic elements of neoliberal policy as the sale of public assets to private corporations (which often raises residents' costs for basic necessities such as water and power), weakening of democratic institutions, deregulation of labor markets (often pushing down wages), reduction in progressive taxation (shifting a greater share of the tax burden to the poor), restrictions on labor organization (making workers generally more vulnerable), and encouragement of competitive relations among society's members.

Neoliberalism promotes self-interest and equates improved human well-being with wealth accumulation (Keddie, 2010). Amanda Keddie noted that believers in neoliberalism oppose "all forms of social solidarity" (that is, groups of people banding together based on shared interests), instead favoring individual "personal responsibility" (p. 139). This follows from the idea that social inequities result from personal choices rather than broader social systems and practices (for example, sexism or racism). Today, neoliberal policies and globalization are often seen as closely linked. Globalization can be defined as "the increased exchange of people, goods, capital, ideas and culture across national boundaries" (H. James, 2010, para 1). Critics of both argue that although poverty has been reduced in some regions (Southeast Asia, for example) and globalization has brought new prosperity to some, poverty rates remain stubbornly high (sub-Saharan Africa's share of global poverty, for example, has actually increased) (Hauge, 2014). Most notably, globalization has not led to a wider distribution of wealth or an increase in social mobility (J. Gilbert). In fact, quite the opposite, according to J. Gilbert: the effect of neoliberal practices has been to consolidate power in those who own businesses and employ workers. Inequality has grown, largely along "racialized, gendered and classed lines" (Keddie, p. 140); this is true in countries of the Global South certainly, but also in the Global North in countries like the United States where wages have been pushed downward by outsourcing, particularly of manufacturing jobs (Madrick, 2014; Stiglitz, 2014).

Underlying this system is what has become known as the **race to the bottom**, the push by transnational corporations to find ever-cheaper sources of labor to produce their goods, often without regard for workers' rights. The race to the bottom means that companies close factories and switch suppliers seemingly overnight, often leaving workers with no jobs and no prospects for recovering wages or benefits due. The predictable result, wrote Bethan Emmett (2009), are ever-more-desperate supply chains, increasing the likelihood of informal and trafficked labor, the latter of which often involves sexual exploitation (see Chapter 10 for a discussion of trafficking).

The transnational feminist Chandra Mohanty (2003) asserted that as a result of neoliberal policies, the lives and bodies of women of color globally are being **recolonized**. By this, C. Mohanty (2003) meant that just as foreign colonial powers of the Global North once exploited the peoples and resources of vast swaths of Africa, Asia, and Latin America, today institutions (like the IMF and World Bank) and transnational corporations dominated by the Global North have reasserted control over significant parts of the political, economic, and social lives of the Global South and its people. (For more on Chandra Mohanty, see Chapter 12, "Feminisms.")

What is to be done? Some have argued that institutions like the World Bank, IMF, and World Trade Organization must change their policies to be more sensitive to the circumstances of the poor and marginalized, particularly women of color. Others, however, have criticized this as a sort of "add gender and stir" approach (for example, see Keddie), noting that even should such organizations become more gender-sensitive, they remain neoliberal institutions, that is, profit-centered systems rather than systems centered on human well-being. It is difficult to imagine these types of institutions undertaking the structural transformations that would be necessary to move from a model based on economic development to one based on human development (a move some feminist economists have advocated). (Human development is broadly focused on improving people's lives through expanded opportunities and freedom, rather than assuming that economic growth will lead to better lives for all.) C. Mohanty (2003) pointed out that although women of the Global South have organized against the devastations of globalization, for women of the Global North, it has not been a locus of organizing. For change to occur, continued C. Mohanty (2003), political solidarity and broad-based social resistance are needed across both the Global South and the Global North.

CONCLUSION

Women, people of color, lesbians, gay men, transgender people, and/or others in the global labor force face many challenges such as unequal pay, unequal power, and discrimination. Women leaders, but not men, may face a series of double binds, or lose–lose situations, where they must choose between work and family and between femininity and competence.

Social policies such as family leave policies, working time regulations, and early childhood care and education are vitally important to facilitating women's participation in the labor force. When such policies lag, as they do in the United States, women's ability to make choices about work and family (and men's too) are limited and work–family tensions increase.

Transnational corporations are a growing presence in the global economy and are a driving force behind the new international division of labor, which is often marked by low-paying, tedious, and hazardous work exported to the Global South, where much of it is performed by women. Although this sort of work has improved the lives of women in some instances, many scholars agree that all too often employees make less than a living wage, have few rights, and have no path to redress exploitative situations. Neoliberal practices promoted by transnational institutions like the World Bank, IMF, and the World Trade Organization undergird and support exploitative labor practices globally.

Key Terms

THINK, LEARN, ACT

The following resources are available on the Student Website: www.oup.com/us/gillis-jacobs

Taking Stock, Taking Action prompts and activities. Apply what you've learned to take action on campus and in the broader community.

Recommended Readings and Multimedia Resources, including scholarly and literary works, documentaries, feature films, podcasts and more, to enrich the in- and out-of-classroom experience.

GENDER-BASED VIOLENCE

Before we begin this chapter, we want to acknowledge that reading and talking about violence is difficult for many of us, perhaps particularly so for those who have experienced violence first- or secondhand. With this in mind, we have chosen not to include graphic descriptions or images of violence in this chapter. Where descriptions are present, as in the opening (to follow), they are fictional and have minimal detail; their purpose is to convey information. But for many, they will evoke an emotional response. This is natural and human. As you discuss this material, we urge you to be aware that the person next to you may be a rape survivor, may have been abused by an intimate partner, or may have survived a hate crime. In fact, it is difficult to imagine a classroom of students in which no one has experienced such violence. Be sensitive to others as they respond and as you respond. Take care of yourself if you or someone you know is a survivor.

(The following scenarios are fictional.) A young woman who has just graduated from college lands a good job in a new city. Out one night, she is introduced to the friend of a coworker. They begin dating and within several months she moves in with him.

She is happy; he is funny and thoughtful and insists that he enjoys "taking care of her." He tells her that when he gets his next promotion, she will no longer need to work. But slowly his taking care becomes controlling. He phones and texts constantly, demanding to know where she is. When she does not respond immediately, he loses his temper. One night when she comes home, he accuses her of cheating on him. He hits her, giving her a black eye, and storms out. When he returns, he cries and tells her he is sorry. She forgives him. For several weeks things go well between them but then the cycle begins again.

Although this is a fictitious scenario, it is not an untruthful one. Many of the details it presents are common in situations of **intimate partner violence,** although given the many forms such violence takes we would hesitate to call it (or any situation) typical. It is the kind of situation that affects millions of women, and to a lesser extent men, each year. Consider another scenario. Two young gay men emerge from a bar holding hands and kissing. They are approached by a group of men who shout anti-gay slurs. The two young men are surrounded and then punched and kicked, sustaining serious injuries. Or another scenario: a young woman is told by her father that he has arranged a marriage for her but she refuses, telling him she wishes to marry someone else. She leaves her home to stay with a friend but within days is confronted by her father and brother, who tell her they have heard rumors she is sleeping with her boyfriend. She refuses to go with them. Saying she has shamed her family, they kill her.

What do these three scenarios have in common? They all involve **gender-based violence**, which we define as violence (or the threat of violence) directed at an individual because of that person's gender, often because of perceived gender nonconformity (failing to meet expectations of gendered appearance and behavior, for example) and as a means to subordinate. In this chapter we will explore different forms of gender-based violence and examine ways in which certain notions of masculinity, femininity, and heteronormativity intersect with, and contribute to, such violence. The forms of violence we will look at include intimate partner violence, sexual violence, stalking, and violence against people in LGBTQQIA communities. We begin our discussion with a (re)definition of gender-based violence.

recap of terms:
Heteronormativity

Berlant and Warner (1998) defined **heteronormativity** as practices and ways of understanding that not only privilege heterosexuality over all other sexual orientations, but also mark heterosexuality as "invisible" or "natural" or give it a "sense of rightness" (p. 548).

From Chapter 4, "LGBTQQIAA Identities and Challenges."

(RE)DEFINING GENDER-BASED VIOLENCE

Gender-based violence has often been defined as violence directed against a woman because she is a woman or violence that disproportionately affects women. The term has commonly been used interchangeably with the term "violence against women." Although it is important to acknowledge that most gender-based violence is directed against women and that it is overwhelmingly perpetrated by men, researchers are increasingly also acknowledging the fact that women are not the only targets of gender-based violence. The equation of gender-based violence with violence against women is problematic in at least two ways.

First, it displays a misunderstanding of gender. To equate gender-based violence with violence against women is to misunderstand gender by conflating it with sex, that is, thinking of sex and gender as one and the same. Violence directed at a woman because she is a woman is, strictly speaking, better defined as sex-based violence. But this conception offers none of the complexity inherent in the term gender or in the idea of gender-based violence. The term violence against women suggests women are targeted because of their biological difference, but the term gender-based violence suggests a more complex idea: that violence directed at women, men, and people of other sex and gender identities (for example, transgender people) is sometimes bound up with the ways that gender is socially constructed, that such violence is both the result of hierarchical conceptions of gender and a way of reinforcing those conceptions. Thus, gender-based violence is a better descriptor and allows us to see links between different forms of violence that the violence against women label does not.

Second, equating gender-based violence with violence against women is at once too narrow and too broad a conception. How is it too narrow? Such an equation renders invisible the fact that all people (women, men, transgender people, third sex/third gender, intersex people, and others) are gendered. When we think of women alone as being gendered, we fail to recognize the dynamic relationship and interdependence among femininity, masculinity, and other conceptions of gender,

> ### recap of terms:
> ### Hegemonic Masculinity and Emphasized Femininity
>
> Multiple masculinities exist and are arranged in a hierarchy, at the top of which is **hegemonic masculinity**, which Connell and Messerschmidt (2005) defined as "the currently most honored way of being a man" (p. 832). Hegemonic masculinity is not the norm but normative, not fixed but changing over time, not universal but "locally specific" (p. 840). The subordination of women is currently central to hegemonic masculinity.
>
> The female companion to hegemonic masculinity, **emphasized femininity** is oriented around the idea that women should accommodate "the interests and desires of [heterosexual] men" (Connell, 1987, p. 183). Central features are "compliance, nurturance and empathy" (Connell, p. 188). Connell wrote that emphasized femininity is given the "most cultural and ideological support at present" (Connell).
>
> From Chapter 3, "Gender and In/Equality."

such as genderqueer. We also fail to recognize that gender expectations can be problematic and a source of vulnerability not only for women (particularly as exemplified by emphasized femininity) but also for men, particularly for men who fail to live up to conceptions of hegemonic masculinity, or, similarly, those who fall outside Audre Lorde's (1978/1984) mythical norm—"white, thin, male, young, heterosexual, christian, and financially secure" (p. 116) and those who have other sex/gender identities. (See Chapters 3 and 6 for discussions of the mythical norm.) Recognizing that men are gendered also reminds us that male perpetrators of violence can be seen (and may see themselves) as playing into gendered expectations of male aggression.

How then is the equation of violence against women with gender-based violence also too broad? In short, not all instances of violence against women are gender based. Think, for example, of a female soldier involved in a firefight with enemy forces. If she is fully integrated into her military unit and if she is indistinguishable from other soldiers in the field, then the violence she faces is not directed against her as a woman but against her as a soldier. The fact that she is a woman, although it is not immaterial, is not salient (that is, it is not the most important factor) in determining why she is subjected to violence in this instance. This is not to say that her experience as a soldier is not gendered; undoubtedly it is. But the violence she experiences in this firefight is not gender based.

There are numerous examples of gender-based violence against women, who make up the group most predominantly affected by such violence. Gender-based violence against women has taken many forms across time and place, including intimate partner violence, rape, female infanticide, dowry-related violence, and "honor" crimes. Instances of gender-based violence directed at women are part of a system that creates and maintains unequal gendered power relations on the individual and societal levels. They are often motivated by a desire for power and control. In instances of gender-based violence, such violence may be influenced not only by local conceptions of gender, but also by numerous other parts of identity including race, ethnicity, class or caste, migrant or refugee status, age, religion, sexual orientation, marital status, dis/ability, HIV status, and/or other factors.

Perhaps the most obvious examples of acts of gender-based violence not directed at women are some instances of violence directed at gay and bisexual men (or men who are perceived to be gay or bisexual) and transgender or third sex/third gender people, who are particularly vulnerable because of their gender nonconformity. In the United States, we identify such violence as bias or hate crimes. It can also be seen as part of a system of heteronormativity, a visceral reminder of the "wrongness" of same-sex desire and the "rightness" of heterosexuality. When anti-LGBTQQIA violence is intended to punish (perceived) gender nonconformity and enforce subordination, it should be understood as gender based. Some heterosexual men (or men who are perceived to be heterosexual) also experience gender-based violence. Men in wartime, both civilians and soldiers, are vulnerable to sexual violence that is sometimes rightly categorized as gender based. Wars in the former Yugoslavia and Congo are two recent examples of conflicts in which military and paramilitary forces have sexually assaulted men as a way to emasculate and stigmatize them. Such violence marks them as less than men; they are, in essence, feminized. Women, of course, have also been the targets of sexual violence in conflict (and make up the overwhelming majority of victims), which is also rightly classified as gender based. It is likely, however, that the intent and effects of sexual violence in conflict are, or at least can be, different for women versus men, so each must be examined in its own right.

Historically, African American men who have been targets of lynching by whites (often justified by trumped-up charges that they had raped a white woman) can also be understood as victims of gender-based violence. In this case, race is also salient and the intersection of gender and race must be examined. For African American men, wrote Brundage (1997), "lynching graphically demonstrated their vulnerability and debasement" (p. 11). Its purpose was often to terrorize, to emasculate (to drive this point home, lynching was sometimes accompanied by sexual mutilation), and to demonstrate white men's intention to "occupy the loftiest position in the racial and gender hierarchy" (Brundage, p. 11). As such, it was a particularly brutal tool in a gendered and racialized honor code that existed most prominently in the American South. As a last example, men who are raped in hypermasculinized settings or institutions—such as the military or men's prisons—may also be victims of gender-based violence if the violence is meant to punish perceived gender nonconformity, undermine a sense of masculinity, and/or reinforce a subordinate status.

What about other forms of violence against men? Men are, after all, not only the most frequent perpetrators of violence globally, but also its most frequent victims. Should all violence against men rightly be called gender-based violence? Recalling Marilyn Frye's (1983) conception of oppression (which we discussed in Chapter 3, "Gender and In/Equality") is helpful here. Frye asserted that oppression is a network of forces that together restrict the freedom of individuals. Frye further explained that oppression can occur only because one is a member of an oppressed class. Similarly, gender-based violence, as we

ON THE

web

Read about **sexual violence in conflict areas** on the Student Website: www.oup .com/us/gillis-jacobs

define it, can occur only when one is being targeted as a member of a gendered class or group. Furthermore, the effect of such violence is to oppress. Many instances of violence against men simply do not meet the definition of gender-based violence (as we define it) because the intent is not to subordinate or oppress based on gender norms.

One final scenario—two men are involved in a minor traffic accident. One confronts the other and a heated discussion turns violent when the first man hits the second. As it turns out, the first man is straight and the second is gay, although neither is aware of the other's sexuality at the time of the assault. Is the violence gender based? No. Although the man who has been hit is gay, he is not in this instance being hit *because* he is gay. The straight man by resorting to violence *is* conforming to traditional gender expectations of male aggression, so in that sense the violence has a gendered aspect. It is likely an enactment of hegemonic male gender norms. In this specific case, however, because there is no intent to maintain or create unequal gendered power relations, this is not gender-based violence

It is important to understand that gender-based violence is a term that is still evolving. We offer our conception here, which retains the notion of subordination present in conceptions of violence against women and hate crimes, while opening up the possibility that some instances of violence against men and third sex/third gender people can also be gender based. We will now move from the theoretical discussion of gender-based violence to an examination of specific forms of such violence.

INTIMATE PARTNER VIOLENCE

If you or someone you know is affected by intimate partner violence, there are resources to help. See the Student Website for more information.

Intimate partner violence—physical, sexual, or psychological harm (including threats of physical or sexual violence) by a current or former partner or spouse—is one of the most common forms of interpersonal violence globally, although prevalence varies widely from one place to another (World Health Organization, 2002). In this section, we will examine intimate partner violence in various settings, but the bulk of our discussion will focus on the Global North, where the majority of research has been conducted.

A brief note about terminology—"intimate partner violence" is now the most commonly used term to refer to a phenomenon that was once better known as "domestic violence" or "wife battering." Intimate partner violence is seen as a more inclusive term and a better descriptor for violence that is enacted between intimates, whether the intimates are married, dating, or acquaintances; gay or straight; old or young; whether the violence is perpetrated by women and/or men; and whether it is perpetrated by one partner or both.

Intimate Partner Violence Globally

Reporting on the global scope of intimate partner violence poses two challenges. First, there is relatively little cross-cultural research. Second, even where such research exists, making comparisons between studies is difficult because researchers often employ widely differing methods to collect and analyze data. (This is also true within the United States, which we will discuss below.) In response, the World Health Organization, in 2006, published a large study of intimate partner violence using data collected from women in 10 countries (men were not surveyed): Bangladesh, Brazil, Ethiopia, Japan, Namibia, Peru, Samoa, Serbia and Montenegro, Thailand, and the United Republic of Tanzania. The researchers found widely varying rates of prevalence in different locations; between 15 and 71 percent of women surveyed reported having experienced intimate partner violence in their lifetimes (Garcia-Moreno et al., 2006). The lowest prevalence was found in Japan among city-dwelling women and the highest prevalence rates were found in rural provinces of Bangladesh, Ethiopia, Peru, and Tanzania. A large proportion of the violence

FIGURE 9.1

An Afghan national policewoman stands at attention. Women's police units have been established in more than a dozen countries. In India, the establishment of women's police stations resulted in an increase in reporting of crime against women and children and a higher conviction rate.

was found to be severe and frequent, particularly in traditional rural settings. The authors reported that this finding mirrored earlier studies by the World Health Organization in Nicaragua and elsewhere. In all but one setting (Japan, city), women were found to be at far greater risk of physical and sexual violence by their partners than from violence by others. Men who were more controlling were also more likely to be violent. The number of women who reported perpetrating violence against men in intimate relationships was small, that is, intimate violence was reported to be predominantly **unidirectional violence**, men against women.

The psychologist John Archer (2006), in a recent meta-analytic review (a study of many studies) of intimate partner violence in 16 countries, found that women's victimization relative to men's was higher where women had less power or lower status. Archer (2006) also found the converse to be true: "across nations, states and cultures, women's empowerment is associated with lower victimization rates from their partners" (p. 147). Archer (2006) reported that in countries where women's empowerment was low, people tended to show considerable approval of wife beating. Taken together, these findings show the important role that cultural or societal norms play in supporting or discouraging intimate partner violence against women.

Intimate Partner Violence in the United States and Other Western Countries

Studies in the United States (and other Western countries) mirror the above findings in important ways. A recent meta-analysis found that between 22 and 42 percent of couples in the United States experience intimate partner violence (Langhinrichsen-Rohling et al., 2012). In the West, numerous studies have shown that women are more likely than men to suffer a spectrum of negative consequences as a result of intimate partner violence. Women are more likely to be injured and go to emergency rooms than men as a result of intimate partner violence. Women also report higher incidences of fear and depression and suffer greater economic losses when compared with male victims of such violence (Langhinrichsen-Rohling, 2010). Women with the fewest resources (e.g., women who are poor) and women who battle discrimination (e.g., women of color) are particularly vulnerable because they face difficult barriers to escaping violent situations (Fagan & Maxwell, 2006). In the West (and globally), men commit more sexual violence and stalking in intimate relationships than women.

Studies have also shown, however, that intimate partner violence in the West differs from intimate partner violence elsewhere in some important ways. For example, the bulk of studies indicate that the most common type of intimate partner violence in the United States and other Western countries is **bidirectional violence**—that is, both partners are violent toward one another—and that roughly equal numbers of women and men perpetrate physical violence in intimate relationships (which researchers call **gender symmetry**) (Archer, 2000; Desmarais et al., 2012; Esquivel-Santoveña et al., 2013; Langhinrichsen-Rohling et al.; Straus, 2008). However, this does not negate the fact that women in the West (like women globally) suffer many more negative outcomes from intimate partner violence than men. As we noted above, women are more likely to be injured, to report feeling fear and depression, and to suffer greater economic losses than men in situations of intimate partner violence.

The finding that intimate partner violence is often bidirectional may surprise you. (It did us.) If your first reaction is skepticism, you are not alone. But we believe there are important reasons to understand this body of research—and to complicate it. This is our goal.

To begin complicating the idea of bidirectional violence, we first draw attention to this assertion: *the bulk of studies indicate that the most common type of intimate partner violence in the United States and other Western countries is bidirectional.* The bulk of studies, but not all. Some well-known national (U.S.) studies record different results. The findings of the National Violence Against Women Survey, for example, contradict those reported above. The survey found women seven more times more likely than men to say they had been assaulted by an intimate partner (Tjaden & Thoennes, 2000). If you know anything at all about intimate partner violence, this may fit more closely with your conceptions. It is not our intention to proclaim one of these results "better" than the other. Rather, we contend it is important to understand what each result seems to tell us about intimate partner violence (namely, that there are different types of intimate partner violence). We will discuss this in detail below.

Where We Get Our Data

Why the different findings regarding intimate partner violence? Much of it seems to come down to who is studied and how. Researchers from diverse fields—from sociology to criminology to public health—conduct research on intimate partner violence, studying different populations and utilizing various measurement tools. Large-scale studies (e.g., utilizing population or community samples), particularly in the West, often fall into two general categories: (1) **family conflict studies** and (2) **victimization and crime studies**.

Because these two types of studies can yield what seem to be conflicting results, comparisons between them can be problematic.

In family conflict studies, researchers ask their subjects to report on a broad range of physically aggressive behaviors (that they perpetrate and that are perpetrated against them), from minor acts—such as throwing an object or pushing—to severe acts—such as kicking, beating up, or using a weapon. Acts need not reach the level of a crime to be included, and in fact, many do not. Family conflict studies often find that roughly equal numbers of women and men commit physical aggression in intimate relationships (symmetry) (Archer, 2000, 2006; Esquivel-Santoveña et al.; Heyman et al, 2001; Langhinrichsen-Rohling et al.).

Family conflict studies often utilize a tool called the Family Conflict Tactics Scale (FCTS) to measure intimate partner violence. One strength of this scale is that it measures a wide range of violent acts. But the FCTS has some key drawbacks. First, it cannot tell researchers the motivations of the perpetrators of violence (e.g., was violence committed to coerce? to control? in self-defense?). Second, the FCTS does not reveal who initiated the violence (in the case of bidirectional violence). Third, the scale does not measure the impact (physical and mental) of the violence (e.g., is the victim intimidated? sustain minor injury? major injury?) (Heyman et al.; Langhinrichsen-Rohling et al.).

Victimization and crime studies, by contrast, examine rates of intimate partner violence reported to police or defined by survey respondents as crime. Such studies often yield far lower numbers of victims overall and show men perpetrating much more violence than women in intimate relationships (gender asymmetry) (Desmarais et al.). Why? Lower numbers overall probably result because victimization and crime studies capture primarily more severe violence, that which is seen to rise to the level of crime. Findings of greater male perpetration may result for at least three reasons. First, males may perpetrate more severe violence than females in intimate partner relationships. Second, men may be less likely to view an assault by a woman as a crime and to report it as such (Dutton, 2006). Third, men's self-reporting might also be suppressed when studies are labeled as being about violence against women (for example, the National Violence Against Women Survey) (Dutton).

Making Sense of the Data: Typologies of Violence

Some researchers have proposed that seemingly disparate findings about intimate partner violence can be better understood if we conceive of intimate partner violence as falling into different typologies or forms. M. P. Johnson

(1995, 2008) proposed three central intimate partner violence typologies: **intimate terrorism**, **violent resistance**, and **situational couple violence**.

Intimate Terrorism—Intimate terrorism is systematic in nature, escalating in frequency and severity over time, and often unidirectional (primarily men using violence against women) (M. P. Johnson, 2008; see also Hines & Douglas, 2010; Langhinrichsen-Rohling). Various researchers have argued that the intent of intimate terrorism is to exert power and control (M. P. Johnson, 2008). Intimate terrorism is thought to make up a relatively small proportion of intimate partner violence incidents. It has been theorized that more of the violence reported in crime and victimization surveys (like the National Violence Against Women Survey) fits into this category (M. P. Johnson, 1995).

Violent Resistance—Violent resistance occurs when victims of intimate terrorism (often women) retaliate with violence. The individual resisting is violent but not controlling and is faced with a partner who is both violent and controlling. The motivations for and intentions of violent resistance are various (M. P. Johnson, 2008).

Situational Couple Violence—Situational couple violence, which is thought to be the most common form of intimate partner violence, is defined as occasional violence; escalation is the exception rather than the rule. It has been theorized that a significant portion of the violence captured in family conflict studies fits into this category and that women and men in the United States and other Western countries are equally likely to perpetrate situational couple violence (M. P. Johnson, 1995, 2008). Motivations for such violence are variable and may or may not include control (M. P. Johnson, 1995, 2008).

Risk Factors Associated With Intimate Partner Violence

Studies suggest that intimate partner violence is a "complex" and diverse phenomenon, driven by multiple factors related to the individual (including beliefs and attitudes), the situation, and the particular relationship (Hamel, 2009). Although the factors associated with perpetration of intimate partner violence are not the same for women and men, studies indicate that they are "far more similar . . . than they are dissimilar" (Hamel, p. 46). Studies have shown that patriarchal beliefs may "be a contributing factor in some male-perpetrated" intimate partner violence, but holding "pro-violent attitudes" is a more important risk factor for men (as well as for women) (Hamel, p. 46). Other risk factors for both women and men include "growing up in a

TABLE 9.1

Recap of How We Study Intimate Partner Violence

Family Conflict Studies	Crime/Victimization Studies
Bidirectional violence most prevalent	**Unidirectional** violence most prevalent (men perpetrate against women)
Symmetry—women and men perpetrate similar amounts of physical aggression	**Asymmetry**—violence is perpetrated predominantly and almost exclusively by men against women
Thought to capture a **wide range of violence**, much of it minor (situational couple violence), but also severe violence (intimate terrorism)	Thought to capture primarily **severe violence** (intimate terrorism), that which is seen to rise to the level of crime
Challenging questions—Why do some studies find men perpetrate more violence against women than vice versa? Why do women suffer more serious injuries and other negative consequences?	**Challenging questions**—Why do many studies find higher rates of prevalence overall and high rates of bidirectional violence?

violent home," having "certain personality traits, such as dependency and jealousy," and having a personality disorder or a "generally aggressive personality" (Hamel, p. 46).

Factors associated with intimate partner violence also include unemployment, low socioeconomic status, youth (being under 30), and being in a dating or cohabitating relationship (as opposed to married) (Capaldi et al., 2012; Hamel; Jewkes, 2002).

Intimate partner violence cuts across all lines—racial, ethnic, national, religious, socioeconomic, sexual orientation, gender identity, age, and others. Some U.S. studies have found that African American, Latina/o, and Native American couples report higher rates of intimate partner violence than white couples (Caetano et al., 2005; Rennison & Welchans, 2000; Tjaden & Thoennes; West, 2012). How do we understand these findings? First, it is important to note that samples from "minority" communities are often small; such findings may therefore be less reliable. Research shows that people of color and people from lower socioeconomic groups (among whom people of color are overrepresented) suffer disproportionately from a myriad of negative social forces, including racism, classism, sexism, and other forms of discrimination committed by individuals and institutions. If we subtract the influence of these factors ("control" for them, in research terms), as well as several other risk factors (youth, urban dwelling), then differences in rates of intimate partner violence among different racial/ethnic groups disappear or become much less pronounced (Rennison & Planty, 2003). What does this mean? The stress that results from multiple forms of discrimination and the attendant struggle just to get by has numerous negative consequences for people with lower incomes and/or people of color, including an increased risk for exposure to many forms of violence. When looked at this way, it becomes clear that broad social influences are implicated in intimate partner violence; we begin to see the problem as much more complicated than simply individual failing.

Based on these findings, it seems clear that broad-based programs are needed to respond to and prevent intimate partner violence, from those focusing on individual perpetrators and survivors, to those aimed at eliminating racism, classism, sexism, and all other -isms, to those that work to ensure equal opportunities in education, employment, and housing, among other things. Much research today points to the fact that addressing economic issues is particularly important to helping survivors leave violent relationships. When women are economically independent, they are much more likely to leave abusers (research on male victims is scarce). Access to affordable housing, child care, transportation, and social support are also major factors.

Same-sex couples in the United States may also be at increased risk for intimate partner violence, although study results have been inconsistent, with some showing comparable rates of intimate partner violence among same-sex couples and heterosexual couples and some showing elevated rates among same-sex couples (Carvalho et al., 2011; West). As we noted above, when higher rates of intimate partner violence have been found, they are largely attributable to stress as a result of societal forces, in this case, discrimination and homophobia (both external and internalized) (West), possibly combined with racism and/or classism for gay people of color and gay working-class people.

Studies also suggest important differences between the ways that heterosexual couples and gay, lesbian, and bisexual couples experience intimate partner violence. The isolation and helplessness that intimate partner violence victims often experience may be exacerbated in the LGBT community, particularly if individuals are closeted. Societal heterosexism may make it more difficult to report intimate partner violence and access services (which often do not serve same-sex victims). LGBT people who experience intimate partner violence may fear seeking assistance from a legal system in which they have few rights and may experience discrimination in dealing with police and health-care workers (Carvalho et al.). Victims of same-sex partner violence may also face the threat or possibility of being "outed" by the perpetrator of the violence, which could result in job loss, loss of child custody, and further damages. Intimate partner violence among transgender people is largely unexamined; there is a great need for more research among all of these groups (West).

Feminist Activism and Intimate Partner Violence

More than 40 years ago, social scientists, many of them feminists, "discovered" intimate partner violence. Prior to this time (and still to some extent today), intimate partner violence was seen as a "private issue" best hidden from public scrutiny. Police ignored the issue. Services for survivors were practically nonexistent. Little was known about the scope or dynamics of intimate partner violence. Feminists, however, insisting that "the personal is political," pushed the issue into public view. They theorized that intimate partner violence was widespread and, like other forms of violence against women, was best seen as a tool used by men to assert and maintain power and control over women. Feminists refuted the idea, prevalent in psychology at the time, that women who stayed in abusive relationships were passive or "masochistic" by focusing attention on the structural obstacles women faced when trying to leave violent situations. The early work of feminists focused primarily on unidirectional violence perpetrated by men and directed at women. "This focus made sense" from a practical standpoint, wrote Langhinrichsen-Rohling et al., given what feminists knew to be true—that women sustained more injuries and more serious injuries, as well as other negative consequences, from intimate partner violence and that men were generally more prone to violence than women (with higher rates of rape, physical assault, and stalking). Forty years later, the work is continuing and our understanding of intimate partner violence is evolving. It now seems clear that no one theory can account for all intimate partner violence; it is a heterogeneous phenomenon. Still, women continue to be disproportionately negatively affected by such violence, and the work of feminists remains as vital today as it was 40 years ago.

Women Advocate for Change

As a result of feminist research, advocacy, and activism, advances have been made both legally and in services available to survivors. However, great challenges remain. Lack of affordable, safe housing is a major reason survivors of intimate partner violence cannot escape abusive situations. In fact, in New York and other major U.S. cities, more than a quarter of families in homeless shelters cite abuse as the cause for their stay (Navarro, 2014). More resources are needed, particularly in marginalized communities. Many advocates also note the need for economically focused programs such as job training and employment assistance to aid victims of intimate partner violence who wish to leave abusive situations but face economic barriers to doing so.

Feminists have also been instrumental in key legislative victories in the United States, including the historic passage of the **Violence Against Women Act** (VAWA). Largely as a result of VAWA, police, prosecutors, and courts are better trained and equipped to deal with situations of intimate partner violence. But legal responses are far from perfect. For example, some advocates question the use of mandatory arrest policies in cases of intimate partner violence, a strategy championed by some and encouraged under VAWA but one that some feminists argue disempowers survivors and may discourage reporting of intimate partner violence under circumstances where victims are reluctant to have perpetrators arrested (for example, when arrest would lead to job loss by the perpetrator and result in economic hardship for the victim). Advocates for survivors

The Violence Against Women Act

In 1994, the U.S. Congress passed the Violence Against Women Act (VAWA), which it reauthorized most recently in 2013, after contentious debate, much of it prompted by the law's expanded protections for Native Americans and LGBT people (more below on those protections). VAWA focuses on multiple areas, including strengthening judicial and law enforcement responses to violence against women, improving services for victims, providing housing and safety for battered women and children, protecting battered and trafficked immigrants, and providing safety for American Indian women (Sacco, 2015).

The 2013 reauthorization strengthened the law in several areas: enhancing the criminal justice response to crimes against women and some men (including providing transitional housing, legal assistance, law enforcement training, and violence hotlines); working to reduce sexual assault on college campuses; adding stalking to the list of crimes that make immigrants eligible for protection; and authorizing programs to reduce the backlog in rape investigations.

VAWA 2013 also expanded protection for Native Americans, giving tribal authorities greater power to prosecute some non-Indians for domestic and dating violence and violations of protection orders committed on tribal lands. Prior to reauthorization of VAWA, the power to prosecute non-Indians for crimes committed on tribal lands rested solely with federal prosecutors, who were often reluctant to prosecute (U.S. Department of Justice, 2013).

VAWA 2013 also expanded protections for gays and lesbians, becoming the nation's second LGBT-inclusive federal law. (The first is the Matthew Shepard and James Byrd Jr. Hate Crimes Prevention Act of 2011.) VAWA contains provisions prohibiting the denial of services to anyone on the basis of race, religion, national origin, sexual orientation, and/or disability (Brydum, 2013).

MORE ABOUT...

of intimate partner violence continue to debate the best approaches to preventing and dealing with intimate partner violence, but broad-based approaches are needed that extend beyond the criminal justice system.

SEXUAL VIOLENCE

If you or someone you know is affected by sexual violence, there are resources to help. See the Student Website for more information.

Sexual violence is a global phenomenon affecting vast numbers of people, the overwhelming majority of them female, but third sex/third gender people and a relatively smaller number of males are also affected. In this section we will discuss sexual violence perpetrated by strangers and nonstrangers, the latter being much more common; indeed just over half of female victims of sexual violence and a third of male victims report being raped by intimate partners (Black et al., 2011).

Sexual violence knows no boundaries. Lalumière et al. (2005) contended that "**rape** is probably universal across societies, but its frequency varies considerably" (p. 13). High-quality research is rare in many places, and even where data do exist, they are unlikely to capture anything like the full extent of the problem because rape is thought to be one of the most underreported crimes.

MORE ABOUT...

The Challenge of Defining Rape

Rape is defined differently in different jurisdictions (for example, in different states, federally, in the military). The U.S. federal definition of rape is "the penetration, no matter how slight, of the vagina or anus with any body part or object, or oral penetration by a sex organ of another person, without the consent of the victim." Many state laws are broader than the federal definition, but they vary on a number of issues (Urbina, 2014). Some statutes require negative consent, a clear sign of "no," whereas a growing number require positive consent, a clear sign of "yes." But in most states, consent is not specifically defined. Some statutes require proof of physical aggression, although a growing number do not. In some states, not only force but also resistance is required for an act to qualify as rape (Urbina). ("Sexual assault" often covers a broader range of nonconsensual acts like kissing and groping that fall short of legally defined rape in most cases.)

In the United States, for example, studies have shown an estimated 64 to 96 percent of all rapes are never reported to police (Lisak & Miller, 2002). It is certain that millions of women and girls (and significant but lesser numbers of men and boys) are subjected to sexual violence each year. In the United States, studies have found that a woman's chances of being raped are between 1 in 6 and 1 in 8 (Black et al.; CounterQuo, 2011). An estimated 1 in 71 men in the United States report being raped (Black et al.). A conservative estimate is that 14.6 million women and 1.6 million men in the United States are living with the consequences of rape.

What Do We Know About Rape?

An overwhelming majority of rapes are committed by males against females, but men rape other men, and women also commit sexual violence against females and males, mostly children. In the United States, young men are overrepresented among individuals charged and convicted of rape, parallel-ing other violent crimes. Most victims of rape are young women between 16 and 24 years old. Most rape is intraracial (involves two people of the same race) (Bryden & Grier, 2011; Lalumière et al.). The LGBT community, people with dis/abilities, prison inmates, and the homeless are victims of sexualized violence at higher rates than are individuals in the general popu-lation (Black et al.). Undocumented immigrants are also vulnerable because their abusers often threaten to have them deported if they seek help. The vast majority of rapes are committed by acquaintances and intimate partners and typically involve no weapons. It is not typical for rape to be reported promptly to police and most rapes are never reported at all (M. J. Anderson, 2005). Rape by a known assailant is the least likely to result in conviction (Brenner, 2013).

How We Study Who Rapes and Why

The reasons for rape and the motivations of rapists, like the dynamics of rape itself, are complex and diverse. Brenner wrote, "The reasons one perpetrator rapes a stranger may be fundamentally distinct from the reasons a perpetra-tor rapes in the commission of another crime, a batterer rapes his or her inti-mate partner, and a person rapes an acquaintance in a quasi-romantic setting" (p. 520).

Research seeking to answer the questions of who rapes and why has gener-ally examined one of two populations: incarcerated rapists or (nonincarcer-ated) young men (often college students). A number of similarities have been found between incarcerated and undetected rapists (that is, those who admit to behavior that is legally defined as rape or attempted rape but who have not been arrested), including high levels of anger at women, a need to dominate women, hypermasculinity, lack of empathy, psychopathy, and antisocial traits (Lisak & Miller). (**Hypermasculinity** is an extreme form of masculinity that often includes "endorsement of stereotypical gender roles, a high value placed on control, power, and competition, toleration of pain, and mandatory heterosexuality" [Turchik & Wilson, 2010].) Incarcerated and undetected rapists are more likely to hold "pro-rape" attitudes and associate sexual activity with domination than men who report being "nonaggressive" (Lalumière et al.).

At least one study has shown that among male college students, a relatively small proportion of men may be responsible for a large number of rapes. In this study, 6.4 percent of college men admitted to committing rape or attempted rape. Of this 6.4 percent, almost two-thirds (63 percent) were repeat offenders who committed nearly six rapes each (Lisak & Miller). How did they escape arrest for their crimes? Most attacked within their social networks and left no visible physical injuries. The takeaway for the researchers: many rape cases that seem "difficult to prove" might not actually be, if peers within the perpetrator's social network and former intimate partners are questioned.

Debunking Rape Myths

Only bad girls get raped.

Any healthy woman can resist a rapist if she really wants to.

Women ask for it.

Women lie about rape.

Rapists are sex starved, insane, or both.

All of the above are **rape myths**, "beliefs about rape and sexual assault that blame the victim, justify the perpetrator's actions, and discount the violence of rape" (Chapleau & Oswald, 2010, p. 68). Rape myths often seek to deflect attention from the act of rape to the actions of the female rape survivor. Some studies have shown a positive link among acceptance of rape myths, the inclination to commit rape, and judgments of victim blame in cases of rape (Bohner et al., 2005; see also Bryden & Grier). Rape myths are powerful and pervasive ideas that reflect and shape how societies think about sexual violence. They run counter to many of the basic facts about sexual violence that we have discussed here, yet they persist, affecting everything from the media's coverage of sexual violence, to a jury's decision to convict an accused rapist, to a rape survivor's self-perception. Feminists have sought to counter rape myths with the complex truth about rape.

Below are two examples:

Sexual assault does not require force on the part of the perpetrator or utmost resistance on the part of the victim to be "real" rape. Although many women physically resist, many women do not because they are too surprised or frightened, because they do not trust their own judgment, because they fear being further injured, or because they are incapacitated. Physically resisting to the utmost is the exception, not the rule (M. J. Anderson, 2005; Lonsway et al., 2009).

Falsely accusing someone of rape is a serious issue but research does not show it to be a widespread problem. When rigorous research methods are applied, estimates of false reports tend to be between 2 and 8 percent, not dissimilar to false reports of other crimes (Lonsway et al.).

Rape myths are not going away anytime soon, but today more and more people understand why they are problematic—and how they distort the truth about rape.

Sexual Assault on Campus

Sexual violence is a serious problem on college campuses. Recent research indicates that in the United States, approximately 1 in 5 women and 1 in 17 men experience attempted or completed sexual assault while in college. (Sexual assault includes a broader range of acts than rape, for example, nonconsensual kissing or groping.) Most victims are assaulted by men they know and trust. The majority of sexual assaults occur when women are incapacitated because of use of substances, primarily alcohol (Krebs et al., 2007).

The Case of Margaux J.—In May 2006, Margaux J., a student at Indiana University, was notified that the male student she had accused of rape had been found "responsible" for nonconsensual "sexual contact" by a university panel, which recommended suspending him for a single summer semester. Margaux, stunned by the light punishment, wrote a letter to the university administration urging a harsher penalty. Her parents did the same. Margaux feared seeing her assailant on campus when they both returned to school in the fall. Eventually, the man accused of raping her did receive a more serious punishment—suspension for two additional semesters—but only after Margaux decided to transfer to another university (Lombardi, 2010/2014).

FIGURE 9.2

A young man taking part in an anti-rape demonstration in Melbourne, Australia.

FIGURE 9.3

On many campuses, students are learning to recognize the potential for sexual assault and how to intervene safely through bystander intervention programs. Safety is key. "We're definitely not looking to create Captain Bystander," said one trainer. The best intervention is often the one the aggressor does not know happened.

The outcome of Margaux's case is not unusual. A study by the Center for Public Integrity revealed that students deemed "responsible" for sexual assaults on college campuses often face little or no consequences for their actions. According to the U.S. Department of Justice (DOJ) Office on Violence Against Women, colleges expel only 10 to 25 percent of such men; most of the disciplinary actions taken by schools in the DOJ database involve only minor sanctions, ranging from social probation (assailants are removed from campus for all nonacademic pursuits) to academic penalties, although the DOJ encourages "appropriate sanctions, such as expulsion." In contrast, survivors' lives, reported Lombardi, are frequently turned "upside down." They can experience depression, post-traumatic stress disorder, sleep disorders, and other conditions. Many leave school before graduation.

Young women like Margaux J. are increasingly speaking out about their experiences of rape on campus and connecting with each other through social media. Because of their activism, there is not only hope, but also evidence of change. For example, the **Campus Sexual Violence Elimination (SaVE) Act**, part of VAWA 2013, affirms that schools are responsible for preventing, not just responding to, sexual assault. The act joins the **Jeanne Clery Act**, landmark federal legislation signed into law in 1990 that requires U.S. colleges and universities to disclose information about crime, including sexual assault, on and around their campuses. Recently, the administration of Barack Obama has announced initiatives to aid colleges in responding to campus sexual violence and to provide greater transparency. The administration has launched a website, notalone.gov, that informs students of their rights and how to file a complaint. The site also includes enforcement actions the government has taken against individual colleges. The DOJ has begun to more vigorously hold schools accountable for their obligations under **Title IX**, federal civil rights legislation that prohibits sex discrimination in education. Title IX stipulates that schools must meet three requirements if they find sexual assault has occurred: (1) end the "hostile environment"; (2) prevent future occurrences; and (3) restore victims' lives. Schools that fail to meet these standards can be denied federal funding. Advocates say many colleges are falling well short of these requirements.

In 2014, California and New York became the first states to institute what has become known as "yes means yes" legislation regarding sexual assaults on campus. (At this writing, New Jersey and New Hampshire, among other states, and many colleges and universities have implemented or are considering implementation of "yes means yes" policies, and many legal experts predict changes to criminal laws in many states are forthcoming [Urbina].) The California law requires colleges in the state that receive state-financed student aid to change the definition of consent in their sexual assault policies, replacing the traditional "no means no" standard with "affirmative consent" or "yes means yes." The effect of the law is to shift the burden to the student initiating sex to obtain a "yes" from the prospective partner, who has traditionally been required to convey a "no." The law defines consent as "affirmative, conscious, and voluntary agreement to engage in sexual activity." Consent need not be spoken. Under the law, in sexual assault proceedings, the accused will bear the primary burden of explaining their actions and what made them think they had received consent, thus minimizing the possibility

Know Your IX

Know Your IX (knowyourix.org) is a campaign to educate U.S. college students about their rights under Title IX if they are sexually assaulted on campus. It provides practical advice about college grievance proceedings and, if necessary, how to file a complaint against a college with the Department of Education's Office for Civil Rights. It also has ideas for campus activism to combat sexual violence. Know Your IX is run by survivor-activists with firsthand experience in the fight to overcome rape on college campuses.

of victim blaming. As the *New York Times* editorial board (2014b) noted, "the new standard won't convince young men intent on getting their way . . . to back down," but it could improve how colleges handle sexual assault allegations.

Sexual Violence by Women

Rape and sexual abuse by females is predominantly, but not exclusively, against family members, intimate partners, and acquaintances, both female and male. Law enforcement data indicate the percentage of female sex offenders is small. In 2000, females accounted for 1 percent of those arrested for rape and 8 percent of those arrested for other sex offenses (not including prostitution) (Levine, 2006).

"It is not uncommon to believe a man cannot be raped by a woman," according to Ybarra and Mitchell (2013, n.p.). Although "gender stereotypes can make it difficult to imagine a dominant woman coercing or forcing an unwilling man to have sex" (Ybarra & Mitchell, n.p.), it does happen, if rarely. (Men can achieve erections without sexual arousal.) Male victims of sexual violence, whether victimized by another male or by a female, may feel constrained by gender expectations and may not view their experiences as abusive or may be reluctant to report them for fear of not being believed (L. Bunting, 2007; Levine).

breaking the frame
Focus on the Perpetrators of Sexual Violence

FIGURE 9.4

Anti-rape activists are changing the discourse about rape. Increasingly, the message "Don't rape" is being heard loud and clear. For advocates, the shift is much more than rhetorical. For too long the attention—and the onus—has been on potential victims, most of them women, to reduce the risk of sexual violence by avoiding certain situations, certain ways of dressing, or certain behaviors. Survivors have been blamed for their own victimization, a phenomenon without parallel for other forms of violence. Feminist advocates are increasingly demanding that the attention shift to perpetrators and the behaviors they should avoid, namely sexual violence. Does this mean that women should abandon measures to reduce the risk of sexual violence? Of course not. Such measures remain necessary. But the shift of focus to perpetrators recognizes that women's actions alone can never solve the problem of sexual violence. The onus must be on potential perpetrators to change their behavior.

The Role of Culture in Sexual Assault

Before turning to our discussion of the anti-rape movement, we want to return to the statement with which we began this section of the chapter—*sexual violence knows no boundaries*. Rape, we reported, is "probably universal across societies" but its prevalence varies from group to group. The anthropologist Peggy Reeves Sanday (2003) similarly found that some cultures or groups are "rape prone," whereas others are comparatively "rape free"—by which she did not mean rape is entirely absent, but that it is both stigmatized and rare in some cultures or groups. Sanday's early work, on which she first based this claim, focused on relatively small indigenous groups, not large, mixed contemporary cultures. She later applied her theory to college campuses and fraternities as well. Sanday's central claim is that there is a "significant correlation between rape and the overall position of women" in many groups. She further explained that in groups marked by equality between women and men and where women have significant power and authority, rape is less prevalent and more stigmatized. By contrast, in groups marked by male dominance and female subordination and where the dominant masculinity is defined by male toughness and interpersonal violence, rape is more prevalent and normalized. In **rape-prone cultures**, wrote Sanday, sexual violence is "an expression of a social ideology of male dominance" (p. 341). Sanday concluded that culture plays an important role in the expression of male sexual aggression. If this is true, then strategies to prevent sexual violence must focus not only on individual men who perpetrate, but also more broadly on cultures that condone or promote sexual violence as man's right and (largely) woman's burden.

Related to Sanday's notion of rape-prone cultures is the idea of compulsive heterosexuality, which builds on Adrienne Rich's idea of compulsory heterosexuality (Chapter 4) and Judith Butler's idea of performativity (Chapter 2). C. J. Pascoe (2007), who spent a year observing students in a California high school, described how the young male students produced their masculinity and heterosexuality through ritualized repetition of hypermasculine behaviors (denigrating young women, boasting of sexual exploits, and calling out other young men as "fags" for the slightest perceived slips in hypermasculine behavior). "Taken together," wrote Pascoe, "these ritualized interactions continually affirm masculinity as mastery and dominance" (p. 87). Those who best conformed to compulsive heterosexuality gained the greatest social status, whereas others were relegated to the "fag position," the bottom of the high school social ladder.

Subgroups that Sanday and others have studied include fraternities and athletic teams, both of which are frequently connected to incidents of sexual violence against women. The bulk of research has found that *some* male fraternities and sports teams are indeed at high risk for committing sexual violence, but not all (Humphrey & Kahn, 2000; Sanday). Among those that are more rape prone, members reported "significantly higher levels of sexual aggression" and hostility toward women and more "male peer support for sexual violence" than among low-risk groups (Humphrey & Kahn, p. 1320). More research is needed to determine whether members of these high-risk groups have high levels of hostility toward women and/or commit sexual violence before joining such groups and/or whether levels of sexual aggression increase after joining such groups.

ON THE
web

Read about **sexual assault in the U.S. military** on the Student Website: www.oup .com/us/gillis-jacobs

Advocates Campaign Against Sexual Violence

In 1975, Susan Brownmiller published *Against Our Will: Men, Women and Rape,* which examines cultural constructions of rape. The book became a central part of a growing feminist critique of rape that, as Estelle Freedman (2013) explained, "explicitly linked the problem of sexual violence to male privilege" and sought to "put women's experience of sexual violence at the center of a new political analysis of rape" (n.p.).

FIGURE 9.5
Take Back the Night marches have been popular on college campuses since the 1970s. The marches, which are held in cities globally, are vigils for those affected by sexual violence and protests against such violence.

Beginning in the early 1970s, women in large numbers began for the first time to share their experiences of sexual violence with each other through consciousness-raising groups that were a feature of second wave feminism in the United States (More on consciousness-raising will come in Chapters 11 and 12.) Women also began to publicly speak out, renouncing rape as a crime of violence. In response, grassroots women's groups devoted to stopping rape "sprang up" across the United States, wrote Freedman (2013). Feminists founded rape crisis hotlines and, by 1976, had opened 400 rape crisis centers (Freedman, 2013). They were critical of police and health-care responses to rape and called for sweeping changes, which have resulted, among other things, in specially trained sexual assault teams and the common use of rape kits. Seeking to empower themselves, feminists encouraged self-defense classes and took to the streets in "Take Back the Night" marches (Figure 9.5).

Women of color in the feminist movement, following in the footsteps of the antilynching activist Ida B. Wells-Barnett and others, "called attention to the intersections of gender, race, and sexual violence" (Freedman, 2013). (For more on Black feminist activists, see Chapters 11 and 12.) African American writers such as Angela Davis and Alice Walker demanded an end to racism in the antiviolence movement. Chicana activists focused on services for Spanish-speaking communities, such as the bilingual rape hotline founded in East Los Angeles in 1976.

Rape law was, and remains, a particular concern of many feminists. U.S. law, and British common law from which it derives, historically viewed rape of white women (those deemed sexually innocent) as a crime against property—the woman, under coverture laws, being the property of her father or husband. (For more on coverture, see Chapter 3.) Black women and women deemed "fallen" found virtually no protection under the law. As recently as 60 years ago, in some Southern and Western states, consensual sexual relations between a Black man and a white woman could be considered rape (Urbina). In 1973, the National Organization for Women created a rape task force to advocate for changes to state rape laws. Although rape laws in the United States in the 1970s were much changed from earlier times, they were still deeply flawed, placing a high burden of proof on rape victims without parallel for other crimes (Sanday). For example, in many U.S. states, to prove rape required the corroborative testimony of a witness, proof of overwhelming force on the part of the perpetrator, and proof of utmost resistance on the part of the victim, none of which was easily fulfilled in the vast majority of rape cases. A rape victim was often blamed for her own victimization and subjected to brutal scrutiny of her prior sexual history in court and the media (M. J. Anderson, 2005). The prior history of the accused, on the contrary, could not be introduced in court on the grounds that it could prejudice the jury—a clear double standard that discouraged many rape survivors from having their day in court (M. J. Anderson, 2005). Until the 1980s, many U.S. jurisdictions did not recognize rape within marriage (Olen, 1991). As late as 1991, two states (North Carolina and Oklahoma) still enabled defendants to use the fact of marriage to the victim as an absolute defense against rape charges (Olen). And in 1998, Mississippi became the last state to stop stipulating that statutory rape was not real rape if the girl was "unchaste" (Urbina).

Thanks to feminist advocates, U.S. rape law today is much changed. Corroboration is no longer required. **Rape shield laws** limit the evidence a defendant is allowed to admit at trial about a victim's sexual history. The marital rape exception has been abolished. Rape laws are now more sex neutral and definitions of rape are broader, including acts beyond penile penetration of the vagina. Still, problems exist, including the fact that there is "little uniformity on how to define rape, which makes counting rapes, and countering and even discussing the issue, difficult," wrote Ian Urbina (SR 12). Many states still require proof of physical aggression on the part of the perpetrator and/or resistance on the part of the victim for the crime to be considered rape, the most serious legal designation, and eligible for the heaviest penalties (M. J. Anderson, 2005; Urbina). Without force, sexual assault remains difficult to prove and prosecutors are often hesitant to bring charges; as a result, many survivors of sexual violence remain reluctant to report (M. J. Anderson, 2005). Exceptions in rape shield laws often fail to protect survivors. And still, whether a rapist is brought to trial and convicted depends largely on perceptions of victim "innocence." Survivors who are seen as engaging in "unacceptable sexual behavior" or who are from marginal communities are less likely to seek or receive justice (Counter-Quo). The modern campaign against sexual violence has "achieved an impressive agenda," asserted Freedman (2013), but given the immensity of the problem still, much work remains. One focal point of activism today is Slut-Walk, a global grassroots movement to challenge rape culture, victim blaming, and slut shaming. (See Chapter 12, "Taking Stock, Taking Action," on the Student Website for more information, including controversy surrounding SlutWalk.)

VIOLENCE AGAINST MEMBERS OF THE LGBT COMMUNITY

"The experience of violence and property crime is disturbingly widespread" among members of the LGBT community (Herek, 2009a, p. 71). In a national sample of lesbians, gay men, and bisexuals in the United States (18 years and older), nearly 20 percent of respondents reported having experienced a personal or property crime in their lifetime motivated by their sexual orientation. Half reported having been verbally harassed, and 1 in 10 said they had been the victim of employment or housing discrimination (Herek, 2009a). But within the group, rates varied widely, with gay men being "significantly more likely than lesbians or bisexuals to experience violence and property crimes" and to be harassed because of their sexual orientation (Herek, 2009a, p. 54). Herek (2009a) asserted that gay men "are at greater risk for antigay victimization" than lesbians and bisexuals for several reasons. First, men are more likely than women to be victims of violent crime in general, especially crime committed by strangers. Second, most crimes are "perpetrated by heterosexually identified men, who tend to hold more hostile attitudes" toward male versus female "sexual minorities." Last, gay men may be more visible targets, particularly if they frequent gay-oriented venues (such as gay bars) (p. 69).

A smaller study has found that lesbians and gay men of color experience more frequent violence compared with white lesbians and gay men (Kidd & Witten, 2007).

There is little research about the transgender community in general and research about violence against members of the transgender community is no exception. Studies tend to be small and localized so cannot be compared with larger national-sample studies such as that cited above. Even given these shortcomings, however, Kidd and Witten concluded that many transgendered people's lives are characterized by systemic discrimination and violence. Several small studies have shown that between 60 and 91 percent of transgender

The Evolution of Gay Rights

The field of gay rights is changing quickly. But positive developments in one part of the world have been offset by negative developments in others. While ever more countries legalize gay marriage, including the United States, others—India, Uganda, Nigeria, and Russia among them—have recently criminalized, or upheld laws criminalizing, behavior or "propaganda" related to homosexuality. Globally, about 80 countries still ban same-sex relations; a handful allow the death penalty for those convicted of having "consensual homosexual relations."

Yet there does seem to be a steady, if difficult, march toward acceptance of LGBTI rights. (LGBTI refers to lesbian, gay, bisexual, transgender and intersex. See Chapters 1, "Sex, Gender, and Social Construction," and 4.) Nepal provides an instructive example. In 2007, Nepal's Supreme Court ruled that LGBTI individuals should have the same legal rights as other citizens of Nepal. Same-sex marriage is now legal in Nepal and third gender national identity cards are available. In 2008, the country elected its first openly gay lawmaker. Many of these changes are the result of Nepal's Blue Diamond Society, a nongovernmental organization working to advocate and provide services for LGBTQQIA people. But progress in Nepal has also met resistance. Violence against LGBTQQIA people continues, including death threats, harassment, and arbitrary arrests of LGBTQQIA activists.

The issue of gay rights globally will certainly remain unsettled for years to come, but greater attention—and compassion—at the highest levels point toward a more hopeful future in many places. (See Chapter 10 for more about human rights and the LGBTI community.)

identified people report having experienced violence and/or harassment in their lifetimes. Elevated rates of violence against transgender people have been found in studies conducted in diverse settings globally, including Buenos Aires, Argentina, India, Nepal, and the United States. Denny (2007) concluded that "violence against transgendered persons . . . is an international [problem]. Death squads in South American countries have executed transsexual persons and crossdressers in large numbers, and police in other countries (especially in the Middle East) harass, torture, and murder transgendered persons with little fear of reprisal" (para. 14). Kidd and Witten noted that the level of aggression in many instances of antitransgender violence is striking and may indicate "a desire to deface and mutilate the bodies of transgender people because they challenge the normative worldview of the perpetrator with respect to gender" (p. 34).

Viviane Namaste (2009), examining the issue from a different perspective, suggested that violence against trans people is not always best understood from a primarily gendered perspective, but instead "as part of a continuum of violence against the poor and the disenfranchised" (p. 23). Namaste noted that many trans people are poor, that a significant number work as prostitutes (particularly trans women of color), and that violence against trans people should be examined within the context of violence against "the homeless, street vendors, and street prostitutes" (p. 23). Namaste argued more generally against "neglecting the specificity" of trans people's lives and cautioned against placing transgender women and transgender men "on the same gender continuum" (p. 27).

Anti-LGBT Violence and Hate Crimes

In the United States under federal legislation, a crime motivated by sexual orientation is considered a **hate crime**, which is defined as a "criminal offense against a person or property motivated in whole or in part by an offender's bias against a race, religion, disability, ethnic origin or sexual orientation" ("Hate Crime—Overview," 2015, para. 2) (sexual orientation was added in 2009 with the passage of the Matthew Shepard and James Byrd Jr. Hate Crimes Prevention Act). As of 2014, more than two dozen states also have laws addressing hate crimes based on sexual orientation or sexual orientation and gender identity (Human Rights Campaign, 2014). Although hate crime legislation varies from state to state, all hate crime statutes recognize that bias-motivated crimes affect not only the victim but also indirectly the entire class of people targeted.

Hate crimes motivated by the (perceived) sexual orientation of the victim are a "manifestation of *sexual stigma*," wrote Herek (2009a, p. 56, italics in original). He defined sexual stigma as society's "negative regard for any non-heterosexual behavior, identity, relationship, or community . . . a system through which homosexuality [or bisexuality] is denigrated, discredited and socially constructed as invalid relative to heterosexuality" (pp. 56, 57). (See Chapter 5 for further discussion about sexual stigma.) Herek's (2009a) description of sexual stigma clearly ties such violence to heteronormative practices, that is, practices that denigrate same-sex relations as "wrong" or "unnatural" and emphasize the "rightness" and "naturalness" of heterosexuality. Because anti-LGBT violence is meant to punish gender nonconformity and preserve the traditional gender binary system, it is rightly categorized as gender-based violence.

The effects of anti-LGBT hate crimes are many. Individuals who experience hate crimes are at greater risk for psychological distress than are people who do not experience such crimes. What seems to set hate crimes apart and make them particularly damaging is the fact that they are aimed at a core aspect of

FIGURE 9.6

The artist Tatyana Fazlalizadeh creates posters using the words and images of real women to hang in public spaces where street harassment occurs. She calls the art series "Stop Telling Women to Smile." Learn more at stoptellingwomentosmile.com.

one's identity. Kidd and Witten reported that studies have also shown that anti-LGBT hate crimes (or even the threat of such crimes) "reinforce adherence to normative gender behaviors in people across the sexual orientation and gender identity spectra because of fear of being perceived as gay or lesbian" (pp. 49–50).

For transgender people, the effects of hate crimes can be especially devastating. Kidd and Witten concluded that such crimes "evoke a sense of fear that percolates throughout the transgender community, encouraging transgender people to renounce open expression of their gender identity lest they face similar violence" (p. 51). Violence, Kidd and Witten noted, is just one part of a "constellation of systemic oppressions" that makes it extremely difficult for transgender people to secure even basic life necessities such as housing, work, and health care. More research and more resources are vitally important to combating anti-LGBT violence.

STALKING

If you or someone you know is affected by stalking, there are strategies that can help. See the Student Website for more information.

Stalking, which is a "pattern of repeated intrusive and intimidating behaviors toward a specific person that causes the target to feel harassed, threatened or fearful" (L. Miller, 2012, p. 496), affects approximately 16 percent of women and 5 percent of men in the United States in their lifetimes (Black et al., 2011). Stalking is thought to be more prevalent among college undergraduates (perhaps 20 percent of undergraduates have been stalked) than among the general population (L. Miller). Women comprise approximately 80 percent of stalking victims and the vast majority of acts of stalking are perpetrated by men (Meloy & Felthous, 2011). Most stalkers know their victims and have had a previous intimate relationship with them; stranger stalking, like stranger rape, is the least common form. The duration of stalking and the likelihood of violence both increase when the perpetrator and victim have been involved in an intimate relationship. By the year 2000, all 50 U.S. states and the federal government had outlawed stalking, along with many other countries. Although definitions of stalking vary by jurisdiction, most statutes include both physical and electronic stalking, also known as **cyberstalking**.

The number of women who stalk is relatively small and female stalkers have been found to be both less threatening and less violent in general than male stalkers (Meloy et al., 2011). Among female stalkers, many seem to stalk celebrities or acquaintances (female and male) rather than former intimate partners. Women who do stalk former partners, however, have been found to be more violent than women who stalk nonintimates (Meloy et al.). Men who report female stalkers to police are often met with indifference, skepticism, or even derision, reported Meloy and colleagues.

Cyberstalking, a pattern of repeated intrusive and intimidating behaviors via computer, phone, or other technology toward a specific person that causes the target to feel harassed, threatened, or fearful, often accompanies other forms of stalking, although sometimes it is the sole method of stalking. In cases of cyberstalking, the stalker's identity may be known or the stalker may remain anonymous. **Textual harassment**, the sending of text messages (sometimes hundreds in the course of a day) to harass and/or threaten, is thought to be particularly prevalent among teens in abusive dating relationships (St. George, 2010). The private nature of texting can make it especially problematic, wrote Donna St. George, because parents and friends may not be aware its happening or take it as seriously as they should. St. George also contended that many teens have difficulty recognizing the behavior as abusive.

The consequences for stalking victims can be severe, including death (although most stalkers do not become physically violent). Because stalking is ongoing and its outcome is unknown, it can take a serious psychological toll on victims that can persist even after stalking ends. All forms of stalking can result in anxiety disorders, depression, and even post-traumatic stress disorder.

CONCLUSION

Gender-based violence—violence directed at a person because of that person's gender (often because of their perceived gender nonconformity)—is part of a system that creates and maintains unequal gendered power relations on the individual and societal levels. It is a global phenomenon directed overwhelmingly at women and girls, but some men, boys, and individuals whose identities fall outside these categories are also at risk.

Intimate partner violence is common globally, although its prevalence varies widely. Women worldwide suffer disproportionately from the effects of intimate partner violence. Sexual violence probably occurs in every society, although, like intimate partner violence, its frequency varies considerably. Although women are the primary victims, a smaller but significant number of men are also victimized by rape, much of it perpetrated by other men. Although rape laws in the United States have undergone dramatic changes, rape remains difficult to prove in a court of law and is vastly underreported to law enforcement. Anti-LGBT violence is widespread but there is little research on the issue globally. Such crimes often reinforce adherence to normative (heterosexual) gender behaviors because of fear of being perceived as gay or lesbian.

THINK, LEARN, ACT

The following resources are available on the Student Website: www.oup.com/us/gillis-jacobs

Taking Stock, Taking Action prompts and activities. Apply what you've learned to take action on campus and in the broader community.

Recommended Readings and Multimedia Resources, including scholarly and literary works, documentaries, feature films, podcasts and more, to enrich the in- and out-of-classroom experience.

HUMAN RIGHTS AND GLOBAL ACTIVISM

Before we begin this chapter we want to acknowledge that some of the topics it covers may be upsetting and/or evoke an emotional response. With this in mind, we have chosen not to include graphic descriptions or images of violence, but we do discuss sensitive topics. If you or someone you know is a survivor of violence, take care of yourself. Be aware that others around you may have experiences similar to those described in this chapter. Be sensitive as you respond.

LA GUERRA DEL AGUA—THE WATER WAR

Cochabamba is a city of 800,000 people perched in the Andes Mountains of Bolivia, South America's poorest country. In the 1980s, Bolivia's government battled hyperinflation that left the economy in ruins. Out of money and options, Bolivia turned to the World Bank and the International Monetary Fund (IMF) for aid, which they received in the form of loans. The World Bank and IMF, in turn, effectively took control of Bolivia's economy (as they have in scores of other countries in the Global South) and imposed "structural adjustment." Bolivia was required to devalue its currency, cut government spending, abolish wage and price controls, and sell off its assets, including its "airline, railroads, mines and electric company," to foreign-owned companies (PBS, 2002a). Inflation was brought under control but a crippling recession and widespread unemployment followed. Foreign investment in Bolivia increased, as the World Bank and IMF had planned, but for poor Bolivians, that investment made hardly a dent in their poverty (Finnegan, 2002). Bolivians were not alone; in Latin America as a whole, poverty was higher in 2002, after 2 decades of free trade and foreign investment, than it had been in 1980 (Finnegan).

Why had trade and investment failed to lift masses out of poverty? The answers are different in different contexts, but often concessions to transnational corporations meant they paid little or no taxes, were subject to few labor regulations (about wages and working conditions, for example), and, since most were foreign-owned, profits were often funneled out of Latin America. In many cases, governments exhausted revenue and loans in the building of infrastructure, like roads, ports, and electrical and water systems, that benefited transnational corporations and factory owners but often bypassed local communities. Government spending on education, health care, and other social programs on which the poor depended was often slashed in the name of cost cutting.

Still cash strapped in the late 1990s, Bolivia was pressured by the World Bank to sell off its water. Cochabamba put its water system up for auction. The U.S.-based Bechtel Corporation, the only bidder, was awarded a 40-year concession to operate the city's water system and was promised at least a 15 percent return on their investment. Four months into the contract, water service had not improved but prices spiked up as much as 400 percent, with some residents forced to spend more than a quarter of their income to buy water (Arnold, 2009).

In response, the people of Cochabamba "took to the streets" (PBS, 2002a). *La guerra del agua*—the water war—drew in tens of thousands of protestors. One Bolivian journalist noted, "I've never seen anything like it in Bolivia. Housewives were throwing stones at the police. It really was a revolt" (PBS, 2002a). From the beginning of the water war, women played a key role, taking to the barricades and making connections between different neighborhoods and rural and urban citizens (Bennett et al., 2008). Many women who participated in the protests experienced "profound changes" in their roles as community members afterward and reported greater participation in activities that once would have been out of reach (Bennett et al.).

Concerned that the government of Bolivia could collapse, officials conceded to protestors' demands and canceled Bechtel's contract. Cochabamba's water system was turned over to a local consortium, including some who had participated in the protests. In addition, the Bolivian government recognized that "water is a fundamental human right and a public trust" (Arnold). The victory in Cochabamba is significant and has inspired others to resist, but it is a partial victory at best. Lacking funds, the local consortium is still working to extend the water system to thousands who remain without a reliable source of clean water.

Water and Gender

What is the connection between water and gender? Of an estimated 200 million hours spent each day globally collecting water, women and girls account for three-quarters of that time (World Health Organization, 2010). Particularly in poor rural communities of the Global South, such as Cochabamba, water is integral to domestic chores performed primarily by females, including cooking, cleaning, laundry, and watering of gardens and animals. (See Appendix B, Names for People and Places for a definition of Global South and Global North.) Because of lack of access to clean water and sanitation, millions of women can do little more than work for the survival of themselves and their families, severely curtailing the time they can spend attending school, earning an income, and participating in community life. Yet in many places, including Latin America, the management of water is "structured as a masculine domain: the domain of engineers, ditch diggers . . . farmers . . . [and] urban planners" (Bennett et al., p. 107). In Cochabamba, as elsewhere, women were prevented by law or custom from being involved in decision making regarding water (Bennett et al.). Yet studies have shown that water projects where women fully participate in the design and implementation are more sustainable and effective than are projects that exclude women (Gross et al., 2001). Many women and girls must travel long distances to collect water or to have access to latrines (or privacy in the absence of latrines), making them more vulnerable to violent attacks, including rape, by men.

Water Privatization Globally

The privatization of water in Cochabamba is not unique. The World Bank has imposed water privatization on dozens of countries in the Global South. Meanwhile, in the Global North, just a few multinational corporations control the water market in France and Britain, making billions in profits (PBS, 2002a). When Britain privatized water in the 1990s, water bills in some cities rose by more than 100 percent and thousands of public-sector jobs were lost. One-third of all community water systems in the United States are owned and/or operated by private corporations (Arnold). The experience in Atlanta, Georgia, is instructive. There, customers suffered through multiple boil orders, fire hydrants that did not work, leaking water mains that went unrepaired for weeks, and lengthy periods without water because of work orders that went unattended after the French-based multinational corporation Suez took over management of Atlanta's water system (Arnold). Suez did succeed at one goal—cutting operating costs—which it achieved by firing a quarter of its workers (Luoma, 2002). The city of Atlanta terminated its contract with Suez after 4 years.

Water as a Human Right

The United Nations (UN) General Assembly in 2010 recognized the human right to water and sanitation. Yet 783 million people have no access to clean water and 2.5 billion lack access to adequate sanitation (UN Water, 2013). The overwhelming majority of these are poor people living in the Third World, but uneven access to water is a global issue. In the United States, for example, 13 percent of Native Americans do not have access to clean water and/or sanitation compared with less than 1 percent of non-Native Americans (Hauter, 2011). Studies have also found that people of color in some cities in the United States (Boston and Detroit are examples) are more likely to be threatened with water shutoffs than white people (Hauter).

Managing Water in the Public Interest

Water availability is falling globally, affecting locations as diverse as northern China, the Western United States, and sub-Saharan Africa. Meanwhile, demand continues to rise, particularly the demand for water to produce food. Climate change is expected to exacerbate the problem, making some areas drier, whereas others, particularly low-lying areas, will get wetter or disappear altogether (UN Water).

A number of thorny questions remain to be answered: How is the public interest in water best protected? When governments lack the funds to build or maintain water systems (as they often do), can private companies effectively and equitably manage water? Arnold suggested "privatization and commodification," which favor short-term profits and immediate consumption, are not viable, long-term strategies (p. 828). Water, wrote Arnold, must be owned, managed, conserved, and supplied in the public interest, "for the public interest" (p. 836). Likewise, water policies must be made through "full, meaningful, and transparent public participatory and deliberative processes" (p. 847), including people—in many cases people of color and in particular women of color—who have historically been marginalized and exploited. Even with comprehensive water stewardship, access to clean water will be one of the most difficult issues facing all nations for the foreseeable future. (See Chapter 8 for more about transnational economic policies that disadvantage people of the Global South.)

A NOTE ABOUT READING THIS CHAPTER

Before we continue our examination of human rights and activism, we wish to briefly discuss the challenge this chapter presents. When writing or reading about experiences that may not be our own, there is great potential to "get it wrong." If you are a person from the Global North (or First World) reading or writing about people from the Global South (or Third World), there are a number of frames you must be aware of. (See Appendix B, Names for People and Places for a definition of First World/Third World.) First, there is a tendency to think of all countries progressing from "primitive" or "backward" to "modern" or "more developed." However, we should remind ourselves that industrialization itself or being part of an industrialized culture is not necessarily better than being part of less industrialized cultures. For example, we noted in Chapter 1 that some early American Indian societies recognized gender diversity in a way that Western societies at the time did not. This suggests cultures can be sophisticated and well suited to people's needs without being industrialized.

Second, Western (that is, European and North American) media tends to exoticize Global South cultures and focus on so-called "primitiveness." Many people from the Global North may be surprised, for example, at the level of urbanization in places like Latin America and Africa, where 75 and 37 percent of the population, respectively, live in cities (UN Population Division, 2002).

Third, when confronted with cultural practices that seem alien and damaging from our own cultural standpoint, it can be easy to slip into othering people, particularly those from the Global South, and to dismiss them as irrational or worse. In point of fact, cultures in the Global North engage in practices that may seem unnecessary, irrational, and damaging from other cultural perspectives, including various forms of cosmetic surgery and male circumcision.

Fourth, there is a tendency to divide the world into a series of binary oppositions, including modern/primitive, civilized/savage, and rational/irrational (Quijano, 2000). Some theorists refer to this use of language as involving a form of discourse, which the French philosopher Michel Foucault (1971/1982) defined as "practices that system-atically form the objects of which they speak" (p. 49). Discourse, in other words, is the use of words (or symbols more generally) in a particular historical and social con-text that generates a way of thinking. Within the context of this chapter, if you find yourself thinking about cul-tural practices that are far removed from your own and slipping into evaluations of societies as either modern/primitive or rational/irrational, a good corrective is to remind yourself that although these binaries may seem convenient, they may obscure a deeper understanding of the cul-tural practices. We should be humble regarding what we do not know. If a cul-tural practice strikes us as bad, we should strive as best we can to understand it from within the other culture's perspective and not be too quick to judge it.

Fifth, there is also the potential for us to think of Third World women (and men, perhaps to a lesser degree) as a "homogeneous 'powerless' group," as Chandra Mohanty (1986) wrote in "Under Western Eyes" (p. 338). When we are involved in First World discourse about human rights, it is easy to slip into the binary of savior/victim, where people in the Global North are perceived to know the right way to proceed and become the heroes, whereas people in the Global South are perceived to lack the answers and are simply victims. As we shall see, however, people within a culture are often best positioned to change it, and those of us outside of a culture often have a great deal to learn (as *la guerra del agua*/the water war example shows).

In the remainder of this chapter we will focus on several major human rights challenges and the work of activists to combat them. The issues we will discuss include human trafficking, genital cutting practices, and violence against LGBT people. We will also feature human rights activists who are working to defend human rights around the globe. Last, we will outline the work of the global community, primarily through the United Nations, in the development of international human rights law.

Although the focus of this chapter is global, we wish to say explicitly that one need not look outside the United States to find human rights abuses. Human Rights Watch (2015) noted, for example, that despite "strong constitu-tional protections for many basic rights . . . U.S. laws and practices routinely violate rights" (para. 1), particularly in the areas of criminal justice, immigration, and national security/privacy. "Often, those least able to defend their rights in court or through the political process—racial and ethnic minorities, immigrants, children, the poor, and prisoners—are the people most likely to suffer abuses" (Human Rights Watch, 2015, para. 1).

HUMAN TRAFFICKING

An adolescent girl living with her family in a poor, remote village is recruited by a woman who used to be a neighbor to work as a waitress in a city hundreds of miles away, but when she arrives, her identification papers are taken and she is sold into domestic servitude. For months she is not allowed to leave the house where she is held and she is beaten if she refuses to work.

The girl is one of millions of victims of human trafficking globally. **Human trafficking** is defined in the Protocol to Prevent, Suppress and Punish Trafficking in Persons, Especially Women and Children (also known as the Palermo Protocol), as "the recruitment, transportation, transfer, harboring or receipt of persons" by the threat or use of force, "abduction," "fraud," "deception," "abuse of power," or payment to another person "for the purpose of exploitation" (Pati, 2011, p. 116). Trafficking comes in many forms. Trafficking for **commercial sexual exploitation** is a severe problem and accounts for slightly more than half of all detected trafficking victims (UN Office on Drugs and Crime, 2014). Trafficking for **forced labor**—victims are forced to work as domestics, agricultural workers, in factories, mines, restaurants, construction, and more—accounts for 40 percent of detected trafficking victims and is growing (UNODC). One recent study, for example, found that nearly one-third of migrant workers in Malaysia's electronics industry were working "under forced labor conditions" (Greenhouse, 2014b, para. 1). They produce electronics for companies such as Apple, Samsung, and Sony (Greenhouse, 2014b). In many cases, those trafficked are enslaved in a system of bonded labor. **Bonded labor** is recognized under international law as a form of slavery. It occurs when a debtor promises their personal services or those of another as security for a debt but the services are undervalued and/or not actually paid or applied toward repayment of the debt. (A note on terminology: Countries report officially "detected" offenders and victims of trafficking to the United Nations, meaning those who have come into contact with the criminal justice system or social services because of their involvement in trafficking. The United Nations notes, however, that "there is a large and unknown 'dark figure' of criminal activity that is never officially detected" (UNODC, p. 18).

Therefore, the reported figures "do not reflect the real extent of trafficking in persons" but are considered a sample that can be used to "analyze patterns and flows of trafficking in persons" (p. 18).)

Human Trafficking Is a Global Problem

Human trafficking affects nearly every country in every region globally (UNODC). The U.S. government, for example, estimates that tens of thousands of individuals are trafficked into the United States each year. In Europe, the number may be in the hundreds of thousands (Flowe, 2010). Seventy percent of the detected victims of trafficking are women and girls, the vast majority of whom are trafficked for sexual purposes; globally, one in three detected victims of trafficking is a child. UNODC reported that "the overall profile of trafficking victims may be slowly changing, however, as relatively fewer women, but more girls, men and boys are detected globally" (p. 9). Men make up nearly three-quarters of those convicted for trafficking in persons (UNODC).

Trafficking in persons is carried out by different types of traffickers, ranging from individuals to organized crime groups. The prime motivation for human trafficking is profit; billions of dollars are reaped by a web of participants, including recruiters, traffickers, agents, those who buy trafficked humans and profit from their labor, police and border agents, and government officials. Because of its highly secretive nature, no one knows for sure how many people are affected by trafficking; the United Nations is currently working to generate a sound estimate of the global number of trafficking victims (UNODC).

Global Trends in Trafficking

Although trafficking is a global phenomenon, its dynamics vary from region to region. Briefly, major trends include the following (UNODC):

South and East Asia and the Pacific—Adults make up approximately two-thirds of detected trafficking victims in this region. Trafficking for forced labor is the "major detected form of trafficking" (UNODC, p. 34), accounting for nearly two-thirds of victims (and more than 80 percent of victims in South Asia). Females make up the majority of detected victims trafficked for forced labor in this region, many probably forced to do domestic work. Southeast Asians, more than any other group, are widely trafficked across the world. Trafficking for forced marriages has been documented in this region.

Africa and the Middle East—Children constitute more than 60 percent of the detected victims of trafficking in this region. In Sub-Saharan Africa some children, mostly boys, are trafficked for armed combat. The majority of the detected victims trafficked for forced labor in this region are females (but poor data make it difficult to draw conclusions); many may be exploited in domestic labor. The Middle East is primarily an area of destination for trafficking victims, more than half of whom are trafficked from other regions (the highest share globally).

Europe and Central Asia—The most common detected victims in this region are adult women. Trafficking for sexual exploitation accounts for more than 65 percent of the victims detected. Males constitute two-thirds of victims of trafficking for forced labor. Trafficking for forced marriages has been documented. Countries in Eastern Europe and Central Asia report high rates of female participation as recruiters, agents, and traffickers.

Americas—Adults comprise approximately two-thirds of the detected victims in this region. However, North and Central America, as well as some countries in South America, have recently registered "clear increases" in the number of children among the detected victims (UNODC, p. 30). Nearly equal numbers of people are trafficked for forced labor and sexual exploitation in this region. (The proportion of detected trafficking for forced labor is likely underestimated in South America because it is unknown how many victims held in slavelike conditions are local and how many are held as a result of trafficking.)

Trafficking for Purposes of Sexual Exploitation

Trafficking for purposes of sexual exploitation happens in every region of the world. The victims are overwhelmingly women and girls; males account for about 3 percent of detected victims (UNODC). Those trafficked for sexual exploitation may be transported to foreign countries, where they do not understand the language or their legal rights. Police and immigration officials may be complicit in the exploitation or seek to arrest or deport exploited individuals, rather than aid them. A number of researchers report that globalization has brought a significant increase in trafficking for sexual exploitation, particularly among children (Estes & Weiner, 2001/2002; Flowe). (As a reminder, globalization is "the increased exchange of people, goods, capital, ideas and culture across national boundaries" [H. James, 2010, para. 1].) Women and girls are trafficked both within the Global North (within and between Europe, Canada, and the United States, for example) and within the Global South and from the Global South to the Global North. A recent nationwide study found that in the

MORE ABOUT...

Activists Combat Trafficking and Forced Labor

Farm workers—women and men—are among the "poorest paid and most exploited workers" in the United States (Anti-Slavery International, 2015, para. 1). Some migrant workers, mainly from Mexico, Guatemala, and Haiti, are lured by traffickers who promise to take them to well-paid jobs on American farms. Instead, workers find themselves caught in a system of debt bondage, allowed to keep only a small portion of their wages or none at all, after "expenses" are deducted to pay for their "debts" and other items such as housing and food. Enslaved workers often labor seven days a week, live in squalid conditions, and are subject to threats and violence. Women in forced labor may be subject to sexual harassment and assault (Anti-Slavery International, 2015).

The situation is often grave, but not without hope. In the United States, for example, the Coalition of Immokalee Workers, a worker-based human rights group in Florida, is educating farm workers and consumers, investigating and exposing farm slavery operations, and developing the Fair Food Program to hold growers and buyers accountable for fair labor practices. They have helped to rescue more than a thousand farm workers from slavery in the United States and have improved wages and working conditions for thousands more through accountability programs with corporations such as Taco Bell, McDonalds, Whole Foods, Burger King, and Subway (Coalition of Immokalee Workers, 2013).

FIGURE 10.1
Migrant workers pick sweet potatoes in Mechanicsville, Virginia. Exploitation of farm laborers is common in the United States but activist organizations, including the United Farm Workers and the Coalition of Immokalee Workers, are working to end forced labor.

United States, a significant number of children and adolescents who were being commercially sexually exploited were runaway or "throwaway" children from working- and middle-class families who had experienced sexual abuse at home (Estes & Weiner). Of these children, some girls (rarely boys) were trafficked across the United States or to other high-income countries such as Canada, Japan, Korea, England, and Germany (Estes & Weiner).

Who Is Vulnerable?

Although trafficking affects many kinds of victims, some patterns are worth noting. The most commonly detected victims of trafficking are those from "relatively poorer countries" or regions, who are exploited in "relatively richer ones" (UNODC, p. 38). Children are more vulnerable to trafficking than adults, largely because they are dependent on adults and tend to be more trusting of people in general. Females are more vulnerable than males, particularly when the threat or use of force is involved. Would-be migrants—those looking to leave their home countries in search of work—and newly arrived

breaking the frame
Male Victims of Trafficking

Male victims of trafficking, although far fewer in number than female victims, can be found globally and their numbers are thought to be increasing. Most detected male victims are trafficked for forced labor (UNODC). For example, in Russia, Central Asian men are victims of forced labor. Boys are forced to labor in illegal drug production in the United Kingdom and Mexico. Male victims of trafficking in South America and Africa can be found in "agriculture, construction, mining and logging" (U.S. Department of State, p. 35). Adolescent boys are vulnerable to sex trafficking in some countries, including the United States and Canada. In Afghanistan and Sri Lanka, boys are more likely than girls to be trafficked for sexual purposes (U.S. Department of State). Men from Cambodia and Myanmar are trafficked in large numbers and sold to captains on Thai fishing vessels for as little as a few hundred dollars each. There they are forced to work long hours for little or no pay in dangerous and miserable conditions, sometimes for years (Service & Palmstrom, 2012).

Although awareness of male victims of trafficking and forced labor is growing, male victims are still too often overlooked. Male victims may be at risk for deportation as undocumented or may be charged with crimes because authorities "fail to recognize" them as exploited (U.S. Department of State, p. 10). There is a great need for more research on the trafficking of boys and men (Laczko, 2005).

immigrants—those without ties or support networks—are often targeted by traffickers. Undocumented immigrants are particularly vulnerable to trafficking because they are often afraid or reluctant to go to local authorities for fear of deportation. Adolescents, particularly girls, living on the streets are vulnerable to trafficking for sexual exploitation, including in countries like the United States and Canada. Persons with disabilities may be targeted for forced begging. Refugees fleeing wars and natural disasters may also be targeted by traffickers (UNODC). LGBT people, because of persistent homophobia and discrimination, may be particularly vulnerable to traffickers who prey on the desperation of those who wish to escape "social alienation and mistreatment" (U.S. Department of State, 2013).

What Are the Causes of Human Trafficking?

There are complex push and pull factors related to trafficking. The most important push factor is poverty, which may be caused or exacerbated by a number of circumstances, including lack of economic opportunity, discrimination (based on race, sex, religion, disability, sexual identity, and/or other variables), armed conflict, and natural disasters in one's place of origin. Pull factors include the demand for labor and promise of a better life in one's intended destination. All of these make people vulnerable to trafficking. The greed that motivates traffickers and their agents is also a major factor, as are lax policies and enforcement, as well as corruption. Underlying these push and pull factors are ideologies and practices, including globalization and neoliberalism, that have contributed to poverty in some places and rising inequality globally, making millions of people vulnerable to trafficking. We discussed these in some depth in Chapter 8, "Work, Inequality, and Neoliberalism," and will recap them here.

Economic policies associated with neoliberalism have been promoted by a number of actors from the Global North, including governments, transnational lending agencies (like the World Bank), and transnational corporations and organizations (like the World Trade Organization). These policies include free trade agreements that limit or abolish regulations meant to protect workers, consumers, the economy, and the environment (Stiglitz, 2014) and may restrict labor unions; loans to "developing" countries that come with many strings attached, frequently including structural adjustment programs that force recipient governments to make deep cuts to social programs like health care, education, and social security; and privatization of public assets such as water, electrical grids, mines, roads, and other resources to for-profit companies in the name of cost cutting and efficiency (we discussed this in the opening of the chapter).

Although globalization has benefited some workers in the Global South, the riches produced have by and large gone to a wealthy elite that controls an ever-expanding proportion of the world's assets. Meanwhile, the poor in many parts of the Global South are left vulnerable to negative consequences such as forced labor and trafficking (C. Thomas, 2000).

GENITAL CUTTING PRACTICES

Genital cutting and modification are practiced worldwide and constitute a wide range of procedures, from male circumcision to intersex and sex reassignment surgeries to female genital cosmetic surgeries to traditional female genital cutting (fgc) practices. Some practices, like male circumcision (mc), are more common and well known. Approximately 30 percent of males globally "have had their genitals surgically modified" as infants, preadolescents, or adolescents (Public Policy Advisory Network, 2012, p. 21); most males in the United States have been circumcised (which most often involves removal of the prepuce or foreskin of the penis), but the prevalence of mc varies dramatically among different groups and overall is dropping in the United States (D. Smith et al., 2010). The American Academy of Pediatrics (2012) acknowledges that the health benefits of infant mc outweigh the risks but says the benefits are not great enough to recommend routine infant mc. Some groups oppose routine infant mc on the grounds that infants cannot consent to the procedure.

Other genital cutting practices are less common and little known, such as intersex surgery. Beginning in the mid-1900s in the United States, infants born with "ambiguous genitalia" were often subject to surgery so as to bring their genitals into conformity with societal norms for female or male genitalia (Intersex Society of North America, 2008a). Many were never told of their medical histories. The Intersex Society of North America (2008a) reported that the care that intersex infants receive even today "varies dramatically" depending on where a child is born. Although there seems to be general movement away from surgical interventions to alter infants' genitals, healthy testes continue to be removed from "female" infants and vaginoplasties continue to be performed on infants and small children in the name of social conformity (a vaginoplasty is surgery to create or "repair" a vagina). Regarding intersex surgery, Milton Diamond and H. Keith Sigmundson (2009), both of whom are doctors, advised that doctors should "perform no major surgery for cosmetic reasons alone; only for conditions related to physical/medical health" (para. 7). They continued,

ON THE web

Read about **what you can do about human trafficking** on the Student Website: www.oup.com/us/gillis-jacobs

This will entail a great deal of explanation needed for the parents who will want their children to "look normal." Explain to them that appearances during childhood, while not typical of other children, may be of less importance than functionality and post pubertal erotic sensitivity of the genitalia. Surgery can potentially impair sexual/erotic function. Therefore such surgery, which includes all clitoral surgery and any sex reassignment, should typically wait until puberty or after when the patient is able to give truly informed consent.

Female genital cosmetic surgeries are a growing practice in the West. In the United States today, such surgeries, marketed as "vaginal rejuvenation" and "designer vaginoplasty," are among the fastest growing cosmetic procedures (Braun, 2005). The procedures, which are largely unregulated, include clitoral reduction (cutting away the clitoral hood or prepuce to reduce its size) and labiaplasty (smoothing, reducing, or otherwise altering the labia minora and majora, the "lips" that make up the vulva, surrounding the clitoris). The American Congress of Obstetricians and Gynecologists (2007) has said that such procedures serve no medical purpose and their safety and effectiveness have not been documented. Complications can include scarring, infection, and altered sensation.

Perhaps the genital cutting practices that have received the widest attention from the media are **traditional female genital cutting practices** (also known as female circumcision or female genital mutilation) common to some groups in parts of Africa (mainly east and west Africa), the Middle East, and Southeast Asia (Figure 10.2). An estimated 200 million females are affected by these customary practices (UNICEF, 2016). Although the Western media has tended to focus on the most radical forms, fgc is made up of a "diverse set of practices," noted Leslye Obiora (1997, p. 52), including symbolic nicking/piercing or removal of the hood of the clitoral prepuce (the latter similar to the Western practice of clitoral reduction), partial or total removal of the clitoris, partial or complete removal of the labia minora and majora, and infibulation, which involves sewing shut the vaginal opening, with or without the removal of the clitoris. Infibulation, the most radical form of fgc, constitutes about 10 percent of all fgc and its prevalence is dropping (Wade, 2012). (We will return to fgc below.)

This is an extremely short survey, and we do not wish to equate all of these practices with each other; to do so would be overly "simplistic" and misleading (Wade, 2012, para. 9). What we do wish to suggest, however, is that genital modification is not unique to a particular region or the Global South, nor are the range of global practices completely unrelated (Wade, 2012). We will return to these ideas at the close of this section.

Traditional Female Genital Cutting

When Bogaletch Gebre was growing up in a village in southern Ethiopia, it was her job to fetch water for her family (Rosenberg, 2013). Each day on her way, however, she would sneak off to spend time at school before collecting the water and returning home. Eventually she became the first girl in her district to go to school beyond the fourth grade. As an adult, she studied abroad in Israel and the United States, before returning home in 1997 to found the organization *Kembatti Mentti Gezzima-Toppe* or KMG, which

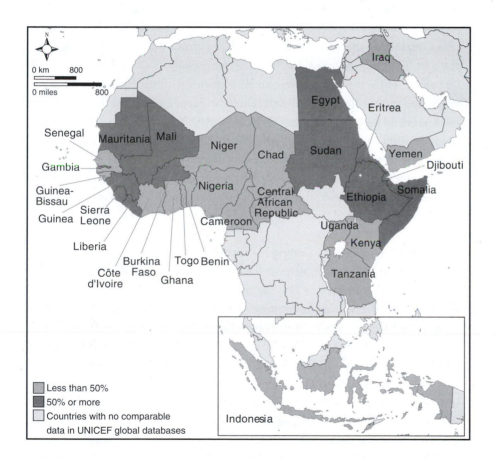

FIGURE 10.2

In the 30 countries where traditional female cutting is concentrated, there are wide variations in the percentages of girls and women cut within and between countries. Nearly half of females who have experienced fgc live in just three countries—Egypt, Ethiopia, and Indonesia (UNICEF, 2016).

means "women of Kembata working together." (Kembata Tembaro is the zone in southern Ethiopia where she grew up.) The organization works to end the practice of fgc. Gebre and her sisters were cut, like virtually all the girls in her district. Today, some 40 years later, female cutting has nearly vanished from Kembata Tembaro, in large part because of Gebre's work.

Fgc, like mc (which is also common where traditional fgc is practiced), occurs across a range of ages from infancy to late adolescence. Although the cutting is mostly carried out by traditional circumcisers, many of whom are female, trained health-care providers perform more than 18 percent of fgc procedures and that number is increasing (World Health Organization, 2013).

The percentage of females aged 15 to 49 who have undergone fgc remains high in some places (more than 90 percent in Somalia, Guinea, and Djibouti, for example), but there has been an overall decline in the prevalence of fgc over the past 30 years. In Egypt, for example, recent surveys found approximately 70 percent of 15- to 19-year-olds had undergone fgc compared with 97 percent of women in their late 40s. Liberia, Burkina Faso, and Kenya have also seen declines of 30 percent or more (UNICEF, 2016). Younger women are also less likely to support fgc than older women. In Egypt, only one-third of girls recently surveyed thought fgc should continue compared with two-thirds of older women (UNICEF, 2013). Although the percentage of females who are cut is declining, the overall number of females affected is still rising because population growth is outpacing the rate of decline (UNICEF, 2016).

The Reasons Why Female Cutting Is Practiced—Traditional fgc is not "a single phenomenon with a single purpose," wrote Ellen Gruenbaum (2000, p. 47). It is practiced for a variety of reasons among different ethnic groups. Among many groups, it marks a rite of passage from girlhood to womanhood and is seen as an integral part of a girl's upbringing. As such, it may be seen as a demonstration of strength and courage and mark a girl's entry into a powerful and secretive female society (Ahmadu, 2001). Among other groups, the primary reason for fgc is to clean, smooth, or beautify a woman's genitals, not unlike the reasons women in the United States give for undergoing labiaplasty or clitoral reduction. (Male circumcision in Africa is often performed for a similar reason.) Among still other groups, its purpose is to ensure a woman's morals or control her sexuality. In these cases, fgc can be a "manifestation of deep-rooted gender inequalities . . . [grounded] in cultural understandings of gender, sexuality, marriage and family" (UNICEF, 2010, p. 1).

In most countries where fgc is practiced, a majority of people think it should end, including nearly two-thirds of boys and men (UNICEF, 2016). Yet the practice persists. Why? The answer seems to lie in the fact that in communities where it is practiced, female cutting is a social norm, that is, it is customary within the group; such practices define who may be part of a group and who may not. In the case of fgc, the practice is seen as a necessary step to raising a girl and making her eligible for marriage. Indeed, the most common reason women give for supporting the practice is to gain social acceptance (UNICEF, 2013). Although many people believe it is religiously mandated, no religious scripts prescribe the practice. The social rewards and sanctions associated with fgc are "powerful," according to UNICEF (2010). Failure to conform can mean a girl is unable to marry, lead to social exclusion, and negatively affect the status of her whole family; conformity can bring social approval, respect, and enhanced social standing. Because of the social aspect of fgc, it is extremely difficult to abandon on an individual basis (UNICEF, 2010).

Consequences of Traditional Female Genital Cutting—The World Health Organization (2013) stresses that there are no health benefits to fgc, but the negative consequences can be far-reaching. Fgc can cause severe pain, shock, hemorrhage, tetanus, and sepsis (bacterial infection). Longer-term consequences can include obstructed menstruation, recurrent bladder and urinary tract infections, increased vulnerability to HIV/AIDS, infertility, and increased risk of childbirth complications (World Health Organization, 2013). It is difficult to assess whether serious negative health consequences related to fgc are the exception or the rule, particularly given the wide variation in the quality of health care throughout the regions where fgc is practiced (see, for example, Public Policy Advisory Network). It would not be surprising if girls and women from different regions are at radically different risk for negative outcomes. More study is warranted.

The sexual consequences of fgc can also be severe—pain during intercourse, significantly less sexual satisfaction, and decreased or no sexual desire (World Health Organization, 2011). There is evidence, however, that some, perhaps many, women, particularly those who have less radical forms of fgc, retain sexual pleasure. This may be because cutting away external tissue leaves erectile material, which lies mostly beneath the surface of the vulva, largely intact (Public Policy Advisory Network).

Although the physical consequences of fgc can be reduced if the procedure is done by a trained medical professional, many anti-fgc advocates oppose this practice, known as the medicalization of fgc. The World Health Organization (2011) noted that health-care providers who perform fgc contribute to the "persistence of the practice," lend it medical legitimacy, and can contribute to

FIGURE 10.3

Doussou Konate (center) campaigns to spread awareness of the harmful effects of female genital cutting in her native Senegal.

its spread (p. 5). No evidence exists to support the idea that medicalization will lead to the abandonment of female cutting. Other advocates, however, support limited medicalization of fgc to prevent infection and other negative outcomes (Ahmadu). This often means ensuring that traditional circumcisers practice under hygienic conditions and can administer local anesthesia.

Combating Female Genital Cutting—There is a significant African grassroots movement to end female cutting (Mgbako et al., 2010). In recent years, more than 5,000 villages in Senegal, Guinea, Gambia, Burkina Faso, and Somalia have pledged to end female cutting (C. Dugger, 2011; Mgbako et al.). Senegal, with the active involvement of government and activist and women's groups, is often considered a model for its comprehensive approach to ending fgc (Figure 10.3).

Much of the credit for progress against female cutting in Senegal goes to the human rights group Tostan (meaning "breakthrough"), which began its work there in 1991. An important component of Tostan's approach is getting entire villages or groups of villages to pledge to abandon the practice together, creating support for and accountability to one another (C. Dugger, 2011). Tostan and *Kembatti Mentti Gezzema-Toppe* (which we discussed earlier) both emphasize cooperation and consensus. "You must allow the community to decide for themselves rather than condemning," said Gebre. These groups have been successful largely because they are homegrown and because they address the social aspect of female cutting.

Critiquing the Western Discourse—Many feminists from the Global South, and increasingly feminists from the Global North, are critical of Western media, academics, and activists for distorted coverage of traditional fgc practices (often called female genital mutilation by groups who are against the practice) (Obiora). Feminists such as Chandra Mohanty, Leslye Obiora, and Fuambai Sia Ahmadu are part of a growing chorus of voices warning against viewing and representing female genital cutting as monolithic, backward, and uniquely Third World. Such views, noted Lisa Wade (2014), are "strongly shaped by racism [and] ethnocentrism" (para. 2). They also caution against the neocolonial perspective that the Global South is a place to be civilized through intervention by the Global North. Women of the Global South have too often been constructed as always victims, wrote C. Mohanty (1986). C. Mohanty (2003) explained that the Global South must not be seen simply through the lens of oppression, "but in terms of historical complexities and the many struggles to change these oppressions" (p. 501). (See Chapter 12, "Feminisms," for more on transnational feminism.)

Where, then, do transnational feminists such as those cited above stand on the issue? They have differing views, but many explicitly recognize the importance of incorporating context and complications. Generally speaking, many oppose routine infant fgc as a violation of girls' rights. More specifically, Leslye Obiora, who is from Nigeria and now teaches in the United States, counseled that where there is *well founded* evidence that the practice causes harm the custom should be challenged" (p. 67, italics in original). Obiora also asserted that local women have the right to initiate and lead anti-fgc strategies and to formulate local solutions.

Fuambai Ahmadu, an anthropologist from Sierra Leone who grew up in the United States and chose to return to Sierra Leone to be circumcised at the age of 21, believes girls should be taught the positives and negatives about fgc and should be allowed to make informed decisions themselves. She has argued that traditionalists must afford uncircumcised women the same status as circumcised women and that abolitionists must stop stigmatizing those who continue the practice. Women, she says, must not be forced "to choose between two extremist positions" (p. 309).

Interrogating Genital Modification Globally

Let us return for a moment to the broader context of genital modification practices with which we opened this section. How should we think about mc? Female genital cosmetic surgeries? Should we oppose such procedures? Some activists question whether mc should be performed on infants who have no ability to consent or refuse. Others point to its cultural and religious importance in their support of the practice.

The issue of genital cosmetic surgeries is similarly complicated. Feminists have theorized that coverage of genital cosmetic surgeries in the media, the mainstreaming of pornography, and the Western veneration of youth have contributed "to the widespread acceptance of a single genital ideal, and the normalization of cosmetic surgery as the solution to deviations from that ideal" (Keil, 2010, p. 12). Yet some women report being better able to enjoy sex after cosmetic surgery because they are no longer self-conscious about the appearance of their genitals (Braun). But how "free" is sexual freedom bought at the price of cosmetic surgery? Is there such a thing as a free and informed decision when Western beauty standards exert pressure on all of us? What about the right to choose what one does with one's own body? If—and we do mean *if*—you come to the conclusion that there is no single right or wrong answer in the case of Western genital modification practices, then you must ask, is there a single right or wrong answer in the case of traditional fgc practices?

When it comes to genital cutting practices, the more you know, the less certain you may feel. That may be unsettling to you, but deep engagement with complex issues often is—and should be. Well-informed and well-intentioned people can and do disagree about this issue (and many others), but as long as they disagree from within nuanced understandings, this is okay. The one answer we know is wrong is the one that is not well considered.

HUMAN RIGHTS AND THE LGBTI COMMUNITY

Recognition of the human rights of those in the LGBTI community is progressing, perhaps even gaining momentum, but tremendous challenges remain. According to the UN High Commissioner for Human Rights (2015), "Hundreds of [LGBT] people have been killed and thousands more injured in brutal, violent attacks" in recent years. The Trans Murder Monitoring project noted that 1,731 trans and gender-diverse people were reported killed from 2008 to 2014 globally ("Transrespect Versus Transphobia," 2015). (More on violence against LGBT people is discussed in Chapter 9, "Gender-Based Violence.")

A number of countries enshrine discrimination against LGBT people in their laws. Those convicted of consensual same-sex sexual activity in Iran, Mauritania, Sudan, Yemen, and portions of Nigeria and Somalia face the death penalty. Homosexuality remains criminalized in 76 countries. There are reports from Iraq and Syria indicating that the Islamic State has executed men for allegedly engaging in sodomy (UN High Commissioner for Human Rights). Uganda, Nigeria, and India have recently taken actions that deny LGBT rights and potentially place LGBT people in danger. Russia is among countries that have adopted "anti-propaganda" laws aimed at LGBT people. The result in Russia has been harassment and violence against LGBT people in a "deteriorating situation of widespread and concerted abuse" (Human Rights Watch, 2014, para. 1). The Russian police response has been unsympathetic or worse. Vigilante groups have attacked gay people in dozens of Russian cities and posted videos of the attacks online, further stigmatizing those targeted. U.S. evangelical Christian groups have promoted efforts to promulgate anti-LGBT laws in Russia, Nigeria, Uganda, Namibia, Malawi, Kenya, Liberia, Zambia, Rwanda, and Zimbabwe (Eichelberger, 2014).

Yet negative developments have been matched by positive developments elsewhere. A number of countries have recently extended rights to LGBT people, including Mozambique, Palau, Sao Tome, and Principe, which have decriminalized homosexuality since 2011. Chile, Cuba, Fiji, and Malta have enacted or strengthened laws prohibiting discrimination based on sexual orientation and gender identity. New Zealand, France, Luxembourg, and the United States are among more than a dozen nations that have extended marriage rights or civil unions to lesbians and gays since 2011. Dutch lawmakers recently approved a bill allowing trans people to legally change their sex on official documents (UN High Commissioner for Human Rights). Trans and intersex people in Australia and New Zealand are able to mark "indeterminate" in the gender category on their passports. Other countries have made a similar shift, including Nepal, which issues citizenship papers with a category for third gender, India, which allows voters to choose "other" as a gender category on voter forms, and Bangladesh, which recognizes *Hijra* as a third gender category on passports. In Germany, parents of intersex children can mark their birth certificates with an X rather than specifying the sex of the child as female or male.

Important steps have been taken to improve the situation of LGBTI people globally, but, as the UN High Commissioner noted, "much, much more needs to be done."

NO COUNTRY IS FREE OF HUMAN RIGHTS ABUSES

It is appropriate to be outraged by the injustices that plague our world. We should all want better for the world's people. But it would be a mistake to think that human rights abuses are perpetrated only by other people or other governments in other places. No country is free from human rights abuses. The United States has been home to some of the most brutal human rights abuses imaginable: the enslavement of Africans, lynching of Blacks, and genocidal campaigns against Native Americans among them. Colonialism by dozens of Western countries exploited the peoples and natural resources of entire countries. Neocolonialist practices continue this legacy. Human rights abuses in the United States—and elsewhere—are not only historical; they are also ongoing. Do American soldiers rape in war? Yes, and as elsewhere, they are rarely prosecuted. Are Americans traffickers? Again, yes. They are also trafficked. Untold thousands of workers in the United States—many undocumented immigrants—are subject to forced labor. In the United States, studies suggest that one in five women experiences attempted or completed sexual assault while in college (Krebs et al., 2007). Some activists have warned that the exceptionally high rate of imprisonment of young men of color in the United States is a contemporary form of Jim Crow. The United States has the largest reported incarcerated population in the world and by far the highest rate of imprisonment among industrialized nations; with about 5 percent of the world's population, the United States imprisons about one-fourth of the world's prisoners (Stiglitz, 2014). It is also the only Western democracy to execute prisoners.

Beyond such abuses, there are plenty of examples of corrosive and harmful social norms in American society. Narrow beauty standards, for example, contribute to low self-esteem, depression, eating disorders, and a growing demand for plastic surgery. America is home to more cosmetic enhancements every year than any other country, including so-called Cinderella surgery, creating "designer feet for designer shoes" by shortening or lengthening toes or other procedures (Stover, 2014).

Your outrage is welcome. Just remember, there are many abuses out there—and some of them are right in front of you.

THE UNITED NATIONS, HUMAN RIGHTS, AND ACTIVISM

Although the idea of human rights has developed over hundreds of years, the idea of the universality of such rights (meaning that rights apply to everyone) gained prominence much more recently, with the establishment of the

ON THE
web

Read about **sexual violence in conflict areas** on the Student Website: www.oup.com/us/gillis-jacobs

United Nations (Briceño, 1998). Three years after its founding, in 1948, the UN General Assembly adopted the Universal Declaration of Human Rights, the most widely recognized statement of human rights globally. Its first article reads, "all human beings are born free and equal in dignity and rights." The rights it enshrines are today widely recognized in theory if not always in practice.

The Universal Declaration of Human Rights and two important human rights covenants that followed—the International Covenant on Civil and Political Rights and the International Covenant on Economic, Social, and Cultural Rights—together form what is known as the international bill of human rights. Their scope is exceptionally broad and their language inclusive. Yet, despite this broad foundation and the thousands of international, regional, and national laws that further enumerate people's rights, abuses persist. Women and girls are particularly vulnerable to such abuses, but not exclusively so. Minorities (racial, ethnic, religious, and others), people with dis/abilities, children (including boys), LGBT people, migrants, refugees, civilians in conflict situations, and/or the poor, among others, are also vulnerable.

In the seven decades since the founding of the United Nations, the body of human rights law has expanded greatly. Conceptions of human rights and their application have evolved. We will turn our discussion particularly to human rights law and women as an illustrative example of the way human rights law has changed and grown largely because of the work of activists. We will also highlight the work of three human rights activists, beginning with Leymah Gbowee (below).

FIGURE 10.4
Eleanor Roosevelt holding a copy of the Universal Declaration of Human Rights in Spanish. Roosevelt chaired the commission that drafted the declaration and was instrumental in shaping its vision of human rights.

Universal and Indivisible?

Human rights are, at least on paper, both universal (that is, they apply to everyone equally) and indivisible (none is to be applied separately or privileged over others); in practice, however, they have too often been neither. Rather than universal, they have privileged male experiences, and rather than indivisible, they have been applied unevenly, often to the detriment of women (among others). The problem is twofold: First, the application of human rights law has

Leymah Gbowee, Liberia

"Sometimes people call my way of speaking ranting," said Leymah Gbowee. "The reason why I rant is because I am a voice for many women. . . . And I will not stop ranting until my mission of equality of all girls is achieved." Gbowee led the women's campaign for peace in Liberia, a small West African nation that had been at war for more than two decades (Figure 10.5). In 2003, campaign members began gathering each day in the capital city of Monrovia at the fish market to demand peace as war lords bore down on the city. Eventually their presence forced the country's president to enter into peace talks. To increase the pressure for peace, they staged a sex strike, reminiscent of Lysistrata (in the classical play of the same name by Aristophanes). With peace talks dragging as violence still raged, Gbowee and hundreds of women barricaded recalcitrant war lords (all men) into a negotiating hall and threatened to remain until a peace deal had been reached. Largely because of their efforts, a peace deal was announced not long after. But the women were not yet satisfied. They turned their sights to ensuring that the country's upcoming presidential election was free and fair. In 2006, Liberia became the first African country with an elected female president, Ellen Johnson Sirleaf.

Leymah Gbowee (2011), in her Nobel acceptance speech, talked about the hard-fought victory the women of Liberia had achieved:

We worked daily confronting warlords, meeting with dictators and refusing to be silenced in the face of AK 47s and RPGs [rocket-propelled grenades]. We walked when we had no transportation, we fasted when water was unaffordable, we held hands in the face of danger, we spoke truth to power when everyone else was being diplomatic, we stood under the rain and the sun with our children to tell the world the stories of the other side of the conflict. Our educational backgrounds, travel experiences, faiths, and social classes did not matter. We had a common agenda: peace for Liberia now.

(The documentary film *Pray the Devil Back to Hell* [2008] tells the story of Leymah Gbowee and the Women of Liberia Mass Action for Peace Campaign.)

FIGURE 10.5
Leymah Gbowee led the Women of Liberia Mass Action for Peace Campaign, which was instrumental in ousting Liberia's corrupt president and ending the civil war that wracked her home country. She won the Nobel Prize in 2011.

focused primarily on persecution in the public realm by governments. The unique abuses that women and girls face simply because they are female, which often take place in private at the hands of family or community members, too often go unrecognized. Second, the part of human rights law that does consider women's rights specifically has often been without teeth or simply ignored by governments. We will take up the first of these problems here and the second in our discussion of the Women's Convention that follows.

Public and Private Rights

Geraldine Ferraro, the first female vice presidential candidate representing a major American political party, dedicated herself to the advancement of women's human rights throughout her life. In 1993, she wrote, "Although the 1948 Universal Declaration of Human Rights nominally includes women, the icon of human rights abuse has been a man behind bars, tortured for speaking his mind." Think Nelson Mandela and Chinese human rights activist Liu Xiaobo. Without a doubt, such men deserve protection. Also without a doubt, women have been detained and tortured for speaking their minds. Aung San Suu Kyi was under house arrest for nearly 15 years in her native Myanmar (Burma) for opposing that country's military junta (Figure 10.6). Such imprisonments are widely recognized as human rights violations and widely condemned.

But what about women who are tortured for speaking their minds at home? What if, wrote Susan Moller Okin (1998), "a husband pays a bride price for his wife or marries her without her adult consent, if he confines her to their home, forbids her to work for pay, or appropriates her wages, if he beats her for disobedience or mishap; these manifestations of slavery would not be recognized in many parts of the world" (p. 35). What if a woman cannot access credit or own property because she is a woman? What if a girl child is not allowed to go to school, fed less than her brothers, and given inferior health care because she is a girl? These are violations that females face because they are females. They occur not in public, but in private, not at the hands of her government, but at the hands of her family and community (although governments often also have a role in condoning them). Among the most likely forms of discrimination and violence that

FIGURE 10.6
Aung San Suu Kyi leads the National League for Democracy in Myanmar (Burma). She spent nearly 15 years under house arrest for supporting democracy in her country. In 2015, her party captured a majority of seats in parliament in the first free elections in 25 years.

women face globally, they are rooted in gendered notions that devalue women and girls. It is these violations that are too often excluded from the human rights arena.

Engendering Human Rights Law Through a Women's Convention

The **UN Convention on the Elimination of All Forms of Discrimination Against Women**, also known as CEDAW or the Women's Convention, is a "landmark in the history of women's human rights," the first human rights treaty to comprehensively address women's rights (Briceño, p. 52). Adopted by the UN General Assembly in 1979, the Women's Convention has been ratified (adopted as law) by all but a handful of countries. The United States is the only country in the developed world not to sign CEDAW into law. U.S. ratification of CEDAW, like all treaties, requires a two-thirds vote of the Senate.

In its preamble, the Women's Convention asserts that "a change in the traditional role of men as well as the role of women in society and in the family is needed to achieve full equality of men and women." Article One defines discrimination against women as "any distinction, exclusion or restriction made on the basis of sex which has the effect or purpose of impairing or nullifying the . . . exercise by women, irrespective of their marital status, on a basis

MORE ABOUT...

The Women's Convention

Governments that have ratified the convention agree to take actions that include the following:

- Passing legislation to modify or abolish customs and practices that discriminate against women;

- Guaranteeing women the rights to vote and to hold office;

- Taking all measures necessary to suppress forced prostitution and trafficking in women;

- Ensuring women equal rights with men in education, employment, health care, property ownership, and all matters relating to marriage and family relations;

- Including advice on family planning in the education process and guaranteeing women's right to decide freely the number and spacing of their children.

(Read the full text at http://www.un.org/womenwatch/daw/cedaw/text/econvention.htm#article1.)

of equality of men and women, of human rights and fundamental freedoms in the political, economic, social, cultural, civil or any other field." The scope of the Women's Convention is not limited to the conduct of the nation state (that is, primarily the government and related entities), but obliges countries to eliminate discrimination wherever it occurs.

Where CEDAW Falls Short—Despite its broad scope, CEDAW has some serious weaknesses, perhaps the greatest of which is that the main body of the text does not address gender-based violence against women, a human rights violation in and of itself, but also a major obstacle to achieving other rights. Although CEDAW is legally binding (countries that ratify it are required to enforce it as law), violence is dealt with only in a nonbinding way, and many countries have chosen to ignore this provision.

Another significant problem is that governments that have ratified CEDAW have made more reservations to its mandates than to any other human rights treaty, thereby signaling they do not intend to uphold certain parts of the treaty. Many of these reservations deal with women's rights within marriage and the family, the root of much discrimination that women face globally, including rights to own property and inheritance rights. Such reservations indicate governments' unwillingness to challenge the most embedded practices of discrimination (Butler & Gillis, 1997).

It is worth noting two other issues on which CEDAW is silent—abortion rights and the rights of lesbians and transgender people. Because abortion is illegal in many countries, no UN treaty to date has included the right to a safe and legal abortion (Howard-Hassmann, 2011). The issue remains too controversial to be addressed in this way. Additionally, no UN treaty addresses discrimination on the basis of sexual orientation or gender identity, although the UN High Commissioner for Human Rights and the UN Secretary-General have expressed their support for protections based on sexual orientation and gender identity.

U.S. Nonratification of CEDAW—Why hasn't the United States ratified CEDAW? The stated reasons vary, but one common objection is to imposing "international law" on the United States. The United States, however, has acceded to dozens if not hundreds of international treaties on issues ranging from conduct in war to disarmament to torture. Another common objection is that U.S. law already guarantees the major provisions of CEDAW. This is largely true, although whether these laws work effectively to combat discrimination is certainly debatable. Think, for example, of the fact that women in

MORE ABOUT...

Tawakkol Karman, Yemen

On a night in January 2011, Tawakkol Karman, a 32-year-old activist and journalist from Yemen, a small country at the southern end of the Arabian Peninsula, gathered with friends in her country's capital city of Sana, sparking a movement that eventually involved millions of protesters (Figure 10.7). Demonstrators demanded the resignation of Yemen's president, Ali Abdullah Saleh, widely seen as heading a corrupt regime that left nearly one-third of Yemenis living in severe poverty and saw Yemen ranked 148th of 148 countries for gender equality (UN Development Programme, 2013). Karman, who became a leader of the movement for democracy in Yemen, was beaten, kidnapped, and, as a woman, singled out for criticism, accused of degrading the morals of Yemeni women. Yet she persisted, declaring, "We will make our revolution . . . or we will die trying." After more than a year of protest, President Saleh resigned. Tawakkol Karman's struggle, as well as that of her country, to complete the democratic revolution continues.

FIGURE 10.7

Tawakkol Karman was a leader in the struggle for democracy in Yemen during the Arab Spring movement in 2011. She is the first Arab woman to win the Nobel Prize.

the United States still earn only 78 cents for every dollar that men earn. (See Chapter 8, "Work, Inequality, and Neoliberalism," for more on the pay gap.) Passage of CEDAW could draw attention to where those laws are working and where they fall short and could be a tool for advocates to pressure for stronger measures to uphold women's human rights. U.S. passage of CEDAW would also be a powerful symbol that the United States is dedicated to ensuring women's rights at home and abroad.

The UN Fourth World Conference on Women

Beginning in 1975 in Mexico City, the United Nations held a series of conferences to address the status of women globally. The **UN Fourth World Conference on Women**, held in Beijing in 1995, marked a significant turning point in the global recognition of women's rights.

"A revolution has begun and there is no going back," declared Gertrude Mongella, secretary-general of the Fourth World Conference on Women at the conclusion of that conference (Butler & Gillis, p. 8). The revolution she spoke of was largely embodied in the conference's Platform for Action, which was agreed on by the 189 countries represented in Beijing at the conference and can be summed up by the phrase that became the unofficial slogan of the conference, "Women's rights are human rights and human rights are women's rights." But not all that was important happened inside the conference hall where governmental delegates met. Arguably as important were the more informal meetings of civil society groups, which offered a venue for women and men from all over the world to educate one another, to strategize together, and to make contacts that have been integral to the development of a global women's movement.

The Platform for Action, which addresses 12 critical areas, represents the most comprehensive agenda on women's rights ever agreed on by governments (although it is not legally binding). Among other things, governments agreed to do the following: modify economic policies to ensure women's advancement, reduce maternal mortality, guarantee the right of women to equal pay for equal work, enact laws to ensure marriage is entered into with free consent, and take steps to abolish traditional practices harmful to girls. The Platform for Action acknowledges that the gap between the existence of women's human rights and their enjoyment stems from a lack of commitment on the part of governments to protect such rights and to inform women and men about them. The platform built on decades of work by advocates for women's rights and signaled the growing strength of a global women's movement working to address the diverse issues that affect women and men worldwide

(Butler & Gillis). In the years since its passage, it has been broadly influential within the UN system and has been used by many women's groups to hold their own governments accountable for protecting women's human rights. *Read the Platform for Action at* http://www.un.org/womenwatch/daw/beijing/platform/.

A Conference of Firsts—The Women's Conference and Platform for Action were notable for their significant firsts.

Sex and Gender—Governmental representatives debated the meanings of the terms sex and gender for the first time, revealing both misconceptions and misgivings. (For a review of the terms sex and gender, see Chapters 1 and 3.) In negotiations, some governmental delegates sought to replace the term gender in the Platform for Action (with its implication of social construction and mutability) with the term sex as traditionally understood (that is, there are two biological sexes, female and male, that are essentially different from one another and lead women and men to play naturally different roles in society) (Bunch & Fried, 1996). Ultimately, conservative forces lost this battle, and the term gender was used hundreds of times throughout the Platform for Action, a significant victory for women's advocates because it recognizes that women's secondary status in so many arenas is not natural but a construction of societies.

Multiple Oppressions—The multiple barriers facing many women, which had been rendered invisible at past women's conferences, were acknowledged in the platform, including discrimination based on race, ethnicity, age, and/or dis/ability. "For . . . women of color, [the Fourth World Conference on Women] marked an historic turning point," wrote Dorothy Gilliam, a columnist for the *Washington Post*. "After four decades since its founding, the U.N. has finally recognized, officially, that gender was not the sole issue for the majority of the world's women" (Butler & Gillis).

Sexual Rights and Sexual Orientation—Also for the first time, governmental delegates openly discussed "sexual rights" and "sexual orientation" in the context of the Platform for Action. Although the phrase sexual orientation was excluded from the Platform, "a door was opened" with the discussions (Bunch & Fried, p. 202). In a positive development, a number of governments, including some from each region of the world, supported inclusion of sexual orientation as a category deserving of protection from discrimination; a number

The Importance of Educating Girls

The number of children not in school has dropped by almost one-third in the past decade, thanks in part to the Beijing Platform for Action and the Millennium Development Goals that followed it, which have prompted more attention to inequality in education. Still, of the 67 million children still out of school, more than half are girls (UN Girls' Education Initiative, 2012). Having an education makes an enormous difference for females. Women with a basic education are much less likely to be poor. An infant born to an educated woman is much more likely to survive into adulthood. Women and girls who are educated are better able to claim other rights (United Kingdom Department for International Development, 2005).

For some girls, getting an education has proven extremely dangerous, as the example of Malala Yousafzai, the young Pakistani activist who was shot by the Taliban, has shown (Figure 10.8). The UN secretary-general Ban Ki-moon, when introducing Malala at the United Nations in 2013, said that by targeting her, "extremists showed what they fear most: a girl with a book."

FIGURE 10.8
Malala Yousafzai of Pakistan advocates for female education and is the youngest ever Nobel Prize laureate. She was 17 at the time of her award.

MORE ABOUT...

of those countries stated that they interpreted the platform to include such protections (Bunch & Fried).

The Platform for Action has had an influential presence at the United Nations, where women are increasingly seen as important partners in peace-making and development, and in the international arena, where a number of laws have been passed since 1995 to ensure women's equality. Post-Beijing, one area of greatest impact, wrote Linda Tarr-Whelan (2010), is women's participation in decision making and governing. The Platform for Action calls on countries to work toward gender balance in government. In response, since 1995, "governments on every continent except North America, 101 in all, have

MORE ABOUT...

Ai-jen Poo, United States

There are an estimated 1–2 million domestic workers in the United States today—housekeepers and caregivers for children, the elderly and people with dis/abilities; nearly all are excluded from federal and state labor laws. These workers, who are overwhelmingly female, have no right to collective bargaining, occupational safety and health protections, sick and vacation pay, or protections from discrimination and sexual harassment (MacArthur Foundation, 2014). Ai-jen Poo and the labor movement she has galvanized are working to change this (Figure 10.9). Poo began her work on Manhattan's Lower East Side, volunteering with immigrant workers.

Soon she was helping domestic workers connect with one another. Poo and the workers she organized fought for passage of the U.S.'s first Domestic Workers Bill of Rights in New York State (enacted in 2010), which entitles domestic workers in New York to overtime, one day off per week, and three days of paid leave per year (Swarns, 2014). Poo also mobilized thousands of domestic workers to successfully lobby the U.S. Department of Labor to include caregivers for the elderly and people with dis/abilities in federal minimum wage and overtime protections.

FIGURE 10.9
Ai-jen Poo is the director of the National Domestic Workers Alliance and has spearheaded creation of a worker-led labor movement to advocate for the rights of domestic workers in the United States. She was awarded a MacArthur Foundation "genius" grant for her work in 2014.

established legal, constitutional or [political] party changes to improve the representation of women in public policy-making" (Tarr-Whelan, para. 14). Some countries have instituted quotas for women, and these countries are seeing major changes in the number of women elected to office, whereas those without quotas are seeing only slow changes (Tarr-Whelan). Two recent studies by the UN Development Fund for Women have shown the possible impact of such changes. In Norway, for example, there is a strong positive correlation between the availability of child care and higher numbers of female representatives on municipal councils. Also, in India, where local village councils have quotas for female participation, women-led councils have seen a 60 percent increase in drinking water projects compared with villages where councils are led by men (Tarr-Whelan). (See the Student Website for more on political quotas.)

The struggle for women's human rights has been long and is far from complete. There are still places in the world where discrimination against women is enshrined in laws (for example, UN Women (2012) reported that 86 countries had discriminatory inheritance practices or laws in 2012), and even where it is not, women have yet to achieve equality with men. But progress has been made, particularly in the recognition at the international level that women's rights are human rights.

CONCLUSION

In 1999, Catharine MacKinnon wrote an essay in which she asked, "Are women human?" In the face of trafficking, rape in wartime, son preference, forced marriage, and other grave violations, "to be a woman is not yet a name for a way of being human," she concluded. "If we measure the reality of women's situation in all its variety against the guarantees of the Universal Declaration [of Human Rights], not only do women not have the rights it guarantees—most of the world's men don't either—it is hard to see, in its vision of humanity, a woman's face" (p. 43). MacKinnon's question is compelling. Although the recognition of women's rights as human rights is emerging, progress is slow and uneven. But there is progress. MacKinnon's almost parenthetical comment—"*most of the world's men don't have the rights guaranteed in the UDHR either*"—should not be ignored. Many men are negatively affected by human rights violations. Immigrant men, those from racial and ethnic minorities, gay men, men with dis/abilities, and/or poor men are particularly vulnerable.

Key Terms

Although the movement for human rights has been ongoing for more than 200 years and work for women's rights nearly as long, the movement for recognition of LGBT rights is by comparison much younger. Globally, the rights of the LGBT community are precarious, newly recognized in some countries, and unrecognized in many others.

When it comes to human rights, it is important to think globally, but it is also important to look and act locally. Human rights abuses happen in every country. We encourage you to critically examine your own country's record on human rights and to act—locally and globally—for a better world.

THINK, LEARN, ACT

The following resources are available on the Student Website: www.oup.com/us/gillis-jacobs

Taking Stock, Taking Action prompts and activities. Apply what you've learned to take action on campus and in the broader community.

Recommended Readings and Multimedia Resources, including scholarly and literary works, documentaries, feature films, podcasts and more, to enrich the in- and out-of-classroom experience.

HISTORY OF WOMEN'S ACTIVISM IN THE UNITED STATES

STRUGGLES AND SOLIDARITIES

In what Jennifer Baumgardner (2011) called a "really,
really short history" of U.S. feminism, she employed the traditional
three "wave" model of the American women's movement to describe feminist activism from the mid-1800s to the present. Of the
first wave of American feminism, which Baumgardner dated from
about 1840 to 1920, she wrote, "If the First Wave had to be boiled
down to one goal, it was rights of citizenship" (para. 10). The first
wave's landmark event was the Seneca Falls conference on

women's rights (1848) and its landmark achievement was suffrage (1920). On the way to the vote, women won property rights and were for the first time admitted to the bar (1870) and elected to Congress (1917). Scores of feminists were arrested while agitating for the right to vote and Margaret Sanger was arrested for distributing birth control information (1914).

Baumgardner dated the **second wave** from about 1960 to 1988. The dominant goal of second wavers, according to Baumgardner, "might be boiled down to equality" (para. 12). Feminists—liberal, radical, socialist, and more—declared that *the personal is political* and connected to other women's experiences through consciousness-raising sessions. Second wavers successfully pushed for laws prohibiting sex and race discrimination in the workplace (1964) and sex discrimination in education (1972 and 1974); 1974 marked the first time a woman in the United States had the right to a credit card in her own name. Women of color, increasingly frustrated with a white, middle-, and upper-class feminist movement, developed theories of multiple, interlocking oppressions.

Baumgardner dated the start of the **third wave** as 1988 (others have cited 1992). Third wavers "rejected the idea of a shared political priority list or even a set of issues one must espouse to be feminist," according to Baumgardner (para. 15); third wave feminism is "portable" and "individually driven" (para. 17). Third wave feminism engages, produces, and critiques popular culture. It is multicultural and genderbending, influenced by postmodern and queer theorists (for postmodern, see Chapter 12; for queer, see Chapters 4 and 12).

RETHINKING THE WAVES

It is important to understand the three waves model of feminism because references to it in accounts of American women's history are plentiful. But we feel it is vital to move beyond what many feminists are recognizing as its exclusionary focus. The historian Julie Gallagher (2010), for example, has noted that the three waves illuminate "only certain kinds of activism that were engaged in by a limited set of historical actors," those actors often being middle- and upper-class white women (pp. 81–82). This model also narrowly focuses on women working within movements or organizations that have considered sex and gender the primary or sole factors oppressing women. Women of color, working-class women, immigrant women, women on welfare, lesbians, transgender people, women with dis/abilities, older women, and/or others who face multiple oppressions are among those whose activism is often rendered invisible in this model. Our goal with this chapter is to make connections across a broad array of American social movements, suggesting what Cobble (2010) called a "long women's movement," echoing historians' conception of a long Black freedom movement (extending both before and after the civil rights movement of the 1960s and 1970s). By doing so, we hope to provide, in Cobble's (2010) words, not "a single vision of sisterhood" but many versions of sisterhoods, with "contingent solidarities and shifting points of convergence" (p. 90).

THE ROOTS OF FEMINIST ORGANIZING IN THE UNITED STATES

Although 1848 and the Seneca Falls conference on women's rights are often pegged as the beginning of the "woman" movement in the United States, there are many reasons to look further back to find the roots of feminist organizing (Hewitt, 2010). Indeed, a number of historians have argued that the antislavery movement is rightly seen as the birthplace of feminist activism in the United States, both because many abolitionists, particularly women, were later involved in the woman movement and because many abolitionist organizations were being pressed by these women to face "the woman question" (Hewitt).

FIGURE 11.1

Angelina Grimké, with her sister Sarah, came from a prominent South Carolina slave-owning family. She and her sister moved to Philadelphia, became Quakers, and were prominent abolitionists and women's rights activists.

The Antislavery Movement and the Woman Question

As early as the latter half of the 1600s, antislavery activists, many of them Quakers, were working in the American colonies to condemn slavery and persuade others of its horrors. The first antislavery society was formed in Pennsylvania as the American Revolution began.

By the early 19th century, a number of women and men, both Black and white, who were active in the antislavery movement regularly spoke out about women's rights, linking "women's exploitation to issues of race and labor" (Hewitt, p. 18). Prominent among them were Angelina and Sarah Grimké and Lucretia Mott (who were white) and Grace Bustill Douglass and Charlotte, Margaretta, and Sarah Louisa Forten (free Black women) (Figure 11.1). These women founded the Philadelphia Female Anti-Slavery Society, the first abolitionist organization in which Black and white women shared leadership. At the

Anti-Slavery Convention of American Women in 1837, Angelina Grimké offered a resolution that said, "The time has come for woman to move in that sphere which Providence has assigned her, and no longer remained (*sic*) satisfied in the circumscribed limits with which corrupt custom and a perverted application of Scripture have encircled her" (as cited in Hewitt). These words resounded 11 years later when repeated nearly verbatim at the Seneca Falls conference on women's rights.

Although the Philadelphia Female Anti-Slavery Society was integrated, many antislavery organizations remained segregated and, as Estelle Freedman (2002) noted, "opposition to slavery did not necessarily translate into a belief in racial equality" among white abolitionists (p. 77). As a result, it was largely left to African Americans to take up the cause of racial justice. From the early 1800s, African American women were important figures in campaigns for racial justice and for women's rights. Women such as Sojourner Truth, who was formerly enslaved, and Maria Stewart, a free-born Black woman, spoke about their experiences, often with heavily religious overtones, to "promiscuous audiences"—mixed audiences of women and men—a rarity at the time. Stewart is thought to be the first African American woman to speak before a mixed audience of women and men and the first recorded African American female journalist ("Maria W. Stewart," 2007; National Women's History Museum, 2007). In 1831, she implored African American women to

> possess the spirit of independence.... Possess the spirit of men, bold and enterprising, fearless and undaunted. Sue for your rights and privileges. Know the reason that you cannot attain them. Weary them with your importunities. You can but die if you make the attempt; and we shall certainly die if you do not. (M. Richardson, 1987, p. 38)

Harriet Tubman, who escaped from slavery, became a "guiding light" of the Underground Railroad, and served in the Union Army as an espionage agent, also worked on behalf of women's rights after the Civil War (Reifer, 2005). Many Black women brought an "immediate, material" focus to the abolitionist movement, advocating for access to education and jobs for Blacks and aid to those who had escaped enslavement (Hewitt, p. 21). Their work raising money, challenging segregated schools, and boycotting goods produced by enslaved persons was vital to the abolitionist movement and their organizing experience was a key to later social movements, including antilynching and labor campaigns.

Although many of the women and men involved in the social movements of the 1800s couched their activism in religious terms, some were decidedly nonreligious. Ernestine Rose, a socialist, was an "other" among others—an Eastern European among Western European Americans, a Jew among Christians, and an atheist among believers (Kolmerten, 2002). Rose arrived in New York from London in 1836 and almost immediately began advocating for passage of a married women's property act in that state, which was achieved a dozen years later. New York's law, which recognized a woman's right to retain control of her property after marriage, became a model for many other states. One of the most important speakers in the early feminist movement, Rose was also one of its most radical members, arguing that organized religion and capitalism were primary contributors to women's inferior status. Because of her identity and her radical views, Rose faced hostility within and outside the movement and is often overlooked in histories of the women's movement, a fact Susan B. Anthony seemed to anticipate when she said, "Mrs. Rose is not appreciated, nor cannot (*sic*) be by this age—she is too much in advance of the extreme ultraists even, to be understood by them" (as cited in Kolmerten, n.p.).

Labor Movements in an Industrializing America

Large-scale labor movements formed during the Industrial Revolution for the first time to demand rights for workers; women were active, although not always welcome, members in these movements. As the center of textile production since the 1820s, Lowell, Massachusetts, was a hub for female labor organizing. For many of the Lowell "mill girls," working in factories was their first experience away from home and a rare chance for a degree of independence from their families (Figure 11.2). To convince New England families of the propriety of mill work, Lowell mill owners enforced "strict regulations and restraints on the moral conduct of the women," including compulsory church attendance, nightly curfews, and sexual abstinence on company property (Leary, 2012, p. 27). The thousands of women who flocked to Lowell were paid the highest wages available to women in the United States at the time, and despite the strict moral code and toil of their labor, they experienced freedom they could have only dreamed of at home (Leary).

But by the 1830s, tough economic times meant deteriorating conditions for many mill workers. The work week averaged 73 hours and workers faced wage cuts and increased production demands amid growing competition (Dublin, 1975). Work that had seemed to offer dignity was increasingly compared with slavery by the workers. When factory management announced

FIGURE 11.2

Lowell mill girls circa 1910–1915. In the first half of the 1800s, Lowell's mills employed 8,000 female workers, three-quarters of the workforce, many doing waged work for the first time. Although they made only half what men did, the wages were still considered good for the time (Leary).

a wage cut in February 1834, 800 of Lowell's women operatives went on strike, an unprecedented action for women workers. The *Boston Evening Transcript* reported that "one of the leaders mounted a pump and made a Mary Woolstonecroft [sic] speech on the rights of women" (as cited in Leary, p. 34) (a reference to the English writer and intellectual Mary Wollstonecraft, 1759–1797, who wrote *A Vindication of the Rights of Woman*). Although the strike lasted only a few days and the wage cut stood, the action itself was important because the women had overstepped "the accepted middle-class bounds of female propriety by participating in public protest" (Dublin, p. 107). Two years later, nearly twice as many Lowell factory girls went on strike to protest an increase in rent for company-controlled housing; they remained off the job for several weeks before the rent hike was abandoned (Lowell.com, 2014).

The "decidedly unfeminine" (according to mill managers) actions of the Lowell mill girls paved the way for the creation of the Lowell Female Labor Reform Association in 1844, a trade union prominent in the struggle for a 10-hour workday (Dublin). The association also advocated for women's rights, including the right of women to speak publicly on their own behalf. Although not all Lowell mill girls were radical, those who were played a key role, laying the groundwork for the later nationwide labor movement "with direct action and a focus on the idea that the interests of workers and their employers were opposed" (Leary, p. 36).

SENECA FALLS, SUFFRAGE, AND BEYOND

Along with workers, women's rights advocates and suffragists were gaining prominence as the 1800s progressed. In 1848, Lucretia Mott and Elizabeth Cady Stanton were among a small cadre of women who called for a women's convention to be held in Seneca Falls, New York. The seed for the convention had been planted 8 years earlier at the World Antislavery Convention, where Mott, Stanton, and other female delegates were refused seats because they were women. The hastily arranged convention in Seneca Falls drew about 300 women and men and culminated in a Declaration of Sentiments modeled on the Declaration of Independence. The Declaration of Sentiments, which reads, "We hold these truths to be self-evident: that all men and women are created equal," called for a range of rights for women, including the right to equal education, equal treatment under the law, and the right to vote. Sixty-eight women and 32 men (including Frederick Douglass, who escaped enslavement to become a prominent writer, orator, and supporter of rights for Blacks and women) signed the declaration (National Women's History Museum). (Read the full text at http://ecssba.rutgers.edu/docs/seneca.html.)

Schism in the Woman Movement

Following the Seneca Falls convention, in the latter half of the 19th century, activists in the woman movement in the United States, particularly white, middle-class women, increasingly viewed the enfranchisement of women as integral to achieving broader social reforms (Tacey, 2003). Supporters of woman suffrage wrote, lectured, organized, marched, and lobbied on behalf of the cause. But shortly after the end of the Civil War, the woman suffrage movement suffered a "great schism," a split over the issue of Black male enfranchisement. Some in the woman movement supported Black male suffrage even at the (temporary) cost of not achieving white female suffrage, whereas others

breaking the frame
Seneca Indians and Spanish/Mexican Women Exercise Their Rights

Long before women and men gathered in Seneca Falls to demand women's rights, women of the Seneca tribe and Spanish/Mexican women on the Mexican frontier enjoyed a variety of rights denied most women in Anglo-American society. The Seneca, who still make their home near Seneca Falls, New York, are part of the Iroquois (or Haudenosaunee) confederacy of tribes. Seneca women (and Iroquois women more generally) held broad powers, including the power to veto declarations of war, remove chiefs, and leave their husbands (Wagner, 1996). Iroquois women also controlled agriculture and economic resources such as crops. This stood in stark contrast to the denial of white women's rights to vote, divorce, or control their own property (Wagner). Three important woman suffrage leaders had significant personal contact with Iroquois women: Matilda Joslyn Gage (who was adopted into the Mohawk wolf clan), Elizabeth Cady Stanton, and Lucretia Mott. Some feminist scholars contend that the Iroquois were an inspirational example for 19th-century women's rights advocates (Figure 11.3; Wagner).

Over time, however, pressure from colonial authorities and Christian missionaries resulted in a slow erosion of Seneca women's authority. In 1848, the Seneca adopted a new

SAVAGERY TO "CIVILIZATION"
THE INDIAN WOMEN: We whom you pity as drudges reached centuries ago the goal that you are now nearing

FIGURE 11.3

A 1914 illustration from *Puck* magazine showing Iroquois women overlooking white women suffragists. The caption reads, "THE INDIAN WOMEN: We whom you pity as drudges reached centuries ago the goal that you are now nearing," a reference to the fact that Seneca women could vote in tribal elections.

constitution that further degraded traditionally held rights for women, although significantly, Seneca women retained the right to vote and to ratify decisions of the legislature, two rights being sought by the women at the Seneca Falls convention.

Spanish/Mexican women on the Mexican frontier (prior to becoming part of the United States in 1848) also had legal rights not afforded their Anglo peers in the United States. For example, married women could buy and sell property, draw up wills, lend and borrow money, and engage in litigation (Ruiz, 1998; "Women—Colonial Spanish America," 2005). In 1848, however, with the conclusion of the Mexican–American War, much of the Mexican frontier was ceded to the United States (525,000 square miles, roughly 50 percent of Mexico's original land mass) (Flores, 2014). In the new U.S. territories, many of the rights Spanish/Mexican women had enjoyed, including the right to own property, were denied (Montoya, 2002).

refused to support voting rights for Black men without simultaneous consideration of female suffrage (although it became clear the two could not be won together). In the ensuing years, the rhetoric of some of those committed to white female suffrage, perhaps most notably Susan B. Anthony, became increasingly racist, asserting that white women were more suitable for citizenship than Black men (O'Brien, 2009). After the great schism, many white suffragists campaigned for their own suffrage and many Black suffragists supported universal suffrage. Ginzberg (2002) noted, however, that the split in the suffrage movement "did not simply divide white women from Black; it also divided white feminists from one another" (p. 425). That is, many white woman suffragists joined Black women and men in supporting Black men's suffrage, having decided that "at least for the moment, the African-American community needed a political voice even at the cost of white women's" (Ginzberg, p. 425).

In 1870, Black men were enfranchised with the ratification of the 15th Amendment. Eventually the two factions of the woman suffrage movement reconciled and by 1910 the fight for women's right to vote had become a mass movement in which "working-class women, Black women, women in the radical left, the young and the upper class joined in force," wrote the feminist historian Nancy Cott (1987, p. 30). Within the suffrage movement, "consciously modern" tactics—public vigils, marches, and protests—were being utilized more

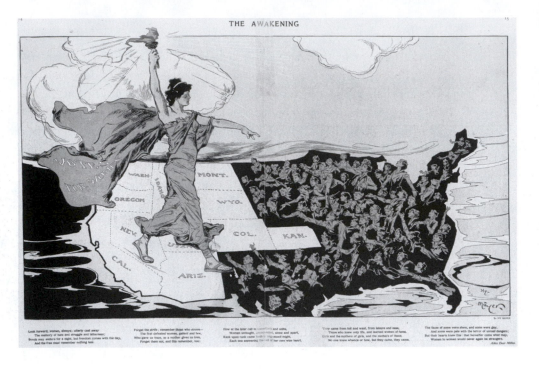

FIGURE 11.4

This poster, published in 1915, shows a torch-bearing female, labeled "Votes for Women," striding across the western United States, where women first achieved the right to vote. By 1915, 5 years prior to women winning the vote on the federal level, 10 Western states had instituted woman suffrage.

frequently, at least in part to appeal to the emerging mass media, which was hungry for sensational news (Cott). Alice Paul and Lucy Burns, who founded the National Woman's Party in 1917, emerged as two key radical figures who embraced militant tactics and proudly bore the label "Feminist."

On January 10, 1917, Paul, Burns, and other members of the National Woman's Party began to picket the White House in support of suffrage, carrying signs that asked, "Mr. President, How Long Must Women Wait for Liberty?" (Figure 11.5). Over months of picketing, women demonstrators were hooted at and mobbed while police mostly stood by (Cott). A number of demonstrators, including Paul and Burns, were arrested; some were force fed in jail when they refused to eat. They persisted in picketing even as the United States entered World War I, a controversial move that alienated some within the suffrage movement and many outside it. Their picket finally ended in 1919, when

FIGURE 11.5

Members of the National Woman's Party picketed in front of the White House beginning in 1917. By 1918, President Woodrow Wilson had announced his support for suffrage, but picketing continued while Congress considered the suffrage amendment.

the Senate passed the suffrage amendment. In August 1920, after the 36th state ratification, the 19th Amendment became law.

Even with the amendment, however, suffrage was hardly universal. Millions remained legally or effectively disenfranchised, including Asian Americans and Mexican Americans, many of whom continued to be denied voting rights until the 1940s. Nearly all Blacks in the South were effectively disenfranchised until passage of the Voting Rights Act in 1965, as were many poor whites in the South who were also subject to literacy tests and poll taxes. Native Americans, who had been unilaterally enfranchised by the 1924 Indian Citizenship Act, had decidedly mixed feelings about enfranchisement; many saw it as a further step toward limiting or denying tribal sovereignty. Some states denied Native Americans suffrage rights until 1948 (Bruyneel, 2002).

Equal Rights for Women

After passage of the 19th Amendment, Alice Paul and the National Woman's Party championed the idea of pursuing legal equality for women, and in 1923, on the 75th anniversary of the Seneca Falls Declaration of Sentiments, they announced the language of an Equal Rights Amendment (ERA). Despite championing women's equality, the ERA was at first opposed by some women's groups and organized labor because they felt it would eliminate hard-won labor protections for women, including state laws limiting the number of hours women could work and setting a minimum wage for women. About a quarter of U.S. women were in the labor force at the time, a number that hardly budged until the 1940s (Cott). Nearly half worked in menial jobs for low pay. For Black women in particular, opportunities were extremely limited and domestic labor was their only real option. Even as new opportunities in clerical and professional areas opened up for white women in the 1930s, the workplace remained largely segregated along lines of sex and race (Cott).

The ERA was introduced into Congress every year from 1923 to 1972, when pressure from a revived women's movement produced lopsided votes in its favor in both the House (354–24) and the Senate (84–8) (a two-thirds vote in favor in both houses of Congress is required, after which the amendment goes to the states for approval). Presidents Richard Nixon, Gerald Ford, and Jimmy Carter supported its passage. Polls at the time showed more than half of Americans also supported ratification (Neale, 2014). But as the amendment was considered in state legislatures (three-quarters of which needed to adopt it for it to be ratified), opposition grew. In the end, only 35 of the required 38 states ratified it during the decade allowed. The ERA had been defeated. Its opponents had argued, among other things, that the ERA dangerously erased all differences between women and men, was antifamily, could be used to force women into combat, and would be used by lesbians and gays to demand equal rights (Sandeen, 2011). Since 1982, there have been regular efforts to introduce the ERA into Congress but no progress toward passage. The Supreme Court Justice Ruth Bader Ginsburg said of the ERA, "If I could choose an amendment to add to the Constitution, it would be the Equal Rights Amendment. I think we have achieved [equal rights] through legislation, but legislation can be repealed, it can be altered."

So what exactly does this radical amendment first introduced (in a slightly different form) by Alice Paul in 1923 say? The following (in total): "Equality of rights under the law shall not be denied or abridged by the United States or by any state on account of sex."

THERE IS NO BREAK IN THE WAVES

After woman suffrage was achieved, the mass movement for women's rights in the United States dispersed, but feminists continued to be actively engaged on a number of fronts, including in the movement against lynching, the labor movement, and the birth control movement.

The Antilynching Movement

Between 1892 and 1940, there were more than 3,000 lynchings in the United States; most happened in the South and most targeted African American males (M. Brown, 2003). (A lynching is a killing, often by a mob, especially by hanging, outside legal authority, for example, without a trial.) Black women, beginning in the 1890s and led by Ida B. Wells-Barnett, the first investigative journalist in the United States, formed the backbone of the early antilynching movement. Wells-Barnett was a fearless advocate whose strategies included investigating incidents of lynching and exposing the true motivations behind the actions. Contrary to public belief, Wells-Barnett found that most men who had been lynched were not accused of—much less guilty of—rape, but instead had been accused of a variety of offenses, real and imagined (M. Brown, 2003). Wells-Barnett and her fellow activist, Mary Church Terrell, were involved in the formation of the National Association of Colored Women's Clubs, which advocated for federal antilynching legislation, and the National Association for the Advancement of Colored People's antilynching campaign, which included women and men, both Black and white. Although the U.S. Congress considered a number of antilynching bills in the 1920s and 1930s, all were defeated, but antilynching drives "hastened the decline of lynchings," the number of which had decreased greatly by the 1930s (M. Brown, 2003, p. 385).

The Rise of Organized Labor

One hundred years after women textile workers in Lowell, Massachusetts, organized to demand better working conditions in textile factories, organized labor was once again on the rise in the United States. But women of all colors, as well as men of color, were still excluded from many labor unions and only rarely served as leaders in the movement. In response, they formed their own unions and demanded their own rights. The International Ladies' Garment Workers' Union, known for its work fighting sweatshops, organized walkouts of New York City shirtwaist makers in 1909 (known as the Uprising of the 20,000) and cloak makers in 1910. Chicanas and Mexicanas conducted strikes

FIGURE 11.6

In 1938, Emma Tenayuca was arrested for leading more than 10,000 pecan shellers in the largest strike in San Antonio history. Tenayuca, a Mexican American, fought for a minimum wage, the right to strike, and equal rights for Mexican-born workers (Vargas, 2004).

in El Paso (laundresses) at the turn of the 20th century, in Texas (pecan shellers) in 1938, in California (cannery workers) in the 1930s and 1940s, and in support of striking miners in the 1950s (Figure 11.6; Rose, 2002). The Brotherhood of Sleeping Car Porters, the first Black labor union, negotiated for better hours and increases in salary for Black railroad porters in the 1930s.

By the 1940s, millions of women had entered the workforce as part of the war effort. Many of them joined unions and their auxiliaries, constituting nearly 20 percent of union members by the early 1950s (Cobble, 2003). Some historians argue they are "America's forgotten wave of feminism," bridging early labor organizing by women, such as that in Lowell, Massachusetts, and later labor and welfare rights advocacy from the 1960s onward (Cobble, 2003; see also Lucander, 2014).

In the 1940s, women also began to assume leadership roles in the labor movement. Among the first to become leaders were both privileged women, like Katherine Ellickson and Esther Peterson (both of whom worked for the American Federation of Labor and Congress of Industrial Organizations and went on to work in the Kennedy administration), and those who worked their way up from shop floors (who constituted a majority of women labor leaders). Dolly Lowther Robinson was an excellent example of the latter, an African American laundry worker who helped unionize 30,000 fellow laundry workers in New York City in the late 1930s (Cobble, 2003). She later joined Peterson at the Women's Bureau, a part of the U.S. Department of Labor charged with advocating for the nation's working women.

Another fierce labor advocate was Layle Lane. A graduate of Howard University, Lane was the first woman and the first African American to serve as vice president of the American Federation of Teachers and was instrumental in pushing for desegregation of the federation's locals in the South (Lucander; Schierenbeck, 2000). She was also a key figure in the March on Washington Movement, which in 1941 planned to bring 100,000 African Americans to Washington to protest widespread discrimination in the defense industry against Black workers (Lucander). To head off the march, President Franklin Roosevelt issued an executive order banning racial discrimination by defense contractors. Lane, a socialist, went on to play a role in the fight to integrate the U.S. armed forces and helped draft the American Federation of Teachers' amicus brief supporting school desegregation in *Brown v. Board of Education of Topeka*.

In the battle for economic justice for women, female labor leaders set out an ambitious agenda, including ending sex discrimination, winning equal job rights for women, achieving equal pay for comparable work, and addressing women's **double work day** on the job and at home (Cobble, 2003). Women in labor unions challenged the idea of the **unencumbered worker**, questioning a system under which all workers were assumed to be available for full-time, long-term, uninterrupted work. Women saw higher wages as the "core ingredient of a family-friendly workplace" (Cobble, 2003, p. 67) and pushed for higher wages as a way to reduce working hours.

In 1945, labor feminists introduced the Equal Pay Bill into the U.S. Congress and reintroduced it every year until 1963, when it finally passed. They also championed the idea of a **provider wage**, a wage high enough to support a family, not solely an individual worker. Although the idea did not prevail, Cobble (2003) pointed to it as a precursor of the contemporary movement for a living wage. (See Chapter 8, "Work, Inequality, and Neoliberalism," for more about women, minimum-wage work, and contemporary labor organizing.)

The Birth Control Movement

At the turn of the 20th century, women in the United States gave birth to between three and four children on average, about half as many as they had just 100 years earlier. Still, many struggled to properly space and care for children, an issue that spurred concern among a number of women reformers. An assortment of birth control devices were available in the United States by the 1870s, including condoms, sponges, and diaphragms. But in 1873, the U.S. Congress passed the **Comstock Laws**, which labeled birth control information and contraceptives as obscene material and outlawed their distribution via the U.S. Postal Service or interstate commerce, making the United States the only Western country at the time to criminalize birth control (others would follow) (PBS, 2002b).

At the center of the birth control movement in the United States was Margaret Sanger, who, in 1916, opened the first clinic in the United States to distribute information about contraception. Sanger went on to found the organization that would become Planned Parenthood. Although Sanger, a nurse, was motivated by real concern about women's health (particularly poor women) in relation to too-frequent pregnancies (many women died for lack of the ability to properly space pregnancies), she also held troubling views influenced by the eugenics movement, which promoted childbearing by the "fit" classes

(Ordover, 2003). The influence of the American eugenics movement on issues related to birth control in the 20th century was broad, including support for compulsory sterilization of those seen as "unfit" to reproduce. Although Sanger was not above appealing to eugenics supporters, some eugenicists, in fact, opposed her work to make birth control accessible, thinking it would "impoverish" the superior classes (Ordover). Sanger's connection to eugenics is troubling; she was nonetheless an important figure whose legacy includes a key role in the development of the **birth control pill**.

Sanger, beginning in the early 1900s, hoped to find a "magic pill" that women could take to prevent pregnancy, but it would take until the 1950s for work to begin on the use of hormones as a contraceptive, the breakthrough that led to the development of the modern-day birth control pill. Sanger, an unflagging advocate for five decades, recruited the wealthy heiress Katharine McCormick to fund her cause and doctors Gregory Pincus and John Rock to develop the pill (Eig, 2014).

The pill's development was not without controversy and some activists assert that women, particularly poor women of color, were deceived and exploited in the process. Early clinical trials were conducted largely, although not exclusively, on poor women of color outside the United States. Because the high dosage of hormones in the earliest version of the pill caused serious side effects, a large number of women left the clinical trials. Three women participating in trials in Puerto Rico died; whether the pill was the cause was not investigated (PBS, 2002b). The doctor conducting the trials in Puerto Rico told Pincus the pill caused too many side effects to be acceptable, but her conclusions were dismissed (Eig). Women in Puerto Rico were not told they were participating in clinical trials (not disclosing such information was common at the time).

Despite wide-ranging and sometimes serious side effects, the pill was approved for sale as a contraceptive in 1960. Four years later, eight U.S. states still prohibited the sale of contraceptives and many single women had a difficult time getting prescriptions; nevertheless, use of the pill exploded. By 1965, 6.5 million women in the United States were taking oral contraceptives, the most popular form of birth control in the country (PBS, 2002b).

A variety of side effects plagued early users of the pill. Less than two years after its release, reports linking the pill to blood clots, strokes, and possibly cancer began to reach the U.S. Food and Drug Administration. Little action was taken to address these issues until the feminist journalist Barbara Seaman brought it to public attention with the publication of *The Doctors' Case Against the Pill* in 1969. As a result, Congress convened hearings on the pill's safety. The docket included a number of male doctors who recounted the pill's potential dangers, but not a single woman was invited to testify. Incensed, members of the feminist group D.C. Women's Liberation led a series of protests and appeared frequently on the nightly news as the hearings continued without women; their grievances gained national attention and startled users, millions of whom quit taking the pill. In the aftermath of the hearings, hormone levels in the pill were reduced dramatically and within several years the number of users rebounded. "The real impact of the hearings was not on Pill usage, but on the nascent consumer health movement," reported PBS (2002b). As a result of feminist activism, the U.S. government began to require pharmaceutical companies to include information about side effects in all medications, changing forever the way Americans take medication.

The pill has proven enormously popular. Four of every five sexually experienced women in the United States have used the pill and approximately 100 million women worldwide take the pill (Daniels et al., 2013; Gibbs, 2010). Partly as a result, birth rates in many parts of the world have tumbled. The pill is revolutionary in a number of ways—it lets sexually active partners avoid the hassles of barrier methods; it puts control of contraception in the hands of women; and, if used properly, it is highly effective. The pill has been a major factor in the huge increase in women's labor force participation over the past half century. However, it is not a panacea. It requires a prescription, does not prevent sexually transmitted diseases, and places the responsibility for birth control on women, among other things.

THE 1950S: EMERGING MOVEMENTS, PIVOTAL MOMENTS

Along with the development of the birth control pill, the 1950s saw key developments in an array of social justice movements. In 1951, for example, Harry Hay, considered by many the founder of the gay rights movement in the United States, formed the Mattachine Society, the first national gay rights organization. Shortly after, the Daughters of Bilitis, a pioneering national lesbian organization, was founded. The year 1954 saw the Supreme Court strike down segregated education in *Brown v. Board of Education,* and the following year, Rosa Parks refused to give up her seat on a Montgomery, Alabama, bus, sparking a year-long African American boycott of the city's bus system.

Although Black men like Martin Luther King Jr. were the face of the civil rights movement, Black women like Parks, Ella Baker, Fannie Lou Hamer, and hundreds more were its "backbone" (V. Crawford et al., 1990). Parks, whose decision not to give up her bus seat is often described as spontaneous, had in fact been involved in her local National Association for the Advancement of Colored People for a dozen years. Far from accidental, her actions were "a deliberate effort to challenge injustice" (Loeb, 2010, para. 3). Another key figure was Ella Baker, who was a founder of the Southern Christian Leadership Conference and was also influential in the founding of the Student Non-Violent Coordinating Committee. The Student Non-Violent Coordinating Committee was instrumental in 1961s Freedom Rides and 1964s Freedom Summer, in which racially integrated groups of college students registered Black voters in America's South. The year 1964 also marked the passage of the Civil Rights Act, which outlawed racial and sex discrimination, and 1965 saw passage of the Voting Rights Act, which outlawed racial discrimination in voting and enabled many Blacks in the South to vote for the first time. Amid these victories, however, Black women began to chafe at the sexism within the civil rights movement (Freedman, 2002).

U.S. FEMINIST ORGANIZING FROM 1960

Accounts of what is traditionally known as the second wave of American feminism sometimes begin with the publication of Betty Friedan's *Feminine Mystique* (1963/1967) in 1963, in which Friedan asserted that American middle-class women suffered from a "problem that has no name," a deep "sense of dissatisfaction, a yearning" (11). Friedan continued:

> *As she made the beds, shopped for groceries, matched slipcover material, ate peanut butter sandwiches with her children, chauffeured Cub Scouts and Brownies, lay beside her husband at night—she was afraid to ask even herself the silent question—"Is this all?" (p. 11)*

(See Chapters 8 and 12 for more.) Although Friedan's book has been credited with exploding "the myth of the happy housewife in the affluent, white, American suburbs" (Walters, 2005, p. 102), it has also been criticized for its narrow focus on middle- and upper-class white women. bell hooks, a feminist, writer, and intersectional theorist, for example, noted that for poorer women, Friedan's advice to women to pursue meaningful work outside the home as a way to personal fulfillment rang hollow. hooks (1984) wrote, "As workers, poor and working-class women knew from their experiences that work was neither personally fulfilling nor liberatory—that it was for the most part exploitative and dehumanizing" (p. 98). Liberation for poorer women, asserted Benjamin Barber, might mean something very different, "the freedom of a

ON THE
web
Read about the **National Welfare Rights Organization** on the Student Website: www.oup.com/us/gillis-jacobs

mother finally to quit her job . . . [to] stay at home. . . . To be able to work and to have to work are two very different matters" (as cited in hooks, 1984, p. 98).

In 1966, Betty Friedan became a founding member of the National Organization for Women (NOW) and drafted its statement of purpose, which reads in part, "The time has come to confront, with concrete action, the conditions that now prevent women from enjoying the equality of opportunity and

FIGURE 11.7

National Welfare Rights Organization march to end hunger, 1968. The organization fought for the rights of people receiving government assistance (welfare). Its members included African Americans, Latinas/os, American Indians, and whites; about 90 percent of its members were women (Kornbluh, 1998).

freedom of choice which is their right, as individual Americans, and as human beings" (NOW, 2014). Pauli Murray was another founding member of NOW. Murray, the granddaughter of an enslaved woman and a mixed-race Union soldier, was a long-time activist. She was arrested 15 years before the Montgomery bus boycott for refusing to sit at the back of a bus. In the 1940s, Murray was active in the March on Washington Movement and participated in restaurant sit-ins. She also helped to found the Congress of Racial Equality and was the first African American woman to obtain a PhD in law from Yale University. Yet when she sought work, no law faculty and only one law firm offered her a permanent position. She coined the phrase "Jane Crow" to refer to racial and sex discrimination faced by Black women (Lucander). Among the 49 founding members of NOW were professional women, labor and civil rights activists, African American, Puerto Rican, and Jamaican American women, and a small number of men (NOW, 2016).

Equality Feminism

NOW and its members, along with *Ms. Magazine,* which Gloria Steinem founded in 1972, championed antidiscrimination laws to guarantee women equal rights in education, work, and access to credit, including the Equal Employment Opportunity Act (1972), Title IX (1972), the Women's Educational Equity Act (1974), the Equal Credit Opportunity Act (1974), and the Equal Rights Amendment. They also encouraged women to run for political office and worked to get them elected. Nancy Fraser (1997) called their approach **equality feminism**; others have termed it liberal feminism. In broad terms, liberal feminists sought to free women of limitations based on sex and traditional views of gender and gender roles. To this end, liberal feminists worked to remove barriers, legal and social, to women's equality and advocated laws and policies to empower women to achieve what men were able to achieve. (See Chapter 12, "Feminisms," for more.)

Difference Feminism

In contrast to liberal feminism, other feminists of the time developed what Fraser called **difference** or essentialist **feminism**, which held that "women are naturally more maternal and nurturing . . . more likely to be peacemakers; more moral . . . better communicators; less violent; less

FIGURE 11.8
Gloria Steinem founded the National Women's Political Caucus, *Ms. Magazine,* and the Ms. Foundation for Women. She has written about and advocated for many feminist issues and for many has been the public face of feminism in the United States.

competitive" (Fudge, 2005). Some radical feminists who fell under this umbrella proclaimed that women and men are essentially different and celebrated women's culture (see Chapter 6, "Beyond the Mythical Norm," for a discussion of essentialism). They saw women's subordination as the primary form of oppression in society and argued that the deeply embedded culture of patriarchy must be uprooted. Further, some radical feminists questioned the work of liberal feminists within what they saw as "male" institutions such as government, the law, and education. Bonnie Kreps summed up the view, saying, "We in [the radical] segment of the movement do not believe that the oppression of women will be ended by giving them a bigger piece of the pie.... We believe that the pie itself is rotten" (as cited in Freedman, 2002, p. 87).

"To have a radical approach," wrote the feminist Kathie Sarachild (1978), "we had to study the situation of women." For many radical feminists, women's lived experiences became the starting point for their discussions in an approach they called **consciousness-raising**. The purpose of consciousness-raising was "to get to the most radical truths about the situation of women in order to take radical action" (Sarachild). Consciousness-raising connected individual experiences to the experiences of women as a group and demonstrated that the personal is political. Through consciousness-raising women realized "that what looked like individual experiences, with little social resonance and certainly no political importance—rape, street harassment, you doing the vacuuming while your husband read the paper—were part of a general pattern of male dominance and female subordination," wrote Katha Pollitt (1999, para. 1). Sarachild noted that consciousness-raising was not an end in itself, but rather a part of uncovering the truth about women's lives "to take radical action."

Radical feminists championed women's liberation, sometimes but not always through a separatist politics that excluded men. Those who advocated separatism included lesbian separatists, many of whom felt sidelined by both the mainstream women's movement and the emerging male gay rights movement. Some lesbians, Rita Mae Brown, Adrienne Rich, and Charlotte Bunch (in her early work) among them, insisted that lesbians should be central to the women's liberation movement because they represented the greatest threat to masculine-centered "compulsory heterosexuality" (Rich's term). In 1970, the group Radicalesbians issued "The Woman Identified Woman," the first lesbian feminist manifesto,

recap of terms:
Compulsory Heterosexuality

The poet and activist Adrienne Rich (1980) noted that society enforces **compulsory heterosexuality** through a variety of economic, social, and political forces that "have enforced or insured the coupling of women with men" (p. 636). Think about the pressure on females to date males and males to date females, or the "traditional" definition of marriage as being between a man and a woman.

From Chapter 4, "LGBTQQIAA Identities and Challenges."

which concluded, "It is the primacy of women relating to women, of women creating a new consciousness of and with each other, which is at the heart of women's liberation, and the basis for the cultural revolution" (Radicalesbians, 1970, p. 4). (See Chapter 12 for more on radical feminism.)

Multiracial Feminism

Although it is useful and convenient to think of 1960s and 1970s feminism in the United States as falling under two broad canopies—equality and difference—this paradigm, like the waves model, obscures the complexity of the women's movement(s) and excludes many who either blended these approaches or stood outside them all together, especially women of color (see Chapter 12 for more forms of feminism). While white feminists were proclaiming sisterhood is powerful, Black, Latina, Asian, and Native American feminists found sisterhood with white feminists was complicated and often problematic. Many women of color who joined NOW and other mainstream feminist organizations felt stranded in a sea of whiteness, dismissed or treated primarily as tokens or bridges.

Women of color had also chafed at sexism within the activist movements in which many took part. Black female members of Students for a Democratic Society, for example, announced they had begun to apply the lessons of the civil rights movement "to their relations with brothers," whom they challenged to deal with male chauvinism (as cited in Walters). In response, women of color championed what Becky Thompson (2002) called **multiracial feminism**. Two of the earliest organizations were founded by Chicanas, *Comisión Femenil Mexicana Nacional* (Mexican Women's National Commission) in 1970 (M. Chávez, 2010) and *Hijas de Cuauhtémoc* (Daughters of Cuauhtémoc) in 1971 (named after a Mexican women's underground newspaper published during the 1910 Mexican Revolution) (B. Thompson, 2002). Chicanas also formed theatrical companies (such as San Francisco's *Las Cucarachas*), publishing houses (such as Mango), and magazines (such as *Third Woman*). The Chicana activist Francisca Flores created the California League of Mexican American Women and Alicia Escalante founded the Chicana National Welfare Rights Organization, which addressed issues such as education, immigration, child care, and reproductive rights (Rosales, 2008). Chicana feminists traced a "long, beautiful

FIGURE 11.9

Dolores Huerta cofounded the National Farmworkers Association (which became the United Farm Workers of America) in 1962 with César Chávez. Huerta was the union's first contract negotiator and directed the grape boycott in New York City. She was awarded the Medal of Freedom in 2011.

history" of social activism among Chicanas reaching back to the Mexican Revolution of the early 20th century (M. Chávez, 2010, p. 77).

At the same time, other women of color were also forming feminist organizations. Asian women founded Asian Sisters in Los Angeles. Another group, the Nisei Women's Forum, began consciousness-raising meetings, including discussions of the Japanese internment camp experience during World War II (see Chapter 6).

Native American women began Women of All Red Nations (WARN), which grew out of the organization the American Indian Movement (B. Thompson, 2002). In the 1970s, WARN took up the issue of forced sterilizations of Indian women and health issues related to the mining and storage of nuclear material on Indian land. WARN remains active, advocating for Native American treaty rights and social, economic, and environmental justice for Native Americans (Thunder Hawk, 2011).

The foremost Black women's organization of the time was the National Black Feminist Organization, which inspired the founding of the Combahee River Collective in 1974 (B. Thompson, 2002). (The collective took its name from the Combahee River in South Carolina, where Harriet Tubman led a successful Union raid in 1863.) Central to the work of many of these organizations was the notion of "double jeopardy," a term introduced by Frances Beale in 1972 to describe the dual discriminations of racism and sexism faced by Black women (King, 1988). Beale also observed that economic disadvantage was often part of Black women's lives. Women of color quickly understood they faced not only double jeopardy, but also **multiple jeopardy**. They also made clear that discrimination does not work like a math problem: "racism plus sexism plus classism" does not simply equal triple jeopardy (King, p. 47). This model wrongly suggests each variable is "single, direct, independent," wrote King, when they are interdependent. Therefore, no single variable can be drawn out of the equation and dealt with separately; all must be considered simultaneously and within a specific context (King).

The Combahee River Collective Statement (1977/2013) clearly articulated the multiple jeopardies faced by the women of that group, who stood outside the liberal-radical paradigm on a number of counts. Early in their statement they explained their intersectional approach, "We are actively committed to struggling against racial, sexual, heterosexual, and class oppression, and see as our particular task the development of integrated analysis and practice based upon the fact that the major systems of oppression are interlocking" (p. 116). The women of the Combahee River Collective identified themselves as Black, lesbian, socialist, and feminist. They called out racism and elitism in the feminist movement, but also sexism within the Black liberation movement. They asserted, "We struggle together with Black men against racism, while we also struggle with Black men about sexism" (p. 118). Declaring a socialist agenda, they wrote that "the liberation of all oppressed peoples necessitates the destruction of the political-economic systems of capitalism and imperialism as well as patriarchy. . . . We are not convinced, however, that a socialist evolution that is not also a feminist and anti-racist revolution will guarantee our liberation" (p. 118). (For more on multiracial feminism, see Chapter 12.)

Feminist Advocacy: 1960–1990

American feminists in the 1960s, 1970s, and 1980s worked on an array of issues, much of that work ongoing today. Below is a thumbnail sketch of many of the major issues (many of which are discussed in greater detail elsewhere in the textbook) and an extended discussion of feminist work on reproductive choice.

Education—Feminists worked to end discrimination through laws such as Title IX and ensure equal access and opportunity, particularly in areas where women were (and continue to be) underrepresented, including science, technology, engineering, and math. (See Chapter 8, "Work, Inequality, and Neoliberalism.")

Work—Feminists advocated for equal pay and an end to job segregation and sexual harassment in the workplace. They worked to break the glass ceiling and promoted family-friendly policies like parental leave and flex time. (See Chapter 8, "Work, Inequality, and Neoliberalism," for more.)

Body Image and Beauty Standards—Feminists critiqued narrow, Western-centric beauty standards, protested the objectification and sexualization of women in the media and popular culture, and raised awareness of disordered eating and its health consequences. (See Chapter 7, "Embodiment, Beauty, and the Viewer.")

Capitalism and Imperialism—Feminists critiqued the exploitation of workers, American consumer culture, and imperialist economic policies such as structural adjustment programs that impoverish poorer nations. (See Chapter 8, "Work, Inequality, and Neoliberalism," Chapter 10, "Human Rights and Global Activism," and Chapter 12, "Feminisms.")

Violence Against Women—Feminists raised awareness of domestic violence and sexual assault, established women's shelters and rape hotlines, and advocated for reform of laws and police procedures regarding rape and domestic violence. (See Chapter 9, "Gender-Based Violence.")

Pornography—Antipornography feminists equated pornography with violence and wrote statutes to outlaw it. Pro-sex and free speech feminists argued that pornography is a potentially positive outlet for viewers as well as those who work in the sex industry. (See Recommended Readings and Multimedia Resources for this chapter on the Student Website.)

Reproductive Health—Feminists were instrumental in the development of the birth control pill, advocated for access to birth control and legalization of abortion, and raised awareness of and sought to end coercive sterilization. (More below.)

Issue Focus: Reproductive Choice

Issues of reproductive choice—including women's access to contraception and safe and legal abortions, the ability to safely space the birth of children, access to infertility options, and access to the choice not to have children—have long been central to the feminist movement. The activist Angela Davis (1981/2003) asserted the importance of these issues when she wrote, "birth control—individual choice, safe contraceptive methods, as well as abortions when necessary—is a fundamental prerequisite for the emancipation of women" (p. 353). It was not until 1965 that contraception was permitted in all U.S. states, and abortion remained illegal until 1967, when some states began loosening restrictions (National Abortion Federation, 2010). As a result of the criminalization of abortion, many women, particularly poor women, were forced to seek abortions from untrained providers often working in unsanitary conditions. The results could be deadly. In the 1960s, an estimated 1 million women may have had illegal abortions annually; up to 1,000 of them died annually from the complications, many of them poor women of color (Freedman, 2002).

In the late 1960s and early 1970s, women increasingly spoke out about the need for safe and legal abortions. As a result of this advocacy, between 1967 and 1973, one-third of U.S. states liberalized or repealed criminal abortion laws (National Abortion Federation). In 1973, the U.S. Supreme Court struck down the remaining restrictive state laws with its decision in *Roe v. Wade*

ON THE
web
Read about **contemporary obstacles to reproductive health care** on the Student Website:
www.oup.com/us/gillis-jacobs

(National Abortion Federation). After the Supreme Court decision, the number of deaths from back-alley abortions fell (as it did in France, West Germany, Italy, and Spain, where laws were also liberalized in the 1970s and 1980s). Currently, more than 60 percent of the world's population lives in countries where abortion is permitted for a wide range of reasons or without restriction; 26 percent of all people reside in countries where abortion is generally prohibited (Center for Reproductive Rights, 2013).

Reproductive choice, however, has always meant more than having the choice not to conceive or having access to contraception and safe and legal abortions. For poor women, particularly poor women of color, reproductive choice also means freedom from coercive sterilization. In 1973, the same year as *Roe v. Wade*, Minnie Lee and Mary Alice Relf, two young Black girls from Montgomery, Alabama, were an integral part of a class action lawsuit demanding the United States stop using government funds to sterilize women and girls. Minnie Lee and Mary Alice's mother had been coerced into signing papers she was told would allow medical staff to administer Depo-Provera (an experimental contraceptive) to her daughters, ages 14 and 12, through a federally funded program. (Depo-Provera was approved for use in the United States in 1992.) What Mrs. Relf, who was illiterate, did not know was that she had in fact "consented" to surgical sterilization for her daughters, which happened a few days after she signed the forms.

The Relf sisters were far from alone. No one knows for sure how many women were involuntarily sterilized in the United States but activists estimate the number to be as high as several hundred thousand between 1950 and 1980. Countless others were forced to agree to sterilization when doctors threatened to terminate their welfare benefits unless they consented to the procedure (Kluchin, 2009). Although some of those targeted were white, "the most systematic campaigns for punitive sterilization were waged against women and girls of color," wrote Nancy Ordover (p. 166). Nearly half those surgically sterilized under government-funded programs were Black; approximately 25 percent of American Indian women were sterilized (Kluchin; Rutecki, 2011). Puerto Rican women in New York and Puerto Rico, Mexican American women in California, and scores of other women of color were also sterilized under government-funded programs, many without full and informed consent (Davis; Ordover). By contrast, many middle-class, white women who wanted to be sterilized had difficulty finding a doctor who would perform the procedure.

In his 1974 ruling, the judge in the Relfs' case barred federally funded sterilization of minors and ordered the development of regulations safeguarding patients against coercion. The case was formally dismissed in 1977 after federal governmental bodies withdrew the challenged regulations on involuntary sterilization. State agencies, however, were unaffected by the rule changes and even at the federal level, flagrant violations were common at least through the 1970s (Davis; Ordover).

The 1980s, Conservatism, and Backlash in the United States

The 1980s in the United States were marked by what Susan Faludi (1991) termed a "backlash" against feminism. Critics attacked feminism on two fronts, on the one hand charging that it was an anachronism and no longer necessary and on the other that it had failed American women and exacerbated their un-

happiness. As a result, antifeminists argued, a new generation had left feminism behind (Figure 11.10). But there was plenty of evidence that the critics were wrong on both counts. Many women had made gains in various areas, thanks in large part to feminist activism, but feminists also understood their work was far from done, as documented in books like Naomi Wolf's *The Beauty Myth* (1990) and Faludi's *Backlash*. Faludi (1991) cataloged the ways the American media had created the myth that "feminism is responsible for making women miserable" (p. 7). The real source of women's unhappiness, asserted Faludi (1991), was not feminism but women's continued inequality. Faludi (1991) identified numerous arenas in which hard-fought feminist gains were slipping away—at school, at home, at work, and in politics, the result of a "powerful counterassault on women's rights" (p. 10). In a similar vein, Wolf took on repressive beauty standards, writing, "The more legal and material hindrances women have broken through, the more strictly and heavily and cruelly images of female beauty have come to weigh on us" (p. 10). She went on to catalog the toll of eating disorders, cosmetic surgery, and pornography and to criticize the fashion and beauty industries for exploiting women. (For more on conservatism and antifeminism, see Chapter 12.)

The Third Wave

Many feminists had a sense of frustration as the 1980s, which had been dominated by the conservative politics that propelled Ronald Reagan into office, came to a close. If it was difficult to catalog major feminist victories during the

FIGURE 11.10

The press has been declaring feminism over since at least 1982, when the *New York Times Magazine* gave us "Voices of the Post-Feminist Generation." In 1998, *Time* magazine asked from its cover, "Is Feminism Dead?" Their answer was yes.

MORE ABOUT...

AIDS Activism in the 1980s and 1990s

In 1981, the Centers for Disease Control reported on what would retrospectively be identified as the first cases of AIDS in the United States. Building on a decade of gay liberation activism, the gay community stepped in quickly and visibly to address the crisis (Bateman, 2011). In 1982, the first AIDS service organizations were formed in New York and San Francisco (Bateman) and became the primary source of medical and social support for people with AIDS. Although government funding for AIDS-related research increased throughout the 1980s, President Ronald Reagan did not say the word AIDS in public until 1985 and did not give a major address on the subject until 1987, with only 19 months left in his second term (Murdock, 2003). Allen White (2004) noted that by that time "36,058 Americans had been diagnosed with AIDS and 20,849 had died" (para. 8).

The founding of the AIDS Coalition to Unleash Power (ACT UP) in 1987 "ignited a new phase of AIDS activism" (Bateman, p. 3). Members of ACT UP, fueled by anger at government indifference to AIDS, engaged in civil disobedience, often aimed at government agencies and the pharmaceutical industry. Activists demanded increased research dollars, more effective treatment options, and streamlined clinical trials to get newly developed drugs more quickly to those who were dying without medication. Although the history of AIDS activism often centers on gay men, lesbians were an integral part of the movement. The women's caucus of ACT UP brought a feminist analysis to the group's work, pushing gay activists to consider AIDS "in the context of a broader movement for social change" (Bateman, p. 4). The women's caucus was instrumental in successfully lobbying for the inclusion of women and people of color in drug trials and in pushing the Centers for Disease Control to change its definition of AIDS to include women (Boehmer, 2000).

Another activist group, Queer Nation, was formed in 1990 to address gay bashing and push for gay visibility. They held kiss-ins, "invaded" straight social spaces, and distributed pro-gay pamphlets in suburban shopping malls (Blotcher, 2011). They also outed gay public figures and were instrumental in pressuring police to investigate the murder of Julio Rivera, a gay man (three were convicted) (Blotcher; Signorile, 2003). Queer Nation made famous the chant "We're here. We're queer. Get used to it!" (Blotcher). This use of the word queer has been identified as part of a new radical activism that moved away from gay identification in favor of an anti-identity that resists what Michael Warner (1993/2007) called "regimes of the normal" (p. xxvi). (See Chapters 4 and 12 for more.)

decade, it was easy enough to name an array of issues in which feminists had actively engaged, including environmentalism, disarmament, antiapartheid campaigns, reproductive rights, affirmative action, and AIDS activism. As noted earlier, the 1980s also marked the height of multiracial feminism and theorizing on the part of women of color about the intersecting oppressions many women faced. (For more on intersectionality see Chapter 3, "Gender and In/Equality," and Chapter 12.) It was within this context that what has become known as feminism's third wave rose.

The term third wave came to public consciousness with Rebecca Walker's essay, "Becoming the Third Wave," published in *Ms.* in 1992 (although Walker was not the first to use the term) (Springer, 2002). Walker wrote her essay in response to Clarence Thomas's Supreme Court confirmation (specifically the discounting by many male senators of Anita Hill's testimony during the confirmation process that Thomas had sexually harassed her). In her essay, Rebecca Walker (1992), who is the daughter of the feminist and writer Alice Walker (who wrote *The Color Purple* and dozens of other fiction and nonfiction works), explained,

> *I write this as a plea to all women, especially women of my generation: Let Thomas' confirmation serve to remind you, as it did me, that the fight is far from over. Let this dismissal of a woman's experience move you to anger. Turn that outrage into political power. Do not vote for them unless they work for us. Do not have sex with them, do not break bread with them, do not nurture them if they don't prioritize our freedom to control our bodies and our lives. I am not a post-feminist feminist. I am the Third Wave. (paras. 12–13)*

Later that year, Rebecca Walker and Shannon Liss founded what would become the Third Wave Foundation. A purpose of the organization was to provide funding and support to young-women-led groups (Third Wave Fund, 2016). If there is a good deal of consensus around the idea that Rebecca Walker helped launched the term third wave, there is less consensus about how to define the third wave and how to differentiate it from the second wave. For some, third wave feminism can be delineated in terms of the calendar. You are a third waver if you were born between 1963 and 1974 (e.g., Heywood and Drake, 1997) or, similarly, if you came of age in the 1980s and 1990s (Gilley, 2005). Others argue that third wavers should be defined by their politics. Falling under the category third wave are diverse forms of feminism. Highlighted below are several forms of feminism that have been (are) influential and speak persuasively to third wave themes.

Transfeminism

Emi Koyama (2003), in "The Transfeminist Manifesto," argued for a broadening of the women's movement to include trans people (see Chapter 4 for more on trans people). "**Transfeminism** embodies feminist coalition politics in which women from different backgrounds stand up for each other," wrote Koyama (p. 245). Transfeminism argues that not only gender is socially constructed, but also sex and that the distinction between sex and gender is "artificially drawn as a matter of convenience" (p. 249). For trans people in particular, argued Koyama, biological sex can feel "artificial and changeable" (p. 249). Transfeminism, then, "views any method of assigning sex as socially and politically constructed, and advocates a social arrangement in which one is free to assign her or his own sex (or non-sex, for that matter)" (p. 250). Transfeminism also rejects that idea that gender and sex " 'naturally' cohere" (p. 251). Ultimately, wrote Koyama, "transfeminism asserts that it is futile to debate intellectually who is and is not included in the category 'woman'; instead, we must act—now—and build alliances" (p. 257).

Hip-Hop Feminism

Gwendolyn Pough and other Black feminists have argued that "rap has political potential" for feminists (Pough, 2003, p. 237). Pough admitted that "this might sound crazy, given rap music's track record of sexism and misogyny." But for Pough, rap music has feminist potential in at least two ways. First, female rappers can "wreck" sexist stereotypes perpetuated in rap lyrics and hip-hop culture more generally (Peoples, 2008, p. 24). Second, hip-hop is a place where young black feminists can "hone their skills of critical analysis" (Peoples, p. 21). To this end, Pough argued that **hip-hop feminism** must give young people the tools to critique and counter rap's negative representations of women.

Riot Grrrl, Zines, and DIY Feminism

The **Riot Grrrl movement** began in the early 1990s largely in response to sexism experienced by the punk band Bikini Kill, whose lead singer, Kathleen Hanna, became the movement's most visible and influential member (Dunn & Farnsworth, 2012). The "Riot Grrrl Manifesto" described the movement as motivated by the desire to "take over the means of production," to foster and support "girl scenes and girl artists," to share information and stay alive "instead of making profits," and to be a "revolutionary soul force that can and will change the world" ("Riot Grrrl Manifesto," 1991). Bands associated with Riot Grrrl expressed feminist and antiracist views in their songs (Feliciano, 2013). Central to Riot Grrrl's goals was the creation of alternative media—zines—and DIY publishing (Dunn & Farnsworth). Members of the movement started Riot Grrrl Press, which for several years gathered and distributed zines, informal magazines written and drawn by girls and women.

Gaga Feminism

Jack Halberstam's (2012) **gaga feminism** is an excellent example of an anti-essentialist, genderbending approach to feminism, which also engages with popular culture, each a hallmark of significant strands of third wave feminism. Halberstam (2012) asserted in "Gaga Feminism for Beginners" that he was "not proposing that there is some kind of clear feminist program for social change in the world of Gaga" (p. 6). Halberstam (2012) explained,

> Gaga is a hypothetical form of feminism, one that lives in between the "what" and the "if"; What if we gendered people according to their behavior? What if gender shifted over the course of a lifetime—what if someone began life as a boy but became a boygirl and then a boy/man? What if some males are ladies, some ladies are butch, some butches are women, some women are gay, some gays are feminine, some femmes are straight, and some straight people don't know what the hell is going on? . . . What if you begin life as a queer mix of desires and impulses and then are trained to be heterosexual but might relapse into queerness once the training wears off? . . . What if girls stopped wearing pink, boys started wearing skirts, women stopped competing with other women, and men stopped grabbing their crotches in public? (p. 8)

Although much of what Halberstam (2012) wrote is playful, he is also making a serious argument for "a feminism that recognizes multiple genders, that contributes to the collapse of our current sex–gender systems, a feminism less concerned with the equality of men and women and more interested in the abolition of those terms as such" (p. 25). Gaga feminism does not have a political agenda, per se. "Gaga feminism is not something to which you will subscribe," wrote Halberstam (2012). "You will not sign up for it, you will not vote for it. Instead, it is something you will do . . . something to be" (p. 26). So how do you go gaga? Let go of your most basic assumptions. Look for transformation on the margins. Do not accept "common sense"; "think counterintuitively, act accordingly" (p. 27). Be outrageous.

Common Themes in Third Wave Feminism

Although third wave feminism is undoubtedly diverse, several themes emerge among its many forms of feminism:

Third Wave Feminists Take a *Feminism Is For Everyone* Approach—Leandra Zarnow (2010) wrote that third wave feminism "cannot be defined by a single identity, practice, or ideology, nor can single individuals, events, and organizations stand for the totality of recent feminisms" (p. 120). R. Claire Snyder (2008) echoed this when she said third wave feminism is "inclusive and nonjudgmental . . . [it] refuses to police the boundaries of the feminist political" (pp. 175–176). A hallmark of third wave feminism, then, is choice. Jennifer Baumgardner and Amy Richards (2003) put it this way, "Feminism isn't about what choice you make, but the freedom to make that choice" (p. 450).

Third Wave Feminists Are Intentionally Multicultural and Coalitional— Building on the work of women of color in particular, third wavers see all identities as "equally valuable in their particularity" (Fraser). As an extension of this, third wave feminism is also coalitional, seeking to build bridges across a variety of issues that include environmental, economic, social, and gender justice (Snyder).

Third Wave Feminists Are Antiessentialist—Third wavers are influenced by postmodern, poststructural, and postcolonial theories. As such, they reject universalist claims that all women share a set of common experiences (Snyder) and universalist explanations, sometimes called grand narratives, that seek to explain all the oppression of all women. Some third wavers reject categories, such as women, men, homosexual, and heterosexual, altogether. (See Chapter 6 for more information on essentialism and Chapter 12 for more on postmodernism, poststructuralism, and postcolonialism.)

Third Wave Feminists Are Genderbending—Third wavers emphasize the fluid nature of gender, sex, sexuality, and sexual identity (Snyder). Third wavers are intentionally boundary crossing and boundary breaking when it comes to gender (Freedman, 2002). Many are influenced by queer theory and the writing of academics such as Eve Kosofsky Sedgwick and Judith Butler, who view gender as performance and performative (see Chapter 2, "Language and Communication," for a discussion of performativity and Chapter 12 for more on Sedgwick and Butler).

Third Wave Feminists Engage Popular Culture—Third wavers are consumers of culture, but more than that, they are also producers and critics of culture. They have set up their own presses, published their own zines, and are astute about online organizing and the use of social media to broadcast their messages.

Third Wave Feminists Are Often Pro-Sex—Many third wavers are "devoted to reducing the stigma surrounding sexual pleasure," wrote Snyder. They

Online Activism

Feministing, Racialicious, Hollaback!, Colorlines, Feministe, Color of Change. Much of the most vibrant feminist activism happening today takes place online on sites such as these—and many more. Here feminists debate, rant, organize, blog, vlog, and petition for change. They have scored some significant victories, including bringing new urgency to the fight against campus sexual violence. As many upsides as there are to online activism, there are some significant downsides, too. "Feminist work online is woefully underfunded," noted Sarah Mirk (2013, para. 8). "Most people writing about feminism online are doing so for free or on miniscule budgets" (para. 8). Burnout and feelings of isolation are common. Mirk and others worry that without stable funding, online activism could become "a province of the already privileged" (para. 9). What is needed? More funding, for sure, but also infrastructure making it easier for individual voices "to come together into an influential feminist force" (Martin & Valenti, 2013, p. 25).

MORE ABOUT...

celebrate sexuality and in some cases girly (girlie) culture, which might include wearing makeup, high heels and short skirts while also being proudly feminist (see, for example, *Manifesta*, Baumgardner & Richards, 2000). Pro-sex feminists (also called sex positive) are distinctly nonjudgmental about sex work and media portrayals of sex. Pro-sex feminists range from sex workers to performers, like Annie Sprinkle, to writers and educators, like Susie Bright, to academics, like Lisa Duggan and Nan Hunter (Fudge, 2005). In response to the antipornography (and what some would call antisex) strain of second wave feminism, many third wavers oppose censorship and see pornography as potentially empowering for everyone if it makes available a range of images, not simply those portraying male dominance and female subordination.

Second Wave Is to Third Wave as Mother Is to Daughter?

Fudge noted that "from its first utterance, the notion of a third wave has generated controversy," particularly among those who conceive of the second wave–third wave split as a sort of "mother–daughter spat" (see, for example Faludi, 2010; Henry, 2004). Others, however, have noted the continuities, particularly between third wavers and second wave feminists of color (Snyder; Springer). Gloria Steinem summed up the frustration of some second wavers at what they felt were unfair criticisms leveled by third wavers, particularly the charge that second wavers did not engage enough with issues like race and sexuality.

Steinem, in a foreword to Rebecca Walker's third wave anthology, *To Be Real*, wrote that when she reads such critiques, she feels "like a sitting dog being told to sit" (p. xxii).

Nevertheless, the idea of a third wave is an important mark of distinction for many feminists. To third wavers, it signals a more intentionally inclusive movement that locates diversity as a source of strength. Declaring a third wave has also been a way to counter the notion of postfeminism, the idea that the feminist movement had, as Fudge wrote, "outlived its usefulness" that popped up in the media throughout the 1980s and 1990s (and to some extent still today) and to declare feminism alive and kicking. Although this discussion of third wave feminism has focused primarily on its theoretical stance, many third wave feminists—and those who would today situate themselves outside the third wave—are activists for whom the advocacy of first and second wave feminists is deeply resonant and inspiring. Feminist activists today can be found working across a huge range of issues: for reproductive rights and against sweatshop labor, for a living wage and against sexual violence on campus, for gay and immigrant rights and against the destructive forces of globalization, for racial justice and against the prison industrial complex, to mention only a few.

Given that more than 20 years has passed since the supposed inception of the third wave, is it time for recognition of a fourth wave? Some feminists have argued yes. Jennifer Baumgardner, for example, argued for recognition of a fourth wave that is "tech savvy and gender sophisticated." What do you think?

CONCLUSION

Although the women's movement in the United States is often periodized into three waves, many scholars suggest this excludes the contributions of many women. Instead, the notion of a long women's movement captures activism that had its roots in 19th-century antislavery and labor activism. The movement for woman suffrage was bolstered by the Seneca Falls convention on women's rights but suffered a great schism over the 15th Amendment granting Black men the right to vote. Women in the United States achieved suffrage with the passage of the 19th Amendment. Following this, women's activism continued in the antilynching, labor, birth control, and civil rights movements.

The beginning of the so-called second wave of U.S. feminism is often marked with the publication of Betty Friedan's *Feminine Mystique*. The 1960s and 1970s saw further articulation of various feminist viewpoints, including equality or liberal feminism and difference feminism. This period also saw the formation of Chicana, Asian American, Native American, and Black feminist groups informed by race, class, and/or gender.

The 1980s and 1990s in the United States were marked by a backlash against feminism and claims in the media that feminism was no longer useful. However, feminist activism and theorizing continued, and the so-called third wave of feminism arose. This period also saw the emergence of AIDS activism with groups like ACT UP and Queer Nation. Third wave feminism included many strains of activism including transfeminism, hip-hop feminism, Riot Grrrl feminism, and gaga feminism. There is talk today of a fourth wave of feminism with a focus on online activism.

THINK, LEARN, ACT

The following resources are available on the Student Website: www.oup.com/us /gillis-jacobs

Taking Stock, Taking Action prompts and activities. Apply what you've learned to take action on campus and in the broader community.

Recommended Readings and Multimedia Resources, including scholarly and literary works, documentaries, feature films, podcasts and more, to enrich the in- and out-of-classroom experience.

Key Terms

Birth control pill 332

Comstock Laws 331

Consciousness-
    raising 337

Difference feminism 336

Double work day 331

Equality feminism 336

First wave 317

Gaga feminism 347

Hip-hop feminism 346

Multiple jeopardy 339

Multiracial feminism 338

Provider wage 331

Riot Grrrl movement 346

Second wave 318

Third wave 318

Transfeminism 346

Unencumbered
    worker 331

FEMINISMS: THEORIES AND PRACTICES

"**Feminists are made, not born,**" wrote bell hooks in *Feminism Is for Everybody* (2000). She continued, "One does not become an advocate of feminist politics simply by having the privilege of having been born female. Like all political positions one becomes a believer in feminist politics through choice and action" (p. 7). What does it mean to be a feminist? To do feminist theory? We have come full circle to ask again, what is feminism? A common dictionary definition of feminism is the belief in and/or advocacy of the political, economic, and social equality of women and men. But as we have noted, feminism often encompasses much more. bell hooks's (2000) definition is both more far-reaching and more open to possibilities: feminism is "a movement to end sexism, sexist exploitation, and oppression" (p. 1).

What would equality or the end of sexist exploitation and oppression entail? Given what we have discussed about intersex people and sex and gender diversity, a fuller articulation of feminism would probably include freedom for people of all sexes (not simply female and male), regardless of gender identification or performance. Given what we have discussed about sexual orientation, it would probably include freedom for people regardless of sexual desire, activity, or relationships. Furthermore, feminism would include attention to differences based on race, ethnicity, and socioeconomic class. The possible intersections with sex and gender are too numerous to list but could also include religion, dis/ability, and age, among others. As with any vibrant belief system, conceptions of feminism are evolving. Since people have different understandings about the world and different value orientations, they have developed different conceptions of feminism to reflect their worldviews. This chapter is devoted to explaining in broad strokes (and primarily from a U.S. perspective) various ways feminists have diagnosed the problem of inequality and/or oppression and the solutions they propose.

ADVANTAGES OF FEMINIST THEORETICAL ANALYSIS

You might wonder why a person would choose to identify as a particular kind of feminist. If we agree that there is inequality or oppression in society, why bother to spend more time discussing it rather than solving the problem? Feminists and other social theorists would say that to properly treat a problem you must first correctly diagnose it. If you simply treat the symptoms, you will not necessarily address the underlying causes. For example, if a person has a headache and takes painkillers, it will reduce the pain, but if the source of the pain is a brain tumor, treating the symptoms alone could lead to the person's health getting worse. The same can be the case with societal problems. It may be the case that we are distracted from the core problems that women and others face because the superficial symptoms are more prominent and tempting to remedy. Having a firm understanding of feminisms helps you keep your eyes on the prize.

However, recognizing an underlying problem does not always mean we should neglect the symptoms. Suppose we all agree that hunger is caused by the way the economic system is structured. Getting at the root of the problem would require changing the economic system rather than feeding the hungry (which is only a symptom). However, it seems reasonable and humane to both make donations to food pantries and work on changing the broader policies that cause hunger in the first place.

Another question often raised is, Why identify as a kind of feminist rather than indicating you are for *all* human beings? Isn't a broader philosophy of action like humanism or one that supports ethical treatment of all living things better than a narrow philosophy of feminism? We agree that broader political or ethical stances are a good thing—and they need not conflict with a stance like feminism. To begin with, feminism is about equality for all people regardless of their sex—meaning it is not as narrow as many may assume. Second, broader political or ethical stances (such as caring for all people) may be achieved only by having more specific philosophies of how to achieve justice for specific subgroups. If women or trans people suffer inequality as women or trans people, we must diagnose and solve these problems to help everyone achieve equality.

UNDERSTANDING FORMS OF FEMINISM

Understanding forms of feminism can be challenging. Here are a few things to keep in mind as you read through this chapter.

Read and Re-Read the Forms of Feminism

To understand one form of feminism, it is helpful to understand other forms. Because many forms of feminism are in dialogue with one another, we have tried to explain each one in part by referencing other forms of feminism. Perhaps more than any other chapter in this book, this chapter is designed to be re-read rather than simply read. You may also want to use Appendix C, Feminisms in Brief, as an added guide.

Understand There Are No Neat Divisions

Because feminist viewpoints are often articulated in response to other important views of the time (feminist and otherwise) or to historical circumstances, they tend to draw on and react to a wide range of ideas and trends. As a consequence, forms of feminist thought bleed into one another in various ways. Instead of focusing only on how the forms of feminism differ from one another, it is useful to think about how each form of feminism developed within a particular intellectual and historical context.

Recognize This Is a Brief Introduction

There are often substantial differences in viewpoints between thinkers and activists who are identified as adhering to the same form of feminism. Because this is a brief introductory survey, we cannot address all the complications, contradictions, and permutations within these forms of feminism. Also, we are not explaining every form of feminism (for example, anarchist feminism is not discussed). We would further note that our schema for categorizing feminisms is not the only approach.

If you are a student who never takes another women's, gender, or sexuality studies course or reads more about feminism, we hope this chapter serves as a rough guide to some of the many and varied forms of feminism. If you are planning on taking upper-level courses or engaging in independent reading in the field, we hope this chapter will help you make some sense of discussions of feminism in your classes and identify some of the forms of feminism you can explore more deeply.

Not Agreeing With Everything Is Okay

You do not have to subscribe to all the elements of a particular form of feminism to identify with it. You may find yourself picking and choosing elements among them—that is okay.

Understand Antifeminism

An important tool for understanding feminism is to understand its opposite, antifeminism. In its simplest form, antifeminism requires rejecting the basic definition of feminism: belief in and advocacy of the political, economic, and social equality of all sexes. Let's briefly examine what rejecting these forms of equality would entail. To reject political equality in a democracy would mean believing women (or men, or those of another sex designation) do not have the same right to participate in politics—such as the right to vote or run for office. To reject economic equality would mean believing women (or men, or others) do not have the same right to participate in the economic sphere—such as the right to jobs outside the home or equal pay or to control property. To reject social equality would mean believing women (or men, or others) do not have the same right to be treated as social equals. There are at least two ways of conceiving of social equality: (1) the right to engage in the same kinds of social activities regardless of sex (such as engaging in premarital sex without more harsh social sanction than another sex) or (2) the equal valuing of separate sex/gender roles (such as the claim of equal status of women and men in some Native American societies that nonetheless had distinct sex/gender roles). Many feminists would claim that it is impossible to equally value different social roles, but in principle, if one could, it is possible to claim this view as a feminist view.

Sometimes people raise objections to feminism that are not objections at all. For example, it is possible to believe that women as a group are less likely to have the physical strength necessary for certain jobs, such as in the military or firefighting. Feminism does not require that all women should be allowed to be firefighters regardless of physical ability, but many forms of feminism would require that all people be given the same opportunity to prove themselves under relevant standards.

One important contemporary antifeminist activist was Phyllis Schlafly, the leader of the successful STOP ERA (Equal Rights Amendment) campaign (Equal Rights Amendment, 2013; "Phyllis Schlafly Explains," 2014). As discussed in Chapter 11, "History of Women's Activism in the United States," the ERA, which reads, "Equality of rights under the law shall not be denied or abridged by the United States or by any state on account of sex," failed to pass in 1982, in part because of Schlafly's efforts.

Schlafly, in keeping with her conservative philosophy, championed traditional gender roles for women and men. A **conservative** is "a person who conserves or preserves something; (now usually) an adherent of traditional values, ideas, and institutions; an opponent of (social and political) change, a conservative person" (OED). Conservatives may be antifeminists, but, as we will discuss, many liberal feminists in the 19th century held conservative views about gender roles. As we will describe, some radical feminists who see women as having superior abilities in child-rearing, nurturing, or concern for the environment may also be considered conservatives but still feminists. In all these cases, recognition of women's unique abilities requires conserving and protecting women's traditional roles and women's spheres of knowledge.

> *recap of terms:*
> ### First, Second, and Third Waves of Feminism
> ---
> U.S. feminist history is often divided into three waves. Although many scholars agree this model oversimplifies and privileges certain forms of activism, it remains a useful shorthand and we will employ these terms throughout this chapter.
>
> **First Wave** (1840—1920). Primary goal is the rights of citizenship (vote, hold office, own property) and landmark achievement is suffrage (1920).
>
> **Second Wave** (about 1960—1980s). Dominant goal, equality. Celebration of women's culture. Achievements include antidiscrimination laws in the workplace and education and legalization of abortion. Women of color developed theories of multiple, interlocking oppressions.
>
> **Third Wave** (1990s—present). Embraces broad range of issues; no political priority list. Intentionally inclusive, diverse, multicultural, and genderbending. Engages, critiques, and creates popular culture. Leverages technology and social media.
>
> From Chapter 11, "History of Women's Activism in the United States."

LIBERAL FEMINIST THEORY

The central characteristic of **liberal feminism** is that it is liberal. Exactly what liberal means can be confusing because the term has been used in contradictory ways over the centuries. Today, conservatives in popular media often use the word liberal as a label to tar Democrats who they feel are too permissive when it comes to morality, crime, and government spending, among other issues, whereas some Democrats use the term as a badge of honor (Beinart, 2014). Regardless of what you think of this current-day political label, it sheds more heat than light on the meaning we will unpack and is best left aside as we explore the evolution of the word.

The word liberal comes from the Latin word *liberalis,* of or relating to a free person (originally a man) (OED). So-called classical liberals such as John Locke (1632–1704) believed that individuals were entitled to certain freedoms such as freedom of thought, freedom of expression, the right to private property, and equality of opportunity—and that these rights should be protected from interference by the state (that is, the government) (Eisenstein, 1998). The U.S. Bill of Rights, which prohibits the state from infringing on rights, including freedom of speech, religion, and assembly, is a good example of classical liberal philosophy in action (Hardin, 2011). Many classical liberals today also believe that freedom should include freedom from economic regulation. Thus they support the so-called "free market" (Gaus & Courtland, 2011; Greenberg, 2010).

Today, classical liberals focus on what philosophers call negative liberty (or negative freedom), the freedom from restraint (Gaus & Courtland). So, for example, freedom from government restrictions on women's rights to vote or own property are examples of negative freedom.

Some liberals, however, would like to guarantee more than negative liberty. For example, just because the United States removed the restriction on the rights of women to vote does not mean all women can effectively exercise this right. If a poor elderly woman cannot walk to her polling place or afford transportation, the *formal* right to vote is meaningless. What is missing is a *substantive* right—the ability to exercise that right (see Mann, 2012). If the government offered free public transportation to polling places to the poor, the elderly, and/or people with disabilities, they could then exercise their right to vote. Some liberals go beyond the support of negative freedom to support (in some circumstances) this more robust freedom to accomplish one's ends—what is known as positive liberty (or positive freedom) (Gaus & Courtland). Positive liberty might include guaranteeing maternity leave or laws like Title IX that require colleges to provide equal opportunity in education, including athletic programs. Both policies go beyond the removal of restraint to the enabling of action; maternity leave makes paid employment by mothers more feasible and requiring support for women's athletics ensures teams exist for women to play on. Policies to secure positive liberty are sometimes called welfare liberalism—and these policies sometimes bleed into socialist policy (which will be discussed later) (Mann). Regardless of whether liberal feminists focus on negative or positive liberty, they generally advocate for the same freedoms that middle-class, straight, white men usually have.

For this reason, liberal feminism is sometimes called equality feminism (see Chapter 11).

History of Liberal Feminism

Before and during the first wave of feminism, female abolitionists recognized that just as Black women and men were not free, white women did not have the freedom of white men (see Chapter 11). Among the many limitations women faced, they could not vote or own property because of the doctrine of coverture (see Chapter 3). Abolition of slavery, woman suffrage (the right to vote), access to education, and reform of property rights were all liberal feminist causes in the first wave of feminism. The temperance movement was still another cause with liberal feminist supporters. The temperance movement began as a campaign for moderation in alcohol consumption but moved to a call for total abstinence and prohibition of alcohol. Although most temperance advocates were not feminists, some were, like the suffragist Susan B. Anthony and Frances Willard, the head of the Women's Christian Temperance Union. They believed that women were too often victimized by husbands who drank (and divorce was not an option), so reducing or eliminating alcohol consumption would free women from abuse and poverty caused by alcoholism (Anthony, 2001; Banks, 1993; Marilley, 1993; Riegal, 1971).

Women dominated many 19th-century social movements, such as the women's club and settlement house movements, in which middle- and upper-class Black and white women worked and even lived (hence the name settlement) in poor communities (primarily in cities) providing education, health care, and child care, as well as fighting for workers' rights and city sanitation (Banks; Mann). Important white figures in these movements included Jane Addams, who founded Hull House settlement, and Florence Kelley, who was a member of Hull House. Important Black figures included Ida B. Wells-Barnett, who created the first Black settlement house, the Negro Fellowship League, and the first Black women's club, and Lugenia Burns Hope, who created the Atlanta Neighborhood Union—a club that functioned as a settlement house (Banks; Mann).

Some liberal feminists, including Willard and Addams, believed that although women should have the same liberties as men, females were naturally

ON THE

web

bell hooks (1984) explains **why feminist activism shouldn't be designated "women's work" and males should "participate equally in revolutionary struggle"** (p. 67).

FIGURE 12.1

Victoria Claflin Woodhull ran for the U.S. presidency in 1872, the first woman to do so. Woodhull believed that because marriage was economically essential for most women, it was akin to prostitution. She and her sister were the first-known women stockbrokers.

different from men and these differences should be celebrated (Banks; Dow, 1991). These feminists contended that women should have the right to vote precisely because women were naturally more patient, gentle, loving, self-sacrificing, religious, morally sensitive, and sexually pure than men—a 19th-century ideology known as the cult of true womanhood (Banks; Dow; Peaden, 1993; Welter, 1966). However, other liberal feminists, such as Mary Wollstonecraft (prior to the first wave), who wrote *A Vindication of the Rights of Woman* (1792), rejected these kinds of essential differences between the sexes (Mann; Tong, 1998).

By the time of second wave feminism, feminists increasingly distinguished between the terms sex and gender, arguing that much of women's oppression was a result of oppressive gender roles. Those who rejected natural differences between the sexes, like Betty Friedan, the author of *The Feminine Mystique* (1963/1967), asserted that girls and women should be encouraged to be androgynous, but other liberal feminists wanted more recognition of female culture and female roles (Mann). These feminists included critics of mainstream culture such as Carol Gilligan (1982), who contended that girls and women develop "a different voice" than males that is not recognized by society.

Second wave liberal feminists supported the ERA to the U.S. Constitution, abortion rights (which resulted in the *Roe v. Wade* Supreme Court decision recognizing the right to abortion), and publicly funded child care and more public support for poor women. These political efforts were advocated by many groups, including the National Organization for Women (NOW) (Bill of Rights, in Jaggar & Rothenberg, 1993).

breaking the frame
Liberal Feminism, A Relatively Conservative Philosophy

Liberal feminists—even if they have been considered extreme in their own times—have often sought the same liberties as white, middle-class, straight men. In this respect, liberal feminism is often viewed as a relatively conservative philosophy of social change that seeks to integrate women and others into the already established system of rights; as such, liberal feminism is a reform ideology rather than a revolutionary ideology (see, for example, Tong).

Current examples of liberal feminist thinkers include Sheryl Sandberg, the chief operating officer of Facebook who wrote *Lean In* (2013) (which provides practical advice for women in how to succeed in their careers), as well as the movement for marriage equality for gay people. In both instances, the move is to work within the established system—the world of work for Sandberg and the established system of marriage for marriage equality advocates—and help women and gay people secure the same liberties as men and straight people, respectively. The theme that connects liberal feminists is advocacy of individual liberty for all—even if they conceive of that liberty differently (and it is also important to recognize that the term liberal feminist is a descriptive term used by theorists today and is not always a name these feminists call(ed) themselves).

RADICAL FEMINIST THEORY

When people hear someone described as radical, they often jump to the conclusion that the person is extreme, wild, or even crazy. However, the word radical comes from the Latin word *radicalis,* which means of or relating to a root or roots. To look at something from a radical point of view, then, is to be concerned with the inherent nature, cause, or basis of something. Paradoxically, radical analysis (such as our analysis of the root meaning of the word radical) can be a conservative project—a return to the roots of something; or such analysis can identify a fundamental problem and formulate a radical change, a change from the roots up.

Thinkers and activists identified with **radical feminism** are a diverse group but tend to share three beliefs about women's oppression: (1) the oppression of women was the first form of oppression—and perhaps also the source of other forms of oppression; (2) women's oppression is nearly universal—existing in most known societies—and causes the most damage of any system of oppression; (3) women's oppression is more deeply rooted in our psychology and social relations than other systems of oppression (Jaggar & Rothenberg; Tong). Radical feminists vary on solutions but agree that until the relationship between women and men is fundamentally altered, women's oppression (and, perhaps, the domination of others) will continue.

Two theorists who influenced many radical feminists were Karl Marx (1818–1883) and Friedrich Engels (1820–1895). Of particular importance was Engels's *The Origin of the Family, Private Property and the State,* first published in 1884 (Figure 12.2; Mann). Engels believed that anthropological research showed that in early societies women were not subordinate to men (Engels,

FIGURE 12.2

Friedrich Engels' work, *The Origin of the Family, Private Property and the State*, was based in part on notes by Karl Marx.

1884/1993). Engels contended that women had status because clan membership was determined by matrilineal descent, inheritance was through the female line, and women "ruled the house" (Engels, p. 735; Mann). Engels contended that with the development of other economic systems (including capitalism), men established control of private property and passed on that property through patrilineal descent (Engels; Mann). Engels believed that the low status of women in Western society was not a result of biology but rather of these historical developments (Engels; Mann). Marx, Engels, and others referred to this sort of concrete historical analysis of how life has been produced through economic arrangements and reproduced through childbirth and family arrangements as historical materialism (Engels; Marx & Engels, 1845–1846/1988; see also for example, Firestone, 1970/1972).

Radical feminists took up this form of materialist analysis and developed it in different ways. Some radical feminists, such as Shulamith Firestone, contended that Marx and Engels did not go far enough in analyzing the oppression of women and that the true root of women's oppression is located in the biology of reproduction and not the economic system. As we will discuss, Firestone advocated, among other things, developing artificial reproduction to free women from birthing and rearing children. Other radical feminists, such as Gayle Rubin, not only built on Marx and Engels's materialist analysis but also combined it with insights from the psychoanalytic perspectives of Sigmund Freud and Jacques Lacan (Rubin, 1984/1993). Rubin argued for eliminating the sexual division of labor and social systems that result in sex/gender differences.

History of Radical Feminism

Many women who later identified as radical feminists began their activism as part of the women's rights movement, the civil rights movement, and/or the anti–Vietnam war movement, which came of age in the 1960s and 1970s and are known collectively as the New Left (Goss, 2005; Mann; Weisbrot, 2010). Women in many New Left groups routinely faced "exclusion from decision-making and . . . relegation to domestic and other auxiliary chores" (Banks, p. 225). When women raised the issue of equal treatment, they were often harshly dismissed. For example, in 1967 the women's caucus at the National Conference for New Politics was refused the opportunity for floor

The Psychoanalytic Perspectives of Freud, Lacan, and Rubin

Freud, who is considered the father of psychoanalysis, theorized that girls, realizing they do not have penises, develop penis envy. To Lacan (and perhaps Freud), girls do not envy the literal penis so much as they envy the male power it represents (which Lacan called the phallus). In Lacan's view, a girl's "penis" envy develops because she recognizes that she will always lack the power her father has in society, power that in turn makes her father pleasing to her mother. Lacking phallic power, the girl cannot "please" her mother (her primary emotional attachment), so she turns away from her mother and toward her father. Thus, according to Lacan, the girl seeks power the only way she can, through attachment to men (Rubin, 1984/2008). Radical feminists such as Rubin argued that psychoanalysis explains how unequal power arrangements between women and men affect psychosexual development, produce different sexes, enforce heterosexuality, and create "deformed gender roles." Lacanian and other psychoanalytic perspectives have influenced liberal feminists, radical feminists, and others.

discussion of a resolution advocating a number of women's issues, including equal pay, child care, and abortion on demand. Five women, including Shulamith Firestone, rushed the podium; in response, a man patted Firestone on the head, referred to her as a little girl, and said, "we have more important things to talk about" (Freeman, 1999/n.d., 2012/n.d.; Hall, 2011).

It was in this context that a number of women began writing and organizing under the banner of radical feminism. Early radical feminist groups included New York Radical Women (founded in 1967), Redstockings, and New York Radical Feminists (both founded in 1969) (Buchanan, 2011; New York Radical Women, 2006; Redstockings, 2006). Radical feminists utilized the practice of consciousness-raising, in which women gathered together to talk about their lives. By sharing their experiences of interpersonal violence, harmful beauty standards, sexual harassment at work, restrictive gender roles at home, and other topics, women realized, as the slogan went, "the personal is political" (Freedman, 2002; Hanisch, 1969/2009).

In 1970, Shulamith Firestone argued in *The Dialectic of Sex* that a materialist analysis of women revealed that their oppression lay in "the biological division of the sexes" rather than the economic system—as Marx and Engels argued (as cited in Firestone, p. 12). Firestone contended that because women

FIGURE 12.3

Radical feminists protested at the Miss America Pageant in 1968. However, plans to burn items like bras, girdles, and high-heeled shoes in a "freedom trash can" were never carried out.

historically have been the ones to birth, nurse, and raise children, they have been relegated to a separate, lower caste from men (Firestone). According to Firestone, women's reproductive capacity resulted in the first division of labor in society and the first form of inequality.

Firestone argued that women must be freed from their biology, which made them dependent on men. To Firestone, liberal feminist solutions like contraception, child-care centers, or even paying women to raise children were not radical solutions because they did not "challenge the basic division of labor" (p. 208). The answer for Firestone was technology that allows for artificial reproduction of children, thus freeing women from the limits of female biology. Firestone also advocated for "economic independence and self-determination" for women and children—through socialism (p. 239) (see "Marxist and Socialist Feminist Theory" in this chapter). She also supported androgyny and suggested pansexuality "would probably supersede hetero/homo/bi-sexuality" once sex was no longer tied to reproduction (p. 11).

In 1975, Gayle Rubin wrote an influential essay, "The Traffic in Women: Notes on the Political Economy of Sex," in which she coined the term sex/gender system (Mann). Rubin combined Marx and Engels's materialist analysis with Lacan's psychoanalytic perspective (both described in the previous section). She also drew on the anthropological work of Claude Lévi-Strauss, who studied the way men in kinship societies built social bonds by exchanging women for marriage (think of how political alliances or peace between tribes was often cemented through marriage). For Rubin (1975/2008), kinship systems use separate sex/gender roles to divide labor and use heterosexual coupling as a way to order society. (See Chapter 5, "Constructions of Homosexualities.") These societal structures are oppressive to women because they create sex and gender, enforce heterosexual coupling, and restrain women sexually. To solve women's oppression, asserted Rubin (1975/2008), we must eliminate the sexual division of labor so that both sexes care equally for children; eliminate the sexual property system where men exchange women for the purposes of male bonding; and eliminate compulsory heterosexuality.

In 1978, the radical feminist Mary Daly took a different tack in her book *Gyn/Ecology*. Daly argued that patriarchy had colonized women's minds and drained them of their "biophilic" (life loving) female energy (p. 12). She asserted that the patriarchal mentality has a love of death, that is, that its natural ends are violence (including war) and ecological destruction of the planet. Daly's goal was to escape from the deception of "male-myth masters," which required understanding patriarchal language, returning to original abandoned meanings of words, and creating new language that expressed a gynocentric (women-centered) value system. She reclaimed words used to denigrate women and referred to her sister feminists as Lesbians, Hags, Spinsters, Crones, and Furies (Daly). Daly asserted that her book was "for the Lesbian imagination in all women" (p. 3) and although she did not insist on women's physical separation from men, she did advocate forms of what Marilyn Frye calls "female yes-saying" where women form primary relationships with other women and become "woman-identified" women (pp. xlvi–xlvii).

Radical feminist activism has spanned a number of issues, notably including engagement against sexual assault and pornography. Susan Brownmiller's *Against Our Will: Men, Women and Rape* (1975), which was enormously influential, credited the movement with creating rape crisis centers, rape legislation study groups, and self-defense classes for women. Brownmiller argued that pornography objectified and dehumanized women and also contended that eliminating prostitution was "central to the fight against rape" because it "institutionalizes the concept that it is a man's monetary right, if not his divine right, to gain access to the female body" (p. 392).

In 1983, the radical feminists Andrea Dworkin and Catharine MacKinnon drew up model antipornography legislation, which treated pornography as sex discrimination. Indianapolis, Indiana, passed legislation based on the model ordinance but it was ruled unconstitutional by the Supreme Court (Strossen, 1995). Not all radical feminists supported antipornography and antiprostitution measures, however, including Gayle Rubin (1984), who in, "Thinking Sex: Notes for a Radical Theory of the Politics of Sexuality," argued against burdening sexual acts "with an excess of significance" (p. 11) and lamented the "need to draw and maintain an imaginary line between good and bad sex" (p. 14).

As this sketch of radical feminism indicates, radical feminists are an enormously diverse group of theorists and activists. They have drawn on a variety of theoretical tools, among them materialist analysis (from Marx and Engels), psychoanalytic approaches (Freud and Lacan), and anthropological analysis (Lévi-Strauss).

MARXIST AND SOCIALIST FEMINIST THEORY

The collapse of the Soviet Union in 1991 is often cited as evidence that Karl Marx's idea of Communism is a failure. If Marxism and Communism have been "disproven," why bother to study Marxism or Marxist feminist theory? We believe an answer requires some unlearning about Soviet Communism and a bit of background about Karl Marx's work.

Marx believed that economic systems, or modes of production, as he called them, change over the course of history and that the current mode of production (capitalism) would be overthrown by a social revolution (A. W. Wood, 1988). Marx encouraged a Communist revolution in Russia but expected it to be accompanied by revolutions in more developed Western European countries—revolutions that never happened (A. W. Wood, 2004). So, Marx's theory of history was wrong (A. W. Wood, 2004). But what about Soviet Communism? In fact, the Soviet Union bore no resemblance to Marx's admittedly vague vision of communism (A. W. Wood, 2004). Among other things, Marx expected democratic rule by the working class, which did not happen in the Soviet Union or so-called Communist Eastern European countries (A. W. Wood, 2004).

Although Marx's Communist revolutions and the end of capitalism never came to pass as he predicted, Marx had many important insights that continue to be relevant (Elster, 1988; Pikkety, 2014; A. W. Wood, 2004). An important component of Marx's thinking is his description of how capitalists exploit workers, which we would describe in brief as follows: Marx used the word capital to describe money that people use to pay workers or invest in a business (or means of production) (Marx, 1891/1978b; A. W. Wood, 1988). A factory is an example of a means of production that may be built through capital invest-ment. When workers work for capitalists, they produce goods in exchange for a wage that is just enough to live on and have nothing left to show for their work. However, capitalists have paid for the production of a good (a product) that can be sold for more than it cost to produce it, thus making a profit, which Marx called surplus value (Marx, 1839–1841/1978; A. W. Wood, 1988). Since capitalists reinvest the surplus value in capital, capital wealth continually grows, whereas workers never accumulate wealth (Marx, 1891/1978b). Marx contended that when capitalists rather than workers receive this surplus value (or control its distribution), workers are exploited. Marx argued there is no reason for corporations to be privately owned by capitalists; rather, workers should own the means of production in common and run them, deciding how the surplus value is to be used or distributed (Marx, 1888/1978, 1891/1978a). Marxists and socialists contend that as long as there is a capitalist class that controls the means of production, the working class will be oppressed (Marx, 1847/1978, 1888/1978)

Marx also contended that the first division of labor was a sexual division of labor between women and men (Engels). Engels, as we noted in the radical feminist theory section, believed that women still had status in early societies in their tribal sex/gender roles but lost it with the development of other modes of production including the capitalist mode (Engels as cited in Jaggar & Rothenberg). Marxist and socialist feminists therefore believe women are ex-ploited because of their lower status in domestic work and reproduction as well as through their waged labor (Engels). Marxist feminists such as Evelyn Reed followed and built on Engels in asserting that sexism (and racism) are perpet-uated by capitalism (Reed 1970/1993). Reed, although acknowledging that sexism is a problem, said that many "downtrodden, exploited men . . . have a stake in the liberation struggle of the women; they can and will become our allies" (p. 173). Reed's thinking is an example of what Jaggar and Rothenberg call "**classical Marxist feminism**" (p. 119) because Reed believed that women should primarily organize with others of the working class to overcome capi-talism rather than as women to overcome women's oppression. By contrast, **socialist feminism** advocates multipronged action on a wider range of op-pressions, including activism as workers against capitalism, activism as women against women's oppression, and possibly on other fronts including racism, homophobia, etc. (Jaggar & Rothenberg; Lorber, 2012; Mann).

Another barrier to understanding Marxism is an issue of terminology: the words Communism and socialism have been used in various and sometimes conflicting ways. Some use the word Communism to denote a classless society

MORE ABOUT...

Marxism and Ecofeminism

Well-known feminists influenced by Marx include Vandana Shiva and Maria Mies, both of whom are associated with **ecofeminism** (a combination of the words ecology and feminism). Ecofeminists analyze the damage done to the earth by human domination by drawing parallels to male domination of women (think, for example, of how we describe the environment as virgin territory or exploitation as the rape of the land, etc.). Although Mies and Shiva draw from Marxist analysis, ecofeminists are a diverse group. Other ecofeminists have a liberal feminist approach (such as Rachel Carson, who wrote *Silent Spring*—which is credited with sparking the 1960s environmental movement) (Mann). Still other ecofeminists are associated with other forms of feminism we have yet to discuss. Shiva and Mies were particularly influenced by Rosa Luxemburg, who in *The Accumulation of Capital* (1913), described the workings of capitalist imperialism. Shiva and Mies build on Luxemburg's ideas to analyze how current-day capitalist imperialism harms the environment and women. They have authored books such as *Staying Alive: Women, Ecology and Development* (1989) by Shiva and *Ecofeminism* (1993) by Shiva and Mies (Mann).

where workers own all the means of production. The word socialism is sometimes used to indicate precisely the same thing (or a transitional phase to Communism), but it is also used to refer to national government ownership of significant segments of (but not all) the means of production, as well as government intervention in the economy—such as government-subsidized universal health care, which is found in every industrialized country except the United States (Universal Health Care, 2004). We would point out that even the United States—which is often called capitalist—has social welfare policies such as a minimum wage, unemployment insurance, social security, and publicly funded education that are also found in socialist systems. Among other things, socialist feminists have advocated for maternity and paternity leave and universal health care, child care, and elder care as rights. Since such policies enable women in particular to take on more high-status work and reduce the sex/gender division of labor roles, they are socialist feminist solutions (Mann).

History of Marxist and Socialist Feminism

One example of a first wave activist in the classical Marxist tradition was Mary Harris "Mother" Jones, a labor activist and self-described "hell-raiser"

(M. H. Jones, 1925/2004). Mother Jones believed working-class women and men should organize against capitalists rather than focus narrowly on women's issues. The wealthy elite, she argued, had "organized their women . . . keep[ing] them busy with suffrage, prohibition and charity" as a distraction from real social change (M. H. Jones). Underpinning Jones's argument was the idea that liberal reforms such as suffrage, prohibition, and charity did not address the root cause of inequality for working-class women and men—capitalist exploitation.

Some first wave socialist feminists disagreed with the idea that eliminating capitalism would in itself free women. For example, the socialist feminist Crystal Eastman, a labor lawyer and suffragist, contended that women's emancipation would take more than the "downfall of capitalism" (Eastman as cited in Mann, p. 123; Figure 12.4). She argued that fighting sexism was equally important and advocated measures such as changing the socialization of girls and boys (Mann).

During feminism's second wave in the United States, whereas some Marxist feminists continued to focus on capitalism as the sole root of women's oppression, others analyzed multiple forms of oppression, including oppression based on class, sex/gender, and race. Heidi Hartmann (1976), for example, argued that it was not only capitalists who benefited from the exploitation of working-class women. Working-class men also benefited, she said, by encouraging the segregation of women into lower paying jobs and unwaged domestic work (thus allowing men to keep more valuable waged work for themselves). Hartmann (1981/1993), riffing off Marx's phrase from the *Communist Manifesto* (1836) that workers "have nothing to lose but their chains," noted that working-class men had "more to lose than their chains" (p. 200), namely the privilege that their sex had brought them.

Nancy C. M. Hartsock (1983/2013), like other socialist feminists, criticized Marx for paying too little attention to the unique position of women in capitalism. Hartsock argued that women, through "[m]enstruation, coitus, pregnancy, childbirth, lactation" (p. 359), experience more fluid boundaries with the external world than men, who experience others, the natural world, and mind and body as separate. Through materialist analysis, said Hartsock, women can come to understand the "partial and perverse" nature of the male view and develop class consciousness as women (p. 354). As a result, women understand that to be free they must struggle for inclusion of their vision of the

FIGURE 12.4

Crystal Eastman (left), a socialist feminist, coauthored the Equal Rights Amendment of 1923 with Alice Paul, founder of the National Woman's Party. Eastman was blacklisted and had difficulty finding work during the Red Scare of 1919–1921 (Eastman, 2001, 2014).

FIGURE 12.5
Angela Davis is a socialist feminist activist. Much of her work is devoted to dismantling the prison–industrial complex as part of what she calls a 21st-century abolitionist movement.

world, which Hartsock called the **feminist standpoint**. She made clear it is not a "woman's standpoint" because not all women have developed class consciousness as women to see the world from this perspective (p. 355).

A well-known example of a socialist feminist who emphasized the multiple roots of oppression (including race, sex, and class) is Angela Davis (Mann; Figure 12.5). An academic and long-time activist, Davis emerged during the second wave (and is still active today). She twice ran for vice president of the United States in the 1980s on the Communist Party line (Rösch, 2005). Davis's sort of analysis will be described at length in the sections on intersectional feminism.

U.S. INTERSECTIONAL FEMINIST THEORY

In 1982, Gloria T. Hull, Patricia Bell Scott, and Barbara Smith published a collection of essays, *All the Women Are White, All the Blacks Are Men, but Some of Us Are Brave: Black Women's Studies*. Kimberlé Crenshaw (1989) noted that this title encapsulated the problem with feminist theory from the perspective of many people of color. When feminists in the movement, many of them white, middle-, and upper-class women, considered the oppression of women, they often assumed that their problems were the problems of all women. In addition, when Black people's oppression was discussed, theorists tended to focus on the position of Black men to the exclusion of Black women. Many feminists, particularly women of color, reacted against this tendency and theorized about how their positions as people of different races, ethnicities, nationalities, socioeconomic classes, sexual orientations, and other factors resulted in their oppression, exploitation, and/or discrimination.

This sort of feminist perspective has often been categorized as multicultural (or multiracial or multiethnic) feminism (Lorber, 2012; Tong). Feminists with a multicultural approach are increasingly identified as intersectional feminists—even if their writing predates the coining of the term intersectionality (in 1989)—and all of our characterizations of multicultural feminism apply to what is now called **intersectional feminism** (see, for example, Mann). We will further discuss intersectionality later in this section.

Multicultural/intersectional feminism is not so much a completely different kind of feminism from liberal, radical, or Marxist/socialist feminisms (although it does reject the narrow focus these feminisms sometimes take) as an expanded or overlapping approach for engaging in feminist analysis and activism. For example, members of the Combahee River Collective identified themselves as socialists but stated they were trying "to address a whole range of oppressions" including oppression based on race, sex, class, and sexual orientation (1977/2013, p. 119). Maxine Baca Zinn and Bonnie Thornton Dill have noted that multicultural feminism "does not offer a singular or unified feminism so much as a method of analysis that takes into account multiple systems of domination" (as cited in Lorber, 2005, p. 202). Becky Thompson (2002) went further, asserting,

> *Multiracial feminism is not just another brand of feminism that can be taught alongside liberal, radical, and socialist feminism. Multiracial feminism is the heart of an inclusive women's liberation struggle. The race–class–gender–sexuality–nationality framework through which multiracial feminism operates encompasses and goes way beyond liberal, radical, and socialist feminist priorities—and it always has. (p. 349)*

Another important feature of many multicultural theorists and activists is their advocacy of forms of communication that are open and accessible and would traditionally be considered less academic. For example, bell hooks (1984) argued that professors should be rewarded for the creation of "translations" of feminist work from highly academic language to more accessible forms (p. 111). She herself wrote a popular work, *Feminism Is for Everybody* (2000). Patricia Hill Collins argued that the inaccessible language of some theoretical writing functions to exclude Black women from intellectual work (Mann). The Combahee River Collective (1977/2013) stated that "even our Black women's style of talking/testifying in Black language about what we have experienced has a resonance that is both cultural and political" (p. 119). Cherríe Moraga and Gloria Anzaldúa, in *This Bridge Called My Back: Writings by Radical Women of Color* (1981/1983), wrote of the need to create theory that takes into account the multiple standpoints of women of color:

> *A theory in the flesh means one where the physical realities of our lives—our skin color, the land or concrete we grew up on, our sexual longings—all fuse to create a politic born out of necessity. Here, we attempt to bridge the contradictions in our experience:*

We are the colored in a white feminist movement.

We are the feminists among people of our culture.

We are often the lesbians among the straight.

We do this bridging by naming our selves and by telling our stories in our own words. (p. 23)

A particularly important issue for multicultural/intersectional feminists is how to theorize identity and oppression. In 1972, Francis Beale coined the term double jeopardy to describe the position of Black women who faced oppression not only as Black people but also as women (King, 1988). Others followed by noting the existence of triple and even quadruple jeopardy, in the case, for example, of a Black woman who must negotiate being lesbian and poor. Barbara Smith (1983/2000) emphasized the simultaneity or interlocking nature of oppressions—that is, the idea that one must "be dealing with race and sex and class and sexual identity all at one time" (Collins, 1990/2002), and Deborah King noted that these categories did not always result in a neat hierarchy of oppression. For example, King pointed out that in the case of income, white males outearned Black males, who earned more than white females, followed by Black females. But in the case of education, white males attained the most years of education, followed by white females, then Black males, and last Black females. (We should note that King was writing in 1988; levels of educational attainment are different today.) King suggested that oppression functions differently in different contexts and coined the term multiple jeopardy to describe this fact.

In 1989, Kimberlé Crenshaw coined the term intersectionality to provide an even more nuanced model of how oppression operates (see recap of terms on this page).

Various theorists (Cho et al., 2013; Walby et al., 2012) have noted that the study of intersectionality must focus not only on identities, but also on the social, legal, and other systems that enable oppression. Social systems

---

recap of terms:

Intersectionality

The term **intersectionality** was introduced in the late 1980s to describe a method of analysis that considers how discrimination can vary depending on "multiple dimensions" (such as race, sex and class) (Crenshaw, 1991, p. 1244). Intersectional theory was meant to counter the tendency to treat race, sex, class and other categories as "mutually exclusive" (Crenshaw, 1989, p. 39). It is useful to recognize that discrimination varies depending on several factors: (1) the unique combination of characteristics of the person or group being discriminated against (their race, sex, class, sexual orientation, etc.); (2) the unique combination of characteristics of the person or group doing the discriminating (their race, sex, class, sexual orientation, etc.); and (3) the context in which the discrimination occurs. Although intersectionality begins with "the infinite combinations and implications of overlapping identities," the more recent work of intersectional theorists moves beyond identity categories and is primarily concerned with processes that advantage some while disadvantaging others (Cho et al., 2013, p. 797).

From Chapter 3, "Gender and In/Equality."

may include stereotypes or what Collins (1990/2002) called controlling images (see Chapter 7, "Embodiment, Beauty, and the Viewer"), and legal systems might include laws regarding segregation or undocumented immigrants. Collins called any such system a matrix of domination. Intersectionality presumes that identities and matrices of domination are not static; they change over time. This led Choo and Ferree (2010) to the insight that intersectionality is about *processes* that advantage or disadvantage particular people within particular contexts. Thus intersectionality is concerned with "racialization more than races, economic exploitation rather than classes, gendering and gender performance rather than genders" (Choo & Ferree, p. 134). (See Chapter 6, "Beyond the Mythical Norm," for more on racialization and Chapter 2, "Language and Communication," for more on gender and performativity.)

History of U.S. Intersectional Feminism

Women of color in the United States have critiqued the conception of women's issues as white women's issues and called for a more complex analysis since before the first wave of feminism. Maria Stewart, the first African American female journalist, focused her attention on the plight of "the fair daughters of Africa" in an 1831 pamphlet (Collins; National Women's History Museum, 2007). Sojourner Truth in her 1851 "Ain't I a Woman?" speech noted the gulf in the treatment of Black and white women (Mann; Figure 12.6). These themes were also taken up by later Black intellectuals and activists, including Ida B. Wells-Barnett and Mary Church Terrell (who opposed lynching and founded the National Association of Colored Women's Clubs), Mary McLeod Bethune (who founded the National Council of Negro Women and what became Bethune–Cookman University), and Anna Julia Cooper (who wrote *A Voice From the South: By a Black Woman of the South* [1892] and earned a doctorate in 1925), among others (M. Brown, 2003; "History of Bethune–Cookman," 2014; Mann).

In feminism's second wave there was a strongly negative reaction on the part of many women of color to the work of Betty Friedan and other white, middle-class liberal feminists, whom they perceived as ignoring issues of race and class. bell hooks remarked in *Feminist Theory: From Margin to Center* (1984) that Friedan's analysis of "the problem that

FIGURE 12.6
Sojourner Truth, who escaped from enslavement in 1826, became a preacher, abolitionist, and women's rights activist. She agitated for the inclusion of Blacks in the Union Army and advocated for woman suffrage.

I SELL THE SHADOW TO SUPPORT THE SUBSTANCE.
SOJOURNER TRUTH.

has no name" (the sense of a lack of fulfillment that middle-class housewives felt) and her proposed solution (careers for women) applied only to white middle-class women:

> [Friedan] did not discuss who would be called in to take care of the children and maintain the home if more women like herself were freed from their house labor and given equal access with white men to the professions. She did not speak of the needs of women without men, without children, without homes. She ignored the existence of all non-white and poor white women. She did not tell readers whether it was more fulfilling to be a maid, a babysitter, a factory worker, a clerk or a prostitute, than to be a leisure class housewife. (1984, pp. 1–2)

Audre Lorde (1978/1984) summed up this critique by saying,

> By and large within the women's movement today, white women focus upon their oppression as women and ignore differences of race, sexual preference, class, and age. There is a pretense to a homogeneity of experience covered by the word sisterhood that does not in fact exist. (p. 116)

The rise of the second wave of feminism coincided with the growth of a number of racial and ethnic group movements, including the Asian American movement, Black civil rights, and Black Power movements, the Chicano movement, and the Native American movement. Feminists from these identity groups all contributed to the critique of liberal, radical, and Marxist and socialist feminisms and attested to the need to develop a consciousness that included their unique experiences and struggles.

In 1971, the Chicana feminist student group *Hijas de Cuauhtémoc* (daughters of Cuauhtémoc, the last Aztec ruler to fight Spanish conquistador Hernan Cortés) was formed and ran a newspaper of the same name in Long Beach, California. *Hijas de Cuauhtémoc* was named after a feminist underground newspaper that supported the Mexican Revolution in 1910 (Cuauhtémoc, 2005; Garcia, 1973/1997; B. Thompson, 2002). The Long Beach newspaper took up a range of issues such as religion, Chicana art and poetry, macho attitudes, and the high dropout rate of Chicanas, including those with high grade point averages who had little support from schools and dropped out because of marriage and pregnancy, among other reasons. Also founded in 1971 was Asian Sisters, which focused on preventing drug abuse in Los Angeles (B. Thompson, 2002). At the Vancouver Indochinese Women's conference in

1971, 150 women gathered to address U.S. imperialism against the Indochinese (which includes people in current-day Vietnam, Cambodia, and Laos). Asian women also worked on issues such as immigration, refugees, and the battering of women (B. Thompson, 2002).

In 1973, the National Black Feminist Organization was formed in response to the male-dominated media's focus on white women in the feminist movement. The organization addressed stereotypes in the media and the minimum wage, was involved with political candidates, and conducted consciousness-raising sessions that focused on Black women and beauty, self-esteem, rape, and discrimination in the workplace (B. Thompson, 2002). In 1974, a group of Black lesbian socialist feminists founded the Combahee River Collective, which was named after the site of a raid by Union troops led by Harriet Tubman that freed 750 enslaved people (Combahee River Collective, 2009; B. Smith). Mann called their work, "A Black Feminist Statement," which was written in 1977, "one of the second wave's major statements of intersectionality theory" (p. 172).

Native American women formed the group Women of All Red Nations (WARN), which grew out of the American Indian Movement, in 1974. Among its members were women who had been present at the Indian occupation of Wounded Knee in 1973. They took up a variety of issues, including forced sterilization of Native American women, forced enrollment of Indian children in boarding schools, domestic violence, substance abuse, and connecting with native people in Nicaragua and Guatemala (Cullen-DuPont, 2000; Means, 1999; B. Thompson, 2002).

Feminists of color also argued that just as European powers colonized, dominated, and exploited people in the Third World, the United States has engaged in internal colonialism of people of color within the United States. Internal colonialism involves (1) being forced into a country; (2) forced assimilation into the dominant language and culture; (3) denial of citizenship rights; and often (4) being channeled into low-paying, low-status jobs (Mann). Mann described three internal colonies in the United States: Native American people who have been forced onto reservation territories that were believed to be the least desirable land; enslaved people who were imported into what is now the United States; and people of the Mexican territory that was annexed by the United States at the conclusion of the Mexican–American War (1846–1848).

Women of color associated with multicultural or intersectional approaches identified in a variety of ways. Some African American women rejected the term feminist because they viewed it as narrowly representing white, middle-class women's interests and instead used the terms womanist and womanism (Mann). Latinas chose terms such as " 'Hispanas,' 'Latinas,' 'Mestizas,' 'Chicana feminists,' and/or 'Xicanistas' " (Mann). Many women of color in the United States also identified as Third World women or U.S. Third World feminists. (See Appendix B, Names for People and Places for definitions of First and Third World.) These terms emphasize that whether they are, say, African American, Native American, or people of Latin American ancestry, they share a common position (despite differences among Third World people) in relation to white America and white feminists.

Many women of color thought of themselves as straddling multiple identities and communities. Gloria Anzaldúa, who grew up on the South Texas border with Mexico, is an excellent example. She wrote in *Borderlands/La Frontera: The New Mestiza* (1987) that Chicanas must develop a new consciousness that "is a consciousness of the borderlands," recognizing Chicana history as a fusion of multiple cultures—Indian, Spanish, Mexican, and U.S.—with movement back and forth between these cultures. Mestiza consciousness, according to Anzaldúa, involves a "plural personality" that does not insist on a single, rigid point of view but tolerates ambiguity, contradictions, and inclusivity.

In 1991, Chela Sandoval (1991/2001) built on this idea, contending that Third World feminists should engage and disengage the gears of various feminist approaches to best move forward. Sandoval also argued that U.S. Third World feminism must struggle to overcome what Gayatri Chakravorty Spivak called **hegemonic feminism**—a dominant form of feminism that currently focuses on white middle-class feminist issues and elides people of color.

TRANSNATIONAL FEMINIST THEORY

Transnational feminism, like U.S. intersectional feminism, takes into account multiple systems of domination. Transnational feminists are particularly concerned with global forces, past and present, that affect women and other marginalized groups of the Global South. (See Appendix B, Names for People and Places for definitions of Global North/Global South.)

The *trans* in transnational comes from Latin and means "across, through, over, to or on the other side of, beyond, outside of, from one place, person, thing, or state to another" (OED). Transnational is not just another word meaning "international," which by contrast means "between, among, in-between, in the midst" of nations and is often used to suggest relations between or on behalf of nations—for example, trade negotiations between China and the United States. Although international relations are still important today, nation-states are neither the sole nor always the most important actors globally. Today there are a variety of agents that go beyond national boundaries—transnational organizations—including economic associations like the European Union, which created a transnational currency, the Euro, that has replaced the national currencies of 28 countries; global terrorist groups such as Al Qaeda, with affiliates around the world; transnational corporations like News Corporation or Ford Motor Company; and nongovernmental organizations like Women's Global Network for Reproductive Rights (European Union, n.d.; Moghadam, 2005). These groups do not simply operate "between" nations (*inter*nationally) but across, through, over, beyond, and outside of nation-states (*trans*nationally) (Mann). Increasingly, such groups can have enormous power in our globalized world. As a reminder, globalization can be defined as "the increased exchange of people, goods, capital, ideas and culture across national boundaries" (H. James, 2010, para 1).

Transnational feminists are concerned with the processes of globalization and particularly its effects on people of the Global South. Transnational feminists argue that globalization has not only accelerated the mixing of the First and Third Worlds but also contributed to the existence of both a capitalist elite and a marginalized poor and working class throughout the world. For example, many countries such as Brazil, the United States, South Africa, or India have industrialized areas inhabited by people who are part of the Global North, whereas other people in the same country are better thought of as part of the Third World or Global South. Transnational feminist networks such as Development Alternatives with Women for a New Era and Women's Environment and Development Organization argue that what is necessary is not simply attempts at so-called "*economic* development," which has decreased poverty globally but left many in the Global South merely subsisting while the those in the Global North accumulate an increasing share of the world's wealth (J. Gilbert, 2013; Moghadam). Instead, these transnational feminist networks advocate for *human* development that focuses on the world's most vulnerable including women, children, and the poor (see Chapters 8 and 10 for a discussion of neoliberalism) (Moghadam).

Another important component of transnational feminist thinking and activism is attention to how language can influence thought. Transnational feminists (and other feminists—especially postmodern/queer theorists, whom we will discuss later) tend to draw from a school of thought known as **poststructuralism**, which (among other claims) contends that words do not have inherent meaning but only signify things in relation to other words (Beasley, 1999; "Poststructuralism," 2004; de Saussure, 1916/1998). For example, think about how many words are part of a binary system of meaning such as woman/man, feminine/masculine, gay/straight, Black/white, etc. As discussed in Chapter 10, "Human Rights and Global Activism," these words are part of what Foucault (1971/1982) and others called discourse: "practices that systematically form the objects of which they speak" (p. 49)—that is, the use of words (or symbols more generally) in a particular historical and social context that generates a way of thinking (J. Richardson, 2005).

As we have discussed, discourses on sex, gender, and sexual orientation tend to enforce a binary (and limiting) way of thinking about these subjects. Transnational feminists apply these ideas to the language we use about our transnational world. For example, the binaries of First World/Third World, North/South, Western/non-Western, developed/less developed all enforce a way of thinking about the world that privileges a Western-centric view and overlook both differences within each category and similarities across these binaries. A source for this critique is Edward Said's book *Orientalism* (1978).

Global feminist discourse has often done the same thing; assumed a white, Western, middle-class perspective that homogenizes and others non-Western people (see Chapters 2 and 6 for a discussion of being other and othering, respectively). Western-centric feminist discourse also tends to place Western feminists in the position of compassionate heroes who describe Third World women's problems and then act to save these victims—what Uma Narayan calls a "missionary framework" (as cited in Mann). This narrative further others Third World women and falsely suggests they are irrational (for allowing their suffering to continue) and lack agency—the power to act themselves (Mann). As we have described in Chapter 10, women's participation in certain practices such as forms of female genital cutting (fgc) may initially appear to some Westerners as irrational and victimizing; however, they may be socially meaningful and/or rational choices in some contexts. Furthermore, as we also show in Chapter 10, Third World women through groups such as Tostan do frequently act to change their position in society.

Transnational feminism, then, can be defined as a form of feminism that rejects a universal or hegemonic Western feminism, considers the varying positions of women and others across the world, and pays attention to global forces (both historical and current) such colonialism, neoliberalism, and hegemonic discourses that affect women and others (Grewal & Kaplan, 1997; Hanak, 2009; Mann; C. Mohanty, 2003).

History of Transnational Feminism

During feminism's first wave, some Western feminists attempted to organize across national boundaries through organizations such as the International

Council of Women (1888), the International Alliance of Women (1904), and the Women's International League for Peace and Freedom (1915 and still active today). Although these organizations welcomed women of all countries, races, religions, and political affiliations, membership remained primarily Western until the years after World War I (Rupp, 2010).

In the mid- to late-19th century, U.S. militarism and imperialism were topics of activist discussion. During this time the United States annexed more than half of Mexico following the Mexican–American War (1848) and took control of Cuba, Puerto Rico, the Philippines, and Guam in 1898 after the Spanish–American War (Buchenau, 1998; "Spanish–American War," 2005). U.S. feminist groups, however, did not have a strong record of opposing such actions. The National American Woman Suffrage Association (NAWSA), for example, often sought to prove women deserved the vote by supporting U.S. imperialism. Elizabeth Cady Stanton, the first president of NAWSA, wrote, "The great public topic just now is 'expansion,' of which I am in favor ... what would this continent have been if we had left it to the Indians?" (as cited in Sneider, 2008, p.102). However, support for U.S. imperialism was not universal among American feminists. Carrie Chapman Catt, a later president of NAWSA, opposed militarism, joined the Women's Peace Party, and supported independence for the Philippines from the United States (Mann).

The second wave of U.S. feminism coincided with the U.S. war in Vietnam, and feminists were increasingly active theorizing and participating in movements against imperialism, militarism, and so-called "development" (Mann). By the early 1980s, a number of feminist writers were publishing books about the exploitation of women in global factory labor, including Annette Fuentes and Barbara Ehrenreich's *Women in the Global Factory,* María Patricia Fernandez-Kelley's *For We Are Sold, I and My People,* both of which documented the experience of Mexican women working in *maquiladoras* (foreign-owned factories in Mexico), and Wendy Chapkis and Cynthia Enloe's *Of Common Cloth: Women in the Global Textile Industry* (Mann). These books connected the problems of women globally with the increasing reach of transnational corporations. These and other writers analyzed a number of actors within the global capitalist system, including: (1) transnational corporations (referred to as multinational corporations at the time) that located factories wherever labor costs, corporate taxes, and labor and environmental regulation were lowest; (2) international lending agencies such as the World Bank that made huge loans to Third World governments to "develop" their countries (including building roads, power plants, and factory facilities) to attract multinational corporations; and (3) Third World elites in government and business (often supported by First World governments) who profited within the system, sometimes through corruption and mismanagement of development aid. (See Chapter 8, "Work, Inequality, and Neoliberalism," for a discussion of neoliberalism and globalization.)

These authors stressed that Third World countries were often unable to pay off their "development" loans and accumulated huge foreign debt, particularly when transnational corporations relocated to other countries where wages, taxes, and environmental and safety regulations were lower. This created a race to the bottom where Third World countries continually lowered wages, taxes, and regulations to compete for jobs. Many feminist critics argued that such a system is rigged for the benefit of the Global North at the expense of the Global South.

In 1987, Charlotte Bunch described the need to speak of global feminism rather than international feminism because, she said, "I see feminism as a movement of people working for change across and despite national boundaries, not of representatives of nation-states or national governments" (as cited in Jaggar & Rothenberg, p. 249). Bunch further contended that "we must move beyond the concept of nation-state, which is another expression of patriarchy whereby groups battle for domination . . . on the basis of geographical territory" (as cited in Jaggar & Rothenberg, p. 249). Bunch argued that feminism must abandon a "laundry list of so-called women's issues such as child care and equal pay" and develop a transformational program aimed at changing institutions and power structures (p. 250). This approach meant developing stances on the international economic order, the nuclear arms race, imperialism, and other issues.

By 1997, feminists such as Inderpal Grewal and Caren Kaplan were using the term transnational feminism rather than international or global feminism as a way to signal an added critique of the traditionally Western-centered approach of feminism that tended to treat the Global North and South as monolithic entities. As a result, Grewal and Kaplan viewed transnational feminism as a counter to a hegemonic Western feminism.

Chandra Talpade Mohanty is a highly influential transnational feminist, whose essays "Under Western Eyes" (1986) and "'Under Western Eyes' Revisited: Feminist Solidarity Through Anticapitalist Struggles" (2003) provided a foundation for transnational feminist practice (Figure 12.7). C. Mohanty, in the latter essay, wrote "my focus now is on . . . anticapitalist transnational feminist practice—and on the possibilities, indeed on the necessities of cross-national feminist solidarity and organizing against capitalism" (p. 509). C. Mohanty engaged in a materialist analysis of women's and men's lives, taking into account globalization and the exploitative nature of capitalism. She argued that despite differences between feminists of the Global South and Global North, alliances can and must be formed—but feminists of the Global North must be careful not to frame issues or engage in activism that recolonizes women and men of the Global South (2003). Instead, they must take a decolonial approach in which activist language and efforts recognize and are genuinely inclusive of the differences and the agency of people of the Global South (see the previous discussion of poststructuralism).

FIGURE 12.7

Chandra Talpade Mohanty, born in Mumbai, India, in 1955, is a transnational and postcolonial feminist theorist. Much of her work today is about capitalist exploitation of the Global South and the complexities of working across lines of race, class, sexuality, and nationality to form feminist alliances.

C. Mohanty's approach, and that of many other transnational feminists, is often called **postcolonial feminism**. Postcolonial feminists not only use poststructuralism's insights to critique the Global North's discourse about the "Third World," but also contend that the oppression of women and men in the Global South has roots in a system created through colonialism that still exists in altered forms in the postcolonial period (Mann). Postcolonial and transnational feminists assert that the end of colonialism has given rise to a new set of oppressive political, economic, social, and cultural conditions. Rather than having a system of colonial domination with exploitation through direct rule of colonies by colonial powers, there is now a postcolonial system in which the Global North, especially through capitalism, continues to dominate and exploit the Global South (Mann). The most marginalized groups, such as women, suffer most and in a variety of ways, including through labor exploitation, violence, environmental degradation and destruction, and sexual exploitation. (See, for example, Chapter 8 and neoliberalism and Chapter 10 and human trafficking.) Transnational feminists argue that addressing these issues requires critical analysis of transnational systems of dominance that give rise to these ills. So for example, labor exploitation in the Global South must be dealt with by addressing the neoliberal economic system that enables transnational corporations to pay workers little and offer little or no health and safety protections for workers. In developing these views, transnational feminists built on theorists such as Aimé Césaire's *Discourse on Colonialism* (1955/2000) and books by Frantz Fanon, including *The Wretched of the Earth* (1961).

MORE ABOUT...

Transnational Feminist Networks

Valentine M. Moghadam (2005) identified several groups she calls transnational feminist networks that are active today, including Development Alternatives with Women for a New Era and Women in Development Europe, both of which are critical of the World Bank, the International Monetary Fund, and the neoliberal economic system. Other transnational feminist groups include MADRE (mother in Spanish), which "works in partnership with community-based women's organizations [in nine countries in Africa, the Caribbean, Central and South America, and the Middle East as well as with the International Indigenous Women's Forum] to address issues of health and reproductive rights, economic development, education and other human rights" (MADRE, 2014). Women Living Under Muslim Laws (WLUML) is still another "international solidarity network" that "extends to more than 70 countries ranging from South Africa to Uzbekistan, Senegal to Indonesia and Brazil to France" (Women Living Under Muslim Laws, n.d.). WLUML's focus includes peacebuilding, resisting the effects of militarization, opposing fundamentalisms, expanding the debate about bodily autonomy (to include such issues as sexual and reproductive rights), and promoting and protecting women's legal equality (WLUML). Additional transnational feminist issues include the environment, the labor movement, and indigenous people's movements. (For a list of organizations divided by their form of advocacy, see the table of more than 35 organizations in Moghadam's book, *Globalizing Women* (pp. 10–11).)

POSTMODERN FEMINIST/QUEER THEORY

In the field of philosophy, **modernism** and the modern period begin with René Descartes and especially his work *Meditations on First Philosophy* first published in 1641 (Cottingham, 1995). Descartes's project was to systematically doubt everything and methodically think through what he could know for certain and build on that firm foundation of knowledge (Descartes, 2012). Modern thinkers believe that we can have firm foundations of knowledge, that reason and science can be used to get at the truth of things—ideas that are also central to the period known as the Enlightenment (Beasley; Cottingham; Magnus, 1995; Norris, 1995). Some but not all theorists distinguish between modern*ity*—referring to a time period and modern*ism*—referring to a body of thought (see for example, Grewal & Kaplan). (We will not make this distinction.)

Although we have been focusing on philosophical notions of modernity, different academic fields define modernity differently (Harrison, 2003). For example, in the field of English, the modern period often refers roughly to the first 20 years of the 20th century (Harrison) and literary modernism refers to a particular literary style and themes developed in that period. Thus in the field of English, literary modernism and the reaction against it, postmodernism, refer to ideas that differ from philosophic notions of modernism and postmodernism.

Philosophic postmodern thinkers reject the central tenets of modernism: the idea that there are foundations to knowledge and precise definitions, as well as the view that reason and science can get us to "happily ever after" (Beasley; Lyotard, 1979/1984; Magnus). Because postmodernists reject the idea that we can definitively categorize things, ideas, or people, they reject essentialism (Beasley; Magnus). (See Chapter 6.) For example, take the idea of categorizing someone by sex. What does it mean to say someone is of the female sex? Consider people who have undergone the sex reassignment process. Are people who have transitioned from "male to female" of the female sex? In some senses they are biologically changed (perhaps in terms of genitalia, breasts, and/or hormones) but their chromosomes remain "male," among other biological characteristics. What about intersex people? Can a person have a penis and be a woman? (See Chapter 1, "Sex, Gender, and Social Construction.") One other example: what does it mean to be homosexual? Can a man have occasional sex with men and still identify as heterosexual? Can a closeted gay man claim to be gay if he has only had sex with his wife? (See Chapter 4.)

Many women's and gender studies theorists would argue that there are no definitive answers to the questions of what it means to be female or homosexual (or other identity categories important to women's and gender studies). If notions of sex, gender, and sexual orientation are not fixed (or lack essential properties), they cannot be "knowable" in the usual sense of the term. Put another way, if these categories do not have firm boundaries, then we cannot say that people fit these definitions. Thus, there are no "women," (or "men"); no "homosexuals" (or "heterosexuals") or "Black" people (or "white" people etc.). Postmodernists would agree that we *treat* people as female or homosexual or as belonging to a racial category but they do not believe there is an essential property or set of properties that makes someone female or gay or of a particular race (see, for example, Foucault, 1976/1980). (See the discussion of racialization in Chapter 6.) Postmodernists would say all social categories are radically indeterminate—free floating and the result of any number of shifting associations rather than fixed or determined by any single factor,

recap of terms:

Essentialism

Essentialism is the belief that a thing is what it is because it has a specific property or set of properties. Put another way, essentialism is the belief that a characteristic or set of characteristics define the thing; constitute the essence of the thing.

From Chapter 6, "Beyond the Mythical Norm."

whether it is biology, psychology, economics, etc. (See also the discussion of poststructuralism in the transnational feminism section.)

Postmodern feminism also rejects the idea that there are universally true statements about all human beings (Beasley). Because we are all different, any attempt to make statements about all people (or even subgroups such as all women or all gay people) invariably overlook important differences between people. If we cannot make universal statements, then we cannot have a single conception of, say, freedom. If we cannot universalize about all women, we cannot have a single ideal that would result in freedom for all women. To put this in concrete terms, let's take a subject like gender. Suppose that the gender binary feminine/masculine systematically reinforces the subordinate position of women (because femininity entails passivity, weakness, and emotionality, as discussed in Chapters 1 and 3). This would lead feminists to want to eliminate the binary to create freedom for women. However, suppose it is also true that some people, such as some trans women and some women who were assigned female at birth, feel most comfortable being highly feminine. For these women to be true to themselves, we would need to keep the gender binary. A postmodern feminist could argue that no universal approach would satisfy the needs of all these women—and that feminism requires pursuing multiple and particular (as opposed to universal) approaches. A postmodern feminist would recognize that all social configurations empower or advantage some at the expense of others. Thus any solution will require continual concern and adjustment.

A perspective that has much in common with postmodernism and postmodern feminist theory is queer theory. Queer theory springs in part from postmodernists' denial of foundations for knowledge, universal categories, that faith in reason or science will give us definitive answers, or that we will reach a happily ever after where everyone is free (Beasley). As the name suggests, queer theory is an outgrowth of the study of queerness—meaning not only homosexuality but also nonnormative categories more generally (although the first major works were concerned with homosexuality). Queer theorists have often argued against modernism by focusing on the incoherence of the category of sexual orientation—as well as the categories of sex and gender (Jagose, 1996). Queer theorists assert that these categories are not stable because people are constantly shifting what it means to be a member of these categories (Beasley; Jagose; Pilcher & Whelehan, 2005). For example, in ancient Rome a man could engage in same-sex sex and still be conceived as adhering to hegemonic masculinity (see Chapter 5). Today, in what we might think of as traditional, middle-class U.S. white culture, male same-sex sexual activity is often perceived as undermining hegemonic masculine identity.

These historical changes suggest that gender, sexual orientation, and other categories or identities are not fixed but performative. (See Chapter 2 for a discussion of performativity.)

Because queer theory is an approach that tries to continually open up possibilities, Annamarie Jagose said that "to attempt an overview of queer theory and to identify it as a significant school of thought . . . is to risk domesticating it, and fixing it in ways that queer theory resists fixing itself" (pp. 1–2). So although queer theory has its roots in the postmodern analysis of sex, gender, and sexual orientation, the methods and content of queer theory are supposed to always remain open.

It is sometimes suggested that queer theory is not necessarily feminist since it rejects the belief in the existence of the category of women and the idea that women (and others) can reach a point of universal freedom. (The same may be said of postmodernism.) Although it may be true that queer theory does not necessitate adherence to feminism, Jagose pointed out that "the most prominent theorists in the area are undoubtedly feminist" (p. 119). So, even if queer theorists do not have to take a feminist approach in principle, they generally do in practice.

Postmodern and queer theoretical approaches may be feminist to the extent that they recognize that social categories such as sex, gender, and sexual orientation *create* women, lesbians, gay men, transgender people, etc. Postmodern theorists include Michel Foucault and queer theorists include Judith Butler (described in Chapters 5 and 4, respectively, and discussed further in the next section). These theorists contend that insisting that people conform to these categories inherently limits people by requiring them to be "normal" women, men, gay men, heterosexuals, etc. By tearing apart or multiplying these categories, we open up possibilities for people to exist in other ways (Jagose; Seidman, 1993). Thus, genderbending and queer identification are examples of postmodern and queer feminist approaches (see Chapters 1, 4, and 11).

History of Postmodernism and Queer Theory

Theorists identified as postmodern feminists often draw on the work of Jacques Derrida, Jacques Lacan, and Michel Foucault. According to Rosemarie Putnam Tong, Derrida's contributions to postmodern feminism include criticism of phallocentrism and dualism, the tendency to think of the world in binary oppositions in Western thought. (See Chapter 5 for more on phallocentrism.) Lacan, as we described in the section on radical feminist theory, drew on Freud's notion of penis envy to describe how girls turned their desire away from their mothers as they grew conscious of male power represented by the

FIGURES 12.8 AND 12.9

Judith Butler (left), philosopher, gender theorist, and professor of comparative literature, and Eve Kosofsky Sedgwick (right), poet, literary, critic and professor of English, were instrumental in the formation of queer theory and queer studies.

phallus. Foucault's analysis in his work *The History of Sexuality Volume I: An Introduction* (1976/1980), contributed to queer theory by describing how the category of the homosexual was constructed in the 19th century (see Chapter 5) and other work by Foucault focused on how our notions of truth and the exercise of power reciprocally create one another.

Three important postmodern theorists who are often associated with postmodern feminism are Julia Kristeva, Hélène Cixous, and Luce Iragaray. These theorists, often referred to as "French feminists," had different views but influenced queer theorists including Judith Butler and Eve Kosofsky Sedgwick (Tong; Figures 12.8 and 12.9). Here is a sampling of their ideas.

Kristeva, in an interview in 1974 entitled "Woman Can Never Be Defined," argued there is no definable category of "woman" and worried that women's activism based on identity could result in a reverse version of the current oppressive male system. Cixous, in her 1975 essay, "Sorties," explored a number of binary terms in Western culture including "Activity/passivity," "Culture/Nature," "Father/Mother," "Head/heart," and "Intelligible/sensitive." She contended that there is a hierarchy of these terms with man represented by the first term and woman by the second. As with many postmodern theorists who reject rigid definitions and essentialism, Cixous was investigating not what women are, but how they are perceived in relation to an other—namely men

(Cixous). Iragaray, in her 1977 essay, "This Sex Which is Not One," detailed how women's sexual experience differs from that of men and critiqued Freud's theory of penis envy. In doing so, Iragaray was following in the postmodern tradition of rejecting a shared, objective reality and argued that people's understanding of the world is shaped by their subjective bodily experience as women or men.

Often overlooked in the history of queer theory is the work of Cherríe Moraga and Gloria Anzaldúa, who together edited *This Bridge Called My Back: Writings by Radical Women of Color* (1981/1983) and Anzaldúa's later work, *Borderlands/La Frontera: The New Mestiza* (1987). In *This Bridge Called My Back,* Moraga (1981/1983) explicitly identified as queer and took up the queer theoretical idea of oppressors projecting their fear "into the bodies of women, Asians, gays, disabled folks, whoever seems most 'other' " (p. 32). Anzaldúa, in *Borderlands/La Frontera: The New Mestiza* (1987), described a new *mestiza* (Latin American woman) who "can't hold concepts or ideas in rigid boundaries," who has "tolerance for contradictions, a tolerance for ambiguity," and has a "pluralistic personality" (p. 79)—all approaches in keeping with postmodernism and queer theorizing about the instability of categories.

Two other works that are more generally noted as founding texts of queer theory are Judith Butler's *Gender Trouble* (1990/1999) and Eve Kosofsky Sedgwick's *Epistemology of the Closet* (1990)—although both were published before the coining of the term "queer theory" by Theresa de Lauretis (Jagose). It is in *Gender Trouble* that Butler introduced the idea of gender as performative and argued that the category of sex is socially constructed. Butler contended that since sex, gender, and sexual orientation (among other categories) are socially constructed, they do not exist. Feminists therefore cannot liberate so-called "women" or "gay people." Building on Foucault, Lacan, the French feminists, and others, she argued that we can overcome the binaries of sex and gender (and the hierarchy they impose) by recognizing the role of performativity in constructing these categories and by subverting these categories through performative acts that create new configurations of sex and gender.

Sedgwick's *Epistemology of the Closet,* which was published just a few months after Butler's *Gender Trouble,* asserted that "many of the major nodes of thought and knowledge in twentieth-century Western culture as a whole are structured—indeed fractured—by" the heterosexual/homosexual binary (p. 1). In part, Sedgwick (1990) was arguing that our conception of heterosexuality is generated by its opposite: homosexuality. Sedgwick (1990) further argued that "homo/heterosexual definition has been a presiding master term of the past century," which has influenced our culture by indelibly marking

FIGURE 12.10

The art collective Gran Fury, who were also ACT UP members, created this ad for ACT UP's day of protest in 1988 (Meyer). ACT UP was influenced by queer theory and utilized ideas of queerness in their politics and activism.

other important binaries in Western thought including knowledge/ignorance, masculine/feminine, innocence/initiation, active/passive, in/out, and art/kitsch to name just a few (p. 11). So, for example, the binary innocence/initiation carries with it the idea that to be innocent is to be innocent of (that is, not knowledgeable about) homosexuality and to be initiated is to be initiated into (have experience of) the world of homosexuality. Sedgwick (1990) considered all these terms to have the "suffusing stain of homo/heterosexual crisis" (p. 73). For Sedgwick (1990), then, understanding the heterosexual/homosexual binary is critical to our understanding of Western knowledge and Western interpretation.

The 1980s and 1990s gave rise to queer activism by groups such as ACT UP (formed in 1987) and Queer Nation (formed in 1990), whose outrageous methods, including shouting "We're here. We're queer. Get used to it" in street demonstrations (Stryker, 2004, para. 4), holding kiss-ins, and creating provocative advertisements, set about to disrupt as Michael Warner (2002) put it, "the idea of normal behavior" (p. 218) (Meyer, 2002). Rather than presenting gay people as a group that should be accepted and assimilated into the broader culture, these groups demanded respect for difference. Following Butler and her notion of subverting categories through performativity, participants in same-sex kiss-ins included "straight and bisexual members of the group" who would kiss a same-sex person. Rather than demonstrating their sexual identity, such acts performed queerness regardless of the sexual desire of the couples (Meyer). (See Chapter 12 for more on ACT UP and Queer Nation.)

One novel application or expansion of queer studies is Elena Levy-Navarro's (2009) contention that queer theory should be applied to fat studies and fat activism. Levy-Navarro stressed that conceptions of fatness (as with homosexuality) have changed over time and that fatness has not always been thought of as "pathological" as it often is today. Levy-Navarro's application of queer analysis demonstrates how queer theory can be applied beyond the category of homosexuality to the more general project of dismantling categories and championing the nonnormative. (See Chapters 5 and 7.)

Postmodern feminist theory and queer theory, then, are broad-ranging approaches used by feminists to critique social norms and develop strategies for opposing them.

CONCLUSION

By now it should be clear why we often speak of feminisms (in the plural) or forms of feminism rather than feminism (in the singular). Despite a common belief in and advocacy of equality for people regardless of sex, the various forms of feminism conceive of problems and solutions in different ways. Sometimes these forms of feminism offer competing perspectives. For example, liberal feminists want to achieve equality by working within the current system, whereas radical feminists want to fundamentally alter the relationship between women and men. Despite these differing perspectives, feminists sometimes agree on goals. For example, liberal and radical feminists sometimes agree on the need to eliminate homophobia, sexist stereotypes, and/or violence against women. Moreover, conservative feminisms sometimes share common perspectives with antifeminists—such as a belief in a unique feminine capacity in certain spheres of activity and thought.

Frequently feminisms overlap, drawing on common methodological approaches. Radical feminists often use Marxist/materialist or psychoanalytic analysis as do Marxist/socialist feminists. Intersectional analysis (both U.S. Third World and transnational feminist analysis) has been utilized especially by those with a Marxist/socialist perspective.

Given the diversity of these forms of feminism and the diversity within them, it is frequently impossible to generalize about them at all. Any assertions about them must be made within a particular historical context and with attention to a particular feminist's philosophical program. Many who write about feminism speak of this as the need to historicize descriptions of feminism.

We hope this chapter also reveals something about the connection between theory and activism within feminism. Frequently the theory or philosophy of a particular subject is studied without reference to activism or how these theories intersect with our lived experience. By contrast, our history of feminist theory is deeply intertwined with people engaged with the "real world" and with activism in particular. We'd like to leave you with the words of 2 thinkers and activists. First, Marx (1845/1978), who wrote, "The philosophers have only *interpreted* the world, in various ways; the point, however, is to *change* it" (p. 145). Next, Ella Baker, who said, "If there is any philosophy, it's that those who have walked a certain path should know some things, should remember some things that they can pass on, that others can use to walk the path a little better" (as cited in Ransby, 2003, p. 357). Marx understood the value of being able to interpret the world but also the necessity of working for change. Ella Baker's words remind us that whatever our path, there are those who have walked that path before us—and that their wisdom can ease our own journey.

Ultimately, we hope this chapter will help you interpret the world and give you tools to change it.

THINK, LEARN, ACT

The following resources are available on the Student Website: www.oup.com/us/gillis-jacobs

Taking Stock, Taking Action prompts and activities. Apply what you've learned to take action on campus and in the broader community.

Recommended Readings and Multimedia Resources, including scholarly and literary works, documentaries, feature films, podcasts and more, to enrich the in- and out-of-classroom experience.

APPENDIX A

Basic Terms

The following terms are basic to women's, gender, and sexuality studies. They are discussed in this textbook in Chapter 1, "Sex, Gender, and Social Construction." Additional chapters where individual terms are discussed at length appear in parentheses after some entries. (Note: In some cases, these terms are also used in biology, where they may have different meanings. We have tried to note this where appropriate.)

Androgynous—The state of having female and male characteristics, interests, etc. To behave and/or appear in both traditionally feminine and masculine ways. (In biology, may mean to have biological sex characteristics of females and males at once.)

Asexual—Someone who "experiences little or no sexual attraction" to other people (AVEN, 2012). (In biology, generally refers to a lack of sex-specific sex organs.) (See also Chapter 4, "LGBTQQIAA Identities and Challenges.")

Assigned sex—Alternative to "biological sex," which recognizes that sexual categorization is not simply a matter of objective biological fact but also a matter of human decision, that is, that sex is to some degree socially constructed.

Butch—Vernacular (informal or colloquial) term frequently used in gay and lesbian subcultures for women who are gender nonconforming (i.e., masculine) and men who are gender conforming.

Cisgender—Term used to describe people whose gender identity is in traditional alignment with their assigned sex at birth (for example, a woman who is traditionally feminine).

Cognitive schema—A mental system of organization. Sex and gender are major cognitive schemas in most societies.

Feminine—A descriptor of gender; traditionally those assigned female at birth are expected or "supposed" to be feminine. Characteristics associated with Western notions of traditional femininity include passive, dependent, and emotional. Traditionally thought of in binary (consisting of two parts) opposition with masculine.

Femme—Vernacular (informal or colloquial) term frequently used in gay and lesbian subcultures for women who are gender conforming (i.e., feminine) and men who are gender nonconforming.

Gender—Less physiological aspects related to femininity, masculinity, androgyny, and other associated categories; ways of presenting oneself that are constructed and reconstructed through what one does, how one looks, how one behaves, etc.

Gender expression (or gender presentation)—One's outward expression of gender. For example, how one dresses or the length of one's hair.

Gender identity—One's perception of the gender that is appropriate to oneself.

Gender ideology—A set of interrelated, internalized beliefs about gender. In Western society, gender ideology is often subdivided into masculinity ideology and femininity ideology (Levant et al., 2007).

Gender polarization—The notion that femininity and masculinity are polar opposites. Defines mutually exclusive scripts for being female and male and defines persons or behaviors that deviate from these scripts as problematic (Bem, 1993).

Gender role—A set of social expectations about the part one should play (including how one "should" appear and behave) within a specific culture based on one's sex and gender. For example, traditionally in Western society women have had the gender role of homemaker and men have had the role of breadwinner.

Gender variant (gender nonconforming)—To have one's gender expression in nontraditional alignment with one's assigned sex at birth. (See also transgender.)

Genderqueer—To express gender nonnormatively; often signals recognition that gender is not a stable or unchanging marker of identity and a rejection of binary notions of gender. Related terms include transgender, genderfluid, and pangender.

Intersectionality—The term intersectionality was introduced in the late 1980s to describe a method of analysis that considers how discrimination can vary depending on "multiple dimensions" (such as race, sex, and class) (Crenshaw, 1991, p. 1244). Intersectional theory was meant to counter the tendency to treat race, sex, class and other categories as "mutually exclusive" (Crenshaw, 1989, p. 39). It is useful to recognize that discrimination varies depending on several factors: (1) the unique combination of characteristics of the person or group being discriminated against (their race, sex, class, sexual orientation, etc.); (2) the unique combination of characteristics of the person or group doing the discriminating (their race, sex, class, sexual orientation, etc.); and (3) the context in which the discrimination occurs. Although intersectionality begins with "the infinite combinations and implications of overlapping identities," the more recent work of intersectional theorists moves beyond identity categories and is primarily concerned with processes that advantage some while disadvantaging others (Cho et al., 2013, p. 797). Thus intersectionality is concerned with "racialization more than races, economic exploitation rather than classes, gendering and gender performance rather than genders" (Choo & Ferree, p. 134). (See also Chapter 3, "Gender and In/Equality," and Chapter 12, "Feminisms.")

Intersex—Having sex characteristics that make one different from predominant notions of biological femaleness and maleness. (See also Chapter 4.)

Masculine—A descriptor of gender; traditionally those assigned the male sex at birth are expected or "supposed" to be masculine. Characteristics associated with Western notions of traditional masculinity include active, independent, and unemotional. Traditionally thought of in binary (consisting of two parts) opposition with feminine.

Sex—The more physiological characteristics used to classify a person as female, male, intersex, third sex, or other related category. Since human choice is always involved, sex classification always involves more than biological characteristics and is always to some degree socially constructed. In recognition of this fact, many have abandoned the term "biological sex" in favor of "assigned sex."

Sex identity—What people understand their sex to be.

Sex reassignment process—Surgery and/or hormone treatment to bring a person's body more into biological alignment with their sex identity. Surgery can include a range of procedures, including "top surgery" (breast augmentation or removal) and "bottom surgery" (altering genitals). Also called gender reassignment and gender-affirming or gender-confirming surgery. In the past, also called sex change surgery, but this term is now considered derogatory by many.

Sexual orientation—An "elusive concept" (Galupo et al., 2014, p. 404). Most simplistically, involves the sexual and/or romantic attraction one has to others based on one's sex and/or gender in relation to another's sex and/or gender. (See also Chapter 4.)

Social construct/socially constructed—"A concept or perception of something based on the collective views developed and maintained within a society or social group . . . as opposed to existing inherently or naturally" (OED).

Third sex/third gender—An umbrella term used to identify people across various cultures who go outside usual (normative) Western sex and gender boundaries. Sometimes also covered under the term transgender. (See also transgender, Chapter 5, "Contructions of Homosexualities"—"India's *Hijras*.")

Transgender—Currah (2006) defined "transgender" (citing Susan Stryker) as an umbrella term that includes people of one sex who choose to have sex reassignment surgery or hormonal treatment to bring their bodies more into alignment with another sex (specifically referred to as transsexuals, although this is an older term that has fallen out of favor). It can also include people of one sex who choose to take on the gender that society generally considers appropriate for another sex. Among other practices, it can include heterosexual cross-dressing and gay drag. It covers identities including butch lesbianism and third sex people, among others. (See Chapter 1, "Sex, Gender, and Social Construction," for a discussion of third sex people.) Because it may not be readily apparent what pronoun trans people prefer, when referring to them, it is sometimes acceptable to ask what their preferred gender pronoun is. Both trans and transgender are adjectives, so they are used in phrases such as trans people or transgender rights, but neither trans nor transgender is used as a stand-alone noun; so one would not say "Transgenders are a diverse group of people" or "Sasha is a transgender" but instead, "Transgender people are very diverse" or "Sasha is a transgender person." (GLAAD, 2015) (Note: these are our examples based on GLAAD's model). (See also Chapter 4 and Appendix B, Names for People and Places.)

Transsexual—GLAAD (2015) noted that "transsexual" is "an older term that originated in the medical and psychological communities" and is "still preferred by some people who have permanently changed—or seek to change—their bodies through medical interventions" such as hormones and/or surgeries. Unlike "transgender," transsexual is "not an umbrella term. Many transgender people do not identify as transsexual" (even if they have had medical interventions) (GLAAD). GLAAD advised that "it is best to ask which term an individual prefers." (We use transsexual when a specific person self-identifies as "transsexual" or when we need to refer in general terms to people who have undergone the sex reassignment process. "Transsexual," like "transgender," is used as an adjective, for example, transsexual woman.) (See also Chapter 4.)

Names for People and Places

NAMING GROUPS

Because meanings reside in people, not words, any individual person's preference for what to be called can vary (see Chapter 2, "Language and Communication"). However, some good rules of thumb on using names are as follows: first, use the names that people say they prefer to refer to themselves; and second, be conservative—be careful about using derogatory names that have been appropriated as badges of pride.

We should be careful about punishing or stigmatizing people for using disfavored names. Wherever possible, we should be generous in assuming the innocent intent of a speaker or writer until there is evidence to the contrary. If our goal is to honestly explore difficult issues such as race, gender, sexual orientation, and/or dis/ability, we must create an atmosphere where people from stigmatized groups feel respected and an environment where well-meaning people from dominant groups feel free to express themselves and learn without fearing they may be violating some unknown rule.

It is important to note that analysis of the appropriateness of names often comes from academics and expert advocates for these groups. Unsurprisingly, textbooks tend to privilege explanations by academics and well-placed advocates over the preferences of the wider public. However, more informal, commonly spoken, and less academic speech, called vernacular speech, should not be dismissed out of hand. Vernacular speech can be more vibrant and may more accurately reflect the priorities of its speakers than language developed by so-called experts. With that caveat, here is a brief guide to preferred American English names for many groups discussed in this text.

African Americans—This term generally refers to Black people in the United States who are the descendants of Africans and who consider

ON THE
web
Read about the **merits of labeling groups** on the Student Website: www.oup.com/us/gillis-jacobs

themselves culturally American—that is, part of U.S. culture ("African American/Afro-American," 2005). Black people who live in the United States but have emigrated from other countries may not consider themselves African American (see, for example, Okpalaoka & Dillard, 2012). For example, Black people from Haiti may refer to themselves as Haitian American rather than African American (NABJ Style Guide A, n.d.). Some scholars use terms such as Black immigrants (which would include Blacks from a number of regions such as the Caribbean and Africa) or African immigrants to distinguish voluntary migrants of African descent from African Americans (those born in the United States or who identify with U.S. culture) (see for example, Greer, 2013; Waters et al., 2014). Afro-American is a dated term and should be avoided ("African American/Afro-American").

Africans—This is a widely accepted umbrella term (an overarching term that includes other terms within it) for people from Africa. Where possible, it is preferable to refer to people's nations of origin (such as Ethiopia, Sierra Leone, or Congo) or their tribal affiliation (such as the Amhara, Igbo, or Luba).

Asians—This is an umbrella term for people from Asia. Although countries in the Middle East have sometimes been included as part of Asia, the word Asian is more likely to refer to people who range from as far west as Afghanistan to as far east as Indonesia ("Asian," 2015). Because of the diversity in Asia, several regional terms are used, including South Asian (for people from places such as India, Pakistan, and Bangladesh), South East Asian (for people from Brunei, Myanmar, Indonesia, Cambodia, Laos, Malaysia, Singapore, the Philippines, Thailand, and Vietnam), and East Asian (for people from countries including China, North and South Korea, and Japan) ("South Asian," OED; "South-East Asia," 2013; Stafford, 2009). As with other groups, it is generally better to refer to people by their nation of origin or ethnic group or another regional umbrella term where possible, rather than as Asian. The term Oriental is no longer an accepted term for Asians (Asian).

Blacks, Black people—These are often used as umbrella terms for people of color who are African or descended from Africans who live in other parts of the world. Often Black and white are used as parallel terms. Some usage guides suggest using a lower case b and w when writing these terms—as one would do with any color as opposed to a proper name (Cohen, 2012b). In this text, Black is always capitalized because Black people frequently think of the term as denoting a racial, ethnic, or cultural group, as well as the closest term to representing a country or tribe of origin—which would be capitalized (Tharps, 2014). White is always lowercase in this text (unless it appears at the beginning of a sentence) because it is generally not conceived as a cultural group by whites themselves (whites usually conceive themselves to be culturally Italian, Hungarian, etc.) and whites often refer to their nationalities of origin in uppercase letters.

First World/Third World—During the Cold War, the term First World was used to refer to the United States and liberal democratic countries in Europe, such as England, France, and West Germany. By contrast, the term Second World referred to the Soviet Union and Communist Eastern European countries ("Third World," 1993). Even before the collapse of the Soviet Union, however, the term Second World fell out of use. The term Third World referred to countries that were not aligned with either the First or the Second World. Although these three terms were initially political designations, the terms First and Third World quickly became economic designations, with First World referring to "industrialized" or "developed" countries and Third World referring to "developing," "less developed," or "underdeveloped" countries (although this classification system does not work well for many countries, for example, China) ("Third World"). Many are critical of First/Third World terminology not only because of the many exceptions to and imprecision of the category system but also because it inappropriately implies economics should be the primary way to classify a country and that all countries should strive for the same industrial economic system. It also "others" Third World countries and people, suggesting they are deviating from the norm or ideal. Nonetheless, these terms remain popular and are even sometimes used by those who find them problematic. The most popular alternative terms are Global North and Global South. Another alternative is One Third/Two Thirds Worlds. (See for example, C. Mohanty, 2003 for a discussion of all three sets of terms.)

Gay people—This is probably the most popular umbrella term for lesbians and gay men, although it is sometimes used to refer only to gay males ("Gay," 2005). Because of this, both the terms lesbian and gay are often used when the intent is to refer to both gay females and males ("Gay"). The word homosexual is often avoided because it was the preferred term during a time when it was popularly associated with mental illness and perversion (Peters, 2014). An umbrella term that includes lesbians and gay men is LGBT (lesbian, gay, bisexual, and transgender). A still more inclusive alphabetic string is LGBTQQIA (lesbian, gay, bisexual, transgender, queer, questioning, intersex, and asexual). Still another term for LGBTQQIA people is gender and sexual minorities—although we avoid it because concentrating on the minority status seems an odd focus (Suresha, 2013).

Global North/Global South—These terms (and also North/South) are generally used to distinguish "high income/high consumption areas of the globe from those characterized as low income/low consumption" (Mann, 2012, p. 356). These terms are an alternative to the terms First World/Third World. The Global North generally corresponds to countries north of the Equator (including the First World or Western countries of Europe and North America, as well as Japan). The Global South generally corresponds to countries south of the Global North (most of Africa, Central and South America, and parts of Asia). However, there are clear exceptions, such as Australia and Hong Kong, which are part of the Global North and many countries that do not fit neatly into the model, such as Brazil, China, India, and South Africa. Arif Dirlik (1994) suggested the terms be used not to refer to specific geographical areas but to people who inhabit and benefit from the industrialized world economy (Global North) and those "marginalized in the new world economy" (Global South), regardless of geographical location (p. 350). So for example, regardless of whether a person lived in New York City, the United States, or Mumbai, India, an investment banker or high-tech worker would be part of the Global North and a person who earns a living by picking recyclables out of the trash would be part of the Global South. We will generally use Global North/Global South in this second sense, although we also use First World/Third World in some contexts. (See also One-Third/Two-Thirds World.)

Latinas/Latinos—These terms refer to females (Latinas) and males (Latinos) residing in the United States who have Latin American ancestry (Central, South, and North America) and who have a history of speaking Spanish (although sometimes Portuguese speakers are also included) ("Latino," OED; Lozada, 2013; Moya, 2001). As with many plural nouns, the masculine plural, Latinos, is used collectively to include Latinas and Latinos. We will often combine the two names as Latinas/os to avoid subsuming females in the masculine term Latino. The term Hispanic is also an umbrella term for "a Spanish-speaking person, esp. one of Latin-American descent, living in the U.S." (OED). This definition excludes people of Latin American descent who are, for example, Brazilian speakers of Portuguese. Both Hispanic and Latina/o are frequently used by Latinas/os—and different terms are preferred in different regions of the United States (Alcoff, 2005). Alcoff argued that "while both the terms 'Latino' and 'Hispanic' have been chosen by various Latin American communities, the term 'Hispanic' has been imposed on us all" (p. 403) by the U.S. federal government, which adopted the term at the suggestion of the king of Spain in 1978.

When possible, it is preferable to refer to people's nationality (such as Dominican, Mexican, Nicaraguan, or Peruvian) since it is more precise. Some people who have lived in the United States for two or more generations may identify as "American" (meaning from the United States) and when descent is relevant, it is preferable to refer to them as Americans (or Californians or Coloradoans, etc.) of Latin American descent (P. B. Corbett, 2009). Latinas/os sometimes distinguish themselves from Anglos—whites of European ancestry other than Spain. Anglos in the United States should be aware that Latin Americans consider themselves American (because they are from the Americas) and many take offense at Anglos from the United States using American as if it referred only to being from the United States (Martinez-Carter, 2013).

Native Americans—This is an accepted umbrella term for indigenous people in North America and is sometimes used for native people throughout the Americas ("Native American," 2005). The terms "indigenous people," "aboriginal people," and "native people" are terms used for any group that is native to a particular area (such as in Australia or Africa). The term First Nations is sometimes used to refer to native people across the globe, but it is also used to refer to indigenous peoples recognized by Canada (Faubion, 2006). In the Canadian context, when Inuit and Métis people are included, the term is First Peoples ("Native American"). The name American Indians or Indians has fallen out of favor in some circles but is still used today by many Native Americans and nonnative people alike ("Native American"). The term Indian is sometimes not used simply to avoid confusion with people from India. In this text we use the terms Native American, Indian people, and indigenous people as umbrella terms. We avoid the term Indians simply to avoid confusion with Asian Indians.

There are hundreds of Native American tribes in the United States, including 566 federally recognized "American Indian and Alaska Native tribal entities" (Toensing, 2014). When possible, it is always preferable to refer to the specific tribal or national affiliation (such as the Karuk Tribe, or Onondaga Nation, or Kaw Nation) rather than to Native Americans more generally (Schaeffer, 2011).

One-Third/Two-Thirds World—These terms are an attempt to move away from First World/Third World terminology (see First World/Third World in this appendix). Esteva and Prakash (1998) used the term One-Third World to refer to the affluent "social minorities" throughout the world who have a high standard of living in the new world economy—those who have high-income jobs and engage in high rates of consumption (p. 16). They used the term Two-Thirds World to describe the "social majorities" throughout the world who do not enjoy the average standard of living that those in industrialized countries enjoy—those who have low incomes and engage in low rates of consumption. The One-Third World includes both people of average income and above in so-called First World or Western countries and high-income people in so-called Third World countries. The Two-Thirds World includes people in both the so-called First World and the so-called Third World who do not enjoy the average industrialized standard of living. One advantage of One-Third/Two-Thirds World over the terms First World/Third World or Global North/Global South (also described in this appendix) is that it highlights that the Two-Thirds World constitutes the majority of the world's population.

Some use the terms One-Third/Two-Thirds World primarily to describe the gap between the global rich and the global poor (see, for example, Mann), but others use the terms in an attempt to highlight the value of traditional societies that are low-income/low-consumption societies. Esteva and Prakash, for example, have described these social majorities as having not a deficient lifestyle, but rather a worthy one. Their conception of the good life is shaped by "local traditions" rather than being based on the model of consumption from the One-Third World. Esteva and Prakash's definition of Two-Thirds World would not include all of the global poor, but only those in traditional societies that reject "the forces [of the One-Third World] encroaching upon their lives and destroying their traditions" (p. 17). Examples of the Two-Thirds World for Esteva and Prakash would presumably include Native people living traditional lifestyles in the Americas, Chinese peasant farmers, and nomadic people in Africa.

> **People of Color**—This is an umbrella term for all people except whites ("Person of Color," 2015). It is preferred over the term nonwhite, because nonwhite implies that white people are the norm and that what distinguishes people of color is their lack of whiteness. This can have the effect of "othering" people of color. (See Chapter 6, "Beyond the Mythical Norm," for a discussion of othering.) The term colored people in the U.S. context has negative connotations because of its use during the period of racial segregation and has fallen out of use ("Person of Color").

> **People with dis/abilities**—Traditionally, "disability" has been defined as "the state of being physically and/or mentally different from some assumed 'norm' of human corporeal and/or psychological functioning" ("Disability," 2009, para. 1). "Disability" has often been framed negatively as a deficit, "loss" or "lack," with little attention paid "to the experiences and aspirations of the people affected" ("Disability," para. 1). For example, Deaf (with a capital D) people do not consider themselves "disabled" (whereas those who do not capitalize the d in deaf do) (Solomon, 1994). American Sign Language and other sign languages are recognized by scholars as linguistically complete languages (Solomon). Not being able to hear may have drawbacks, but it also comes with advantages, such as being able to communicate easily in a noisy room via sign language. Deaf people who are fluent in one sign language can learn basic communication in other sign languages in a few days, which is usually impossible in spoken languages (Solomon). Given these advantages, hearing people can be said to be "handicapped" by their reliance on oral communication.

Theorists in the field of disability studies often argue that rather than conceiving of people as inherently disabled, it is more useful to think of "social and environmental barriers" that disable people. For example, if we construct a house with steps leading up to the entrance, we enable people who can walk to enter the house. Absent the steps, the house may be inaccessible to many, regardless of whether one can or cannot walk. If we construct a ramp instead of steps, we enable people who can use wheelchairs as well as those who can walk to enter the house. Another example: audible doorbells enable hearing people to be alerted to the presence of visitors; "doorbells" that flash a light enable Deaf people to be alerted to the presence of visitors. In these examples, so-called able-bodied people are enabled by technologies (steps, ramps, audible doorbells) and so-called disabled people are enabled by technologies (ramps and visual doorbells). So-called able-bodied people are often blind to how assistive technologies enable them and view assistive technologies for so-called disabled people as special. Once we understand that much of our built environment disables some and enables others, we can understand how dis/ability is a product of our design and other human choices. It is the result of a "mismatch" between the characteristics of a person with dis/abilities and "the physical and social environment" (Wasserman et al., 2013, para. 12). Put another way, dis/ability is socially constructed (Annamma et al., 2013). From this perspective we can see that "disability is a universal human condition . . . that all human beings have physical or mental variations that can become a source of vulnerability or disadvantage in some settings" (Wasserman et al., para. 12).

Like Annamma and colleagues, we use "dis/ability" (with a slash) to draw attention to the ways in which the term disability (with no slash)

> overwhelmingly signals a specific inability to perform culturally-defined expected tasks (such as learning or walking) that come to define the individual as primarily and generally "unable" to navigate society. We believe the " / " in disability disrupts misleading understandings of disability, as it simultaneously conveys that mixture of ability and disability. (p. 24)

Annamma et al. warned that dis/ability should not be seen as creating a "universal experience" but rather one "mediated by the particular social, historical and political context" (p. 19). People's experiences of "dis/ability" and the impact of being labeled "disabled" also vary depending on many personal factors, including race, ethnicity, class, sex, age, and/or other characteristics. Thus an intersectional approach is needed when studying dis/ability (Annamma).

The term "people with dis/abilities" is preferred to simply "disabled" because it makes the person rather than the disability the central characteristic. The American Psychological Association (2011) called this phrase or locution "people-first language" (sec. 3.15).

Transgender people—Currah (2006) defined "transgender" (citing Susan Stryker) as an umbrella term that includes people of one sex who choose to have sex reassignment surgery or hormonal treatment to bring their bodies more into alignment with another sex (specifically referred to as transsexuals, although this is an older term that has fallen out of favor). It can also include people of one sex who choose to take on the gender that society generally considers appropriate for another sex. Among other practices, it can include heterosexual cross-dressing and gay drag. It covers identities including butch lesbianism and third sex people, among others. (See Chapter 1, "Sex, Gender, and Social Construction," for a discussion of third sex people. See Chapter 4, "LGBTQQIAA Identities and Challenges," for a more complete discussion of the word transgender.) Sometimes transgender people are referred to as trans people. Another term often used interchangeably with transgender is gender variant. Because it may not be readily apparent what pronoun trans people prefer, when referring to them, it is sometimes acceptable to ask what their preferred gender pronoun is. Some trans people do not want to be referred to by gendered pronouns and prefer gender-neutral terms such as ze/zir instead. So one might say, "Ze is transgender" or "That's zirs backpack." Both trans and transgender are adjectives, so they are used in phrases such as trans people or transgender rights, but neither trans nor transgender is used as a stand-alone noun; so one would not say "Transgenders are a diverse group of people" or "Sasha is a transgender" but instead, "Transgender people are very diverse" or "Sasha is a transgender person." (GLAAD, 2015) (Note: these are our examples based on GLAAD's model).

Western/Non-Western—The West is typically defined as Europe and North America (OED). By extension, Western is "of or relating to the Western part of the world" (OED). Non-Western is generally used to mean of or relating to the rest of the world. Because the terms Western/non-Western make the West central and "other" the rest of the world, many are critical of these terms. (See Chapter 6, "Beyond the Mythical Norm," for a discussion of othering.) However, even some critics such as Chandra Talpade Mohanty (2003) say it has "political and explanatory value" (p. 505) and still use the term. C. Mohanty probably means that since the West has such enormous power politically, economically, and socially, it is useful to use the term Western in many contexts (although she uses Third World rather than non-Western as the opposite term). We will use the term Western when it seems descriptively most apt (often when referring to Western culture) but we agree that its use can be problematic. The most popular alternative terms are Global North (and its opposite, Global South). Another alternative is One-Third World (and its opposite, Two-Thirds World). (See for example, C. Mohanty, 2003, for a discussion of all three sets of terms.) However, these alternatives suggest a broader geographical scope than Western and sometimes are not good substitutes. (See also Global North/Global South in this appendix.)

Feminisms in Brief

This appendix offers a brief introduction to the following forms of feminism: liberal, radical, Marxist/socialist, U.S. intersectional, transnational, and post-modern/queer theory. Please note that although this appendix shares some material in common with Chapter 12, "Feminisms," it is not a wholesale recap of that chapter.

For each form of feminism we include the following:

- "**Thumbnail Description**" and "**Sources of Inequality**" (condensed from "Feminist Theory" sections of Chapter 12)
- "**Some Problems and Solutions**" and "**Advances Toward Feminist Goals**" (these sections go beyond material in Chapter 12)

Moreover, the "History of Feminist Theory" sections from Chapter 12 are not recapped here. This appendix is designed to be used in combination with Chapter 12 or as a stand-alone resource.

Given the brevity of the appendix, we cannot address all forms of feminism or all the complications, contradictions, and permutations within each form of feminism. There is much more to know; this is just a beginning. Also keep in mind that although it may be convenient to think of feminist viewpoints as in opposition to one another, they are more often in conversation with one another and often share elements, methods, and goals, which you will see as you read this appendix. Finally, many feminists find themselves straddling multiple forms of feminism or find that elements of many different forms of feminism resonate with them, and you may do the same.

LIBERAL FEMINISM

Liberal feminism is concerned with freedom and equal rights for women—and for all people regardless of sex.

Thumbnail Description

Women—and all people regardless of sex—should be free and should have equality of rights with white, middle-class, straight men. Women (and all people) should be free—in particular, not limited by political, economic, and social conditions, especially related to sex, gender, gender roles, and sexual orientation. Some would go further and say women (and all people) should be empowered to substantively exercise their liberties.

Sources of Inequality

Women are not treated as equal members of society (politically, economically, and socially) because of their sex and gender. Historically, women have faced legal discrimination, such as the denial of the right to vote, own property, and serve in the military, and today women's equality under U.S. law is still not explicitly guaranteed. Women also continue to face a great deal of unequal social treatment, which limits their success in realms such as politics and the workplace.

Some Problems and Solutions

1. **Problem**: The subtle influence of language reinforces traditional gendered thinking or results in male-only thinking. **Solution(s)**: Adopt gender-neutral language in place of male generic language (such as people or humanity for words like mankind) and other language that reduces traditional gendered assumptions about women. (See Chapter 2, "Language and Communication.")

2. **Problem**: Gender stereotypes and gender roles limit women's power. **Solution(s)**: Adopt gender-neutral child rearing and socialization of girls and boys. (See Chapter 1, "Sex, Gender, and Socialization," and Chapter 3, "Gender and In/Equality.")

3. **Problem**: Stereotypes about being female (including regarding marriage and motherhood) reduce career opportunities of women but stereotypes about being male (including regarding marriage and fatherhood) generally do not. **Solution(s)**: Eliminate obstacles that keep women from achieving workplace goals, such as negative perceptions of women in leadership roles, disproportionate responsibility on women for child care, and the presumption by employers that child-care responsibilities will fall on their women employees. Policy answers include affirmative action and other workplace measures such as parental leave policies and workplace child care. (See Chapter 8, "Work, Inequality, and Neoliberalism.")

4. **Problem**: Inequality for LGBTQQIA people including lack of same-sex marriage and/or ability to choose a sex designation beyond female or male.

Solution(s): Support rights for LGBTQQIA people such as same-sex marriage or the right to choose a sex designation other than female or male on birth certificates and other government documents. (See Chapter 1, Chapter 4, "LGBTQQIAA Identities and Challenges," and Chapter 5, "Constructions of Homosexualities.")

5. **Problem**: Little or no recognition of reproductive freedom (including contraception, freedom from nonconsensual sterilization, and abortion access). **Solution(s)**: Adopt laws that guarantee reproductive freedom. (See Chapter 11, "History of Women's Activism in the United States.")

6. **Problem**: Gender-based violence—especially against women and gender nonconforming people. **Solution(s)**: Create women's shelters, anti-rape campaigns, and reform of laws regarding sexual violence (including rape and hate crime laws to include LGBTQQIA people). (See Chapter 9, "Gender-Based Violence.")

Advances Toward Liberal Feminist Goals

1. Woman suffrage (the right to vote) and an end to laws related to coverture, including women's right to own property, sign contracts, expansion of divorce, and recognition of marital rape. (See Chapters 3, 9, and 11.)

2. Major publication guidelines in academia (such as the American Psychological Association and Modern Language Association) and in journalism require gender-neutral language and make attempts to eliminate stereotypical language. (See Chapter 2.)

3. Affirmative action, which has increased the hiring of women and people of color and reduced unequal pay.

4. Title IX legislation protecting equal access to education regardless of sex has been particularly beneficial to women's sports programs and is now part of a campaign to eliminate sexual violence on campuses. (See Chapter 9.)

5. Birth control, comprehensive sex education, and abortion rights have reduced unwanted pregnancy and allowed women to plan pregnancy and space births in a way that enables them to attain higher levels of education and have more power over their lives and careers.

6. Record number of women elected to the U.S. Congress in 2014. (See Chapter 3.)

RADICAL FEMINISM

Radical feminism is concerned with uprooting patriarchy to end the subordination of women as women.

Thumbnail Description

The oppression of women is primary: it is the first form of oppression in history and some say it is central to all other forms of oppression. Until the relationship between women and men fundamentally changes, not only will women not be free but also some say the male pattern of domination will continue to form the basis of the domination of other groups such as LGBTQQIA people and people of color.

Sources of Inequality

Patriarchy is the problem. Radical feminists vary in their understanding of the origins of patriarchy but agree that the deeply embedded culture of patriarchy must be uprooted in people of all sexes. To achieve this, radical feminists argue that one or more of the following must change: (1) women's relationship to sexual reproduction; (2) social relationships between women and men; (3) patriarchal thinking; and (4) the economic system, which limits and devalues women's labor.

Some Problems and Solutions

1. **Problem**: Women's reproduction and sexuality is controlled by men. **Solution(s)**: Destroy sex difference in a radical way (perhaps including the option of artificial reproduction or forms of child care that free women from traditional sex roles). (See Chapter 12.)

2. **Problem**: Patriarchal thinking and behavior are to blame for women's oppression, which is the primary form of oppression. **Solution(s)**: Focus on women's oppression first and foremost and oppose patriarchy, including patriarchal language, thinking, and behavior. Some advocate the abandonment of heterosexuality (lesbian separatism). (See Chapters 2, 3, 4, and 12.)

3. **Problem**: Society does not value women's sexualities and sexual orientations. **Solution(s)**: Advocate for LGBTQQIA rights. (See Chapter 4.)

4. **Problem**: Women's bodies are not valued. **Solution(s)**: Value women's bodies regardless of dis/ability or size and free women from harmful beauty standards. Oppose harmful imagery in the media (advertising, movies, etc.). (See Chapter 7, "Embodiment, Beauty, and the Viewer.")

5. **Problem**: Gender-based violence—especially against women and gender nonconforming people. **Solution(s)**: Create women's shelters, anti-rape campaigns, and reform of laws regarding sexual violence (including rape and hate crime laws to include LGBTQQIA people). (See Chapter 9.)

6. **Problem**: The capitalist economic system creates a sexual division of labor that exploits women. **Solution(s)**: Develop a socialist system that allows women more freedom to do waged work. (See Chapter 12.)

7. **Problem**: Patriarchy fosters militarism. War is a threat to human well-being and to women in particular. **Solution(s)**: Participate in the peace movement.

8. **Problem**: Patriarchy fosters environmental destruction. **Solution(s)**: Participate in the ecofeminist (feminist environmental) movement and support policies such as those to stop climate change, species destruction, reduce consumption, and promote recycling.

Advances Toward Radical Feminist Goals

1. Anti-rape and anti–domestic violence movements have raised awareness, founded rape hotlines and battered women's shelters, and led to reform of rape and domestic violence legislation. (See Chapter 9.)

2. The LGBTQ movement has promoted lesbian acceptance and the critique of heterocentrism. (See Chapters 4, 5, and 11.)

3. Substantial body of work critiques misogynist imagery, including pornography (although some radical feminists support sexually explicit imagery). (See Chapters 7 and 11.)

4. Legal recognition of abortion rights. (See Chapter 11.)

5. Less rigid definitions of masculinity and femininity in U.S. society today.

6. The sexual division of housework has been eroded. In the United States, men today are more likely to share household chores, including child care (although women still do more care and housework than men). (See Chapter 8.)

7. Various movements, including fat acceptance movement, have raised awareness of the harmful effects of Western beauty standards and fat shaming. (See Chapter 7.)

8. Growth of the environmental movement, which has been informed by ecofeminist criticisms of patriarchy and capitalism. (See Chapter 12.)

MARXIST/SOCIALIST FEMINISM

Marxist/socialist feminism is concerned with ending the exploitation of women workers (and all workers) under capitalism.

Thumbnail Description

The subordination of women is caused at least in part by the economic order of society (today that order is capitalism). Women will not be free and equal to men until an egalitarian economic system is put into place. Many Marxist/socialist feminists say women's emancipation will take more than a change to the economic order; it requires an intersectional approach focusing on issues such as race, gender, and class.

Sources of Inequality

Workers are exploited under capitalism, which requires an unequal division of labor. Therefore, as long as capitalism exists, someone will be unequal. Why? Because under capitalism, the worker class produces goods but does not receive or control the distribution of profits from those goods (called surplus value). Instead, workers receive wages, which may be enough to live on but little else. The capitalist class, by contrast, accumulates wealth by collecting or controlling profits from the goods produced by workers. Under a Marxist or socialist system, workers would own the means of production (such as a factory) and collect or control profits themselves. Women are not only exploited like male workers, but also generally have lower status than men in waged labor. Women are further exploited because they bear primary responsibility for unwaged domestic work and reproduction (bearing and caring for children). Some Marxist/socialist feminists go further and say the sources of inequality go beyond the economic order and include many other independent factors such as racism, sexism, and homophobia.

Some Problems and Solutions

1. **Problem**: There is an unequal division of labor resulting in the exploitation of all workers, including women. **Solution(s)**: Eliminating or significantly curtailing capitalism and instituting an egalitarian economic order are essential. (See Chapter 12.)

2. **Problem**: Women's domestic labor is not valued and reduces their power in society. **Solution(s)**: Reduce the unpaid private service work of women through government-sponsored child care, legal rights to maternity and paternity leave, and changes to Social Security so unpaid domestic labor counts toward retirement benefits. (See Chapter 8.)

3. **Problem**: Women's waged labor globally is devalued. **Solution(s)**: Raise the minimum wage, support unionization, and fight the world economic order that reduces wage, health, safety, and environmental protections for women and other vulnerable workers. (See Chapter 8, Chapter 10, "Human Rights and Global Activism," and Chapter 11.)

4. **Problem**: Capitalism perpetuates patriarchal thinking and economic policies that lead to the oppression of women, environmental destruction, and war. **Solution(s)**: Be critical of language that can reinforce patriarchal thinking, oppose neoliberal economic policies that foster environmental destruction and harm the welfare of women, and participate in the peace movement. (See Chapters 2, 8, 10, 11, and 12.)

5. **Problem**: Capitalism harms the welfare of women and other vulnerable groups (such as people of color). **Solution(s)**: Support social welfare programs that protect the welfare of women and other vulnerable groups such as government-supported universal health care and free universal education and oppose the privatization of public utilities such as water and electricity. (See Chapters 10 and 11.)

6. **Problem**: Capitalism causes or perpetuates racism, homophobia, and discrimination against people who are regarded as other in society. **Solution(s)**: Oppose transnational capitalism, which has resulted in growing inequality among people (including free trade zones and agreements that lack adequate protections for workers and the environment), oppose the prison–industrial complex, which disproportionately incarcerates people of color in the United States, oppose transnational corporate attempts to enforce hegemonic white beauty standards, and support indigenous conceptions of sex/gender and homosexualities. (See Chapters 1, 5, 7, 8, and 10.)

(See also Some Problems and Solutions in Transnational Feminism.)

Advances Toward Marxist/Socialist Feminist Goals

1. Legislation for a 40-hour work week, child labor laws, minimum wage laws, the creation of Medicare, Medicaid, and Social Security, and the formation of unions (including among female workers and people of color) in the early 20th century. (See Chapter 8.)

2. Advocacy by the reproductive rights movement for birth control and sex education. (See Chapter 11.)

3. Passage of the U.S. Affordable Care Act (known as Obamacare).

4. Local living wage laws that require pay above minimum wage. (See Chapter 8.)

5. Fair trade and "no-sweat" goods created by workers who earn higher wages under safer work conditions.

6. Awareness of exploitative work conditions in free trade zones and pressure on transnational corporations to end exploitative labor practices. (See Chapters 8 and 10.)

U.S. INTERSECTIONAL FEMINISM

U.S. intersectional feminism is concerned with processes that advantage or disadvantage groups based on factors such as sex, gender, race, class, sexual orientation, ethnicity, religion, age, language, immigration status, etc.

Thumbnail Description

Discrimination is based on (1) the unique combination of characteristics of the person or group being discriminated against (their race, sex, class, sexual orientation, nationality, ethnicity, age, etc.); (2) the unique characteristics of the person or group doing the discriminating; and (3) the context in which the discrimination occurs. Intersectional analysis focuses on the processes that advantage or disadvantage groups, such as racialization or economic exploitation, and systems or matrices of domination. It is not so much a distinct form of feminism as a mode of analysis for understanding and resisting oppression. It may combine with other feminist approaches.

Sources of Inequality

The sources of women's inequality are varied and multiple. For example, a middle-class Asian American female may face discrimination at home from her husband because he wants her to conform to traditional conceptions of femininity and female gender roles and also face sexual harassment from her white boss, who stereotypes Asian American women as sexually exotic. At the same time, this woman might discriminate against lesbians and gay men in her own hiring decisions. In combination with discrimination at the individual level, institutions and processes (legal, social, economic, political) advantage some groups (often men, white people, able-bodied people, the young, and/or financially secure people, etc.) and disadvantage others (often women, people of color, LGBTQQIA people, poor people, people with dis/abilities, and/or older people, etc.) For example, the Asian American woman may face systematic institutional bias in the context of promotion or may be sexually objectified in part through the process of racialization as an Asian American woman.

Some Problems and Solutions

1. **Problem**: Groups are treated as monolithic, possessing a single set of characteristics. **Solution(s)**: Recognize how intersectionality operates and be attentive to how various characteristics can advantage or disadvantage people in different circumstances. (See Chapter 3.)
2. **Problem**: The dominant system advantages particular people—white, male, financially secure, heterosexual, and/or abled, etc. **Solution(s)**: Empower people by providing substantive access to high-quality education, jobs that provide a living wage, and the political process. (See Chapter 11.)
3. **Problem**: The standpoints of many kinds of people are not represented or misrepresented in the dominant culture. **Solution(s)**: Recognize, value, and include the voices of traditionally underrepresented perspectives such

as through courses and scholarship that represent marginalized stand-points (for example, Latino/a studies, dis/ability studies, women's studies, and classes in history, literature, social sciences, etc.), include the work of marginalized groups in museums, discourage stereotyping and promote inclusion of diverse viewpoints in the media and popular culture, and advocate for political inclusion. (See Chapters 4–11.)

4. **Problem**: Theory and activism often exclude marginalized groups (even groups that such theory and activism act "on behalf of"). **Solution(s)**: Write theory in an accessible way and/or translate theory into language that is accessible to broader groups of people and build inclusive activist movements initiated and guided by marginalized people; welcome forms of communication that come from marginalized cultures and subcultures. (Chapter 12.)

5. **Problem**: The justice system discriminates against people of color, including through racial profiling and higher rates of arrest, conviction, and incarceration. **Solution(s)**: Reform the justice system by raising awareness of bias, reform the training of police, prosecutors, and judges, and overhaul the penal code and prison system to reduce rates of incarceration and focus more on rehabilitation. (See Chapter 6, "Beyond the Mythical Norm.")

6. **Problem**: Systems of domination exist, including racial systems, economic systems, and gender systems. **Solution(s)**: Oppose systems of racialization, economic exploitation, and gender exploitation. (Chapters 4–11.)

(See also: Some Problems and Solutions in Transnational Feminism.)

Advances Toward Intersectional Feminist Goals

1. Advances in legal equality throughout the 20th century to address discrimination against people of color, women, LGBTQQI people, people with dis/abilities, older people and/or others, including suffrage, civil and voting rights, workplace rights (affirmative action), hate crimes legislation, legal steps to end discrimination in education, housing, employment, marriage, etc. (See Chapter 11.)

2. Increased understanding of and attention to intersectional issues, including in academia and social justice movements. (See Chapters 3 and 12.)

3. Growth of activism based on identity, such as Black activism, Latina/o activism, American Indian activism, dis/ability rights activism, women's activism, etc. (See Chapters 11 and 12.)

4. Growth of the movement to address immigrant rights. (See Chapter 6.)

5. Growth of the living wage movement and efforts to address wealth and income inequality. (See Chapters 6 and 8.)

TRANSNATIONAL FEMINISM

Transnational feminism is concerned with global forces that disadvantage people of the Global South and advantage people of the Global North.

Thumbnail Description

Transnational feminism rejects the idea that there is a universal form of feminism. Instead, transnational feminists argue that feminisms must be the outgrowth of the standpoints of women and others across the world. They are critical of Western hegemonic feminism—a form of feminism that has historically been formulated by Western feminists that reflects their experiences and interests while marginalizing global feminist viewpoints. Transnational feminism pays attention to global forces (historical and current) such as colonialism, globalization, and neoliberalism that systematically disadvantage people of the Global South and advantage people of the Global North. Another important force is discourse—the use of language that generates a way of thinking. Transnational feminism critiques hegemonic feminist discourse in an attempt to decenter Western feminist thought. Both forces of domination and forces resisting domination (such as transnational feminist networks and counterhegemonic discourse) do not simply operate at the level of nation-states (*inter*nationally) but through, over, and beyond nation states (*trans*nationally). Like U.S. intersectional feminisms, they may combine with other feminist approaches. (We use Global South and Global North not in the strictly geographic sense. See Appendix B, Names for People and Places, for a more complete discussion.)

Sources of Inequality

Women and other people of color in the Global South and the environment have been exploited by those in the Global North through colonialism, neocolonialism, neoliberalism, and discourse practices. These practices perpetuate racism, classism, homophobia, and other supremacist ideologies in myriad ways across the globe.

Some Problems and Solutions

1. **Problem**: Exploitation of the people and resources of the Global South historically through colonialism. **Solution(s)**: Oppose the legacies of colonialism, including neocolonial practices. (See Chapters 8 and 12.)
2. **Problem**: Exploitation of the people and resources of the Global South through neoliberal practices, including free trade zones and agreements.

Solution(s): Oppose free trade zones and agreements and/or demand inclusion of protective measures for workers, the environment, etc. Demand a focus on human development and locally sustainable industries. (See Chapters 8, 10, and 12.)

3. **Problem**: "Development" loans and structural adjustment programs imposed on the Global South have resulted in growing inequality globally. **Solution(s)**: Oppose "development" loans and structural adjustment programs and support human development. (See Chapters 8, 10, and 12.)

4. **Problem**: The demand for cheap consumer goods in the Global North and the drive for higher profits on the part of transnational corporations have fueled the growing problem of trafficking of persons and exploitative labor practices, particularly in the Global South. **Solution(s)**: Oppose rampant consumerism, support living wages and decent work conditions, and fight slave labor. (See Chapters 8 and 10.)

5. **Problem**: Privatization of public assets in the Global South such as water, electricity, mines, and airlines has often resulted in skyrocketing prices for vulnerable people, with little or no improvement in access or service. **Solution(s)**: Oppose privatization of public assets and demand adequate funding of public services. (See Chapters 8 and 10.)

6. **Problem**: Discourse originating in the Global North about the Global South has advantaged white, Western perspectives, othered and homogenized the people of the Global South, and portrayed them as irrational, backward, and perpetually victimized. This discourse has also placed Westerners (including Western feminists) in the position of compassionate heroes set to "save" Third World women. **Solution(s)**: Oppose binary thinking (such as East/West or primitive/modern), decenter hegemonic viewpoints and practices, and demand recognition of the rationality and agency of women (in particular) in the Global South. (See Chapters 6, 10, and 12.)

7. **Problem**: Lack of engagement in activism by Global North feminists, particularly regarding economic exploitation. **Solution(s)**: Advocate for constructive engagement by feminists in the Global North in partnership with feminists in the Global South. (See Chapters 10 and 12.)

Advances Toward Transnational Feminist Goals

1. Growing awareness of and movement against exploitative labor practices globally, including trafficking and forced labor. (See Chapters 8 and 10.)
2. Local labor movements and transnational nongovernmental coalitions are demanding safer work conditions, living wages, and environmental protections in the Global South. (See Chapters 8 and 10.)

3. Significant body of scholarly work countering hegemonic discourse practices. (See Chapters 10 and 12.)
4. Growing calls for human and sustainable development practices including within the United Nations community. (See Chapter 8.)
5. Increased visibility and availability of fair trade and "no-sweat" goods created by workers who earn higher wages under safer conditions. (See Chapter 8.)
6. Growing numbers of transnational feminist networks, such as Women Living Under Muslim Laws and Development Alternatives With Women for a New Era, that empower local feminist activism.

POSTMODERN FEMINISM/QUEER THEORY

Postmodern feminism and queer theory insist that all categories are socially constructed, resist categorical thinking, and oppose essentialism.

Thumbnail Description

The belief in universal truths about social categories (such as "women," "men," and "gay people") is without philosophical foundation. Therefore, any universal statement about women, men, or gay people (or other social categories) will always be wrong, at least about some members of these so-called groups. In this sense, women as a universal group do not really exist. It follows then that the "emancipation of women" is a nonsensical solution—albeit to an actual problem. Individual women are indeed oppressed, but not necessarily in the same way, and the solution to each woman's problem may be different. The idea of emancipation is also problematic. It suggests that history can march toward a heroic conclusion (where everyone lives "happily ever after"), which is a fictional idea. Emancipation is also problematic because it assumes there is a one, true kind of freedom, but every social order imposes restraints on freedom and there is no ideal position from which to evaluate the best way to be free (so even if there was a "best way to be free" for one person, it would not necessarily be best for everyone else). Despite the *problematique* (or complex of issues) of "women's emancipation" or "gay liberation" or "racial equality," people are nonetheless treated as women and are disadvantaged as women (and/or gay, Black, Latina/o, etc.).

Sources of Inequality

Women (and others) are limited by social categories and by political, economic, and social practices. Other feminisms have identified actual sources of oppression (and there will undoubtedly be many more perspectives that identify real sources of unfreedom). In some places at some times, women (and others) face common enemies and share common interests, but these commonalities are not universal and there are often deep differences among so-called women (and others); any alliance between identity groups will require negotiating inevitable differences and dealing with inevitable conflicts.

Some Problems and Solutions

There are no solutions in the sense that no actions will result in everyone being absolutely free. However, "problems" and "solutions" might be formulated in the following way:

1. **Problem**: Many fail to recognize that there are no philosophical foundations for belief in social categories. **Solution(s)**: Oppose foundationalism (the idea that there can be a universally recognized foundation for belief). Rather than looking for foundations, understand how beliefs are justified in relationship to other beliefs (for example, we "know" what women are in relation to what men are). Oppose existing networks of meaning that produce these so-called "truths" (See Chapters, 2, 4, and 12.)

2. **Problem**: Acceptance of categories (whatever they are) limits people's freedom and gives power to those who are at the top of the category hierarchy. **Solution(s)**: Resist categorical thinking (including binary categories such as female/male, feminine/ masculine, gay/straight) and oppose essentialism, which gives rise to categories. One could refuse to identify as female, male, gay, straight, etc., or oppose the use of categories to box people (e.g., oppose bathrooms labeled by sex). Identify as queer or subvert or queer categories—for example, act in ways that do not conform to others' conceptions of your sex, gender, sexual orientation, class, etc. (See Chapters 1, 3, 4, 5, and 11.)

3. **Problem**: Unity is not possible; individuals do not share a set of interests in common. This means, for example, not all gay people will have the same interests in common, nor will different groups be able to perfectly unite around a common goal. **Solution(s)**: Make alliances with other groups but do not strive for a "unity" that papers over inevitable differences. (See Chapters 6 and 11.)

Advances Toward Postmodern Feminist/Queer Theory Goals

1. Scholarly, artistic, and pop culture understandings of sex, gender, sexual orientation, and other categories has shifted. Postmodern feminism and

queer theory have provided a rationale for seeing all three of these categories as fluid. This has helped create an environment that is supportive of intersex rights and identity, transgender rights and identity, and fluid or queer conceptions of sexual orientation. (See Chapter 4.)

2. Scholarly methods in collecting data on identity groups have shifted. Researchers now recognize they cannot presume that categories such as sex, gender, sexual orientation, race, and/or class are defined by various cultures in the same ways (or consistently within cultures). So, for example, it has influenced the study of the history of same-sex relations where researchers do not assume that modern conceptions of lesbianism or male homosexuality existed across time and cultures. Much research explicitly recognizes that identities are performative. (See Chapters 2, 5, and 6.)

3. There is heightened awareness that norms such as maleness, masculinity, heterosexuality, middle-class identity, and/or whiteness are fragile constructions created through opposition to a series of "others" such as femaleness, femininity, homosexuality, lower-class identity, and/or Blackness. (See Chapters 2, 3, 6, 7, and 12.)

The forms of feminism discussed here are all discussed in greater detail in Chapter 12, "Feminisms: Theories and Practices."

Glossary

These are key terms from the chapters or terms from the appendices. The numbers that appear after each definition indicate the chapter(s) in which the term appears. When more than one number is listed, numbers with asterisks indicate more in-depth discussions of the terms.

Accidental property—Inessential property, a property that is not necessary for an entity to be what it is. (See also essential property.) (6)

***Activo* sex role**—Term used to refer to men who play the insertive role among men who have sex with men in some Latin American cultures. (See also *pasivo* sex role.) (5)

Aesthetics—Ideas about what is beautiful or tasteful. (7)

African Americans—See Appendix B, Names for People and Places. (6)

Africans—See Appendix B, Names for People and Places.

Ally—Non-LGBTQQIA people who are supporters of LGBTQQIA rights (represented by a second "A" in the alphabetic string). (4)

Androcentric—Focused on males or men. (2)

Androgynous—The state of having female and male characteristics, interests, etc. To behave and/or appear in both traditionally feminine and masculine ways. (In biology, may mean to have biological sex characteristics of females and males at once.) (1)

Asexual—Someone who "experiences little or no sexual attraction" to other people (AVEN, 2012). (In biology, generally refers to a lack of sex-specific sex organs.) (1, 4*)

Asians—See Appendix B, Names for People and Places.

Assigned sex—Alternative to "biological sex," which recognizes that sexual categorization is not simply a matter of objective biological fact but also a matter of human decision, that is, that sex is to some degree socially constructed. (1)

***Bagburu* relationship**—A practice among the Azande people (from parts of Africa) in which a woman was given permission to enter into a formal bond of friendship with another woman, sometimes providing "respectable cover" for female same-sex sexual activity (Edward Evans-Pritchard). (5)

Bamboo ceiling—Obstacles to Asian American advancement to managerial or executive positions in the workplace. (6)

Benevolent sexism—Prejudice based on sex that may appear to be affectionate or chivalrous in nature, for example, believing women are morally superior to men or that women are deserving of men's protection; underpinned by the idea of masculine dominance. (See also hostile sexism.) (3)

Bidirectional violence (intimate partner violence)—Intimate partner violence in which both partners are violent toward one another. (9)

Birth control pill—Pill utilizing hormones as a contraceptive for women approved for sale as a contraceptive in the United States in 1960. (11)

Bisexual—Attraction or the potential to be attracted to people of one's own sex and other sexes (Ochs, 2014). Originally used to refer to people attracted to their own sex and the "opposite" sex. (4)

Blacks/Black people—See Appendix B, Names for People and Places. (6)

Bonded labor—A form of slavery that occurs when debtors promise their personal services or those of another as security for a debt but the services are undervalued and/or not actually paid or applied toward repayment of the debt. (10)

Boston marriage—A practice in late-19th-century New England in which two women lived together in a long-term relationship; it seems some were sexually intimate but others were not. (5)

Boy-wife—A practice among the Azande people (parts of Africa) in which men were allowed to pay a lower bride price for a male youth who would take on the gender role of wife; boy-wives and male husbands practiced intercrural sex and often married female wives later in life. (5)

Butch—Vernacular (informal or colloquial) term frequently used in gay and lesbian subcultures for women who are gender nonconforming (i.e., masculine) and men who are gender conforming. (1)

Caballerismo—A code of conduct (within Latino culture) for men marked by respectful manners and chivalry; derived from the Spanish word *caballero*, meaning horseman. (6)

Campus Sexual Violence Elimination (SaVE) Act—Part of the Violence Against Women Act (2013); affirms that schools are responsible for preventing sexual assault. (9)

Chaste femme love—Term coined by Valerie Traub (2002) to refer to the idea (common in 17th-century England) that women's close and sometimes sexual relationships were accepted as a way of preserving the chastity of women with regard to men. (5)

Cisgender—Term used to describe people whose gender identity is in traditional alignment with their assigned sex at birth (for example, a woman who is traditionally feminine). (1)

Classical Marxist feminism—Form of feminism that holds that women should primarily organize with others of the working class to overcome capitalism (rather than as women to overcome women's oppression). (12, Appendix C, Feminisms in Brief)

Cognitive schema—A mental system of organization. Sex and gender are major cognitive schemas in most societies. (1)

Colorism—Differential treatment based on skin tone that generally (but not always) manifests itself as a preference for lighter-colored skin. (7)

Commercial sexual exploitation—Commercial transaction involving the sexual exploitation of a child or adult, often through prostitution or pornography. (10)

Commodification—The act of turning something or someone into or treating something or someone as an object to be bought, sold, or traded. (7)

Communication—"The process of creating meaning through symbolic interaction" (Adler et al., 2012). Meaning is not found in words; it is created through our understanding of one another in a particular context. Communication occurs through symbolic interaction: words, fashion, movement, etc. (2)

Communities of practice—A group of people "who come together around mutual engagement in some common endeavor" (Eckert & McConnell-Ginet, 2011). (2)

Compulsory heterosexuality—Term coined by Adrienne Rich (1980) to refer to the fact that economic, social, and political forces "have enforced or insured the coupling of women with men." (4)

Comstock laws—Passed by U.S. Congress in 1873, labeled birth control information and contraceptives as obscene material and outlawed their distribution via the U.S. Postal Service or interstate commerce. (11)

Consciousness-raising—Practice of women sharing their personal experiences to connect them to women as a group and demonstrate that the personal is political. (11, 12)

Conservative—"A person who conserves or preserves something; (now usually) an adherent of traditional values, ideas, and institutions; an opponent of (social and political) change" (OED). (12)

Cool pose—The appearance of aloofness and superiority among young Black males, meant to convey pride, strength, control, and emotionlessness; a coping strategy used in the face of racism or as a way to express contempt toward the dominant society (Majors & Billson, 1992). (6)

Coverture—Doctrine of English common law on which U.S. laws were based, under which female persons have no legal identity. The male (father or husband) exercises rights on behalf of the female, who is under his legal cover; she has no legal right to act independent of his control (e.g., she cannot own property, enter into contracts, or gain custody of her children). (3)

Cyberstalking—Pattern of repeated intrusive and intimidating behaviors via computer, phone, or other technology toward a specific person that causes the target to feel harassed, threatened, or fearful. (9)

Cycles of salience—Valerie Traub's (2002) term to describe how different aspects of female same-sex relationships become more prominent in specific historical periods. As a result, sometimes female same-sex relationships are seen as acceptable and other times as suspect. (5)

Defensive-expressive homophobia—A type of homophobia in which individuals (men) express homophobia as a way to cope with anxiety over their own heterosexual masculinity (Herek, 1986). (4)

Difference feminism—Form of feminism that holds that women are different from men and celebrates women's difference and culture. Also called essentialist feminism. (See also radical feminism.) (11, 12)

Different cultures thesis—Claim that many (but not all) females and males are socialized into two fairly distinctive groups that often have different goals when communicating, different strategies for achieving those goals, and different approaches to interpreting communication. (2)

Differential treatment—Unequal treatment of a class of people, for example, banning gay marriage. (6)

Dis/ability/people with dis/abilities—See Appendix B, Names for People and Places.

Discrimination—Often, unequal treatment of a class of people. (6)

Disparate impact—When the "equal" treatment of people according to a set of rules or procedures disadvantages one class of people versus another (e.g., voter identification laws that require state-issued identification to vote, which can disadvantage poor people, older people, people with dis/abilities, and others who find it more difficult to obtain such identification). (6)

Domestic heterosexuality—The notion that marriage should involve both love and erotic desire on the part of a husband and wife for each other, and that such domestic partners should "invest more of their emotional life into [each other] and express it through sex" (Traub, 2002, p. 269). (5)

Double bind—A lose–lose situation. (3)

Double standard—A rule or set of standards that applies differently to different groups (e.g., different standards of acceptable sexual behavior for women and men). (3)

Double work day—The idea that women labor at both paid work outside the home and unpaid work within the home, often creating a longer total workday than that of men. (11)

Ecofeminism—Form of feminism that analyzes damage done to the earth by human domination drawing parallels to male domination of women. May be Marxist, liberal, radical, etc. (12)

Elide—"To strike out, suppress or pass over in silence" (OED). (2)

Embodiment—The way our bodies are and interact with the world to create social meaning. (7)

Emphasized femininity—The female companion to hegemonic masculinity. Oriented around the idea that women should accommodate "the interests and desires of [heterosexual] men" (Connell, 1987, p. 183). Central features are "compliance, nurturance and empathy" (p. 188). Connell wrote that emphasized femininity is given the "most cultural and ideological support at present" (Connell). (See also hegemonic masculinity and patriarchal bargain.) (3)

Environmental racism—Term used to describe the connection between racism and disproportionate environmental degradation in communities of color. As a result, many people of color bear the costly burdens of environmental hazards on their health and well-being, while elites benefit through profit and protection. (8)

Equality feminism—Form of feminism that seeks to free women—and all people regardless of sex—of limitations based on sex and traditional views of gender and gender roles. (Sometimes also called liberal feminism.) (11, 12*)

Essence—"Property of a thing without which the thing could not be what it is" ("Essence," 2004). (6)

Essential property—A fixed and unchanging property or set of properties that necessarily make something or some organism what it is. (6)

Essentialism—Doctrine that at least some things have a common nature; a fixed and unchanging property or set of properties that necessarily make something or some organism what it is. (6)

Ethnic group—Any "group of people who set themselves apart and/or are set apart by others with whom they interact or co-exist on the basis of their perceptions or cultural differentiation and/or common ancestry" (as cited in Baumann, 2004, pp. 12–13). Cultural elements that set ethnic groups apart from others often include religion, language (or varieties of language), and customs. (6)

Exoticize—To view as exotic, foreign, or unusual in an interesting way. Women outside the racial norm are often exoticized in sexual ways. (7)

Family conflict studies—Intimate partner violence studies in which researchers ask participants to report on a broad range of physically aggressive behaviors; often find that roughly equal numbers of women and men commit physical aggression in intimate relationships (symmetry). (9)

Fat—Although terms such as "overweight" and "obese" are often considered more acceptable or polite, fat activists and scholars are reclaiming "fat" as a preferred term because, unlike overweight and obese, there is no assumption about an abstract ideal weight for all people. (7)

Fatherhood premium—Phenomenon in which fathers are often paid more and rated more highly than nonfathers at work. (8)

Female genital cosmetic surgeries—Surgery performed on female genitals for cosmetic purposes only, including clitoral reduction (cutting clitoral hood or prepuce to reduce its size) and labiaplasty (smoothing, reducing, or otherwise altering the labia minora and majora), practiced primarily in the West. (10)

Feminine—A descriptor of gender; traditionally those assigned female at birth are expected or "supposed" to be feminine. Characteristics associated with Western notions of traditional femininity include passive, dependent, and emotional. Traditionally thought of in binary (consisting of two parts) opposition with masculine. (1)

Feminine mystique—The idea, promoted by popular culture and psychology, that women are naturally fulfilled by devoting themselves to wife- and motherhood; coined by Betty Friedan (1963) in book of the same name. (8, 11, 12)

Femininity Ideology Scale—Scale measuring adherence to five norms of traditional femininity ideology: (1) stereotypic image and activities, (2) dependence/deference, (3) purity, (4) caretaking, and (5) emotionality (Levant et al., 2007). (1)

Feminism/feminist—The belief in (one who believes in) and/or advocacy of the political, economic, and social equality of people regardless of sex. A "movement to end sexism, sexist exploitation, and oppression" (bell hooks, 2000/2014). (3, 12*)

Feminist standpoint—Term developed by Nancy Hartsock (1983/2013) (a socialist feminist) to describe the perspective of women who have developed class consciousness as women, which allows them to understand that to be free they must struggle for inclusion of their vision of the world. (12)

Femme—Vernacular (informal or colloquial) term frequently used in gay and lesbian subcultures for women who are gender conforming (i.e., feminine) and men who are gender nonconforming. (1)

First wave of feminism—(approx. 1840–1920). U.S. feminist movement, landmark achievement is women's suffrage (19th Amendment). (11*, 12)

First World—See Appendix B, Names for People and Places.

Forced labor—Work or services people are forced to perform against their will under the threat of some form of punishment; forced labor is a form of slavery. (10)

Fragmentation—The reduction of a person to a particular body part while neglecting the person as a whole; a strategy sometimes used by advertisers. (See also objectification.) (7)

Free trade zone (special export zone)—Geographical areas set up to attract transnational corporations, often subject to little or no taxation and regulation. (8)

Gaga feminism—Antiessentialist, genderbending, "hypothetical" form of feminism that engages with pop culture; coined by Jack Halberstam (2012). (11)

Gay people—See Appendix B, Names for People and Places. (4, 5)

Gender—Less physiological aspects related to femininity, masculinity, androgyny, and other associated categories; ways of presenting oneself that are constructed and reconstructed through what one does, how one looks, how one behaves, etc. (1)

Gender expression (or gender presentation)—One's outward expression of gender. For example, how one dresses or the length of one's hair. (1)

Gender identity—One's perception of the gender that is appropriate to oneself. (1)

Gender ideology—A set of interrelated, internalized beliefs about gender. In Western society, gender ideology is often subdivided into masculinity ideology and femininity ideology (Levant et al., 2007). (1)

Gender polarization—The notion that femininity and masculinity are polar opposites. Defines mutually exclusive scripts for being female and male and defines persons or behaviors that deviate from these scripts as problematic (Bem, 1993). (1)

Gender role—A set of social expectations about the part one should play (including how one "should" appear and behave) within a specific culture based on one's sex and gender. For example, traditionally in Western society women have had the gender role of homemaker and men have had the role of breadwinner. (1)

Gender schematic—Imposing a gender-based (or gender polarizing) classification system. (3)

Gender symmetry (in intimate partner violence)—The finding that roughly equal numbers of women and men perpetrate physical violence in intimate relationships; mostly a Western phenomenon. (9)

Gender variant (gender nonconforming)—To have one's gender expression in nontraditional alignment with one's assigned sex at birth. (See also transgender.) (1)

Gender-based model of sexual identity—A model where sexual orientation is determined based on the gender presentation (rather than sex) of the people who are attracted to each other. For example, in some communities in Mexico, a man who is macho can have sex with either a woman (presumed feminine) or a feminine man and be thought of as *normal* (akin to heterosexual) and not homosexual. (5)

Gender-based violence—Violence or the threat of violence directed at an individual because of that person's gender, often because of gender nonconformity and as a means to subordinate. (9)

Gender-neutral terms—Terms that do not make specific reference to females or males, such as humankind (for mankind), police officer (for policeman), or postal worker (for postman). (Strictly speaking, these are *sex* neutral terms, but the term "gender neutral" was created before the distinction between sex and gender was widely used.) (2)

Genderqueer—To express gender nonnormatively; often signals recognition that gender is not a stable or unchanging marker of identity and a rejection of binary notions of gender. Related terms include transgender, genderfluid, and pangender. (1)

Generic he—The use of the pronoun "he" as a default term to refer to a non-specific subject who could be any sex/gender. Also called universal he. (2)

Genital cutting/modification practices—Variety of cutting and modification practices including male circumcision, intersex surgery, sex reassignment surgery, female cosmetic surgeries, and traditional female genital cutting, practiced globally. (10)

Glass ceiling—Invisible barrier preventing women from reaching the highest levels of the corporate ladder. (8)

Glass cliff—The phenomenon whereby women are more likely to break through to senior leadership positions if an organization is in crisis; such situations are inherently risky and female leaders in these positions may find themselves more isolated and less able to rally support than male leaders. (8)

Glass escalator—Invisible advantage that some white men enjoy, leading to quicker advancement up the corporate ladder than female and other male employees. (8)

Global North—See Appendix B, Names for People and Places.

Global South—See Appendix B, Names for People and Places.

Golden Orchid Associations—Practice in Pearl River delta region of China in 19th and early 20th century in which unmarried women (many working in the silk industry) became "sworn sisters." These relationships were sometimes sexual in nature. (See also *sou hei* ceremony.) (4)

Great Masculine Renunciation—Beginning in 1666, England's King Charles II set out to create a new restrained fashion in men's clothing, ushering in the era of the three-piece suit and modern masculinity, which "has been associated with modesty and plainness in dress" (Kuchta, 2002, p. 2). Upper- and middle-class men came to renounce conspicuous consumption in dress. (7)

Gynocentric—Focused on females or women. (2)

Hate crime—Under U.S. federal law, defined as a "criminal offense against a person or property motivated in whole or in part by an offender's bias against a race, religion, disability, ethnic origin or sexual orientation" ("Hate Crime—Overview," 2015, para. 2). (9)

Health at Every Size (HAES)—A public health model to which many fat scholars and activists subscribe, which emphasizes that there are healthy people at every size (but not that everyone is healthy at any size). The HAES movement is not concerned with gaining or losing weight so much as developing "long-term health-enhancing behaviors" (Burgard, 2009, pp. 49.) The HAES model also advocates, among other things, "an end to weight bias" and "size and self acceptance" (Shuman & Kratina, cited in Burgard, p. 43). (7)

Hegemonic feminism—A dominant form of feminism that currently focuses on white, middle-class feminist issues and elides (strikes out, passes over) people of color (Spivak as cited in Sandoval [1991/2001]). (12)

Hegemonic masculinity—Multiple masculinities exist and are arranged in a hierarchy, at the top of which is hegemonic masculinity, which Connell and Messerschmidt (2005) defined as "the currently most honored way of being a man" (p. 832). Hegemonic masculinity is not the norm but normative, not fixed but changing over time, not universal but "locally specific" (p. 840). The subordination of women is currently central to hegemonic masculinity. (See also emphasized femininity.) (3)

Heterocentrism—The belief that heterosexuality should be central and normal in contrast to other sexual orientations that are marginal, abnormal, and inferior. (See heteronormativity.) (4)

Heteronormativity—A term coined by Michael Warner (1993/2007) to stand for the idea that "heterosexual culture thinks of itself as the elemental form of human association." (See heterocentrism.) (4)

Heterosexism—Prejudice, stereotyping, or discrimination on the basis of not being heterosexual. "The belief in the inherent superiority of one pattern of loving and thereby its right to dominance" (Lorde, 1978/1984). (4)

Hijra (in the context of India)—People, mostly assigned male at birth, who adopt female dress (at least on some occasions) and ideally renounce sexual desire and sex and undergo the removal of their penis and testicles in a sacrifice to the Hindu goddess Bahuchara Mata. However, some *Hijras* do engage in sex with men. (5)

Hip-hop feminism—Form of feminism that engages with rap music and other elements of hip-hop culture to counter and critique negative representations of women; developed primarily by young Black women (Pough, 2003). (11)

Historicism—The belief that social and cultural phenomena should be understood within their historical circumstances or contexts (OED). (5)

Homonegativity—Negative attitudes about gay people. (See homophobia.) (4)

Homophile organizations—Early name for gay rights organizations prior to Stonewall uprising, most notably the Mattachine Society and the Daughters of Bilitis in the United States. (5)

Homophobia—"Fear or hatred of homosexuals and homosexuality" (OED) or, more broadly, negative attitudes about gay people. (See homonegativity.) (3, 4*)

Homosexual identity as a movement—The emergence of the idea of homosexuals as a group with their own cultural norms and practices and, by extension, the idea that gay people deserve equality. (5)

Homosexualities—The idea that there are varying ways of schematizing same-sex desire, same-sex sexual activity, and same-sex relationships across time and cultures (rather than a universal, unchanging category of homosexuality). (5)

Homosocial—A descriptor of the social bonds between persons of the same sex; applied to "female bonding" or "male bonding" activities such as sorority activities, fraternity activities, or same-sex sports activities. May occur in homosexual or nonhomosexual contexts. (4)

Hostile sexism—Overt prejudice based on sex and grounded in the belief that men are more competent than women and therefore deserve higher status and more power than women, for example, sexist name-calling, sexual harassment, and employment discrimination based on sex. (See also benevolent sexism.) (3)

Human trafficking—"Recruitment, transportation, transfer, harboring or receipt of persons" by "the threat or use of force," "abduction," "fraud," "deception," "abuse of power," or payment to another person "for the purpose of exploitation" (Pati, 2011, p. 116). (10)

Hypermasculinity—Extreme form of masculinity that often includes "endorsement of stereotypical gender roles, a high value placed on control, power and competition, toleration of pain, and mandatory heterosexuality" (Turchik & Wilson, 2010). (9)

Ideal viewer—A specific imagined viewer, often (but not necessarily) white, male, and heterosexual. (7)

(Im)possibility—Valerie Traub's (2002) idea that in early modern England the very notion of lesbian sexual activity was at times conceived as a possibility and at other times an impossibility. It was sometimes considered impossible because women lacked a phallus and sometimes considered possible when in the popular imagination women could be thought of as tribades or users of dildos or when women assumed masculine gender roles. Traub's notion of (im)possibility can be applied to other sexual activity beyond women and beyond early modern England. (5)

In(significance)/in(visibility)—Valerie Traub's (2002) idea that certain forms of sexual activity are at times considered trivial and therefore rendered invisible and at other times are important and become visible. Used by Traub in reference to lesbianism in early modern England. (5)

Institutional homophobia/heterosexism—A cultural ideology that is embodied in institutional practices that disadvantage sexual minority groups even in the absence of individual prejudice or discrimination. For example, the denial of same-sex marriage rights by law does not require prejudice against gay people by an individual judge who might otherwise marry a gay couple. (See homophobia and heterosexism.) (4)

Internalized homophobia—Homonegative attitudes directed toward oneself. (4)

Intersectional feminism—An inclusive approach for engaging in feminist analysis and activism, considering a wide range of interlocking oppressions, including those based on race, sex, class, and sexual orientation. (See also intersectionality and transnational feminism.) (12)

Intersectionality—The term intersectionality was introduced in the late 1980s to describe a method of analysis that considers how discrimination can vary depending on "multiple dimensions" (such as race, sex and class) (Crenshaw, 1991, p. 1244). Intersectional theory was meant to counter the tendency to treat race, sex, class and other categories as "mutually exclusive" (Crenshaw, 1989, p. 39). It is useful to recognize that discrimination varies depending on several factors: (1) the unique combination of characteristics of the person or group being discriminated against (their race, sex, class, sexual orientation, etc.); (2) the unique combination of characteristics of the person or group doing the discriminating (their race, sex, class, sexual orientation, etc.); and (3) the context in which the discrimination occurs. Although intersectionality begins with "the infinite combinations and implications of overlapping identities," the more recent work of intersectional theorists moves beyond identity categories and is primarily concerned with processes that advantage some while disadvantaging others (Cho et al., 2013, p. 797). Thus intersectionality is concerned with "racialization more than races, economic exploitation rather than classes, gendering and gender performance rather than genders" (Choo & Ferree, p. 134). (1, 3*, 12*)

Intersex—Having sex characteristics that make one different from predominant notions of biological femaleness and maleness. (1, 4*)

Intimate partner violence—Physical, sexual, or psychological harm (including threats of physical or sexual violence) by a current or former partner or spouse. (9)

Intimate terrorism—Intimate partner violence that is systematic in nature, escalating in frequency and severity over time, and often unidirectional (primarily men using violence against women). (9)

(In)visibility—See (In)significance/(in)visibility. (5)

Jeanne Clery Act—1990 federal legislation requiring U.S. colleges and universities to disclose information about crime, including sexual assault, on and around their campuses. (9)

Kinsey Scale—Seven-point scale to measure sexual orientation developed by Alfred Kinsey in which individuals are assigned ratings from exclusively heterosexual (0) to exclusively homosexual (7). Asexuality was later acknowledged and denoted by an X. (4)

Klein Grid—A tool to measure sexual orientation developed by Fritz Klein in which seven dimensions are assessed during the past, the present, and the person's ideal: (1) sexual attraction, (2) sexual behavior, (3) sexual fantasies, (4) emotional preference, (5) social preference, (6) self-identification, and (7) heterosexual/homosexual lifestyle. (4)

Language— A "collection of symbols, governed by rules, and used to convey messages between individuals" (Alder et al., 2012, p. 98).

Latinas/Latinos—See Appendix B, Names for People and Places. (6)

Latino Threat Narrative—The notion that "illegal aliens" are flooding across the border into the United States. Despite the focus on undocumented immigrants, this perspective casts people of Latin American descent as an undifferentiated group with little attention to their birthplace or legal status. In this view, immigrants pose a threat to "traditional American identity," (Samuel Huntington's phrase, as cited in L. R. Chavez, 2013, p. 24) and their goal is *la reconquista*—reconquering the Southwest United States, which the United States won in the Mexican–American War. (6)

Lesbian continuum—A term coined by Adrienne Rich (1980), "a range—through each woman's life and throughout history—of woman-identified experience." Inclusive of homosocial bonds both sexual and nonsexual—everything from heterosexual friendship to "bonding against male tyranny" to lesbian sexual relationships (Rich, p. 649). (4)

Liberal feminism—Form of feminism that seeks to free women—and all people regardless of sex—of limitations based on sex and traditional views of gender and gender roles. (Sometimes also called equality feminism.) (11, 12*, Appendix C, Feminisms in Brief)

Love Jones cohort—Black people who are single and living alone (predominantly female and professional), named after the romantic comedy of the same name (Marsh, 2012). (6)

Machismo—Measure of (Latino) manhood based on inner strength, personal daring, bravado, and sexual prowess that stresses the role of the man as provider and protector within the (Latino) family and culture. (Counterpart to *marianismo*.) (6)

Male gaze—Looking or viewing from the perspective of an ideal male viewer which can result in the objectification of women. (7)

Male generic terms—Sex (male) -specific terms that are used to apply to people regardless of sex. For example, the word "guy," as in "Hey, guys!" (2)

Male Role Norms Inventory—Revised—Scale measuring adherence to seven norms of traditional masculinity ideology: (1) avoidance of femininity, (2) negativity toward sexual minorities, (3) self-reliance through mechanical skills, (4) toughness, (5) dominance, (6) importance of sex, and (7) restrictive emotionality (Levant et al., 2010). (1)

Malinche (La)—Indigenous woman who acted as a translator for Spanish conquistador Hernán Cortés in his conquest of Mexico beginning in 1519 and who bore his son. (6)

Maquiladora—Factory located in free trade zones in Mexico and Central and South America. (8)

Marianismo—Idealized image of the Latina as "submissive, self-sacrificing, humble" and virginal before marriage (Torres et al., 2002, p. 166); the term is derived from the Virgin Mary. (Counterpart to *machismo*.) (6)

Marked—Group that because of distinguishing characteristics is conceived of as outside the norm, different, other (often lesser) (e.g., women as opposed to men, working-class people as opposed to middle-class people). (2)

Marriage premium—Phenomenon in which married men are often paid more and rated more positively than nonmarried men at work. (8)

Masculine—A descriptor of gender; traditionally those assigned the male sex at birth are expected or "supposed" to be masculine. Characteristics associated with Western notions of traditional masculinity include active, independent, and unemotional. Traditionally thought of in binary (consisting of two parts) opposition with feminine. (1)

Metrosexual—Model of masculinity that emerged in the 1990s and early 2000s; a kind of modern day dandy, typically a "single" man with a "high disposable income, living or working in the city" (Coad, 2008, p. 19). The term was created by marketers as a strategy to get male consumers to act more like female consumers. Appeal is limited by associations with homosexuality. (7)

Microaggressions—"Brief and commonplace daily verbal, behavioral, or environmental indignities, whether intentional or unintentional, that communicate hostile, derogatory, or negative slights and insults" (Sue et al., 2007, p. 271). (4)

Misogyny—"Hatred or dislike of, or prejudice against women" (OED). Misogynists do not usually avoid women. A misogynist might marry a woman or be attracted to women but simultaneously think less of women than men. (3)

Model minority—Stereotype of Asian Americans as hard working, academically superior, and professionally successful. (6)

Modern regime of sexuality—Modern Western conception of homosexuals as a type of person (as opposed to earlier conceptions of same-sex sexual activity as an act anyone might commit). (5)

Modernism—In the field of philosophy, modernism and the modern period begin with René Descartes and especially his work *Meditations on First Philosophy*, first published in 1641 (Cottingham, 1995). Philosophic modernism should not be confused with literary modernism of the early 20th century (Harrison, 2003). Modern thinkers believe that we can have firm foundations of knowledge, that reason and science can be used to get at the truth of things—ideas that are also central to the period known as the Enlightenment (Beasley; Cottingham; Magnus, 1995; Norris, 1995). (12)

Monosexuals—People with a sexual orientation toward only one sex (e.g., homosexual or heterosexual). (4)

Motherhood penalty—Phenomenon in which mothers are often paid less and rated more poorly than nonmothers at work. (8)

Multiple jeopardy—The idea that women of color (and many others) experience multiple forms of prejudice and discrimination (oppression) simultaneously. (11, 12)

Multiracial feminism—Forms of feminism championed by women of color that stresses the importance of understanding the multiple oppressions faced by women of color and others. (See also intersectional feminism and transnational feminism.) (11, 12)

Mummy–baby relationships—Modern practice in certain African countries between adolescent girls and young women in which one takes on the role of "mommy" and the other of "baby." Often emotionally and physically intimate, sometimes sexual/erotic. (5)

Mythical norm—Audre Lorde (1984) coined the term to refer to those considered the social norm; Lorde said the mythical norm in America is usually defined as "white, thin, male, young, heterosexual, christian [sic] and financially secure." (3, 6*)

Native Americans—See Appendix B, Names for People and Places. (6)

Neoliberalism—Ideology that prioritizes profit, equates human well-being with wealth accumulation, discourages government regulation, and encourages competition over social solidarity. (8, 10)

New international division of labor—Term coined by Barbara Ehrenreich and Annette Fuentes (1984) to refer to a system under which industrial production was moved to different parts of the "Third World" whereas the technology and control (and much of the profits) stayed in the "First World." (8)

New male mystique—Pressure felt by some men to be their families' financial providers while also being more involved at home; counterpart to Friedan's feminine mystique. (8)

Object choice model of sexual identity—Model in which sexual orientation is determined by the sex of the person who is attracted to another and the sex of the person one is attracted to. (See also gender-based model of sexual identity.) (5)

Objectification—"Seeing and/or treating a person, usually a woman, as an object" (Papadaki, 2012, para. 1). (7)

Occupational feminization—Movement of women into an occupational field in greater numbers, often accompanied by diminishing pay. (8)

One-Third World—See Appendix B, Names for People and Places.

Oppression—According to Marilyn Frye (1983), a network of forces that together restrict the freedom of individuals. According to Wendy Kaminer (1997), the denial of basic civil rights and liberties. (3)

Other—Group that exists in opposition to the norm and/or that exhibits difference. (See also marked.) (2)

Othering—"Perception or representation of a person or group of people as fundamentally alien from another, frequently more powerful, group" (OED). (6)

Pansexual—"A person who is sexually attracted to people regardless of their gender identity, gender expression or biological sex" ("Bisexual/Pansexual Basics," 2015, p. 18). (4)

Parallel terms—Words that are supposed to be equivalent in denotation (dictionary definition) and connotation (cultural meaning). So-called parallel terms are often not parallel in connotation (e.g., ladies and gentlemen for females and males). (2)

Part-time pay penalty—Part-time workers earn less per hour than full-time workers on average; affects women to a greater extent than men. (8)

***Pasivo* sex role**—In many Latin American cultures, among men who have sex with men, the man who is penetrated. May be considered effeminate and be stigmatized for role. (See *activo* sex role.) (5)

Paternity quota—Parental leave that can be used only by fathers and is lost if not used; implemented to encourage fathers to utilize paternity leave. (8)

Patriarchal bargain—"A decision [by females] to accept gender rules that disadvantage women in exchange for whatever power one can wrest from the system" (Wade, 2010, para. 4). In such bargains, an individual woman benefits at the expense of women generally (such as a woman who gains celebrity and money by being a sex object, but by doing so furthers the objectification of women generally who are then disadvantaged). (3)

Patriarchy—A rough definition of patriarchy is a system under which women are subordinated to men in society. A more nuanced definition is "a sociopolitical system in which men and their experience have power over women and their experience" (Basow, 2001). For example, a 40-hour work week without a parental leave benefit was designed with men's experience in mind. However, such a work structure disadvantages women who often have primary caretaking responsibilities for children and other family members. Although patriarchy generally advantages men over women, not all men benefit equally and people of any sex can oppose patriarchy. (3)

Patrilocality—The practice or custom of married couples residing with the husband's family. (4)

Pay gap—Women are paid less than men on average for waged work. (8)

Pederasty—Ancient Greek tradition of relationships between adult males (20 to 30 years old) and male youth (around 14 years plus), including educational guidance and military training, sometimes sexual in nature. (5)

People of color—See Appendix B, Names for People and Places.

People with dis/abilities—See Appendix B, Names for People and Places.

Performativity—Idea developed by Judith Butler (1990/1999) that a person's identity is created through "a stylized repetition" of conventional or widely accepted acts. A person doesn't have preformed identity; rather a person's identity comes into being by "doing" the identity. A popular misunderstanding of performativity is that it means gender is simply a performance—a role that one takes on as one would take on a role in a play. This misconception assumes that gender is, to use Butler's (1990/1999) word, "exterior" to us and masks our true selves. Butler (1990/1999) rejected the notion that we have a one, true self; performativity relies on the notion that we are a sum of our actions, which have symbolic meaning. These acts then are not a false performance, but that does not imply these acts are "natural" or inevitable. (2)

Personification of homosexuality—Modern Western conception of an individual who engages in same-sex sexual activity as being a kind of person, a homosexual (Msibi, 2011). (See modern regime of sexuality.) (5)

Perversion of lesbian desire (the)—Process by which intense romantic relationships between women came to be seen as improper and threatening to new visions of marriage that emerged in the late 17th century in Europe (Traub, 2002). (See also chaste femme love.) (5)

Phallocentrism—Attitude in which attention revolves around the phallus or penis (to the exclusion of women and their experiences). (5)

Phenotypical traits—Observable physical characteristics and behaviors of an organism. (6)

Politics of respectability—A term coined by Evelyn Brooks Higginbotham (1993) to describe African American campaign at the turn of the 20th century to "earn . . . a measure of esteem from white America" by inculcating in lower-class Blacks "allegiance to temperance [abstaining from drinking], industriousness, thrift, refined manners, and Victorian sexual morals" (p. 14). The politics of respectability in altered forms continues to be used as a middle-class strategy by some African Americans. (7)

Postcolonial feminism—Form of (transnational) feminism that contends that the oppression of women and men in the Global South has its roots in a system created through colonialism. The exploitation of the Global South continues, especially through capitalist and neoliberalist practices. (See transnational feminism.) (12)

Postmodern feminism—Form of feminism that rejects the notion of universal foundations for knowledge, universal categories and definitions, and faith in reason and science to give us definitive answers. Individual women (and individual members of other social groups such as gay people) are oppressed but not necessarily in the same way. The solution to each person's problem is different and there is no ideal position from which to evaluate the best way to be free. Postmodern feminists would agree that enforcing any rigid system of categories (such as precise definitions of sex, gender, and sexual orientation) is oppressive and all systems of categorization must be opposed. (12*, Appendix C, Feminisms in Brief)

Poststructuralism—School of thought that contends (among other things) that words do not have inherent meaning but signify things only in relation to other words. Theory often employed by those who analyze discourse. (12)

Prime directive of masculine sexual behavior—Ancient Roman rule of sexual conduct in which the man (to remain masculine) must always give the appearance of playing the insertive role in penetrative sex acts (with female or male partners) (C. A. Williams, 2010). (5)

Provider wage—A wage high enough to support a family, not just an individual worker. (11)

Queer theory—"An approach to social and cultural study which seeks to challenge or deconstruct traditional ideas of sexuality and gender, especially the acceptance of heterosexuality as normative and the perception of a rigid dichotomy of male and female traits" (OED). (4, 12*)

Questioning—From the alphabetic string LGBTQQIAA; used to identify people who are seeking to explore their identification with regard to sexual orientation. (4)

Race—Concept that traditionally has been used to refer to a group of people who all share inherited biological features not shared by others. Many scholars today believe there are no essential properties (i.e., shared biological features) related to race. Thus, "race" does not exist. (See also racialization.) (6)

Race to the bottom—Push by transnational corporations to find ever-cheaper sources of labor to produce goods, often without regard for work conditions or workers' rights. (8)

Racialization—The act of categorizing someone or being marked by "race," which recognizes that becoming marked by race is something that happens to people rather than something they are. (6)

Racism—"The belief that all members of each race possess characteristics, abilities, or qualities specific to that race, especially so as to distinguish it as inferior or superior to another race or races" (OED). (6)

Radical feminism—Form of feminism concerned with uprooting patriarchy to end the subordination of women as women. Until the relationship between women and men fundamentally changes, not only will women not be free but also some say the male pattern of domination will continue to form the basis of the domination of other groups such as LGBTQQIA people and people of color. (See also difference feminism.) (11, 12*, Appendix C, Feminisms in Brief)

Rape—Under U.S. federal law, rape is "the penetration, no matter how slight, of the vagina or anus with any body part or object, or oral penetration by a sex organ of another person, without the consent of the victim." State laws vary and some offer broader definitions than this. (9)

Rape myths—"Beliefs about rape that often blame the victim, justify the perpetrator's actions and discount the violence of rape" (Chapleau & Oswald, 2010, p. 68). (9)

Rape shield laws—Laws that limit the evidence a defendant is allowed to admit at trial about a victim's sexual history. (9)

Rape-prone cultures—The idea that some cultures are more prone to rape whereas others are comparatively rape free. In rape-prone cultures sexual violence is "an expression of a social ideology of male dominance" (Sanday, 2003, p. 341). (9)

Reception theory—Study of how symbols or messages are received. (2)

Recolonized—Idea that international institutions (like the World Bank) and transnational corporations are asserting control over significant parts of the political, economic, and social lives of the "developing" world and its people and exploiting them in much the same way that foreign colonial powers did in the past. (8)

Reverse discourse—An oppositional way of naming or valuing things (Foucault, 1976/1980). For example, the appropriation or use of terms like "bitch" and "slut" to reclaim stigmatized identities. (2)

Rigid regulatory frame—A set of social conventions operating at any given moment that limit what is acceptable to do (e.g., how one can enact one's gender) (Butler, 1990/1999). (2)

Riot Grrrl movement—Form of feminism that emerged in the early 1990s growing out of the punk music scene; supports "girl artists" producing and distributing their own art, especially associated with the production and distribution of zines ("Riot Grrrl Manifesto," 1991). (11)

Rule of masculine self-restraint—Ancient Roman rule of sexual conduct in which a free-born man (to remain masculine) should limit sexual activity to his wife or, if outside of marriage, to noncitizens (female or male) such as slaves or prostitutes (C. A. Williams, 2010). (5)

Second sex—Term used by Simone de Beauvoir (1953/1989) to refer to women so as to assert that men are seen as the norm or primary (first), but women are seen as different or other (second). (See also marked and unmarked.) (2)

Second wave of feminism—(approx. 1960–1988). U.S. feminist movement with focus on equality, women's culture, and theories of multiple oppressions (among other things). Achievements include antidiscrimination laws in the workplace and education and legalization of abortion. (11*, 12)

Semantic change—The idea that words develop new meanings and associations and lose old meanings and associations. (2)

Service work—Work that women are expected to perform for men, including personal service, sexual service, and ego service (Frye, 1983). (3)

Sex—The more physiological characteristics used to classify a person as female, male, intersex, third sex, or other related category. Since human choice is always involved, sex classification always involves more than biological characteristics and is always to some degree socially constructed. In recognition of this fact, many have abandoned the term "biological sex" in favor of "assigned sex." (1)

Sex identity—What people understand their sex to be. (1)

Sex reassignment process—Surgery and/or hormone treatment to bring a person's body more into biological alignment with their sex identity. Surgery can include a range of procedures, including "top surgery" (breast augmentation or removal) and "bottom surgery" (altering genitals). Also called gender reassignment and gender-affirming or gender-confirming surgery. In the past, also called sex change surgery but this term is now considered derogatory by many. (1)

Sex segregation (in employment)—Women and men tend to be concentrated in different fields of work that often correspond to stereotypical gender roles. (8)

Sex stratification (in employment)—Women and men within the same occupational field tend to be employed at different levels, with men overrepresented in the top tier and women often clustered in the middle and bottom. For example, in education women are more likely to be elementary school teachers and men university professors. (8)

Sexism—Prejudice based on sex. (3)

Sexual orientation—An "elusive concept" (Galupo et al., 2014, p. 404). Most simplistically, involves the sexual and/or romantic attraction one has to others based on one's sex and/or gender in relation to another's sex and/or gender. (See also gender-based model of sexual identity and object choice model of sexual identity. See Chapter 4 for more.) (1, 4*, 5)

Sexual stigma—"Negative regard, inferior status, and relative powerlessness that society collectively accords to any nonheterosexual behavior, identity, relationship, or community" (Herek, 2007, pp. 906-907). (4)

Situational couple violence—Intimate partner violence that is occasional and often not escalating. (9)

Social construct/socially constructed—"A concept or perception of something based on the collective views developed and maintained within a society or social group . . . as opposed to existing inherently or naturally" (OED). (1)

Social-expressive homophobia—A type of homophobia in which individuals try to gain the approval of others and enhance their own self-esteem by expressing homophobia (Herek, 1986). (4)

Socialist feminism—Form of feminism that advocates multipronged action on a wide range of oppressions, including activism against capitalism, against women's oppression, and possibly on other fronts, including racism and homophobia. (12*, Appendix C, Feminisms in Brief)

Socioeconomic status—"Social standing or class of an individual or group . . . often measured as a combination of education, income and occupation" (American Psychological Association, 2014). (6)

***Sou hei* ceremony**—Performed in the Pearl River Delta region of China in the 19th and early 20th centuries as an alternative to a marriage ceremony in which a female took a vow to remain celibate and unmarried. The women often joined sisterhoods, worked in the silk industry, and contributed financially to their families. (See Golden Orchid Associations.) (4)

Speech community—"A group of people who share norms about communication" (J. T. Wood, 2013, p. 126). (2)

Stalking—"Pattern of repeated intrusive and intimidating behaviors toward a specific person that causes the target to feel harassed, threatened or fearful" (L. Miller, 2012, p. 496). (9)

Storms's Scale—Scale developed by Michael D. Storms to measure sexual orientation based on the type, extent, and frequency of a person's erotic fantasies. Classifies people as relatively homosexual, bisexual, asexual, or heterosexual. Homoeroticism and heteroeroticism are independent variables, so a person can be high in both (bisexual), low in both (asexual), or high in one and low in the other (homosexual or heterosexual). (4)

Strategic essentialism—Use of essentialist labels although they are recognized to be inaccurate because they help achieve important short-term objectives (term used by Gayatri Spivak.) (Heyes, 2012). (6)

***Sumangali* system**—System under which young female workers in India are paid only a small wage during their contract period from which money is deducted by the employer to pay for food and housing, with the promise of a lump sum when the contract is complete; considered a form of slavery. (8)

Textual harassment—Repeated sending of text messages to a specific person to harass or threaten. (9)

Third sex/third gender—An umbrella term used to identify people across various cultures who go outside usual (normative) Western sex and gender boundaries. Sometimes also covered under the term transgender. (See also transgender.) (1*, 5*—"India's *Hijras*")

Third wave of feminism—(1990s–present). Embraces a broad range of issues; no political priority list. Intentionally inclusive, diverse, multicultural, and genderbending. Engages, critiques, and creates popular culture. Leverages technology and social media. (11*, 12).

Third World—See Appendix B, Names for People and Places.

Title IX—Federal civil rights legislation that prohibits sex discrimination in education. (9)

Total discrimination—Effect of current and past discrimination. (6)

Traditional female genital cutting/female circumcision—Diverse set of practices from symbolic piercing or removal of the hood of the clitoral prepuce to partial or complete removal of the clitoris, labia minora, and/or labia majora, practiced primarily in East and West Africa, the Middle East, and Southeast Asia (also called female genital mutilation). (10)

Trans—See transgender.

Transfeminism—Form of feminism that argues for inclusion of trans people in feminist movement; argues that sex (like gender) is socially constructed (Koyama, 2003). (11)

Transgender—See Appendix B, Names for People and Places. (1, 4*)

Transnational feminism—A form of feminism that is particularly concerned with global forces, past and present (such as colonialism, globalization, and neoliberalism), that affect women and other marginalized groups of the Global South. Takes into account multiple systems of domination that perpetuate sexism, racism, classism, homophobia, and other supremacist ideologies. Employs poststructuralism to critique Western discourse. (12*, Appendix C, Feminisms in Brief)

Transphobia—"Societal discrimination and stigma of individuals who do not conform to traditional norms of sex and gender" (Sugano et al., 2006, p. 217). (4)

Transsexual—GLAAD (2015) noted that "transsexual" is "an older term that originated in the medical and psychological communities" and is "still preferred by some people who have permanently changed—or seek to change—their bodies through medical interventions" such as hormones and/or surgeries. Unlike "transgender," transsexual is "not an umbrella term. Many transgender people do not identify as transsexual" (even if they have had medical interventions) (GLAAD). GLAAD advised that "it is best to ask which term an individual prefers." (We use transsexual when a specific person self-identifies as "transsexual" or when we need to refer in general terms to people who have undergone the sex reassignment process. "Transsexual" like "transgender" is used as an adjective, for example, transsexual woman.) (See transgender.) (1, 4*)

Tribade—Term used in early modern Europe to describe a woman with an unusually large clitoris. Some might have been what we call intersex today. In other time periods, tribades could be anatomically "normal" women who engaged in same-sex sexual activity. (5)

Two-Spirit—Umbrella term used by modern Native people in North America to describe Native people who identify variously as lesbian or gay, belonging to contemporary Native gender categories, belonging to traditional Native third sex categories, belonging to third sex categories beyond Native American culture, and transgender people. (1)

Two-Thirds World—See Appendix B, Names for People and Places.

Unencumbered worker—The idea that workers are assumed to be available for full-time, long-term, uninterrupted work. (11)

Unidirectional violence (**intimate partner violence**)—Intimate partner violence in which only one partner is violent toward the other. (9)

UN Convention on the Elimination of All Forms of Discrimination Against Women (CEDAW)—Adopted by the UN General Assembly in 1979, the first international human rights treaty to comprehensively address women's rights. (Also called the Women's Convention.) (10)

UN Fourth World Conference on Women—UN-sponsored conference held in Beijing in 1995 to address the rights of women globally; adopted a nonbinding Platform for Action that addresses 12 critical areas. (10)

Unmarked—Group that is conceived of as the norm and thought to lack distinguishing characteristics (e.g., to be without ethnicity or distinctive culture); "normal" or "regular" (e.g. men as opposed to women, white people as opposed to people of color). (2)

Value-expressive homophobia—A type of homophobia in which individuals express homophobia as part of a broader value system of right and wrong, such as a conservative religious ideology (Herek, 1986). (4)

Vendida—Sellout; used to describe Latinas who stray outside the prescriptive bounds of *marianismo*. (6)

Victimization/crime studies—Studies that examine rates of intimate partner violence reported to police or defined by survey respondents as crime; often find that men perpetrate much more violence than women in intimate relationships (gender asymmetry). (9)

Violence Against Women Act (VAWA)—U.S. law first passed in 1994 that comprehensively addresses violence against women; among other things, VAWA strengthens law enforcement responses to crimes against women and some men, improves victims' services, and provides resources for battered women and children. (9)

Violent resistance—Occurs when victims of intimate terrorism (often women) retaliate with violence. (9)

Virgjinesha—Literally, sworn virgin. An Albanian third sex category in which a female would adopt a masculine gender role (and swear to abstain from sex), sometimes when there was no other male in the family. Although some virgjinesha may still be living, it is thought that no more girls are becoming virgjinesha. (1)

Voyeur—Someone who takes sexual pleasure in looking (often male). (7)

Walking while Black—The practice of racially profiling Black people while they are walking; treating Black pedestrians as suspicious simply for the act of walking. Spin-off of term "driving while Black." (6)

Western/non-Western—See Appendix B, Names for People and Places.

White privilege—Advantages (often invisible) that white people enjoy simply because they are white. (6)

References

10 Pictures that changed America. (1989, January). *American Photographer, 22*(1), 30–36. The 70's. (2014, December 2). *Idealist Style*. Retrieved from http://www.idealiststyle.com/blog/beauty-ideal-over-the-decades-part-6-the-70s

The 80's. (2014, February 2). *Idealist Style*. Retrieved from http://www.idealiststyle.com/blog/beauty-ideal-over-the-decades-part-5-the-80s

The 90's. (2014, January 25). *Idealist Style*. Retrieved from http://www.idealiststyle.com/blog/beauty-ideal-over-the-decades-part-4-the-90s

The 2000's. (2013, December 14). *Idealist Style*. Retrieved from http://www.idealiststyle.com/blog/beauty-ideal-over-the-decades-part-3-the-2000s

2013. (2013, November 27). *Idealist Style*. Retrieved from http://www.idealiststyle.com/blog/beauty-ideal-over-the-decades-part-2-right-now-2013

Adler, R. B., Rodman, G., with Hutchinson, C. C. (2012). *Understanding human communication* (11th ed.). New York, NY: Oxford University Press.

African American/Afro-American. (2005). In *The American Heritage guide to contemporary usage and style*. Boston, MA: Houghton Mifflin. Retrieved from http://ezproxy.sunyrockland.edu:2048/login?qurl=http%3A%2F%2Fsearch.credoreference.com%2Fcontent%2Fentry%2Fhmcontempusage%2Fafrican_american_afro_american%2F0

Ahmadu, F. (2001). Rites and wrongs: An insider/outsider reflects on power and excision. In B. Shell-Duncan & Y. Hernlund (Eds.), *Female "circumcision" in Africa: Culture, controversy and change* (pp. 283–312). Boulder, CO: Rienner.

Alcoff, L. M. (2005). Latino vs. Hispanic. *Philosophy & Social Criticism, 31*(4), 395–407.

Alderman, L., & Greenhouse, S. (2014, October 28). Living wages, rarity for U.S. fast-food workers, served up in Denmark. *The New York Times*, Retrieved from http://www.nytimes.com/2014/10/28/business/international/living-wages-served-in-denmark-fast-food-restaurants.html?_r=0&gwh=8CF162408F774B775D030AFFFB35BB11&gwt=pay&assetType=nyt_now

Allen, P. G. (2005). Where I come from is like this. In R. Fiske-Rusciano & V. Cyrus (Eds.), *Experiencing race, class and gender in the United States* (4th ed., pp. 82–86). New York, NY: McGraw-Hill.

Allgor, C. (n.d.). Coverture—The word you probably don't know but should. National Women's History Museum. Retrieved from http://www.nwhm.org/blog/coverture-the-word-you-probably-don%E2%80%99t-know-but-should/

American Academy of Pediatrics. (2012). New evidence points to greater benefits of infant circumcision but final say is still up to parents, says AAP. Retrieved from http://www.aap.org/en-us/about-the-aap/aap-press-room/Pages/New-Benefits-Point-to-Greater-Benefits-of-Infant-Circumcision-But-Final-Say-is-Still-Up-to-parents-Says-AAP.aspx

American Association of University Women. (2016, Spring). The simple truth about the gender pay gap. Retrieved from http://www.aauw.org/files/2016/02/SimpleTruth_Spring2016.pdf

American Congress of Obstetricians and Gynecologists. (2007). ACOG advises against cosmetic vaginal procedures due to lack of safety and efficacy data. Retrieved from http://www.acog.org/About-ACOG/News-Room/News-Releases/2007/ACOG-Advises-Against-Cosmetic-Vaginal-Procedures

American Psychological Association. (2011). *Disabilities* (sec. 3.15). Washington, DC: Author.

American Psychological Association. (2014). Socioeconomic status. Retrieved from http://www.apa.org/topics/socioeconomic-status Anderson, E. (2011). Inclusive masculinities of university soccer players in the American Midwest. *Gender and Education, 23*(6), 729–744.

Anderson, M. J. (2005). All-American rape. *St. John's Law Review, 79*(3), 625–644.

Andreasen, R. O. (2005, February). The meaning of "race": Folk conceptions and the new biology of race. *The Journal of Philosophy, 102*(2), 94–106.

Annamma, S., Connor, D., & Ferri, B. (2013). Dis/ability critical race studies (DisCrit): Theorizing at the intersections of race and dis/ability. *Race, Ethnicity and Education, 16*(1), 1–31.

Anthony, Susan B. (2001). In *Encyclopedia of women social reformers*. Retrieved from http://ezproxy.sunyrockland.edu:2048/login?qurl=http%3A%2F%2Fsearch.credoreference.com%2Fcontent%2Fentry%2Fabcwsr%2Fanthony_susan_b%2F0

Anti-Slavery International. (2012, June). Slavery on the high street: Forced labour in the manufacture of garments for international brands. Retrieved from http://www.antislavery.org/includes/documents/cm_docs/2012/s/1_slavery_on_the_high_street_june_2012_final.pdf

Anti-Slavery International. (2015). Forced labour in the United States agricultural industry. Retrieved from http://www.antislavery.org/english/who_we_are/our_history/english/what_we_do/antislavery_international_today/award/forced_labour_in_the_united_states_agricultural_industry.aspx

Antoine, D. M. (2011). Unethical acts: Treating native men as lurking threat, leaving native women without voice. *Journal of Mass Media Ethics, 26*(3), 243–245.

Antonopoulos, R. (2009). *The unpaid care work–paid work connection* (International Labor Office Working Paper No. 86). Geneva, Switzerland: International Labor Organization. Retrieved from http://www.ilo.org/wcmsp5/groups/public/---dgreports/---integration/documents/publication/wcms_119142.pdf

Anzaldúa, G. (1987). *Borderlands/La frontera: The new mestiza.* San Francisco, CA: Aunt Lute Books.

Archer, J. (2000). Sex differences in aggression between heterosexual partners: A meta-analytic review. *Psychological Bulletin, 126*(5), 651–680.

Archer, J. (2006). Cross-cultural differences in physical aggression between partners: A social-role analysis. *Personality & Social Psychology Review, 10*(2), 133–153.

Arciniega, G., Anderson, T. C., Tovar-Blank, Z. G., & Tracey, T. G. (2008). Toward a fuller conception of Machismo: Development of a traditional Machismo and Caballerismo Scale. *Journal of Counseling Psychology, 55*(1), 19–33.

Arnold, C. A. (2009). Water privatization trends in the United States: Human rights, national security, and public stewardship. *William and Mary Environmental Law and Policy Review, 33*(3/4), 785. Retrieved from scholarship.law.wm.edu/wmelpr/vol33/iss3/4/

Arreola, C. (2014, September 15). Latina's 2014 sexiest men awards. *Latina.* Retrieved from http://www.latina.com/entertainment/celebrity/sexy-latino-men-awards-2014#1

Asian. (2005). In *The American Heritage guide to contemporary usage and style.* Boston, MA: Houghton Mifflin. Retrieved from http://ezproxy.sunyrockland.edu:2048/login?qurl=http%3A%2F%2Fezproxy.sunyrockland.edu%3A2103%2Fcontent%2Fentry%2Fhmcontempusage%2Fasian%2F0

Aumann, K., Galinsky, E., & Matos, K. (2011). The new male mystique. *Families and Work Institute.* Retrieved from http://familiesandwork.org/site/research/reports/newmalemystique.pdf

AVEN: The Asexual Visibility and Education Network. (2012). *Asexuality.org.* Retrieved from http://www.asexuality.org

Azande. (2003). In *The Macmillan encyclopedia.* Retrieved from http://ezproxy.sunyrockland.edu:2048/login?qurl=http%3A%2F%2Fwww.credoreference.com/entry/move/azande

Bajaj, V. (2015, March 17). Venture Capital's Boys' Club on trial. *The New York Times,* A26.

Bakhtin, M. (1929/1990). Marxism and the philosophy of language. In P. Bizzell & B. Herzberg (Eds.), *The rhetorical tradition: Readings from classical times to the present* (pp. 932–934). Boston, MA: Bedford Books.

Balsam, K. F., Molina, Y., Beadnell, B., Simoni, J., & Walters, K. (2011). Measuring multiple minority stress: The LGBT People of Color Microaggressions Scale. *Cultural Diversity and Ethnic Minority Psychology, 17*(2), 163–174.

Banks, O. (1993). *Faces of feminism.* Cambridge, MA: Blackwell.

Banner, L. W. (1984). *American beauty.* Chicago, IL: University of Chicago Press.

Barlow, R. (2014, January 16). BU research: A riddle reveals depth of gender bias. *Boston University Today.* Retrieved from http://www.bu.edu/today/2014/bu-research-riddle-reveals-the-depth-of-gender-bias/

Bartky, S. L. (1990). *Femininity and domination: Studies in the phenomenology of oppression.* New York, NY: Routledge.

Basow, S. (2001). Androcentrism. In J. Worell (Ed.), *Encyclopedia of women and gender: Sex similarities and differences and the impact of society on gender* (pp. 125–135). San Diego, CA: Academic Press.

Basow, S. A., & Johnson, K. (2000). Predictors of homophobia in female college students. *Sex Roles, 42*(5/6), 391–404.

Bateman, G. W. (2011). AIDS activism. *GLBTQ Social Sciences,* 1–5.

Baumann, T. (2004, September). Defining ethnicity. *The SAA Archaeological Record, 4*(4), 12–14.

Baumgardner, J. (2011). Is there a fourth wave? Does it matter? *Feminist.com.* Retrieved from http://www.feminist.com/resources/artspeech/genwom/baumgardner2011.html

Baumgardner, J., & Richards, A. (2000). *Manifesta: Young women, feminism, and the future.* New York, NY: Farrar, Straus & Giroux.

Baumgardner, J., & Richards, A. (2003). The number one question about feminism. *Feminist Studies, 29*(2), 448–452.

BBC. (2014, February 10). Where is it illegal to be gay? Retrieved from http://www.bbc.com/news/world-25927595

Beasley, C. (1999). *What is feminism? An introduction to feminist theory.* Thousand Oaks, CA: Sage.

Beauboeuf-Lafontant, T. (2009). *Behind the mask of the strong Black woman: Voice and the embodiment of a costly performance.* Philadelphia, PA: Temple University Press.

Beaumont, L. A. (2006). Family. In N. G. Wilson (Ed.), *Encyclopedia of Ancient Greece*. New York, NY: Routledge/Taylor & Francis.

Becker, J. C., & Wright, S. C. (2011). Yet another dark side of chivalry: Benevolent sexism undermines and hostile sexism motivates collective action for social change. *Journal of Personality and Social Psychology, 101*(1), 62–77.

Beery, A., & Zucker, I. (2011, January). Sex bias in neuroscience and biomedical research. *Neuroscience and Biobehavioral Reviews, 35*(3), 565–572.

Beinart, P. (2014, February 5). Liberal is good. *The Atlantic.* Retrieved from http://www.theatlantic.com/politics/archive/2014/02/liberal-is-good/283617/

Bem, S. L. (1981). Gender schema theory: A cognitive account of sex typing. *Psychological Review, 88*(4), 354–364.

Bem, S. L. (1993). *The lenses of gender.* New Haven, CT: Yale University Press.

Bennett, V., Davila-Poblete, S., & Rico, M. (2008). Water and gender: The unexpected connection that really matters. *Journal of International Affairs, 61*(2), 107–126.

Benshoff, H., & Griffin, S. (2009). *America on film: Representing race, class, gender, and sexuality in the movies.* Malden, MA: Wiley.

Berger, J. (n.d.). *Ways of seeing.* New York, NY: Penguin.

Berlant, L., & Warner, M. (1998). Sex in public. *Critical Inquiry, 24*(2), 547–566.

Berman, E. (2014, March 25). Why women still suffer from the Ally McBeal effect [Web log post]. Retrieved from http://www.huffingtonpost.ca/erica-berman/beauty-ideals_b_5030288.html

Bernard, T. (2013, February 22). In paid family leave, U.S. trails most of the globe. *The New York Times,* Retrieved from http://www.nytimes.com/2013/02/23/your-money/us-trails-much-of-the-world-in-providing-paid-family-leave.html?pagewanted=all&_r=0

Best, D. (2002). Cross-cultural gender roles. In J. Worell (Ed.), *Encyclopedia of women and gender: Sex similarities and differences and the impact of society on gender, A-P/Volume 1* (pp. 279–290). San Diego, CA: Academic Press.

Best, D. (2004). Gender roles in childhood and adolescence. In U. P. Gielen & J. Roopnarine (Eds.), *Childhood and adolescence: Cross-cultural perspectives and applications* (pp. 199–228). Westport, CT: Praeger.

Best, D. (2009). Another view of the gender-status relation. *Sex Roles, 61*(5/6), 341–351.

Biernat, M., Tocci, M. J., & Williams, J. C. (2012, March). The language of performance evaluations: Gender-based shifts in content and consistency of judgment. *Social Psychological and Personality Science, 3*(2), 186–192.

Bisexual/pansexual basics. (2015). *Empty Closet, 486,* 18–19.

Bitchmedia. (2015). About us. Retrieved from https://bitchmedia.org/about-us

Black lives matter. (2015). State of the Black union. Retrieved from http://blacklivesmatter.com

Black, M., Basile, K., Breiding, M., Smith, S., Walters, M., Merrick, M., . . . Stevens, M. (2011). *The National Intimate Partner and Sexual Violence Survey 2010: A summary report.* Arlington, VA: National Center for Injury Prevention and Control, Centers for Disease Control and Prevention.

Blanco, J. F., Leff, S., Kellogg, A. T., & Payne, L. W. (2008). *The Greenwood encyclopedia of clothing through American history 1900 to the present. Vol. 2 1950–Present.* Westport, CT: Greenwood Press.

Blau, F., & Kahn, L. (2016, January). The gender wage gap: Extent, trends, and explanations. *Institute for the Study of Labor.* Retrieved from http://ftp.iza.org/dp9656.pdf

Blotcher, J. (2011). Queer nation. In D. A. Gerstner (Ed.), *Routledge international encyclopedia of queer culture* (pp. 475–476). New York, NY: Routledge.

Blundell, S. (1995). *Women in Ancient Greece.* Cambridge: MA: Harvard University Press.

Boehmer, U. (2000). *The personal and the political.* Albany, NY: SUNY Press.

Bogaert, A. F. (2004). Asexuality: Prevalence and associated factors in a national probability sample. *Journal of Sex Research, 41*(3), 279–287.

Bogaert, A. F. (2006). Toward a conceptual understanding of asexuality. *Review of General Psychology, 10*(3), 241–250.

Boggs, J. (1996, January/February). What about men's oppression? [Letter to the editor]. *The Humanist, 56*(1), 2.

Bogle, D. (1973). *Toms, coons, mulattoes, mammies, and bucks: An interpretive history of Blacks in American films.* New York, NY: Viking Press.

Bogle, K. (2008). *Hooking up: Sex, dating and relationships on campus.* New York, NY: New York University Press.

Bohner, G., Jarvis, C., Eyssel, F., & Siebler, F. (2005). The causal impact of rape myth acceptance on men's rape proclivity: Comparing sexually coercive and noncoercive men. *European Journal of Social Psychology, 35,* 819–828.

Bolt, C. (1995). *Feminist ferment: The "woman question" in the USA and England, 1870–1940.* London, United Kingdom: University College London Press.

Bordo, S. (1999). Gay men's revenge. *Journal of Aesthetics & Art Criticism, 57*(1), 21.

Boswell, H. (1991, Summer). The transgender alternative. *Transgender Tapestry, 98.* Retrieved from http://www.ifge.org/index.php?name=News&file=article&sid=58&theme=Printer

Braun, V. (2005). In search of (better) sexual pleasure: Female genital "cosmetic" surgery. *Sexualities, 8*(4), 407–424.

Brekhus, W. (1998, March). A sociology of the unmarked: Redirecting our focus. *Sociological Theory, 16*(1), 34–51.

Brannon, T. (2011). Media representations of Michelle Obama. *UCLA Center for the Study of Women*. Retrieved from http://escholarship.org/uc/item/1kg651b3

Brenner, A. (2013). Resisting simple dichotomies: Critiquing narratives of victims, perpetrators, and harm in feminist theories of rape. *Harvard Journal of Law & Gender, 36*(2), 503–568.

Briceño, R. (1998). Reclaiming women's human rights. In N. Stromquist (Ed.), *Women in the Third World* (pp. 49–58). New York, NY: Garland.

Bridgeman, B., Dugan, A., Lal, M., Osborne, M., & Villones, S. (2012, May). Accounting for household production in the national accounts, 1965–2010. *Survey of Current Business, 92*(5), pp. 23–36. Retrieved from http://www.bea.gov/scb/pdf/2012/05%20May/0512_household.pdf

Brotto, L. A. (2010). The DSM diagnostic criteria for sexual aversion disorder. *Archives of Sexual Behavior, 39*(2), 271–277.

Brown, H. (2012, September 17). "Obesity paradox," thinner may mean sicker. *The New York Times,* Retrieved from http://www.nytimes.com/2012/09/18/health/research/more-data-suggests-fitness-matters-more-than-weight.html

Brown, M. (2003). Advocates in the age of jazz: Women and the campaign for the Dyer anti-lynching bill. *Peace & Change, 28*(3), 378–419.

Brownmiller, S. (1975). *Against our will: Men, women and rape.* New York, NY: Simon & Schuster.

Brundage, W. (1997). *Under sentence of death: Lynching in the South.* Chapel Hill, NC: University of North Carolina Press.

Bruyneel, K. (2002). *Ambivalent Americans: Indigenous people and U.S. citizenship in the early 20th century.* Conference Papers—American Political Science Association, 1–40.

Bryden, D. P., & Grier, M. M. (2011). The search for rapists' "real" motives. *Journal of Criminal Law & Criminology, 101*(1), 171–278.

Brydum, S. (2013, February 28). Advocacy Orgs. Applaud house passage of LGBT-inclusive Violence Against Women Act. *Advocate.* Retrieved from http://www.advocate.com/politics/2013/02/28/advocacy-orgs-applaud-house-passage-lgbt-inclusive-violence-against-women-act

Buchanan, P. D. (2011). *Radical feminists: A guide to an American subculture.* Santa Barbara, CA: ABC-CLIO.

Buchenau, J. (1998). Guadalupe Hidalgo, treaty of. In *Encyclopedia of Mexico: History, society & culture.* London, United Kingdom: Routledge. Retrieved from http://ezproxy.sunyrockland.edu:2048/login?qurl=http%3A%2F%2Fezproxy.sunyrockland.edu%3A3959%2Fcotent%2Fentry%2Froutmex%2Fguadalupe_hidalgo_treaty_of%2F0

Budig, M., & England, P. (2001). The wage penalty for motherhood. *American Sociological Review, 66,* 204–225.

Bullock, H. E. (1995). Class acts: Middle-class responses to the poor. In B. Lott & D. Maluso (Eds.), *The social psychology of interpersonal discrimination* (pp. 118–159). New York, NY: Guilford.

Bunch, C., & Fried, S. (1996). Beijing 95: Moving women's human rights from margin to center. *Signs, 22*(1), 200–204.

Bunting, L. (2007). Dealing with a problem that doesn't exist? Professional responses to female perpetrated child sexual abuse. *Child Abuse Review, 16*(4), 252–267.

Bunting, M. (2011, April 28). Sweatshops are still supplying high street brands. *The Guardian.* Retrieved from http://www.theguardian.com/global-development/poverty-matters/2011/apr/28/sweatshops-supplying-high-street-brands

Burgard, D. (2009). What is "Health at Every Size?" In E. Rothblum & S. Solovay (Eds.), *The fat studies reader* (pp. 42–53). New York, NY: New York University Press.

Burgess, N. (1994). Gender roles revisited: The development of the "woman's place" among African American women in the United States. *Journal of Black Studies, 24*(4), 391–401.

Butler, J. (1990/1999). *Gender trouble: Feminism and the subversion of identity.* New York, NY: Routledge.

Butler, J. (2006). Undiagnosing gender. In P. Currah, R. M. Juang, & S. P. Minter (Eds.), *Transgender rights* (pp. 274–298). Minneapolis, MN: University of Minnesota Press.

Butler, J., & Gillis, M. (1997). *When we are all strong together.* Louisville, KY: Presbyterian Peacemaking Program.

Butrica, J. L. (2005). Some myths and anomalies in the study of Roman sexuality. *Journal of Homosexuality, 49*(3/4), 209–269.

Caetano, R., Ramisetty-Mikler, S., & Field, C. A. (2005). Unidirectional and Bidirectional intimate partner violence among white, Black, and Hispanic couples in the United States. *Violence & Victims, 20*(4), 393–406.

Campbell, D. A. (Trans.). (1982). *Greek lyric* (Vol. 1, pp. 79–81). Cambridge, MA: Harvard University Press.

Campos, P., Saguy, A., Ernsberger, P, Oliver, E., & Gaesser, G. (2006). The epidemiology of overweight and obesity: Public health crisis or moral panic? *International Journal of Epidemiology, 35,* 55–60.

Canary, D., & Hause, K. S. (1993). Is there any reason to research sex differences in communication? *Communication Quarterly, 41*(2), 129–144.

Capaldi, D. M., Knoble, N. B., Shortt, J., & Kim, H. K. (2012). A systematic review of risk factors for intimate partner violence. *Partner Abuse, 3*(2), 231–280.

Carmichael, S. (1966, October). Black Power address at U.C. Berkeley. *Americanrhetoric.com*. Retrieved from http://www.americanrhetoric.com/speeches/stokely carmichaelblackpower.html

Carrillo, H. (2002). *The night is young: Sexuality in Mexico in the time of AIDS*. Chicago, IL: University of Chicago Press.

Carter, D. (2009). What made Stonewall different. *Gay & Lesbian Review Worldwide, 16*(4), 11–13.

Carter, D. (2010). *Stonewall: The riots that sparked the gay revolution*. New York, NY: St. Martin's Griffin.

Carvalho, A., Lewis, R., Derlega, V., Winstead, B., & Viggiano, C. (2011). Internalized sexual minority stressors and same-sex intimate partner violence. *Journal of Family Violence, 26*(7), 501–509.

Cashmore, E. (Ed.). (2003). Beauty. *Encyclopedia of race and ethnic studies* (pp. 50–51). Florence, KY: Routledge.

Casselman, B. (2014). Race gap narrows in college enrollment but not in graduation. *Fivethirtyeight.com*. Retrieved from http://fivethirtyeight.com/features/race-gap -narrows-in-college-enrollment-but-not-in-graduation/

Castillo, L. G., Perez, F. V., Castillo, R., & Ghosheh, M. R. (2010). Construction and initial validation of the Marianismo Beliefs Scale. *Counselling Psychology Quarterly, 23*(2), 163–175.

Castle, S. (2012, September 18). Proposed quota for women in boardrooms is at risk. *The New York Times,* p. B4.

Catalyst. (2007). The double-bind dilemma for women in leadership: Damned if you do, doomed if you don't. Retrieved from http://www.catalyst.org/knowledge/double-bind -dilemma-women-leadership-damned-if-you-do -doomed-if-you-don%E2%80%99t-0

Catalyst (2013, December 10). 2013 Catalyst census: *Fortune 500* women board directors. Retrieved from http://www .catalyst.org/knowledge/2013-catalyst-census-fortune -500-women-board-directors

Catalyst (2014, November 7). Women CEOs of the Fortune 1000. Retrieved from http://www.catalyst.org/knowledge/ women-ceos-fortune-1000

Catalyst. (2016). Womens CEOs of the S&P 500. *Catalyst*. Retrieved from http://www.catalyst.org/knowledge/women -ceos-sp-500

Center for Reproductive Rights. (2013). The world's abortion laws map 2013 update. Retrieved from http://www .reproductiverights.org/sites/crr.civicactions.net/files/ documents/AbortionMap_Factsheet_2013.pdf

Césaire, A. (1955/2000). *Discourse on colonialism* (J. Pinkham, Trans.). New York, NY: Monthly Review Press.

Cha-Jua, S. K. (2008). Black audiences, blaxploitation and kung fu. In P. Fu (Ed.), *China forever: The Shaw brothers and diasporic cinema* (pp. 199–223). Chicago, IL: University of Illinois Press.

Chan, J. (2000, April). Bruce Lee's fictional models of masculinity. *Men and Masculinities, 2*(4), 371–387.

Chang, K. (2012, September 25). Bias persists for women of science, a study finds. *The New York Times*, D1, D6.

Chapleau, K., & Oswald, D. (2010). Power, sex, and rape myth acceptance: Testing two models of rape proclivity. *Journal of Sex Research, 47*(1), 66–78.

Chare, N. (2009). Sexing the canvas: Calling on the medium. *Art History, 32*(4), 664–689.

Charlie's Angels. (2009). In A. Room & E. Brewer (Eds.), *Brewer's dictionary of modern phrase and fable*. London, United Kingdom: Cassell.

Chavez, L. R. (2013). *The Latino threat: Constructing immigrants, citizens, and the nation*. Stanford, CA: Stanford University Press.

Chávez, M. (2010). We have a long, beautiful history: Chicana feminist trajectories and legacies. In N. A. Hewitt (Ed.), *No permanent waves: Recasting histories of U.S. feminism* (pp. 77–97). New Brunswick, NJ: Rutgers University Press.

Chenoune, F. (1993). *A history of men's fashion*. Paris, France: Flammarion.

Chinese, Mandarin. (2015). *Ethnologue.com*. Retrieved from http://www.ethnologue.com/language/cmn

Cho, S., Crenshaw, K., & McCall, L. (2013). Toward a field of intersectionality studies: Theory, applications, and praxis. *Signs, 38*(4), 785–810.

Choo, H. Y., & Ferree, M. M. (2010). Practicing intersectionality in sociological research: A critical analysis of inclusions, interactions, and institutions in the study of inequalities. *Sociological Theory, 28*(2), 129–149.

Chu, T., & Kwan, V. Y. (2007). Effect of collectivistic cultural imperatives on Asian American meta-stereotypes. *Asian Journal of Social Psychology, 10*(4), 270–276.

Chyten-Brennan, J. (2014). Surgical transition. In L. Erickson-Schroth (Ed.), *Trans bodies, trans selves: A resource for the transgender community* (pp. 265–290). New York, NY: Oxford University Press.

Cixous, H. (1975/1980). Sorties. In E. Marks & I. deCourtivron (Eds.), *New French feminisms* (pp. 90–98). New York, NY: Shocken Books.

Clarke, J. R. (2005). Representations of the Cinaedus in Roman art: Evidence of "gay" subculture? *Journal of Homosexuality, 49*(3/4), 271–298.

Clifford, S. (2011, August 4). Even marked up, luxury goods fly off shelves. *The New York Times*, A1, A3.

Coad, D. (2008). *The metrosexual: Gender, sexuality and sport.* Albany, NY: SUNY Press.

Coalition of Immokalee Workers. (2013). Anti-slavery campaign. Retrieved from http://ciw-online.org/slavery/

Cobble, D. S. (2003). Halving the double day. *New Labor Forum, 12*(3), 62–72.

Cobble, D. S. (2010). The long history of women's freedom struggles. In K. Laughlin, J. Gallagher, D. Cobble, & E. Boris (Eds.), Is it time to jump ship? Historians rethink the waves metaphor. *Feminist Formations, 22*(1), 86–90.

Cock, J. (2003). Engendering gay and lesbian rights: The equality clause in the South African constitution. *Women's Studies International Forum, 26*(1), 35–45.

Cohen, P. (2012a, March). What if women were in charge? In *Gender revolution symposium.* Symposium conducted online by the Council on Contemporary Families. Retrieved from https://contemporaryfamilies.org/gender-revolution-symposium/

Cohen, P. (2012b, April 5). Black is not a color. *Family Inequality.* Retrieved from https://familyinequality.wordpress.com/2012/04/05/black-is-not-a-color/

Cohen, P. (2012c, June 25). Do Asians in the U.S. have high incomes? *Family Inequality.* Retrieved from https://familyinequality.wordpress.com/2012/06/25/do-asians-in-the-u-s-have-high-incomes/

Cohen, P. (2015, 15 September). Lifetime chance of marrying for Black and white women. *Family Inequality.* Retrieved from https://familyinequality.wordpress.com/

Cokal, S. (2000). Supermodels. In T. Pendergast & S. Pendergast (Eds.), *St. James encyclopedia of popular culture.* Detroit, MI: St. James Press.

Cole, S. (2008). Butch queens in macho drag: Gay men, dress, and subcultural identity. In A. Reilly & S. Cosbey (Eds.), *The men's fashion reader* (pp. 279–294). New York, NY: Fairchild Books.

Collins, P. H. (1990/2002). *Black feminist thought: Knowledge, consciousness and the politics of empowerment* (2nd ed.). New York, NY: Routledge.

Combahee River Collective. (1977/2013). A Black feminist statement. In C. R. McCann & S-K. Kim (Eds.), *Feminist theory reader: Local and global perspectives* (pp. 116–122). New York, NY: Routledge.

Combahee River Collective. (2009). In *Encyclopedia of African-American writing.* Retrieved from http://ezproxy.sunyrockland.edu:2048/login?qurl=http%3A%2F%2Fsearch.credoreference.com%2Fcontent%2Fentry%2Fghaaw%2Fcombahee_river_collective_crc%2F0

Connell, R. W. (1987). *Gender and power: Society, the person and sexual politics.* Stanford, CA: Stanford University Press.

Connell, R. W., & Messerschmidt, J. W. (2005). Hegemonic masculinity: Rethinking the concept. *Gender & Society, 19*(6), 829–859.

Coontz, S. (2013a, February 17). Why gender equality stalled. *The New York Times,* pp. SR1, SR7.

Coontz, S. (2013b, June 8). Progress at work, but mothers still pay a price. *The New York Times,* Retrieved at http://www.nytimes.com/2013/06/09/opinion/sunday/coontz-richer-childless-women-are-making-the-gains.html

Corbett, C., & Hill, C. (2012). Graduating to a pay gap: The earnings of women and men one year after college graduation. *American Association of University Women.* Retrieved from http://www.aauw.org/files/2013/02/graduating-to-a-pay-gap-the-earnings-of-women-and-men-one-year-after-college-graduation.pdf

Corbett, P. B. (2009, June 9) Hispanic Latino or what. *The New York Times,* Retrieved from http://afterdeadline.blogs.nytimes.com/2009/06/09/hispanic-latino-or-what/

Correll, S., Benard, S., & Paik, I. (2007). Getting a job: Is there a motherhood penalty? *American Journal of Sociology, 112*(5), 1297–1339. Retrieved from http://www.jstor.org/stable/10.1086/511799

Cortese, A. J. (2007). *Provocateur: Images of women and minorities in advertising* (3rd ed.). Blue Ridge Summit, PA: Rowman & Littlefield.

Cosbey, S. (2008). Something borrowed: Masculine style in women's fashion. In A. Reilly & S. Cosbey (Eds.), *The men's fashion reader.* New York, NY: Fairchild Books.

Cott, N. F. (1987). *The grounding of modern feminism.* New Haven, CT: Yale University Press.

Cotter, D., Hermsen, J., Vanneman, R. (2012, March). Is the gender revolution over? In *Gender revolution symposium.* Symposium conducted online by the Council on Contemporary Families. Retrieved from https://contemporaryfamilies.org/gender-revolution-symposium/

Cottingham, J. (1995). Descartes, René. In T. Honderich (Ed.), *Oxford companion to philosophy* (p. 583). New York, NY: Oxford University Press.

CounterQuo. (2011). The prevalence of rape in the United States. Retrieved from http://www.icasa.org/docs/misc/cq%20rape%20stats%2012-11%20final.pdf

Craig, M. L. (2002). *Ain't I a beauty queen? Black women, beauty and the politics of race.* New York, NY: Oxford University Press.

Crawford, M., & Popp, D. (2003). Sexual double standards: A review and methodological critique of two decades of research. *Journal of Sex Research, 40*(1), 13–26.

Crawford, V., Rouse, J., & Woods, B. (Eds.). (1990). *Women in the civil rights movement: Trailblazers and torchbearers, 1941–1965.* Bloomington, IN: Indiana University Press.

Crenshaw, K. (1989). Demarginalizing the intersection of race and sex: A Black feminist critique of antidiscrimination doctrine, feminist theory and antiracist politics. *The University of Chicago Legal Forum, 140*, 139–167.

Crenshaw, K. (1991, July). Mapping the margins: Intersectionality, identity politics, and violence against women of color. *Stanford Law Review, 43*(6), 1241–1299.

Crenshaw, K., & Ritchie, A. (2015). Say her name: Resisting police brutality against Black women. *African American Policy Forum*. Retrieved from http://www.aapf.org/sayhernamereport/

Crompton, L. (2003). *Homosexuality & civilization.* Cambridge, MA: Belknap Press/Harvard University Press.

Cuauhtémoc. (2005). In *The crystal reference encyclopedia.* Retrieved from http://ezproxy.sunyrockland.edu:2048/login?qurl=http%3A%2F%2Fsearch.credoreference.com%2Fcontent%2Fentry%2Fcre%2Fcuauht%25C3%25A9moc_c_1495_1525%2F0

Cullen-DuPont, K. (2000). Women of All Red Nations (WARN). In *Encyclopedia of women's history in America* (p. 277). New York, NY: Facts on File.

Currah, P. (2006). Gender pluralisms under the transgender umbrella. In P. Currah, R. M. Juang, & S. P. Minter (Eds.), *Transgender rights* (pp. 3–31). Minneapolis, MN: University of Minnesota Press.

Daly, M. (1978/1990). *Gyn/ecology: The metaethics of radical feminism.* Boston, MA: Beacon Press.

Dane, S. K., & MacDonald, G. (2009). Heterosexuals' acceptance predicts the well-being of same-sex attracted young adults beyond ingroup support. *Journal of Social and Personal Relationships, 26*(5), 659–677.

Daniels, K., Mosher, W. D., & Jones, J. (2013, February 14). Contraceptive methods women have ever used: United States, 1982–2000. *National Health Statistics Reports, 62.* Hyattsville, MD: National Center for Health Statistics.

Dardenne, B., Dumont, M., & Bollier, T. (2007). Insidious dangers of benevolent sexism: consequences for women's performance. *Journal of Personality and Social Psychology, 93*(5), 764–779.

David Agbodji: Model profile (n.d.). *New York Magazine.* Retrieved from http://nymag.com/fashion/models/dabodji/davidagbodji/

Davis, A. (1981/2003). Racism, birth control and reproductive rights. In R. Lewis & S. Mills (Eds.), *Feminist postcolonial theory: A reader* (pp. 353–367). New York, NY: Routledge.

Davison, H. K., & Burke, M. J. (2000). Sex discrimination in simulated employment contexts: A meta-analytic investigation. *Journal of Vocational Behavior, 56*, 225–248.

de Beauvoir, S. (1949/1989). *The second sex.* New York, NY: Vintage Books/Random House.

de Saussure, F. (1916/1966). C. Bally & A. Sechehaye in collaboration with A. Riedlinger (Eds.), *Course in general linguistics.* New York, NY: McGraw-Hill.

de Saussure, F. (1916/1998). *Course in general linguistics.* Chicago, IL: Open Court.

Delaney, L. (2014). Trans*missions. *Empty Closet, 474*, 24.

DeMello, M. (2007). *Encyclopedia of body adornment.* Westport, CT: Greenwood Press.

DeNavas-Walt, C., & Proctor, B. (2014, September). Income and poverty in the United States: 2013. *U. S. Census Bureau.* Retrieved from http://www.census.gov/content/dam/Census/library/publications/2014/demo/p60-249.pdf

Denny, D. (2006). Transgender communities of the United States in the late twentieth century. In P. Currah, R. M. Juang, & S. P. Minter (Eds.), *Transgender rights* (pp. 171–191). Minneapolis, MN: University of Minnesota Press.

Denny, D. (2007). Transgendered youth at risk for exploitation, HIV, hate crimes. Retrieved from http://dallasdenny.com/Writing/2011/11/05/transgendered-youth-at-risk-for-exploitation-hiv-hate-crimes-2003/

Descartes, René. (2012). In *Britannica concise encyclopedia.* Retrieved from http://ezproxy.sunyrockland.edu:2048/login?qurl=http%3A%2F%2Fezproxy.sunyrockland.edu%3A3959%2Fcontent%2Fentry%2Febconcise%2Fdescartes_rene%2F0

Desmarais, S., Reeves, K., Nicholls, T., Telford, R., & Fiebert, M. (2012). Prevalence of physical violence in intimate relationships, Part I: Rates of male and female victimization. *Partner abuse, suppl. The Partner abuse state of knowledge project: Part I, 3*(2), 140–169.

Desmond, M. (2009). Bottoms up. *Contexts, 8*(1), 69–71.

Devor, H. (1992). Becoming members of society: Learning the social meanings of gender. In M. Schaum & C. Flanagan (Eds.), *Gender images* (pp. 23–33). Boston, MA: Houghton Mifflin.

Dey, J. G., & Hill, C. (2007). Behind the Pay Gap. *American Association of University Women.* Retrieved from https://www.aauw.org/files/2013/02/Behind-the-Pay-Gap.pdf

Diamond, M., & Sigmundson, H. K. (2009). Management of intersexuality: Guidelines for dealing with individuals with ambiguous genitalia. *Pacific Center for Sex and Society.* Retrieved from http://www.hawaii.edu/PCSS/biblio/articles/1961to1999/1997-management-of-intersexuality.html

Dibb, M. (Producer & Director). Berger, J. (Writer). (1972). *Ways of seeing.* Episode 2. United Kingdom: BBC.

Dirlik, A. (1994). The postcolonial aura: Third World criticism in the age of global capitalism. *Critical Inquiry, 20*(2), 328–356.

Disability. (2009). In D. Gregory (Ed.), *The dictionary of human geography.* Oxford, United Kingdom: Blackwell. Retrieved from http://ezproxy.sunyrockland.edu:2048/login?qurl=http%3A%2F%2Fezproxy.sunyrockland.edu%3A2103%2Fcontent%2Fentry%2Fbkhumgeo%2Fdisability%2F0

Domhoff, G. W. (2013). Wealth, income, and power. *Who rules America?* Retrieved from http://www2.ucsc.edu/whorulesamerica/power/wealth.html

Dominguez, E., Icaza, R., Quintero, C., López, S., & Stenman, A. (2010). Women workers in the maquiladoras and the debate on global labor standards. *Feminist Economics, 16*(4), 185–209.

Don't ask, don't tell: Policy perspectives on the military ban. (2014). In C. Rimmerman (Ed.), *The lesbian and gay movements.* New York, NY: Westview Press.

Douglass, F. (1892/2001). Life and times of Frederick Douglass written by himself. Retrieved from http://docsouth.unc.edu/neh/dougl92/dougl92.html

Dow, B. J. (1991). The "womanhood" rationale in the woman suffrage rhetoric of Frances E. Willard. *Southern Communication Journal, 56*(4), 298–307.

Dowley, E. (2011). Early childhood in the shipyards. In A. Gordon & K. Browne (Eds.), *Beginnings and beyond: Foundations in early childhood education* (8th ed., pp. 68–70). Wadsworth Cengage Learning.

Downs, K. (2008). Mirrored archetypes. *Western Folklore, 67*(4), 397–414.

Dube, A. (2013, November 30). The minimum we can do. *The New York Times,* Retrieved from http://opinionator.blogs.nytimes.com/2013/11/30/the-minimum-we-can-do/

Dublin, T. (1975). Women, work and protest in the early Lowell Mills: "The oppressing hand of avarice would enslave us." *Labor History, 16,* 99–116.

Dugger, C. (2011, October 15). Senegal curbs a bloody rite for girls and women. *The New York Times,* Retrieved from http://www.nytimes.com/2011/10/16/world/africa/movement-to-end-genital-cutting-spreads-in-senegal.html

Dugger, K. (1991). Social location and gender-role attitudes: A comparison of Black and white women. In J. Lorber & S. Farrel (Eds.), *The social construction of gender* (pp. 38–59). Newbury Park, CA: Sage.

Dunn, K., & Farnsworth, M. (2012). "We are the revolution": Riot Grrrl Press, girl empowerment, and diy self-publishing. *Women's Studies, 41*(2), 136–157.

Dutton, D. (2006). *Rethinking domestic violence.* Toronto, Canada: UBC Press.

Eagly, A., & Carli, L. (2007). Women and the labyrinth of leadership. *Harvard Business Review, 85*(9) 62–71.

Eaklor, V. (2008). *Queer America: A GLBT history of the 20th century.* Westport, CT: Greenwood Press.

Earp, B. D. (2012). The extinction of masculine generics. *Journal for Communication & Culture, 2*(1), 4–19.

Eastman, Crystal. (2001). In *Encyclopedia of women social reformers.* Retrieved from http://ezproxy.sunyrockland.edu:2048/login?qurl=http%3A%2F%2Fezproxy.sunyrockland.edu%3A3959%2Fcontent%2Fentry%2Fabcwsr%2Feastman_crystal%2F0

Eastman, Crystal. (2014). In *The reader's companion to American history.* Boston, MA: Houghton Mifflin. Retrieved from http://ezproxy.sunyrockland.edu:2048/login?qurl=http%3A%2F%2Fsearch.credoreference.com%2Fcontent%2Fentry%2Frcah%2Feastman_crystal%2F0

Eckert, P. (2011). Gender and sociolinguistic variation. In J. Coates & P. Pichler (Eds.). *Language and gender: A reader* (pp. 57–66). Malden, MA: Wiley–Blackwell.

Eckert, P. (2012). Three waves of variation study: The emergence of meaning in the study of sociolinguistic variation. *Annual Review of Anthropology, 41,* 87–100.

Eckert, P., & McConnell-Ginet, S. (2011). Communities of practice: Where language, gender and power all live. In J. Coates & P. Pichler (Eds.), *Language and gender: A reader* (pp. 573–582). Malden, MA: Wiley–Blackwell.

Edin, K., & Nelson, T. J. (2014). *Doing the best I can: Fatherhood in the inner city.* Berkeley, CA: University of California Press.

Ehrenreich, B., & Fuentes, A. (1984). Life on the global assembly line. *Ms. Magazine.* Retrieved from http://www.msmagazine.com/spring2002/ehrenreichandfuentes.asp

Eichelberger, E. (2014, March 13). You thought it was tough being gay in Uganda. "It's hell in Nigeria." *Mother Jones.* Retrieved from http://www.motherjones.com/politics/2014/03/nigeria-anti-gay-law-hiv

Eig, J. (2014). *The birth of the pill: How four crusaders reinvented sex and launched a revolution.* New York, NY: Norton.

Eisenstein, Z. (1998). Liberalism. In *The reader's companion to U.S. women's history.* Retrieved from http://ezproxy.sunyrockland.edu:2048/login?qurl=http%3A%2F%2Fsearch.credoreference.com%2Fcontent%2Fentry%2Frcuswh%2Fliberalism%2F0

Eisikovits, E. (2011). Girl-talk/boy-talk: Sex differences in adolescent speech. In J. Coates & P. Pichler (Eds.). *Language and gender: A reader* (pp. 38–48). Malden, MA: Wiley–Blackwell.

Elborgh-Woytek, K., Newiak, M., Kochhar, K., Fabrizio, S., Kpodar, K., Wingender, P., . . . Schwartz, G. (2013). Women, work, and the economy: Macroeconomic Gains from gender equity. *International Monetary Fund*. Retrieved from https://www.imf.org/external/pubs/ft/sdn/2013/sdn1310.pdf

Elizabeth, A. (2013). Challenging the binary: Sexual identity that is not duality. *Journal of Bisexuality, 13*(3), 329–337.

Elster, J. (1988). *An introduction to Karl Marx*. New York, NY: Cambridge University Press.

Emmett, B. (2009, March). Paying the price for the economic crisis. Oxfam International. Retrieved from http://oxfam.org

Engels, F. (1884/1993). Origin of the family, private property, and the state. In A. M. Jaggar & P. S. Rothenberg (Eds.), *Feminist frameworks: Alternative theoretical accounts of the relations between women and men* (pp. 160–170). New York, NY: McGraw-Hill.

English. (2015). *Ethnologue.com*. Retrieved from https://www.ethnologue.com/language/eng

Epprecht, M. (2005). "Hidden" histories of African homosexualities. *Canadian Woman Studies, 24*(2/3), 138–144.

Epprecht, M. (2008). *Heterosexual Africa? The history of an idea from the age of exploration to the age of AIDS*. Athens, OH: Ohio University Press.

Equal Rights Amendment. (2013). In R. Chapman & J. Ciment (Eds.), *Culture wars in America: An encyclopedia of issues, viewpoints, and voices*. Retrieved from http://ezproxy.sunyrockland.edu:2048/login?qurl=http%3A%2F%2Fsearch.credoreference.com%2Fcontent%2Fentry%2Fsharpecw%2Fequal_rights_amendment%2F0

Escoffier, J. (1998). *American homo: Community and perversity*. Berkeley, CA: University of California Press.

Esquivel-Santoveña, E., Lambert, T., & Hamel, J. (2013). Partner abuse worldwide. *Partner Abuse, 4*(1), 6–75.

Essence. (2004). In N. Bunnin (Ed.), *Blackwell dictionary of Western philosophy* (p. 223). Malden, MA: Blackwell.

Estes, R., & Weiner, N. (2001/2002). The commercial sexual exploitation of children in the U.S., Canada and Mexico. *University of Pennsylvania*. Retrieved from http://www.thenightministry.org/070_facts_figures/030_research_links/060_homeless_youth/CommercialSexualExploitationofChildren.pdf

Esteva, G., & Prakash, M. S. (1998). *Grassroots postmodernism: Remaking the soil of cultures*. New York, NY: Palgrave.

European Union. (n.d.). Europa. Retrieved from http://europa.eu/about-eu/countries/member-countries/

Evans-Pritchard, E. E. (1970). Sexual inversion among the Azande. *American Anthropologist, 72*, 1428–1434.

Faderman, L. (1981). *Surpassing the love of men: Romantic friendship and love between women, from the Renaissance to the present*. New York, NY: Morrow.

Faderman, L. (1993). Nineteenth-century Boston marriage as a possible lesson for today. In E. D. Rothblum & K. A. Brehony (Eds.), *Boston marriages: Romantic but asexual relationships among contemporary lesbians* (pp. 29–42). Amherst, MA: University of Massachusetts Press.

Fagan, J., & Maxwell, C. (2006).Integrative research on intimate partner violence. *Public Health Report, 121*(4), 358–359.

Faludi, S. (1991). *Backlash: The undeclared war against American women*. New York, NY: Crown.

Faludi, S. (2010, October). American Electra. *Harper's*. Retrieved from http://susanfaludi.com/americanelectra.pdf

Fanon, F. (1961). *The wretched of the earth* (C. Farrington, Trans.). New York, NY: Grove Press.

Faubion, J. D. (2006). First nations. In B. Turner (Ed.), *Cambridge dictionary of sociology*. Cambridge, United Kingdom: Cambridge University Press. Retrieved from http://ezproxy.sunyrockland.edu:2048/login?qurl=http%3A%2F%2Fezproxy.sunyrockland.edu%3A2103%2Fcontent%2Fentry%2Fcupsoc%2Ffirst_nations%2F0

Fausto-Sterling, A. (2000). The five sexes, revisited. (Cover story). *The Sciences, 40*(4), 18–23.

Feagin, J. R., & Feagin, C. B. (2011). *Racial and ethnic relations* (9th ed.). New York, NY: Prentice Hall.

Federal Bureau of Investigation. (2013). 2012 Hate crime statistics. Retrieved from http://www.fbi.gov/about-us/cjis/ucr/hate-crime/2012/topic-pages/victims/victims_final

Feliciano, S. (2013, June 19). The Riot Grrrl movement. *New York Public Library*. Retrieved from http://www.nypl.org/blog/2013/06/19/riot-grrrl-movement

Ferdman, R. (2014, July 1). The great American Hispanic wealth gap. *Washington Post*. Retrieved from http://www.washingtonpost.com/news/wonkblog/wp/2014/07/01/hispanics-make-up-more-than-16-of-the-u-s-population-but-own-less-than-2-3-of-its-wealth/

FIDM Museum. (2010, September 14). 1890s shirtwaist. *FIDM Museum & Galleries*. Retrieved from http://blog.fidmmuseum.org/museum/2010/09/1890s-shirtwaist.html

Fingerhut, A. W., Peplau, L., & Gable, S. L. (2010). Identity, minority stress and psychological well-being among gay men and lesbians. *Psychology & Sexuality, 1*(2), 101–114.

Finkel-Konigsberg, M. (2010). Homophobia. In C. S. Clauss-Ehlers (Ed.), *Encyclopedia of cross-cultural school psychology*. New York, NY: Springer Science + Business Media

Finnegan, W. (2002, April 8). Leasing the rain. *The New Yorker*. Retrieved from www.newyorker.com/magazine/2002/04/03/leasing-the-rain

Firestone, S. (1970/1972). *The dialectic of sex: The case for feminist revolution*. New York, NY: Bantam Books/Morrow.

Fleras, A., & Dixon, S. (2011). Cutting, driving, digging, and harvesting: Re-masculinizing the working-class heroic. *Canadian Journal of Communication, 36*(4), 579–597.

Flores, C. (2014). Guadalupe Hidalgo, treaty of. In S. Bronner (Ed.), *Encyclopedia of American studies*. Baltimore, MD: Johns Hopkins University Press. Retrieved from http://ezproxy.sunyrockland.edu:2048/login?qurl=http%3A%2F%2Fezproxy.sunyrockland.edu%3A2103%2Fcontent%2Fentry%2Fjhueas%2Fguadalupe_hidalgo_treaty_of%2F0

Florido, A. (2015, September 8). Mass deportation may sound unlikely, but it's happened before. *National Public Radio*. Retrieved from http://www.npr.org/sections/codeswitch/2015/09/08/437579834/mass-deportation-may-sound-unlikely-but-its-happened-before

Flowe, M. (2010). The international market for trafficking in persons for the purpose of sexual exploitation: Analyzing current treatment of supply and demand. *North Carolina Journal of International Law & Commercial Regulation, 35*(3), 669–721.

Flugel, J. C. (1930/1950). *The psychology of clothes*. London, United Kingdom: Hogarth Press.

Folbre, N. (2012, May 28). Valuing domestic product [Web log post]. Retrieved from http://economix.blogs.nytimes.com/2012/05/28/valuing-domestic-product/

Forbes 400. (2014). *Forbes.com*. Retrieved from http://www.forbes.com/forbes-400/list/#tab:women

Ford, T. C. (2013, August). SNCC women, denim, and the politics of dress. *Journal of Southern History, 89*(3), 625–658.

Foucault, M. (1971/1982). *The archeology of knowledge and the discourse on language*. New York, NY: Pantheon Books.

Foucault, M. (1976/1980). *The history of sexuality: Volume I: An introduction*. Hurley, R. (Trans.). New York, NY: Vintage Books/Random House.

Franklin, B. (1751/1936). Observations concerning the increase of mankind, peopling of countries, etc. In F. L. Mott & C. E. Jorgenson (Eds.), *Benjamin Franklin: representative selections, with introduction, bibliography and notes*. New York, NY: American Book Company. Retrieved from http://www.gutenberg.org/ebooks/35508

Frantz, S. (2003). Jane Austen's heroes and the great masculine renunciation. *Persuasions: Journal of the Jane Austen Society of North America, 25*, 165–175.

Fraser, N. (1997). *Justice interruptus: Critical reflections on the "postsocialist" condition*. New York, NY: Psychology Press.

Freedman, E. (2002). *No turning back: The history of feminism and the future of women*. New York, NY: Ballantine Books.

Freedman, E. (2013, August 25). Feminism's amazing achievement: Changing the conversation—and laws—about rape. *Salon*. Retrieved from http://www.salon.com/2013/08/25/how_feminism_redefined_rape/

Freeman, J. (1999/ n.d.). On the origins of social movements. *Jofreeman.com*. Retrieved from http://www.jofreeman.com/socialmovements/origins.htm

Freeman, J. (2012, September 2/n.d.) In memory of Shulamith Firestone. *JoFreeman.com*. Retrieved from http://www.jofreeman.com/feminism/firestone.htm

Freson, T. S., & Arthur, L. B. (2008). Fashioning men's bodies: Masculinity and muscularity. In A. Reilly & S. Cosbey (Eds.), *The men's fashion reader* (pp. 337–354). New York, NY: Fairchild Books.

Freud, S. (1916/1920). *Three contributions to the theory of sex*. A. A. Brill (Trans.). Retrieved from http://www.gutenberg.org/files/14969/14969-h/14969-h.htm

Freud, S. (1933/1994). Femininity. In C. Roman, S. Juhasz, & C. Miller (Eds.). *The women and language debate: A sourcebook* (pp. 20–36. New Brunswick, NJ: Rutgers University Press.

Friedan, B. (1963/1967). *The feminine mystique*. New York, NY: Dell.

Frye, M. (1983). *The politics of reality: Essays in feminist theory*. Berkeley, CA: Crossing Press.

Fudge, R. (2005). Everything about feminism you wanted to know but were afraid to ask. *Bitch*. Retrieved from http://bitchmagazine.org/article/everything-about-feminism-you-wanted-to-know-but-were-afraid-to-ask

Fussell, E. (2000). Making labor flexible: The recomposition of Tijuana's maquiladora female labor force. *Feminist Economics, 6*(3), 59–80.

Gailey, C. W. (1987). Evolutionary perspectives on gender hierarchy. In B. B. Hess & M. M. Ferree (Eds.), *Analyzing gender: A handbook of social science research* (pp. 32–67). Newbury Park, CA: Sage.

Gallagher, J. (2010). Revisiting constructs and their tyrannical inclinations. In K. Laughlin, J. Gallagher, D. Cobble, & E. Boris (Eds.), Is it time to jump ship? Historians rethink the waves metaphor. *Feminist Formations, 22*(1), 81–86.

Gallup. (2014, May 8–11). Gay and lesbian rights. Retrieved from http://www.gallup.com/poll/1651/gay-lesbian-rights.aspx

Galupo, M. P., Mitchell, R. C., Grynkiewicz, A. L., & Davis, K. S. (2014). Sexual minority reflections on the Kinsey Scale and the Klein Sexual Orientation Grid: Conceptualization and measurement. *Journal of Bisexuality, 14*(3–4), 404–432.

Garcia, A. M. (1973/1997). Introduction to Encuentro Femenil. In A. M. Garcia (Ed.), *Chicana feminist thought: The basic historical writings* (pp. 113–116). New York, NY: Routledge.

Garcia-Moreno, C., Jansen, H., Ellsberg, M., Heise, L., & Watts, C. (2006). Prevalence of intimate partner violence:

findings from the WHO multi-country study on women's health and domestic violence. *Lancet, 368*(9543), 1260–1269.

Garland-Thomson, R. (2004). Integrating disability, transforming feminist theory. In B. G. Smith & B. Hutchison (Eds.), *Gendering disability* (pp. 73–103). Piscataway, NJ: Rutgers University Press.

Gaus, G., & Courtland, S. D. (2011, Spring). Liberalism. In E. N. Zalta (Ed.), *The Stanford encyclopedia of philosophy.* Retrieved from http://plato.stanford.edu/archives/spr2011/entries/liberalism/

Gay. (2005). In *The American Heritage guide to contemporary usage and style.* Boston, MA: Houghton Mifflin. Retrieved from http://ezproxy.sunyrockland.edu:2048/login?qurl=http%3A%2F%2Fsearch.credoreference.com%2Fcontent%2Fentry%2Fhmcontempusage%2Fgay%2F0

Gay, J. (1986). "Mummies and babies" and friends and lovers in Lesotho. *Journal of Homosexuality, 11*(3-4), 97–116.

Gbowee, L. (2011). Nobel lecture. *Nobelprize.org.* Retrieved from http://www.nobelprize.org/nobel_prizes/peace/laureates/2011/gbowee-lecture_en.html

Gibbs, N. (2010, April 22). The pill at 50: Sex, freedom and paradox. *Time.* Retrieved from http://content.time.com/time/magazine/article/0,9171,1983884,00.html

Gilbert, J. (2013). What kind of thing is "neoliberalism"? *New Formations, 80/81,* 7–22.

Gilbert, M. A. (2009). Defeating bigenderism. *Hypatia, 24*(3), 93–112.

Gilley, J. (2005). Writings of the third wave. *The Alert Collector, 44*(3), 187–198.

Gilligan, C. (1982). *In a different voice: Psychological theory and women's development.* Cambridge, MA: Harvard University Press.

Ginzberg, L. (2002). Re-viewing the first wave. *Feminist Studies, 28*(2), 418–434.

GLAAD. (2015). GLAAD media reference guide—Transgender issues. *Glaad.org.* Retrieved from http://www.glaad.org/reference/transgender

Glauber, R. (2007). Marriage and the motherhood wage penalty among African Americans, Hispanics, and whites. *Journal of Marriage and Family, 69*(4), 951–961.

Glauber, R. (2008). Race and gender in families and at work: The fatherhood wage premium. *Gender and Society, 22*(1), 8–30.

Glenn, E. N. (2009). Consuming lightness: Segmented markets and global capital in the skin-whitening trade. In E. N. Glenn (Ed.), *Shades of difference: Why skin color matters* (pp. 166–187). Stanford, CA: Stanford University Press.

Glick, P., & Fiske, S. T. (1996). The ambivalent sexism inventory: Differentiating hostile and benevolent sexism. *Journal of Personality and Social Psychology, 70*(3), 491–512.

Glick, P., Fiske, S. T., Mladinic, A., Saiz, J. L., Abrams, D., Masser, B., & López, W. (2000). Beyond prejudice as simple antipathy: Hostile and benevolent sexism across cultures. *Journal of Personality and Social Psychology, 79,* 763–775.

Godayol, P. (2012). Malintzin/La Malinche/Doña Marina: Re-reading the myth of the treacherous translator. *Journal of Iberian & Latin American Studies, 18*(1), 61–76.

Gonel, A. H. (2013, February). Pansexual identification in online communities: Employing a collaborative queer method to study pansexuality. *Graduate Journal of Social Science, 10*(1), 36–59.

Gornick, J., & Meyers, M. (2003). Supports for working families: Work and care policies across welfare states. *Munich Society for the Promotion of Economic Research.* Retrieved from http://www.cesifo.de/pls/guestci/download/CESifo%20DICE%20Report%202003/CESifo%20DICE%20Report%204/2003/dicereport4-03-forum-3.pdf

Goss, V. (2005). *The movements of the New Left, 1950–1975: A brief history with documents.* New York, NY: Bedford/St. Martin's.

Gould, L. (1992). X: A fabulous child's story. In M. Schaum & C. Flanagan (Eds.), *Gender images: Readings for composition* (pp. 9–16). Boston, MA: Houghton Mifflin.

Graeco-Roman heritage, the. (2005). In *Chambers dictionary of world history.* Retrieved from http://ezproxy.sunyrockland.edu:2048/login?qurl=http%3A%2F%2Fezproxy.sunyrockland.edu%3A3959%2Fcontent%2Fentry%2Fchambdictwh%2Fgraeco_roman_heritage_the%2F0

Graff, E. J. (1993, October 17). The double bed principle. Hers column. *New York Times Magazine,* 14, 16.

Graham, S. (2004). It's like one of those puzzles: Conceptualizing gender among Bugis. *Journal of Gender Studies, 13*(2), 107–116.

Green, L. (2000). Pornographies. *The Journal of Political Philosophy, 8*(1), 27–52.

Greenberg, C. (2010). Liberalism. In *Encyclopedia of American studies.* Retrieved from http://ezproxy.sunyrockland.edu:2048/login?qurl=http%3A%2F%2Fsearch.credoreference.com%2Fcontent%2Fentry%2Fjhueas%2Fliberalism%2F0

Greenhouse, S. (2014a, September 4). Hundreds of fast-food workers striking for higher wages are arrested. *The New York Times,* Retrieved from http://www.nytimes.com/2014/09/05/business/economy/fast-food-workers-seeking-higher-wages-are-arrested-during-sit-ins.html

Greenhouse, S. (2014b, September 17). Report cites forced labor in Malaysia's electronics industry. *The New York Times,* Retrieved from http://www.nytimes.com/2014/09/17/business/international/report-cites-forced-labor-in-malaysia.html?_r=0

Greenhouse, S. (2014c, November 22). The fight for $15.37 an hour. *The New York Times,* Retrieved from http://www.nytimes.com/2014/11/23/business/how-a-coalition-pushed-for-a-hotel-workers-minimum-wage.html

Greer, C. M. (2013). *Black ethnics: Race, immigration, and the pursuit of the American dream.* New York, NY: Oxford University Press.

Grewal, I., & Kaplan, C. (1997). *Scattered hegemonies: Postmodernity and transnational feminist practices.* Minneapolis, MN: University of Minnesota Press.

Grimshaw, D., & Rubery, J. (2007). Undervaluing women's work (European Opportunities Commission Working Paper Series No. 53). Retrieved from http://docplayer.net/111843-Undervaluing-women-s-work.html

Gritz, J. R. (2012). But were they gay? The mystery of same-sex love in the 19th century. *The Atlantic.* Retrieved from http://www.theatlantic.com/national/archive/2012/09/but-were-they-gay-the-mystery-of-same-sex-love-in-the-19th-century/262117/

Gross, B., van Wijk, C., & Mukherjee, N. (2001). Linking sustainability with demand, gender and poverty. Water and sanitation program. Retrieved from www.wsp.org/sites/wsp.org/files/publications/global_plareport.pdf

Grossman, J. R. (1991). *Land of hope: Chicago, Black Southerners, and the Great Migration.* Chicago, IL: University of Chicago Press.

Gruenbaum, E. (2000). *The female circumcision controversy: An anthropological perspective.* Philadelphia, PA: University of Pennsylvania Press.

Gullah. (2008). In *Africa and the Americas: Culture, politics, and history.* Retrieved from http://ezproxy.sunyrockland.edu:2048/login?qurl=http%3A%2F%2Fwww.credoreference.com/entry/abcafatrle/gullah

Gunkel, H. (2009) "What's identity got to do with it?" Rethinking intimacy and homosociality in contemporary South Africa. *NORA–Nordic Journal of Feminist and Gender Research, 17*(3), 206–221.

Hafen, S. (2004) Lesbian history and the politics of identities. In M. Fong & R. Chuang (Eds.), *Communicating ethnic and cultural identity* (pp. 179–196). New York, NY: Rowman & Littlefield.

Halberstam, J. (1998). *Female masculinity.* Durham, NC: Duke University Press.

Halberstam, J. J. (2012). *Gaga feminism: Sex, gender, and the end of normal.* Boston, MA: Beacon Press.

Hall, S. (2011). *American patriotism, American protest: Social movements since the sixties.* Philadelphia, PA: University of Pennsylvania Press.

Halperin, D. M. (2003). The normalization of queer theory. *Journal of Homosexuality, 45*(2), 339–343.

Hamel, J. (2009). Toward a gender-inclusive conception of intimate partner violence research and theory: Part 2—New directions. *International Journal of Men's Health, 8*(1), 41–59.

Hanak, I. (2009). *Language, discourse and participation: Studies in donor-driven development in Tanzania.* New Brunswick, NJ: Transaction.

Hanisch, C. (1969/2009). The personal is political: The women's liberation movement classic with a new explanatory introduction. Retrieved from http://carolhanisch.org/CHwritings/PIP.html

Hannon, L., & DeFina, R. (2014, November 7). When whites are guilty of colorism. *Washington Post.* Retrieved from https://www.washingtonpost.com/opinions/african-americans-still-face-colorism-based-on-their-skin-tone/2014/11/07/8a2ac124-607e-11e4-9f3a-7e28799e0549_story.html

Hardin, R. (2011). Liberalism. In *International encyclopedia of political science.* Retrieved from http://ezproxy.sunyrockland.edu:2048/login?qurl=http%3A%2F%2Fsearch.credoreference.com%2Fcontent%2Fentry%2Fsageieps%2Fliberalism%2F0

Harper, C. (2007). *Intersex.* New York, NY: Berg–Oxford University Press.

Harrison, C. (2003). Modernism. In R. S. Nelson & R. Shiff (Eds.), *Critical terms for art history.* Retrieved from http://ezproxy.sunyrockland.edu:2048/login?qurl=http%3A%2F%2Fsearch.credoreference.com%2Fcontent%2Fentry%2Fuchicagoah%2Fmodernism%2F0

Hartman, J. E. (2013). Creating a bisexual display: Making bisexuality visible. *Journal of Bisexuality, 13,* 39–62.

Hartmann, H. (1976, Spring). Capitalism, patriarchy, and job segregation by sex. *Signs, 1*(3), 137–169.

Hartmann, H. (1981/1993). The unhappy marriage of Marxism and feminism: Towards a more progressive union. In A. M. Jaggar & P. S. Rothenberg (Eds.), *Feminist frameworks: Alternative theoretical accounts of the relations between women and men* (pp. 191–202). New York, NY: McGraw-Hill.

Hartsock, N. C. M. (1983/2013). The feminist standpoint: Toward a specifically feminist historical materialism. In C. R. McCann & S. Kim (Eds.), *Feminist theory reader: Local and global perspectives* (3rd ed., pp. 354–369). New York, NY: Routledge.

Hate Crime—Overview. (2015). *Federal Bureau of Investigation.* Retrieved from https://www.fbi.gov/about-us/investigate/civilrights/hate_crimes/overview

Hauge, J. (2014, September 3). Africa's economic "rise" does not reflect reality. *The Guardian*. Retrieved from http://www.theguardian.com/global-development/poverty-matters/2014/sep/03/africa-economic-rise-does-not-reflect-reality

Hauter, W. (2011, March 8). America's poor and the human right to water. *Food and Water Watch*. Retrieved on 4 December 2014, from http://www.huffingtonpost.com/wenonah-hauter/americas-poor-and-the-hum_b_833614.html

Heath, M., & Mulligan, E. (2008). "Shiny happy same-sex attracted woman seeking same": How communities contribute to bisexual and lesbian women's well-being. *Health Sociology Review*, 17(3), 290–302.

Hegewisch, A., & Hartmann, H. (2014, September). The gender wage gap 2013. *Institute for Women's Policy Research*. Retrieved from http://www.iwpr.org/publications/pubs/the-gender-wage-gap-2013

Hegewisch, A., Williams, C., & Harbin, V. (2012, April). The gender wage gap by occupation (Fact Sheet IWPR #C350a). *Institute for Women's Policy Research*. Retrieved from http://www.iwpr.org/publications/pubs/the-gender-wage-gap-by-occupation-1

Hegewisch, A., Williams, C., Hartmann, H., & Hudiburg, S. (2014, March). The gender wage gap: 2013; Differences by race and ethnicity, no growth in real wages for women. Retrieved from http://www.iwpr.org/publications/pubs/the-gender-wage-gap-2013-differences-by-race-and-ethnicity-no-growth-in-real-wages-for-women

Heilman, M. E., Block, C. J., Martell, R. E., & Simon, M. C. (1998). Has anything changed? Current characterizations of men, women, and managers. *Journal of Applied Psychology*, 74, 935–942.

Heilman, M. E., & Wallen, A. S. (2010). Wimpy and undeserving of respect: Penalties for men's gender-inconsistent success. *Journal of Experimental Social Psychology*, 46, 664–667.

Hellerstein, J., & Neumark, D. (2008). Workplace segregation in the United States: Race, ethnicity, and skill. *The Review of Economics and Statistics*, 90(3), 459–477.

Henry, A. (2004). *Not my mother's sister: Generational conflict and third-wave feminism*. Indianapolis, IN: Indiana University Press.

Herdt, G. (Ed.). (1994). *Third sex, third gender: Beyond sexual dimorphism in culture and history*. New York, NY: Zone Books.

Herek, G. M. (1986). On heterosexual masculinity. *American Behavioral Scientist*, 29(5), 563.

Herek, G. M. (2002). Heterosexuals' attitudes toward bisexual men and women in the United States. *Journal of Sex Research*, 39(4), 264.

Herek, G. M. (2004). Beyond "homophobia": Thinking about sexual prejudice and stigma in the twenty-first century. *Sexuality Research & Social Policy*, 1(2), 6–24.

Herek, G. M. (2007). Confronting sexual stigma and prejudice: Theory and practice. *Journal of Social Issues*, 63(4), 905–925.

Herek, G. M. (2009a). Hate crimes and stigma-related experiences among sexuality minority adults in the United States: Prevalence estimates from a national probability sample. *Journal of Interpersonal Violence*, 24(1), 54–74.

Herek, G. M. (2009b). Sexual prejudice. In T. D. Nelson (Ed.), *Handbook of prejudice, stereotyping and discrimination* (pp. 441–468). New York, NY: Taylor & Francis.

HerStory: 1971–present. (n.d.). *Ms. Magazine*. Retrieved from http://www.msmagazine.com/about.asp

Hewlett, S. A. (2008, August 5). The glass cliff: Are women leaders often set up to fail? *Harvard Business Review*. Retrieved from https://hbr.org/2008/08/are-women-leaders-often-set-up&cm_sp=Article-_-Links-_-End%20of%20Page%20Recirculation

Hewitt, N. A. (2010). Seneca Falls to suffrage? Reimagining a "master" narrative in U.S. women's history. In N. A. Hewitt (Ed.), *No permanent waves: Recasting histories of U.S. feminism* (pp. 15–38). New Brunswick, NJ: Rutgers University Press.

Heyes, C. (2012, Spring). Identity politics. In E. N. Zalta (Ed.), *The Stanford encyclopedia of philosophy*. Retrieved from http://plato.stanford.edu/archives/spr2012/entries/identity-politics/

Heyman, R. E., Feldbau-Kohn, S. R., Ehrensaft, M. K., Langhinrichsen-Rohling, J., & O'Leary, K. (2001). Can questionnaire reports correctly classify relationship distress and partner physical abuse? *Journal of Family Psychology*, 15(2), 334–346.

Heywood, L., & Drake, J. (1997). *Third wave agenda: Being feminist, doing feminism*. Minneapolis, MN: University of Minnesota Press.

Higginbotham, E. B. (1993). *Righteous Discontent: The Women's Movement in the Black Baptist Church 1880–1920*. Cambridge, MA: Harvard University Press.

Hill, J. H. (1994). Women's speech in modern Mexicano. In S. U. Philips, S. Steele, & C. Tanz (Eds.), *Language, gender, and sex in comparative perspective* (pp. 121–162). New York, NY: Cambridge University Press.

Hill, M. E. (2002, March). Skin color and the perceptions of attractiveness among African Americans: Does gender make a difference? *Social Psychology Quarterly*, 65(1), 77–91.

Hines, D. A., & Douglas, E. M. (2010). Intimate terrorism by women towards men: Does it exist? *Journal of Aggression, Conflict and Peace Research*, 2(3), 36–56.

Hinkle, C. E., & Viloria, H. (n.d.). *10 Misconceptions about Intersex.* Organisation Intersex International. Retrieved from http://oii-usa.org/1144/ten-misconceptions-intersex/

History of Bethune–Cookman. (2014). Bethune–Cookman University. Retrieved from http://www.cookman.edu/about_BCU/history/index.html

Hobson, J. (2012, September 7). "Respectability" politics: Michelle Obama vs. Nicki Minaj [Web log post]. Retrieved from http://msmagazine.com/blog/2012/09/07/respectability-politics-michelle-obama-vs-nicki-minaj/

Holdcroft, A. (2007, January). Gender bias in research: How does it affect evidence based medicine? *Journal of the Royal Society of Medicine, 100*(1), 2–3.

hooks, b. (1984). *Feminist theory: From margin to center.* Boston, MA: South End Press.

hooks, b. (1989). *Talking back: Thinking feminist, thinking Black.* Boston, MA: South End Press.

hooks, b. (2000). *Feminism is for everybody: Passionate politics.* Cambridge, MA: South End Press.

hooks, b. (2000/2014). *Feminism is for everybody: Passionate politics.* Cambridge, MA: South End Press.

Howard-Hassman, R. (2011). Universal women's human rights since 1970: The centrality of autonomy and agency. *Journal of Human Rights, 10*, 433–449.

Hubbard, T. K. (2004). The varieties of Greek love. *Gay & Lesbian Review Worldwide, 11*(3), 11–12.

Human Rights Campaign. (2014). State hate crimes laws. Retrieved from http://hrc-assets.s3-website-us-east-1.amazonaws.com//files/assets/resources/hate_crimes_laws_022014.pdf

Human Rights Watch. (2014). Russia: Sochi Games highlight homophobic violence. Retrieved from http://www.hrw.org/news/2014/02/03/russia-sochi-games-highlight-homophobic-violence

Human Rights Watch. (2015). World report 2015: United States. Retrieved from https://www.hrw.org/world-report/2015/country-chapters/united-states

Humes, K. R., Jones, N. A., & Ramirez, R. R. (2011, March). Overview of race and Hispanic origin: 2010. *2010 Census briefs.* U.S. Census Bureau. Retrieved from http://www.census.gov/prod/cen2010/briefs/c2010br-02.pdf

Humphrey, S. E., & Kahn, A. S. (2000). Fraternities, athletic teams, and rape: Importance of identification with a risky group. *Journal of Interpersonal Violence, 15*(12), 1313–1322.

Hunter, M. L. (2005). *Race, gender and the politics of skin tone.* New York, NY: Routledge.

Intersex Society of North America. (2008a). What do doctors do now when they encounter a patient with intersex? Retrieved from http://www.isna.org/faq/standard_of_care

Intersex Society of North America. (2008b). What is intersex? Retrieved from http://www.isna.org/faq/what_is_intersex

Iragaray, L. (1977/1998). This sex which is not one. In D. H. Richter (Ed.), *The Critical tradition: Classic texts and contemporary trends* (pp. 1466–1471). Boston, MA: Bedford Books.

Jacobs, A. T. (2002). Appropriating a slur: Semantic looping in the African American usage of "Nigga." *M/C: A Journal of Media and Culture.* Retrieved from http://journal.media-culture.org.au/0208/semantic.php

Jacobs, S. E., Thomas, W., & Lang, S. (Eds.). (1997). *Two Spirit people: Native American gender identity, sexuality and spirituality.* Chicago, IL: University of Illinois Press.

Jaffe, S. (2013). Trickle down feminism. *Dissent.* Retrieved from www.dissentmagazine.org/article/trickle-down-feminism

Jaggar, A., & Rothenberg, P. S. (1993). *Feminist frameworks: Alternative theoretical accounts of the relations between women and men.* New York, NY: McGraw-Hill.

Jagose, A. (1996). *Queer theory: An introduction.* New York, NY: New York University Press.

James, H. (2010). Globalization. In S. Bronner & J. Haddad (Eds.), *Encyclopedia of American studies.* Retrieved from http://ezproxy.sunyrockland.edu:2048/login?qurl=http%3A%2F%2Fsearch.credoreference.com%2Fcontent%2Fentry%2Fjhueas%2Fglobalization%2F0

James, M. (2012, Winter). Race. In E. N. Zalta (Ed.), *The Stanford encyclopedia of philosophy.* Retrieved from http://plato.stanford.edu/archives/win2012/entries/race/

Jamieson, K. H. (1995). *Beyond the double bind: Women and leadership.* New York, NY: Oxford University Press.

Jewkes, R. (2002). Violence against women III: Intimate partner violence: Causes and prevention. *Lancet, 359*(9315), 1423–1429.

Johnson, A. G. (2004). Patriarchy, the system: An it, not a he, a them, or an us. In G. Kirk & M. Okazawa-Rey (Eds.), *Women's lives: Multicultural perspectives Third Edition* (pp. 25–32). New York, NY: McGraw-Hill.

Johnson, M. P. (1995). Patriarchal terrorism and common couple violence: Two forms of violence against women. *Journal of Marriage and the Family, 57,* 283–294.

Johnson, M. P. (2008). *A typology of domestic violence.* Boston, MA: Northeastern University Press.

Jones, E. M. (1995). One small step. Retrieved from http://www.hq.nasa.gov/alsj/a11/a11.step.html

Jones, M. H. (1925/2004). *The autobiography of Mother Jones.* Mineola, NY: Dover.

Jones, N., & Bullock, J. (2013). Understanding who reported multiple races in the U.S. Decennial Census: Results from

Census 2000 and the 2010 Census. *Family Relations, 62*(1), 5–16.

Kaminer, W. (1997, September). A civic duty to annoy. *Atlantic Monthly*, 16.

Kanter, R. (1977). *Men and women of the corporation*. New York, NY: Basic Books.

Kaplan, K. (2013). Did Neil Armstrong really say, "That's one small step for a man"? Retrieved from http://www.latimes.com/news/science/sciencenow/la-sci-sn-neil-armstrong-one-small-step-for-a-man-20150605,0,1063827.story

Karimi, F., & Thompson, N. (2014). Uganda's President Museveni signs controversial anti-gay bill into law. *CNN.com*. Retrieved from http://edition.cnn.com/2014/02/24/world/africa/uganda-anti-gay-bill/

Katz, J. N. (1997). "Homosexual" and "heterosexual:" Questioning the terms. In M. Duberman (Ed.), *A queer world: The Center for Lesbian and Gay Studies reader*. New York, NY: New York University Press.

Keating, A. (2009). Introduction. In A. Keating (Ed.), *The Gloria Anzaldúa reader* (pp. 1–18). Durham, NC: Duke University Press.

Keddie, A. (2010). Neo-liberalism and new configurations of global space: Possibilities, tensions and problematics for gender justice. *Journal of Gender Studies, 19*(2), 139–152.

Keil, A. (2010). Genital anxiety and the quest for the perfect vulva: A feminist analysis of female genital cosmetic surgery. Retrieved from http://www.anthropology.uci.edu/files/docs/2010_benedict_keil.pdf

Keiller, S. W. (2010). Masculine norms as correlates of heterosexual men's attitudes toward gay men and lesbian women. *Psychology of Men & Masculinity, 11*(1), 38–52.

Keith, V. M. (2009). A colorstruck world: Skin tone, achievement, and self-esteem among African American women. In E. N. Glenn (Ed.), *Shades of difference: Why skin color matters* (pp. 25–39). Stanford, CA: Stanford University Press.

Kidd, J. D., & Witten, T. M. (2007). Transgender and transsexual identities: The Next strange fruit-hate crimes, violence and genocide against the global trans-communities. *Journal of Hate Studies, 6*(1), 31–63.

Kiesling, S. F. (1998). Men's identities and sociolinguistic variation: The case of fraternity men. *Journal of Sociolinguistics, 2*(1), 69–99.

Kim, J. Y. (2012, July). *Evidence and impact: Closing the gender gap*. Paper presented at a U.S. State Department/Gallup event. Washington, DC.

Kimmel, M. (2013). *The gendered society* (5th ed.). Oxford, United Kingdom: Oxford University Press.

Kimmel, M. S. (2003). Consuming manhood: The feminization of American culture and the recreation of the male body,

1832–1920. In S. Ervø & T. Johansson (Eds.), *Bending bodies: Moulding masculinities* (Vol 2., pp. 47–76). Burlington, VT: Ashgate.

King, D. K. (1988). Multiple jeopardy, multiple consciousness: The context of a black feminist ideology. *Signs: Journal of Women in Culture & Society, 14*, 42–72.

Kinsey, A. C., Pomeroy, W. B., & Martin, C. E. (1948/1998). *Sexual behavior in the human male*. Bloomington, IN: Indiana University Press.

Kinsman, G. (1987/1992). Men loving men: The challenge of gay liberation. In M. Schaum & C. Flanagan (Eds.), *Gender images: Readings for composition* (pp. 84–98). Boston, MA: Houghton Mifflin.

Kite, L. & Kite, L. (2011, February 1). Beauty whitewashed: How white ideals exclude women of color [Web log post]. Retrieved from http://www.beautyredefined.net/beauty-whitewashed-how-white-ideals-exclude-women-of-color/

Kite, M. (2001). Gender stereotypes. In J. Worell (Ed.). *Encyclopedia of women and gender* (Vol. 1, pp. 560–570). New York, NY: Academic Press.

Klein, F. (1993). *The bisexual option*. New York, NY: Haworth Press.

Klinck, A. L. (2005). "Sleeping in the bosom of a tender companion": Homoerotic attachments in Sappho. *Journal of Homosexuality, 49*(3/4), 193–208.

Kluchin, R. (2009). *Fit to be tied: Sterilization and reproductive rights in America, 1950–1980*. New Brunswick, NJ: Rutgers University Press.

Kolmerton, C. (2002, Summer). Ernestine L. Rose: Freethinking rebel. *Free Inquiry, 22*(3).

Kornbluh, F. (1998). The goals of the national welfare rights movement: Why we need them thirty years later. *Feminist Studies, 24*(1), 65–78.

Koyama, E. (2003). The transfeminist manifesto. In Dicker, R. C., & Piepmeier, A. (Eds.), *Catching a wave: Reclaiming feminism for the 21st century* (pp. 244–259). Boston, MA: Northeastern University Press.

Krebs, C. P., Lindquist, C. H., Warner, T. D., Fisher, B. S., & Martin, S. L. (2007). *The Campus Sexual Assault (CSA) Study* (221153).Washington, DC: National Institute of Justice, U.S. Department of Justice.

Kristeva, J. (1974/1980). Woman can never be defined. In E. Marks & I. deCourtivron (Eds.), *New French feminisms* (pp. 137–141). New York, NY: Shocken Books.

Krogstad, J. M., & Lopez, M. H. (2014, April 29). Hispanic nativity shift. *Pew Research Center*. Retrieved from http://www.pewhispanic.org/2014/04/29/hispanic-nativity-shift/

Krugman, P. (2014, May 8). Why we're in a new gilded age. *The New York Review of Books*. Retrieved from http://www.nybooks.com/articles/archives/2014/may/08/thomas-piketty-new-gilded-age/

Kuchta, D. (2002). *The three-piece suit and modern masculinity*. Berkeley, CA: University of California Press.

La Ferla, R. (2009, November 18). It's all a blur to them. *The New York Times*, Retrieved from http://www.nytimes.com/2009/11/19/fashion/19ANDROGYNY.html?pagewanted=all&_r=0

Labov, W. (1966/2006). *The social stratification of English in New York City*. New York, NY: Cambridge University Press.

Lacey, N. (2009, June 20). "Tits out girls": but this is M&S. What's going on? Blog. Retrieved from https://wgoinmedia.wordpress.com/2009/06/20/tits-out-boys-but-this-is-ms/

Laczko, F. (2005). Introduction: Data and research on human trafficking. In Laczko, J. & Gozdziak, E. (Eds.), *Data and research on human trafficking: A global survey* (pp. 5–16). Geneva, Switzerland: International Organization for Migration. Retrieved from http://lastradainternational.org/lsidocs/282%20IOM%20survey%20trafficking%20(Global).pdf

Lakoff, R. (1975). *Language and woman's place*. New York, NY: Harper/Colophon Books.

Lalumière, M., Harris, G., Quinsey, V., & Rice, M. (2005). *The causes of rape: Understanding individual differences in male propensity for sexual aggression*. New York, NY: American Psychological Association.

Lamarche, B., Després, J. P., Pouliot, M. C., Moorjani, S., Lupien, P. J., Thériault, G., & . . . Bouchard, C. (1992). Is body fat loss a determinant factor in the improvement of carbohydrate and lipid metabolism following aerobic exercise training in obese women? *Metabolism: Clinical and Experimental, 41*(11), 1249–1256.

Lancaster, R. N. (1988). Subject honor and object shame: The construction of male homosexuality and stigma in Nicaragua. *Ethnology, 27*(2), 111–125.

Landrine, H. (1985). Race X class stereotypes of women. *Sex Roles, 13*(1-2), 65–75.

Langhinrichsen-Rohling, J. (2010). Controversies involving gender and intimate partner violence in the United States. *Sex Roles, 62*(3/4), 179–193.

Langhinrichsen-Rohling, J., Misra, T. A., Selwyn, C., & Rohling, M. L. (2012). Rates of bidirectional versus unidirectional intimate partner violence across samples, sexual orientations, and race/ethnicities: A comprehensive review. *Partner Abuse, suppl. The Partner Abuse State of Knowledge Project, Part 1, 3*(2), 199–230.

Laughlin, K. A., Gallagher, J., Cobble, D. S., & Boris, E., (2010, Spring). Is it time to jump ship? Historians rethink the waves metaphor. *Feminist Formations, 22*(1), 76–135.

Leary, C. (2012). Gold watches and old maids: The Lowell offering's role in the emerging social consciousness of 19th century factory girls, 1840–1845. *Atlanta Review of Journalism History, 10*(1), 26–40.

Leinbach, M., & Fagot, B. (1993). Categorical habituation to male and female faces: Gender schematic processing in infancy. *Infant Behavior & Development, 16*(3), 317–332.

Leit, R. A., Pope H. G., Jr., & Gray, J. (2001). Cultural expectations of muscularity in men: The evolution of playgirl centerfolds. *The International Journal of Eating Disorders, 29*(1), 90–93.

Lenehan, S. (2011, Spring). Nose aesthetics: Rhinoplasty and identity in Tehran. *Anthropology of the Middle East, 6*(1), 47–62.

Leon, A. (2011, 27 October). Slideshow: Top 10 Black stars at the box office. *The Grio.com*. Retrieved from http://thegrio.com/2011/10/27/top-grossing-aas-in-hollywood/

Levanon, A., England, P., & Allison, P. (2009). Occupational feminization and pay: Assessing causal dynamics using 1950–2000 U.S. Census data. *Social Forces, 88*(2), 865–892.

Levant, R. F., Hall, R. J., & Rankin, T. J. (2013). Male Role Norms Inventory–Short Form (MRNI-SF): Development, confirmatory factor analytic investigation of structure, and measurement invariance across gender. *Journal of Counseling Psychology, 60*(2), 228–238.

Levant, R., Rankin, T., Williams, C., Hasan, N., & Smalley, K. (2010). Evaluation of the factor structure and construct validity of scores on the Male Role Norms Inventory-Revised (MRNI-R). *Psychology of Men & Masculinity, 11*(1), 25–37.

Levant, R. F., & Richmond, K. (2007). A review of research on masculinity ideologies using the male role norms inventory. *Journal of Men's Studies, 15*(2), 130–146.

Levant, R., Richmond, K., Cook, S., House, A., & Aupont, M. (2007). The Femininity Ideology Scale: Factor structure, reliability, convergent and discriminant validity, and social contextual variation. *Sex Roles, 57*(5–6), 373–383.

Levine, K. (2006). No penis, no problem. *Conference Papers—Law & Society, 1*.

Levy-Navarro, E. (2009). Fattening queer history: Where does fat history go from here? In E. Rothblum & S. Solovay (Eds.), *The fat studies reader* (pp. 15–22). New York, NY: New York University Press.

Li, P. (2014). Recent developments hitting the ceiling: An examination of barriers to success for Asian American women. *Berkeley Journal of Gender, Law & Justice, 29*(1), 140–167.

Lincoln, A. E., & Allen, M. (2004). Double jeopardy in Hollywood: Age and gender in the careers of film actors, 1926–1999. *Sociological Forum, 19*(4), 611–631.

Lips, H. (2005). *Sex and gender: An introduction* (5th ed.). New York, NY: McGraw-Hill.

Lisak, D., & Miller, P. (2002). Repeat rape and multiple offender among undetected rapists. *Violence and Victims, 17*(1), 73–84.

Littlewood, R. (2002). Three into two: The third sex in Northern Albania. *Anthropology & Medicine, 19*(1), 37–50.

Loeb, P. (2010). The Real Rosa Parks. Retrieved from http://www.paulloeb.org/articles/rosaparks.htm

Lombardi, K. (2010/2014). A lack of consequences for sexual assault. *The Center for Public Integrity.* Retrieved from https://www.publicintegrity.org/2010/02/24/4360/lack-consequences-sexual-assault

Lonsway, K., Archambault, J., & Lisak, D. (2009). False reports: Moving the issue to successfully investigate and prosecute non-stranger sexual assault. *The Voice, 3*(1). Retrieved from http://www.ndaa.org/pdf/the_voice_vol_3_no_1_2009.pdf

Lopez, M. H., & Fry, R. (2013, September 4). Among recent high school grads, Hispanic college enrollment rate surpasses that of whites. *Pew Research Center.* Retrieved from http://www.pewresearch.org/fact-tank/2013/09/04/hispanic-college-enrollment-rate-surpasses-whites-for-the-first-time/

Lorber, J. (2005). *Gender inequality: Feminist theories and politics* (3rd ed.). Los Angeles, CA: Roxbury Publishing Co.

Lorber, J. (2012). *Gender inequality: Feminist theories and politics* (5th ed.). New York, NY: Oxford University Press.

Lorde, Audre. (1978/1984). *Sister outsider.* Berkeley, CA: Crossing Press.

Lott, B., & Saxon, S. (2002). The influence of ethnicity, social class, and context on judgments about U.S. women. *Journal of Social Psychology, 142*(4), 481–499.

Louderback, L. A., & Whitley, B. E., Jr. (1997). Perceived erotic value of homosexuality and sex-role attitudes as mediators of sex differences in heterosexual college students' attitudes toward lesbian and gay men. *Journal of Sex Research, 34*(2), 175.

Lovelock, J. M. (2014) Using the Klein Sexual Orientation Grid in sociological studies. *Journal of Bisexuality, 14*(3–4), 457–467.

Lowell.com. (2014). Lowell Mill girls. Retrieved from http://www.lowell.com/lowell-mill-girls/

Lozada, C. (2013, June 21). Who is Latino? *Washington Post.* Retrieved from https://www.washingtonpost.com/opinions/who-is-latino/2013/06/21/bcd6f71a-d6a4-11e2-b05f-3ea3f0e7bb5a_story.html

Lucander, D. (2014). *Winning the war for democracy: The March on Washington Movement, 1941–1946.* Chicago, IL: University of Illinois Press.

Ludwig, P. W. (1996). Politics and Eros in Aristophanes' speech: Symposium 191E-192A and the comedies. *American Journal of Philology, 117*(4), 537–562.

Luoma, J. (2002, December). Water for profit. *Mother Jones.* Retrieved from www.motherjones.com/politics/2002/11/water-profit

Lurie, A. (1981). *The language of clothes.* Illustrations assembled by Palca, D. New York, NY: Random House.

Lynda Carter Biography. (n.d.). IMDB.com. Retrieved from http://www.imdb.com/name/nm0004812/bio?ref_=nm_ov_bth_nm

Lyons, P. (2009). Prescription for harm: Diet industry influence, public health policy, and the "obesity epidemic." In E. Rothblum & S. Solovay (Eds.), *The fat studies reader.* (pp. 75–87). New York, NY: New York University Press.

Lyotard, J. (1979/1984). *The postmodern condition: A report on knowledge* (G. Bennington & B. Massumi, Trans.). Minneapolis, MN: University of Minnesota Press.

MacArthur Foundation. (2014). MacArthur Fellows Program. Retrieved from http://www.macfound.org/fellows/924/

MacGeorge, E. L., Graves, A. R., Feng, B., Gillihan, S. J., & Burleson, B. R. (2004). The myth of gender cultures: Similarities outweigh differences in men's and women's provision of and responses to supportive communication. *Sex Roles, 50*(3/4), 143–175.

MacKinnon, C. (1999). *Are women human?: And other international dialogues.* Cambridge, MA: Harvard University Press.

MacRuairc, G. (2011). They're my words—I'll talk how I like! Examining social class and linguistic practice among primary-school children. *Language and Education, 25*(6), 535–559.

Madden, J. (2012). Performance-support bias and the gender pay gap among stockbrokers. *Gender & Society, 26,* 488–518.

MADRE. (2014). Who we are and our partners. Retrieved from http://www.madre.org/index/meet-madre-1/who-we-are-49.html

Madrick, J. (2014, October 5). Our misplaced faith in fair trade. *The New York Times,* SR5.

Magnus, B. (1995). Postmodern. In R. Audi (Ed.), *Cambridge dictionary of philosophy.* New York, NY: Cambridge University Press.

Majors, R., & Billson, J. (1992). *Cool pose: The dilemmas of Black manhood in America.* New York, NY: Lexington Books.

Malcolm, A. (2009, February 22). Michelle Obama's first White House state dinner: Behind the scenes. *Los Angeles Times.* Retrieved from http://latimesblogs.latimes.com/washington/2009/02/michelle-obam-1.html

Malveaux, J. (1984). *The status of women of color in the economy: The legacy of being other.* Retrieved from EBSCO. (Document number ED246210).

Manchel, F. (2007). *Every step a struggle: Interviews with seven who shaped the African-American image in movies.* Washington, DC: New Academia Publishing.

Mankiller, W., Navarro, M., & Steinem, G. (1998). Feminism and feminisms: Feminism. In *Reader's companion to U.S. women's history* (pp. 187–192). New York, NY: Houghton Mifflin Harcourt.

Mann, S. A. (2012). *Doing feminist theory: From modernity to postmodernity.* New York, NY: Oxford University Press.

Manning, A., & Petrongolo, B. (2006, November). *The part-time pay penalty for women in Britain.* (IZA Discussion paper 2419). Institute for the Study of Labor/IZA. Retrieved from http://ftp.iza.org/dp2419.pdf

Maria W. Stewart (1803–1879). (2007). In J. Rodriguez (Ed.), *Slavery in the United States: A social, political, and historical encyclopedia.* Santa Barbara, CA: ABC-CLIO. Retrieved from http://ezproxy.sunyrockland.edu:2048/login?qurl=http%3A%2F%2Fezproxy.sunyrockland.edu%3A2103%2Fcontent%2Fentry%2Fabcslavery%2Fmaria_w_stewart_1803_1879%2F0

Marilley, S. M. (1993). Frances Willard and the feminism of fear. *Feminist Studies, 19*(1), 123–146.

Marlboro Man. (2003). In *American masculinities: A historical encyclopedia.* Retrieved from http://www.credoreference.com/entry/sageam/marlboro_man

Marsh, K. (2012, Jan 4). *Opinion: Where is the Black middle class? You don't have to look far.* In America. [CNN blog]. Retrieved from http://inamerica.blogs.cnn.com/2012/01/04/where-is-the-black-middle-class-you-dont-have-to-look-far/

Marsh, K., Darity, W. A., Jr., Cohen, P. N., Casper, L. M., & Salters, D. (2007). The emerging Black middle class: Single and living alone. *Social Forces, 86*(2), 1–28.

Martin, C., & Valenti, V. (2013). #Femfuture: Online revolution (Vol. 8). Retrieved from http://www.thenation.com/wp-content/uploads/2015/03/NFS8-FemFuture-Online-Revolution-Report-April-15-20131.pdf

Martinez-Carter, K. (2013, June 19). What does "American" actually mean? *The Atlantic.com.* Retrieved from http://www.theatlantic.com/national/archive/2013/06/what-does-american-actually-mean/276999/

Marx, K. (1839–1841/1978). The *Grundrisse.* In R. C. Tucker (Ed.), *The Marx–Engels reader* (2nd ed., pp. 221–293). New York, NY: Norton.

Marx, K. (1845/1978). Theses on Feuerbach. In R. C. Tucker (Ed.), *The Marx–Engels reader* (2nd ed., pp. 143–145). New York, NY: Norton.

Marx, K. (1847/1978). The coming upheaval. In R. C. Tucker (Ed.), *The Marx–Engels reader* (2nd ed., pp. 218–219). New York, NY: Norton.

Marx, K. (1888/1978). Manifesto of the Communist Party. In R. C. Tucker (Ed.), *The Marx–Engels reader* (2nd ed., pp. 469–500). New York, NY: Norton.

Marx, K. (1891/1978a). Critique of the Gotha Program. In R. C. Tucker (Ed.), *The Marx–Engels reader* (2nd ed., pp. 525–541). New York, NY: Norton.

Marx, K. (1891/1978b). Wage labour and capital. In R. C. Tucker (Ed.), *The Marx–Engels reader* (2nd ed., pp. 203–217). New York: Norton.

Marx, K., & Engels, F. (1845–1846/1988), The German ideology (1845–1846) (Selections). In A. W. Wood (Ed.), *Marx: Selections.* New York, NY: Macmillan.

Masini, B. E., & Barrett, H. A. (2008). Social support as a predictor of psychological and physical well-being and lifestyle in lesbian, gay, and bisexual adults aged 50 and over. *Journal of Gay & Lesbian Social Services, 20*(1/2), 91–110.

Maume, D. (1999). Glass ceilings and glass escalators: Occupational segregation and race and sex differences in managerial promotions. *Work and Occupations, 26,* 483–509.

McIntosh, P. (1988). White privilege and male privilege. In S. Shaw & J. Lee (Eds.), *Women's voices, contemporary visions* (pp. 75–82). New York, NY: McGraw-Hill.

McShane, L. (2009, June 25). "Charlie's Angels" actress Farrah Fawcett dies from cancer at 62; Longtime love Ryan O'Neal at side. *New York Daily News.* Retrieved from http://www.nydailynews.com/news/charlie-angels-actress-farrah-fawcett-dies-cancer-62-longtime-love-ryan-o-neal-side-article-1.197019

Means, L. D. (1999). Women of All Red Nations. In A. M. Josephy, J. Nagel, & T. R. Johnson (Eds.), *Red power: The American Indians' fight for freedom* (pp. 51–52). Lincoln, NE: University of Nebraska Press.

Meerkamper, S. T. (2013). Contesting sex classification: The need for genderqueers as a cognizable class. *Dukeminier Awards: Best Sexual Orientation Law Review Articles,* 121–23.

Meloy, J., & Felthous, A. (2011). Introduction to this issue: International perspectives on stalking. *Behavioral Sciences & the Law, 29*(2), 139–140.

Meloy, J., Mohandie, K., & Green, M. (2011). The female stalker. *Behavioral Sciences & the Law, 29*(2), 240–254.

Mendible, M. (2009) Big booty beauty and the new sexual aesthetic. *Alternet.org.* Retrieved from http://www.alternet.org/story/117518/big_booty_beauty_and_the_new_sexual_aesthetic

Metzger, S. (2014). *Chinese looks: Fashion, performance and race.* Bloomington, IN: Indiana University Press. Retrieved from http://muse.jhu.edu/books/9780253015686

Meyer, R. (2002). *Outlaw representation: Censorship and homosexuality in twentieth-century American art.* Boston, MA: Beacon Press.

Mgbako, C., Saxena, M., Cave, A., Farjad, N., & Shin, H. (2010). Penetrating the silence in Sierra Leone: A blueprint for the eradication of female genital mutilation. *Harvard Human Rights Law Journal, 23*, 111–140.

Miller, C. (2014a, July 17). Some universities crack code in drawing women to computer science. *The New York Times,* Retrieved from http://www.nytimes.com/2014/07/18/upshot/some-universities-crack-code-in-drawing-women-to-computer-science.html?_r=0&abt=0002&abg=1

Miller, C. (2014b, November 9). The leave seldom taken. *The New York Times,* pp. B1, B6.

Miller, C., & Alderman, L. (2014, December 14). The flexibility gap. *The New York Times,* pp. BU1, BU5.

Miller, C., & Swift, K. (1976). *Words and women.* Garden City, NY: Anchor Press/Doubleday.

Miller, C., & Swift, K. (2000). *The handbook of nonsexist writing: For writers, editors and speakers.* Lincoln, NE: iUniverse.com.

Miller, L. (2012). Stalking: Patterns, motives and intervention strategies. *Aggression and Violent Behavior, 17*, 495–506.

Milligan, L. (2012, March 1). Who's who: Hedi Slimane. *Vogue.* Retrieved from http://www.vogue.co.uk/spy/biographies/hedi-slimane-biography

Minter, S. P. (2006). Do transsexuals dream of gay rights? Getting real about transgender inclusion. In P. Currah, R. M. Juang, & S. P. Minter (Eds.), *Transgender rights* (pp. 141–170). Minneapolis, MN: University of Minnesota Press.

Mirk, S. (2013). Where are the young feminist leaders? For now, right here online. *Bitch Media.* Retrieved from https://bitchmedia.org/post/where-are-the-young-feminist-leaders-for-now-right-here-online

Mirza, H. (1999). Black masculinities and schooling: A black feminist response. *British Journal of Sociology of Education, 20*(1), 137–147.

Mishkind, M. E., Rodin, J., Silberstein, L. R., & Striegel-Moore, R. H. (1987). The embodiment of masculinity: Cultural, psychological and behavioral dimensions. In Changing M. Kimmel (Ed.), *Changing men: New directions in research on men and masculinity.* (pp. 37–52). Newbury Park, CA: Sage.

Misra, J., Budig, M., & Moller, S. (2005). Employment, wages, and poverty: Reconciliation policies and gender equity. *Academia.edu.* Retrieved from http://umass.academia.edu/JoyaMisra/Papers/656877/Employment_Wages_and_Poverty_Reconciliation_Policies_and_Gender_Equity

Mixon, B. (2008, April 28). Chore wars: Men, women and housework. *National Science Foundation.* Retrieved from https://www.nsf.gov/discoveries/disc_summ.jsp?cntn_id=111458

Moghadam, V. (2005). *Globalizing women: Transnational feminist networks.* Baltimore, MD: Johns Hopkins University Press.

Mohanty, C. (1986). Under Western eyes: Feminist scholarship and colonial discourses. *Boundary 2, 12/13*(3/1) (Spring/Fall 1984, actual pub date 1986), 333–358.

Mohanty, C. (2003). "Under Western eyes" revisited: Feminist solidarity through anticapitalist struggles. *Signs, 28*(2), 499–535.

Mohanty, L. (2014, April 17). 10 most expensive women shoe brands in the world. *Fashionlady.* Retrieved from http://www.fashionlady.in/10-most-expensive-women-shoe-brands-in-the-world/9058

Montoya, M. (2002). *Translating property: The Maxwell Land Grant and the conflict over land in the American West, 1840–1900.* Los Angeles, CA: University of California Press.

Mooney, A., & Evans, B. (Eds.). (2015). *Language, society and power: An introduction* (4th ed.). New York, NY: Routledge.

Moore, R. (2003). Racialization. In *Dictionary of race, ethnicity & culture.* Retrieved from http://ezproxy.sunyrockland.edu:2048/login?qurl=http%3A%2F%2Fsearch.credoreference.com%2Fcontent%2Fentry%2Fsageukrace%2Fracialization%2F0

Moradi, B., Mohr, J. J., Worthington, R. L., & Fassinger, R. E. (2009). Counseling psychology research on sexual (orientation) minority issues: Conceptual and methodological challenges and opportunities. *Journal of Counseling Psychology, 56*(1), 5–22.

Moraga, C. (1983). I come from a long line of Vendidas. *Loving in the war years: Lo Que nunca paso por sus labios.* Cambridge, MA: South End Press.

Moraga, C. (2000). Interview with Rosemary Weatherston. In Boon, J. A. et al. (Eds.), *Queer frontiers: Millennial geographies, genders and generations* (pp. 64–83). Madison, WI: University of Wisconsin Press.

Moraga, C., & Anzaldúa, G. (1981/1983). *This bridge called my back: Writings by radical women of color.* New York, NY: Kitchen Table/Women of Color Press.

Morton, P. (1991). *Disfigured images: The historical assault on Afro-American women.* New York, NY: Praeger.

Moya, P. (2001, Spring). Why I am not Hispanic: An argument with Jorge Gracia. *APA Newsletter, 00*(2), 100–105.

Msibi, T. (2011). The lies we have been told: On (homo) sexuality in Africa. *Africa Today, 58*(1), 55–77.

Muehlehard, C. L., & Peterson, Z. D. (2011). Distinguishing between sex and gender: History, current conceptualizations, and implications. *Sex Roles 64*, 791–803.

Mulvey, L. (1975/1997). Visual pleasure in narrative cinema. In R. R. Warhol & D. P. Herndl (Eds.), *Feminisms: An anthology of literary theory and criticism* (pp. 439–448). New Brunswick, NJ: Rutgers University Press.

Murdock, D. (2003, December 3). The truth about Reagan and AIDS. *Independent Gay Forum*. Retrieved from http://igfculturewatch.com/2003/12/03/the-truth-about-reagan-and-aids/

Murnen, S. K. (2011) Gender and body images. In T. Cash & L. Smolak (Eds.), *Body image: A handbook of science, practice, and prevention* (2nd ed., pp. 173–179). New York, NY: Guilford Press.

Murray, D. (2001). Representation and cultural sovereignty: Some case studies. In G. Bataille (Ed.), *Native American representations: First encounters, distorted images, and literary appropriations* (pp. 80–99). Lincoln, NE: University of Nebraska Press.

Murray, S. O. (1995). Southwest Asian and North African terms for homosexual roles. *Archives of Sexual Behavior, 24*(6), 623–629.

Muslimah Media Watch. (2008, 28 January). Oooh, baby, Put it on: Ripping up veil fetish art. Retrieved from http://www.patheos.com/blogs/mmw/2008/01/oooh-baby-put-it-on-ripping-up-veil-fetish-art-2/

NABJ Style Guide A. (n.d.). *National Association of Black Journalists*. Retrieved from http://www.nabj.org/?styleguideA

Nagoshi, J., Adams, K., Terrell, H., Hill, E., Brzuzy, S., & Nagoshi, C. (2008). Gender differences in correlates of homophobia and transphobia. *Sex Roles, 59*(7/8), 521–531.

Namaste, V. (2009). Undoing theory: The "transgender question" and the epistemic violence of Anglo-American feminist Theory. *Hypatia, 24*(3), 11–32.

Nanda, S. (1993). Hijras as neither man nor woman. In H. Abelove, M. A. Barale, & D. M. Halperin (Eds.), *The lesbian and gay studies reader* (pp. 542–552). New York, NY: Routledge.

Nanda, S. (2014). *Gender diversity: Crosscultural variations*. Long Grove, IL: Waveland Press.

Nanda, S., & Warms, R. (2010). *Cultural anthropology* (10th ed.). New York, NY: Cengage.

National Abortion Federation. (2010). History of abortion. Retrieved from http://prochoice.org/education-and-advocacy/about-abortion/history-of-abortion/

National Women's History Museum. (2007). Women with a deadline. Retrieved from https://www.nwhm.org/online-exhibits/womenwithdeadlines/wwd17.htm

National Women's Law Center. (2015, May 13). Fair pay for women requires a fair minimum wage. Retrieved from http://nwlc.org/resources/fair-pay-women-requires-a-fair-minimum-wage/

Native American. (2005). In *The American Heritage guide to contemporary usage and style*. Boston, MA: Houghton Mifflin. Retrieved from http://ezproxy.sunyrockland.edu:2048/login?qurl=http%3A%2F%2Fsearch.credoreference.com%2Fcontent%2Fentry%2Fhmcontempusage%2Fnative_american%2F0

Navarro, M. (2014, November 11). Homeless, because they are abused at home. *The New York Times*, A1, A27.

Neale, T. H. (2014, April 8). The proposed Equal Rights Amendment: Contemporary ratification issues. Congressional Research Service, doc. no. 7-5700. Retrieved from http://www.equalrightsamendment.org/misc/CRS%20ERA%20report%204-8-14.pdf

Negrón-Muntaner, F. (2004). *Boricua pop: Puerto Ricans and the Latinization of American culture*. New York, NY: New York University Press.

Nesvig, M. (2001). The complicated terrain of Latin American homosexuality. *Hispanic American Historical Review, 81*(3–4), 689–729.

New York Radical Women. (2006). In *From suffrage to the Senate: America's political women*. Retrieved from http://ezproxy.sunyrockland.edu:2048/login?qurl=http%3A%2F%2Fsearch.credoreference.com%2Fcontent%2Fentry%2Fghssapw%2Fnew_york_radical_women%2F0

New York Times Editorial Board. (2014a, October 4). Silicon Valley's diversity problem. *New York Times*. Retrieved from http://www.nytimes.com/2014/10/05/opinion/sunday/silicon-valleys-diversity-problem.html

New York Times Editorial Board. (2014b, September 9). When yes means yes. *The New York Times*, A28.

New York Times Editorial Board. (2015, September 15). How segregation destroys black wealth. *New York Times*. Retrieved from http://www.nytimes.com/2015/09/15/opinion/how-segregation-destroys-black-wealth.html?_r=0

Ng, V. (1997). Looking for lesbians in Chinese history. In Duberman, M. (Ed.), *A queer world: The Center for Lesbian and Gay Studies reader* (pp. 199–204). New York, NY: New York University Press.

Ngai, M. (2004). *Impossible subjects: Illegal aliens and the making of modern America*. Princeton, NJ: Princeton University Press.

Nichols, P. C. (2011). Black women in the rural South: Conservative and innovative. In J. Coates & P. Pichler (Eds.). *Language and gender: A reader* (pp. 49–56). Malden, MA: Wiley–Blackwell.

Niemann, Y. F. (2001). Stereotypes about Chicanas and Chicanos: Implications for counseling. *The Counseling Psychologist, 29*, 55–90.

Norris, C. (1995). Modernism. In T. Honderich (Ed.), *Oxford companion to philosophy* (p. 583). New York, NY: Oxford University Press.

Norton, R. (1997). *Myth of the modern homosexual*. London, England: Continuum.

NOW. (2014). Statement of purpose. Retrieved from http://now.org/about/history/statement-of-purpose/

NOW. (2016). Honoring our founders and pioneers. Retrieved from http://now.org/about/history/honoring-our-founders-pioneers/

O'Brien, C. C. (2009). "The white women all go for sex": Frances Harper on suffrage, citizenship, and the reconstruction South. *African American Review, 43*(4), 605–620.

O'Neill, A., & O'Reilly, C. (2011). Reducing the backlash effect: Self-monitoring and women's promotions. *Journal of Occupational and Organizational Psychology*, 1–8. Retrieved from http://www.alphagalileo.org/AssetViewer.aspx?AssetId=40772&CultureCode=en

Obiora, L. (1997). The little foxes that spoil the vine: Revisiting the feminist critique of female circumcision. *Canadian Journal of Women & the Law, 9*(1), 46–73.

Ochs, R. (2014). Bisexual. RobynOchs.com. Retrieved from http://robynochs.com/bisexual/

Okin, S. (1998). Feminism, women's human rights, and cultural differences. *Hypatia 13*(2), 32–52.

Okpalaoka, C. L., & Dillard, C. B. (2012). (Im)migrations, relations, and identities of African peoples: Toward an endarkened transnational feminist praxis in education. *Educational Foundations, 26*(1–2), 121–142.

Olen, H. (1991). The law: Most states now ban marital rape. *Los Angeles Times*. Retrieved from http://articles.latimes.com/1991-10-22/news/mn-163_1_current-laws

Olson, M., Diekema, D., Elliott, B., & Renier, C. (2010). Impact of income and income inequality on infant health outcomes in the United States. *Pediatrics 126*(6), 1165–1173.

O'Neal, W. J. (1993). The status of women in ancient Athens. *International Social Science Review, 68*(3), 115.

Ong, P., & Hee, S. (1993). Work issues facing Asian Pacific Americans: Labor policy. In *The state of Asian Pacific America: A public policy report: Policy issues to the year 2020* (pp. 141–152). Los Angeles, CA: LEAP Asian Pacific American Public Policy Institute and UCLA Asian American Studies Center.

Ordover, N. (2003). *American eugenics: Race, queer anatomy, and the science of nationalism*. Lincoln, NE: University of Minnesota Press.

Orenstein, P. (2011). *Cinderella ate my daughter: Dispatches from the front lines of the new girlie-girl culture*. New York, NY: HarperCollins.

Organisation Intersex International Australia. (2014). *Intersex for allies*. Retrieved from https://oii.org.au/wp-content/uploads/key/OII-Australia-Intersex-Ally.pdf

Organization for Economic Cooperation and Development (OECD). (2016). OECD. Stat: Employment: Time spent in paid and unpaid work, by sex. *OECD*. Retrieved from http://stats.oecd.org/index.aspx?queryid=54757

Padavic, I., & Reskin, B. (2002). *Women and men at work*. Thousand Oaks, CA: Pine Forge Press/Sage.

Pager, D., & Shepherd, H. (2008, January 1). The sociology of discrimination: Racial discrimination in employment, housing, credit, and consumer markets. *Annual Review of Sociology, 34*, 181–209.

Painter, N. I. (2010). *The history of white people*. New York, NY: Norton.

Pais, J. (2011). Socioeconomic background and racial earnings inequality: A propensity score analysis. *Social Science Research, 40*, 37–49.

Paludi, M. A. (Ed.). (2004). *Praeger guide to the psychology of gender*. Westport, CT: Praeger.

Papadaki, E., (2015, Winter). Feminist perspectives on objectification. In E. N Zalta (Ed.), *The Stanford encyclopedia of philosophy*. Retrieved from http://plato.stanford.edu/archives/win2015/entries/feminism-objectification/

Parrillo, V. N. (2011). *Strangers to these shores* (10th ed.). New York, NY: Allyn & Bacon.

Pascoe, C. J. (2007). *Dude you're a fag: Masculinity and sexuality in high school*. Los Angeles, CA: University of California Press.

Pati, R. (2011). States' positive obligations with respect to human trafficking: The European Court of Human Rights breaks new ground in *Rantsev V. Cyprus and Russia. Boston University International Law Journal, 29*(1), 79–142.

Patterson, M., & Elliott, R. (2002). Negotiating masculinities: Advertising and the inversion of the male gaze. *Consumption, Markets and Culture, 5*(3), 231–246.

Paul Robeson (1898–1976). (2012). In P. Dreier (Ed.), *The 100 greatest Americans of the 20th century: A Social Justice Hall of Fame*. New York, NY: Nation Books. Retrieved from http://ezproxy.sunyrockland.edu:2048/login?qurl=http%3A%2F%2Fezproxy.sunyrockland.edu%3A3959%2Fcontent%2Fentry%2Fpersgreatest%2Fpaul_robeson_1898_1976%2F0

PBS. (1999). Internment history. *Children of the camps*. Retrieved from http://www.pbs.org/childofcamp/history/index.html?PHPSESSID=032e01e0d9275e2e1d447e604074cc9c

PBS. (2002a). Bolivia: Leasing the rain. *Frontline World*. Retrieved from http://www.pbs.org/frontlineworld/stories/bolivia/thestory.html

PBS. (2002b). The pill. Retrieved from http://www.pbs.org/wgbh/amex/pill/

Peaden, C. (1993). Jane Addams and the social rhetoric of democracy. In G. Clark & S. M. Halloran (Eds.), *Oratorical culture in nineteenth century America: Transformations in the theory and practice of rhetoric* (pp. 184–207). Carbondale, IL: Southern Illinois University Press.

Pedriana, N., & Abraham, A. (2006). Now you see them, now you don't: The legal field and newspaper desegregation of sex-segregated help wanted ads 1965–75. *Law & Social Inquiry, 31*(4), 905–938.

People Magazine's Sexiest Man Alive Through the Years. (2016). *ABC News*. Retrieved from http://abcnews.go.com/Entertainment/photos/people-magazines-sexiest-man-alive-years-12024905/image-14962368

Peoples, W. A. (2008). "Under construction": Identifying foundations of hip-hop feminism and exploring bridges between Black second-wave and hip-hop feminisms. *Meridians: Feminism, Race, Transnationalism, 8*(1), 19–52.

Percy, W. A., III. (2005). Reconsiderations about Greek homosexualities, *Journal of Homosexuality, 49*(3), 13–61.

Perez, B. (2003). Woman warrior meets mail-order bride: Finding an Asian American voice in the women's movement. *Berkeley Women's Law Journal, 18*, 211–236.

Person of color. (2005). In *The American Heritage guide to contemporary usage and style*. Boston, MA: Houghton Mifflin. Retrieved from http://ezproxy.sunyrockland.edu:2048/login?qurl=http%3A%2F%2Fsearch.credoreference.com%2Fcontent%2Fentry%2Fhmcontempusage%2Fperson_of_color%2F0

Peters, J. W. (2014, 21 March). The decline and fall of the "H" word: For many gays and lesbians, the term "homosexual" is flinch-worthy. *The New York Times,* Retrieved from http://www.nytimes.com/2014/03/23/fashion/gays-lesbians-the-term-homosexual.html

Phenotype. (2012). In *Saunders comprehensive veterinary dictionary*. Retrieved from http://ezproxy.sunyrockland.edu:2048/login?qurl=http%3A%2F%2Fsearch.credoreference.com%2Fcontent%2Fentry%2Fehsvetdict%2Fphenotype%2F0

Phillips, C. M., Brown, T. L., & Parks, G. S. (2011). Barack, Michelle, and the complexities of a Black "love supreme." In G. S. Parks & M. W. Hughey (Eds.), *The Obamas and a (post) racial America?* (pp. 135–162). New York, NY: Oxford University Press.

Phyllis Schlafly explains why feminism has made women unhappy. (2014). *Tell Me More. National Public Radio*. Retrieved from http://www.npr.org/2014/07/21/333582322/phyllis-schlafly-explains-why-feminism-has-made-women-unhappy

Piketty, T. (2014). *Capital in the twenty-first century* (A. Goldhammer, Trans.). Cambridge, MA: Belknap Press of Harvard University Press.

Pilcher, J., & Whelehan, I. (2005). *50 key concepts in gender studies*. Thousand Oaks, CA: Sage.

Pitts, M., & Phillips, K. (1998). Social circumstances, inequalities and health. In K. Phillips & M. Pitts (Eds.), *The psychology of health: An introduction* (2nd ed.) (pp. 314–328). New York, NY: Routledge.

Pollitt, K. (1999, April 18). The solipsisters. *The New York Times,* Retrieved from http://www.nytimes.com/books/99/04/18/bookend/bookend.html

Porter, E. (2014, March 25). Income equality: A search for consequences. *New York Times*. Retrieved from http://www.nytimes.com/2014/03/26/business/economy/making-sense-of-income-inequality.html?_r=0

Porter, S., & Parks, G. (2011). Michelle Obama: Redefining images of black women. In G. Parks & M. Hughey (Eds.), *The Obamas and a (post) racial America?* (pp. 116–132). New York, NY: Oxford University Press.

Poststructuralism. (2004). In *Sage dictionary of cultural studies*. Retrieved from http://ezproxy.sunyrockland.edu:2048/login?qurl=http%3A%2F%2Fsearch.credoreference.com%2Fcontent%2Fentry%2Fsageukcult%2Fpoststructuralism%2F0

Pough, G. (2003). Do the ladies run this?: . . . Some thoughts on hip hop feminism. In R. Dicker & A. Piepmeier (Eds.), *Catching a wave: Reclaiming feminism for the 21st century* (pp 232–243). Boston, MA: Northeastern University Press.

Poverty in the United States: Frequently asked questions. (2016). *National Poverty Center/University of Michigan*. Retrieved from http://www.npc.umich.edu/poverty/

Prashad, V. (2003). Bruce Lee and the anti-imperialism of kung fu: A polycultural adventure. *Positions, 11*(1), 51–90.

Public Policy Advisory Network. (2012). Seven things to know about female genital surgeries in Africa. *The Hastings Center Report, 42*(6), 19–27.

Quijano, A. (2000). Coloniality of power, Eurocentrism, and Latin America. *Nepantla: Views from South, 1*(3), 533.

Quinn, J. (2014, January 24). Gays in Africa face rise in state-sponsored homophobia. Retrieved from http://www.thestar.com/news/world/2014/01/24/gays_in_africa_face_rise_in_statesponsored_homophobia.html

Radicalesbians. (1970). The woman identified woman. Duke University Archives. Retrieved from http://library.duke.edu/rubenstein/scriptorium/wlm/womid/

Ransby, B. (2003). *Ella Baker and the black freedom movement: A radical democratic vision*. Chapel Hill, NC: University of North Carolina Press.

Reddy, G. (2005). *With respect to sex: Negotiating Hijra identity in South India*. Chicago, IL: University of Chicago Press.

Redstockings. (2006). In *From suffrage to the Senate: America's political women*. Retrieved from http://ezproxy.sunyrockland.edu:2048/login?qurl=http%3A%2F%2F

search.credoreference.com%2Fcontent%2Fentry%2Fghssapw%2Fredstockings%2F0

Reed, E. (1970/1993). Women: caste, class, or oppressed sex? In A. M. Jaggar & P. S. Rothenberg (Eds.), *Feminist frameworks: Alternative theoretical accounts of the relations between women and men* (3rd ed., pp. 170–173). New York, NY: McGraw-Hill.

Reeser, T. (2010). *Masculinities in theory: An introduction.* Edison, NJ: Wiley–Blackwell.

Reifer, T. (2005). Tubman, Harriet. In *Encyclopedia of intelligence & counterintelligence.* Retrieved from http://ezproxy.sunyrockland.edu:2048/login?qurl=http%3A%2F%2Fezproxy.sunyrockland.edu%3A3959%2Fcontent%2Fentry%2Fsharpint%2Ftubman_harriet%2F0

Reinholtz, E. (2013). Thalberg, Irving. In R. C. Sickles (Ed.), *100 entertainers who changed America: An encyclopedia of pop culture.* Santa Barbara, CA: ABC-CLIO.

Rennison, C., & Planty, M. (2003). Nonlethal intimate partner violence: Examining race, gender, and income patterns. *Violence and Victims, 18*(4), 433–443.

Rennison, C. M., & Welchans, S. (2000). Intimate partner violence. *Bureau of Justice Statistics Special Report.* Retrieved from http://www.bjs.gov/content/pub/pdf/ipv.pdf

Rice, E. (2008). Greece: Ancient. *GLBTQ Social Sciences,* 1–9.

Rich, A. (1980, Summer). Compulsory heterosexuality and lesbian existence. *Signs: Journal of Women in Culture & Society, 5*(4), 631–660.

Rich. A. (1995). *On Lies, Secrets, and Silence.* New York, NY: W. W. Norton.

Richardson, J. (2005). Discourse. In *Key concepts in journalism studies.* Retrieved from http://ezproxy.sunyrockland.edu:2048/login?qurl=http%3A%2F%2Fsearch.credoreference.com%2Fcontent%2Fentry%2Fsageukjour%2Fdiscourse%2F0

Richardson, M. (1987). *Maria W. Stewart, America's first Black woman political writer: Essays and speeches.* Indianapolis, IN: Indiana University Press.

Richlin, A. (1992). *The garden of Priapus: Sexuality & aggression in Roman humor.* New York, NY: Oxford University Press.

Riegal, R. E. (1971). *American women: A story of social change.* Rutherford, NJ: Fairleigh Dickinson University Press.

Riot Grrrl Manifesto. (1991). *Bikini Kill Zine 2.* Retrieved from http://onewarart.org/riot_grrrl_manifesto.htm

Risen, C.(2004). Pedophilia. In *Encyclopedia of women's health.* Retrieved from http://ezproxy.sunyrockland.edu:2048/login?qurl=http%3A%2F%2Fezproxy.sunyrockland.edu%3A3959%2Fcontent%2Fentry%2Fsprwh%2Fpedophilia%2F0

Robehmed, N. (2014, November 11). Andreja Pejic and the rise of transgender models. *Forbes.* Retrieved from http://www.forbes.com/sites/natalierobehmed/2014/11/11/andreja-pejic-and-the-rise-of-transgender-models/

Robeson, Paul. (2014). In E. Foner & J. Garraty (Eds.), *The reader's companion to American history.* Boston, MA: Houghton Mifflin. Retrieved from http://ezproxy.sunyrockland.edu:2048/login?qurl=http%3A%2F%2Fezproxy.sunyrockland.edu%3A3959%2Fcontent%2Fentry%2Frcah%2Frobeson_paul%2F0

Rockquemore, K., & Brunsma, D. (2008). *Beyond Black: Biracial identity in America.* New York, NY: Rowman & Littlefield.

Rodríguez, C. E. (2004). *Heroes, lovers and others: The story of Latinos in Hollywood.* Washington, DC: Smithsonian Books.

Rohlinger, D. A. (2002, February). Eroticizing men: Cultural influences on advertising and male. Objectification. *Sex Roles, 46*(3/4), 61–74.

Roman empire. (2002). In *The new dictionary of cultural literacy.* New York, NY: Houghton Mifflin. Retrieved from http://ezproxy.sunyrockland.edu:2048/login?qurl=http%3A%2F%2Fezproxy.sunyrockland.edu%3A3959%2Fcontent%2Fentry%2Fhmndcl%2Froman_empire%2F0

Rondilla, J. L. (2009). Filipinos and the color complex: Ideal Asian beauty. In E. N. Glenn (Ed.), *Shades of difference: Why skin color matters* (pp. 63–80). Stanford, CA: Stanford University Press.

Rondilla, J. L., & Spickard, P. R. (2007). *Is lighter better?: Skin-tone discrimination among Asian Americans.* New York, NY: Rowman & Littlefield.

Rosales, F. (2008). Chicana liberation. In N. Kanellos (Ed.), *The Greenwood encyclopedia of Latino literature.* Santa Barbara, CA: ABC-CLIO. Retrieved from http://ezproxy.sunyrockland.edu:2048/login?qurl=http%3A%2F%2Fezproxy.sunyrockland.edu%3A2103%2Fcontent%2Fentry%2Fabclatlit%2Fchicana_liberation%2F0

Rösch, C. (2005). Davis, Angela Yvonne. In *Germany and the Americas: Culture, politics, and history.* Retrieved from http://ezproxy.sunyrockland.edu:2048/login?qurl=http%3A%2F%2Fezproxy.sunyrockland.edu%3A3959%2Fcontent%2Fentry%2Fabcgeamrle%2Fdavis_angela_yvonne%2F0

Roscoe, W. (1994). How to become a berdache: Toward a unified analysis of gender diversity. In G. Herdt (Ed.), *Third sex, third gender: Beyond sexual dimorphism in culture and history* (pp. 329–372). New York, NY: Zone Books.

Rose, M. (2002). Traditional and nontraditional patterns of female activism in the United Farm Workers of America, 1962 to 1980. In Y. F. Niemann (Ed.), *Chicana leadership:*

The frontiers reader (pp. 202–220). Lincoln, NE: University of Nebraska Press.

Rosenberg, T. (2013, July 17). Talking female circumcision out of existence. *The New York Times,* Retrieved from http://opinionator.blogs.nytimes.com/2013/07/17/talking-female-circumcision-out-of-existence/?_php=true&_type=blogs&_php=true&_type=blogs&_r=1

Rothblum, E., & Solovay, S. (2009). Introduction. In E. Rothblum & S. Solovay (Eds.). *The fat studies reader* (pp. 1–7). New York, NY: New York University Press.

Rubin, G. (1975/2008). The traffic in women: Notes on the political economy of sex. In A. Bailey & C. Cuomo (Eds.), *The feminist philosophy reader* (pp. 13–41). New York, NY: McGraw-Hill.

Rubin, G. (1984/1993). Thinking sex: Notes for a radical theory of the politics of sexuality. In H. Abelove, M. A. Barale, & D. M. Halperin (Eds.), *The lesbian and gay studies reader* (pp. 3–44). New York, NY: Routledge.

Rudman, L. A., & Phelan, J. E. (2008). Backlash effects for disconfirming gender stereotypes in organizations. *Research in Organizational Behavior, 28,* 61–79.

Ruiz, V. (1998). Chicanas and Mexican American women. In W. Mankiller (Ed.), *The reader's companion to U.S. women's history.* Boston, MA: Houghton Mifflin. Retrieved from http://ezproxy.sunyrockland.edu:2048/login?qurl=http%3A%2F%2Fezproxy.sunyrockland.edu%3A2103%2Fcontent%2Fentry%2Frcuswh%2Fchicanas_and_mexican_american_women%2F0

Rupp, L. J. (2009). *Sapphistries: A global history of love between women.* New York, NY: New York University Press.

Rupp, L. J. (2010). Constructing internationalism: The case of transnational women's organizations, 1888–1945. In K. Offen (Ed.), *Globalizing feminisms, 1789–1945: Rewriting histories* (pp. 139–152). New York, NY: Routledge.

Rutecki, G. W. (2011). Forced sterilization of Native Americans: Later twentieth century physician cooperation with national eugenic policies? *Ethics & Medicine: An International Journal of Bioethics, 27*(1), 33–42.

Rutherford, J. (1988). Who's that man? In R. Chapman & J. Rutherford (Eds.), *Male order: Unwrapping masculinity.* (pp. 21–67). London, United Kingdom: Lawrence & Wishart.

Ryan, H. (2014, January 10). What does trans* mean, and where did it come from? *Slate.com.* Retrieved from http://www.slate.com/blogs/outward/2014/01/10/trans_what_does_it_mean_and_where_did_it_come_from.html

Ryle, R. (2015). *Questioning gender: A sociological exploration.* Los Angeles, CA: Sage.

Sacco, L. N. (2015, May 26). The Violence Against Women Act: Overview, legislation, and federal funding. *Congressional Research Service.* Retrieved from https://www.fas.org/sgp/crs/misc/R42499.pdf

Said, E. (1978). *Orientalism.* New York, NY: Pantheon Books.

Saint Louis, C. (2015, March 25). Longtime nursing pay gap hasn't budged, study says. *The New York Times,* A20.

Sanday, P. R. (2003). Rape-free versus rape-prone: How culture makes a difference. In C. Travis (Ed.), *Evolution, gender, and rape* (pp. 334–361). Cambridge, MA: MIT Press.

Sandberg, S. (2013). *Lean in: Women, work, and the will to lead.* New York, NY: Knopf.

Sandeen, A. (2011). What arguments against the renewed ERA could feminists face? *Feministing.* Retrieved from http://feministing.com/2011/08/10/what-argument-against-the-renewed-era-could-feminists-face/

Sandoval, C. (1991/2001). U.S. Third World feminism: The theory and method of oppositional consciousness in the postmodern world. In K-K. Bhavnani (Ed.), *Feminism and "race"* (pp. 261–280). New York, NY: Oxford University Press.

Sankar, A. (1986). Sisters and brothers, Lovers and enemies: Marriage resistance in Southern Kwangtung. In E. Blackwood (Ed.), *Anthropology and homosexual behavior* (pp. 69–83). East Sussex, United Kingdom: Psychology Press.

Sappho. (1999). In *The Cambridge guide to women's writing in English.* Retrieved from http://ezproxy.sunyrockland.edu:2048/login?qurl=http%3A%2F%2Fezproxy.sunyrockland.edu%3A3959%2Fcontent%2Fentry%2Fcamgwwie%2Fsappho%2F0

Sarachild, K. (1978). "Consciousness-raising, a radical weapon." In Redstockings (Eds.), *Feminist revolution.* New York, NY: Random House.

Saulny, S. (2011, January 29). Black? White? Asian? More young Americans choose all of the above. *The New York Times,* Retrieved from http://www.nytimes.com/2011/01/30/us/30mixed.html?pagewanted=1&%2359;gwt=pay&%2359&_r=0

Schaefer, R. T. (2011). *Racial and ethnic groups* (12th ed.). Saddle River, NJ: Prentice Hall.

Schierenbeck, J. (2000). Lost and found: The incredible life and times of (Miss) Layle Lane. *American Educator.* American Federation of Teachers.

Schmitt, J., & Woo, N. (2013, December). *Women workers and unions.* Center for Economic and Policy Research. Retrieved from http://www.cepr.net/documents/union-women-2013-12.pdf

Scott, J. W. (1986, December). Gender: A useful category of analysis. *The American Historical Review, 91*(5), 1053–1075.

Scully, P., & Crais, C. (2008, April). Race and erasure: Sara Baartman and Hendrik Cesars in Cape Town and London. *Journal of British Studies, 47*(2), 301–323.

Seaman, B. (1969). *The doctors' case against the pill.* New York, NY: P. H. Wyden.

Sears, B., & Malloy, C. (2011, July). Documented evidence of employment discrimination and its effects on LGBT people. *Williams Institute.* Retrieved from http://williams institute.law.ucla.edu/wp-content/uploads/Sears-Mallory -Discrimination-July-20111.pdf

Sedgwick, E. K. (1985). *Between men: English literature and male homosocial desire.* New York, NY: Columbia University Press.

Sedgwick, E. K. (1990). *Epistemology of the closet.* Berkeley, CA: University of California Press.

Seidman, S. (1993). Identity and politics in a "postmodern" gay culture. In M. Warner (Ed.), *Fear of a queer planet: Queer politics and social theory* (pp. 105–142). Minneapolis, MN: University of Minnesota Press.

Sell, R. L. (1997). Defining and measuring sexual orientation: A review. *Archives of Sexual Behavior, 26*(6), 643–658.

Semyonov, M., & Lewin-Epstein, N. (2009). The declining racial earnings' gap in the United States: Multi-level analysis of males' earnings, 1960–2000. *Social Science Research, 38,* 296–311.

Serbin, L. A., Poulin-Dubois, D., Colburne, K. A., Sen, M. G., & Eichstedt, J. A. (2001). Gender stereotyping in infancy: Visual preferences for and knowledge of gender-stereotyped toys in the second year. *International Journal of Behavioral Development, 25*(1), 7–15.

Service, S., & Palmstrom, B. (2012, June 19). Confined to a Thai fishing boat, for three years. *National Public Radio.* Retrieved from http://www.npr.org/2012/06/19/155045295/ confined-to-a-thai-fishing-boat-for-three-years

Shannon, B. (2006). *The cut of his coat: Men, dress, and consumer culture in Britain, 1860–1914.* Athens, OH: Ohio University Press.

Shemar Moore. (2015). *People.* Retrieved from http://www .people.com/people/package/gallery/0,,20237714_ 20159879_20366818,00.html

Sheridan, P. (2015, March 20). Lynda Carter: After Wonder Woman I became an alcoholic. *Express.co.uk.* Retrieved from http://www.express.co.uk/news/showbiz/563789/ Lynda-Carter-on-being-beauty-queen-playing-Wonder -Woman-her-alcoholism

Sherman, A., & Zurbriggen, E. (2014). "Boys can be anything": Effect of Barbie Play on girls' career cognitions. *Sex Roles, 70,* 195–208.

Shih, M., & Sanchez, D. T. (2009). When race becomes even more complex: Toward understanding the landscape of multiracial identity and experiences. *Journal of Social Issues, 65*(1), 1–11.

Shiva, V. (1989). *Staying alive: Women, ecology and development.* Boston, MA: South End Press.

Shiva, V., & Mies, M. (1993). *Ecofeminism.* London, United Kingdom: Zed Books.

Shuster, R. (1987). Sexuality as a continuum: The bisexual identity. In Boston Lesbian Psychologies Collective (Eds.), *Lesbian psychologies: Explorations and challenges* (pp. 56–71). Chicago, IL: University of Illinois Press.

Shuttleworth, R., Wedgwood, N., & Wilson, N. J. (2012). The dilemma of disabled masculinity. *Men and Masculinities, 15*(2), 174–194.

Signorile, M. (2003). *Queer in America: Sex, the media, and the closets of power.* Madison, WI: University of Wisconsin Press.

Silva, C., Carter, N., & Beninger, A. (2012). Good intentions, imperfect execution? Women get fewer of the "hot jobs" needed to advance. Catalyst. Retrieved from http://www.catalyst.org/ knowledge/good-intentions-imperfect-execution-women -get-fewer-hot-jobs-needed-advance

Simpson, M. (2002, July 22). Meet the metrosexual: He's well dressed, narcissistic and obsessed with butts. But don't call him gay. *Salon.com.* Retrieved from http://www.salon .com/2002/07/22/metrosexual/

Slaughter, A. (2015, September 20). A toxic work world. *The New York Times,* SR 1, SR 6.

Smith, B. (1983/2000). Introduction. In B. Smith (Ed.), *Home girls: A Black feminist anthology* (pp. xxi–lviii). New Brunswick, NJ: Rutgers University Press.

Smith, C. S. (1997). Women, weight, and body image. In J. C. Chrisler, C. Golden, & P. D. Rozee (Eds.), *Lectures on the psychology of women* (pp. 113–125). Boston: McGraw-Hill. In McGraw-Hill Primis Online Coursepack (2001).

Smith, D., Taylor, A., Kilmarx, P., Sullivan, P., Warner, L., Kamb, M., . . . Mastro, T. (2010). Male circumcision in the United States for the prevention of HIV infection and other adverse health outcomes: Report from a CDC consultation. *Public Health Reports, 125*(Suppl. 1), 72–82. Retrieved from http:// www.ncbi.nlm.nih.gov/pmc/articles/PMC2788411/

Sneider, A. L. (2008). *Suffragists in an Imperial age: U.S. expansion and the woman question, 1870–1929.* New York, NY: Oxford University Press.

Snyder, R. (2008). What is third-wave feminism? A new directions essay. *Signs: Journal of Women in Culture & Society, 34*(1), 175–196.

Soffer, O., Adovasio, J. M., & Hyland, D. C. (2000). The "Venus" figurines: Textiles, basketry, gender, and status in the upper Paleolithic. *Current Anthropology, 41*(4), 511–537.

Solomon, A. (1994, August 28). Defiantly Deaf. *The New York Times,* Retrieved from http://www.nytimes.com/1994/08/28/ magazine/defiantly-deaf.html?pagewanted=all

Soto. S. K. (2013). Queerness. In S. Bost & F. R. Aparicio (Eds.), *The Routledge companion to Latino/a Literature* (pp. 75–83). New York, NY: Routledge.

South-East Asia. (2013). In S. Butler (Ed.), *The Macquarie dictionary.* South Yarra, Australia: Macquarie Dictionary. Retrieved from http://ezproxy.sunyrockland.edu:2048/login?qurl=http%3A%2F%2Fsearch.credoreference.com%2Fcontent%2Fentry%2Fmacqdict%2Fsouth_east_asia%2F0

Southern Education Foundation. (2015). A new majority research bulletin: Low income students now a majority in the nation's public schools. Retrieved from http://www.southerneducation.org/Our-Strategies/Research-and-Publications/New-Majority-Diverse-Majority-Report-Series/A-New-Majority-2015-Update-Low-Income-Students-Now

Spanish. (2015). *Ethnologue.com.* Retrieved from http://www.ethnologue.com/language/spa

Spanish–American War. (2005). In *Iberia and the Americas: Culture, politics, and history.* Santa Barbara, CA: ABC-CLIO. Retrieved from http://ezproxy.sunyrockland.edu:2048/login?qurl=http%3A%2F%2Fezproxy.sunyrockland.edu%3A3959%2Fcontent%2Fentry%2Fabcibamrle%2Fspanish_american_war%2F0

Spence, J. T. (1984). Gender identity and its implications for concepts of masculinity and femininity. In T. B. Sonderegger (Ed.), *Nebraska Symposium on Motivation: Psychology and gender, 32,* (pp. 59–96). Lincoln, NE: University of Nebraska Press.

Springer, K. (2002). Third wave black feminism? *Signs: Journal of Women in Culture & Society, 27*(4), 1059.

St. George, D. (2010, June 21). Text messages become a growing weapon in dating violence. *The Washington Post.* Retrieved from http://www.washingtonpost.com/wp-dyn/content/article/2010/06/20/AR2010062003331.html

Stabiner, K. (1982, May 2). Tapping the homosexual market: For the first time advertisers are . . . *The New York Times,* Retrieved from http://www.nytimes.com/1982/05/02/magazine/tapping-the-homosexual-market.html

Stafford, C. (2009). Asia: East. In A. Barnard & J. Spencer (Eds.), *Encyclopedia of social and cultural anthropology.* London, United Kingdom: Routledge. Retrieved from http://ezproxy.sunyrockland.edu:2048/login?qurl=http%3A%2F%2Fsearch.credoreference.com%2Fcontent%2Fentry%2Froutencsca%2Fasia_east%2F0

Stanfield, K. (2011). Persistent racial disparity, wealth and the economic surplus as the fund for reparations in the United States. *Journal of Economic Issues, 45*(2), 343–352.

Staples, B. (1998, February). Just walk on by: A Black man ponders his power to alter public space. *Literary Cavalcade, 50*(5), 38–41.

Steil, J. (2001). Family forms and member well-being: A research agenda for the decade of behavior. *Psychology of Women Quarterly, 25,* 344–363.

Steinem, G. (1995). Foreword. In R. Walker, *To be real: Telling the truth and changing the face of feminism* (p. xxii). New York, NY: Anchor Books.

Stewart, M. (1999). *The Spanish language today.* New York, NY: Routledge.

Stewart, S. (2009, 26 June). Farrah Fawcett dies of cancer at 62. *The New York Times,* Retrieved from http://www.nytimes.com/2009/06/26/arts/television/26fawcett.html?pagewanted=all&_r=0

Stiglitz, J. (2014, June 29). Inequality is not inevitable. *The New York Times,* SR 1, SR 7.

Stockard, J., & Johnson, M. M. (1992). *Sex and gender in society.* Englewood Cliffs, NJ: Prentice Hall.

Stoljar, N. (1995). Essence, identity and the concept of woman. *Philosophical Topics, 23*(2), 261–293.

Storms, M. D. (1980). Theories of sexual orientation. *Journal of Personality and Social Psychology, 38*(5), 783–792.

Stotko, E. M., & Troyer, M. (2007). A new gender neutral pronoun in Baltimore, Maryland: A preliminary study. *American Speech, 82*(3), 262–279.

Stover, L. (2014, April 22). Make them fit, please! *The New York Times,* Retrieved from http://www.nytimes.com/2014/04/24/fashion/foot-surgeries-so-women-can-wear-designer-shoes-in-comfort.html?_r=0

Straus, M. (2008). Dominance and symmetry in partner violence by male and female university students in 32 nations. *Children and Youth Services Review, 30*(3), 252–275.

Streitfeld, D. (2015, March 25). At Kleiner trial's close, a battle of powerhouse lawyers. *New York Times.* B1, B2.

Strossen, N. (1995). *Defending pornography: Free speech, sex and the fight for women's rights.* New York, NY: Scribner.

Stryker, S. (1994). My words to Victor Frankenstein above the village of Chamounix: Performing transgender rage. *GLQ: A Journal of Lesbian and Gay Studies, 1,* 237–254.

Stryker, S. (2004). *Glbtq.com.* Retrieved from http://www.glbtq.com/social-sciences/queer_nation.html

Stryker, S. (2008). *Transgender history.* Berkeley, CA: Seal Press.

Student Non-Violent Coordinating Committee. (2014). In E. Foner & J. Garraty (Eds.), *The reader's companion to American history.* Boston, MA: Houghton Mifflin. Retrieved from http://ezproxy.sunyrockland.edu:2048/login?qurl=http%3A%2F%2Fsearch.credoreference.com%2Fcontent%2Fentry%2Frcah%2Fstudent_non_violent_coordinating_committee%2F0

Sue, D., Capodilupo, C. M., & Holder, A. B. (2008). Racial microaggressions in the life experience of Black Americans. *Professional Psychology: Research and Practice, 39*(3), 329–336.

Sue, D., Capodilupo, C. M., Torino, G. C., Bucceri, J. M., Holder, A. B., Nadal, K. L., & Esquilin, M. (2007). Racial microaggressions in everyday life: Implications for clinical practice. *American Psychologist, 62*(4), 271–286.

Sugano, E., Nemoto, T., & Operario, D. (2006). The impact of exposure to transphobia on HIV risk behavior in a sample of transgendered women of color in San Francisco. *AIDS & Behavior, 10*(2), 217–225.

Sundbye, A., & Hegewisch, A. (2011, May). Maternity, paternity and adoption leave in the United States (Fact Sheet IWPR #A143). *Institute for Women's Policy Research*. Retrieved from http://www.iwpr.org/publications/pubs/maternity-paternity-and-adoption-leave-in-the-united-states

Superville, D. (2015, April 27). Michelle Obama designs new White House china set. *Christian Science Monitor*. Retrieved from http://www.csmonitor.com/USA/Politics/2015/0427/Michelle-Obama-designs-new-White-House-china-set-video

Suresha, R. (2013). "Diversities" may enrich "LGBTQIAP" alphabet soup. *Huffington Post*. Retrieved from http://www.huffingtonpost.com/ron-suresha/diversities-may-enrich-lgbtqiap-alphabet-soup_b_3929870.html

Swami, V., & Abbasnejad, A. (2010). Associations between femininity ideology and body appreciation among British female undergraduates. *Personality & Individual Differences, 48*(5), 685–687.

Swarns, R. (2014, September 21). A capstone in career spent fighting for the rights of domestic workers. *The New York Times*, Retrieved from http://www.nytimes.com/2014/09/22/nyregion/a-capstone-in-a-career-spent-fighting-for-the-rights-of-domestic-workers.html?_r=1

Syfers, J. (1990, July). Why I (still) want a wife. *Ms. Magazine*, 17.

Tacey, E. (2003). Women's movement: First wave/suffrage. In *Propaganda and mass persuasion: A historical encyclopedia, 1500 to the present*. Retrieved from http://ezproxy.sunyrockland.edu:2048/login?qurl=http%3A%2F%2Fezproxy.sunyrockland.edu%3A3959%2Fcontent%2Fentry%2Fabcprop%2Fwomen_s_movement_first_wave_suffrage%2F0

Tafolla, C. (1993). La Malinche. In T. Rebolledo & E. Rivero (Eds.), *Infinite divisions: An anthology of Chicana literature* (pp. 198–199). Tucson, AZ: University of Arizona Press.

Tannen, D. (1990). *You just don't understand*. New York, NY: HarperCollins.

Tarr-Whelan, L. (2010). The impact of the Beijing Platform for Action 1995–2010. *Human Rights, 37*(3), 2.

Tharps, L. L. (2014, November 18). The case for Black with a capital B. *The New York Times*, Retrieved from http://www.nytimes.com/2014/11/19/opinion/the-case-for-black-with-a-capital-b.html?_r=0

Theodore, P. S., & Basow, S. A. (2000). Heterosexual masculinity and homophobia: A reaction to the self? *Journal of Homosexuality, 40*(2), 31.

Thesander, M. (1997). *The feminine ideal*. London, United Kingdom: Reaktion Books.

Thing, J. (2010). Gay, Mexican and immigrant: Intersecting identities among gay men in Los Angeles. *Social Identities, 16*(6), 809–831.

Third Wave Fund. (2016). Third wave history. Retrieved from http://thirdwavefund.org/history-past-initiatives.html

Third World. (1993). In *Bloomsbury guide to human thought*. Retrieved from http://ezproxy.sunyrockland.edu:2048/login?qurl=http%3A%2F%2Fsearch.credoreference.com%2Fcontent%2Fentry%2Fbght%2Fthird_world%2F0

Thomas, A. J., Hacker, J. D., & Hoxha, D. (2011). Gendered racial identity of black young women. *Sex Roles, 64*, 530–542.

Thomas, C. (2000). *Global governance, development and human security: The challenge of poverty and inequality*. London, England: Pluto Press.

Thomas, L. (1990, December). "In my next life I'll be white." *Ebony, 46*(2), 84.

Thompson, B. (2002). Multiracial feminism: Recasting the chronology of second wave feminism. *Feminist Studies, 28*(2), 334–360.

Thompson, C. (1992). A new vision of masculinity. In M. Schaum & C. Flanagan, (Eds.), *Gender images: Readings for composition* (pp. 77–83). Boston: Houghton Mifflin.

Thompson, G. (2011). How the right made racism sound fair—and changed immigration politics. *Colorlines*. Retrieved from http://colorlines.com/archives/2011/09/how_the_right_made_racist_rhetoric_sound_neutral--and_shaped_immigration_politics.html

Thompson, M. S., & Keith, V. M. (2001, June). The blacker the berry: Gender, skin tone, self-esteem and self-efficacy. *Gender & Society, 15*(3), 336–357.

Thunder Hawk, M. (2011). Women of All Red Nations. In D. Wishart (Ed.), *Encyclopedia of the Great Plains*. Retrieved from http://plainshumanities.unl.edu/encyclopedia/doc/egp.pd.059

Tjaden, P., & Thoennes, N. (2000). Full report of the prevalence, incidence, and consequences of violence against women: Findings from the National Violence against Women Survey Research. *National Institute of Justice*. Retrieved from www.ncjrs.gov/pdffiles1/nij/183781.pdf

Toensing, G. C. (2014, February 10). Updated federally recognized tribes list published. *Indian Country Today Media*

Network. Retrieved from http://indiancountrytodayme
dianetwork.com/2014/02/10/updated-federally
-recognized-tribes-list-published-153459

Tong, R. P. (1998). *Feminist thought: A more comprehensive introduction*. Boulder, CO: Westview Press.

Topley, M. (1975). Marriage resistance in rural Kwangtung. In M.
Wolf, R. Witke, & E. Martin (Eds.), *Women in Chinese society*
(pp. 67–88). Stanford, CA: Stanford University Press.

Torres, J. B., Solberg, V. H., & Carlstrom, A. H. (2002). The
myth of sameness among Latino men and their machismo.
American Journal of Orthopsychiatry, 72(2), 163–181.

Tortora, P. G., & Eubank, K. (1998). *Survey of historic costume: A
history of Western dress* (3rd ed.). New York, NY: Fairchild.

Transrespect Versus Transphobia Worldwide. Alarming figures:
Over 1,700 trans people killed in the last 7 years. (2015).
Retrieved from http://www.transrespect-transphobia
.org/en_US/tvt-project/tmm-results/idahot-2015.htm

Traub, V. (2002). *The renaissance of lesbianism in early modern
England*. Cambridge, United Kingdom: Cambridge
University Press.

Trebay, G. (2008, February 7). The vanishing point. *The
New York Times*, Retrieved from http://www.nytimes
.com/2008/02/07/fashion/shows/07DIARY.html?_r=0

Trepanier, D. (2015, January 12). A brief history of men's style.
ArticlesofStyle.com. Retrieved from http://articlesofstyle
.com/56239/a-brief-history-of-mens-style

Trudgill, P. (1972). Sex, covert prestige and linguistic change in
the urban British English of Norwich. *Language in Society,
1*(2), 179–195.

Tully, C. T. (2000). *Lesbians, gays, & the empowerment perspective*. New York, NY: Columbia University Press.

Turbin, C. (2002, November). Fashioning the American man:
The Arrow Collar Man, 1907–1931. *Gender & History,
14*(3), 470–491. Retrieved from http://ezproxy.sunyrock
land.edu:2320/ehost/pdfviewer/pdfviewer?vid=4&hid=
110&sid=02a0b193-0ee9-4b9d-ac66-42e82a
32ef0b%40sessionmgr114

Turchik, J., & Wilson, S. (2010). Sexual assault in the U.S. military: A review of the literature and recommendations for
the future. *Aggression and Violent Behavior, 15*(4), 267–277.

UN Water. (2013). Facts and figures. Retrieved from http://www
.unwater.org/water-cooperation-2013/water-cooperation/
facts-and-figures/en/

UN Women. (2012, July 5). Discrimination against women persists around the globe hampering development. Retrieved
from http://www.unwomen.org/en/news/stories/2012/7/
discrimination-against-women-persists-around
-the-globe-hampering-development

UN Women. (2014). Facts and figures: Leadership and political participation. United Nations. Retrieved from http://
www.unwomen.org/en/what-we-do/leadership-and
-political-participation/facts-and-figures

UNICEF. (2010). The dynamics of social change: Towards the
abandonment of female genital mutilation/cutting in five
African countries. Retrieved from http://www.unicef-irc
.org/publications/pdf/fgm_insight_eng.pdf

UNICEF. (2013). Female genital mutilation/cutting: A statisti-
cal overview and exploration of the dynamics of change.
Retrieved from http://www.unicef.org/cbsc/files/UNICEF
_FGM_report_July_2013_Hi_res.pdf

UNICEF. (2016). *Female genital mutilation/cutting: A global
concern*. New York, NY: UNICEF.

United Kingdom Department for International Development.
(2005). Girls' education: Towards a better future for all.
Retrieved from http://www2.ohchr.org/english/issues/
development/docs/girlseducation.pdf

United Nations. (2010). *The world's women 2010: Trends and statistics*. New York, NY: Author.

UN Development Programme. (2013). *Human development
report 2013*. New York, NY: Author.

UN Girls' Education Initiative. (2012). *Engendering empowerment: Education and equality*. Retrieved from http://www
.ungei.org/resources/files/EngenderingEmpowerment
_WebVersion.pdf

UN High Commissioner for Human Rights. (2015, May 4).
*Discrimination and violence against individuals based on
their sexual orientation and gender identity*. A/HRC/29/23.
Retrieved from http://www.hrc.org/blog/entry/un-human
-rights-office-releases-report-detailing-violence-and
-discrimi

UN Office on Drugs and Crime. (2014). Global report on trafficking in persons 2012. Retrieved from https://www
.unodc.org/documents/data-and-analysis/glotip/
GLOTIP_2014_full_report.pdf

UN Population Division. (2002). *World urbanization prospects:
The 2001 revision*. Retrieved from http://www.un.org/esa/
population/publications/wup2001/WUP2001_CH1.pdf

U.S. Bureau of Labor Statistics. (2012). *Women in the labor force*.
Retrieved from http://www.bls.gov/opub/ted/2011/
ted_20111223.htm

U.S. Bureau of Labor Statistics, U.S. Department of Labor. (2013).
Labor force statistics from the current population survey. Retrieved from http://www.bls.gov/cps/cpsaat37.htm

U.S. Census Bureau. (2011a). *America's families and living arrangements 2011, Table FG8*. Retrieved from http://www
.census.gov/hhes/families/data/cps2011.html

U.S. Census Bureau. (2011b, October). *Maternity leave and employment patterns of first-time mothers: 1961–2008.* Retrieved from http://www.census.gov/prod/2011pubs/p70-128.pdf

U.S. Census Bureau. (2013, February 20). American Indian and Alaska Native poverty rate about 50 percent in Rapid City, S.D., and about 30 percent in five other cities, Census Bureau reports. *US Census Bureau Newsroom.* Retrieved from https://www.census.gov/newsroom/press-releases/2013/cb13-29.html

U.S. Department of Justice. (2013). *Tribal jurisdiction over crimes of domestic violence.* Retrieved from http://www.justice.gov/tribal/vawa-tribal.html

U.S. Department of State. (2013). *Trafficking in persons report.* Retrieved from http://www.state.gov/j/tip/rls/tiprpt/2013/index.htm

U.S. Government Accounting Office. (2003, October). *Women's earnings: Work patterns partially explain differences between men's and women's earnings* (GAO-04-35). Retrieved from http://www.gao.gov/assets/250/240547.pdf

U.S. House of Representatives. (2015). Women of color in Congress. Retrieved from http://history.house.gov/Exhibitions-and-Publications/WIC/Historical-Data/Women-of-Color-in-Congress/

Universal Health Care. (2004). In *The concise Corsini encyclopedia of psychology and behavioral science.* Retrieved from http://ezproxy.sunyrockland.edu:2048/login?qurl=http%3A%2F%2Fsearch.credoreference.com%2Fcontent%2Fentry%2Fwileypsych%2Funiversal_health_care%2F0

Urbina, I. (2014, October 12). The challenge of defining rape. *The New York Times*, SR 12.

Valdeón, R. A. (2013). Doña Marina/La Malinche: A historiographical approach to the interpreter/traitor. *Target: International Journal on Translation Studies, 25*(2), 157–179.

Valdivia, A. (2007). Is Penélope to J.Lo as culture is to nature?: Eurocentric approaches to "Latin" beauties. In M. Mendible (Ed.), *From bananas to buttocks: The Latina body in popular film and culture* (pp. 129–148). Austin, TX: University of Texas Press.

Vargas, Z. (2004). Tenayuca, Emma. December 21, 1916–July 23, 1999. In S. Ware & S. Braukman (Eds.), *Notable American women: Completing the twentieth century.* Cambridge, MA: Harvard University Press. Retrieved from http://ezproxy.sunyrockland.edu:2048/login?qurl=http%3A%2F%2Fezproxy.sunyrockland.edu%3A2103%2Fcontent%2Fentry%2Fhupnawiii%2Ftenayuca_emma_december_21_1916_july_23_1999%2F0

Varma, R. (2004), Asian Americans: Achievements mask challenges. *Asian Journal of Social Science, 32*(2), 290–307.

Veblen, T. (1912). *The theory of the leisure class: An economic study of institutions.* New York, NY: Macmillan Company.

Vega, C. B. (2010). *Spanish–English grammar: Pocket dictionary.* Hauppauge, NY: Barron's Educational Series.

Venus, L. R. (2011). Transgenderism. In D. A. Gerstner (Ed.), *Queer culture* (pp. 567–570). New York, NY: Routledge.

Vernon, P. (2010, June 26). Thin is in: In search of the perfect male body. *The Guardian.* Retrieved from http://www.theguardian.com/lifeandstyle/2010/jun/27/mens-health-weight

Victor, D. (2106, February 9). Women in company leadership tied to stronger profits, study says. *The New York Times*, Retrieved from http://www.nytimes.com/2016/02/10/business/women-in-company-leadership-tied-to-stronger-profits.html?src=me&_r=0

Voter ID is the real fraud. (2014, April 29). [Editorial]. *The New York Times*, Retrieved from http://www.nytimes.com/2014/04/30/opinion/voter-id-is-the-real-fraud.html

Wade, L. (2010, December 21). Why is Kim Kardashian famous? *Sociological Images.* Retrieved from http://thesocietypages.org/socimages/2010/12/21/why-is-kim-kardashian-famous/

Wade, L. (2012, December 10). A balanced look at female genital "mutilation." *Sociological Images.* Retrieved from http://thesocietypages.org/socimages/2012/12/10/a-balanced-look-at-fgm/

Wade, L. (2014, February 19). Rethinking a zero tolerance approach to "female genital mutilation." *Sociological Images.* Retrieved from http://thesocietypages.org/socimages/2014/02/19/rethinking-a-zero-tolerance-approach-to-female-genital-mutilation/

WAGE Project. (2012). What are the costs of the wage gap? Retrieved from www.wageproject.org/files/costs.php

Wagner, S. R. (1996). The untold story of the Iroquois influence on early feminists. *Feminist.com.* Retrieved from http://www.feminist.com/resources/artspeech/genwom/iroquoisinfluence.html

Walby, S., Armstrong, J., & Strid, S. (2012). Intersectionality: Multiple inequalities in social theory. *Sociology, 46*(2), 224–240.

Walker, R. (1992). Becoming the third wave. Retrieved from http://www.msmagazine.com/spring2002/BecomingThirdWaveRebeccaWalker.pdf

Wallace, M. (1978/1999). *Black macho and the myth of the superwoman.* New York, NY: Verso.

Walters, M. (2005). *Feminism: A very short introduction.* New York, NY: Oxford University Press.

Wann, M. (2009). Forward: Fat studies: An invitation to revolution. In E. Rothblum & S. Solovay (Eds.), *The fat studies reader* (pp. xi–xxv). New York, NY: New York University Press.

Ward, E. (2005). Homophobia, hypermasculinity and the U.S. Black church. *Culture, Health and Sexuality, 7*(5), 493–504.

Warner, M. (1993/2007). *Fear of a queer planet: Queer politics and social theory,* (7th printing). Minneapolis, MN: University of Minnesota Press.

Warner, M. (2002). *Publics and counterpublics.* New York, NY: Zone Books.

Wasserman, D., Asch, A., Blustein, J., & Putnam, D. (2013, Fall). Disability: Definitions, models, experience. In E. Zalta (Ed.), *The Stanford encyclopedia of philosophy.* Retrieved from http://plato.stanford.edu/archives/fall2013/entries/disability/

Waters, M. C., Kasinitz, P., & Asad, A. L. (2014). Immigrants and African Americans. *Annual Review of Sociology, 40,* 369–390.

Wax, E. (2008, May 4). In India, fairness is a growth industry; men buy skin-lighteners in growing numbers as a path to love, wealth. *Washington Post,* A17.

Way beyond the binary. (n.d.) Bisexual Resource Center. *Bire source.net.* Retrieved from http://www.biresource.net/waybeyondthebinary.shtml

Weedon, C. (1987). *Feminist practice and poststructuralist theory.* Cambridge, MA: Blackwell.

Weil, J. (2008). Transcending the reification of "old women's" bodies: Some sociological theorists' views. *Journal of Aging, Humanities & the Arts, 2*(1), 50–61.

Weinberg, T. (2015). Introduction. In T. Weinberg & S. Newmahr (Eds.), *Selves, symbols, and sexualities: An interactionist anthology* (pp. xiii–xxii). Thousand Oaks, CA: Sage.

Weinberger, C. (2011). In search of the glass ceiling: Gender and earnings growth among U.S. college graduates in the 1990s. *Industrial and Labor Relations Review, 64*(5), 949–980.

Weinger, S. (2000). Children's perceptions of class differences: Worries and self-perceptions. *Journal of Poverty, 4*(3), 99.

Weinrich, J. D. (2014a). Multidimensional measurement of sexual orientation: Ideal. *Journal of Bisexuality, 14*(3–4), 544–556.

Weinrich, J. D. (2014b). Multidimensional measurement of sexual orientation: Past. *Journal of Bisexuality, 14*(3–4), 314–332.

Weisbrot, R. (2010). New left. In R. Chapman (Ed.), *Culture wars: An encyclopedia of issues, viewpoints, and voices.* Retrieved from http://ezproxy.sunyrockland.edu:2048/login?qurl=http%3A%2F%2Fsearch.credoreference.com%2Fcontent%2Fentry%2Fsharpecw%2Fnew_left%2F0

Welter, B. (Summer, 1966). The cult of true womanhood: 1820–1860. *American Quarterly, 18*(2), Part 1, 151–174.

West, C., & Zimmerman, D. H. (1987). Doing gender. *Gender & Society, 1*(2), 125–151.

West, C. M. (2012). Partner abuse in ethnic minority and gay, lesbian, bisexual, and transgender populations. *Partner Abuse, 3*(3), 336–357.

White, A. (2004). Reagan's AIDS legacy/Silence equals death. *SFGate.* Retrieved from http://www.sfgate.com/opinion/openforum/article/Reagan-s-AIDS-Legacy-Silence-equals-death-2751030.php

Wilder, J. (2010). Revisiting "color names and color notions": A contemporary examination of the language and attitudes of skin color among young black women. *Journal of Black Studies, 41*(1), 184–206.

Wilhoit, F. (1979). *The quest for equality in freedom.* New Brunswick, NJ: Transaction Books.

Williams, C. (1992). The glass escalator: Hidden advantages for men in the "female" professions. *Social Problems 39*(3), 253–267.

Williams, C. (2013). The glass escalator, revisited: Gender inequality in neoliberal times. *Gender & Society, 27*(5), 609–629.

Williams, C. A. (2010). *Roman homosexuality.* New York, NY: Oxford University Press.

Williams, J., & Bennett, S. (1975). The definition of sex stereotypes via the adjective check list. *Sex Roles, 1*(4), 327–337.

Williams, J., & Best, D. (1982/1990). *Measuring sex stereotypes: A multination study.* Newbury Park, CA: Sage.

Williams, J., Satterwhite, R., & Best, D. (1999). Pancultural gender stereotypes revisited: The five factor model. *Sex Roles, 40*(7/8), 513–525.

Willis, D., & Williams, C. (2002). *The Black female body: A photographic history.* Philadelphia, PA: Temple University Press.

Wilson, W. J. (2011). Being poor, Black, and American: The impact of political, economic, and cultural forces. *American Educator, 35*(1), 10–23.

Wingfield, A. (2009). Racializing the glass escalator: Reconsidering men's experiences with women's work. *Gender and Society, 23*(1), 5–26.

Witt, C. (1989). *Substance and essence in Aristotle: An interpretation of metaphysics VII–IX.* Ithaca, NY: Cornell University Press.

Wittig, M. (1992/2002). *The straight mind and other essays.* Boston, MA: Beacon Press.

Wolf, N. (1990). *The beauty myth.* London, United Kingdom: Chatto & Windus.

Women Living Under Muslim Laws. (n.d.). About WLUML. Retrieved from http://www.wluml.org/node/5408

Women—Colonial Spanish America. (2005). In J. Francis (Ed.), *Iberia and the Americas: Culture, politics, and history*. Santa Barbara, CA: ABC-CLIO. Retrieved from http://ezproxy.sunyrockland.edu:2048/login?qurl=http%3A%2F%2Fezproxy.sunyrockland.edu%3A2103%2Fcontent%2Fentry%2Fabcibamrle%2Fwomen_colonial_spanish_america%2F0

Wong, Y., Owen, J., Tran, K. K., Collins, D. L., & Higgins, C. E. (2012). Asian American male college students' perceptions of people's stereotypes about Asian American men. *Psychology of Men & Masculinity, 13*(1), 75–88.

Wood, A. W. (1988). Introduction. *Marx selections*. New York, NY: Macmillan Publishing.

Wood, A. W. (2004). *Karl Marx* (2nd ed.). New York, NY: Routledge.

Wood, J. T. (2002, Winter). A critical response to John Gray's Mars and Venus portrayals of men and women. *Southern Communication Journal, 67*(2), 201–210.

Wood, J. T. (2013). *Gendered lives: Communication, gender and culture*. Boston, MA: Wadsworth/Cengage.

Woods-Giscombé, C. (2010). Superwoman schema: African American women's views on stress, strength, and health. *Qualitative Health Research, 20*(5), 668–683.

World Health Organization. (2002). World Report on Violence and Health—Summary. Retrieved from http://www.who.int/violence_injury_prevention/violence/world_report/en/summary_en.pdf

World Health Organization. (2010). Progress on sanitation and drinking-water: 2010 Update. Retrieved from http://www.wssinfo.org/fileadmin/user_upload/resources/1278061137-JMP_report_2010_en.pdf

World Health Organization. (2011). An update on WHO's work on female genital mutilation. Retrieved from http://whqlibdoc.who.int/hq/2011/WHO_RHR_11.18_eng.pdf

World Health Organization. (2013). Female genital mutilation: Key facts. Retrieved from http://www.who.int/mediacentre/factsheets/fs241/en/index.html

Yancy, G. (2013). Walking while Black in the "White Gaze." *The New York Times*, Retrieved from http://opinionator.blogs.nytimes.com/2013/09/01/walking-while-black-in-the-white-gaze/

Yardley, J. (2013, July 14). Bangladesh pollution, told in colors and smells. *The New York Times*, Retrieved from http://www.nytimes.com/2013/07/15/world/asia/bangladesh-pollution-told-in-colors-and-smells.html?pagewanted=all&_r=0

Ybarra, M., & Mitchell, K. (2013). Prevalence rates of male and female sexual violence perpetrators in a national sample of adolescents. *JAMA Pediatrics 167*(12), 1125–1134.

Yoshino, K. (2000). The epistemic contract of bisexual erasure. *Stanford Law Review, 52*(2), 353.

Young, A. (2000). *Women who become men: Albanian sworn virgins*. Oxford, United Kingdom: Berg.

Zarnow, L. (2010). Bringing the third wave into history. In K. Laughlin, J. Gallagher, D. Cobble, & E. Boris (Eds.), Is it time to jump ship? Historians rethink the waves metaphor. *Feminist Formations, 22*(1), 111–120.

Zea, M., Reisen, C. A., & Poppen, P. J. (1999). Psychological well-being among Latino lesbians and gay men. *Cultural Diversity and Ethnic Minority Psychology, 5*(4), 371–379.

Zeshan, U. (2002). Towards a notion of "word" in sign languages. In R. W. Dixon & A. I. Aikhenvald (Eds.). *Word: A cross-linguistic typology* (pp. 153–179). Cambridge, United Kingdom: Cambridge University Press.

Credits

IMAGE CREDITS

Chapter 1

Figure 1.1: OUP; **Figure 1.2:** OUP; **Figure 1.3:** Photo courtesy of Tony Briffa—www
.briffa.org; **Figure 1.4:** National Anthropological Archives, Smithsonian Institution, GN
02235A; **Figure 1.5:** AP Photo/Hektor Pustina

Chapter 2

Figure 2.1: iStock/Rich Legg; **Figure 2.2:** OUP; **Figure 2.3:** OUP; **Figure 2.4:** https://
commons.wikimedia.org; **Figure 2.5:** © 2011 The University of Wisconsin–Milwaukee
LGBT Resource Center; **Figure 2.6:** © Jeff Shesol; **Figure 2.7:** OUP; **Figure 2.8:** Re-
printed by permission of *Ms.* magazine, © 2013; **Figure 2.9:** Photo by Andrew T. Jacobs;
Figure 2.10: iStock/Hulton Archive; **Figure 2.11:** All Star Picture Library/Graham
Whitby Boot; **Figure 2.12:** All Star Picture Library/Graham Whitby Boot

Chapter 3

Figure 3.1: Courtesy of Martha Gradisher, Funny Times; **Figure 3.2:** iStock/EdStock;
Figure 3.3: Collection of the U.S. House of Representatives; **Figure 3.4:** John D. &
Catherine T. MacArthur Foundation; **Figure 3.5:** Wikipedia. David Shankbone;
Figure 3.6: iStock/EdStock; **Figure 3.7:**; Library of Congress, LC-USZ62-15887
Figure 3.8: Official White House Photo by Pete Souza

Chapter 4

Figure 4.1: Courtesy of the Kinsey Institute; **Figure 4.2:** Fritz Klein. The Klein Sexual Orientation Grid is reproduced by permission of the American Institute of Bisexuality, Inc.;
Figure 4.3: istolethetv/Flickr; **Figure 4.4:** Photo by Andrew T. Jacobs; **Figure 4.5:**
lev radin/Shutterstock.com; **Figure 4.6:** Photo by Andrew T. Jacobs; **Figure 4.7:** Photo by
Rosemary, courtesy of Lesbian Herstory Archives; **Figure 4.8:** Thomas Victor, Schlesinger
Library, Radcliffe Institute, Harvard University; **Figure 4.9:** Hong-Kong c. 1880: women un-
winding silk cocoons/Photo © PVDE/Bridgeman Images; **Figure 4.10:** Queer Patterns;
Figure 4.11: Library of Congress, LC-U9- 10332-11 **Figure 4.12:** Photo by Andrew T. Jacobs

Chapter 5

Figure 5.1: Wikipedia. Museo Archeologico Nazionale; **Figure 5.2:** Wikipedia;
Figure 5.3: National Archives War and Conflict Number 1272; **Figure 5.4:** Manuscripts
and Archives Division, The New York Public Library. "Silence = Death" The New York

Chapter 6

Chapter 7

Chapter 8

Chapter 9

Chapter 10

Figure 10.4: National Archives 195981; **Figure 10.5:** Photo courtesy of Michael Angelo; **Figure 10.6:** Simon Davis/DFID; **Figure 10.7:** Wikipedia, Frank Plitt; **Figure 10.8:** Russell Watkins/Department for International Development; **Figure 10.9:** John D. & Catherine T. MacArthur Foundation

Chapter 11

Figure 11.1: Angelina Emily Grimké 1805 to 1879. [No Date Recorded on Caption Card] Image. Retrieved from the Library of Congress, https://www.loc.gov/item/2003653379; **Figure 11.2:** Bain News Service, Publisher. Lowell—Portuguese mill girls. [between and Ca. 1915, ca. 1910] Image. Retrieved from the Library of Congress, https://www.loc.gov/item/ggb2004010358; **Figure 11.3:** Keppler, Udo J., Artist. Savagery to "civilization"/Keppler; drawn by Joseph Keppler. New York: Published by Puck Publishing Corporation, 295 309 Lafayette Street, 1914. Image. Retrieved from the Library of Congress, https://www.loc.gov/item/97505624; **Figure 11.4:** Mayer, Henry, Artist. The awakening/Hy Mayer. New York: Published by Puck Publishing Corporation, 295 309 Lafayette Street, 1915. Image. Retrieved from the Library of Congress, https://www.loc.gov/item/98502844; **Figure 11.5:** Harris & Ewing, Washington, D.C. [PennSylvania on the Picket Line—1917]. 1917. Image. Retrieved from the Library of Congress, https://www.loc.gov/item/mnwp000212; **Figure 11.6:** Creekmore Fath Papers, e_rap_0105, The Dolph Briscoe Center for American History, The University of Texas at Austin; **Figure 11.7:** Jack Rottier photograph collection, Collection #C0003, Special Collections Research Center, George Mason University Libraries; **Figure 11.8:** Gloria Steinem at news conference, Women's Action Alliance. 1972. Image. Retrieved from the Library of Congress, https://www.loc.gov/item/2004672751; **Figure 11.9:** © epa european press photo agency b.v./Alamy Stock Photo; **Figure 11.10:** OUP

Chapter 12

Figure 12.1: Wikipedia, C.D. Fredericks & Co.; **Figure 12.2:** Wikipedia, William Elliott Debenham (1839–1924); **Figure 12.3:** AP Photo; **Figure 12.4:** Bain News Service, Publisher. Crystal Eastman, Amos Pinchot. [between and Ca. 1920, ca. 1915] Image. Retrieved from the Library of Congress, https://www.loc.gov/item/ggb2005021957; **Figure 12.5:** Boris Roessler/picture-alliance/dpa/AP Image; **Figure 12.6:** Library of Congress, LC-USZ62-119343 **Figure 12.7:** Wikipedia. Provided by Dr. Chandra Mohanty; **Figure 12.8:** Andrew Rusk, www.flickr.com/photos/74098208@N00/5513754235; **Figure 12.9:** Wikipedia, Eve Kosofsky Sedgwick by David Shankbone; **Figure 12.10:** Manuscripts and Archives Division, The New York Public Library. "Read My Lips (Boys) (Postcard)" The New York Public Library Digital Collections. http://digitalcollections.nypl.org/items/510d47e3-5349-a3d9-e040-e00a18064a99

TEXT CREDIT

Chapter 7

More About Veiling as Fetish Art: Muslimah Media Watch, Fatemeh Fakhraie http://www.muslimahmediawatch.org/2008/01/28/oooh-baby-put-it-on-ripping-up-veil-fetish-art-2/

Index

Note: Page numbers in *italics* indicate images, tables, and charts.

See also the Glossary for all key terms and Appendix C, Feminisms in Brief, for more on forms of feminism.